PRAISE FOR JEFFREY M. DUBAN'S
HOMER'S ILIAD IN A CLASSICAL TRANSLATION

"Those who know Jeffrey Duban's translations and original poetry, *The Shipwreck Sea: Love Poems and Essays in a Classical Mode* (2019), and *The Lesbian Lyre: Reclaiming Sappho for the 21st Century* (2016), will be little surprised to have his *Iliad* now as well. This, as Duban explains, is not just another *Iliad* 'in a new translation' but a new *Iliad* 'in a Classical translation'; that is, an attempt to communicate in English the archaic, ornamental, and artificial qualities of Homer's language. He employs a once-traditional poetic diction, an elegant twelve-syllable line, principally iambic. Homeric poetry is at once archaic and new, traditional and surprising. Readers of Greek will here rediscover the *Iliad* in translation, while those without Greek will acquire a sense of the beauty of Homer's language."

– Pura Nieto Hernández, Brown University, Distinguished Senior Lecturer in Classics, Author, "Reading Homer in the 21st Century," Contributor, *The Homer Encyclopedia*

"Translation is a high calling of the classics scholar, an endeavor undertaken only by classicists of the highest order. Following in a nearly four-century tradition of reverence for the beauty of ancient languages and for the lessons antiquity offers to contemporary society, Dr. Duban hails from a long line of Boston Latin School educated scholars. His new translation of the Iliad brings to life a familiar epic that bursts with fresh vigor like the heroes whose journey and travails it recounts. With the achievement of this work, Dr. Duban brings great credit to the Latin School educators of days gone by and to the traditions and curricular rigor that persist today in the nation's oldest and most historic institution of secondary learning."

– Sherry Lewis-da Ponte '88, Chair of the Classics Department, The Boston Latin School

Homer's Iliad in a Classical Translation

faciebat

Jeffrey M. Duban

Achilleid Books
The Stuyvesant
258 Riverside Dr.
New York, NY 10025

and

Clairview Books Ltd.
Russet, Sandy Lane, West Hoathly
W. Sussex, RH19 4QQ

www.poemoftroy.com
www.jeffreyduban.com
www.clairviewbooks.com

Published by Achilleid Books and Clairview Books 2025

© Jeffrey M. Duban 2025

This book is copyright under the Berne Convention. All rights reserved. Apart from any fair dealing for the purpose of private study, research, criticism or review, no part of this publication may be reproduced, stored in a retrieval system, or transmitted in any form or by any means, electronic, electrical, chemical, mechanical, optical, photocopying, recording or otherwise, without the prior written permission of the copyright owner. Inquiries should be addressed to the Publishers

The right of Jeffrey M. Duban to be identified as the author of this work has been asserted by him in accordance with sections 77 and 78 of the Copyright, Designs and Patents Act, 1988

A CIP catalogue record for this book is available from the British Library

Print book ISBN 978 1 912992 65 2
Ebook ISBN 978 1 912992 66 9

Designed and typeset by Rachel Trusheim
Printed and bound in Malta by Gutenberg Press Ltd.

To the Memory of

Paul Petrek-Duban
(1989–2019)

ἠΰς τε μέγας τε

My son, my hero,
and best boy.

Now eve is manifest,
And Homeward lies our way:
Behold the weary West!

Tired flower! upon my breast,
I would wear thee alway:
Come hither, Child! be blessed,
My boy, my ever-joy confest!

– ERNEST DOWSON / JMD

~ Contents ~

Acknowledgments	xiii
Abbreviations	xv
Persons, Places, Regions, and Relationships	xvi
Pronunciation, Principal Characters	xxi
Preface	xxxix

I:
Commentary

Introduction

I.	A Personally Taken *Iliad*	3
II.	Homeric Language: As Rich as English Might Aspire to Become	14
III.	Dactylic Hexameter: The Meter of Homer and Classical Epic (in Brief)	27
IV.	Homeric Artificiality in Translation: Rightness of Result	
	1. Alliteration: Roots and Reason	39
	2. Making a Translation: Freedom in Constraint	42
	3. Inflection, Particles, Dialect Forms	44
	4. Rhetorical Artificiality	48
	5. Alliteration: Artificiality's Case in Point	50

II:
Homer's Iliad in a Classical Translation
(Each book preceded by a summary)

Prologue: Mythological Background	59
Book 1	Achilles and Agamemnon Quarrel, Achilles Withdraws from Battle, Thetis Implores Zeus to Avenge Achilles by Favoring the Trojans	63

Book 2 | Zeus Sends Agamemnon a False Dream, Agamemnon Tests the Army, the Rowdy Thersites, the Catalogue of Ships   83

Book 3 | The Parties Declare a Truce, the View from the Wall, the Single Combat Between Menelaus and Paris   113

Book 4 | The Trojans Breach the Truce, Agamemnon Marshals the Forces, the First Day of Battle   129

Book 5 | The Battlefield Excellence (or "Aristeia") of Diomedes, His Wounding of Aphrodite and Ares   149

Book 6 | Diomedes and the Lycian Glaucus Exchange Armor in a Chivalrous Gesture, the Parting of Hector and Andromache   181

Book 7 | The Single Combat between Hector and Ajax, the Dead are Buried, the Greeks Build a Wall to Protect Their Encampments and Ships   201

Book 8 | The Trojans Advance to the Wall and Encamp, the Greeks Beleaguered, the Second Day of Battle   219

Book 9 | The Embassy to Achilles: Agamemnon Seeks to Reconcile Achilles with Gifts   239

Book 10 | The Night Raid, Diomedes and Odysseus Capture and Kill the Trojan Spy Dolon   265

Book 11 | The Savagery and Wounding of Agamemnon, Patroclus Seeks to Identify a Wounded Greek and (at Nestor's Urging) Will Seek to Impersonate Achilles, the Third Day of Battle   285

Book 12 | Hector Storms the Barricade and Enters the Greek Camp, the Fourth Day of Battle   315

Book 13 | Battle is Waged for the Greek Ships, Poseidon Aids the Greeks, Mayhem Reigns, Idomeneus Deters the Trojan Advance   331

Book 14 | The Deception of Zeus: Aphrodite and the God Sleep Assist Hera in Seducing Zeus Who Then Slumbers as Hera Aids the Greeks   361

Book 15 | Zeus Awakens and Chastises Hera, the Greeks are Repulsed to Their Ships, the Doings of Ajax, the Fifth Day of Battle   379

Book 16 | Deeds and Deaths of Sarpedon, Cebrionēs, and Patroclus,
      the Sixth Day of Battle   405

Book 17 | Fight for the Body of Patroclus, Deeds of Ajax and Menelaus,
      the Seventh Day of Battle   435

Book 18 | Achilles' Anguish for Patroclus, Thetis and the Nereids
      Mourn, Hephaestus Forges New Armor for Achilles   463

Book 19 | Achilles and Agamemnon Reconciled, Briseis Restored   487

Book 20 | The Gods Prepare for Battle, Achilles Returns to the Plain   503

Book 21 | Achilles Battles the River Scamander, Hephaestus Checks
      the River's Advance   521

Book 22 | The Death of Hector: Hector Dragged by the Heels Behind
      Achilles' Chariot Around the Barrow of Patroclus   543

Book 23 | The Immolation of Patroclus, the Games in His Honor   563

Book 24 | The Ransoming of Hector's Body, the Immolation of Hector   595

Additional materials can be found at www.poemoftroy.com: Artwork Sources, Appendix I, II, III, Endnotes, Principal Works Consulted, and Index of Extended Similes

~ Acknowledgments ~

My sincerest thanks and appreciation to:

JAYNE CONNELL, dearest wife, who read and reread each page of this book and each line of this translation. To this labor she brought a consummate appreciation of poetry and of the English nineteenth century and its novels. This was especially helpful in the framing and use of the stylized diction with which I sought to infuse this translation, though more than once did I decline an archaism from her lavish store.

Above and beyond all this, and as the work approached finality, we took turns reading the entire translation aloud—an exuberant exercise that yielded unexpectedly valuable results, good fellowship, and cheer. It is amazing how differently the work "sounded" when encountered on the computer screen or in hard copy versus oral delivery (Homer's medium, of course). Each of these reviews and edits—the oral in particular—brought improvement and, hopefully, luster and "rightness of result" to every line.

James Diggle, for probing comment on front matter, introduction, and translation excerpts with an attentiveness past anything deserved; for corrections and bibliography and, not least, for urging constraint vis-à-vis materials deemed tangential or political.

Harmar Brereton, MD, Homer enthusiast, scholar and gentleman, for his friendship and generous introduction to James Diggle.

Richard Janko, for his review in near final form of preface, introduction, and translation excerpts, and for insightful comment, correction, and bibliography.

Dana Gioia, Steven Shankman, and Reginald Gibbons, for cordial and instructive correspondence that encouraged the development and fine-tuning of this work.

James Duban, for his review of the several initial drafts and encouragement from that point onward; for his wisdom in conscripting me, after the death of my son, into the co-authorship of James Duban and Jeffrey M.

Duban, "From Iliadic Integrity to Post-Machiavellian Spoils: James's *The Ambassadors*," Philosophy and Literature 47.1 (2023), 1–23.

Jake Bonar, for his acute editorial eye and suggestions.

Rachel Trusheim, for her invaluable editorial and design expertise over the years.

Chris Hobbick and Morgan Creative for their acute sensibility in the cover design.

Michael Putnam, undergraduate advisor, mentor, lifesaver in time of crisis, lifetime supporter, and friend.

Alfred Runte, author of enduring books on America's national parks and railroads, steadfast friend, support, and advisor.

Sevak Gulbekian (Chief Editor, Clairview Books), publisher of my earlier books, for his confidence, discernment, independence, and old-world gentlemanliness.

And a posthumous thanks to:

Charles Fornara (Department of Classics, Brown University) who, when I sought freshman enrollment in his Advanced Homer, kindly (though skeptically) allowed me to attend on a trial basis. We read the entire *Odyssey*. Returning to him in my senior year to direct my Master's thesis, I read the entire *Iliad* and wrote on its major duel sequences, work which in time was published.

Patrick ("Oki") O'Callaghan, my Greek teacher, grades ten through twelve, at The Boston Public Latin School (est. 1635)—an endearingly eccentric, devoted, and learned man who demanded and got much from his students.

Wilfred O'Leary (BLS Headmaster) who, when second-language elective students were insufficient to warrant starting a new class in French, German, Russian, or Greek, brought us together, prevailing on all to take Greek. As important in its way, he instituted a dress code for the then all-boys school: jackets and ties (with consequences for omissions). Many the patch and tear in many the jacket, for we were all from middle and lower-middle income families, and *those* were the only jackets we had. Proper dress, attitude, and comportment thus complemented an extraordinarily rich and purposeful curriculum. Teachers were referred to as "masters." We rose from our seats when addressing them and called them "Sir" (consequences for omissions).

Abbreviations

Eng.	English
Fr.	French
Ger.	German
Gr.	Greek
Lat.	Latin

acc.	accusative (case)
c.	abbreviation, Lat. *circa* 'around'
cf.	abbreviation, Lat. *confer* 'compare' (imp.)
dat.	dative (case)
gen.	genitive (case)
lit.	literally
masc.	masculine
nom.	nominative (case)
part.	participle (mood)
pass.	passive (voice)
perf.	perfect (tense)
pl.	plural
pron.	pronounced
sing.	singular

Classical

Aen.	*Aeneid*
Il.	*Iliad*
Met.	*Metamorphoses*
Od.	*Odyssey*
Th.	*Theogony*
KJB	King James Bible
TLL	*The Lesbian Lyre: Reclaiming Sappho for the 21st Century* (Clairview Books, 2016)
TSS	*The Shipwreck Sea: Love Poems and Essays in a Classical Mode* (Clairview Books, 2019)

Persons, Places, Regions, and Relationships

Iliad line references in parentheses (here and throughout) are to this translation; in brackets, to the original text. In rare cases lacking either brackets or parentheses, references are determined by context. Line references to the *Odyssey* and *Theogony* are in parentheses. My translation is based on HOMERI OPERA, David B. Monroe and Thomas W. Allen, eds., 2 Vols. (Oxford, 1920, 3d ed.). Citations to the *Odyssey* are to THE ODYSSEY OF HOMER, W. B. Stanford, ed., 2 Vols. (Macmillan, 1965, 2d ed.). Citations to the *Theogony* are to M. L. West, HESIOD THEOGENY (Oxford, 1966). The following are discussed below.

Homer's "Greeks"	Homer's "Greece"	Homer's Trojans	Post-Homeric Greeks
Achaea	Hellas	Dardania	Greaci
Achaeans	Hellen	Dardanians	Greacia
Achaeus	Hellenes	Dardanian Priam	Graecus
Argives	Panhellenes	Dardanus	Magna Graecia
Argos	Panachaean(s)	Ilos, Ilion/Ilium	
Danaans	*Panachaiōn* [gen.]	*Iliad*	
Danaus	*Panachaious* [acc.]	Tros, Troy	
Mycenae	*pantes Achaioi* [nom.]	Troad (Peninsula)	

Descendant	District	People	Dialect
Aeolus	Aeolia	Aeolians	Aeolic
Dorus	Doria	Dorians	Doric
Ion	Ionia	Ionians	Ionian
(Atthis)	Attica	(indigenous)	Attic/classical Greek

Homer never refers to the Greeks at Troy as *Greeks* but as **Achaeans**, **Argives**, and **Danaans**. The choice is largely determined by meter—meter

xvi

being determinative both in Homer and metered translation. The Trojans, for their part, go by the sole designation **Trōes**. Whatever the Greek, I use the three designations interchangeably, occasionally resorting to *Greeks*.

Homer's **Achaea** constituted the northern part of the Peloponnese, extending the length of the Gulf of Corinth. At Achaea's eastern extremity lay the principal site of **Mycenae** and, nearby it, Argos, one of the foremost Mycenaean cities—whence Achaeans and Argives as two of the three collective designations for the Greeks at Troy (but never "Mycenaeans"; though we find "Mycenae" and "the Mycenaean city of Argos"). The third designation, **Danaans**, derives from an Argive foundation myth involving the Libyan King Danaus. His fifty daughters—the *Danaïdes**—fleeing marriage from their cousins—are the subject of Aeschylus' *Suppliants*. Though Homer, as noted, uses **Achaeans**, **Argives**, and **Danaans** interchangeably, **Achaeans** predominates. They are often called **eüknēmides Achaioi** 'well-greaved Achaeans' (greaves = shin armor).

Danaans is not to be confused with **Dardanians**, a Trojan-related clan from the city of **Dardania**, north of Troy—the city founded by **Dardanus**, a son of Zeus. **Dardania** and **Troy** shared power on the **Troad Peninsula**. Homer clearly distinguishes **Dardanians** and **Trojans**, though by Virgil's time the two had become synonymous. Also on the **Troad**—south and far eastward of Troy at the terminus of its principal river, Scamander—lies **Mt. Ida**. This is Zeus' "getaway" from the frequent ruckus on Mt. Olympus (northern Greek mainland at the border of Thessaly and Macedonia). Ida allows Zeus, as it were, a closer vantage point for the war. The Judgment of Paris (pp. 59–60), giving rise to the war, occurs on the slopes of Ida.

Erichthonius, a mythical king of Dardania, begot **Tros**, the eponym of **Troy** (Gr. Troiē), also called **Ilion** (Lat. Ilium) after Tros' son **Ilos** (Lat. Ilus), whence Iliad (the story of Ilion). Ilus begot Laomedon, father and predecessor to Priam, king of Troy (the genealogy in greater detail at *Il*. 20.224-267 [203-241]). Homer sometimes refers to Priam as **Dardanian Priam**. As with Troy/Ilion, there are alternate names for the Trojan prince Paris/Alexander, and for the river Scamander/Xanthus. Alternate names, as seen, are used interchangeably *metri gratia* (Lat. 'for the sake of meter'). Scamander's companion river is Simoeis (or Simoïs).

I generally Latinize Greek names, following English translation practice. Thus **Ilus** for **Ilos**, **Ilium** for **Ilion**, **Cronus** for **Kronos**, **Ajax** for **Aias**,

Hephaestus for Hephaistos, etc. Where I do not—e.g., Gr. Heracles instead of Lat. Hercules—it (again) reflects translation practice or personal preference. But such instances are rare. The translation never alternates between Greek and Latin names for the sake of meter or otherwise. It does not use Jupiter/Jove for Zeus; Juno for Hera; Minerva for Athena. It does not refer to Zeus or any other god as God—though Homer frequently refers to a god or some god to indicate divine agency.

Ancient Greece was known as Hellas—derived from the mythological Hellen, son of Deucalion and Pyrrha, survivors of the great deluge (analogous to the biblical flood). Hellen was father to Aeolus and Dorus—progenitors of two of the principal Greek tribes, the Aeolians and Dorians. Hellen was also father to Xuthus, whose sons, Achaeus and Ion, were progenitors of the two other principal tribes, the Achaeans (see Achaea, above) and Ionians. The Aeolians, Ionians, and Dorians principally extended north to south along the coast of Asia Minor and its adjacent islands, whence three of the principal Iliadic dialects: Aeolic, Ionic, and Doric. The fourth, Attic, predominated on the Attica Peninsula (Greek mainland), with its principal city of Athens facing the islands of Salamis and Aegina to the west; and further west, Mycenae. Attic flourished during the classical period (c. 450 BC), aka the Age of Pericles, becoming the principal Greek dialect thereafter. It was, among much else, the dialogue dialect of Greek tragedy, while tragedy's choral odes retained earlier dialectical forms.

According to the Greek historian Thucydides (c. 460–400 BC), the different tribes of Greece/Hellas all eventually took the designation Hellenes—(Gr. pron. Hel'-len-es; Eng. Hel'-lenes)—in deference to the increasing power of Hellen and his sons. Homer, he continues, nowhere refers to the land's inhabitants as **Hellenes** but uses the terms Achaeans, Argives, and Danaans (as noted). Homer only once uses Hellenes, referring to Achilles' men (*Il.* 2.715 [684])—the original Hellenes—because the sons of Hellen came to power in Phthiotis, i.e., the region of Phthia (Gr. *Phthiē*) in Thessaly (northern Greece) where Homer locates Achilles (*Il.* 1.159 [155], 174 [169]):

> Now those inhabiting Pelasgian Argos,
> And dwelling in Alus, Alopē and Trachis,
> And holding Phthia and Hellas—the land of fair
> Womankind—Myrmidons, Hellenes, and Achaeans

Were called; of these Achilles captained fifty ships.

(*Il.* 2.712-716 [681-685])

The various Hellenic enclaves took no collective action prior to the Trojan War. The war, whatever its initial cause, size, or purpose—historically and archaeologically debated, but fixed for posterity by Homer and the Homeric tradition—became the focal point of Greek and Roman mythology, heroism, religion, precept, literature, and history; in sum, the Greeks' mytho-historical nation-forging enterprise and, subsequently, through Virgil, the focal point of Western Civilization.

A nation-forging endeavor, the war, as related by Homer, involved *all* Hellenes, incorporating the principal Hellenic dialects and, through the famed Catalogue of Ships (*Il.* 2.493-940 [484-877]), purporting to identify and number the expedition's aggregate force. The *Iliad* was thus intended to have a unifying **Panhellenic** appeal. Only in the Catalogue of Ships does Homer refer to *Panhellenes*, equating them with Achaeans: *Panhellēnas kai Achaious* [acc.] [*Il.* 2.530]. Homer elsewhere refers to *Panachaeans* (typically a line-final genitive: *aristēres/aristēras* [nom./acc.] *Panachaiōn* 'the best **of all the Achaeans**', lit. 'the best **of the All-Achaeans**'), the compound more frequently appearing as *pantes Achaioi* [nom.] '**all the Achaeans**'. Homer regularly mentions the **Hellespont** (the waterway on the eastern entrance of which stood Troy); the Hellespont today known as the **Dardanelles** (after Dardanus, above).

The designation **Greece** comes from Lat. *Graecia* 'Greece', in turn derived from Gr. *Graikos*, Lat. *Graecus*. Graecus, a nephew of Hellen, was the eponymous founder of the tribe of *Graeci* 'Graecians'. These were the first Hellenic peoples to colonize southern Italy, also known as Lat. *Magna Graecia* 'Great(er) Greece'. Because they were the first Hellenes with whom the ancient Latins had contact, the Romans called *all* Hellenes *Graeci* 'Greeks'. The Trojan Aeneas, arriving at Latium (the future site of Rome) encounters the Latians, later *Latins*, ruled by King Latinus (putative brother of Graces).†

†For the above references and genealogies, See H. G. Evelyn-White, *Hesiod, The Homeric Hymns, and Homerica* (Harvard Univ. Press, Loeb Classical Library, 1914, 1974), xxii, 154–157: §§ 1, 2, 4, 5; Glenn W. Most, *The Shield, Catalogue of Women, Other Fragments* (Harvard Univ. Press, Loeb Classical Library, 2007), 41–49: §§ 1, 2, 3, 4, 9; and Thucydides, 1.3.1-4, in *Thucydides: History of the*

Peloponnesian War, Rex Warner, tr. (1954, rev. 1972), 36–37. Parts of the same information may be found in the run of mythology handbooks. For more detailed treatment, see Robert Fowler, "Genealogical Thinking, Hesiod's *Catalogue*, and the Creation of the Hellenes," *Proceedings of the Cambridge Philological Society*, 44 (1988) 1–19; and Benjamin Sammons, *The Art and Rhetoric of the Homeric Catalogue* (Oxford Univ. Press, 2010).

Pronunciation, Principle Characters

A DETAILED GUIDE to the pronunciation of classical names appears in *TLL* xvii–xxii. For present purposes, I offer an abbreviated version, owing to limitations of space and the uncertainties of the pronunciational endeavor itself. Indeed, questions enough exist concerning the pronunciation of Homer's Greek in its own time, let alone the pronunciation of Homeric names in English millennia later. The English pronunciation of classical names is, in sum, variable, notwithstanding consensus in the most prominent cases. Few will argue the pronunciations of Achilles, Helen, Hector, and Agamemnon. But practice may differ, e.g., as to Priam (*Prī'-am* preferred; sometimes *Pree'-am*). An approach differing from that set forth in *TLL* may, in any event, be helpful.

The complexity of the issue may be garnered from Help:IPA/Greek: the pronunciation key for IPA transcriptions of Greek on Wikipedia (IPA = International Phonetic Alphabet). See also "Patroclus" (Wikipedia: 1. "Pronunciation of name"), and *TLL* 118 (on the multi-dialectical spellings and pronunciations of "Sappho"). Bypassing the IPA, as we did in *TLL*, we prefer to think that a good reading habit, a feel for language (*Sprachgefühl*), and reliance on the metrical scheme of this translation will render pronunciation generally manageable. The "intake" of multiple names in catalogue form will remain challenging, though one must appreciate the oral compositional skill involved and the original audiences' delight in the poet's command of the "catalogue subgenre" of epic poetry. Be that as it may, the following is intended to familiarize readers with the most probable pronunciations of the *Iliad*'s key characters and locations, many such pronunciations settled by usage and consensus.

⁂

To transliterate is to express the sounds of one language in the alphabet of another. In English, as well as in transliterated Greek, a disyllabic name is typically stressed on the first syllable. Trisyllabic names are typically stressed on the first (and sometimes second) syllable; quadrisyllabic names, e.g., Tal-thy'-bi-us, on the second or third. The following line (divided by types of English poetic feet) would read as follows:

/ / / ⌣ ⌣ / ⌣   ⌣ / ⌣ ⌣ /

And Eu | rybatēs | beckoned, Tal | thybius too.

spondee   dactyl   dactyl   choriamb

(*Il.* 1.329)

[For types of poetic feet, see further Part III.]

Given the meter and requisite sensibility, one would be disinclined to read the names with third-syllable stresses, e.g., Tal-thy-bi'-us and Eu-ry-ba'-tēs (though that is how the latter name is stressed in Greek). Thus does the translation's meter, for all else it does, aid in pronunciation. The name Πάτροκλος 'Patroclus' (see above) is yet more illustrative. The name is most often pronounced *Pa-tro'-clus*, although *Pa'-tro-clus* (as in Greek) is also common. However, in each instance of this translation, rhythm renders *Pa-tro'-clus* inevitable, as noted by the stress marks and bolded syllables below:

⌣ / ⌣ / ⌣ ⌣ / ⌣ / ⌣ / ⌣

But come, Pa | **tro**clus, di | vinely born, | relinquish

amphibrach   dactyl   amphibrach   amphibrach

(*Il.* 1.346)

/ ⌣ / ⌣ ⌣ / ⌣ ⌣ / ⌣ ⌣ /

Thus he | spoke, and Pa | **tro**clus his | dear friend obeyed.

Trochee   dactyl   dactyl   choriamb

(*Il.* 1.354)

The metrical disposition of "Patroclus" thus aids in the name's consistent pronunciation. Other consistently scanned names could be adduced. Challenges, however, remain, especially where the name appears but once, e.g.,

(... had not their stepmother)

/ ‿ ‿ / ‿ ‿ / ‿ ‿ / / /

Beauteous | Ēeri | boea, beseeched | Hermes

 dactyl dactyl choriamb spondee

(*Il.* 5.432)

In such cases (pron. *Ay'-eh-ri-bee'-a*), don't be discouraged. Give it a try and move on.

 One further notes that ancient Greek names, when transliterated, are typically Latinized: Gr. υ to Lat./Eng. y (as in Eurybates and Talthybius, above); Gr. *k* to Lat./Eng. *c*; Gr. *os* to Lat./Eng. *us*. For example, the name "Heracles" (Eng. pron. *Heh'-ra-cleez*) is the Latinized transliteration of Ἡρακλῆς (Gr. pron. *Hay-ra-klace'*). The difference in transliterated pronunciation aside—*Heh'-ra-cleez* versus *Hay-ra-klace'*—there is a Greek-to-English change in syllabic stress from the last to first syllable (as there was in "Eurybates" from the third to the second). In fact, Greek names typically change accentuation when transliterated and pronounced in English. That, however, is of no concern to the Greekless reader, whose reading and common sense will result in a certain habituation to the pronunciation of names. (One may further consult Andrew Collins, "The English Pronunciation of Latin: Its Rise and Fall," *The Cambridge Classical Journal*, 58 [2012], 23–57.)

❧

The Greek vowels, from which derive English *a-e-i-o-u*, are: α (alpha), ε (epsilon), ι (iota), ο (omicron), and υ (upsilon). Speakers of English know when an English vowel is long or short (e.g., "sat" versus "say"). The ancient Greeks would know the same concerning alpha/α, iota/ι, and upsilon/υ. However, long epsilon/ε is represented as eta/η (ā as in *say*); and long omicron/ο as omega/ω (ō as in *old*).

 One thus notes in the name Ἡρακλῆς two eta/H-η sounds, in the opening and final syllables. The opening uppercase eta/η is preceded by what is called a rough breathing, or aspiration, with an *h*-sound—the aspirated eta pronounced *(h)ē*. Thus, when Ἡρακλῆς is more precisely transliterated as *Hēraclēs*, the *ē* (with *ā* sound) properly represents similarly sounded Gr. eta/η.

Or, because eta/η is lengthened epsilon/ε, transliterated *e* instead of *ē* creates an ε sound. At the same time, however, *ē* is often pronounced as either *ay* or *ee* by one or another speaker, from one name to another or with reference to the same name (see *Alcmēnē*, below). In the translation that follows (but rarely in the introduction or endnotes), I indicate Greek eta/η as *ē*, and Greek omega/ω as *ō* in proper names containing them, excepting those otherwise familiar to English readers, e.g., Hector (not Hectōr); Poseidon (not Poseidōn), Hermes (not Hermēs), Peleus (not Pēleus). This is not typically done in Homeric translation, but I do it here to "authenticize"—even exoticize—the text with a hint of original name pronunciations. The long marks—call them vowel elongations—are, nonetheless, largely for flavor.

Reviewing selected other usages, we note:

> HĒRA ("Ηρα [Attic dialect]; "Ηρη [Ionic/Homeric]): variously pronounced *Hera, Hē'-ra,* or *Hee'-ra.*

> ALCMĒNĒ (Ἀλκμήνη): variously pronounced *Alc-mee'-nee, Alc-mē'-nē,* or *Alc-mee'-nē.*

> HĒBĒ ("Ηβη): pronounced *Hee'-bee.*

> MĒRIONĒS (Μηριόνης): variously pronounced *Me-ri-ō'-nace* (preferred, though the original has omicron/o not omega/ω), *Me-ri-ō'-nees, Me-ri-o'-nes, Me-ri-o'-nēs, Mē-ri-o'-nēs,* or *Mē-ri-o'-nees,* etc.

The IPA notwithstanding, there is no formula governing these usages. Pronunciations thus often puzzle and seem to lack consistency. Pronunciations may further vary from one to another speaker, owing to habit, education, region, or English-speaking country of origin.

Seeking to streamline the inquiry, I offer a brief guide to vowel and other selected sounds. There follows a list of principal characters and places with recommended pronunciations where needed.

Vowels

a	as in *are* or *at*
ā	as in *say*
e	as in *elf* or *see*
ē	as in *say*
i	as in *it*

ī	as in *size*
o	as in *on*
ō	as in *zone*
u	as in *us*
ū	as in loose

Diphthongs

ae	as in *aisle* or *see*; sometimes a *u* sound as in *sun*, e.g., Aeneas (pron. *A-nee'-as/U-nee'-us*)
ai	as in *aisle*
au	as in *owl*
ei	as in *freight*
eu	as in *food* or *you*
oe	as in *see*
oi	as in *soy*
ou	as in *food*

The letters *c* and *g* are always hard in classical Latin; and are hard in English, except when followed by *i* or *e* (omitting *g*-words of Germanic origin, e.g., get, gift, girl, begin). There is no equivalent in Homeric or classical Greek to hard/soft *c*. Soft *c* is represented by sigma σ/ς, hard *c* by kappa/κ. At the same time, gamma/γ is always hard. These peculiarities give further rise to uncertainties in the pronunciation of transliterated Greek. For example, the *Iliad*'s Nestor, though mostly associated with Pylos in the southern Peloponnese, also has ties to the town of Γερηνία/*Ge-rē-ni'-a*; hence his epithet "Gerenian Nestor." Not knowing that Greek gamma/Γ—here uppercase γ—is always hard, speakers of English will pronounce it soft because followed by transliterated *e*. So also Μελέαγρος/*Me-le'-a-gros*, which drops the final-syllable ρ/*r* sound to become "Me-le-a'-ger," hero of the pre-Iliadic Calydonian Boar Hunt. The name should be pronounced with hard *g*, but the same *g*-pronunciational confusion here occurs as with *Gerenian* (hard *g* mistakenly pronounced soft). Yet even when the hard *g* is retained, the name is variously pronounced: *Me-lē-ā'-ger* (preferred), *Me-le-ā'-ger*, *Me-lē-ah'-ger*, and even

Me-li-ah'-ger. Also pronounced with hard *g* is the epithet Argeïphontes (*Ar-ge-i-phon'-tēs*; see Hermes, below).

Gr. chi/χ is a gutturalized *k* sound (pron. *ch* as in Ger. *Buch*). It is sometimes transliterated as *kh*, but more often as *ch* pronounced simply as *k*, e.g., Ἀχιλλεύς, Achilles; Ἀρχίλοχος, Archilochus. It is further noted that Gr. thēta/θ is pronounced *th* as in *thin* (not as in *the*).

&

The following is a list of gods and goddesses, characters, and place names most often appearing in the *Iliad*. For purposes of the list, read:

ā as in *say*; *ē* as in *they*; *ī* as in *price*; and *ō* as in *low*.

GODS AND GODDESSES

(Roman names in brackets)

APHRODITE [Venus]: Daughter of Zeus and Diōnē. Goddess of love. Also referred to as Cypris/Cyprian because of her birth onto Cyprus. **Favors the Trojans.**

APOLLO [Apollo]: Son of Zeus and Leto. God of archery, music, dance, and poetry; prophecy, diseases, and healing; sun and light; twin of Artemis. **Favors the Trojans.**

ARES [Mars]: Son of Zeus and Hera. God of war. **Favors the Trojans.**

ARTEMIS [Diana]: Daughter of Zeus and Leto. Virgin goddess of the hunt, the wild, and the moon. Twin sister of Apollo. **Favors the Trojans.**

ATHENA [Minerva]: Daughter of Zeus (born fully grown and armed from his forehead). Virgin goddess of wisdom and war, sharing thoughts and counsel with Zeus. Frequent wielder of the aegis (Zeus' fearsome shield). **Favors the Greeks.**

DIONE (*Di-ō'-nē*): Parentage uncertain. Consort of Zeus. Mother of Aphrodite.

HADES [Pluto]: Son of the Titans Cronus and Rhea. Brother of Zeus and Poseidon. Ruler of the underworld. **Favors the Trojans.**

HEPHAESTUS (*He-phais'-tus*) [Vulcan]: Son of Zeus and Hera. God of fire; fashioner of crafts and armaments; architect of Zeus' palace and the gods' residences on Olympus. **Favors the Greeks.**

HERA [Juno]: Daughter of Cronus and Rhea. Wife and sister of Zeus. Queen of the gods. Goddess of childbirth and the sanctity of marriage. **Favors the Greeks.**

HERMES [Mercury]: Son of Zeus and Maia. Wing-sandaled messenger of the gods. Go-between of heaven and earth, earth and Hades (and guide of souls to Hades). God of those who traverse spaces, including travelers, merchants, and thieves. Also god of boundaries. Often referred to in Homer as *Argeïphontes* (*Ar'-ge-i-phon'-tēs*) (with hard g) 'slayer of Argos' (the hundred-eyed giant). **Favors the Trojans.**

IRIS (*Ī'-ris*): Daughter of Thaumas and the ocean nymph Electra. Goddess of the rainbow. Messenger of the gods. Personal attendant of Hera.

POSEIDON [Neptune]: Son of Cronus and Rhea. Brother of Zeus and Hades. Ruler of the liquid element. **Favors the Greeks.**

THETIS [Thetis]: Daughter of Nereus (the Old Man of Sea) and Dōris. Foremost of the sea nymph or Nereïdes (*Ne-re'-i-des* 'daughters of Nereus'). Married by Zeus to the mortal Peleus (lest union with Thetis produce offspring greater than himself). Doting and mournful mother to Achilles.

ZEUS [Jupiter, Jove]: Son of Cronus and Rhea. King of the gods. Ruler of Olympus, the Olympian gods, the heavens and upper air (including clouds, thunder, rain, and storm). Arbiter of human destiny. His will is fate. **Favors neither Greeks nor Trojans.** Though his plan or intent is the demise of Troy, he intermittently favors the Trojans for reasons made clear in Book 1.

Greeks

ACHILLES: Son of Peleus and the sea nymph Thetis. Grandson of Aeacus (a son of Zeus). From Phthia in northern Greece. Leader of the Myrmidons (see below). Protagonist of the *Iliad*. The embodiment of epic heroism and excess alike. As noted by artist Henry Fuseli (1778–1825), "Each individual of Homer forms a class, expresses and is circumscribed by one quality of heroic power; Achilles alone unites their various but congenial energies. The grace of Nireus, the dignity of Agamemnon, the impetuosity of Hector, the magnitude, the steady prowess of the greater, the velocity of the lesser Ajax, the perseverance of Ulysses, the intrepidity of Diomede, are emanations of energy that reunite in one splendid centre fixed in Achilles." *The Life and Writings of Henry Fuseli, Esq. M.A.R.A.*, John Knowles F. R. S., ed. (Henry Colburn and Richard Bentley, 1831), Vol. II, Lect. I, 38–39.

AGAMEMNON: Son of Atreus. Ruler of the Greek strongholds of Mycenae and Argos. Brother of Menelaus. Leader of the Greek expedition to Troy.

AIANTES (*Ī-an'-tes*): The two Greek warriors named Ajax; often paired, though quite different in aspect and effectiveness.

AJAX: Son of Telamon. Ruler of Salamis. The "greater" Ajax.

AJAX: Son of Oïleus. Ruler of Locris. The "lesser" Ajax.

ANTILOCHUS (*An-til'-o-chus*): Son of Nestor.

DIOMĒDĒS (*Dī-o-mee'-dees*): Son of Tydeus (*Tee'-dyus*). Youthful, valiant, and lethal Greek warrior.

EURYBATES (*Eu-ri'-ba-tees*): Greek herald.

HECAMĒDĒ (*He-ca-mee'-dee*): Serving woman (possibly concubine) of the aged Nestor.

HELEN: Daughter of Tyndareus and the princess Leda. Other legends make her daughter of Leda and Zeus (Zeus, in the form of a swan, seducing Leda). The most beautiful woman in the world. Wife of Menelaus, king of Sparta, who wins her in exchange for the most bountiful bridal gifts. Seduced by the Trojan Paris and brought to Troy, thus precipitating the war. Referred to as Spartan or Argive Helen; subsequently, and most famously, as "Helen of Troy."

IDOMENEUS (*I-doh-meen'-eus*): Son of Deucalion and (according to a late source) an otherwise unknown Cleopatra. King of Crete. Leader of the Cretan contingent. A foremost fighter and advisor to Agamemnon. A principal defender when leading Greek fighters are wounded.

KALCHAS: Son of Thestor and Polymēlē. Greek seer and interpreter of omens.

MACHAON (*Ma-cha'-ōn*): Son of Asclepius, Greek god of medicine. Physician to the Greeks at Troy.

MENELAUS (*Men-e-lā'-us*): Son of Atreus. King of Sparta. Brother of Agamemnon. Husband of Helen.

MERIONES (*Mē-ri-ō'-nēs*): Son of Molus. Comrade and squire of Idomeneus.

NESTOR: Son of Neleus. Aged king of Pylos. The *Iliad*'s sole multigenerational fighter. Father of Antilochus.

ODYSSEUS: Son of Laërtes and Anticlea. Husband of Penelope. King of Ithaca. Protagonist of the *Odyssey*. Prominent in the *Iliad*.

PATROCLUS (*Pa-tro'-clus*): Son of Menoetius (mother uncertain). Childhood friend and companion to Achilles. A largely shadowy figure in the *Iliad*, with the exception of his impersonating Achilles and dying in battle as his "alter ego."

PĒLEUS (see Thetis): Father of Achilles.

PHOENIX: Son of Amyntor. Foster son of Peleus. Childhood mentor to Achilles.

STHENELUS: Son of Capaneus. Comrade of Diomedes.

TALTHYBIUS: Greek herald.

TEUCER (*Too'-sur*): Illegitimate son of Telamon. Half brother of Telamonian Ajax. Famed Greek archer.

THERSITĒS (*Ther-sī'-teez*): Ugliest and most intemperate of the Greek host.

Trojans and Allies

AENEAS (*A-nee'-as*): Son of Aphrodite and the mortal Anchises. Prominent Trojan warrior. Bravely engages Achilles. Distant ancestor of Romulus and Remus, founders of Rome (cf. Virgil's *Aeneid*).

AGENOR (*A-gee'-nōr*): Son of Poseidon. Trojan warrior who engages and almost wounds Achilles. The Agenor-impersonating Apollo allows Hector to pursue him. The diversionary tactic allows the Trojans to complete their flight into Troy while isolating Hector for his final encounter with Achilles.

ANDROMACHĒ (*An-dro'-ma-chee*): Daughter of Ēëtion (*Ē-ee'-shun*), king of Thebe(s). Wife of Hector and mother of their infant son, Astyanax. (This "Thebe/Thebes" on the Troad Peninsula, not to be confused with Thebes in Boeotia [*Bee-ō'-sha*] on the Greek mainland north of Attica/Athens. There is also an Egyptian Thebes.)

ANTENOR (*An-tee'-nōr*): Aged counselor to Priam and the Trojans.

CASSANDRA (*Cas-san'-dra*): Daughter of Priam and Hecuba. Maddened prophetess.

DEÏPHOBUS (*Dē-ee'-pho-bus*): Son of Priam and Hecuba. Leads the charge against the newly built Greek wall fortification. Husband of Helen following Paris' death (both events outside of the *Iliad*).

DOLON (*Doh'-lōn*): Son of Eumēdēs. Trojan spy killed on a night raid by Odysseus and Diomedes.

GLAUCUS (*Glau'-cus*): Son of Hippolochus. Second to Sarpedon as leader of Troy's Lycian allies. Famously encounters Diomedes, the two discovering their ancestral friendship.

HECTOR: Son of Priam and Hecuba. Commander of the Trojans and principal defender of Troy. His death, as he and all acknowledge, is the death of Troy itself.

HECUBA (*Heh'-coo-ba*): Wife of Priam. Queen of Troy. Mother of Hector.

HELENUS (*He'-len-us*): Son of Priam and Hecuba. Soothsayer of Troy.

IDEAUS (*I-dee'-us/I-dī'-us*): Trojan herald. Priam's charioteer.

LYCAON (*Ly-cā'-ōn*): Son of Priam. Previously captured and sold on Lesbos by Achilles. Returning from Lesbos to Troy, Lycaon is identified and, despite his offer of ransom, ironically slain by Achilles.

PANDARUS (*Pan'-da-rus*): Son of Lycaon. Trojan archer. Treacherously breaks an early truce, wounding Menelaus.

PARIS: Also called Alexander. Son of Priam. Seducer of Helen. Slackard. Effeminate. More lover than fighter.

POLYDAMAS (*Pol-y'-dam-as*): Son of Panthous. Trojan warrior and counselor. At odds with Hector.

PRIAM: Son of Laomedon (predecessor king of Troy). Descendant of Tros, founder of Troy. Father of Hector, Paris, Helenus, and many others.

SARPEDON (*Sar'-pe-don/Sar-pē'-dōn*; Gr. Σαρπηδών): Son of Zeus and Laodamia. Leader of Troy's Lycian allies. His death (which Zeus would vainly forestall) and the fight for his body are major events anticipating Patroclus' and Hector's deaths and, outside of the *Iliad*, Achilles' own.

OTHERS

AEACIDES (*Ee-a'-ci-deez*)*: "Son of Aeacus" (technically Peleus). Patronymic sometimes designating Achilles.

AEACUS (*Ee'-a-cus*): Son of Zeus. Grandfather (through Peleus) of Achilles.

AEGEUS (*Ee'-gee-us/Ee'-jus*): King of Athens. Father of Theseus.

AEGIS (*Ee'-jis*): Zeus' tasseled fear-inspiring shield.

ATĒ (*A'-tē*): Madness (personified).

ATREIDĒS/ATREÏDĒS (*A-trei'-deez/A-tre'-i-deez*): "Son of Atreus." Patronymic designating Agamemnon (and sometimes Menelaus).

ATREÏDAI: Patronymic designating both Agamemnon and Menelaus (plural of Atreïdēs).

BRISĒÏS (*Brī-see'-is*): "Daughter of Briseus." Spear bride awarded Achilles. Agamemnon's taking of Brisēïs incites Achilles' wrath and fateful withdrawal from the fighting.

BRISEUS (*Bri'-seus*): Father of Brisēïs.

CHIRON/CHEIRON (*Kī'-rōn/Kei'-ron*): Centaur supervising Achilles' boyhood training.

CHRYSĒ (*Chrī'-see*): Town believed located in the southwest Troad.

CHRYSĒÏS (*Chrī-see'-is*): "Daughter of Chrysēs." Spear bride of Agamemnon returned to Chrysēs and inciting Agamemnon's theft of Brisēïs.

CHRYSES (*Chrī'-seez*): Father of Chryēïs. Priest of Chrysē.

CLYTEMNESTRA (*Cly-tem-nes'-tra*): Wife of Agamemnon.

CRONIDĒS (*Cro-nee'-deez/Cron-ī'-deez*): "Son of Cronus." Patronymic designating Zeus.

CRONION (*Crō-nee'-ōn*): "Son of Cronus." Patronymic designating Zeus.

CRONUS (*Cro'-nus*): Son of Ouranos and Gaia. King of the Titan generation of gods. Father of Zeus.

ĒĒTION (*Ā-ee'-shun*): Andromache's father. Slain by Achilles before her marriage to Hector.

ENYALIUS (*En-ee-al'-ius*): Little distinguished from Ares. Byname of Ares.

ERINYES (*Eh'-rin-eez*): The Furies. Venerable female goddesses of vengeance.

EURYSTHEUS (*Eu-ris'-thee-us*): Son of Sthenelus. Grandson of Perseus (legendary slayer of the Gorgon Medusa). Exacted the Twelve Labors of Heracles as the latter's penance for slaying family members in a fit of rage.

GAIA (*Gī'-a*): Earth. Mother Earth.

GANYMĒDĒ (*Gan-i-mee'-dee*): Lovely Trojan youth swept up by Zeus in the form of an eagle to serve as his cupbearer.

HELLESPONT (*Hel'-les-pont*): Narrow waterway between the Aegean and the Sea of Marmara and, via the Bosphorus, to the Black Sea. Symbolic divide between Asia and Europe. Troy located at the southeast mouth of the Hellespont.

HĒRACLĒS (*Heh'-ra-cleez*): Son of Zeus and Alcmēnē. Mightiest of an earlier generation of civilization-founding heroes. Slayer of monsters and aberrant nature. Model for Achilles.

IDA (*Ī'-da*): Mountain in the south Troad to which Zeus often retreats (from Mt. Olympus on the Greek mainland) to survey the war.

LACEDAEMŌN (*La-ce-dī'-mōn*): Sparta. Home of Menelaus and Helen.

LAOMEDON (*Lā-o'-me-dōn*): Priam's father. Predecessor king of Troy. Known for deceit in cheating Heracles of his compensation for building a protective fortification for Troy. Heracles returns and sacks Troy with a six-vessel contingent.

LYRNESSUS (*Lyr-nes'-sus*): Home of Brisëis. Believed located in the southeast Troad in the vicinity of Mt. Ida.

MELEAGER (*Mel-e-ā'-ger*): Hero of the famed Calydonian Boar Hunt (a predecessor excursion to the Trojan War). Paradigm for Achilles.

MENOETIUS (*Meh-nee'-shus*): Father of Patroclus.

MYCĒNAE (*My-see'-nee*/*My-see'-nī*): Major center of Greek civilization in the second millennium BC (middle to late Bronze Age, c. 2000–1001 BC). A military stronghold dominating much of southern Greece, Crete, the Cyclades (island group southeast of mainland Greece), and parts of southwest Asia Minor (Turkey) and its adjacent islands. The period of Greek history from c. 1600–1200 BC—late Bronze Age—is called Mycenaean, and the Mycenaeans are considered the first Greeks. The period includes the generally accepted date of the Trojan War, c. 1250 BC. In Homer, Mycenae "rich in gold" is Agamemnon's capital city. It is strongly associated and confederated with nearby Argos. As the then seat of power and wealth, Mycenae is a stand-in designation for Greece/Hellas itself.

MYRMIDONS (*Mir'-mi-dons*): The followers of Achilles, lit. "ant men" (derivation uncertain).

NEOPTOLEMUS (*Ne-op-tol'-e-mus*): Son and sole offspring of Achilles (with Deidamia of Scyrus, an island where Achilles disembarked en route to Troy). Does not appear in the *Iliad*. Kills Paris following the fall of Troy.

NEREUS (*Nēr'-eus*): The Old Man of the Sea. Father of Thetis.

NĒRĒÏDES/NĒREIDS (*Nē-re'-i-des*/*Nēr'-eids*): The fifty sea-nymph daughters of Nereus. Sisters of Thetis, their leader.

OCEANUS (*O-ke-an'-us*/*O-kē'-an-us*): The mythical river encircling—and remotest from—earth. The origin of all earthly waterways. Sometimes referred to as "Ocean"—but not to be confused with "the ocean," for which Homer uses the word *thalassa*.

OÏLEUS (*O-ïl'-eus*): Father of the "lesser," or Oïlean, Ajax.

PALLAS: An epithet of Athena (derivation uncertain). Thus, Pallas Athena or simply "Pallas."

PĒLEUS (*Pee'-lyoos*). Mortal father of Achilles. Wed to the sea nymph Thetis.

PĒLIAN (*Pee'-lian*): Adjectival form of (Mt.) Pelion, from the peak of which Chiron cut an ashwood shaft for Peleus, Achilles' father. Hephaestus fashioned and fitted it with a head, whence the Pelian ash spear (or Pelian ash). Peleus gives the spear to Achilles, who uses it at Troy. Uniquely associated with Achilles; only he can heft it.

PĒLEÏDĒS/PĒLEIDĒS (*Pē'-le-ï-dēs'*/*Pē'-lei-dēs'*): "Son of Pēleus." Patronymic designating Achilles (both forms hypothetical, i.e., based on analogous Homeric formations).

PERSEUS (*Per'-seus*/*Per'-see-us*): Son of Zeus and the mortal Danaë (*Da'-na-ee*). Legendary founder of Mycenae. With Cadmus and Bellerophon, the greatest slayer of monsters before Heracles. Famously slays the Gorgon. Rescues Andromeda from the sea beast Cetus.

PHOEBUS: Light-associated epithet of Apollo. Thus, Phoebus Apollo or simply "Phoebus."

PHTHIA (*Phthee'-a*): Town in Thessaly (northern Greece). Home to Achilles.

PLYLOS: City in the Peloponnese (southern Greece). Home to Nestor. Thus, Pylian Nestor.

SCAEAN GATES (*See'-an* or *Scī-an*). Principal entrance to Troy.

SCAMANDER (*Sca-man'-der*): Principal river of Troy (also called Xanthus).

SIMOEIS/SIMOÏS (*Si-mo-eis'/Sim-o'-is*): Lesser river of Troy, flowing southward of Scamander.

TELAMON (*Tel'-a-mōn*): Father of (the greater) Ajax. Thus, Telamonian Ajax (versus Oïlean Ajax). Though Telamon is the elder brother of Peleus and uncle to Achilles, nothing is made of these relationships in the *Iliad*. Participants in earlier heroic exploits—Telamon in the Calydonian Boar Hunt; Telamon and Peleus as Argonauts in Jason's quest of the Golden Fleece—they provide paradigmatic authority for the taking of Troy.

THESEUS (*Thees'-yus/Thee'-see-us*): Son of Aegeus (*Ee'-jus*). Earlier generational hero. Mythic king of Athens. Slayer of Amazons and centaurs. Famously slays the Cretan Minotaur with the help of Ariadne. Undertakes—like Heracles—various civilization-stabilizing labors.

TETHYS (*Te'-thees*): Titan goddess. Sister and wife of Oceanus/Ocean.

THĒBĒ: See Andromache.

TROAD (*Trō'-ad*): Peninsula on which Troy is located. The Troad is bound by the Hellespont to the north, the island of Lesbos to the south, the Aegean to the west, Phrygia to the east, and Mt. Ida to the southeast. The kingdom ruled by Priam.

TYDEUS (*Teed'-yus/Tee'-dee-us*): Father of Diomedes.

XANTHUS (*Zan'-thus*): Alternate designation for Scamander.

> *Patronymic (Gr. *patēr* 'father' + *onuma* 'name'). A form, usually ending in *-idēs* (nom.), used to designate offspring by their father's name. Thus, Pēleidēs or Pēleïdēs ("son of Peleus" or Achilles); Danaïdēs ("Daughters of Danaus"); Nēreïdēs "Daughters of Nēreus"). For the pervasive use of patronymics, see pp. 33–36.

But my grandmother would have thought it sordid to concern herself too closely with the solidity of any piece of furniture in which could still be discerned a flourish, a smile, a brave conceit of the past. And even what in such pieces supplied a material need, since it did so in a manner to which we are no longer accustomed, was as charming to her as one of those old forms of speech in which we can still see traces of a metaphor whose fine point has been worn away by the rough usage of our modern tongue. In precisely the same way the pastoral novels of George Sand, which she was giving me for my birthday, were regular lumber-rooms of antique furniture, full of expressions that have fallen out of use and returned as imagery such as one finds now only in country dialects. And my grandmother had bought them in preference to other books, just as she would have preferred to take a house that had a gothic dovecote, or some other such piece of antiquity as would have a pleasant effect on the mind, filling it with nostalgic longing for impossible journeys through the realms of time.

– MARCEL PROUST, *SWANN'S WAY*, OVERTURE
(C. K. Scott Moncrieff, tr.)

~ Preface ~

> [T]ell your non-literate countrymen that Shakspere is Homeric, and they will get none the clearer idea of Shakspere; tell them that Homer is Shaksperean and they will comprehend more about Homer than if they turned over a shelf-full of his commentators.
>
> – EDMUND LENTHAL SWIFTE,
> *Homeric Studies* (1868)

THIS AS I DETERMINE, is the first translation of Homer into a twelve-syllable—dodecasyllabic, iambic hexametric—line. It further appears to be the most sustained dodecasyllabic work in English. The translation, as much by requirement of meter as by design, is intermittently archaic, i.e., "licensed" (as in poetic license). As with Homer's dactylic hexameter, meter here also commands, and much is done in its name. However, the line between metrical requirement and design is—as it should be—fine.

The resultant idiom, without seeking to replicate Homer, yet provides whatever sense can be recovered or supposed of the *Iliad*'s manner, antiquity, and peculiarities of style. The work is not "Homer's *Iliad* in a New Translation"—as most new Iliads are styled—but "Homer's *Iliad* in a Classical Translation." By its title and execution, it reflects the emphases and ethos of my two prior publications, the second styled: *The Shipwreck Sea: Love Poems and Essays in a Classical Mode* (Clairview, 2019). This *Iliad* translation and the emphases of its introduction are without precedent in the long annals of Homeric translation.

This work is an outgrowth of my *The Lesbian Lyre: Reclaiming Sappho for the 21st Century* (Clairview, 2016)—a book as much about the translation of Homer and epic as of Sappho and lyric. It is an outgrowth of that book's preoccupation with the manner of translation and its programmatic impetus, i.e., how a translation of Greek or Latin poetry should be made and why. The manner of this *Iliad* is traditional and, for that reason, formal.

More specifically, my earlier translations of Sappho and other Greek lyric poets were rhymed and metered. The present work, by contrast, is in a twelve-syllable predominantly iambic ($\smile$ /) line, highlighting poetic diction (i.e., the selection and arrangement of words) and select archaisms (i.e., the "old-fashionedness" of word and word arrangement). The work's metrical analogue is the infrequently used iambic hexameter (iambic pentameter the norm). The meter chosen, if not created, for this translation thus complements its purposefully unusual and archaic/venerable qualities. In fact, the meter, exceeding the more traditional iambic pentameter by two syllables per line, allows for a robust polysyllabism reflecting Homer's own. A reproach to characteristically sparse (i.e., excessively monosyllabic) and often unimaginative (or too imaginative) modern, modernist, or post-modern idiom, the present translation seeks to recall and find a place in the estimable literary past.

The four-part introduction makes the case for the translation's customized diction and idiom. These are designed to elevate the language of Homeric translation from the banalities of the past seventy years and more (in effect, since Lattimore's *Iliad*, 1951). "Banality" includes flatness of expression, most often marked by excessive monosyllabism. It results from lack of effort, imagination, and often of the Greek language itself in those who purport to translate. Excessive monosyllabism has also been the fate of recent translations of Homer's *Odyssey* and Virgil's *Aeneid*.

I. A Personally Taken Translation serves as predicate for the translation anew of a work perhaps more frequently translated than any other. Such a translation necessarily offers something noteworthy, even remarkable: here a regularized style-elevating meter and, for all of that, novelty other than for its own sake. Unlike recent Iliads "in a new translation," this "in a classical translation" offers newness in venerability. It is a translation newly allegiant to what is properly antique (and so viewed) but, for the past three generations at least, never rendered as such. "Old enough to be new," the work is intermittently antique and *artificial*—in the root sense of *art-making*. It thus conveys something of the nature of Homer's original—be it so faint, yet clearly audible, as the cosmic microwave background trailing the Big Bang. Homer's Greek, to be sure, is artificial through and through; considered archaic even in its own time. These qualities have been consistently acknowledged and appreciated by readers of Homer in Greek. Since Lattimore and, arguably, Pope, they have been all but lost to readers in translation.

A substantial part of this work was completed in 2020, the apocalyptic year of COVID and its anarchic racial-warfare and Cancel Culture companions. The work's conclusion in 2023–2024 amid the Israel-Hamas War bore witness throughout the world to harrowing on-campus displays of anti-semitism, anti-Americanism, and the assault on Western values. Yet, in my every rendered line I felt the world, like the *Iliad* itself, reconstituted and preserved. Such was my "personally taken" response to the dissolution from which this *Iliad* emerged—a work, like its original, seeking the fixity and order of art, even as all crumbled about me. This is what art does, as they who most value it know.

II. Homeric Language: As Rich as English Might Aspire to Become proposes an English translation reflecting, without seeking to imitate, the richness of Homeric idiom. Toward that end, Part II makes the case for an intermittently archaizing diction and style responsive to the extreme antiquity of Homeric materials, including: the Greek language and its Indo-European provenance, multi-generational characters, internally recounted legends, physical objects (some validated by archaeological finds), and the ubiquitous evocation of "time out of mind" via references to Oceanus/Ocean. The Titan son of primordial Earth (Gaia) and Heaven (Ouranos), Oceanus is an earth-encircling flow. He and wife Tethys are parent to all earthly waters and water divinities. The *Iliad*'s gods frequently pay visits to Oceanus. Oceanus prominently encircles the all-encompassing Shield of Achilles. And the Trojan river Scamander, son of Oceanus, supernaturally battles with Achilles. Such materials seek the translation idiom best reflecting them. The idiom here used is thus stylized, reverential. It eschews the hip, the colloquial, and the common. It is yet contemporary to the considerable extent that regularized meter and poetic license allow. The result is an elevation of language and style, a decided turnaround from translational decline, again, since Lattimore.

III. Dactylic Hexameter: The Meter of Homer and Classical Epic (In Brief) explains the workings of dactylic hexameter and the kindred formularity of Homeric language. Part III further touches on Homeric meter vis-à-vis English meter, noting that iambic pentameter, the heroic meter of English, is not necessarily best suited to the translation of dactylic hexameter, the heroic meter of Greek. Metrical language, whether in Greek or English is, again, and from start to finish, artificial—a *Kunstsprache* 'art language'— which is to say a self-referential, metrically dictated, artistically wrought construct. We recall in this connection the root etymological meaning of "art" (Gr. root **ar-* / Lat. *art-*): 'fix, fasten, fashion, place, position, set in order' (e.g., Eng. articulate).

By its nature then, Homeric language gives further credence to this translation's ideolect, illustrating author William Fitzgerald's dictum that "poetry is the place where language performs, and so poetry shows us most clearly what a language can do, and what it likes to do." The question, then, is whether one wants a translation of Homer that reads like poetry, in a suitable register exhibiting the incidents of poetry, or like an appliance-installation manual. The issue is one of *decorum*. This is not a revisionary but a *reversionary* translation, one old enough to be new, restoring a certain translational authority, as befits him, to Homer.

IV. Homeric Artificiality in Translation: Rightness of Result uses Homeric meter, dialogue, character posturing, and the *Iliad*'s pervasive alliteration as cases in point. As Part II makes the case for an archaic idiom based on Homer's essential antiquity, Part IV makes the case for a relatedly artificial—i.e., *art-making*—idiom based on the wealth of the *Iliad*'s stylized speeches (especially in battlefield contexts) and other linguistic contrivance, including word order and alliteration. As alliteration is a pervasive Homeric device, it behooves the translator to *make* something of it, as in Gr. *poieō/poiētēs* 'make'/'maker, poet'. Such making resides in a comparably alliterative translation—not, to be sure, in each instance where Homer is alliterative, but wherever resourceful English allows, with the net result of Homeric effect overall. That in fact is the overall goal of this translation: Homeric effect occasioning English poetic appreciation.

– JMD, NEW YORK CITY, 2025

I.
Commentary

I

COMMENTARY

~ Introduction ~

I. A Personally Taken *Iliad*

In the introduction to his translation of Virgil's pastoral poetry—*Virgil: The Eclogues* (1980)—Cambridge University classicist Guy Lee (1918–2005) observes that "at all events the [translated] English line must have a certain strangeness, not to say awkwardness, about it. Poetry is often the unfamiliar, the different, the mysterious, even the slightly odd." By the same token, a twelve-syllable line, as here, not necessarily divisible into discrete four- or six-syllable phrases (or words)—i.e., into thirds or halves—stands on what may called a "metric periphery." It is the first prescription, that of difference, that guides my work; and the second, that of metric reach, that characterizes it. Otherwise, *Homer's Iliad in a Classical Translation* would have been but another *Homer's Iliad in a New Translation*, had it been at all. "The different . . . even the slightly odd" in translation is what a Homer-reflective *Kunstsprache* 'art language' rightly includes; while "on the periphery" is where artful usage—and *Kunstsprache* itself—properly resides. The idea of strangeness hearkens back to Aristotle's *Poetics* where τὸ ξενικόν (pron. *to xe-ni-kon'*) 'that which is strange' is deemed an essential incident of poetry. The path here taken thus appears more untrodden than initially imagined: the first rendering of Homer into a twelve-syllable (dodecasyllabic) line, the line itself uncommon to English epic translation and, even then, testing rhythmic expectation.

Lee further notes that "a translation of poetry is open to objection at virtually any point; it can always be criticized for not being the original"—or for being, or not, much else besides. Responding to what is "not . . . the original," critics inveigh against what is both too greatly or too little colorful—as they have done from Chapman, Pope, Dryden, and onward.

"Colorful" is, of course, to be distinguished from careless, erroneous, willfully idiosyncratic, or decidedly bad.

This translation will escape neither censure nor praise. Reflecting my vision of the need at hand, the work is, in both senses, "visionary." Alternatively, as Homer's archaism did not trouble his own or long-subsequent audiences, *this* Homer troubles today's reader to bear that in mind. Thus, a modicum of curiosity-rousing strangeness, including elevated language, the judicious use of archaisms, and sometimes inverted word order, are much what an evocative translation of epic poetry requires (both aesthetically and metrically). The need at hand further includes the translator's creating the meaning and manner of Homer "in himself, and then . . . creat[ing] an audience like himself to hear him." It is a matter of cumulative argument (think Lucretius). Indeed, the welcome rein of a fixed meter offers what Robert Bridges (Poet Laureate, 1913–1930) calls "desirable irregularities" and "opportunities for unexpected beauties." We recall in this connection the delights taken by the young Marcel in the archaizing style of his idolized Bergotte:

> I could not, it is true, lay down the novel of his which I was reading, but I fancied that I was interested in the story alone, as in the first dawn of love, when we go every day to meet a woman at some party or entertainment by the charm of which we imagine it is that we are attracted. Then I observed the rare, almost archaic phrases which he liked to employ at certain points, where a hidden flow of harmony, a prelude contained and concealed in the work itself would animate and elevate his style; and it was at such points as these, too, that he would begin to speak of the "vain dream of life," of the "inexhaustible torrent of fair forms" . . . . I now no longer had the impression of being confronted by a particular passage in one of Bergotte's works . . . but rather of the "ideal passage" of Bergotte common to every one of his books. . . . Like Swann, they would say of Bergotte: "He has a charming mind, so individual, he has a way of his own of saying things, which is a little far-fetched [*un peu cherchée*] but so pleasant."

Bergotte's style, says Proust, is instantly known; one need not consult the title page for the author's name. Are we surprised? It is reverence for the bygone, for what is lost, that signals Proust's own enterprise—a remembrance of things past (or the search for lost time). That past or loss is intimately deep—chasmic—whether psychologically, archeologically, or philologically determined. The search involves signals for which we listen and expect to hear.

The warriors of Homer's *Iliad*, with discernible origins in the courtly settings and storytelling traditions of Mycenaean palace culture (c. 1500–1200 BC), are singularly savage and fury-driven. They are narcissistic, rapacious, acquisitive, and gluttonous. They delight in slaughtering both foe and hecatomb—nominally an offering of a hundred cattle (or other beast)—and as readily promise hecatombs in furtherance of wish-fulfillment. Pray or pledge, and out shambles a beast for sacrificial slaughter (and dinner). Consider the extreme case of Achilles' heaping the pyre of Patroclus with cloven carcasses, beast and human alike (*Il.* 23.185-202).

At the same time, the *Iliad*'s warrior class possesses, and is redeemed by, a refined sense of beauty, be it of the female body or material objects in their vast array, the objects typically described in minute and appreciative detail, with an emphasis on provenance. The warriors, moreover, are often deeply sympathetic, ennobled by both loyalty to one another and an understanding of life's inevitable and brutal brevity. They thus ever strive for something greater and longer-lived than themselves. They fixate on *kleos* 'glory, fame'—*kleos aphthiton* 'imperishable glory' in the singular case of Achilles (*Il.* 9.464 [413]). I say *fixate* because their preoccupations are what ultimately render their lives *artistic*, i.e., fixed, enduring. It is for fixity of remembrance—to be fixed in memory—that the *Iliad*'s heroes strive, the battlefield the forge on which their teeming mettle is quickened, pounded, and shaped. As American poet and essayist Jones Very (1813–1880) observes, "We respect that grandeur of mind in the heroes of Homer which led them to sacrifice a mere earthly existence for the praise of all coming ages. They have not been disappointed."

The hero's need for remembrance is foil to his mortality. If, like the gods, he had eternal life, he would not need eternal remembrance (see *Il.* 12.340-346). Moreover, the *Iliad*'s heroes are prodigious *talkers*—over sixty percent of the *Iliad* consisting of directly quoted speech. They voice their passions and pains, reproaches and praises, might and misgivings, descents and ancestral deeds. They reflect "addressing their own great-hearted spirits." Never at a loss for words, they reveal their humanity and seek to grasp and vindicate the present and its transience. This, too, is mitigation of savagery. As Thomas Mann has said, "Gigantic courage is barbaric without a well-articulated ideal to guide it. Only the word makes life worthy of a human being. To be without word is not worthy of human being, is inhumane."

Homer's heroes are ξενικοί 'strange' to us for these reasons as well, however much we empathize with their ultimately mortal and immediately understandable conditions and concerns. The means by which they are dissimilar and removed yet require recognition. Indeed, the *Iliad*'s archaic language, even if not entirely understood by the *Iliad*'s original audiences, has been recognized as a common feature of the poem's distancing effect. For our purposes, dissimilarity and distance are conveyed through an English idiom "customized" to both the poem's milieu and its protagonists' manner and circumstance—an idiom here formal in diction and generally exhibiting incidents of high style. The case, in more recent literary guise, is made by poet-author Dana Gioia vis-à-vis Longfellow's *The Song of Hiawatha* (1855), where Longfellow tries to invent a medium in English (including meter) to register the irreconcilably alien cultural material he presents.

These devices remind the listener that *Hiawatha*'s mythic setting is not of this world. There are other devices, including syntax, lineation, diction, and rhetoric that give *Hiawatha* its distinctive style. So also this translation of the *Iliad*. Generally elevated diction, intermittent archaisms, and occasionally inverted word order seek to convey—by their strangeness, glancing off-centeredness, or peripherality—the distance and idiosyncrasy of Homer's Greeks, in time and manner of expression. As linguist-Homerist Geoffrey Horrocks has observed, "Archaic rules of syntax in the language of epic are due entirely to the fact that they are absolutely fundamental to the art of oral composition of dactylic verse." A similar rule should inform the language of epic in translation, if it is somehow to reflect or intimate the original. In dactylic verse, as here, it is meter that governs. The present translation, through such moderately Englished devices, seeks to convey a sense of Homeric *tone* which seeks, if you will, to make a "fit" between Homer's Greek and the English of this translation. The metrically conditioned English of this translation effects an enlargement of usage, reflecting what meter either prompts or requires.

My twelve-syllable line, an enlargement of the more customary ten-syllable pentameter, is unconventional, even as it is original to Homeric translation. To be sure, it is *centered*—between a sometimes short-ended pentameter (often epithet-omitting) and long-ended heptameter, or "fourteener"—the latter given to unwieldiness (as with Chapman, due both to line length and Chapman's own lack of restraint). Also original/inventive is my blend of metrical feet within the line—e.g., iambs (⌣ /), trochees (/ ⌣), spondees (/ /), dactyls (/ ⌣ ⌣), anapests (⌣ ⌣ /), etc.—from phrase to phrase and pause to pause, though iambs predominate (English being English). It is the phrasing itself, often enjambed, and its regulating pauses that allow or even encourage such variations within lines of a predetermined length. However original or inventive the blend, the resultant regulation is decidedly traditional; *this* at a time when there is no longer agreement concerning what, in fact, constitutes an English poetic line. Thus, Charles Stein's *Odyssey* (Berkeley, 2008), with "lines" ranging anywhere from three to twenty syllables and back again. Subsequent translations of Homer (and Virgil), while not as aggravated, show a similar disregard of form, rhythm, and sound. The variable feet of this translation assure a changeable and lively step (if you will), preventing the lockstep of metrical form as traditionally used, e.g., the nearly unbroken trochaic tetrameter of *Hiawatha* (splendid epic that it is) and the uniformity, predictable enough, of iambic pentameter no less than of regularized iambic *hex*ameter: ⌣ / ⌣ / ⌣ / ⌣ / ⌣ / ⌣ /. Variable feet within an exacting twelve-syllable "fix" acquire an aggregate uniformity. They are conceptually tantamount to a publisher's right-justified margin, creating the false but agreeable impression of uniform spacing between words, whether in a line or on the page.

Disavowing a common or quotidian Homer, I have, in Thoreauvian manner—as an expression of "men's second thoughts"—made a classical translation, endowing it with what I believe to be the finesse, elevation, and authority of the original. Such translation further bespeaks a vision and temperament nowadays begging to incur disfavor. So be it. Speaking of the creative impulse, American painter Washington Allston (1779–1834) admonished: "Trust to your own genius, listen to the voice within you, and sooner or later... she will enable you to translate her language to the world, and this it is that forms the only merit of any work of art." More colloquially put, as there is yet no definitive English translation of Homer, this *Iliad* may seek advantage among the contenders.

That the *Iliad* has never been translated into a twelve-syllable line is not necessarily the reason for my choice of meter. Rather, when I initially tried my hand at the poem's opening seven lines—for illustrative purposes in *The Lesbian Lyre*—a twelve-syllable line resulted. Satisfied with that much, I resolved to continue. Indeed, I hold it as an article of faith—reversing the poet Horace's precept concerning the story-telling start of an epic poem—that in judging epic translation one does *not* begin *in medias res* 'in the midst of things' but *ab initio* 'from the start'. An epic translation's start is the bellwether. As goes the start, so goes the rest. Thus encouraged by my rendering of lines 1–7, I was keen to sustain the endeavor. Moreover, as *The Lesbian Lyre* combatively took other epic translations to task, I determined to show how the *Iliad* might be differently or better done, though translating the entire work was far from my initial intent.

Here, then, is my opening:

> SING, Goddess, the wrath of Achilles, Peleus' son,
> The cause accursed of Achaean pains uncounted.
> Many a hero's mighty soul did it hurl down
> To Hell, the mighty themselves making meal for dogs
> And banqueting for birds. Thus Zeus' intent advanced,
> From when the two contending parted first as foes,
> Agamemnon, king of men, and dread Achilles.

The point of such translation is a matter of *decorum*—i.e., the language appropriate or *fit* to the manner of the original (see further Appendix I at www.poemoftroy.com). In sum, the language of translated archaic Greek epic is *fittingly* neither common nor colloquial—notwithstanding the practices of modern translators and their approving reviewers—any more than is the language of Homer's own Greek. No "Yo, Achilles" here. The language of Homer is stylized, lapidary, and transporting. It should thus be rendered. We further note, as especially concerns diction, that poets tend ever to "denigrate what has gone before, suggesting that poetry before theirs was not only dull and wrong but also especially artificial [in the pejorative sense] and falsely poetic. The negative epithet 'poetic diction' tends always to be applied to the poetry preceding one's own."

Wanted for the decorous translation of Homer is less dumbing down and more a sense of what appealed to both Homer's audience (c. 750 BC) and those able to appreciate his language and the language of his adapters for nearly a thousand years thereafter. I refer to the Greek poet Quintus of

Smyrna (3d or 4th century AD) (Smyrna now Izmir, Turkey), who composed an extant *Posthomerica (After Homer)* in fourteen books, starting from where the *Iliad* left off (the funeral of Hector) and continuing to the end of the Trojan War (Quintus likely intending to replace earlier accounts lost by his time). The *Posthomerica* is written in the dactylic hexameter of Homer and very much in Homer's idiom. Nothing dated or out of style about Homeric usage close to a thousand years after the Homeric heyday. Given the unparalleled artistic afterlife of Homer in Homer-imitative Greek, it befits Homeric translation to convey what aspects of Homer it may.

My translation of the *Iliad*'s opening lines differs somewhat from that offered in *The Lesbian Lyre*. This is consistent with the premise that works of art are essentially works ever in progress, even when seeming finished or perfected (Lat. *perficio/perfectum* 'accomplish/accomplished through'). A comparable situation, as we suppose, inhered in the *Iliad*'s own extensive oral development, through to its written transcription and textual codification. In a computer glitch occurring in Book 15, the present author lost some twenty-five "completed" lines, from the document itself and from all backup. They were of course redone, approximating but hardly duplicating the original. More broadly speaking, revision was the constant companion of this translation.

In a lengthy poetic translation, the process of revision, before and possibly even after publication, bespeaks the constant give and take between (1) fidelity to the original; (2) the contending dictates of one's chosen form (assuming form in the first instance); and (3) finish or finesse in translation. A translation *can*, within limits, be at once faithful and beautiful. Indeed, an excellent translation is, in its own right, an excellent poem, conveying the sense of excellence in its source or of the ancient poet's composing likewise in English today. Accordingly, the language of Greek epic translation—as I endeavor to make the language of this translation—should seek to be rich, resourceful, and entertaining, recommending its original as such.

Praising the landmark *Iliad* of Richmond Lattimore (1951), classicist and translator William Arrowsmith (1924–1992) tellingly notes that

> this is to my mind the finest translation of Homer ever made in the English language. It could be improved only by Lattimore's revision of his work, a revision which I very much hope he will have the opportunity to make. For the meantime, it is quite enough that

> we should have an Iliad which again and again gives one the feeling of the Greek on the page, which, when it reads itself, is a creation as exciting as we can hope for in translation and which allows us to have the *Iliad* as a classic in the English language.

Thus, and for as consummate as Arrowsmith deemed Lattimore's *Iliad*, he yet allowed for its imperfections, for the prospect of its revision—the endeavor ever ongoing, the give and take unceasing, the work ever in progress. We note in this connection that poet William Cowper (1731–1800) undertook—for worse more than better—a substantial "revisal" of his 1791 blank-verse translation of the *Iliad*, beginning the second edition (according to his second Preface) almost immediately after publication of the first. Similarly, the dictionally elevated and archaizing Robert Bridges published his greatest work, *The Testament of Beauty* (a poem in four books), in 1929. It was followed in 1930, the year of his death, by a second revised edition.

Arrowsmith's appraisal of Lattimore, without overt reference, reflects the thinking of the Roman author and natural philosopher Pliny the Elder (23–79 AD), who notes in the preface to his multivolume *Natural History* that he

> should like to be accepted on the lines of those founders of painting and sculpture who, as you will find in these volumes, used to inscribe their finished works, even the masterpieces which we can never be tired of admiring, with a provisional title such as *Worked on by Apelles* or *Polyclitus*, as though art was always a thing in process and not completed, so that when faced by the vagaries of criticism the artist might have left him a line of retreat to indulgence, by implying that he intended, if not interrupted, to correct any defect noted.... Not more than three, I fancy, are recorded as having an inscription denoting completion—*Made by* so-and-so.... This made the artist appear to have assumed a supreme confidence in his art, and consequently all these works were very unpopular.

Apelles was the most famous painter in antiquity; Polyclitus, a famed sculptor. The words "worked on by Apelles or Polyclitus" render Pliny's *Apelles faciebat aut Polyclitus* 'Apelles or Polyclitus was making/creating it' (*faciebat* the imperfect or past *continuous* action tense of Lat. *facere* 'to make'). Thus, the artist *was making it, was in the process of making it, was working on it*, when he deemed it finished; the imperfect tense indicating, if you will, that the work remained *imperfect*, i.e., unperfected, incapable of perfection, or necessarily incomplete, regardless the extent worked on. Works of art (in Platonic terms) thus always fall short of their fully expressive potential—unknown upon the work's commencement or putative completion—which is to say, fall short of their heavenly paradigm. They thus remain unfinished—as even the most consummate artist appreciates.

In the present work, there is an epic amount and variety requiring finish. The shorter a translation or original work, the more resistant to disfavor. Imperfections need otherwise be indulged, that the forest be not missed for the trees. In the sole masterpiece that Michelangelo ever signed—his *Pietà* (1498–1499)—we find on the sash across Mary's chest MICHAEL-A[N]GELUS BONAROUS FLOREN[TINUS] FACIEBA[T] ('Michelangelo Buonarroti, the Florentine, was making this'.) By the same token, one opines that Leonardo notoriously left so many of his works unfinished, realizing he would never bring them to perfection. Only in the rarest case, continues Pliny, does one encounter the inscription *ille fecit* 'he made it, finished it' (*fecit* the perfect or past *completed* action tense of *facere* 'to make'). This, opines Pliny, bespeaks a supreme artistic confidence in the finished (supposedly truly finished) work. Of such a kind is the meticulously described Hephaestus-wrought Shield of Achilles (*Il*. 18.534-691). Otherwise, as poet and Homer translator William Cowper colloquially insists, refusing to have his work tidied to modern tastes, "Give me a manly, rough line, with a deal of meaning in it. . . . There is a roughness on a plum, which nobody who understands fruit would rub off, though the plum would be much more polished without it."

This, for present purposes, is to say that in a roughly 2,700-year-old epic poem of 15,693 lines, composed in a *Kunstsprache*—by definition entirely artificial, yet as entirely perfect as any language might be—translation invites an entirely artistic approach and necessarily imperfect result. It is a matter of similitude, no different in its way from the cinematographic re-creation of earlier times via period costumes, re-created sets, modes of transportation, manners and manners of speaking, and all manner of appurtenance. To such *veri*similitude—to such *deception*—we time and again submit. Judiciously used archaisms and related idiosyncrasies are, in fact, verbal *costume*—*mise-en-scène*—distancing and lending credence to period and character; and, incident to character, dialogue. For Milman Parry (1902–1935), whose researches revolutionized our understanding of the oral formulaic nature of

Homeric poetry, Homer was "almost unapproachably strange and distant. Only by recognizing that distance could he be understood." For Parry, "distance and inaccessibility stood at the root of Homer's meaning."

On the other hand, when translators "contemporize" with anachronistic daring or idiosyncrasy—Logue's *Iliad*, Headley's *Beowulf*—they are deemed devilishly clever. The critics, intent on displaying their own flamboyance, parse and parade the peculiarities for all to gawk at. The difference in response reflects modernist preference: out with old, however appropriate; in with new, however outrageous. *Il faut épater le bourgeois*—today as during the birth of modernism in the early twentieth century. A 2020 review article of *The Lesbian Lyre* concludes that "Duban's insistence upon discipline, decorum, and formality in poetry is part of his philosophy of life." It would need be, as such notions are nowadays deemed quaint, regressive, or simply obsolete. But let that be. I have sought to create a work "old enough to be new"—new by virtue of its datedness. Indeed, something of what is now considered dated need be preserved, as older, yet serviceable, uses succumb to the social media juggernaut. The rule is time-honored: when something is replaced, it is all too often lost—if not recollected with scorn.

As Bertrand Russell (1872–1970) states in an essay titled "On Being Modern-minded" (1950), "We imagine ourselves at the apex of intelligence, and cannot believe that the quaint clothes and cumbrous phrases of former times can have invested [Lat. *vestis* 'clothing'] people and thoughts that are still worthy of our attention." A little humility is in any event required, given the more or less recently settled state of "modern" English vis-à-vis the millennia-old perfections and preservations of an archaic Greek *Kunstsprache*. "The desire to be contemporary," says Russell, "is of course new only in degree; it has existed to some extent in all previous periods that believed themselves to be progressive.... The modern-minded man ... has no wish ... to have emotions which are not those of some fashionable group, but only to be slightly ahead of others in point of time." Declining both the modern and modish, the fashionable or contemporary, this work draws on a larger store, judiciously harvesting diction and syntax from the historical trove of English-poetic usage. "Judicious" is the operative term, signaling a language "in the idiom and word-store of our forefathers, and their self-suggested nationality of phrase; with no more Archaism [sic] than has been time woven round Him [i.e., Shakespeare] whose language will never be archaic in English ears." By "judiciously harvesting diction" (above), I mean diction that is largely understandable to twenty-first century readers. Thus, e.g., "despite" but never "maugre"; "erstwhile" but never "whilom"; "azure," "empyrean," or "firmament" for heaven(s) but never "welkin."

So also in the description of the rebellious commoner, Thersites, "despite" appears (archaically) as a noun. Thersites was

> Disdained of the Danaans, held in their despite

(*Il.* 2.228)

I could as readily have written:

> Disdained by the Danaans who quite despised him

or

> Disdained by the Danaans, for they despised him.

The diction is virtually identical. However, I reject these formulations because the one chosen is more archaic-sounding and, thus, dictionally heightened. "Despite" (the noun) is archaic but, again, judiciously so, especially as it contributes to an alliterative pattern, while the participial balance—"Disdained . . . held"—helps order and facilitate the syntax. So, which shall it be in the matter of current versus archaizing word order: *Tender Is the Night* or *The Night Is Tender*? Sufficient Iliads "in a new translation" are readily available. This is not one of them.

This work, as earlier noted, stands as a reproach to Cancel Culture, the movement as of early 2020, gaining apace under the hashtag #DisruptTexts, tweeting its successes as they accrue. "Very proud to say we got the Odyssey removed from the curriculum this year," tweets a Lawrence High School English teacher—*this* in response to a tweet from her friend and colleague, "Be like Odysseus and embrace the long haul to liberation (and then take the Odyssey out of your curriculum because it's trash)." Lawrence High School (as *this* Boston boy has known) is one of the traditionally poorest performing schools in Massachusetts. It is thus, unsurprisingly, pleased to jettison the ballast that would steady it. In the larger picture, its actions are the trickle-down of a now decades-long curricular decline in colleges and universities, where courses of once-recognized formational value are swept aside by the outpour of identity and oppression faddism. "Who kills Homer?" indeed.

II. Homeric Language:
As Rich as English Might Aspire to Become

> It is in the power of language that Jefferson was perhaps most impressed by Homeric song. Homeric language he instinctively felt to be as rich as English might aspire to become: "it is not that I am merely an enthusiast for Paleography. I set equal value on the beautiful engraftments we have borrowed from Greece and Rome, and am equally a friend to the encouragement of a judicious neology; a language cannot be too rich."
>
> – EMILY TOWNSEND VERMEULE,
> "Jefferson and Homer"

THE INTERMITTENTLY ARCHAIC quality of this translation falls, thus far, to the strangeness of the Homeric hero, and the disparity of his world and outlook from those of succeeding ages into our own. Also key is the antiquity of the *Iliad* and its materials—its vast antiquity, its own self-cognizant antiquity and timelessness, and that of the Greek dactylic-hexametric tradition in which it resides. "Homer's age of heroes," says Roderick Beaton, "cannot be a realistic depiction of any world that actually existed. Rather, it incorporates elements drawn from many different times, that range across a span of astonishing depth from the sixteenth to the eighth centuries BCE." Homer's past has similarly been deemed a "bottomless well." As concerns the dactylic hexameter, the specialized diction and formulas embedded within it evoke "a context that is enormously larger and more echoic than the text or work itself, that brings the lifeblood of generations of poems and performances to the individual performance or text." The near clockwork regularity of the hexametric close: — ⏑ ⏑ | — — rolling forth line after endless—or theoretically endless—line, bespeaks the constancy and depth of time itself. It is thus both archaic register and unfailing rhythm that conjure the sense of Homeric alterity—the otherness of epic perception, manner, and compositional style itself. Such factors warrant a translation "old enough to be new." It is ultimately a matter of structure and aesthetic, of a translation, as in the case of Pope, "irradiated by the poetry of the past" and thus "reworking" it into a new-old language of epic poetry.

Homer, as further shown below, was archaic in his own time and appreciated as such. The same applies to Spenser's *The Fairie Queene*, glorifying Elizabeth I ("Gloriana"), whose putative ancestor, the mythologically remote King Arthur, is Spenser's perfected paradigm of the twelve moral virtues. As articulated by Shakespeare scholar Lucy Munro, with precept for the present work, the high style entails, e.g., the self-conscious incorporation into imaginative texts of linguistic or poetic styles that would have registered as outmoded or old-fashioned to the audiences or readers of the works in which they appear; a deliberately old-fashioned style as a "calculated continuity or re-evocation"; and the archaizing writer's effort "to reshape the past, to mould the present, and proleptically to conjure times yet to come . . . creat[ing] a temporal hybrid that looks forward to its own incorporation into a national and literary future." So B. R. McElderry, again as applied to the present work: Spenser's English is "largely the English of his day, enriched from legitimate sources and by legitimate methods. His vocabulary is largely the vocabulary of his contemporaries. His archaic and dialect forms belong to no specific age or section. They color but do not obscure the diction, and many unusual forms appear but once." And so Coleridge—punning, perhaps, on the extent of Spenser's poetic license—calling Spenser "licentiously careless . . . in the orthography of words, varying the final words as the rhyme requires." But no matter. Coleridge and all posterity affirm Spenser, Coleridge adverting to "the indescribable sweetness and fluent projection of his verse, very clearly distinguishable from the deeper and more interwoven harmonies of Shakespeare and Milton."

Archaism and a well-researched antiquarianism pervade Scott's *Ivanhoe* (1819) (the Robin Hood legend), as antique diction sets the tone for Tennyson's *Idylls of the Kings* (1859) (the Arthurian legend, as with Spenser). Medievalism—its chivalry, knight errantry, courtliness, spiritual quests, and magnanimity—has its conceits and expectations: the contemporary or colloquial are not among them. The same may be said of English poet Ernest Dowson's one-act fantasy, *The Pierrot of the Moment* (1897). How else capture, but by archaism and poetic diction, the exquisite disquisition on love between Lady Moonbeam and a stock character of *commedia dell'arte*? The work is in winsome rhymed pentameters, out-Shakespearing the *Dream*—art language through and through. On these and other grounds the present translation is itself a latter-day *Kunstsprache* 'art language' consonant with the language that was Homer's, which I have elsewhere described as "an artificial idiom constructed out of archaic, dialectal, and invented forms, used both for their metrical utility and to give the effect of distancing the poetic language from everyday speech." Spenser, Shakespeare, and Milton are *Kunstsprachen* (pl.). Monumental poetry (and often prose) in any language is a *Kunstsprache*, the art of its language being what makes poetry monumental. Nor is art language an attribute of epic poetry alone. In sum, the Homer of this translation is *fixed* or *set* in the idiom of no particular time. It is thus a work for any time, even as the confection that is Homer makes him "a poet for all ages." If, as Pound submits, "a civilization was founded on Homer," the least a translation can do for Homer is afford him a modicum of aplomb.

Though Greek dialect forms or their likeness defies imitation, and my invented forms (or coinages) are few, metrical utility, as in Homer, dominates. As early recognized, "In verse the thought is wedded to a certain cadence, rhythm, meter, perhaps even rhyme. The metrical system used is actively determinant of the course of thought." And further, "translation is inseparable from measure. In translation from one language to another, a measure must govern the transference that occurs across the interval separating the languages. It is in reference to this measure that a translation can be judged good or bad or even not a translation at all." And finally, the great biographer and arbiter of poets and poetry, Johnson: "To write verse is to dispose syllables and sounds harmonically by some known and settled rule—a rule however lax enough to substitute similitude for identity, to admit change without breach of order, and to relieve the ear without disappointing it." This is further to signal that the present translation is not "like any cultural artifact . . . inevitably and specifically located in [its] own contemporary context"; is not "the product of the age into which [it is] born"; and cares not for the "demands of a contemporary audience." Its concern is not the contemporary concern of "updating," but the opposite—the reasonable extent and desirability of purposeful stylization.

Indeed, the literary translator discards "unnecessary considerations of an identifiable 'target' audience whose needs the translated text is hypothetically designed to meet." Moreover, "because no poet is ever 'a man speaking to men' [Wordsworth], nor any poem nothing more than a 'voice' articulating a 'meaning', so likewise is it impossible to justify a translated poem appealing to the 'reader' for its currency, its validation, or its continuing life." Finally, "there are translations . . . which 'do not so much serve the work as owe their existence to it'"—which I take to mean that certain translations (few, to be sure) seek to meet not the expectations of person or period but the translator's own, given his own disposition and particular sense of the author and his style. This is especially true amid the ongoing artistic debasement early encouraged by twentieth-century modernism. To tailor the adage, one must be true to oneself, even if born to the wrong century.

Reverting from the current and past centuries to those of Greek epic development, it cannot be my purpose to remake or even rehearse the arguments for the divers and thoroughgoing antiquity, and levels of antiquity, of Homer—dating to 3,500 years ago, at the earliest. This has been cumulatively established from the early nineteenth century to date by comparative literary/linguistic, archeological/historical, artistic, and oral-compositional analyses—to say nothing of once customarily intuitive or concordance-aided endeavors. The convergence of such approaches is compelling, whatever the residual issues. The inquiry has exponentially advanced with the aid of computer and algorithmic analyses, by which any element of Homeric composition—formulaic usage and its variants; alternate case endings in line-specific positions; types and lengths of enjambment—may be statistically determined. The findings in their graphed or variously schematized layouts are dizzying. My purpose, then, is to offer salient indications of Homeric antiquity, most derived from the *Iliad* and *Odyssey* themselves, whereby to account for my own "antique" manner. While likely known to the specialist, such points will be welcome to the newcomer, for whom this introduction to an "oldly" translated *Iliad* is largely intended.

Antiquity here keeps company with prominence, perpetuation. We recall that Troy, controlling access to the Hellespont and beyond (see map), was a strategic commercial center and military stronghold—the Hellespont forming part of the continental boundary between Europe and Asia Minor (modern-day Turkey), and later forming the de facto divide between the two. Troy was the greatest and most fabled city of antiquity, a magnet for conquest, the contest for its taking inevitable. Herodotus, at the outset of his *Histories* (5th century BC), views the Trojan War as the official cause of enmity between Asia and Europe, East and West. Indeed, the Trojan War, in its ten-year duration, multitude of combatants, divine machinery, and associated legends, is antiquity's world-cataclysmic event, involving the clash of wealth-fabled civilizations—Mycenae/Europe/the West; Troy/Asia/the East—and of divine, semidivine, and superhuman protagonists of times long past. The Trojan War is also a quasi-historical event in classical Greek thought, the focal point of its mythology and ever the referential and imaginative source of Western literary thought. To the extent the *Iliad* has ever been viewed as a life's guide to valor, self-sacrifice, enmity, reconciliation, compassion, and religious devotion, it is catechism and cataclysm both. In having Agamemnon, King of Mycenae, lead the gathered hosts of Greece in a united cause, Homer "established the foundation of Hellenic nationality; in short, he invented Greece"—even as Greece through Roman assimilation shaped Europe and inspired Western civilization (Greek-permeated Latin the language of Europe for a thousand years). Accordingly, the modern, modernist, colloquial, or bloodlessly monosyllabic translation of Homer—a certain "just nowness"—little serves.

Homer, by *our* reckoning, is an archaic Greek poet (his *floruit* c. 750 BC). His subject matter, the Trojan War (mid-13th century BC), was to Homer himself remote—the "days of yore," as it were (as was medieval knighthood to Spenser). Indeed, and by degree, much of the material in the intervening five centuries of oral epic development was also remote: the stories, their characters, and the ever-changing language in which they were conveyed. The closer to Homer's own time, doubtless the less archaic; though archaic elements, long layered in, would survive for metrical, stylistic, or other reasons. But it is not solely the Trojan War and its mythologically imputed cause— the abduction of Helen—that are at play. An earlier Homeric consciousness, reflected in courtly comportment and aesthetic sensibility, may be traced to the Mycenaean Age of Greece (16th–13th centuries BC), also known as the Late Bronze Age. It was during this period that Mycenae (see map), a military stronghold in southern Greece and then-regional center of Greek civilization, held sway—as far south as Crete and westward to parts of Asia Minor.

The back-reaching antiquity of Homer includes principal and ancillary stories and characters (often recounted in "epic digressions"); the detailed descriptions of physical objects unknown to Homer's (or later) time; set or "formulaic" descriptions of activities or procedures recurring from time immemorial; and especially the conduct and accoutrements of war (so much of the poem describing combat). These are variously mirrored in the diction and syntax of Homer's Greek—conditioned, in turn, by epic meter en route to the perfections of Homeric poetry as eventually codified. As Richard Janko explains:

> Since the oral tradition admitted change and new creation to supplement what was lost as it was handed down through the generations, the amount of archaism having its origin at any specific date will fall as innovations increase—innovations that will in their turn eventually become archaisms if the tradition persists. The rate of innovations might be altered by factors such as dialect or methods of training bards, but short of memorisation some would be inevitable.

There is, in sum, a constant, though never total, changing of the archaic guard throughout the process of epic generation—throughout any bard's *faciebat* to the epic tradition's *fecit*. Archaisms, adopted or displaced during centuries of oral recitational development, are a function of dialect or related factors such as word formation or morphology. Thus, the more *serviceable* an archaism to meter, formulaic expression, or other poetic consideration, the more likely to keep its place, to be layered in or embedded, however old.

As renowned archaeologist Emily Vermeule has noted, with precept for the present effort:

> Each poet learned the traditional phrases of singers before him, often extremely archaic, for it is one function of epic to maintain and transmit an archaic heritage for the next generation. . . . The multiple voices that sound to us out of an epic like the *Iliad* bring a huge vocabulary, layers of new language piled on old language, former dialects and modern dialects, and the sense of many trained and probing minds. . . .

While we are accustomed to crediting Homer with Achilles as the story's overwrought protagonist and consider this the developmental acme of an earlier more basic tale, we do not imagine the *Iliad*'s ancillary detail—including its ample digressions and *their* ancillary detail—spun of whole or recent cloth. These include the heroic reminiscences of the *Iliad*'s own heroes. They also include the lovingly profuse descriptions of both utilitarian and precious objects, whether of human or divine craftsmanship—these the ancestral pride (and sources of authority) of their epic-heroic possessors.

Thus, even as the *Iliad* describes a time far preceding that of Homer and his audience, the poem's characters delight in recollecting times earlier yet, the specifics allusive and elusive both. The past, itself the predicate for storytelling, has a past or past-perfect, or pluperfect, of its own. It is in this sense that the *Iliad* is "soaked in retrospect," showing no clear division between present and past, but a recurring notion of the concurrency of time. As one scholar notes: "elements of the so-called heroic past were juxtaposed with elements of the contemporary world or even recreated in the present. In this manner, the elite created a 'supra-quotidian' world and a timeless order that transcended the differences between past and present." To take a prominent example, Agamemnon—imaginatively quoting Zeus and Hera in a rare instance of retrojective speech within a speech—conjures matter of epic-present importance. Agamemnon thus makes his case: Zeus, ruler of men and gods, was himself once deluded by *Atē* 'Madness' upon the births of Eurystheus and Heracles—the former birth hastened, the latter delayed. This serves as paradigm for what Agamemnon, ruler of men, claims was his own *Atē* in dishonoring Achilles (*Il.* 19.105-152). Heracles, the son of Zeus and Alcmene, is here described as one of Zeus' own generation, bringing the timeless past into the epic-present; Heracles, the mightiest of the first generation of heroes and exemplum for Achilles himself. Reference to Heracles occurs throughout the *Iliad*, thus his paradigmatic and ultimately Troy-related feats. These include an earlier sack of Troy with a band of six vessels after Laomedon, Priam's predecessor, cheats Heracles of wages (Poseidon earlier cheated). A latter-day Heracles, Achilles strives (by other means) for the *kleos* 'glory' of Heracles, i.e., for Hera's *kleos* = Heracles.

Homer and his characters, including the gods, further delight in describing physical objects of great antiquity (or recent manufacture, as the case may be), e.g., Achilles' description of the tree-cut sceptre (*Il.* 1.239-245); Homer's description of the Hephaestus-made sceptre passed through generations of gods and men to Agamemnon (*Il.* 2.103-113) (discussed below); Nestor's antique "Dove Cup" (*Il.* 11.696-711) (discussed below); and, in a category of its own, the ekphrastic Shield of Achilles (*Il.* 18.522-702), newly made by Hephaestus. By the same token, Homer's characters revel in tracing ancestry itself. Even while boasting valor and self-worth in the midst of combat, they engage in detailed genealogical accounts of heroic ancestors and former comrades-in-arms (e.g., *Il.* 6.130-234, 20.224-267). Nor is combat the sole—and realistically unlikely—occasion for recollection. War councils, with their meal settings and exhortations, also serve. The audiences closest to Homer doubtless greeted these accounts, or digressions, with varying degrees of familiarity, while we—and the centuries preceding ours—have encountered them with a certain bewilderment. Make what we may of them—with the help of scholarly notation—they create a deep and florid mytho-historical mise-en-scène.

Nestor, oldest and most garrulous of the Greeks at Troy, is a multi-generational warrior: "Already had / He seen two mortal generations come and gone, / Earl'er flourished and prosp'rous in sandy Pylos. / Amid the third he ruled . . ." (*Il.* 1.256-259). During his extensive lifetime, Nestor associated and fought with an earlier-storied generation of heroes—including Theseus, mythical king and co-founder of Athens; and Theseus' companion Perithous (*Il.* 1.270), king of the legendary Lapiths, whose son Polypoetēs leads a contingent to Troy (*Il.* 2.777-784). Nestor's ramblings, whatever their deeper relevance to the immediate story, reinforce the sense of both Nestor's old age and the deep and eventful antiquity of his experience. Not least, they invest a crusty long-winded but advice-esteemed warrior with entertainment value for the epic audience. Nestor at times recounts his "days of yore" in mind-numbing detail (e.g., *Il.* 11.744-919). Otherwise, he comes across as a long-winded and officious Polonius (*Il.* 23.342-388). We thus have Nestor— himself an "archaic relic," if you will—relating matter archaic to his Iliadic comrades, doubly archaic to Homer's audience, and by multiples more archaic to listeners since. In other cases, a days-of-yore digression is of immediate relevance to the story, as in Phoenix's lengthy parable of Meleager and the Calydonian Boar Hunt, providing a paradigm for Achilles' renouncing his rage and returning to battle (*Il.* 9.589-679).

Epic also has proximate means for conjuring a past more legendary and revered than its own present. Thus, the emphasis on heightened strength—as when a fighter wields a stone that no two men "nowadays" (i.e., in Homer's own time) might lift:

> And Hector grasped and uplifted a stone, lying
> Before the gate, thick at the base, but deadly sharp;
> Not readily might any twain, the best about,
> Have hefted it, a wagon's load, from off the ground,
> As nowadays men are, but blithely he handled
> It, quite alone; and crooked-counseling Cronus'
> Son disburdened it.
>
> (*Il.* 12.475-481, also 20.314-317; cf. 21.449-453)

Such is Homer's recollection of the *Iliad*'s heroes and their aggregate past—the more remote, the worthier. The epic past thus self-referentially unfolds: the performance-present audience admiring remote epic heroes, themselves admiring heroes remoter yet, along an ever retrojected and ultimately mythological continuum, the lines blurred between epic poetry, history, mythology, and evanescent fairy-tale elements.

It is through Agamemnon's capital city, Mycenae "rich in gold," that deep time in the *Iliad* is most apparent (see *Il.* 7.209, 9.49-50, 11.47-48). As the seat of royal power, Agamemnon's Mycenae serves as metonym for all Greece (*Il.* 12.75-76). Owing to its fabled supremacy, "Mycenae" came to designate the age in which it prospered—the Mycenaean Age being a late Bronze Age civilization that flourished in Greece between 1600 and 1200 BC. The period includes the generally accepted date of the Trojan War itself, c. 1250 BC. Mycenaean civilization was the first distinctively Greek civilization, with what excavations and archeological remains show were palaces exhibiting elements of "life at court" and high artistic achievement. The *Iliad* itself suggests that king and palace, like medieval lord and manor, parceled lands on a feudal model (e.g., *Il.* 6.212-217, 9.323-332.). Mycenaean civilization also had a writing system called Linear B, used largely for administrative or record-keeping purposes. In seeking to take Troy, Mycenae sought to take its Asian counterpart.

It was Heinrich Schliemann who, in 1876, having already identified and excavated the site of Troy, turned to Mycenae. There he unearthed dozens of treasure-laden grave shafts in and around the citadel (which he identified as the burial sites of Agamemnon and his followers). Discoveries included, among much else, skeletons, swords, daggers, arrowheads, vases, boar-tusk helmet remains, metal vessels (gold, silver, and bronze), and enumerated objects of jewelry. Most famously discovered was an electrum-made death mask which came to be known as the Death Mask of Agamemnon (displayed at the National Archaeological Museum of Athens).

Linear B has been preserved on thousands of unearthed clay tablets and tablet fragments discovered not only in Mycenae but elsewhere in the Peloponnese, including palace excavations at Pylos (home of the *Iliad*'s Nestor) and in the vicinity of Sparta (home of Menelaus and Helen); also north of the Peloponnese in Thebes (home to the myths of Cadmus, Oedipus, Dionysus, and Heracles); and on the Island of Crete at the royal palace at Knossos. Knossos was the center of the yet earlier Minoan Civilization, 3000–1450 BC, named after Minos, mythical King of Crete; Crete home to the myth of the Minotaur ("Minos' bull"), the Labyrinth, Theseus, and Ariadne.

The *Gilgamesh* epic attests to the vast antiquity not only of Homeric themes but also of Homeric style. We thus learn that Standard Babylonian is "a literary version of Akkadian . . . used to write poetry and royal inscriptions; it has a free word order, and archaizing grammar, and rarefied vocabulary." Poetic license and specialized diction, including archaisms, were thus innate to *Gilgamesh*, often called "the first poem." Free word order and poetic diction, including archaisms, are also apparent in Homer, as noted— the emphasis we here give it fully apparent in a yet older, Mesopotamian source: "Even for the Babylonians, Gilgamesh was a figure of great antiquity . . . liv[ing] around 7800 BC . . . show[ing] that even four thousand years ago, Gilgamesh was thought to have lived four thousand years before that. . . . Gilgamesh himself travels further back in time, to meet what was even for him a figure of great antiquity: Uta-napishti, etc." Accordingly, it is art-language embellishment which, from the millennia-old commencement of literature itself, conveys and reinforces a sense of remote, remoter, and remotest time. What do we possibly garner of a time-immemorial style— Mesopotamian or Greek—in a contemporary, colloquial, or simplified translation idiom?

As further evidence of Homer's archaeological antiquity, we look to the heirloom Dove Cup of old Nestor—an item far predating the *Iliad*'s own time—brought to the dinner table set by Hecamēdē (pron. *Heh-ka-mee'-dee*). She is Nestor's serving woman, likely enough his concubine despite his advanced age:

> First she set for them a smoothly burnished table,
> Crafted with cobalt feet, and thereon a brazen
> Basket set, with an onion to flavor the drink
> And pale honey and cakes of sacred barley meal,
> And aside them stationed a comely cup, studded
> With rivets of gold, from home by the elder brought.
> Four were its handles, twin the doves feeding at each,
> While from under, and twin to the handles upraised,
> Ran buttressing. Scarce might another man avail

> To lift from off the counter the cup fully brimmed;
> But easily would Nestor the elder lift it.
>
> <div align="right">(<i>Il.</i> 11.696-706)</div>

This chronologically distant importation—no mere table utensil—immediately finds epic context through humorous variation on the "which-no-two-men-today" trope, distancing and exalting Iliadic warriors over the men of Homer's own time (see *Il.* 12.475-481, 20.314-317). The cup is further humorous in being so heavy an object, the likes of which Nestor and other Greeks brought from home for merely ceremonial or recreational use. If Hecamede had no trouble bringing it to the table, it was doubtless empty when she did, though we have no description of Nestor's actually "fully brim[ming]" the cup before lifting it. As epic "older" typically signifies bigger and stronger, Nestor, the oldest Greek at Troy, may be credited with "residual strength" in Iliadic old age, comparable to the strength of "age-appropriate" fighters at Troy—despite his protestations of age-related failings. The same would validate Hecamede's status as concubine rather than serving woman. By its description, moreover, the cup presents as an unusual un-Hellenic *objet d'art*—un-Hellenic and pre-Hellenic both—subject to archaeological placement in the sixteenth century BC.

Another notably prized or pedigreed object—many could be adduced, including the Shield of Achilles (*Il.* 18.534-702 [468-617])—is the sceptre of Agamemnon, symbol of his Zeus-sanctioned kingship; this, unlike Nestor's cup, reflecting no archeological find, but antique literary imagination:

> Among them arose wide-ruling Agamemnon,
> Grasping the sceptre the smithy lord had labored
> Making. And on Zeus, lord Cronión, Hephaestus
> Conferred it; and Zeus on his messenger, Hermes,
> Slayer of Argos, bestowed it; the which Hermes
> To lord Pelops presented, whipper of horses;
> And from Pelops to Atreus, the people's shepherd,
> It passed, entrusted thereafter to Thyestēs,
> Flocked with lambs; he to Agamemnon leaving it
> To raise o'er many ships and rule the Argives all.
>
> (*Il.* 2.103-112)

Kings, relates Hesiod, are from Zeus, ruling as Zeus' temporal counterpart on earth and assuring its stability (as Zeus assures stability on Olympus). The provenance of Agamemnon's sceptre is reckoned, in both immortal and mortal generations, from the time of its divine manufacture, which is to say from time immemorial. The *Iliad*'s chronology thus reckoned becomes the less exact—the more nebulous—the closer it approaches to divinity (to which time is meaningless). The duration of sceptre possession, with its successive ownerships, can be only relatively imagined. By such devices, the *Iliad* can be as early, old, or archaic as one likes.

Antiquity, remote antiquity, and primordial antiquity are thus writ large over archaic Greek epic, over the Greek epic tradition—its subject matter, reference points, and style. All of it, with the Muses' cataloging and other resources, recollectable and immediately transmittable; the catalogs an exhaustive table of contents, reference resource, or "search engine." The timelessness of such matter need somehow be reflected in epic translation of any age—now, a hundred years ago, or hence—even as it was reflected and remains enshrined in the epochal translation known as the King James Bible/Version (KJB), aka the Authorized Version (1611). As Matthew Arnold urges, "the Bible is undoubtedly the grand mine of diction for the translator of Homer; and, if he knows how to discriminate truly between what will suit him and what will not, the Bible may afford him also invaluable lessons of style."

Time and space do not allow for discussion of the KJB (1611) as a model for Homeric translation (1611 also marking the first complete translation of the *Iliad* into English by George Chapman). I have, in any event, elsewhere engaged with the topic. Suffice it for now that the Old Testament, both because of its acknowledged sacrosanctity and translators' knowledge of Hebrew, escaped the trespass too often inflicted on Homer by those misguidedly seeking to do him service (their Greek or imaginations sparse). Not that scripture was ultimately spared the like fate in "contemporary" or otherwise simplified post-KJB editions.

Though our concern is the poetic, not prose, translation of Homer, the Victorian prose *Iliad* by Andrew Lang (Books X–XVI), Walter Leaf (Books I–IX), and Ernest Myers (Books XVII–XXIV) (1882) merits comment. The work was conscientiously modeled on the then-familiar diction of the KJB, and frequently disparaged on that account. And yet—surprisingly or not—its assessment a century since has proven more enthusiastic: the work "looks here not like pious embalming but an unusually well-defined stylistic experiment, executed with resource and conviction and capable of delivering the intended effect: 'So they fought like unto burning fire.'" The internally quoted locution, and others like it, can be found in my own translation which, borrowing a page from Arnold, is a variously Hebraicized Homer—this time poetic rather than prose, and as indifferent to time period or age as the *Iliad* itself.

More recently, classicist Mark Edwards (1929–2016) has noted that Homeric language is "dignified, distinct from normal speech, archaic, and very rich in vocabulary, producing something like the effect on us of the familiar archaism of the [KJB] and the enormous vocabulary and metrical form of Shakespeare's plays." What Edwards calls "the familiar archaism" of the KJB connotes a pervasive approach, whereas this translation conveys an "intermittently archaic quality" among other decorum or metrically dictated usages. If Edwards' assessment be accepted, a twenty-first–century Homer in a strictly metered English verse translation should produce effects comparable to those of the KJB and Shakespeare, fulfilling Vermeule's desideratum that Homer in translation be "as rich as English might aspire to become." And why should it not, as the Greek *Iliad*, the Hebrew Bible, the KJB, and this very translation are all *Kunstsprachen* 'art languages'?

III. Dactylic Hexameter:
The Meter of Homer and Classical Epic (in Brief)

> Meter is an ancient, indeed primitive, technique that marks the beginning of literature in virtually every culture. It dates back to a time, so different from our specialized modern era, when there was little, if any, distinction among poetry, religion, history, music, and magic. All were performed in a sacred, ritual language separated from everyday speech by its incantatory metrical form. Meter is also essentially a preliterate technology, a way of making language memorable before the invention of writing.
>
> – DANA GIOIA, "Notes on the New Formalism"

> A metrical form of unsurpassed flexibility and beauty, the heroic hexameter had been wrought out . . .
>
> – JOHN W. MACKAIL, "How Homer Came into Hellas"

FOR THE *ILIAD* AND THE *ODYSSEY* to have developed orally and been performed extemporaneously by the thousands of lines, a performance-facilitating language and meter were needed. The poems in their present form could not have been recited in full by a single bard, in one or consecutive sessions; more likely was their presentation in festival settings, over several days, by teams or relays of singers. The meter was dactylic hexameter, also known as epic, heroic, or Homeric meter. Over the course of its unattested oral development, Homeric meter provided the formulaic yet highly fluid locutions resulting in the *Iliad* and *Odyssey* as we have come to know them.

Greek dactylic hexameter—and Latin hexameter, as adapted—run as follows:

$$\begin{array}{cccccc} 1 & 2 & 3 & 4 & 5 & 6 \\ — & — & — & — & (—) & (\smile) \\ \end{array}$$
$$— \smile \smile \mid — \smile \smile \mid — \smile \smile \mid — \smile \smile \mid — \smile \smile \mid — —$$

NOTE: A dash indicates a long syllable; $\smile$, a short. A dash above two shorts indicates the possible replacement of two shorts by a long. A dash in parentheses above two shorts signifies that replacement is rare. A ⌣ atop a dash represents a variable syllable (long or short). Vertical lines mark poetic feet. In what follows, the need to place long and short marks directly above vowels or diphthongs can create the appearance of uneven spacing.

The meter is dactylic because it consists of six "finger-shaped" units (Gr. *daktulos* 'finger'), the basic unit, or foot, being one long and two short syllables. It is "hexameter" because there are *hex* 'six' feet to the metrical line. Lines typically exhibit a pause, or caesura (Lat. *caesum* 'cut'), often at word end *within* a foot, which strategically both pauses and varies the rhythm. Here is the first line of Virgil's *Aeneid*, known to many, and the first line of the *Iliad* (transliterated):

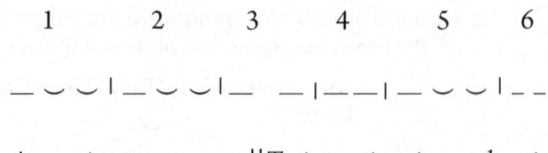

$$\underset{1}{-\smile\smile} | \underset{2}{-\smile\smile} | \underset{3}{-\ |\ -} | \underset{4}{-\ -} | \underset{5}{-\smile\smile} | \underset{6}{-\ -}$$

Arma vir umque cano ||*Troi ae qui primus ab oris*

Arms and the man I sing, who first from shores of Troy

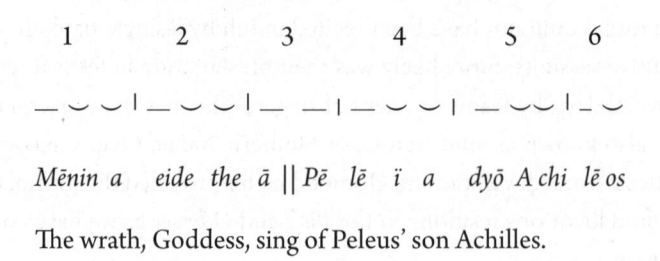

$$\underset{1}{-\smile\smile} | \underset{2}{-\smile\smile} | \underset{3}{-\ |\ -} | \underset{4}{-\smile\smile} | \underset{5}{-\smile\smile} | \underset{6}{-\ \smile}$$

Mēnin a eide the ā || *Pē lē ï a dyō A chi lē os*

The wrath, Goddess, sing of Peleus' son Achilles.

The two are identical but for the substitution by Virgil in the fourth foot of a final long "—" for two shorts. A long syllable may replace any two shorts, as a matter of metrical equivalence. The resultant foot, a "spondee," may occur anywhere but in the fifth foot (with occasional exceptions). The final foot is always disyllabic, with a variably long or short final syllable. Thus, the last syllable of *Aen.* 1.1 is long (-*is*); that of *Il.* 1.1, short (-*os*). The line-ending rhythm is thus invariably: — ⌣ ⌣ | — —, adding a determined finality throughout. However passing and uncertain life itself, however suddenly unsparing the battlefield, the hexameter contains, regularizes, and carries all forward within a set rhythmic design. At the same time, the invariable two-foot hexametric close has been deemed the ancient equivalent of rhyme.

Depending on the number of substitutions of two shorts by a long, a dactylic line contains anywhere from twelve to seventeen syllables; although in practice, thirteen to seventeen, as fully spondaic lines are rare (only five—and all in the *Odyssey*—one of them repeated). For this reason, rhyming "fourteeners" have sometimes been thought the appropriate meter for translating classical epic into English: by Arthur Golding in his highly influential *Metamorphoses* (1567), read by Spenser and Shakespeare; by George Chapman in the first complete translation of the *Iliad* (1611); by William Morris, *Aeneid* (1875); and more recently by A. E. Stallings, *De Rerum Natura (The Nature of Things)* (2007). The operative term, however, is sometimes, as fourteeners have no monopoly.

Dactylic hexameter, to result in an Iliad or Odyssey, would need be highly flexible: the result of (1) protracted development allowing the substitution at will of two shorts by a long; and (2) flexible rules for determining short- and long-vowel lengths in the first instance. A syllable is thus long/weighted either "by nature," containing a naturally long vowel or diphthong, or "by position," containing a short vowel followed by two consonants in the same or adjoining words. A syllable with a short vowel followed by two consonants—one or both of them a "liquid" (*l, m, n, r*) in the same or adjoining words—is either long/weighted or short/light, depending on need. Thus, a short-vowel syllable, though naturally light, acquires metrical quantity or weight when followed by two consonants. A word-final diphthong (otherwise long) scans short (or may be dropped/elided) when the next word begins with a vowel. Conversely, a mid-word diphthong (or long vowel), expectedly weighted for metrical purposes, is not necessarily stressed outside of verse (as the imperative *sing!*—*Il*.1.1: *aeíde*; prose *áeide*). In such a case, metrical quantity supersedes the natural, i.e., assumedly spoken, stress. The interplay between natural stress and metrical weight is essential to ancient Greek (and Latin) poetry. It is this, in significant part, that makes the poetry *poetry*. We mention in passing that natural or spoken stress was likely more a matter of variable vocal pitch or intonation than of emphasis as such.

The interplay between spoken stress and metrical quantity is key, because if metrical weight excessively coincided with spoken stress, the rhythm would be predictably prosaic. This is the danger inherent in English and other poetry based on spoken stress (typically iambic ⌣ /), barring such bravura or finesse of poetic incident as may be brought to bear. Such incidents may include stately diction, including alliteration and assonance; figures of speech and syntax; resourceful imagery; and flexible word order (a challenge in English)—the match of any expressive need. A case in point is Swinburne's *Tristram of Lyonesse* (1882), an epic of 4,488 lines in highly enjambed (and thus flowing) rhymed pentameters, its white heat radiant from within. The poet considered it his best work. So also Keats' *Endymion*. For the lush effectiveness of classicizing diction, imagery, and word order in a twelve-syllable line, one may consider Poet Laureate Robert Bridges (1844–1930):

> ... As when a high moon thru' the rifted wrack
> gleameth upon the random of the windswept night;
> or a sunbeam softly, on early worshippers
> at some rich shrine kneeling, stealth thru' the eastern apse
> and on the unclouded incense and the fresco'd walls
> mantleth the hush of prayer with a vaster silence,
> laden as 'twer with the unheard music of the spheres....
>
> (*The Testament of Beauty*, II.166-172).

Dactylic hexameter encouraged the ready memorization and/or impromptu creation of metrical phrases or units. It was thus that oral composition proceeded, rather than word by word. The singer could think ahead, facilitating performance. A developed example appears in *kleos* 'glory, fame' formulations:

⌣ ⌣ | _ _ ⌣ ⌣ | _ _

κλέος ἄφθιτον ἔσται
kleos *aphthiton estai*
to be imperishable glory

*

⏑ ⏑ | _ _ ⏑ ⏑ | _ ⏑

κλέος ἐσθλὸν ἄροιτο
***kleos** esthlon aroito*
He would gain fine glory.

*

_ _ ⏑ ⏑ | _ ⏑ ⏑ | _ ⏑ ⏑ | _ _

σευ **κλέος** οὐρανὸν εὐρὺν ἱκάνει
*seu **kleos** ouranon eurun (h)ikanei*
Your glory reaches broad heaven.

Somewhat more familiar, perhaps, are such metrical phrases, or formulas, as: "Rosy-fingered Dawn":

⏑ ⏑ | _ _ ⏑ ⏑ | _ _

ῥοδοδάκτυλος Ἠώς
(h)rododactulos Ēōs [nom.]

The "wine-dark" (lit. "wine-faced") sea:

_ ⏑ ⏑ | _ ⏑

οἴνοπα πόντον
oinopa ponton [acc.]

"Earth-encircling" and/or "earth-shaking Poseidon":

_ | _ ⏑ ⏑ | _ ⏑ ⏑ | _ ⏑

γαιήοχος ἐννοσίγαιος
***gai**ēochos ennosi**gaio**s* [nom.] (*gai-* 'earth')

*

⏑ | _ _ | _ _ | _ ⏑ ⏑ | _ ⏑ ⏑ | _ ⏑

Ποσειδάων γαιήοχος ἐννοσίγαιος
Poseidaōn gaiēochos ennosigaios [nom.]

The metrical rhythm for the famed "swift-footed Achilles" is:

⏑ ⏑ | — ⏑ ⏑ | — —
πόδας ὠκὺς Ἀχιλλεύς

The formulas, occupying any number of metrical feet (or partial feet) could be relied on, without forethought, to fill that much of a line. Though some formulas have fixed positions ("swift-footed Achilles" always at line end), others, with or without variation, might be variously placed. Formulaic flexibility is here yet apparent in the variant "swift-footed Iris":

⏑ ⏑ | — ⏑ ⏑ | — ⏑
πόδας ὠκέα Ἶρις

Compare (above):

⏑ ⏑ | — ⏑ ⏑ | — —
πόδας ὠκὺς Ἀχιλλεύς

Here the adjective, in its trisyllabic feminine form ὠ-κέ-α 'swift' modifies the disyllabic Ἶ-ρις 'Iris', whereas the disyllabic masculine ὠ-κὺς 'swift' modifies the trisyllabic Ἀ-χιλ-λεύς 'Achilles'. Then there is "king of men, Agamemnon."

⏑ | — — | — ⏑ ⏑ | — —
ἄναξ ἀνδρῶν Ἀγάμεμνον
(ϝ)anax andrōn Agamemnōn

[The digamma in (ϝ)anax, di(ϝ)os, and numerous other words, with sound approximating the letter w, was (re)discovered by famed British classicist Richard Bentley (1662–1742). Bentley intuited its presence where needed because its absence left the meter defective (an issue glossed by Homer's transcribers over the centuries). **Residual digamma is but one of a number of features attesting to Homer's extreme antiquity.** The letter v or w continues, these millennia later, to reflect the digamma: Gr. di(ϝ)os, Lat. divus 'divine'; Gr. (ϝ)oinos, Lat. vinum 'wine'.]

The formula, occupying three and one-third metrical feet, could be relied on for mention of Agamemnon in the appropriate metrical position. Note that initial *alpha* in *andrōn* and medial *epsilon* in *Agamemnōn* are both naturally short vowels scanned long because followed by double consonants in each instance. Nor is Agamemnon exclusively "king of men, Agamemnon." An alternative formula of comparable metrical length, beginning with a long syllable, makes him "wide-ruling Agamemnon":

$$-\,|\,-\ -\,|\,-\ \ \smile\smile\,|\,-\,-$$
εὐρὺ κρείων Ἀγαμέμνων

Such are the simplest formulaic variations, consisting of noun or proper noun plus stock modifier or epithet (Gr. *epi* 'upon' + root *the-* 'put, place'). This is in no way to understate the intricacy of formulaic usage overall, the ultimate result of which are the *Iliad* and *Odyssey* entire. With certain phrasings and recurrent descriptions largely predetermined—be they two or three words, an entire line, or group of lines—the poet could think ahead, focusing on elaboration, variation, and nuance.

In a category of their own, being a staple of Homeric diction, are formulaic variations consisting of proper name and patronymic (or patronymic alone in lieu of proper name). In Homer's Greek, name-forms ending primarily in disyllabic *-idēs* are patronymics, i.e., offspring designated by the father's name (Gr. *patēr* 'father' + *onuma* 'name'). Thus, *Cronidēs* 'son of Cronus' is Zeus, also referred to (circumventing the patronymic) as *kronou (h)uios* 'of Cronus the son' or 'son of Cronus'. The patronymic *Atreïdēs* 'son of Atreus' designates Agamemnon (sometimes his brother, Menelaus); *Atreïdai* (pl.) 'sons of Atreus' designates Agamemnon and Menelaus. Agamemnon can thus be designated, depending on metrical need, by name Agamemnon; by patronymic *Atreïdēs/Atreidēs* ('son of Atreus'); or both, *Atreïdēs Agamemnōn* ('Atreus' son, Agamemnon').

Atreïdēs Agamemnōn (nom.), scanning $-\ \smile\ \smile\ |\ -\ \ -\ \smile\ \smile\ |\ -\ \ -$ is a Homeric formula, filling three poetic feet (or half a line). Similarly, *Tydeïdēs* 'son of Tydeus' is Diomedes; more expansively, *Tydeïdēn Diomēdea* (acc.) (patronymic and name), scanning $-\ \smile\ \smile\ |\ -\ \smile\ \smile\ |\ -\ \smile\ \smile$. Circumventing the patronymic but using his name is *Tydeos (h)uion . . . Diomēdea* 'of Tydeus (gen.) the son (acc.) . . . Diomedes' (acc.). The metrical flexibility of such naming variations significantly facilitates oral composition. Indeed, patronymic naming constructions exhibit the same flexible word order as any other Homeric phrasings. Thus, e.g., *Hector . . . Priamidēs* 'Hector Priam's son', the two words appearing as the first words in two consecutive lines [*Il*. 13.802-803].

Then there are the special cases of *Telamoniadēs* 'Telamon's son' (the Greater Ajax) and *Oïliadēs* 'Oïleus' son' (the Lesser Ajax). The former, from Salamis (an island facing the port of Piraeus south of Athens), is the bravest and most stalwart of the Greeks after Achilles (serving as his stand-in, as does Diomedes, during Achilles' absence). The latter, from Locris (northwest of Athens to the immediate north of the Peloponnese), is a middling warrior often paired with his superior counterpart. However, unlike the stolid Telamonian Ajax (*Il*. 11.619-628), Oïlean Ajax is especially swift of foot (*Il*. 14.551-554). Their peculiar name-prompted relationship is an Iliadic conceit. As Telamonian Ajax himself urges,

> . . . but back of you will we
> Twain contend 'gainst goodly Hector and the Trojans,
> One in spirit as in name, even we that are
> Wont to stand stoutly erect in dreaded assault,
> Each to the other's side entrusted.
>
> (*Il*. 17.811-815; cf. 2.539-544, 13.789-798)

"Ajax" in Homer's Greek is "*Aias*," and the two heroes, when together, are referred to as the "*Aiantes*" (never Eng. "Ajaxes"). Being of "twin" nature, they are also referred to as the "Aiantes twain" (so in this translation) instead of, e.g., "the two Aiantes." The archaic "twain" reflects frequent Homeric reference to the Aiantes in the Greek *dual*, a form specifically designating two of anything rather than one (singular) or more than two (plural). Dual verbal endings are used from the outset to describe the separation of Agamemnon and Achilles: *diastētēn erisante* 'they [the two] stood apart quarreling' (dual finite verb plus participle). Duals are pervasive in Homer, adding a precision to subject-verb and noun-adjective numeration unknown to Latin or English. Translation of this feature via postpositive "twain" captures Homeric usage with the right archaic flavor.

Achilles was the son of the sea goddess Thetis and the mortal Peleus.

His patronymic *Pēleidēs* 'son of Peleus' is dramatically enshrined—*and archaized*—together with his name, in the poem's opening line:

μῆνιν ἄειδε θεὰ **Πηληϊάδεω Ἀχιλῆος**
The wrath sing, Goddess, **of Peleus' son Achilles**.

[The quinquisyllabic *Πηληϊάδεω/Pē-lē-ï-a-dyō* [gen.] is an old double-suffixed form of patronymic. See *The Iliad, Vol. 1, Books 1–XII*, Walter Leaf, ed. (Macmillan, 1900), 3 (at 1.1). It is, further, the only form of the patronymic in any grammatical case lengthening the second syllable from epsilon (ε) to eta (η), and inserting a penultimate alpha (α). The form is otherwise *Πηλεΐδεω/Pē-le-ï-dyo* (*Il.* 15.64, 17.195, 20.85), typically at line-opening position, and once at line-end, see νεῖκος Ὀδυσσῆος καὶ **Πηλεΐδεω Ἀχιλῆος** (*Od.* 8.75). The unique form of patronymic in the opening line strikes a solemn, authoritative, and markedly archaic note—an indication of the mannered diction to come. To similar archaizing effect is τῶν ἁμόθεν/*tōn ((h)amothen*) (*Od.* 1.10) 'from some one of these matters' (p. 54). For other elements of the *Iliad*'s marked opening line, see W. B. Stanford, "Sound, Sense and Music in Greek Poetry," *Greece & Rome*, 28.2 (1981), 135–136.]

A patronymic is sometimes formed with alternative suffix -*iōn*: *Kroniōn* (= *Kronidēs*) 'son of Cronus' (Zeus); *Pēleïōn* (= *Pēleïdēs*) 'son of Peleus' (Achilles) (nom. *Pēleïōn* not appearing in the *Iliad*). The occasional feminine patronymic is formed with suffix -*ïs*. Βρισηΐς 'Brisēïs'. Achilles' concubine or "spear bride" is thus the daughter of Briseus. Her seizure by Agamemnon triggers the action of the *Iliad*. Χρυσηΐς 'Chrysēïs', Agamemnon's concubine, is the daughter of Χρύσης 'Chrysēs' (priest of Apollo) from Χρύση 'Chrysē' (a town near Troy). Distinguishing such names is the beginner's first challenge. The required return of Chrysēïs to her father sets the stage for Agamemnon's seizure of Brisēïs. The patronymics "Brisēïs" and "Chrysēïs" are the two women's sole designations. Their names, one might say, are patronymically circumscribed. Brisēïs is sometimes called *kourēn brisēos* 'girl, maiden, daughter [acc.] of Briseus,' yet lacks a given name of her own. Her imagined likeness, in a sculpture by Paul Manship (1885–1966), graces the dust jacket of this volume.

In this translation I mix and match patronymic usages for metrical and other reasons. Thus, where Homer designates Agamemnon by name, the translation might use a patronymic and vice versa. Where Homer designates him by formulaic phrase, the translation might resort to simple name or patronymic. By the same token, and depending on metrical need, *Atreïdēs* (pron. *A-tre'-i-dēs*—four syllables) may appear as *Atreidēs* (pron. *A-trē'-dēs*—three syllables). The practice is consistent with Homer's own use of diphthongs (two vowels pronounced as one), which may be separated by dieresis (Gr. *dia* 'apart' + (*h*)*aireo* 'pull, draw'), e.g., *Atreïdēs*, which creates an additional syllable. Whatever the possibilities, the translation on balance retains patronymic flavor vis-à-vis Agamemnon and others.

The reader should be especially alert to the following patronymics appearing throughout this translation:

 Cronidēs — Zeus
 Atreïdēs — Agamemnon, sometimes Menelaus (in this translation sometimes Atreidēs)
 Pēleïdēs — Achilles (in this translation sometimes Pēleidēs)
 Aeacidēs — Achilles (patronymic on the name of Achilles' grandfather Aeacus)
 Telamoniadēs — the Greater Ajax

For purposes of this translation, naming formations have an analogue in noun-epithet combinations, e.g., ship(s) + epithet(s). Homeric ships are regularly "dark," "hollow," "curved," "curve-beaked," "well-benched," "well-balanced," or "rapid-running." The translation, regardless the original, freely chooses from among the alternatives for metrical and other reasons. Similarly, for the Greek alternative-lacking *naus* 'ship', the translation alternates between "ship," "hull," "bow/prow," and "vessel" ("galleon," "barque," "craft," and "keel" but rarely; never "boat")—e.g., "hollow hulls," "well-benched vessels." The nature and balance of Homeric *ship*-formularity is thus preserved in translation, as it is for the Homeric formulary overall. It is further noted that a formula is not rendered identically to each identical Greek usage. However, and as pertains to ships and other objects, the formulaic range or import is always apparent.

As further concerns syllabification, a "curved" ship may become a "curvèd" ship by metrical need comparable to that requiring dieresis, i.e., the need of an extra syllable. In fact, syllable-added accentuation appears in moderation throughout, e.g., "the agèd one," "here gatherèd," "unransomèd," "preferrèd" (usually at or toward line-end). Conversely, vowel elisions occur when one less syllable is wanted. Thus, scanned as either three or two syllables are: "chariot," "warrior," "Ilium"; and comparatives and superlatives such as "earlier," "mightiest." The word "ivory" is properly either two or three syllables, while the word "every" is properly two, but scanned as three where needed. The following are also scanned as two or three, by either (1) synizesis (Gr. *syn* 'with' + *idzō* 'sit'), e.g., "alien," "beauteous" (and other such -eous words), "champion," "devious" (and other such -ious words), "Phrygia," "radiant," etc. or (2) "e"-vowel roll, e.g., "answering" (and other such participial forms), "boisterous," "corselet," "reverent," "sovereign." At the same time, an apostrophe sometimes appears for clarity, e.g., "reverent" or "rev'rent" (both disyllabic). The following may be scanned as three or four syllables, e.g., "charioteer," "Dardania(n)," "Olympian," "pitifully," "superior." "Telamonian" may be scanned as four or five; so also "immediately," "invariably." Words such as "field," "layer," "lion," "power," "tower," "ruin," etc. are here scanned as either one or two syllables; "ruinous" as two or three (but "prayer" always as one). Frequently used trisyllabic "corselet" (above)—always so spelled here (but also spelled "corslet" and "corselette")—is pronounced, according to need, as three or two syllables.

Names ending in *-eus* regularly retain the ending as monosyllabic: "Peleus," "Atreus" (disyllabic); "Otrynteus" (trisyllabic), "Idomeneus" (quadrisyllabic). By contrast, names ending in *-aus* regularly retain the ending as disyllabic: "Menelaus, Agelaus; Oenomäus" (all quadrisyllabic, the last dieresized for clarity), and "Protesiläus (five syllables). Names ending in *-ius* are variable: "Axius, Imbrius" (two or three), "Acrisius" (three or four), "Erichthonius" (four or five). Dieresis also has its uses: thus "Atreïdēs" (four syllables, as seen), but "Atreidēs" (three) (cf. Pēleïdēs/Pēleidēs); also "Oïleus" (three syllables), but "Oileus" (two). Otherwise, contraction occurs primarily through omission of medial *v* or *e*, e.g., "e'er," "o'er." Such uses often appear in alliterative combination:

> ... Fast descending the rugged mount, forth
> Strode he on steadfast step, the lofty mountain **peaks**
> And woodlands **apprehensive** neath th' immortal foot
> Of **Poseidon's o'erpow'ring pace.**
>
> (*Il.* 13.18-21)

Elided "the" (th') before a word-initial vowel is frequent, e.g., "th' Achaeans," "th' Aiantes," "th' immortal," "th' other." Though here marked, such elision in traditional English poetry is frequently implied (the "e" retained but unpronounced). An archaic flavor results from a sometimes-shortened passive participle, e.g., "exasperate" for "exasperated":

> Thus prayed the priest, and Phoebus Apollo heard him.
> From Olympus' summit he pounced, exasperate ...
>
> (*Il.* 1.43-44)

Other examples include "inundate" for "inundated" and "infuriate" for "infuriated" ("infuriate" either three or four syllables).

In some cases, an epithet is supplied for meter's sake, though absent in the original; or is otherwise omitted when present in the Greek. Epithets, though sometimes interchanged when the person or object is known by more than one, are occasionally omitted. Again, it is not the individual instance, but the aggregate of the translation's epithets and other conventions that conveys the tenor of Homeric formularity and style. The reader in translation little cares whether Achilles retires to his "dark ships" or "hollow vessels," any more than did Homer's own listeners. Nor did they (or we) object to a *seated* "swift-footed Achilles." As meter drives every aspect of Homeric poetry, so does it drive this translation—more a *Homeric* translation than merely a translation of Homer. Indeed, there is nothing ultimately new in such once anticipated and appreciated English poetic conventions, however distant (but not remote) from contemporary sensibility. It is in this sense as well that the translation is "in a Classical Mode"—just old enough to be new.

Finally, and so as not to grate with excessive antiquity of diction or style, I have tended toward reduction of Homeric pleonasm (Gr. *pleo* 'fill'; Eng. plenty, replete, replenish). Such usages are in their own right part of the Homeric formulary and, as such, aid oral composition. Homer will thus pleonastically say, e.g., "engage in dread strife and hateful war," "mingle in bed and in love," "speak and address," "order and command," "in spirit and in mind," "heard with his ears," etc. The reduction of such usages—e.g., "when he noted" instead of "when he saw with his eyes"—is as much a concession to meter as to contemporary sensibility.

IV. Homeric Artificiality in Translation: Rightness of Result

> Dante is given the privilege of inventing his own language as he proceeds, freely changing his vowels, genders, and participles to eke out his rhymes, and throwing in words of his own manufacture according to inner sentiment and personal fancy. The freedom enjoyed by writers before the invention of punctuation (which came in with printing) can, of course, never be recovered—a freedom in which Dante revels; for commas and colons are leaden pellets hung on the wings of inspiration. The translator, however . . . must punctuate in such a manner as to show which of the possible interpretations he adopts; he must avoid solecisms and, of course, must never be obscure or hieratic.
>
> – JOHN J. CHAPMAN, *Dante* (1927)

1. *Alliteration: Roots and Reason*

ALLITERATION (LAT. *LITERA* 'letter of the alphabet') occurs when consecutive or closely positioned words begin with the same consonant or consonant sound. More broadly, it occurs when the consonant or consonant sound is initial, medial, and/or final (though the latter two are technically "consonance"). There is also assonance, the recurrence of vowels sounds. For economy's sake, I refer to all three as "alliteration." Homeric alliteration, with examples provided below, occurs at all levels: two- and three-word combinations, full lines, numbers of lines, and entire passages, often with more than a single consonant or vowel sound in play. Alliteration in oral poetry does not surprise, both because oral poetry exists for the ear rather than the eye and because similarities of sound aid memory and recitation. Homeric alliteration is more pervasive than currently recognized, and significantly more integrated or *textured* than the stark word-initial alliterations of *Beowulf* and other early English poetry—stark, because in largely mono- and disyllabic Old English, alliteration falls predominantly at word beginning, whereas in polysyllabic Greek it appears distributively. Little better reveals the signature artificiality of Homeric Greek than its insistent, yet often surprising, alliterations. These bind and secure the poetic line, line group, or passage, often creating or reinforcing meaning (the sound-sense corollary). Alliteration enhances phrase and passage movement. It is ornamental but never trivial, gratuitous, or tongue-twisting, e.g., of the "Peter Piper" or "seashells by the seashore" variety. Artistically done, it delights; and the better done, the less apparent, as the art in art is concealment. The present translation, where and insofar as English allows, is decidedly alliterative—as seen from the outset in my opening seven lines (see Appendix I at www.poemoftroy.com).

Alliteration at its best is an adjunct of meaning—a matter of "poetic decorum," a means by which sound reflects and reinforces sense. Well-known Homeric examples include the Cyclops' dashing of Odysseus' companions' brains against the floor of his cave—with its repeated "κ/k" and "χ/kh" sounds—before dismembering and devouring them (*Od.* 9.287-291); conversely, the liquid-flowing sounds of the Sirens' song, resisted by the mast-bound Odysseus (*Od.* 12.184-191). In both cases, sound reflects and reinforces sense. The technique *analogizes* sound and sense, creating coherence between them. As Pope famously observes in his *An Essay on Criticism:*

> The sound must seem an echo to the sense.
> Soft is the strain when Zephyr gently blows,
> And the smooth stream in smoother numbers flows;
> But when loud surges lash the sounding shore,
> The hoarse, rough verse should like the torrent roar.
> When Ajax strives some rock's vast weight to throw,
> The line too labours, and the words move slow;
> Not so, when swift Camilla scours the plain,
> Flies o'er th' unbending corn, and skims along the main.

Alliteration, to change the metaphor, is a root system throughout the poetic landscape, retaining the soil and making it firm—giving it *grip*—where it would otherwise be crumbly and scatter. Alliteration has its method, capitalizing on the intuited or suggestible kinship among words—words alike in sound or somehow liking one another in context. The technique both secures the soil and advances passage across it.

Or, alliteration is to poetry (and, in its way, to prose) what harmony is to music. The coincident sounds create a pleasurable sense of *rightness*, of inevitability, and thus of purposeful design. As alliteration pleases, so does it persuade. The technique may reflect the gift of an individual poet, or as in the case of Homer and other ancient traditional poetries, the endpoint or summation of countless recitations, each developmental in its way, each lighting on more dictionally decorative and alliteratively pleasing expression. Indeed, the Homeric examples here briefly reviewed could little have leapt to the fore in any initial recitation. They are simply too ingrained with sound-sense and/or ornament, too "rooted" in the poetry, to have sprung extempore. This results from the richly polysyllabic nature of Homeric Greek. The greater the number of syllables, the greater the alliterative potential. The credible translation of Homer reasonably no less than necessarily reflects what is the essence of Homer.

Toward that end, each line of this translation contains at least one di- or polysyllabic word, even if only a disyllabic conjunction or preposition, as sometimes occurs. Most lines contain at least two polysyllabics; many, more than two. Entirely monosyllabic lines are rare, appearing with less frequency than spondaic line closings in Homer. In such a case, the result appears inevitable, e.g., the description of the soothsayer Kalchas in Book 1:

ὃς ᾔδη τά τ' ἐόντα τά τ' ἐσσόμενα πρό τ' ἐόντα
(h)os eidē ta t' eonta ta t' essomena pro t' eonta
Who knew what was, knew what had been and was to be.

(*Il*. 1. 69 [70])

The increased polysyllabism of this translation heightens rhythmic movement, even as it increases alliterative potential. Polysyllabism further signals prosodic maturity. Indeed, from the mid-twentieth century to date, the principal disappointment of Homeric (and Virgilian) free-verse (and even blank-verse) translation has been a deadening mono- and disyllabism. There is, of course, no fully Greek-replicating polysyllabism in English—largely because English is, or has evolved into, a non-inflected language. Which is to say, English is scant in word endings that signal grammatical function (word order serving that end). It is also less compound-prone and very much simpler than Greek (archaic, classical, or contemporary). English, moreover, retains its original Anglo-Saxon/Germanic stock of mono- and disyllabic words. Polysyllabism is yet possible, thanks largely to numerous loan words from Greek and Latin. Thus, to take the readiest examples: luminous/bright; finale/end; antipathy/dislike; amicable/friendly;

appellation/name, domicile/house; deceased/dead. Polysyllabism in the English translation of Greek and Latin is thus a kind of "giveback" to the languages through which English has largely developed, the circle coming round. Of course, there are numerous Greek- and Latin-derived English words that lack Anglo-Saxon–based alternatives. This only increases the case for a robust polysyllabism, though one would not know it from the current state of epic in translation. Whether through lack of initiative or imagination, many a line of classical epic translation appears—in medical parlance—to flatline.

2. Making a Translation: Freedom in Constraint

Translation of the epic-poetic—of all classical poetry, in fact—is thus expected to be more than mere transference or rendering of meaning, but something actively of the translator's own *making* (Gr. *poieō* 'make', *poiētēs* 'maker, poet'; Eng. poet, poetry). It is expected to show invention: (Lat. *in* 'in, into' + *venio* 'I come') and, not least, contrivance (Med. Lat. *contropare* 'compare'; Old Fr. *controver/contreuv-* 'imagine, invent'; Fr. *trouver* 'find'; It. *trovare* 'find, discover'; Eng. trove, contrive, troubadour; cf. *Il Trovatore* 'The Minstrel, Singer, Poet'). Poetic usage thus stands opposed to the pedestrian (Gr. *pod-* / Lat. *ped* 'foot'), which is to say it does more than merely tread or plod. It sooner marks its pace by all available means—by judicious archaisms and alliteration (as argued); a regularized yet varied rhythm (lacking in everyday speech); and various figures of syntax, e.g., inversions (other than expected word order for metrical, ornamental, or archaizing effect). All such devices may be subsumed beneath the heading of *invention*, including the resourceful creation of new words (neologisms), word forms, or compounds—again, for metrical, ornamental, or archaizing effect. The mandate is especially compelling where the original language, here Homer's Greek, abundantly exhibits all such features. Conversely, the mandate—call it poetic license—*decreases* when the translation, as so often during the past one hundred years, is free verse. Where there is no constraint, there is no need for constraint-circumventing devices. In such a case, invention tends more to traduce than translate the original.

Homeric Greek is artificial through and through, a metrically governed and formulaically tailored language at no time ever spoken—yet with an imposing capacity as much for consummate character and story development as for the singular and seemingly microscopic treatment of ancillary matter. Homeric Greek is, further, extremely nuanced, as determined by its use of particles (see below). Therein lie both the majesty and magic of Homer's language. It is a long-developed and eventually consummate invention. It is, in the culinary sense, a *confection* (Lat. *conficere/confectum* 'prepare/prepared'). Being a confection, it is spun like cotton candy; it is the smile on the Cheshire Cat, the absent presence. It can and will do anything for the sake of the meter that drives it. More conventionally put, Homer's language is a centuries-long–developed and perfected artifact (Lat. root *art-* 'art', from Gr. **ar-* 'to fit, make fit, harmonize' + Lat. *facere/factum-* 'make/made'). A poetic translation of Homer should thus also be an artifact—as artificial as it need or dare be. Otherwise much is "lost in translation."

Homeric poetry—as any metrically regulated verse—is at once a competition and compromise between what need be said and how. As meter governs, it significantly shapes the message. This is especially so in Homer where meter, as seen, consists of an ordered alternation of long and short syllables. Think of it: *every syllable of every word* must fit the pattern. The result is like nothing ever spoken or speakable. Moreover, and as also seen, the pattern significantly overrides spoken stress with metrical weight (or quantity), their too frequent coincidence being prosaic in effect. Which is, again, to say Homeric Greek was and could never have been colloquial. It was and remains a *Kunstsprache*, with all the inbuilt and self-glorying artificiality that marked the starting point and, to this day, the highpoint of Western literature. Like armed Athena, sprung fully grown from the forehead of Zeus, Homeric epic, c. 750 BC, made its full and consummate epiphany after an undocumented, oral, centuries-long gestation.

Freedom resides in constraint, in that to which we choose to submit—here, poetic form. And no language has been freer in constraint than Homeric Greek. Such language, at the cost of repetition, is the invitingly unnatural and *sui generis* outgrowth of a meter that requires not only the sequencing of long and short syllables but also the preponderant avoidance of spoken stress and metrical weight—the two in purposeful "conflict." *That*, in significant part, is what makes Homeric poetry *poetry*, and that much is irreplicable in English. Homeric poetry further involves imaginative uses of diction, formulae, figures of speech and syntax, and a preponderantly pliant word order. In English poetry, by contrast, spoken stress and poetic weight/beat necessarily coincide, because English poetry, knowing little of vowel quantity, follows spoken speech. To that extent, English poetry commands fewer artifice-making resources than classical poetry. At its call, however, are meter, rhyme (if used), the apt and imaginative uses of diction, figures of speech and syntax, and a sometimes pliant word order (collectively, the "incidents" of poetry). The result, in the best—i.e., premodern—hands, is metrical and/or rhymed constraint in the service of meaning, a literary yin and yang. English poetry, moreover, has developed from and within a predominantly written tradition, lacking both the accretions and stratifications of oral development, including the in- and intermixing of dialect forms. For this reason, English poetry has no need of the myriad verbal alterations and inventions found in Homer *metri gratia*. Rather, and in a way largely inapplicable to Homer, English—because non-inflected—must deal with expressed personal pronouns, prepositions, auxiliary verbs, and—for other reasons—definite and indefinite articles. Such uses tend toward the monosyllabic piling-up of little words, so much flotsam impeding poetic flow. In sum, and by contrast to classical poetry, English poetry at its art-language best will yet conform to the norms of spoken use.

3. *Inflection, Particles, Dialect Forms*

Ancient Greek (as Latin) is an inflected language (Lat. *in* 'in, inward'+ *flecto* 'turn, bend, curve'; cf. Eng. reflect). Which is to say, a language whose forms inwardly turn or curve to designate grammatical function, e.g., *polemos* 'war' (nom.), *polemoio* 'of war' (gen.) (often contracted to *polemou*); *polemō(i)* 'to or for war' (dat.), *polemon* 'war' (acc.). Words thus change to indicate specific grammatical functions or aspects, here case (nom.), number (sing.), and gender (words ending in -*os* masculine). This feature significantly obviates the need for express prepositions (e.g., *of, to, with, by, in*, etc.). Similarly, ancient Greek verbs exhibit personal endings, i.e., endings added to designate grammatical (1) person (*I, you, he, she*, or *it*, etc.); (2) number (singular, plural, etc.) (3) tense (present, future, etc.), (4) voice (active, passive, etc.), and (5) mood (indicative, subjunctive, etc.). Such endings signal a verb subject absent the use of an express personal pronoun, e.g., *poieō/poiō* 'I make', *poieis* 'you make', etc. (the subject being "contained" in the verb).

Greek verbs further have tense-indicating stems, e.g., *poiēsō* 'I will make' and, in past tenses, past stems together with syllabic augment and/or reduplication, e.g., *epoiēsa* 'I made'; *pepoiēka* 'I have made'; *epepoiēkē* 'I had made', obviating the need for auxiliary verbs (i.e., *am, is, will, did, have, had,* etc.). Inflection results not only in polysyllabism but also in a concision of verbal form and flexibility of word order unthinkable in English and most European languages. Because Greek word endings signal which words "go together," words, especially in poetry, can be loosely distributed over two or three lines—nouns separated from adjectives, adverbs from verbs, and so on. Word endings thus also obviate the need for punctuation (no dangling participles in Greek). Uninflected English, by contrast, relies on a largely predictable word order: subject and verb, adverb and verb, noun and adjective typically within close proximity.

The marked flexibility of Greek word order and of epic word formation and variability is a key element in the artificiality of Homeric Greek, such artificiality having artificialities of its own. Thus, for example, where the meter will not accommodate a past-tense augment, the augment is dropped, augment being "not merely an artistic option but rather an archaic and rule-governed phenomenon." The personal ending may drop as well. Thus, disyllabic *tiei* 'he pays', can appear in the Homeric imperfect tense as

> trisyllabic *etie* 'he was paying'
> [*e*-augment],

> disyllabic *tie* 'he was paying'
> [augment dropped], or

> monosyllabic *ti'* 'he was paying'
> [augment dropped, *e*-ending elided before
> word beginning with a vowel].

Metrical accommodation further occurs in subjunctive endings, which (by rule) are long, e.g.,

> *pempomen* 'we send'
> [with omicron]

45

>   *pempōmen* 'we may send'
>   [with omega].

But the subjunctive stem is regularly shortened if a short syllable is needed. Thus,

>   *pempomen* 'we send *or* 'we may send'
>   [as determined by context].

Such sleights of hand, metrical and otherwise, allow great flexibility within an otherwise regulated line. Need a long syllable where one does not properly exist? Double the *s* (*sigma*) or *l* (*lambda*) without essentially changing the word or its sound; or double an already present *e* (*epsilon*) with something of a "hiccup" effect, e.g., *epesi, epessi,* or *epeessi* 'with words' (the last form both adding an extra short—the first *e*—and then treating the second *e* as long, or weighted, because followed by two consonants). The very name "Achilles" (Ἀχιλεύς / Ἀχιλλεύς) is sometimes spelled with one *lambda*, sometimes two—depending on whether a weighted *iota* syllable is needed. The variants, in fact, appear in the name as twice appearing in the first seven lines of the *Iliad*. In the same metrically accommodating vein, the Homeric infinitive "to be" may appear in five different forms, each suited to different metrical need: *einai, emen, emmen, emenai, emmenai* (to say nothing of other forms of the verb "to be"). So also with other verbs, e.g., 'to go': *elthein, eelthein, elthemen, elthemenai.*

Exerting immense metrical influence—i.e., making meter work—are the Greek "particles," bane of translators and source of lengthy discussion. Particles, as their name implies, are recurring "little words"—often two- and three-letter vowel-final monosyllables. Dropping the final vowel when followed by a vowel-initial word—*de* to *d'* ('but'); *te* to *t'* ('and'); *ge* to *g'* ('at least'); also *kai* ('and') to *k'* (*kai* a conjunction, not a particle)—particles are often reduced to non-syllabic consonant sounds, pronounced as part of the word that follows. Thus, omitting one or more syllables in lines where they occur, elided particles enable and critically regulate meter—so much so that one can find a repeated particle in the same line, once elided and once not—the former a *non-syllabic* consonant sound exerting metrical regulation, e.g., by preventing hiatus [*Il.* 16.30: *mē eme **g'** oun (h)outos **ge** laboi cholos* 'may no such anger in any case take me']. Or, particle repetition may simply enhance alliterative effect while providing a needed final syllable [*Il.* 16.445: (*h*)*on de domon de* 'to his house'; or (*h*)*onde domonde*].

Add to this the Homeric mix, again largely *metri gratia*, of the then four major Greek dialects: Ionic, Aeolic, Doric, and Attic (see map), with forms of the same word differing from one dialect to the other. Thus, the epithet of Apollo—*paiān* 'healer' (and later, the celebratory hymn, a paean):

> *Paiēōn* (Ionic/Homeric)
> *Pāōn* (Aeolic)
> *Paiān* (Doric)
> *Paiōn* (Attic).

I elsewhere provide a list of key Ionic/Homeric vs. Aeolic forms appearing in Homer. One thus sees at a glance the different metrical possibilities and nuances for which dialect-mixing allows. Relatedly, the numerous Homeric (*h*)*apax legomena* 'once spoken' words (sing. *legomenon*). These are words, or word forms, appearing only once in Homer, early estimated at about two thousand.

The ancient Greek dialects, though quite marked in their differences, were still mutually comprehensible, at least in literary contexts. Alternatively, the dialects as literary languages were, collectively, the Greek language itself. Numerous dialect-mixing examples appear in [Plutarch] *Essay on the Life and Poetry of Homer* (1st–2d centuries AD), §§8–14, 71–81. Says [Plutarch]:

> It is clear, then, that in mustering [*apergazetai* 'he works up'] all the dialects [*phōnas*, 'voices, sounds'] of the Greeks, he creates a richly varied discourse [*poikilon . . . logon*] and sometimes uses dialect expressions . . . and sometimes archaic ones, as when he says *aor* [sword] and *sakos* [shield], though in some places he uses the common and ordinary words for those same things, *ksiphos* and *aspis*. One might wonder at the way even everyday words sustain the elevation of Homeric discourse. . . . Studied diction loves to escape the ordinary and thus become more vivid and in general more pleasing. . . . ([Plutarch] §§14–15; Greek transliterated)

It is in this spirit, to be sure, and for metrical and/or alliterative reasons, that this translation alternates between *shield/buckler, belt/baldric, spear/lance, reck/consider, assay/attempt,* among other helpful or simply decorative usages, e.g., *'til/till* for *until*; *scape* for *escape*; and various final *d-* or *ing-*truncated participles, e.g., *situate, infuriate,* and *excruciate* for *situated, infuriated,* and *excruciating.* Subjunctives appear with a frequency and flavor reflecting pre-twentieth century usage, e.g., "If he be," and infinitives are frequently "pruned" for metrical reasons, e.g., "If he prefer await." There are occasional second- and third-person archaic verb endings, e.g., *thinkest/thinkst, thinketh*; even, e.g., *thinkst thou*...? (in a challenge issued by a god). Such usages are assessed, first, by *rightness of result* in context; and second, by the determined style or programmatic dictates of the translation itself. Archaism, as [Plutarch] indicates, is a subset of diction (word choice and disposition). When such diction is "studied" (Gr. *eng-kataskeu[ast]os*, lit. 'thoroughly prepared', i.e., 'created through and through'), it is man-made or *artificial.*

4. Rhetorical Artificiality

The artificiality of Homer, as now seen, begins with the demands and peculiarities of Homeric meter and the allowances and sleights of hand that serve and make it possible. The resultant idiom is unique—no more so than in the poem's direct discourse, i.e., its speeches. Over sixty percent of Homer consists of quoted conversation—introduced by such formulaic lines as these: "And thus answering in turn, he spoke, responding"; or "And looking askance, he thus addressed him, saying"; or "And thus responding, he addressed him wingèd words." Other speeches include prayers to gods, and battlefield exhortations, including self-exhortations—the last introduced by, e.g., "And thus he addressed his own great-hearted spirit"—articulating and allowing the listener to track the speaker's thoughts. There is also imagined or hypothetical speech/reflection introduced by, e.g., "And thus might an Argive address his companion." Speeches give the Homeric poems a highly *dramatic* quality, making Homer the primary source of Greek drama—vis-à-vis medium and plot alike—in which dialogue predominates. But while characters will speak, they do not necessarily or at all speak in dactylic hexameter. *That* is a matter of Homeric artificiality. For as influenced as Greek drama was by Homer, it uses iambic trimeter for dialogue, which tracks the natural rhythms of speech.

Were such manner of speech not artifice enough, Homeric warriors, even when on the battlefield, address one another in the most deferential, even chivalrous, terms, e.g., *daimónie* 'My good sir'/ 'My dear fellow'; *Ō pepon* 'O, my friend' (also *daimoníē* 'My dear lady' in various contexts). There are also chivalrous gestures, as when Diomedes and the Lycian Glaucus, about to engage in combat, realize they and their fathers enjoyed a guest-host relationship. They thus cease fighting and exchange armor to commemorate and perpetuate the tie (*Il.* 6.235-262). Another such gesture appears in Agamemnon's foregoing competition and yielding first prize to his competitor (*Il.* 23.974-984). Warriors, moreover, even while facing foes in mortal combat, pause to boast of prior exploits, these laced with genealogical digressions containing digressions of their own—all by way of establishing lineage and credentials (e.g., *Il.* 5.697-712, 6.130-262, 20.224-267). Anterior to such encounters, warrior and charioteer—even while awaiting their counterparts—will discourse at length on tactics, past personal history, and even the pedigree of horses (*Il.* 5.289-304), the possession or acquisition of which redounds to their glory.

Equally action-arresting, and thus artificial, are the frequent and seemingly frame-by-frame descriptions of an arrow or spear released, flying forward, and penetrating—first through a shield's surface, next through the protective hide and metal layers behind it, next through the warrior's mail-corseleted garment or belt, next through the skin itself, and finally into whichever body part or organ takes the blow (*Il.* 3.377-382). So also a biographical vignette of the intended target after the arrow's release but before its strike (*Il.* 13.742-757). A detailed death throe might ensue, including dying words, or a narrative reflection on the cruelty of death. Prior to the weapon's release, the attacker might voice the intent of taking his adversary's *meliēdea thumon* 'honey-sweet life' (*Il.* 17.20 [17])—the adjective elsewhere used of wine, food, fodder, sleep, and homecoming. In the famous wounding-of-Menelaus scene, description of the arrow-nocking and bow-drawing takes a seeming eternity before the string is actually released (*Il.* 4.120-136; cf. 8.367-374). This is neither how combatants speak nor how combat itself occurs. It is *artifice*—a highly artistic evocation of war in the service of greater-than-life portrayal and effect. It is the millennia-old precursor to the cinematographic slow-motion portrayal of high points or crucial events, as much artifice as artificial.

5. Alliteration: Artificiality's Case in Point

While other examples of artificiality exist, none better serve for illustration than Homer's patterns of alliteration, consonance, and assonance (collectively "alliteration," as noted above). This is not the accent-indicating and thus heavily apparent alliterative scheme of *Beowulf* and other early English poetry, but something far more finely developed and distributive. And it is entirely artificial, judging from its inevitable absence from spoken language. In conversation, even passing alliteration raises eyebrows for its often comic or suggestive effect. In fact, we generally consign alliteration to aphorisms, brand names, and advertising slogans. Conversely, a phrase becomes noteworthy for its alliterative contrivance. In Homer, however, alliteration is a cohesive skein capturing and aligning similar sounds in the service of meaning, finesse, or simple delight. Considerations of space require that we limit discussion to selected examples from which others might be deduced. Noteworthy are letter θ/*thēta* alliterations. The language of translation should, again, reflect this key element of Homeric composition—not on an impossibly case-by-case basis, but on balance, being alliterative where and however English might reasonably allow.

Homeric alliteration runs the gamut. It starts with two-word combinations, e.g.,

>εἰν ἐνὶ δίφρῳ ἐόντας ...
>***ein** (h)**eni** diphrō(i) **e**ontas*
>***in one** chariot being*
>[*ein* a lengthening *metri gratia* for *en* 'in']
>
>[*Il.* 5.160, 11.103]

Alliteration is highly apparent in formulaic phrases, the same often formulaic for that very reason, e.g.,

>ἐπὶ (ϝ)οἴνοπα πόντον
>*epi oinopa ponton*
>upon the wine-dark (lit. wine-faced) sea.
>
>[*Il.* 1.350]

It is also apparent in purposefully contrived (non-formulaic) phrases, e.g.,

δοιὼ δ' οὐ δύναμαι ἰδέειν κοσμήτορε λαῶν
doiō d' ou dunamai ideein kosmētore laōn
But I am not able to see the two shepherds of the people

[*Il.* 3.236]

χύντο χαμαὶ χολάδες
chunto chamai cholades
Spilled to the ground his intestines

[*Il.* 4.526]

Entire lines are often alliterative:

ὣς εἰπὼν ἔμπνευσε μένος μέγα ποιμένι λαῶν.
(*h*)*ōs eipōn empneuse menos mega poimeni laōn*
Thus speaking he inspired great strength into the shepherd of the host.

[*Il.* 15.262]

The step from isolated lines, to two or more lines, to entire passages is small—but with telling effect. Such instances establish semantic, i.e., signaling or signifying, associations (Gr. *sēmainō* 'show', Lat *signum* 'sign'), which is to say sense *rooted* in sound. The most significant instance of sound-sense correlation in archaic Greek poetry appears in the epic *Theogony* (*Birth of the Gods*) by Homer's successor Hesiod. It is of a kind readily found in Homer, and with an actual Homeric parallel. The parallel is no mere borrowing or coincidence, but evidence of powerfully associative thought in poetic time and milieu.

The Muses in Hesiod's *Theogony* descend Mt. Helicon amid their own singing and dance. With a prototypically enigmatic utterance, they inspire the then-shepherd Hesiod with the divine gift of epic poetry. The lines, addressed to the shepherds in mock contempt, signal the ultimate lack of verifiability in any mythic account:

ποιμένες ἄγραυλοι, κάκ' ἐλέγχεα, γαστέρες οἶον,
ἴδμεν ψεύδεα πολλὰ λέγειν ἐτύμοισιν ὁμοῖα,
ἴδμεν δ', εὖτ' ἐθέλωμεν, ἀληθέα γηρύσασθαι.

*poimenes agrauloi, kak' elenchea, gasteres oion,
idmen pseudea polla legein etumoisin (h)omoia
idmen d', eut' ethelōmen, alēthea gērusasthai.*

> Rustic Shepherds, sordid disgraces, stomachs all,
> Many lies to truth likened we know how to tell;
> We know, when so wishing, to speak true things as well.
>
> (*Th.* 26-28)

We note the triple-alliterative *thēta* (θ/th) and the twice alliterative *lambda* (λ/l) in the bolded transliterated phrase—the words meaning: 'we wish' (*ethelōmen*), 'true things' (*alēthea*), 'to speak' (*gērusasthai*). The alliteration signals the association in archaic Greek thought between truth and volition—*truth* uttered when the speaker *wishes* to speak it, i.e., is so inclined, perceives advantage, or is otherwise intent on falsehood. The uncertainty of truth in an oral pre-literate society gives rise to 'many lies resembling the truth' (*pseudea polla . . . etumoisin (h)omoia*), which is to say, to verisimilitude (Lat. *verum* 'true' + *simile* 'like, similar to'). A good liar—one whose story "adds up"—will thus be taken at his word. Such is Odysseus par excellence, of whom Homer says, following one of Odysseus' grand mendacities,

> ἴσκε ψεύδεα πολλὰ λέγων ἐτύμοισιν ὁμοῖα·
> *iske pseudea polla legōn etumoisin (h)omoia*
> Speaking many falsehoods, he likened them to truths.
>
> (*Od.* 19.203; cf. *Th.* 27, above)

But for the change of (1) verb—*iske* 'he likened' for *idmen* 'we know' and (2) participle *legōn* 'speaking' for infinitive *legein* 'to speak', the two contexts are one and the same.

We further note that Homeric *alēthea muthēsasthai* 'to tell the truth', with internally alliterative *muthēsasthai* 'to tell', is used in lieu of Hesiodic *alēthea gērusasthai* 'to utter, speak'—both words emphatic as spondaic line endings: — — | — — (fifth and sixth feet), instead of the typical: — ⏑ ⏑ | — —. One such Homeric context, most approximating Hesiod, is as follows:

> ψεύδοντ᾽, οὐδ᾽ ἐθέλουσιν ἀληθέα μυθήσασθαι
> *pseudont', oud' ethelousin alēthea muthēsasthai*
> They falsely speak, **nor wish they to utter the truth**.
>
> (*Od.* 14.125)

The Muses speak the truth "when they wish" because in archaic Greek thought, as today, the presence or intervention of divinity—including the Muses—is deemed dependent on divine will (cf. "God willing"). What happens *happens* apparently because a god has wished or willed it. Having willed it, the god then arrives to accomplish it (not that arrival is actually needed, though epiphany is always impressive). This creates and further strengthens an alliteratively pronounced association between true things/ the truth (*alēthea*), divinity (*theos*), arrival (*elthōn*), volition (*ethelōn*), and accomplishment or placement (*theiē*).

That gods 'arrive' (*elthein*) among men is an epic commonplace, even as that which the gods 'place', 'position', or 'accomplish' among men is signaled by the soundalike *thēta* root: *θε- 'place, put' (Gr. *tithēmi* 'I place, put'). So also Gr. Θέμις (*themis* 'law, custom, adjudication, appropriate[ness]'—that which is *placed* or *established*—personified as the goddess Θέμις), Thus, Odysseus to Penelope, concerning the riddle of their marital bed:

ὅτε μὴ **θεὸς** αὐτὸς **ἐπελθὼν**
ῥηϊδίως **ἐθέλων θείη** ἄλλῃ ἐνὶ χώρῃ.

(h)ote mē **theos** *autos* **epelthōn**
(h)rēïdiōs **ethelōn theiē** *allē(i) eni chōrē(i)*

Unless a **god**, himself **coming on**,
easily—**wishing** [to do so]—**placed** [the bed] in another place.

(*Od.* 23.185-186)

There are, however, any number of alliterations that are largely ornamental, playful, or purposefully punning. The following line, emphatic in *thēta* sound, is, more than anything else, playful or high-spirited:

μή με **θεὰ Θέμι** ταῦτα διείρεο: **οἶσθα** καὶ αὐτὴ
mē me **thea Themi** *tauta dieireo:* **oistha** *kai autē*
Do not, **goddess Themis**, ask me these things; yourself you **know**.

[*Il.* 15.93]

Here, the alliterative **thea Themi** 'goddess Themis' creates a diminutive or endearing tone, e.g., "Themis, my dear" or "Themis, dearie." We further note a devilishly clever play on verb and apostrophized god:

ἔγνως ἐννοσίγαιε ἐμὴν ἐν στήθεσι βουλὴν
egnōs ennosigaie emēn en stēthessi boulēn
You know, O Earthshaker, the plan within my breast

[Note verb **e-g-n-ō-s** and addressee **e-n-o-s**-i-**g**-ai-e; also *emēn en stēthessi boulēn*]

[*Il.* 20.20]

Space allowing, we would have proceeded to lengthier bravura passages containing *theta* and other alliteration. These appear in the discussion at www.poemoftroy.com. Their purport may, however, be deduced from the alliterative operations as seen above.

We conclude with a *theta* alliteration of purposefully archaizing intent, appearing as it does at the very start of the *Odyssey*. It sends an unequivocal message—as if to say, this is, and will be treated as, an antique poem, even in these, our putatively "modern" times. The poet begins by invoking the Muse to tell of Odysseus, the "man of many turns," who suffered much both on land and sea upon his return from Troy. The adventures are many, so the poet ends the invocation as follows:

τῶν **ἁμόθεν** γε, **θεά**, **θύγατερ** Διός, εἰπὲ καὶ ἡμῖν
tōn (h)amothen ge theā, thugatēr, Dios eipe kai (h)ēmin
From some one of these (events), **goddess, daughter** of Zeus, tell us also

(*Od.* 1.10)

The second word ἁμόθεν ((h)amothen) is compounded of **(h)amos** 'some, someone, some one' (archaic equivalent of otherwise Homeric and classical *tis* 'some, someone') and the archaic suffix **-θε(ν)** (with "**ν/n**" because the next word begins with a vowel). The doubly marked archaic compound signals a plentiful antiquity, even as it sounds alliteratively smart or up to date with the addition of two further θ/*th* sounds in the same line (*tōn (h)amothen ge theā, thugatēr*). Such contrivance is all in an epic's "day's work," this one appearing emphatically at the outset. Homer thus exploits alliteration not only for its own sake but also to announce, in his own time, how remarkably an archaic/archaizing poet he is—in diction, style, and theme. It behooves any translation of Homer to convey whatever modicum of this it might, albeit faint, yet clearly audible, as the cosmic microwave background trailing the Big Bang.

Alliterative examples—beyond two-to-four-word combinations—that lack Homeric counterpart but are yet true to Homeric usage, are:

>   and the old man,
> Peleus, chariot lord, was **offering** a **fattened**
> **Thigh of bull**, to Zeus **thunderbolt** rejoicing,
> Within the **court's enclosure**, and **clasped** a **golden**
> **Goblet**, whence **flowed** as **fellow** to the **offering**
> A **fiery** wine.
>
> (*Il.* 11.864-869 [772-755])

> So we departed, much **aggrieved**, **angered** for the **gain**
> **Agreed** to but **given** not.
>
> (*Il.* 21.511-512 [456-457])

Most extensive yet is the description of Thersites:

> Then were the others still, throughout their ranks restrained,
> But Thersites alone, intemperate of tongue,
> Yet scoffed and bawled, disorderly, obstreperous;
> Convulsed was his vernacular, availing not.
> With kings inclined to quarrel, intoxicate he,
> Danaan dullard and simpleton, reprobate
> Of Troy, blighted his breeding; bandy-leggèd, lame
> Of foot, his shoulders inward shunted to his chest;
> Pointy-headed, and sparse the tuft upon his pate;
> Despisèd of Odysseus he, to Achilles
> Loathsome most, for he ever importuned the two
> And against Agamemnon relentlessly railed,
> Disdained of the Danaans, held in their despite.
>
> (*Il.* 2.216-228 [211-223])

The Thersites rendering is as artificial in its way as any of the *theta*-driven alliterations above. The latter are too intrinsically Greek-contrived to yield gold in translation. Conversely, the Thersites passage in Greek lacks the alliterative fullness given it here. The result nonetheless seems right; and Homer's technique, on balance, retained.

From such passages as these, the reader senses what Homeric language is like and can do—whether by formulaic occurrence or otherwise—in any given phrase, line, lines, or line-sequence. The gold, whether panned from the stream's surface or mined from deep within, is there for the finding. Such specifics as I have highlighted cannot be comparably rendered in translation. However, the nature and effect of such language can be comparably suggested to the extent English alliteration, diction, meter, and ingenuity allow, i.e., wherever it is possible to approximate the resources of one language with those of another. It is ultimately a matter of *rightness of result* on a line-by-line, passage-by-passage basis; and that assessment will surely vary. I have, of course, sought right result throughout (see further Appendix II at www.poemoftroy.com).

II.
Translation

~ Prologue ~

Mythological Background

THE TROJAN WAR BEGINS with the marriage of the mortal Peleus, Achilles' father, and the sea goddess Thetis. Zeus would himself have married Thetis but for the prophecy of an offspring greater than its sire. Zeus had himself been an offspring greater than his sire, the Titan Cronus (whom he dethroned). Zeus thus refrains from wedding Thetis to avoid generational recurrence. Moreover, had Achilles been born a son of Zeus and Thetis, he would have been born a god instead of a demigod. Assuming, next, his own marriage to a mortal woman, Achilles' children would have been demigods. Yet it is sooner a purpose of the Trojan War, or "meta-purpose," to end divine-human marriage, extinguish the race of demigods (a concern paralleled in Genesis 6), and achieve ultimate separation of men and gods. Demigods want nothing more than to be gods, or be considered their equal. The continued existence and propagation of demigods is a threat to established divinity. Thus, the need for demigod extinction. Though not part of the *Iliad*'s story, the matter of demigods is yet written into the story's DNA: Achilles *knows* his divinity has been thwarted. This contributes to his μῆνις 'wrath', which is the poem's opening word and theme.

Peleus was the son of Aeacus, son of Zeus, making Achilles a great-grandson of Zeus. The status is alluded to in Homer (*Il.* 21.213-217), and Homer refers to Achilles as both *Aeacidēs* 'son of Aeacus' and *Pēleïdēs* 'son of Peleus'. The genealogical distancing of Zeus and Achilles mitigates Achilles' threat to Olympus, leaving him threat enough to himself and to the Greeks and Trojans at Troy.

The goddess *Eris* 'Strife' is alone uninvited to the wedding of Peleus and Thetis. In response, and as cause of strife and dissension, she casts an apple into the hall, inscribed "to the fairest." Hera, Athena, and Aphrodite all claim the apple, whereupon Paris, the Trojan prince (handsomest of Trojans), is chosen to adjudicate. The contest, pervasively depicted in works of art, occurs on the foothills of Mt. Ida near Troy, to which Zeus frequently "escapes" to watch the war, away from the to-do on Mt. Olympus on the Greek mainland. Hera promises Paris power; Athena, wisdom; and Aphrodite, the most beautiful woman alive: Helen, already married to Menelaus, king of Sparta. Choosing love over all, Paris declares Aphrodite fairest.

On a visit to Sparta, Paris abducts Helen (she quite willing) and returns with her, her possessions, and treasures to Troy. The Greeks, under the leadership of Agamemnon, Menelaus' brother, amass their combined forces in an expedition to regain Helen. It is noteworthy that Menelaus, though the aggrieved husband, does not lead the troops. This signals Menelaus' lack of leadership (reflected in the inability to retain his own wife). As seen throughout the *Iliad*, he is actually quite mediocre—though he does have his moment in the defense of the fallen Patroclus' corpse. We know from other sources that Menelaus won Helen as wife, over her many suitors throughout Greece, solely by excess of gifts.

Helen's father, Tyndareus, knowing that any choice of husband would cause discord among the remaining suitors, made them all swear the "Oath of Tyndareus," whereby they pledged their support to whoever of them suffered injury. This, perforce, would maintain the peace. The oath thus precipitated the muster of troops for Troy, serving as rationale for the first purposeful alliance of all Hellenes, or Greeks. Indeed, those who wooed Helen from every part of Greece would now fight on her behalf. Hence, the Panhellenic intent of Homer's *Iliad*—a poem with incipient national appeal for all Greeks. The appeal is further apparent in the "Catalogue of Ships" listing the far-ranging Greek contingents that sailed for Troy. Also Panhellenic is the *Iliad*'s freely blended use of dialects from the major regions of Homer's Greece: Aeolic, Ionic, Doric, and Attic (see map). The differing dialect forms also (and more immediately) serve to facilitate Homeric meter. Where the meter does not accommodate one dialect form, it does another. However, Ionic, also known as epic or Homeric Greek, predominates.

Homer's *Iliad* does not begin with the Judgment of Paris, the theft of Helen, the muster of troops, or even the start of the war itself. It begins, according to the Roman poet Horace's dictate, *in medias res* 'in the midst of things', creating a coherent self-contained whole from a given starting point—the procedure approved by Aristotle (Poetics)—and ending with the death and funeral of Hector, the Trojan defender and mainstay. The ending, though neither necessary nor inevitable, is appropriate to Homer's chosen part of the story. Poets of lesser rank dealt with episodes and events pre- and postdating Homer's *Iliad*—the so-called "cyclic" poets. Very little of their work survives, though known by reference and summary—and known to be inferior to that of Homer.

~ Book I ~

Achilles and Agamemnon Quarrel, Achilles Withdraws from Battle, Thetis Implores Zeus to Avenge Achilles by Favoring the Trojans

THE *ILIAD* BEGINS AT a point toward the end of the ten-year siege of Troy, with an argument between Agamemnon and Achilles. Achilles is the mightiest and most beautiful of the Greeks at Troy. Being too young at the time to woo Helen, he is not bound by the Oath of Tyndareus (p. 60) as he takes pains to explain. He fights not to vindicate Menelaus but to ensure his own enduring glory—the promised reward for the brief life allotted him.

To sustain their siege over a ten-year period, the Greeks raid neighboring towns and islands, both for supplies and women to serve as concubines. Two such captives (or "spear brides") are Brisēïs, awarded Achilles; and Chrysēïs, awarded Agamemnon. At the start of the poem, Chrysēs, priest of Apollo and the father of Chrysēïs, comes to the Greek camp to ransom his daughter. But Agamemnon refuses and insolently sends him away. Chrysēs seeks Apollo's vengeance. The god inflicts a nine-day plague on the camp, and the Greeks perish in droves (the plague reflecting, on a different level, the squalor of a ten-year beach encampment).

Achilles calls a council, encouraging the soothsayer Kalchas to explain the plague. Acquiring a promise of protection from Achilles, Kalchas reluctantly blames Agamemnon's refusal to return Chrysēïs. Thus required, Agamemnon focuses on Achilles, whose idea it was to involve Kalchas; and the two quarrel over issues of hierarchy, namely, whether Zeus-granted governance and rule over multitudes (Agamemnon) merit deference to inherent bravery and moral superiority (Achilles). Nestor intervenes to end the dispute, but not before Agamemnon announces he will take Brisēïs as compensation for the surrendered Chrysēïs (which he does).

An outraged Achilles withdraws himself and his troops from battle, since Agamemnon's dishonor of Achilles nullifies his glory (public humiliation being inimical to glory). Achilles will thus have the worst of both worlds: neither glory (the reward for dying young at Troy) nor longevity (the reward for having stayed at home). That is the dilemma and crisis of his withdrawal from battle—with grievous consequence for his companions in arms. He entreats his mother, Thetis, to petition Zeus for Greek defeat in vindication of the affront to his honor. Zeus agrees, inciting Hera to argument (Zeus and Hera regularly arguing throughout the poem). The dispute comically mimics that of the Greek protagonists. The lame smithy god, Hephaestus, seeks to reconcile his arguing parents, complaining their discord will spoil supper. "Unquenchable laughter" seizes the gods at the sight of Hephaestus hobbling about. Dinner concludes, and the gods retire to bed.

μῆνιν ἄειδε θεὰ Πηληϊάδεω Ἀχιλῆος
οὐλομένην, ἣ μυρί' Ἀχαιοῖς ἄλγε' ἔθηκε,
πολλὰς δ' ἰφθίμους ψυχὰς Ἄϊδι προΐαψεν
ἡρώων, αὐτοὺς δὲ ἑλώρια τεῦχε κύνεσσιν
οἰωνοῖσί τε δαῖτα, Διὸς δ' ἐτελείετο βουλή,
ἐξ οὗ δὴ τὰ πρῶτα διαστήτην ἐρίσαντε
Ἀτρεΐδης τε ἄναξ ἀνδρῶν καὶ δῖος Ἀχιλλεύς.

SING, Goddess, the wrath of Peleus' son Achilles,
The cause accursed of Achaean pains uncounted.
Many a hero's mighty soul did it hurl down
To Hell, the mighty themselves making meal for dogs
And banqueting for birds. Thus Zeus' intent advanced   5
From when the two contending parted first as foes,
Agamemnon, king of men, and dread Achilles.

Which, then, of the gods, conjoined the two discordant?
The offspring of Leto and Zeus, the archer god,
Apollo. Enraged at the king, he confounded   10

BOOK I

The camp with pestilence, and the people perished
For Chrysēs' sake, whom Agamemnon dishonored;
For Chrysēs had come to the swift Achaean ships,
Arrayed in the robes of the archer Apollo,
With plentiful spoils, the ransom for his daughter.   15
And he beseeched the Achaeans, especially
Those twain of Atreus sprung, orderers of the ranks:
"Atreus' sons, and you other well-greaved Achaeans!
May the Olympian gods procure your plunder
Of Priam's town and your coming home thereafter,   20
But this ransom accept for my daughter's return,
Respecting the rights of far-shooting Apollo."

Then agreed the Argives all, voicing their assent,
To respect the priest and take the teeming treasure;
But how this rankled Agamemnon, king of men!   25
Roundly he rebuked him, adding this reproval:
"Be ever gone, old grizzled one, your distance keep,
That I no more encounter you, either dawdling
Here aside these hollow hulls or reappearing
Afterward. Forsworn the god's insignia then,   30
Not worth the thread. Your darling girl I'll not release,
'Til senescence be her lot, at my dwelling place
In Argos, far from her fatherland, plying my
Loom and bestriding my bed. But leave, no longer
Anger me, that you depart the more securely."   35
Thus he spoke, and fear unsettled the agèd one.
Silently to the seashore's seething strand he went
And, at a distance removed, beseeched Apollo:
"O god of plague, if e'er to you I've sacrificed
The crackling hinds of bulls or consecrated goats,   40
Then this of my god I devotedly implore:
Let the Argives by your arrows repay my tears."
Thus prayed the priest, and Phoebus Apollo heard him.
From Olympus' summit he pounced, exasperate,
Bearing his bow and quiver covered end to end,   45

And the arrows clanged to the angered god's descent—
Veiled his advance, masked his visage with midnight's dread.
Apart the ships applied he plenteous weapons.
First among the mules, then 'mid rav'nous dogs he ranged,
Then on the soldiery itself the deluge drove 50
Unending. The pyres raged, corpse on corpse compacted.

Thus decimated, nine days long the men endured.
But thereafter Achilles assembled the host,
Beholding, distressed, the soldiers' devastation.
And they, to their stations once gathered and convened, 55
Attended Achilles, who spoke among them thus:
"Sons of Atreus, now I suspect that, driven back,
Will we homeward flee, if disease not triumph first,
Or battle and plague not destroy us every one;
But come, let us some soothsaying counselor seek, 60
Or priest, or bird interpreter—for visions too
Derive from Zeus—to disclose the god's displeasure;
Whether he our ritual offerings resent,
Our sacrifices full; or heartily greeting
The redolence of flawless goats or roasted lambs, 65
He disavow this evil and deliver us."

Thus speaking was he seated, and among them rose
Kalchas, Thestōr's son, bird augur preeminent,
Who knew what was, knew what had been and was to be;
To Troy had he delivered the Danaan ships 70
By seercraft, gift of the archer god Apollo.
Intending them well, he thus intoned among them:
"O Achilles, beloved of Zeus, you bid me speak
The wrath of Apollo, far-shooting archer god.
Declare it, then, I will. But devoutly swear you 75
Yourself, in my need, to render me assistance.
For I shudder to think of distressing the man
Who rules the Argives all, and whom they all obey.
Greater a king when angered at a commoner;

For though he promptly digest his indignation,
Yet nurtures he within distemper unsubdued,
Until it be attained. So, pledge me your support"!
Answering him, swift-footed Achilles proclaimed:
"Nay! Courage taking, speak what prophecy you know.
For not by Apollo, dear to Zeus, to whom you,
Kalchas, praying, divulge your divinations true;
Not whilst I draw breath, beholding the earth entire,
Will anyone on you beside these hollow hulls
Lay heavy hands, of this Greek host assembled here.
Not even should you mention Agamemnon, who
Much proclaims himself the best of the Achaeans."
Directly, then, proclaimed the blameless prophet thus:
"Nor ritual nor sacrifice does he reprove,
But Agamemnon, for his treatment of the priest,
That he released not the daughter nor ransom took,
For which Apollo vexes him and ever will.
Nor exiting the Argive camp will plague depart
Until the lovely-lidded girl delivered be
Unto her sire, unpurchasèd, unransomèd,
And sacrifice to Chrysē brought. Thus mollified
Might Apollo grant remission, his rage renounced."

Thus speaking he retired, and among them up stood
The warrior, wide-governing Agamemnon
Atreïdēs, aggrieved, darkly addled his heart,
His eyes aglare, the likeness of conflagration.
Bleakly regarding Kalchas, he rebuked him thus:
"Unprincipled prophet, so you pontificate,
A derelict, disdaining candor evermore,
Planning villainy beloved of your prophet's craft,
Never speaking soundly nor virtue displaying.
So, now among the Argives give you vatic voice,
That lord Apollo by design undoes us quite,
Since for the girl Chrysēïs I declined accept
The ransom's trove, since greater my inclination

To convey her home, more fully preferring her 115
To my lawful wedded consort, Clytemnestra,
As she in countenance, figure, disposition,
And industry her equal is. But, nonetheless,
Surrendered shall she be, advantaging our cause;
I sooner the men protected than perishing. 120
But rally you, some other prize prepare for me,
That I alone amid the host not prizeless be.
Unfit the thought, well mark it: my prize goes elsewhere!"
Then replied Achilles, the godlike, swift of foot:
"Agamemnon, for greed and gain preeminent, 125
What prize from the great-hearted Greeks will you garner,
Such benefits in short supply obtainable?
Those pillaged hereabouts are allocated all
And, allocated, poorly reapportionèd.
To Apollo deliver the maiden apace! 130
Then from the Argives garner you countless glories
If Zeus to ruin e'er topple towering Troy."
Wide-ruling Agamemnon, scolding, thus replied:
"Inveigle me not, Achilles, however good
And godlike; not thus will you win or elude me. 135
Think you, whilst you possess your battle prize, that I,
As you command, will countenance the girl's return?
So be it, were the Greeks, great-spirited, to gift
Me in return, as due, assigning just reward.
But should they nothing give, then I myself shall take, 140
Escorting her, Odysseus' prize or Ajax's;
Or even yours, Achilles, shall I confiscate,
And much dispirited whome'er I thus approach—
My full intention, as befits, in time disclosed.
But, come now, to the godlike sea a galleon draw, 145
With oarsmen aptly numbered and with hecatomb,
Embarking the fair-favored Chrysēïs thereon.
And more, let one sound-minded man commander be,
Idomeneus, Ajax, or divine Odysseus,
Or, Pēleïdēs, you, most prodigious of men, 150

BOOK I

That Apollo, respected thus, be pacified."

With dour regard the fleet Achilles answered him:
"Villain, alas, appareled in rapacity,
How will the Argives, rank and file, disposèd be
To rally 'gainst the foe, when you command them fight?   155
Not for Trojan spearmen's trespass am I present
Here nor on warfare's whim. Why count them culpable?
Never once upon my livestock have they fallen,
Nor on my hearth in fertile man-fost'ring Phthia,
Nor afflicted my yield, since interposed between   160
Are shade-ensconcèd peaks and coasts far-echoing.
For you alone we came, great contumacious one,
Reaping plaudits for reprobates, dog-countenanced
Menelaus and yourself, from the Trojans all.
This do you allow, oblivious, insensate,   165
Shamelessly proposing to pillage the prizes
For which I battled and which th' Achaeans conferred.
Not once have I reward received the equal yours,
Whene'er the Greeks attack a prosp'rous Trojan town:
A pitiful combat's yield is thus by myself   170
Alone collected, while of parceled prizes all
Is each the greatest granted you; the trifling, me,
Despite my fame, alone to fondle by my ship.
To Phthia I now return, since preferable
My seaborne faring home than biding—scoffed at here—   175
Your fecklessness and prodding your intemperance."

To him responded Agamemnon, king of men:
"Depart then, should your spirit thus command, since I,
On my account, will not entreat you stay. Others
There are to honor me, Zeus counselor most of all.   180
Abhorred to me of Zeus-belovèd lords are you,
Forever discord's darling, drenched in blood and gore.
Be you mightier adjudged? Thus gracious the gods.
Hurried homeward with your vessels and companions,

Commands give to the Myrmidons, damned if I care. 185
Your tantrums I discount, my declaration thus:
As archer Apollo reclaims my Chrysēïs,
I return her, by vessel with warrior escort;
But your prize, fair-featured Brisēïs, I demand,
Myself upon your tent descending, that you mark 190
How much the greater than you I be, and others
Shun to challenge me, deeming them my equal born."
So he spoke, and rose the gall in Achilles' gorge,
And sundered was the heart within his tousled chest:
Whether, from aside his thigh the deft sword wielding, 195
He despatch Agamemnon, provoking the host;
Or arrest his mettle and his choler constrain.
The choices thus within himself considering—
The sharpened sword from out its scabbard drawn—arrived
Athena from high Olympus, by the white-armed 200
Goddess Hera sent, caring alike for them both.
Athena from behind took hold his tawny hair,
By him alone observed, to others unbeknownst.
Wheeling thunderstruck about, Achilles perceived
The goddess proximate—her vision penetrant! 205

Thus fulminating, declared he in wingèd words:
"Why come you, progeny of aegis-bearing Zeus,
To observe Agamemnon Atreïdēs' pride?
But this I prophesy, and promptly transpire it:
His infatuate life to my compulsion lost." 210
Him did the grey-eyed goddess Athena advise:
"From high heaven I come to inhibit your rage—
Should you relent—sent by Hera the white-armed queen,
Solicitous, committed to your well-being.
From dissension now ceasing, your weapon repose 215
And ringingly rebuke him with protestation.
For thus I declare, and the like betide it true:
That magnificent gifts, amends for this misuse,
Will you three-fold amass; but bend you and obey."

BOOK I

Thus responding swift-footed Achilles replied: 220
"Goddess, befits it I follow your counsels twain,
However much irate at heart; far better thus.
Who abides the gods will by gods abetted be."
Thus saying, to its hilt applied he heavy hand,
Scabbardward plunging the ample sword, attending 225
Athena's word; but she Olympus-bound withdrew,
Where aegis-bearing Zeus and th' other gods abide.
Achilles continued, caustically addressing
Agamemnon, nor ever did his dudgeon dim:
"Grape-soaked sovereign, agape your canine countenance, 230
Your heart the darting deer's—never once accoutred
Dare you be, when Danaans for combat convene,
Nor geared be for ambush amid the Argive best,
For that to you were death assured, doubt not. Sooner
You ransack the Achaeans hereabouts, to pounce 235
Plundering his prize, whenever a man protests.
Despot feeding on your folk, worthless willings all,
Elsewise were such affront assuredly your last.
Thus I pronounce and promise true, my pledge aright:
That by this sceptre, bearing leaf no more nor branch, 240
Since from its wooded mount detached—nor will it bloom,
For 'round about the axe has shorn it, branch and bark—
And now the sons of the Achaeans carry it,
Law-givers, in their hands, who guard the precedents
By Zeus pronounced; be this my affirmation sworn: 245
If e'er to the Achaean camp come need of famed
Achilles, doomed be the Danaans—however
Much you agonize—fallen lifeless to Hector,
Slaughterer of men. Then burst your breast asunder,
To have thus abused the best of the Achaeans." 250
So spoke Achilles, downward casting his sceptre,
With golden nailings jeweled, and resumed his seat;
And, sitting across him, Agamemnon railed on.

Stood next among them Nestor, sweet-tongued orator

71

Of Pylos, polished his speech, from whose very lips 255
Pronouncement poured the honey's like. Already had
He known two mortal generations come and gone,
Prior flourished and prosp'rous in sandy Pylos.
Amid the third he ruled. And with good intention
Toward Atreus' son and Achilles proclaimed he thus: 260
"Alack the day, in dread by all Achaeans held!
Let Priam sure and Priam's progeny rejoice,
Let celebrate the Trojans all within their hearts,
Acknowledging this your dire contention, for shame,
Who in counsel and in combat surpass the Greeks. 265
By me persuaded be, and mind my counsel sure.
Aforetime with your betters kept I company,
Nor ever was I once demeaned in doing so,
Valiants the lot of them, none better anywhere;
Perithous one, also Dryas the protector, 270
Kaineus, Exadius, godlike Polyphēmus,
Theseus, good Aegeus' son, like to the immortals.
Prospered they, mightiest nurtured of earthborn men.
Mightiest nurtured and most mightily matched, fought
They feral mountain tribes, annihilating them. 275
With such consorted I, decamping from Pylos,
Far distant the land, for they themselves had summoned.
And well did I acquit myself. But gone today
The earthborn mortal men to join their company;
Yet to my guidance gave they heed and due regard; 280
So heed you both, thereby better deemed obeying.
Do not, however nobly bred, appropriate
His prize, the girl the Argives first afforded him.
Admit his right. And you, Achilles, covet not
To vie with kings, provoking them, since never once 285
Do sceptred kings, on whom Zeus confers eminence,
Apportion their prestige. If you be mightier,
A goddess mother gave you birth. But better he
Since ruling over multitudes. Desist from force,
Atreïdēs, while I entreat him rest his rage, 290

BOOK I

Who of the Greeks in barb'rous clash our bulwark is."

Thus answering, spoke Atreïdēs Agamemnon:
"Indeed, old man, such matter you proclaim aright!
But this man wishes to outdo us every one.
He craves command, desires to be superior, 295
Directives gives—the likes of which I reckon not
To follow. If the gods a fighter fashioned him,
So licensed they his insolence and calumny."
Sidelong viewing him, averred divine Achilles:
"Indeed, a ne'er-do-well and coward would I be, 300
Capitulating to your orders, all of them.
Compliance from these others wrest, but not from me
Intending most your biddings all to disregard.
But this too I declare; attend you and take heed:
My hands from battle dormant lie—idle their use 305
To you or any other on the girl's account,
Since, given, is she taken back. And of the stores
That I possess aside my rapid ship, would you
Against my will take nothing, bearing it away;
Just go ahead and try, that these bear witness true— 310
Your blackened blood a'trickle dripping from my spear."
With words impassioned thus, the twain contending fought,
And the Argive assembly, uprising, adjourned,
Whereat Achilles to his tents and balanced ships
Retired, with Patroclus and their companions all. 315

But Atreïdēs seaward drew a speedy ship,
Equipped with twenty oarsmen, and within it placed
A hecatomb unto the god, himself taking
And seating Chrysēïs, fair-countenanced, within,
And many-minded Odysseus captained the ship. 320
Ascending the vessel they voy'ged the water's way,
But Atreïdēs bid the men self-purify,
And purged they to seaward their contaminations,
And to Apollo offered perfect hecatombs

Of bulls and goats aside the shoreline's restless strand,   325
And the smoke-woven savor suffused high heaven.
Thus labored they about the camp, but Atreidēs
Remained livid, as when first threat'ning Achilles,
And beckoned Eurybates, Talthybius too,
Achaean messengers and bustling henchmen both: 330
"Approach you the tent of Pēleidēs Achilles,
And by her hand fair-featured Brisēis reclaim.
If he deny me, myself will I reclaim her,
With companions approaching, the worse for him yet."
So speaking he despatched them, precise his command.   335
And the twain unwilling walked the restless seashore's
Strand, to the Myrmidon ships and tents arriving,
And found Achilles sitting aside his quarters
And dark vessel; nor viewing them delighted he;
And they, unnerved, attended deferentially,   340
Eyes downward cast, nor ventured nor addressed him aught.
But knowing the matter within his heart, he spoke:
"Greetings both, Zeus' messengers and heralds of men,
Draw near. Not you but Agamemnon is to blame
Who sends you on the maiden Brisēis' account;   345
But come, Patroclus, divinely born, relinquish
The girl, deliver her, that they witnesses be
Before the illustrious gods and mortals all,
And before the remorseless king, if ever need
Of me again arise, some ruin to forestall.   350
With what malefic mind he makes his offerings!
Caution knows he not, nor knows he circumspection,
That the Argives aside their vessels safely fight."

Thus he spoke, and his dear friend Patroclus obeyed.
From the tent conveyed he fair-visaged Brisēis,   355
And gave her for the taking; and the two repaired
From Achilles' camp, and the woman, unwilling,
Followed them. And Achilles, disgusted, withdrew
In tears, far distant from his companions sitting

By the breaking brine, beholding its vast domain;   360
And with palms uplifted, his mother much implored:
"Mother, because to life foreshortened I was born,
Olympian Zeus high-thundering should rightly have
Granted me honor, but misuses me instead;
And now Agamemnon Atreïdēs wide-ruling   365
Derides me, determined to commandeer my prize."
So shedding a tear he spoke, and his reverent
Mother, deep-fathomed in salts below, alongside
Her senescent sire, attended him, and quickly
From the rimy brine uprose, most resembling mist,   370
And aside her heart-stricken offspring sat weeping.
Gently she stroked him, this wingèd word addressing:
"Why weep you, dear child, what misfortune besets you?
Speak, revealing your sorrow, that we know it both."
Deep groaning, swift-footed Achilles responded: 375
"This know you already! Wherefore renew the tale?
To Thebes we came, Eëtion's inviolate town,
Pillaged it through, uprooting it from bottom up;
And among themselves the sons of the Achaeans
Apportioned the take—befittingly—fair-visaged   380
Chrysēïs on lordly Atreïdēs conferring.
But Chrysēs, the priest of far-shooting Apollo,
Approached the ships of the bronze-chitoned Achaeans,
Arrayed in the robes of the archer Apollo,
With plentiful spoils, the ransom for his daughter.   385
He beseeched the Achaean host, especially
The twain of Atreus sprung, orderers of the ranks.
The other Greeks then fully voiced their approvals,
To reverence the priest and take the teeming trove.
But how this rankled Agamemnon, king of men!   390
Roundly he rebuked him, adding a reprimand.
And the old man retired, enraged, and Apollo
Remarked his prayer, loving the priest steadfastly.
Amid the Greeks the god's merciless missiles sped,
And perniciously perished the soldiers away.   395

So sped the god's arrows throughout the encampment.
And to us the seer, well knowing it, prophesied
Divine decree, and I urged the god's appeasement;
But Agamemnon fulminated, fast rising
To his feet, threateningly, as is now fulfilled. 400
The Argives to Chrysē now circumspectly take
The girl, by ship with sacrificial offerings.
Come heralds too, Brisēïs taking from my tent,
The girl the Argives gave me, most deservèd gain.

But fittingly attend, provide your son support, 405
Olympus-bound imploring lord Zeus, if ever
You declared or undertook whate'er promoted
His devisings. For often have I heard you boasting
In your father's halls, when recollection prevailed,
How, alone of the immortal gods, you stymied 410
Unseemly misadventure from cloud-gath'ring Zeus,
When certain deities devised to fetter him:
Poseidon, and Hera, and Pallas Athena;
But you, O goddess, arrived, unmanacled him,
Swift summ'ning the hundred-hander to Olympus 415
Whom gods call Briareus, but men name Aegaeōn,
Abundant his power, quite surpassing his sire's,
And proximate Zeus he exulted in glory,
And cowed were the gods, daring not to constrain him.
The likes of which reminding Zeus, approach and clasp 420
His very knees, that Trojan mettle be unleashed,
Repulsing the Argives proward to their vessels,
Confounded in the fray—thus profit them their king—
And wide-ruling Agamemnon know his madness,
That he dishonored the best of the Achaeans." 425

His dear mother, shedding a tear, responded thus:
"O child of mine, to what nurture, what advantage
Was your dreadful birth decreed? Better far your fate
Afore the ships, stranger to despair, unweeping,

BOOK I

Since desperately foreshortened your life, not lasting. 430
Now stand you most swiftly fated and pitiful
Among mankind, and thus for naught beneath my roof
Were you begot. Myself, then, on your behalf, will
I to thunder-delighting Zeus this plaint propound,
Going to snowbound Olympus, persuading him. 435
But you the while aside the quick-prowed ships abide,
From battle forbear; and bane be to the Argives.
To blameless Aethiop Zeus yesterday repaired
To feast; the other gods comprised his retinue.
Olympus-bound upon the twelfth day he returns, 440
Whereon shall I importune him, overstepping
The brazen portal of his opulent palace
And with genial persuasions fasten to his knees."
Thus conversing she departed, there leaving him
Indignant within on the well-girt girl's account, 445
Whom they coercively reclaimed.
                              Then to Chrysē
Came Odysseus, the sacred hecatomb in tow,
Ship's oarage to the harbor's rippled depth applied.
Gathered they the sails, storing them in the vessel,
Inserted the mast to the crutch, by the forestays 450
Quickly lowering it; and the vessel itself
Its oarsmen hefted forward into harborage.
Anchoring stones were cast, to stern-cables attached,
The men, wading a'front the tide's eddying froth,
Disembarked the hecatomb, meet for Apollo 455
Far-shooting. And forth from the seafaring vessel
Came Chrysēïs; and many-minded Odysseus
Returned her, by the altar, to her father's most
Longing embrace, respectfully addressing him:

"O Chrysēs, now has Agamemnon, king of men, 460
Despatched me with your child, and to lord Apollo
Proffers this sacred hecatomb for sacrifice
On th' Achaeans' account to placate Apollo,

Who imposes upon us a plenteous ruin."
Thus speaking he returned her, and the priest rejoiced   465
Receiving his dear child. Next, aside the well-built
Altar, straightway positioned they unto the god
The holy hecatomb aright. And cleansing hands,
They next uplifted bristled barley groats on high
And o'er the lowing cattle's foreheads scattered them,   470
And midst them all did Chrysēs supplication make:
"Hear me, O Silverbow, who frequentest Chrysē
And sacred Killa, and ruleth Tenedos Isle:
If ever aforetime you attended my prayer,
And favoring me hard burdened the Danaans,   475
Then presently this prayed-for dispensation grant,
Foreclosing further devastation from the Greeks."
Thus speaking he implored, and Apollo heard him.
The prayers completed, and barley sprinkled forth,
They uplifted the necks, slaughtered and flayed the beasts,   480
Apportioned the pieces of thigh, fat enfolded—
The raw flesh laid within—cooked through on wooden stakes.
With glistering wine the elder made libation,
And youths with five-pronged forks arrayed about him stood.
Their endeavors concluded, they lavished a feast,   485
Nor of dining was any want unsatisfied.
Cresting the craters with vintage aswirl, the lads
First proffered libations, apportioning the rest.
Then, the daylong dancing, honored they Apollo,
Sang a paean to Apollo's praises cadenced,   490
And the deity, viewing it, gladdened at heart.
And as Helios yielded to darkness' descent,
The men by their stern-cabled vessels reposed them.
And as rosy-fingered Dawn fast-risen ensued,
For th' Achaean encampment they charted their course,   495
And regaled them Apollo with gladdening gusts.
Upraising the mast, unfurled they the whitened sail,
To favoring winds responsive; and resounded
The foam hard pounding 'bout the briny-balanced prow,

And the hull hastened onward incising the swell. 500
And gaining th' extensive Achaean encampment,
They drew the ship landward, high-seating it in sand,
Stanchioned the stays, and to his own tent scattered each.

But ever he raged by his swift-running vessels,
Zeus-born Pēlëidēs, swift-footed Achilles, 505
Nor ent'ring upon the ennobling assembly
Nor engaging fight, but wilted at heart away,
Keeping to himself, craving war's clamor and clash.

As the hours in cycles passed, and the twelfth day dawned,
The gods ever-living returned to Olympus, 510
Ahead them, assembled all, loud-thundering Zeus;
Nor did Thetis forget her Achilles' commands,
But directly ascended the undulate tide,
Coming early to vast heaven and Olympus,
Encountering there wide-countenanced Cronidēs, 515
Apart, his own counsel keeping, astride a peak
Of many-pinnacled Olympus. And settling
Before him—his knees in her right arm enfolding,
Her left hand caressing his chin—she coyly coaxed
Lord Zeus Cronidēs, addressing him this remark: 520
"Father Zeus, if e'er I have benefit bestowed
On you amid th' immortal gods in word or deed,
Afford this dispensation: sustain my offspring,
Acknowledged most lamentably fated of men,
For Agamemnon Atreidēs disparages 525
Him, commandeering his prize and possessing it;
But honor you him, Olympian counselor Zeus,
The Trojans augmenting, 'til all the Achaeans
Proclaim him preeminently honor-possessed."
So she spoke, and cloud-gathering Zeus kept quiet, 530
And long sat saying nothing; and Thetis, closely
The while adhering to his knees, importuned him
A second time: "So signal and assurance nod,

Or deny me—you clearly may—that I discern
How much of all the gods I stand discredited." 535

Greatly angered, cloud-gathering Zeus responded:
"Dreadful these doings, indeed; the like driving me
To vie with taunting Hera—vexing her retort—
Who even presently among th' immortal gods
Berates me, averring I abet the Trojans. 540
But be you away, lest Hera here behold us.
To this will I attend 'til seeing it attained.
My forehead will I now incline, signifying
These my assurances provided, unswerving,
Dispositive, token undying acknowledged— 545
That word of mine will never uneffected be,
Nor vain, nor mere invention, once I intervene.
Thus speaking, Cronidēs acquiesced, lowering
Darkened brows, the long ambrosial locks cascading
From his kingly head, and lofty Olympus quaked. 550
Their counsel taken, retired the twain, she leaping
From high Olympus downward the fathomless deep;
Lord Zeus to his residence gone. And together
Rose the seated gods, anticipating thund'ring
Zeus, their sire. Nor did any, reposing abide 555
His approach, but together instantly upstood
Who reposing had earlier sat. Nor had furtive
Hera failed to heed how silver-footed Thetis,
Begotten child of the sea-born ancient Nēreus,
Connived with thund'ring Zeus, and straightaway addressed 560
Derisive words to her lord consort, Cronus' son:
"With which duplicitous goddess intrigue you now?
Forever you delight to plot, deluding me,
And thus stands your disinclination apparent,
To disseminate your inwardly made design." 565
Then to her replied the father of gods and men:
"Hera, tempt not to interpret my every word,
Toilsome the process, though you be my wedded spouse.

BOOK I

But what befits to be known, none sooner of gods
Or men will be acquainted with than you. But what   570
I please, from th' immortals apart to implement,
Seek not conclusively to query or survey."
To him reposted the lady ox-eyed Hera:
"Cronidēs, most respected, what utterance this?
Ne'er aforetime have I queried you unduly   575
Nor enquired. Of your own volition you decide
What most avails be done. Now stands my mind dismayed
That silver-footed Thetis, child of the sea-born
Ancient Nēreus, has cajoled you; that risen Dawn
Discovered her aside your throne reposed, firmly   580
Enfolding your knees, you promising to favor
Achilles and destroy Danaans by their ships."
Addressing her, lord Zeus, cloud-gathering, answered:
"Dear lady, ever distrusting me! I never
Escape you! This will you haplessly hasten: my   585
Total estrangement, your lasting disadvantage.
But being seated, contain your tongue and attend,
Lest all the Olympian gods avail you not,
When these my hands inviolable outstretched lay hold."
Thus he spoke, and his consort ox-eyed Hera cringed   590
Quieted, enduring her lord husband's rebuke.
But wroth about the hearth of Zeus, th' Immortal gods
Demurred; whereat Hephaestus th' artificer spoke,
Easing the heart of his mother white-armed Hera:
"Destructive doings these and unendurable,   595
Whene'er you twain contend on mere mortals' account,
Dispensing dissension among the immortals.
Then blight plagues our banqueting, since evil prevails.
My mother, herself e'er mindful, I admonish
And advise to deal good-naturèdly with Zeus,   600
Lest by his upbraidings supper be disrupted.
And should the lord of lightning inclination have
From out our chairs to chasten us—the stronger he!
But swaddle Zeus with sympathetic words about,

Intent on his demeanor, affably disposed."   605
So he spoke, and speedily into Hera's hand
Delivered he her drinking cup, continuing:
"Undaunted be, dear mother mine, and persevere,
Though woesome this grief lest, witness to your whipping
I avail you not, much vexed, howe'er attentive   610
My regard. Displeased is Olympian Zeus opposed.
To your assistance hastened I once aforetime,
But father Zeus, fast clasping my heels, propelled me
From heaven's preeminent threshold, long hurtling
'Til landing on Lemnos, with daylight in decline,   615
Of life all but bereft, the locals lending aid."
Thus he spoke, and the goddess white-armed Hera smiled,
And pleasantly took hold the proffered drinking cup.
Then left to right among the gods Hephaestus poured
Sweet-nectared wine from the crater overflowing,   620
And amid the gods rose laughter unquenchable,
Undying, the lame Hephaestus hobbling about.

When the igneous globe horizonward had waned,
The immortals departed, decamping to bed,
Where the crippled craftsman, skill-famed lord Hephaestus,   625
Had with deft facility built abodes for each.
Strode to his bed Olympian lord of lightning Zeus,
Where he, when wearied, sought repose. Upstepping, lay
He down, aside him sleeping Hera gold-enthroned.

~ Book II ~

Zeus Sends Agamemnon a False Dream, Agamemnon Tests the Army, the Rowdy Thersites, the Catalogue of Ships

THE GREEKS WILL NOW begin paying the price for the insult to Achilles. At Thetis' request, Zeus sends Agamemnon a deceptive dream, urging him to lead the army into battle, for Troy will surely be taken. However, the dream's real purpose is to highlight the implications of Achilles' absence. Deluded into thinking he can take Troy without Achilles, even while fearing the army's despair over Achilles' withdrawal—to say nothing of the recent plague and length of the siege itself—Agamemnon contrives a plan to test the army's loyalty. He first tells his counselors he will propose flight and a return home, but instructs them to halt the flight should the soldiers actually make off. Assembling the Greeks, he thus urges a return home, saying that his dream, promising victory, was false. He expects the rejection of his proposal, but the scheme of course backfires. The Greeks immediately run en masse toward their ships, their multitudes conveyed in a series of vivid similes (these preparatory to the enumeration in the Catalogue of Ships). However, they are stopped and resettled by Odysseus, the craftiest and most persuasive of the Greeks.

Next, in a scene unique to the *Iliad*—one of bathos and humor both—the commoner Thersitēs, the ugliest man who ever came to Troy, stands forth and rebukes Agamemnon. But he is promptly silenced by Odysseus' reprimand and a blow about the shoulders. The troops sympathize with Thersitēs, though believing his punishment just. Various voices are heard, and the advice of Nestor prevails: that the troops muster and divide into clans, preparatory to battle. From this follows the famous Catalogue of Ships, enumerating the forces that came to Troy. Catalogues are a frequent feature of archaic Greek poetry, with structural, storytelling, and entertainment value. An ideal aide-memoire and organizational device, meter-driven catalogues are of the essence of heroic poetry—be they of ships, the slain, material goods, denizens of the deep, famous women or lovers, suitors, or what have you. If it exists in multiples, it is grist for catalogue.

The Catalogue of Ships, though logically belonging to a much earlier point in the story, is one of several such inclusions providing a sense of the *Iliad*'s greater scope and action—a sense of "from start to finish"—even though Homer's theme is far more circumscribed. (Homer elsewhere, and to the same effect, is *forward* looking or anticipatory.) Other such retrospective incidents, i.e., those made part of Homer's narrative present, though logically belonging to an earlier phase of the war, include Helen's identification of Greek heroes in "The View from the Wall" (Book 3), the single combat between Menelaus and Paris (Book 3), the single combat between Ajax and Hector (Book 7)—both duels anticipating the fatal encounter between Hector and Achilles (Book 22)—and the night raid (Book 10).

Now were the other gods and horse-marshaling troops
Fast slumbered the nighttime through. But lacking slumber's
Balm did Zeus devise deft counsel—to high acclaim
Achilles, crushing th' Achaeans aside their ships.
And within his plotting spirit appeared this best: 5
To send lord Atreïdēs a menacing dream.
And thus addressing it in wingèd words, he spoke:
"Go, speed thee, menacing dream; and sped to the tent
Of Atreïdēs Agamemnon, this proclaim
My true design. Order him immediately 10
By rank and file to arm the flowing-haired Argives
To conquer the high-turreted city of Troy,
For the gods dwelling on Olympus determined
Stand, since agonies beleaguer the Trojan lines
And Olympian minds to Hera's pleas respond." 15
Thus he spoke, and mindfully departed the dream.
Quickly it came to the swift-shipped Achaean camp
And advanced to Atreïdēs Agamemnon,

BOOK II

Finding him a'slumber in his tent—ambrosial
The sleep suffusing him—and stood nigh o'er his head, 20
In likeness unto Nestor, Neleus' son, whom most
Of elders Atreïdēs esteemed. His semblance
Assuming, expounded the godly presence thus:
"You sleep, Atreïdēs, horse-taming, wise of heart;
But a counsel-bearing man sleeps little the night, 25
To whom the people entrusted stand and many
The matter preoccupies. But consider this—
A messenger from Zeus I come who, from afar
Compassionate, takes pity and would comfort you.
Bids he the flowing-haired Achaeans quickly armed, 30
Troy's tow'ring citadel and teeming streets to take.
The Olympian gods, now firmly determined, stand
United in resolve since forcefully Hera
Prevails, and by Cronidēs' command the Trojans
Fall beleaguered. Of this, awakened, mindful be." 35
The dream, thus speaking, disappeared, leaving the king
With futile designs ill-fitted to fulfillment;
For adjudged he that day Troy's citadel to take,
The fool, divining naught of Cronidēs' design,
How there boded for Argives and Trojans alike 40
The bellow and bane of tenacious encounter.
Waking from sleep—the voice divine suffusing him—
He sat erect and donned his chiton—downy, soft,
New made—and atop it his stately mantle cast
And fastened decorate sandals to lustrous feet, 45
And 'round his shoulder slung his silver-nailèd sword
And seized th' ancestral sceptre, imperishable,
And advanced to the bronze-chitoned Achaean ships.

Goddess Dawn o'er ample Olympus ascendant
Declared daybreak to Zeus and th' other immortals; 50
And messengers, full clarion-voiced, commanded
The hair-flown Argives to assemble and convene.
These their summons made, and quickly those assembled.

First convened he a counsel of great-souled elders
By the vessel of Nestor, king Pylian-born,   55
And convening them proffered a fast-fitting plan:
"Hear me, friends. A dream divine attended my sleep
This past ambrosial night. Resembling the godly
Nestor—in nature, mien, and countenance—it came,
Standing above my head, a'whisper with this word: 60
'You sleep, horse-taming wise-hearted Atreïdēs,
But a counsel-bearing man sleeps little the night,
To whom the people entrusted stand and many
The matter preoccupies; but consider you this—
A messenger from Zeus I come who, from afar   65
Compassionate, takes pity and would comfort you.
Bids he flowing-haired Achaeans quickly armed,
Troy's teeming streets and tow'ring citadel to take.
The Olympian gods, now firmly, determined stand,
United in resolve, since forcefully Hera   70
Prevails; and by Cronidēs' command the Trojans
Fall beleaguered. Of this be mindful.' Thus speaking
The dream flew off, and fragrant sleep unfettered me.
But come now, attend to armoring the Argives.
But first with words assaying them, as may befit,   75
Will I urge retreat in their sturdy benchèd ships.
But restrain them, you, from each and every quarter."
Thus speaking he sat down, and among them Nestor
Arose, sovereign most astute of sandy Pylos
And, well disposed to them, thus answered and declared: 80
"Dear comrades, Danaan lords and commanders all,
Had some other Achaean recounted this dream,
Falsehood would we deem it, taken aback in scorn;
But dreamed it who boasts the Achaeans' best to be.
So come, be the Achaeans awakened to arms."   85

Thus having spoken, he disbanded the council,
And the sceptre-bearing lords uprose, obeying
The people's shepherd, and followed the host bestirred.

As billowing bees, ever streaming forth afresh,
Their creviced quarters quit, circumnavigating   90
Springtime shoots en masse, veering panoplied o'erhead,
Cascading this way some, others that way swarming;
So quitting tents and ships amassed the swarms of men,
Full-mustered rank and file a'front the teeming strand.
And through the ranks ran Zeus' unbridled messenger—   95
Rumor—to rally them, and rallied were they all.
The meeting ground stretched staggering, and groaned the earth
As crowding down they sat themselves; and loud the din.
And nine the heralds nigh—tenacious, thunderous—
To calm the commotion, that they attend their kings,   100
Zeus-nurtured, speaking. The men sat hastily down,
And sitting were they stayed, their hubbub abated.
Among them arose wide-ruling Agamemnon,
Grasping the sceptre the smithy lord had labored
Making. And on lord Zeus Cronidēs Hephaestus   105
Conferred it; and Zeus on his messenger, Hermes,
Slayer of Argos, bestowed it; the which Hermes
To lord Pelops presented, whipper of horses;
And from Pelops to Atreus, the people's shepherd,
It passed, entrusted thereafter to Thyestēs   110
Flocked with lambs; he to Agamemnon leaving it
To raise o'er many ships and rule the Argives all.
On the sceptre propped, to the Argives spoke he thus:
"O friends, Argive heroes, stout henchmen of Ares,
In falsehood has Zeus Cronidēs encompassed me,   115
Stubborn god, who previously nodded and declared
That o'erwhelming well-walled Troy would I homeward speed.
Now evilly devises Zeus who returns me
Bootless, Argos-bound, with many an Argive gone.
Thus mockingly thundering Zeus somehow intends,   120
Who topples the turrets of innum'rable towns
And the more will topple yet, for ample his might.
And shamefully by men to come will it be known
That so many and so manly were the Argives

Courting conflict who thus for nothing vainly vied, 125
Reviled and gloryless against a lesser foe.
For were we thus inclined, Trojans and Danaans,
Faithful oaths to forge, our forces then to tally,
The Trojans, by as many having homes in Troy,
And the Greeks by groups of ten ordained—a Trojan 130
Designated to every ten its wine to serve—
Many the tens unserved for want of attendant,
So much the greater reckon I th' Achaeans ranged
Than Trojans tallied throughout the town. But many
The allies they conscript, spear-brandishing forces 135
From cities far dispersed, to frustrate my design
To dash Troy's towering turrets, to dust returned.
Nine circling years of mighty Zeus by seasons turn,
Ships decimated by decay, their ropes a'rot,
And somewhere our unwavering wives and offspring 140
Brood, haunting our hallways, awaiting our return;
Yet nonetheless the day drags undeliverèd
That drew us here; but rally each obediently
To my behest, to Argos homeward voyaging,
For capacious Troy defying plunder persists." 145

Thus he proclaimed arousing the multitudes all,
As many as knew naught of the council's design.
The men poured forth en masse as puissant waves upswept
Across th' Icarian main by winds southeastern
Lashed, from father Zeus cloud-gathering fomented; 150
Or as when whooshing winds o'erblown the bounteous
Grain awaken it, ruffled and flattened forward.
Thus disheveled the multitude a'rush the ships,
Its shout triumphant and the dust, beneath its feet
Dispersed, ascending; and to one another nigh 155
Exhorted they the ships, unanchored, be launched. Cleansed
Were the launch grooves, the blocks dislodged beneath; ever
Seaward ventured they home, their clamor heavenbound.
Then were the Argives prematurely homeward come,

Undestined, had not Hera addressed Athena: 160
"For shame, tenacious child of aegis-bearing Zeus!
Braving the brine to their fatherlands far distant
Will the Argives return, relinquishing Helen
To King Priam and Troy—contention's trophy she—
On whose account are many Achaeans reckoned 165
Dead, sundered from distant homesteads? But depart you,
Attend the bronze-chitoned Achaean formations,
With heartening utterance restraining each man,
Nor seaward allow their vessel-balanced voyage."

Thus she spoke, nor refused her grey-eyed Athena, 170
But fast dashing descended th' Olympian mount,
And next, at the curvèd Argive ships arrived, there
Encount'ring Odysseus the gods' equal in craft;
Nor approached he his vessel, sorrow encircling
His spirit and heart. And standing aside him spoke 175
Grey-eyed Athena: "Godly born Laërtes' son,
Much-devising Odysseus, departing in flight
To your fatherland adored, issue you command
To your darkly oar-locked ships? Wouldst unto Priam
And the Trojans proffer Argive Helen, a prize 180
In which to glory, on whose account are many
Achaeans reckoned dead, wasted in the maelstrom,
Of kin bereft? But go now among the Argive
Bronze-chitoned formations, and with utterance true
Giving pause to each man, reverse you their retreat." 185
Thus the goddess, and Odysseus heeded her word.
Off he went running, offcasting his cloak—retrieved
By the herald attending him, Eurybatēs
Of Ithaca—and gaining on Agamemnon
Atreïdēs, commandeered th' ancestral sceptre 190
Sempiternal, tending toward the Achaean ships;
And chancing upon some sovereign or notable,
Stood opposite him, detaining him gently thus:
"Dear sir, alack my alarming you trembling thus,

A shirker; sit down and settle you the others.   195
Little know we Atreïdēs' disposition:
Now made he trial, but will soon turn to tyranny;
Heard we not his directive, issued from council?
Thus prove his spleen not prelude to Danaan pain.
Unequaled the eminence of Zeus-nurtured kings,   200
Comes their honor from Cronidēs, who sanctions them."
But when he chanced upon some commoner yowling
Aloud, he smote him with sceptre and reprimand:
"Sit, sirrah, and keep quiet, paying attention
To others far your better, you simpering wimp,   205
Never of account in council or encounter.
For ne'er were we Achaeans all to kingship born;
Cursed a quantity of kings, let but one command,
One sovereign be, whom crooked-minded Cronus' son
Grants sceptre and decree aright, that he might rule."   210

Thus he charged, bestriding the encampment. But they,
All thickly thundering from out vessels and tents,
Descended on the meeting place, as when a wave
Loud-gurgling grown assaults the surf and, shoreward washed,
Is seething spent, and resolutely roars the brine.   215
Then were the others still, throughout their ranks restrained,
But Thersitēs alone, intemperate of tongue,
Yet scoffed and bawled, disorderly, obstreperous;
Convulsed was his vernacular, availing not,
With kings inclined to quarrel; intoxicate he,   220
Danaan dullard and simpleton, reprobate
Of Troy, blighted his breeding; bandy-leggèd, lame
Of foot, his shoulders inward shunted toward his chest;
Pointy-headed, and sparse the tuft atop his pate;
Despisèd of Odysseus he, to Achilles   225
Loathsome most, for he ever importuned the twain
And against Agamemnon relentlessly railed,
Disdained of the Danaans, held in their despite.
Bellowing forth he berated Agamemnon:

"Fault-finding Atreïdēs, what, pray, is your beef? 230
Your tents with bronze abound, and many the woman
Awarded you whene'er we Argives raze a town.
Are you desperate for gold, that some horse-taming
Trojan might fetch you from Troy, a son's ransom, whom
I or another Danaan deliver bound, 235
Or for some winsome girl to gratify your groin,
Whom you cravenly fondle and maul? How grievous
When Argive leaders heap toil on the Argive host!
For pity! Reproaches all, Achaean women,
No longer men! But here do let's abandon him, 240
Prognosticating on his gains, that he perceive
Whether we promote his enterprise or not who
Has thus dishonored Achilles, a better man
By far than he, having pilfered and impounded
His prize. But truly is Achilles unperturbed, 245
Uncaring quite, or this your final insult were."

Thus spoke Thersitēs, shaming the people's shepherd,
But divine Odysseus deftly strode aside him
And, warily glancing, thus castigated him:
"Thersitēs, tart of tongue, resilient orator, 250
Thou! Refrain, these quarrels with kings relinquishing!
For no worse a man, I reckon, has ever come
To Troy than you, of the multitudes gone Troyward
With Atreïdēs. So, not with kings upon your
Lips shouldst reprimand, nor alone reproaches heap, 255
Nor contemplate return, nowise knowing we how
Stand these matters destined: whether we Danaans
Favored or ill-fated shall homeward be returned.
Your untiring diatribe assaults Atreïdēs
Our king, because the acclaimèd Achaean host 260
Allots him ample prizes whilst you prattle on.
But this I confirm, and concluded shall it be:
Should I again accost you, thus witless as now,
May Odysseus' head from his shoulders disconnect

And to Telemachus be he father forpassed, 265
If I not strip and confiscate your clothing all,
Cloak and chiton, protectors of your private parts—
And you yourself thwack shipward weeping blow by blow."
Thus he spoke and with golden sceptre smartly struck
About his back and shoulders; and doubled over, 270
Thersitēs shed a tender tear: bloody the weal
That welled, to the wallop's warrant true testament.
Pummeled he sat, unnerved, affrighted, despairing,
Tears dampening him. But the men, on his account
Though pained, laughed affably, and furtively peering 275
Addressed their neighbors each: "Lord what wonder betides!
Myriad goods has Odysseus undertaken,
Plans deftly devising and waking men to war,
But best of blessings on the Argives now bestows
Who bridles this blundering lout, unbearable. 280
Certain will testy Thersitēs never again
Be predisposed to clash disdainfully with kings."

As thus the host discoursed, upright stood Odysseus,
Sacker of citadels, sceptre in hand; grey-eyed
Athena aside him in herald's guise, bidding 285
The ranks be quieted, that frontward and aback
The Danaan soldiery heed and comprehend.
And he, to them well-minded, proclamation made:
"Now, O king, the Danaans deem to render you
Most abhorrent of mortal men, voided the vow 290
They took, from horse-nurturing Argos assembled,
That you would homeward turn, Troy's tow'ring walls awaste.
But now like callow lads or widowed wives they weep
For their return. Trouble enough it were to send
A man disheartened home who from his wife afar 295
The month-long endures his bench-fitted craft's constraint,
Whom winter winds immure and swollen waves detain;
But on us here detained a ninth full-year devolves,
Wherefore no mortification imputed be

BOOK II

To Achaean heartache beside their balanced prows. 300
Most shameful nonetheless is it to languish long
With naught to show. Take courage, friends, and yet attend
That we discern if Kalchas prophesied aright;
For this at heart we know, witnesses one and all,
As many as abide the while unclaimed by death, 305
When at Aulis those many yesterdays ago
Achaean prows assembled—for mayhem gathered
Against Priam and his folk—we, about a stream,
To altars sacred to the gods our hecatombs
Consigned, beneath a pliant plane tree, whence chilly 310
Rippling waters ran, when presently a portent
Grimly seen: a snake blood-red its back, and dreadful—
By Cronidēs from neath the altar upward drawn—
Darted slith'ring up the plane tree to the topmost
Bough, where tender sparrows numbering eight recoiled 315
Beneath the frond, and ninth the flittering mother;
Them grievously warbling it ingested, and their
Mother circled 'round bewailing her dear offspring;
But the serpent, upcoiling, caught her wing, and when
The young were swallowed and also the sparrow dam, 320
The god, who had first unearthed the serpent, rendered
It a monument—for crook-minded Croniōn
Converted it to stone; and we, to this very
Wonder witnesses, aghast at the gods' daunting
Portent—signaling our hecatomb's transgression— 325
Wanted augury from Kalchas, who thus proclaimed:
'Ah, fall you quiet, you flowing-haired Achaeans?
To us from counselor Zeus this portent stands disclosed,
Late occurring, the later done, report of which
Will e'er endure: As the serpent downs the sparrow's 330
Young, downs the sparrow too—all eight entire and ninth
The brood-begetting dam—these many years the like
Shall we, contending here, in the tenth wide-highwayed
Troy o'erturn.' Thus Kalchas proclaimed, and thus is it
Accomplished. So persist, you well-greaved Achaeans, 335

Until high-towering Troy be reduced to dust."
Thus he proclaimed, and a deafening din arose
Amid the Danaan ships, the cries resounding
Wondrous and reverberant, lavishly lauding
Divine Odysseus' words, when horseman Nestor spoke: 340

"For woe, alas! Like peabrained children bicker you,
Purblind to combat's bidding. Where, tell me, will our
Bonds and compacts go? Will the plans and thoughtfulness
Of men to flame be flown? What then our offerings
Of unmixed wine, our hands fast bound in stalwart trust? 345
Futile this dissension, unfit to fortify
Resolve for Danaans long fatigued. Atreïdēs,
Rule you now as earlier, ever steadfast your plan;
Arouse the Argives to fearsome fray, and damned be
They, the Danaans—the few of them—mindlessly 350
Devising against your plan. Be their faithlessness
Their folly; fly they to Argos ere we confirm
If aegis-bearing Zeus has pledged aright or not.
For mighty Cronidēs, I vow, did grant consent,
When the Achaeans in their crook-necked ships embarked, 355
To wreak slaughter unrelenting on the Trojans;
And lightning glistered to the right, a singular
Omen manifest. Thus be no one homeward gone
Ere fully gratified atop some Trojan wife,
Well guerdoned for the groans and heavings Helen spawned. 360
Should anyone for Hellas prematurely leave,
Let him thus in his fitted vessel buoyant fare
And despair become his solitary comrade.
But you, O king, be canny and from another
Counsel take, my counsel perdurable adjudged. 365
Select you men by clans and tribes, Atreïdēs,
That clan close-counsel clan, and tribe abet tribe true;
And if the Greeks admit your means, apparent 'tis
Who thus amid the captaincy and thronging ranks
Impedes and who amid them lends support, for each 370

BOOK II

Clan for itself will fight, whilst you affirm whether
Troy by Zeus' ordinance endure the decade through
Or by madness of war or cowardice of men.
Then responding, spoke Agamemnon Atreïdēs:
"Indeed, old sir, again in speech do you surpass   375
The Argives all. Yea, by father Zeus, Athena,
And Apollo, were there even ten Achaean
Counselors your like, then decimate were Priam's town,
By these very hands marauded and ravaged through;
But aegis-bearing Zeus bewilders me, casting   380
A'fore me disputation and discordances;
For Achilles and I did grapple for the girl
With contumacious words, and first to anger I.
But were our purposes conjoined, the Trojan host
Would not be spared misfortune's least impediment.   385
To dinner now disperse, that we to fight be fit;
Sharpen his spear each man and marshal him his shield
And to his horses fleetly hooved their feed allot.
Let each man scrutinize his chariot 'round about,
For battle and in battle's brawn each resolute;   390
For no deferral nor adjournment shall there be
'Til sidling darkness separate the might of men.
Be drenched in sweat about the breast of every man
The baldric of his man-enveloping buckler,
And weary grown the grip about his weighted spear,   395
His team a'sweat, straps taut connected to their cart.
And whom I espy remiss afar from warfare,
By his crook-beaked keel malingering—renounced be
His fate to savage curs and feathered foragers."

Thus he spoke, and th' Argives roared aloud, as a wave   400
By hurricane hurled against high-rearing breakers,
Even some precipice unceasingly pounded
By wat'ry wind-distracting scourge, whence winds arise
Wheresoever arbitrarily. So shipward
Bound, beseeched they this or another deity   405

For rescue from carnage and the war god's travail.
Then king of men, Atreïdēs, made offering:
A fattened ox, five years pastured, to mighty Zeus.
And 'round about himself gathered the noblest all
Of the Achaean host: foremost Nestor and lord   410
Idomeneus, th' Aiantes twain, and Tydeus' son,
Odysseus sixth, the like to lord Zeus counselor;
And of his own accord came Menelaus, war
Cry's voice incarnate, his brother's cares well knowing.
Circling the ox, they raised the scattering barley,   415
And among them declaimed Agamemnon in prayer:
"Zeus, mightiest and most revered, concealed in cloud,
Heaven-inhabiting, let the sun not descend
Nor night upon us fall ere headlong Priam's halls
Be encompassed by blackened smoke, their portals steeped   420
In desperate flame, and by my spearpoint Hector's
Chiton cloven rest across his chest in tatters,
And his companions in their dozens driven through,
Each headlong through his teeth consuming gritty earth."
Thus he spoke, but Cronidēs enabled it not,   425
Taking the gift in return for unending toil.
Then, once they had prayed, scattering the barley grain,
They slaughtered the beast, forward by the throat updrawn,
And flayed it, the thighs to pieces cut, wrapped double-
Blanketed in fat, thereupon raw flesh arranged,   430
And skewered the portions on branchless spits, the innards
Also skewered and for the roasting dispositioned.
And when cooked the meat and savored were the innards,
They pierced the remaining portions, cooking them through,
Attentively, the roast removing piece by piece.   435
Their exertions completed, the supper prepared,
They banqueted, nor was anyone bereft of
Fairly furnished quantity. Then, when the desire
Of drink and dining had among them been allayed,
Spoke Nestor Gerēnian horseman accordingly: 440
"Agamemnon, most glorified, sovereign of men,

Delay we here no longer, nor longer postpone
The outcome by heaven's approval authorized;
But onward! Be all the battalions assembled
Of bronze-chitoned Achaeans dawdling by their ships, 445
And then traverse we the encampments, one by one,
The better battle's tribulation to awake."

Thus he spoke, nor did Agamemnon, king of men,
Delay but directed the resonant heralds
To muster the hair-flown Achaeans to conflict; 450
And muster they did, and the summoned fast complied,
And about Atreidēs discerningly hastened
The Zeus-begotten lords, and grey-eyed Athena
Among them, high bearing the aegis—protective,
Imperishable, unremitting, trailing its 455
Hundred golden-braided tassels, the each of them
A hundred oxen's worth; and with it she darted,
Inducing the Danaans, goading their advance,
In each man's breast engendering the tolerance
For labor unrelenting, relentlessly borne. 460
And thus to them was battle become more honeyed
Than home, than fatherlands from ships well-fashioned viewed.
And as forests ablaze atop a mountain peak
Scrub the teeming woodlands bare, the rage stoked high,
So was radiance of bronze divine, of Danaans 465
Undeterred, through aether directed heavenward.
And as great as wingèd flocks of long-necked swans, wild
Geese, and pinion-pleasured cranes as on the Asian
Pasture by Caystrius' streams fly tumbling about,
Full gloried in their strength of wing and, with loud cries 470
Perching, ever onward press, and resounds the mead,
Thus numerous the Argives on Scamander's plain;
Countless the clans convening from vessels and huts,
And terribly trembled the earth beneath the tread
Of horses and men, the fearsome hordes assailing 475
Scamander's beauteous dappled mead, in numbers

Like to nature's bloom beneath governance of spring.
And as flies abuzz beset the farmer's acreage,
Bestirrèd all, come springtime's lustrous spell—just then
Splats the jettied milk a'bottom the joyful pail— 480
Thus aggregate the Argives grew, unruly-maned,
Intently grown throughout their ranks to ravage Troy.
And as goatherds quickly discern the goats their own
Haphazardly mixed on the mountainside a'graze,
Thus their leaders marshaled them, Greeks from every side, 485
For battle's broil. And among them Agamemnon—
Comely his countenance, alike to thund'rous Zeus,
His girth the war god Ares', his chest Poseidon's—
Stood supreme, a bull unequaled, conspicuous,
Compassed by kine the likeness of his own breeding. 490
Upon that day did Zeus appoint Atreïdēs
Vaunted of multitudes, a hero exalted.

Tell me now, Muses, in Olympian precincts
Reposed—for you are gods, are present, and know all,
But we report alone perceive and nothing know— 495
Who the Danaan leaders were and who their lords;
For nary their numbers would I intone or name
If tenfold tongues I had and ten again the mouths,
If indestructible my voice and bronze my heart,
Unless the Olympian Muses, of aegis- 500
Bearing Zeus the brood, the like recalled, as many
As neath Ilium came. Now the ships' captains will
I recount, and of the ships themselves make tally.

Leïtus and Pēneleōs the Boeotians led,
Arcesilaus, Prothoēnōr, and Clonius 505
Sharing the command—dwellers of Hyria, craggy
Aulis; of Schoenus, Scōlus, and many-ridgèd
Eteōnus; of Graea, Thespeia, and vast
Mycalēssus. These by Harma and Hylē dwelt;
Holding Eilesium, Erythrae, Medeōn's 510

High-mounted citadel, Eleōn, Peteōn,
Ocalea, Cōpae, Eutresis, and Thisbē,
Dwelling place of doves; inhabiting the grassy
Haliartus, Corōneia, and spread afar
Through Glisas and Plataea; possessing lower   515
Thebes, the well-constructed stronghold, and sanctified
Onchestus, Poseidon's splendid precinct; holding
Vine-lavished Arnē, Mideia, hallowed Nisa,
And Anthēdōn farthest off. Of these came fifty
Craft, and boarding each one hundred men and twenty, 520
The mightiest these, the boast of the Boeotians.
And to those dwelling in Asplēdōn and Minyan
Orchomenus, strong Ascalaphus issued command,
And Ialmenus, Ares' sons whom in Actōr,
Azeïdēs' abode, Astyochē—modest   525
Maiden—conceived of mighty Ares when, having
Entered her upper chamber he furtively lay
With her. And vessels thirty accompanied these.
Schedius and Epistrophus, spirited sons
Of Iphitus Naubolidēs, ruled the Phōcians.   530
These controlled Cyparissus and rocky Pythō,
Sanctified Crisa and Daulis and Panopeus;
And well they inhabited Anemōreia
And Hyampolis, o'erlooking Cēphisus' stream,
And held Lilaea by Cephisus' sacred source.   535
With these followed forty black ships. And their leaders
Bustled marshaling the Phōcian ranks, preparing
For battle, hard alongside the Boeōtian left.
And the Locrians as leader had the lesser
Ajax, swift son of Oïleus, in no manner   540
Like unto Ajax, son of Telemon, but much
The less; slight of stature, with corselet of linen,
But who with spear surpassed the Panhellenic host
And Argives. In Cynus they dwelt; and Opoeis;
In Calliarus and Bēssa; Scarphē, lovely   545
Tarphē, and Thronion, and Augeiae—the streams

Of Boagrius about. With Ajax followed
Forty dark vessels of Locrians, their dwelling
Past sacred Euboea.
     They that held Euboea
Were the rage-breathing Abantes that also held   550
Chalcis, Eiretria and Histiaea, rich
In vines, and Cērinthus adjacent the breakers,
Steep fortress of thund'ring Zeus, and that Carystus
Held and dwelt in Styra—these again were ordered
By Elephēnōr, scion of Ares, begotten   555
Son of Chalcōdōn and captain of the great-souled
Abantes, to whom the swift-paced Abantes pledged,
Their hair fast-flown behind them, spearmen impatient
To sunder with outstretched ashen spear the foeman's
Fitted Corselet. And with him forty vessels.   560

And they that held Athens the well-built citadel,
Land of great-hearted Erechtheus whom Athena,
Zeus' daughter, aforetime had parented once grain-
Dispensing earth had borne him; and she settled him
In Athens within in her lavish sanctuary   565
Where Athenian youth, the years within their orbits
Full circling about, appease him with sacrifice
Of bulls and rams—of these had Menestheus command,
Son of Peteōs, nowhere existent his like
Upon earth for the summoning of chariots   570
And buckler-bearing men. Nestor alone his like,
Earlier begotten. And followed him fifty ships.
And Ajax led twelve ships from Salamis, stationed
Where the Athenian battalions steadfastly stood,
And they that came from Argos and tow'ring Tiryns,   575
From Hermionē and Asinē, enfolding
The great gulf, from Troezen, Ēionae and vined
Epidaurus—the sum of Achaean manhood—
From Masēs and Aegina too. These again war-
Crying Diomēdēs led, also Sthenelus,   580

BOOK II

Dear offspring of undaunted Capaneus, and third
Came Euryalus, a godlike warrior, offspring
Of kingly Mēcisteus Talaïonidēs.
But commanding them all was Diomēdēs good
At battle cry. And with them eighty black vessels. 585

And they that held Mycēnae, well-built citadel,
And prosperous Corinth, and well-built Cleōnae,
And dwelt in Orneiae and Araethyrea
And Sicyōn, where earlier Adrastus had ruled,
And they that Hyperēsia held, Pellēnē, 590
And steep Gonoessa, and that inhabited
Aegium and most bounteous Aegialus,
And lived about broad Helicē—these Atreidēs
Agamemnon with a hundred ships commanded,
Bearing the flower of fabled Argive valor; 595
And 'mid them he gloried, donning his splendid bronze,
Their king fully acclaimed, best among all warriors,
Being noblest and leading the greatest numbers.

And those holding ravine-hollowed Lacedaemōn,
And Pharis and Sparta and Messē haunt of doves, 600
Dwelling in Bryseiae and lovely Augeiae;
Who held Amyclae and Helus, a citadel
Hard by the sea, and occupied Laäs, and dwelt
About Oetylus—these Agamemnon's brother

Ordered, even Menelaus good at warcry; 605
Sixty vessels his, and they apart were marshaled.
And he himself among them strode, in his prowess
Exultant most, urging his men to fight; wanting
Beyond others all full acquittal and revenge
For the moans and motions Helen had excited. 610
And they that held Pylos and lovely Arēnē,
And Thryum, the ford of Alpheius, and well-built
Aepy, and those with homes in Cyparissēïs,

101

And in Amphigeneia, Pteleos, Helus,
And Dōrium, where the Muses encountering   615
Thracian Thamyris, discontinued his singing
As he journeyed from Oechalia, from the house
Of Oechalian Eurytus, for he boasted
Proposing to vanquish the Muses, the daughters
Of aegis-bearing Zeus, were they ever to sing   620
Against him; but angered, they maimed and deprived him
Of wondrous song, canceling minstrelsy from his mind;
These followed the horseman Gerēnian Nestor,
And with him assembled were ninety hollow ships.

And they that held Arcadia beneath the steep   625
Mountain of Cyllēnē, aside Aepytus' tomb
Where dwell combatants who grapple at close quarters,
And those that in flock-rich Orchomenus settled,
And in Rhipē, Stratia, and wind-swept Enispē
And in Pheneus; and held Tegea and lovely   630
Mantinea; and that held Stymphēlus and dwelt
In Parrasia—all these led Ancaeus' son,
Lord Agapēnor, with sixty ships; and on each
Embarked full many an Arcadian combatant,
Expert in battle. For Agamemnon himself,   635
King of men, had provided them well-benched vessels,
Even lord Atreïdēs, wherewith to traverse
The wine-dark sea, for of seafaring knew they naught.

And they inhabiting Buprasium and Ēlis—
As much thereof as Hyrminē and seaboarded   640
Myrsinus, Alesium and Olen's outcropping
Between them enclose—were marshaled by leaders four,
And ten the vessels that followed each, with many
Epeians embarked thereon. Of these were some led
By Amphimachus and Thalpius, Actor's kin,   645
Sons of Cteatus one, of Eurytus th' other;
And of some was Amarynceïdēs captain—

The mighty Diorēs—and of the faction fourth
Was the godlike Polyxeinus captain, of king
Agasthenēs born, the son of Augeias he. 650
And those from Dulichium come and the Echinae,
Sacred islands facing Ēlis across the sea,
These again had Megēs, Ares' peer, as leader—
Megēs Phyleïdēs, whom the horseman Phyleus
Beloved of Zeus begat, who aforetime had gone 655
Into Dulichium to dwell, vexed by his father.
And attending Megēs were forty black vessels.

Odysseus led the great-souled Cephallēnians
Inhabiting Ithaca and leaf-quivering
Neritum, that occupied rugged Aegilips 660
And Crocyleia and that dwelt in Zacynthus
Near to Samos, and that occupied the mainland
Ashore, o'erlooking the islands. These Odysseus
Zeus' equal in counsel commanded, and with him
Coming Troyward were vessels twelve vermilion-prowed. 665

And the Aetolians were by Thoas assembled,
Andraemōn's son, even they that dwelt in Pleurōn,
Ōlenus, Pylēnē, and Chalcis by the sea,
And rocky Calydōn. For the sons of mighty
Oeneus were no longer alive, nor he himself, 670
And blond-haired Meleager had departed earth,
To whom directives had been issued to command
The Aetolians; and with Thoas forty black ships.
And the Cretan troops were led by Idomeneus,
Spear-famed, even those that held Cnossus and sturdy- 675
Walled Gortys, Milētus, Lyctus, and chalk-whitened
Lycastus, and Phaestus, and Rhytium—cities
Handsomely Inhabited—and th' others dwelling
In hundred-citied Crete. Them did Idomeneus,
Spear-famed, lead as commander with Mērionēs, 680
Warlike slayer of men. Eighty the black ships theirs.

And goodly and great Tlēpolemus, Heracles'
Son, from Rhodes led ships numbered nine of courageous
Rhodians, of those inhabiting Rhodes by thirds
Divided: Lindus, Ialysus and white-chalked 685
Cameirus—these spear-applauded Tlēpolemus
Led, whom Astyocheia bore to Heracles,
She a prize whom he abducted from Ephyra,
From the river Sellēeis after sacking towns
Aplenty of warlike men belovèd of Zeus. 690

But when in the well-built palace Tlēpolemus
Had to manhood grown, he then murdered his uncle,
Licymnius, of Ares descended, advanced
In years. So hurriedly he assembled him ships
And, convening cohorts, sought the sea's asylum— 695
Heracles' children threatening retribution—
And wandering arrived at Rhodes, woes suffering,
And there settled his people by tribes, divided
By thirds, there living of wide-ruling Zeus beloved
Who profited them with prosperity outpoured. 700

From Symē did Nireus three shapely ships command,
Nireus, offspring of Aglaea and king Charops,
Nireus, handsomest man of the Achaeans all
Who e'er beneath Trojan parapets appearèd
Excepting fearless Achilles, but stamina 705
Eluded him, and meager the host he managed.

And they that in Nisyrus dwelt, and Crapathus,
And Casus, and Cos, city of Eurypylus,
And the isles Calydnian—these Pheidippus led,
And Antiphus, the offspring twain of Thessalus, 710
To Heracles born. And thirty the ships with them.

Now those inhabiting Pelasgian Argos,

BOOK II

And dwelling in Alus, Alopē and Trachis,
And holding Phthia and Hellas—the land of fair
Womankind—Myrmidons, Hellenes, and Achaeans   715
Were called; of these Achilles captained fifty ships.
But they of abhorrent war no cognizance took,
For none was there to champion their ranks. But sooner
Idled he by the ships, the divine swift-footed
Achilles, wrathful over fair-haired Brisēis,   720
The maiden he had seized from Lyrnessus, toiling
Greatly for her when he had leveled Lyrnessus
And the walls of Thebes, and laid low Epistrophus
And Mynēs, spear-empowered warriors, sons of king
Evēnus, Selepius' son. Thus grieving for her   725
Achilles lay idle, though soon to rise again.

They that held Phylacē and flowered Pyrasus,
Demeter's precinct, and Itōn, mother of flocks,
And sea-shored Antrōn, and Pteleus meadow-couched,
These, moreover, proclaimed the command of warlike   730
Prōtesilāus, while living; though now black earth
Encompassed him about. Torn her cheeks with wailing,
Abode his wife in Phylacē, his legacy
But half established. But him a Trojan fighter
Slew when leaping from his ship, of the Danaans   735
Foremost leaping. Yet not leaderless his command—
Though much missing its commander—for marshaled them
Podarcēs, scion of Ares, in flocks o'erflown,
Son of Iphiclus, son of Phylacus in turn,
The brother of great-hearted Prōtesilāus,   740
And the younger born, though better born the elder,
That same hero, the warlike Prōtesilāus.
Thus lacking not for leadership, yet longed his men
For their leader aforetime—and with Podarcēs
Forty the hollow ships that Troyward followed him.   745
They dwelling in Pherae beside Boebēis lake,
In Boebē, Glaphyrae, and well-built Iolcus—

105

These Eumelus led, dear offspring of Admetus,
Eleven his ships, whom Alcestis, celestial
Of women, bore Admetus, she the comeliest 750
Of Pelias' daughters.
                 And those in Mēthōnē
And Thaumacia, and those that held Meliboea
And rugged Olizōn—these with their seven ships
Philoctētēs mustered, expert in archery,
And fifty the oarsmen on each ship embarked, skilled 755
In the bow's harsh employment. But Philoctētēs
Prostrate lay, island-bound, enduring grievous pains,
Bereft on sacred Lemnos, where the Achaeans
Had left him pained, with malignancy inflicted
By a lethal watersnake. There disconsolate 760
He lay; yet shortly would the shipbound Achaeans
Bethink themselves of lord Philoctētēs. His men,
However, lacked not for a leader, though longing
For their lord. But Medōn commanded them, bastard
Son of city-sacking Oïleus whom Rhēnē, 765
Lain beneath him bore.
                      And they in Trickē dwelling,
In craggy Ithōmē and in Oechalia,
City of Oechalian Eurytus—again
Were these by Asclepius' offspring, two sons, led,
Podaleirius and Machāōn, skilled healers, 770
And marshaled with these were thirty hollow vessels.

And they that settled Ormenius and the fountain
Hypereia, and that possessed Asterius
And the white crests of Titanus—Eurypylus
Assembled these, acclaimed offspring of Euaemōn, 775
And came forty black ships accompanying him.

And they that held Argissa, and had Gyrtōnē,
Orthē, and Ēlōnē, and the city of white
Oloössōn—these prince Polypoetēs marshaled,

BOOK II

Valiant in fight—son of Peirithous begot by 780
Immortal Zeus—whom glorious Hippodameia
Conceived beneath Peirithous after requiting
The shaggy Centaurs, routing them from Pēlium
The distance to Aethicēs. Nor was he alone,
But with him partnered Ares' offshoot, Leonteus, 785
Son of Coronus, Caenus' son, mighty of heart,
And with them followed dark vessels forty-numbered.

Gouneus from Cyphus two and twenty vessels led,
And attending him the Eniēnes tribesmen
And Perrhaebians, steadfast both, making their homes 790
About wintry Dōdōna and inhabiting
The ploughland about the river Titarēssus—
Its fair-flowing streams to Pēneius releasing;
Commingling not, howe'er, with the silver eddies
Of Pēneius, but o'er flowing his waters forth, 795
Like unto olive oil, being tributary
To Stygian waters, the dreaded river of oath.

Tenthrēdōn's son, Prothoös, led the Magnetians,
These dwelling about Pēneius and leaf-bristling
Pēlion. These did the swift Prothoös captain; 800
And forty the black ships accompanying him.

And these were the Danaan leaders and their lords.
But the best of them relate, O Muse, of warriors
And snorting steeds attending the Atreïdai.
The best steeds, pinion-paced, belonged to Pherēs' son 805
Eumēlus, by him driven, like of coat and age,
Plumb-level their backs in height. These Apollo reared,
God of the silver bow, upon Mount Pēreia,
Mares the twain, conveying battle's consternation.
And of fighters far best was Telamonian 810
Ajax—the while Achilles raged; for Achilles
Was mightiest far, he and the horses that bore

The peerless offspring of Peleus. But he remained
Amid his beakèd seafaring ships, perfectly
Enragèd at Agamemnon Atreidēs, shepherd 815
Of the host; and his soldiers along the seashore
Made amusement of discus-toss and javelin,
Of archery too. And the horses all, their carts
Nearby, stood sluggish, chomping marsh-nurtured parsley
And lotus, while the chariots in their leaders' tents 820
Stood downward tilted and draped. But the men, longing
For their leader, belovèd of Ares, loitered
Idly about the camp, unthinking of battle.

And so they advanced, as though earth entire were scourged
With flame; and the earth beneath them groaned, like unto 825
Zeus when, with rage of lightning's joy, he decimates
Typhoeus' habitat amid the Arimi
Where men report Typhoeus keeps his berth. The ground
Thus greatly groaned beneath their march unstoppable,
And full swiftly they traversed the plain.
       And Iris 830
To the Trojans passed, a wind-swift speedy-footed
Messenger form aegis-bearing Zeus, grievous her
Message. These gathered in conference at lord Priam's
Portal, together arrayed, young and old alike;
And standing aside them swift-footed Iris spoke, 835
Lik'ning her voice to the voice of Politēs, son
Of Priam, who as Trojan outlook sat the while
Atop the tow'ring mound of agèd Asyētēs,
On swiftfootedness reliant, to indicate
Whene'er the Argives from their ships might disembark; 840
Likening herself to him, swift-footed Iris
Thus addressed Priam: "Old sir, interminably
And ever belovedly you prattle; peacetime
Imagine you this when war reigns unabated?
Many the time aforetime have I fastened ranks 845
Of warriors, but ne'er aforetime have I seen

BOOK II

A host so goodly and so great; for numbering
Leaves or grains of sand advance they resolutely,
On the town intent. Hector, you distinctly I
Enjoin, and do you accordingly—for allies 850
Aplenty inhabit Priam's town, differing
Tongue by tongue throughout their dispersèd multitudes.
Let every man o'er those he captains give the word,
And those let him attend, having marshaled his own."

So she spoke, and Hector straightaway recognized 855
The goddess' voice, and the gath'ring immed'ately
Disbanded, and they hastened to arms. All the gates
Were opened wide, and forth advanced the men, footmen
And charioteers, and great the tumult arising.

Stands a gradient upward from Ilium risen, 860
Apart set on the plain, approachable this way
And that: by men called Batieia, but by gods
The acrobat Myrinē's tomb. There on that day
Did the Trojans and their allies fully tally
Their contingents: the Trojans by stalwart Hector 865
Led, great glimmer-helmeted scion of Priam,
And with him, fully armed, the greatest hosts by far
And the goodliest, raging with their armaments.

Aeneas the illustrious Dardanians
Deployed—Aeneas, whom winsome Aphrodite 870
Delivered to Anchises upon Ida's spurs,
A goddess having intercourse with mortalkind—
Not alone; with him were Antēnōr's offspring twain,
Archelochus and Acamas, accomplished they
In fighting's every turn.
                  And they that resided 875
In Zeleia beneath Mt. Ida's lowest slope,
Wealthy men, drinking the dark flow of Aesēpus,
Trojans themselves—these by the glorious Pandarus,

Offspring of Lycaōn, were assembled, on whom
Lord Apollo, the god himself, bestowed the bow.   880

And they that held Adrasteia and Apaesus,
And inhabited Pityeia and the steep
Mount of Tēreia—these by Adrastus were led
And by Araphius, his corselet linen-made,
Sons the twain of Percōtian Merops: expert he,   885
Surpassing all others in prophesy, suffered
Not his sons' engagement in man-withering war,
But they, by black death seduced, were unpersuaded.

They that dwelt about Percōte and Practius,
And held Sēstus, Abydus, and bright Arisbē—   890
These by the forefighting Asius Hyrtacidēs
Were led—Asius, Hyrtacus' son, whom his tawny
Upright horses had transported from Arisbē
And from the river Sellēeis.
                          And Hippothous
Led the Pelasgians, spear-raging tribesmen all,   895
Even them inhabiting deep-soiled Larisa—
Of these were Hippothous and Pylaeus leaders,
The latter Ares' scion, sons twain of Lethus,
Son of Teutamus. And Acamas the Thracians
Led, and the warrior Peirous led the multitudes   900
By the Hellespont's ravenous surges enclosed.

And Euphemus led the Ciconian spearmen,
The son of Ceas' son, Zeus-nurtured Troezēnus.
But the bow-curved Paeonians Pyraechmēs controlled,
Afar out of Amydōn and the wide-flowing   905
Axius, its waters flowing comeliest of earth.
And the Paphlagonians did shaggy-hearted
Pylamenēs lead from the Eneti's domain,
Whence the rampant race of she-mules. These tenanted
Cytōrus and dwelt about Sēsamus, famous   910

Their dwellings alongside the river Parthenius,
And about Crōmna, Aegialus, and lofty
Erythini. But the Halizoni were led
From afar by Epistrophus and Odius,
From Alybē the very birthplace of silver. 915

And the Mysian force did Chromis and Ennomus,
Bird augur, command; however, his auguries
Availed him not in circumventing grievous fate,
But by Aeacidēs swift-footed he perished,
By Achilles 'mid the river, 'mid his slaughter 920
Of Trojans one and all. And Phorcys and godlike
Ascanius from faraway Ascania
Commanded the Phrygians eager for engagement.
And the Maeonians had commanders twain, Mesthlēs
And Antiphus, twain offspring of Talaemenēs, 925
Born to the maiden nymph of the Gygaean lake.
Marshaled they the Maeonians neath Tmōlus begot.
And Nastēs commanded the Carians, uncultured
Their discourse, holding Milētus, the leaf-deepened
Mountain of Phthirēs, the outflowing Maeander, 930
And Mycalē's ascending crests. These had leaders
Twain, Nastēs and Amphimachus—Amphimachus
And Nastēs, Nomīōn's glorious progeny.
And cretin Nastēs entered battle decked in gold,
Girlishly; gold availing not to circumvent 935
Calamity; no, riverside was he butchered
By Achilles, by swift-footed Aeacidēs,
And sagacious Aeacidēs managed the gold!
And Sarpēdōn and peerless Glaucus commanded
The far-distant Lycians by eddying Xanthus. 940

~ Book III ~

*The Parties Declare a Truce, the View from the Wall,
the Single Combat Between Menelaus and Paris*

With the armies prepared to engage, Paris, dressed in unheroic leopard's pelt, challenges the Greeks to a war-determinative duel. Panicked that the aggrieved Menelaus himself accepts the challenge, Paris seeks to make himself scarce, only to be upbraided for cowardice by his brother, Hector. Paris reasserts his preparedness, and Hector rejoices to announce the contest. Agamemnon stays the belligerent Greeks, allowing Hector to announce the contest and propose its terms. Menelaus urges sacrifices to Zeus and the presence of Priam for increase of solemnity.

The messenger goddess, Iris, arrives summoning Helen to watch the fight. Arriving at the rampart, she is warmly greeted by her father-in-law Priam, who uses the occasion to absolve her of blame for the war: it is both the gods and Helen's irresistible beauty that are to blame. The town's elders endorse the sentiment, exemplifying the folly and lack of judgment that will ultimately result in Troy's destruction. All are besotted with Helen. Priam asks Helen to point out and identify the Greek chieftains. Among them she identifies her husband, Menelaus. For all the devastation her adultery has caused, she wishes she had never left him. The occasion allows for an extended comparison—made by the Trojan Antenor—between Menelaus and Odysseus. The comparison is based on Antenor's impressions when the two earlier come on a truce, seeking terms for Helen's return. The "View from the Wall" thus references earlier negotiations for Helen's return—an episode preceding the Book 3 duel, itself logically occurring toward the poem's start. All are synthesized into the epic storytelling present.

Priam is brought from Troy at Menelaus' request, participates in the sacrifices and oaths, and at his own request is returned to Troy, declining to witness the fight. The arming of Paris is described in detail; that of Menelaus, in a single "did-likewise" line. The duel then comedically follows between the ineffectual Paris—effete lover more than fighter—and middling Menelaus. The combatants' spears are thrown to no avail. Menelaus then lowers his sword on Paris' helmet, only to have it shatter in his hand. He grabs Paris by his helmet's plume and drags him about, only to have the chinstrap break, leaving him with an empty casque which he tosses aside amid imprecations.

Aphrodite then whisks her favorite away, concealing him in a cloud of dust—i.e., Paris somehow gives Menelaus the slip—and delivering him to Helen's bedroom (Helen returned from the wall and her conversation with Priam). Helen berates Paris for the slacker he is, but makes love to him anyway—for Helen the compulsive behavior of one whose existence is charged and defined by erotic attachment; for Paris, the arousal and lust for life following escape from death. Helen's sharp exchange with Aphrodite, as the latter announces Paris' presence, is paradigmatic self-loathing.

The scene reverts to the battlefield, where Menelaus prowls animal-like in search of Paris, while Paris makes love to Helen, Menelaus' wife. It is a scene played for laughs and bitter irony. Believing themselves cheated under the terms of the parties' oaths, the Greeks demand the return of Helen and all her possessions.

Book 3, in sum, plays "catch-up" to much of the story known, but not told, in Homer's *Iliad*. The Greek chieftains' names, already known when Priam inquires of them, are reasserted in "real time." Indeed, fruitless outcome-determinative duels had surely occurred on more than one occasion. The duel is nonetheless here introduced to create a durational sense of the war's entirety, i.e., what logically happened earlier now unfolding in the storytelling present.

❧

When the forces each were gathered, their commanders
Leading them, the Trojans descended with a whoop
And birdlike clamor, as riotous cranes—aloft
A'front heaven's face, retreating from wintry wind
And unsparing storm—strident their passage, their flight 5
Toward Ocean bound, visiting daybreak destruction

BOOK III

On the Pygmy men; vexatious the conflict quite.
But the Danaans silently advanced, fury-
Infused, each ardent for his fellow's benefit.
Even as when the South Wind mists a mountain peak—   10
Mist unliked by shepherd, better than night to thief—
And a man before him sees but a stone's throw off,
Just so from underfoot rose dense the dusty cloud,
And never-ending their advance across the plain.
When close opposite come, convening host on host,   15
The godlike Alexander advanced as Trojan
Champion, on his shoulders sporting panther's pelt,
A curvèd bow, and sword—twain the spears brandishing,
Tipped with bronze—and spurred the best of the Achaeans
To battle him in brutal combat face to face.   20

But when Menelaus beloved of Ares saw
Paris, wide-stridden, advancing a'front the throng,
He delighted, as a lion on a mighty
Carcass lighting, finding a goat or antlered stag,
The lion full-famished, eagerly approaching,   25
Voraciously guzzles it down, swift the sturdy
Youths and hounds that harry it. Thus Menelaus,
While leaping armored from his chariot to the ground,
Viewed godlike Alexander, anticipating
Assurance of vengeance for Paris' transgression.   30
But struck to the quick was godlike Alexander
Seeing Menelaus, staunch his heroic mien,
And aback to the ranks of his comrades withdrew,
Averting fate. And even as one starts aback
Glimpsing a snake in the mountain's glade—a'tremble   35
His limbs throughout, suffused the pallor o'er his cheeks
As he decamps—even so did godlike Paris,
Dire his premonition of Atreidēs, retreat
Within the lordly ranks of gathered Trojans all.
But noting it did Hector scold with shaming words: 40
"Pestilent Paris, fairest most to view, woman-

115

Frenzied, philanderer! Better far had you never
Lived, or died unmarried, as I myself would wish;
Better that by far than living e'er mistrusted,
Rebuked of multitudes. The long-haired Achaeans,   45
Rest assured, will laugh aloud, concluding we boast
A prince by looks alone our defender, lacking
Heft and heart. Of such strength did you avail yourself
That day when—in seafaring vessels o'ercrossing
The boundless brine with the host of your companions—   50
You arrived, accosting an alien people,
And pilfered a beauty, pride of distant domains,
Daughter of weaponed warriors, but dolorous bane
To your father, your entire folk, and teeming town,
To your enemies, delight; to yourself, despair?   55
Will you elude the measure of Menelaus,
Dear to Ares, evade the man whose flow'ring wife
You have stolen? Then will your lyre assist you not,
Nor Aphrodite's gifts, nor locks, nor comeliness—
When with dust commixed. Assuredly be Trojans   60
Cowards, else had you sooner worn a cloak of stone
For the countless evils credit to your account.
And to him the godlike Alexander replied:
"Hector, Your reprimand is fully justified,
Nor idle. Ever tireless your heart, as an axe   65
That a ship-building man, his brawn fully employed,
Wields cleaving vessel plank and board; thus the spirit
Within your breast, unflagging. Example me not
The radiant Aphrodite, her gifts sublime;
Nor dismissive be of the gods' distinguished gifts,   70
As many as they themselves confer, which no man
For the asking takes. But now, be you determined
To see me bellicose, have the other Trojans
Seated, and the Achaeans too, and between us
Set me and Menelaus beloved of Ares   75
To engage for Helen and all her possessions;
And whichever of the twain prevail, thus proving

BOOK III

The better man, homeward let him lead her, claiming
Her and hers entire; but you others swear friendship
And faithful oaths in solemn sacrifice. Then dwell   80
We on Troy's rich acreage and they in horse-grazing
Achaea and in Argos of fabled women."

So he spoke and Hector, hearing his words, rejoiced
Greatly, bestriding the midst, checking the Trojan
Ranks, his spear to middleward grasped, and seated were   85
They all. But the long-haired Achaeans sought the while
To strike at him, aiming their shafts and casting stones;
But lord Agamemnon, king of men, protested:
"Refrain, you Argives and Danaan youths; cast not,
For flashing-helmeted Hector would something speak."   90
So he said and, refraining from blows, silently
They desisted, and Hector made this pronouncement:
"Trojans and well-greaved Achaeans, learn you from me
The word of Alexander, on whose account is
Kindled our contention. The other Trojans all   95
And the Danaans bids he undo their goodly
Battle gear, lowered to bounteous earth, himself
And Menelaus dear to Ares in the midst
Engaging for Helen and all her possessions.
And whichever of the twain prevail and prove him   100
The better man, homeward let him lead her, taking
Her and hers entire; but we others friendship swear
And faithful oaths in consecrated offerings."
So he spoke, and the hosts to muted silence fell,
And then said Menelaus master of warcry: 105
"Attentive be you now to me, whose heart sorrows
Most beyond all others; for I think a parting
Approaches of Argives and Trojans for the pains
Aplenty you have suffered from this my grievance,
At the start whereof stands foremost Alexander.   110
And to whome'er of us be death and fate decreed,
Thus settled his demise, and you others disperse.

Gather two lambs, one white, one black, for Earth and Sun,
And for Zeus obtain we another; and summon
Mighty Priam, that he himself proclaim an oath   115
In sacrifice, since his sons are impertinent,
Duplicitous; lest any impropriety
Profane the vows of Zeus. Ever unavailing
Are youthful minds; but when an elder intercedes,
Afore he looks and aft, for all a trusted tower."   120
So he spoke, and the Trojans and Argives rejoiced,
Wanting respite from wearisome war. And they stayed
Their chariots rank by rank, and themselves stepped forth,
Removing their armor, setting it down; crowded
All, and meagre the ground between them. And Hector   125
To the city quickly sent two heralds to fetch
The lambs and summon Priam; and Talthybius,
By Agamemnon sent to the hollow ships, was
Ordered to bring a lamb, nor failed he to comply.

But Iris as courier to white-armed Helen   130
Sped, likened to her sister-in-law the consort
Of Antēnōr's son Helicaōn to whom wed,
Laodicē, most lovely of Priam's daughters.
She found Helen in the central hall, there weaving
A resplendent textile double-plied, porphyreus,   135
Within it stitched the melee, immeasurable,
For her endured at the war god Ares' behest
By horse-taming Trojans and bronze-clad Achaeans.
Stealing upon her the fleet-footed Iris spoke:
"Hither, dear lady, come; the wondrous doings see   140
Of horse-taming Trojans and bronze-clad Achaeans.
They who aforetime contended so, desiring
Tearful strife on the battlefield—spirits in dire
Discord conjoined—in silence sit, their fighting ceased,
Enclasped their bucklers, groundward embedded their spears.   145
With deadly weaponry will Alexander now
And warlike Menelaus fight for you. And wife

BOOK III

Be you acknowledged of whosoever prevails."
So speaking, the goddess instilled in Helen's breast
Sweet longing for her former lord, for her parents 150
And dear abode; and she, fast enveiling herself
In linen's glint, descended her chamber, letting
Slip a tender tear; nor alone, for two servants
Accompanied her, Aethra, daughter of Pittheus,
And ox-eyed Clymenē; and hasty their footsteps 155
Attaining the Scaean Gates.
                        And with King Priam,
And Panthous and Thymoetēs and Hicataōn,
Scion of Ares, and Lampus, and Clytius,
And Antēnōr and Ucalegōn, prudent both,
Were seated the elders all at the Scaean Gates. 160
Though in their infirmity finished with warfare,
Yet deftly they discoursed like unto tree-ensconced
Cicadas, cascading their lilylike counsel.
Just so the Trojan leaders at the parapet;
But when observing Helen approaching the wall, 165
Soft each to his fellow this wingèd word declared:
"No fault is it that Trojans and greaved Achaeans
Endure the worst for such a woman evermore:
Supernal she—semblance of godhead incarnate!
But homeward be she sooner boarded and embarked, 170
Burden no longer to our children and ourselves."

So they spoke, but Priam summoned Helen aloud:
"Hhither come, dear child, be seated here beside me
That you may view your lord aforetime, your kinsfolk,
And your family. You are not to blame; sooner 175
The gods be blamed who against me raised this Argive
Trial of tears. Relate then: Who might this tow'ring
Warrior be, this colossal man of Achaea—
A tower, though taller by a head the others?
So conspicuous a man have I never seen, 180
Neither one so royal nor kingly in likeness."

Then Helen, godlike of women, responding said:
"Most revered are you, dear father-in-law, and dread.
Would my delight had been a heinous death, when first
I accompanied your offspring here, forsaking   185
My bridal chamber and relations, my cherished
Daughter and beloved companions, the girls my age.
Nor was it thus to occur, for which tearfully
I dissolve. But this will I relate since you ask,
Inquiring. That man is Atreus' son wide-ruling   190
Agamemnon, a righteous ruler, a sturdy
Spearman too, my shameless self's own brother-in-law,
Did such a one exist."
                So she spoke, and Priam
Stood amazed and said: "Ah, happy son of Atreus,
Fortune's offspring, of blessèd lot; now Achaean   195
Youth abundantly acknowledges your person.
Aforetime to vine-rich Phrygia have I ventured
And Phrygian warriors in their multitudes observed,
Masters of glancing steeds, even Otreus' forces
And godly Mygdōn's on Sangarius' levee   200
Encamped; for I too was considered an ally
That day when the man-equaling Amazons neared,
But many the fewer than these bright Argives here."
Next seeing Odysseus the agèd lord inquired:
"Come, lovely child, inform me now also of him,   205
Whoever he be. Less by a head than Atreus'
Son Agamemnon he stands, but broader chested
And shouldered to behold. His battle gear lies placed
Upon bountiful earth, but the man himself steps
Large, the herd's bellwether, amid the ranks of men.   210
Like to a ram he presents to me, thickly fleeced,
Surveying snowy ewes in their capacious span."

Answered him Helen of thundering Zeus begot:
"This again is Laërtes' son, resourceful most,
Odysseus, reared within Ithaca's rugged realm;   215

Crafty most, quick-witted, uncanny in tactics."
And to her responded the sage Antēnōr thus:
"Lady, wisely asserted this statement of yours;
For goodly Odysseus upon a time came here
On your account, on an embassy with warlike   220
Menelaus, and graciously I played them host
And most welcome they were. And I grew familiar
With their forms, demeanors, and close contrivances.
Now, when amid the Trojans they had intermixed,
Then, where they stood, Menelaus overtopped him,   225
His shoulders expansive; but when seated the two,
More striking was Odysseus. But when, all present,
Propounded they their woven web of words and plans,
Menelaus more promptly to the matter spoke,
Succinct but lucid, a speaker stinting of words,   230
His speech precise notwithstanding his younger age.
But many-wiled Odysseus, whene'er he uprose,
Would stand staring, eyes downward fastened to the ground,
His staff neither backward nor forward situate
But motionless held, as by a witless being—   235
A surly, simpering sort would you surmise him.
But whensoe'er his voice cascaded from his chest,
Like snowdrift his words on winter's winds descendent,
Then never with Odysseus could a mortal vie.
Then less our wonder, observing his comportment."   240

And thirdly viewing Ajax, the elder inquired:
"Who, tell, is this other Achaean, masterful,
Imposing, his head o'er the multitude risen,
His shoulders broad?" And to him replied trailing-robed
Helen, fair among women: "This is huge Ajax,   245
Bulwark of the Achaeans, with Idomeneus
Standing near, amid the Cretans, like to a god,
The Cretan captaincy about him collected.
Often did warlike Menelaus entertain
Him in our residence, whene'er arrived from Crete.   250

Now discern I the remainder all of bright-eyed
Danaans, whom I could designate naming each,
But twin marshalers of the army see I not:
Castōr tamer of horses, and Polydeucēs,
Excellent boxer—even my very brothers, 255
Twins of one mother born—either following not
From lovely Lacedaemōn or in seafaring
Vessels arrived, indifferent to the fighting,
Shamed by scandalous me and my immodesty."
So she spoke, but aforetime had Lacedaemōn 260
Reclaimed them, to their dearest native soil returned.
Throughout the town the couriers carried offerings
For the gods' sacred pledges: two lambs, and vintage
In a goatskin flask, heart-gladdening yield of earth;
And the herald Idaeus bore a golden bowl 265
And gilded cups and, aside the elderly king,
Said, rousing him: "Son of Laomedōn, rally!
The best of the horse-taming Trojans and bronze-mailed
Danaans summon you now to the Trojan plain,
That you aver your faith with sacrificial oaths; 270
Then Alexander or warlike Menelaus,
Stoutly battling for Helen with unyielding spears,
Will take her and her possessions, whoso prevail,
Th' others to oaths of friendship fairly pledged. Then dwell
We in Troy's rich acreage, and they in horse-grazing 275
Argos and in Achaea of storied women.
So he spoke, and the old man shuddered, ordering
His companions to couple his team, and quickly
They complied. Priam mounted, drawing back the reins,
And on the floorboard aside him Antēnōr stepped. 280
Stately their conveyance, and rapid the passage
The twain traversed from the Scaean Gates to the plain.
But arrived to the Trojan and Argive ranks, they
Dismounted to bountiful earth, thence proceeding
To midway between the opposing positions. 285
Then bestirred themselves Agamemnon, king of men,

BOOK III

And many-wiled Odysseus; and noble heralds
Together brought the sacrificial offerings,
And blended wine withal and o'er king Priam's hands
Poured water. And Agamemnon accessed the knife   290
E'er suspended aside his sword's great sheath, with it
Cutting head hairs from the lambs; and the messengers
Apportioned strands to the Trojan and Argive chiefs.
Then in their midst Agamemnon wide-ruling king
Prayed loudly, his hands upraised: "Father Zeus who rules   295
From Ida, greatest and most regarded, and you,
O Sun, perceiving all and ever circumspect,
And you river streams and earth, and you avengers
Of men outworn in the underworld—whoever's
Pledge be perjured, to our avowals witness be.   300
If Alexander slay Menelaus, retain
He then Helen and all her possessions; and we
In our seafaring ships will depart. But if blonde
Menelaus his rival slay, let the Trojans
Restore Helen and her trove, and to the Argives   305
Befitting value give as shall in memories
Remain, including generations yet to come.
But should Priam and Priam's sons unwilling be
To offer compensation, Alexander slain,
Then for recompense remaining will I battle   310
On hereafter, 'til battle's end determined be."

He spoke, the lambs' throats op'ning with pitiless bronze,
And groundward they dropped, gasping and gulping for breath,
Their strength by the bronze purloined; then drawing vintage
Into cups from mixing bowls, he decanted it,   315
To the immortals praying. And thus of Argives
And Trojans would one declaim: "Zeus, magnificent
Acclaimèd most, and you other gods immortal,
Whoever of these two transgressor proves to oaths'
Solemnities, o'er the ground be his brains bestrewn   320
Like wine, his and his children's; and his faithful wife

Beneath the force and weight of others lie subdued."
So they conversed, but Zeus the while denied the oaths'
Fulfillment. And Priam, Dardanus' son, to them
Next spoke: "Hear me, you Trojans and well-greaved Argives.   325
At once will I to windswept Troy return, these eyes
Inadequate to my offspring's confrontation
With warlike Menelaus; but Zeus, to be sure,
Discerns, and the other immortal gods, to which
The twain be dismal death ordained." Discoursing thus,   330
The godlike king commanded the lambs uploaded
To his vehicle and, himself ascending, drew
The reins; and aside him within the conveyance
Ascended Antēnōr, the two to Troy returned.

But Hector, Priam's son, and goodly Odysseus   335
First measured the space; and shaking lots, reposed them
In a bronze-cast helm, resolving which of the twain
His brazen spear should first discharge. And the people
To th' immortals prayed, extending their hands; and thus
Would a Trojan or Achaean speak: "Father Zeus,   340
Ruling from Ida, greatest, most revered, whoe'er
Has visited these troubles on both our peoples,
Grant he perish below, in Hades' house interred,
But for us prevail friendship, our devotions pledged."
So they spoke, and Hector gleaming-helmed commingled   345
The lots, looking sideways, and the lot of Paris
Outleapt forthwith; th' others throughout their ranks becalmed,
Where each man's windy-footed horse and dazzling arms
Reposed. 'Round his shoulders goodly Alexander,
Spouse to fair-haired Helen, affixed wondrous armor,   350
Upon his legs fastening decorative greaves,
Attached to which were silver-studded ankle clasps;
Next about himself, adjusted he the corselet
Of Lycaōn his kin, fit to himself as well;
And about his shoulders cast his silver-studded   355
Brazen sword; next setting his protective buckler;

BOOK III

And on his mighty head a well-wrought helmet laid,
Horsehair its crest—and dauntingly nodded the plume
On high; and took he a stalwart grip-fitted spear;
And likewise warlike Menelaus armed himself. 360

But once arming themselves at the hosts' either side,
They strode—glaring grimly—the space between Trojans
And Achaeans; and awe gripped the gawking gathered:
Both Trojans tamers of horses and Achaeans
Well-greaved. But the twain, near together, positioned 365
Themselves in the measured space, each at the other
Wrathfully thrusting his spear. First Alexander
Despatched his far-shadowing spear, smiting the shield
Of Atreïdēs, roundedly balanced about;
But the point, in the buckler lodged, was arrested. 370
Next with spear rushed Atreïdēs Menelaus,
Hard praying to father Cronidēs: "Zeus, father,
Vengeance vouchsafe against him first injuring me,
Even valiant Alexander. Deliver him
Into my hand, that someone of men yet to come 375
May shrink from violating hospitality."
Thus he declared, with sturdy spearshaft taking aim,
And resolutely cast on Alexander's shield
Balanced roundedly about; and through the buckler
Advanced the spear, and sped through the corselet richly 380
Dight, and through the tunic aside his flank traversed.
But he, sideward inclining, avoided dark death.
Then drew Menelaus his silver-studded sword
And, hoisting it high, thwacked the horn of Paris' helm;
But on it was the sword to pieces three and four 385
Fragmented from his hand. Then unyielding the cry
That Menelaus, looking heavenward, unloosed:
"Father Zeus, none the god more malignant than you!
Here I thought to avenge Alexander's offense,
But the weapon within my grip to pieces wastes; 390
And hopelessly amiss the spear departs my palm."

125

So saying sprang he forth and, grabbing Paris fast
By his helm's thick horsehair crest, updragged and spun him
'Round toward the well-greaved Argives; and the bright-broidered
Band hard-throttled his tender throat, there drawn a'stretch   395
Beneath his chin the helmet to secure. And now
Had Menelaus hauled him off, gaining glory
Everlasting had not Aphrodite daughter
Of Zeus, wary observer, to his detriment
Severed the hide-hewn strap of sacrificial ox;   400
And fruitless the helm that trailed in his sturdy fist.
This, held aloft, to the Danaans well-armored
Hurled the hero, and steadfast they carried it off.
Then instantly tore he back, on carnage intent,
To slaughter his rival with brazen spear; but seized   405
Him Aphrodite, deftly as goddesses do,
Secreting him in teeming mist and setting him
Within his redolent chamber, fragrance-wafted;
While she, summoning Helen, departed, finding
Her on the rampart, the Trojan women crowded   410
About her. And the goddess extended her hand,
Tugging at Helen's ambrosial attire, and spoke,
Like to a veilèd carder of wool, loved of old,
Who for Helen, dwelling in Sparta, combed fine wool;
And Helen especially loved her. To her thus   415
Likening herself spoke Aphrodite: "Here come,
Alexander bids you homeward, himself reposed
Well appareled on his apartment's inlaid bed,
Radiant his aspect; nor would you imagine
Him from mortal combat come, but sooner dancing   420
Gone or, having danced, reposed."
                                    Thus spoke the goddess
And roused the spirit within her breast. And seeing
Aphrodite's comely neck, her beauteous breasts,
And dazzling eyes, she stood amazed, thus calling her:
"Dear goddess mine, determined to deceive me thus!   425
Will you somewhere now transport me? To a far-famed

Phrygian city, to enchanting Maionia,
Or wherever your preferrèd of mortal souls
Reside? But now, having bested Alexander,
Menelaus wishes my scandal to Sparta   430
Restored. Thus disposed on that account, O goddess,
Do you deceive me? By Paris sit; abandon
Godly doings, disdain Olympus' parapet;
And attentively ever for Paris lament
Until proclaimed his lawful wife—his slave at least.   435
But none of it will I! The more distressing yet
My tending to his bed, as all the Trojan wives
Will reckon me hereafter scorned and scandalized,
And incalculable will my affliction be."
And indignantly the goddess addressed her thus: 440
"Obdurate woman, incite me not lest angered
I spurn you, loathing you even as aforetime
I have prized you, and incite contention between
Trojans and Argives, and perish you more aggrieved
Than ever." Thus she declared, and Zeus-born Helen   445
Recoiled and, in glistening garments enfolded,
Strode silently, by the Trojan women unseen.

She came to Alexander's splendid residence,
The servants with tasks preoccupied; but Helen,
Wondrous of women, to her high-roofed room retired;   450
And the goddess laughter-loving Aphrodite
Positioned a chair for her opposite Paris,
There seating Helen born of aegis-bearing Zeus.
And looking askance, she rebuked her husband thus:
"So, from war you return. Would you had perished there,   455
Vanquished by a valiant man, my husband erstwhile!
And yet earlier you boasted yourself better
Than Menelaus, Ares-beloved, in sinew,
Hand, and spear. But away, summon Menelaus,
Ares-favorèd, to fight yet again with you;   460
But no, I forbid your continued encounter

With flaxen Menelaus and your fool-hearted
Truculence, lest you somehow succumb to his spear."
To Helen then did Paris responding declare:
"With revilements, dear lady, admonish me not;   465
Menelaus, my better the while, is aided
By Athena. But routed will he someday be,
So help us heaven. But come, to bedded dalliance
Be we sped, for never aforetime has desire
Thus tormented me—not even from the outset,   470
When we absconded from lovely Lacedaemōn
And, in seafaring ships athwart the wayward winds
To Cranae, finally mingled—as now I languish
For you, and acute the craving consuming me."
He spoke, and to the bedstead Helen followed him.   475
Thus lay the twain, upon the corded couch entwined;
But midst the throng ranged Menelaus resembling
A savage beast, if he might somewhere discover
The godlike Alexander; but none the Trojan
Nor any ally to report his whereabouts   480
To Ares-beloved Atreïdēs. Through no love
Would they willingly the least conceal him—had they,
Any, descried him—like unto black death despised.

Then Agamemnon, king of men, among them spoke:
"Hearken unto me, you Trojans, you Dardanians,   485
And allies: unequivocal the victory
Of Ares-beloved Atreïdēs. Surrender
You fair Argive Helen and her all possessions
And proffer merited compensation, payment
Such as men to come shall acclaim and recollect."   490
Thus Agamemnon, and the Argives all agreed.

~ Book IV ~

The Trojans Breach the Truce, Agamemnon Marshals the Forces, the First Day of Battle

THE GODS FROM OLYMPUS follow and comment on the events below, Hera and Zeus, as usual, arguing. Zeus acknowledges Hera's savagery toward the Trojans—she would devour them alive. At the same time, Zeus avers he will destroy what cities he will, though Troy presently merits reprieve for the regularity of its ritual sacrifices and because of Zeus' promise to Thetis to punish the Greeks. Zeus has sometimes even yielded to Hera concerning the destruction of cities. Her expectations must, however, be tamed since Zeus' will, i.e., fate itself, is absolute.

Contemplating the war's further course, Zeus sends Athena to break the truce. She persuades Pandarus, best of the Trojan archers, to shoot at Menelaus. Menelaus is wounded but handily attended by the physician Machaon. The incident highlights Homer's imagistic sensibility and technique. Menelaus' blood-stained thigh is compared to a horse's dye-stained ivory cheekpiece—the treasure by many desired, but concealed in a chest within a chamber, the chamber deep within the household. It also shows Agamemnon's touching concern for his brother, fearful he might have been slain. Meanwhile, a number of Trojans, incited by Pandarus' treachery, attack the Greeks.

Playing the good general, Agamemnon reviews the troops and encourages their leaders, some by praise, others by reproof for substandard performance. Given the Trojans' treachery, the Cretan leader, Idomeneus, swears a special vow of allegiance. The Aiantes are especially commended, as is the elderly Nestor, who urges a workaday approach over showmanship in the fighting to come, even while lamenting the ills of old age.

Agamemnon next reproves Odysseus as a slacker but immediately retracts when Odysseus takes exception. He next comes to the young

Diomedes, claiming him not half the man his father, Tydeus, was and continuing with a digression into Tydeus' earlier heroism. The perfectly chivalrous Diomedes accepts the criticism, not daring to argue with the commander-in-chief. When his comrade Capaneus speaks up on his behalf, Diomedes seeks to contain him, again in deference to Agamemnon. The "interview" between Agamemnon and Diomedes is preparatory to the latter's battlefield excellence in the following book. Though Telamonian Ajax is officially designated best after the absent Achilles, Diomedes is as equally worthy.

Following extended Homeric similes, the two sides join in battle and many on both sides perish. Foremost among the casualties is the Trojan youth Simoeisius, tragic for reasons elsewhere explained (see *TSS* 88–89). Book 4 occurs on the twenty-third day of the *Iliad*, continuing nearly to the end of Book 7.

᛫

Now the gods at Zeus's domicile were gathered
O'er the golden floor; and mistress Hēbē poured them
Godly Nectar, and with golden goblets toasted
They one another, surveying all Troy's expanse.
And next Cronidēs Zeus endeavored to quarrel   5
With Hera, speaking spitefully with taunting words:
"Two are the goddesses aiding Menelaus,
Even Argive Hera and guardian Athena.
Resolutely apart they sit, and as viewers
Only, while Alexander absconds to laughter-   10
Loving Aphrodite's retreat, forestalling fate;
His surety she when looms darkest his demise.
But roundly has warlike Menelaus prevailed.
Let us then consider how best these things betide,
Whether we again rouse ruinous war and harsh   15
Battle's bruit, or foster friendship between the hosts.
Should all in this assent, then might Priam's city
Thrive and Menelaus reclaim his Argive wife."

So he spoke, whereupon Athena and Hera
Whispered, seated side by side, devising Trojan 20
Setback. But Athena, self-restrained, kept quiet,
Saying naught, infuriated with father Zeus,
Her spirit with wrath o'erwrought. However, Hera's
Breast with umbrage burst, and she remonstrated thus:
"Dreadest son of Cronus, what counsel now announced? 25
How contrive you, countermanding my enterprise
And the sweat I sweated toiling? And my horses—
Look!—Both exhausted as I goad the Argive host,
A plague to Priam and his progeny. Go on!
But know we other gods entirely object." 30
Then greatly angered, cloud-gathering Zeus replied:
"Strange lady mine, what plenteous pains do Priam
And Priam's son impose on you that this your pique
Persists, wanting ruin for well-built Ilium?
Were you to enter the gates and towering walls 35
Of Troy, feasting on flesh of Priam and Priam's
Offspring and of Trojans one and all, your outrage
Were then perhaps assuaged. As you wish! But let this
Clash not grievous grow to grim discord between us.
And this my pronouncement also heed, and heed well: 40
Whene'er strong-willed I wish to lay a city waste
Wherein dwell men who worship you, ponder nowise
To impede my rage, but suffer me; since freely
At times have I fully favored you, my spirit
The while unwilling. For of cities all where men 45
Beneath the sun and starry heavens dwell, of these
Within my heart is hallowed Troy most treasurèd,
And Priam proudly ashen-speared and Priam's folk.
For at no time has altar of mine lain bereft
Of fitting feast, libation, or burnt offering, 50
Prerogatives of which, as gods, we stand possessed."

Responding then did queenly ox-eyed Hera speak:
"In truth, three cities deem I dearest to my heart:

Argos, Sparta, and broad-pavemented Mycenae.
Go ravish them whene'er vilest to you they be.　　　　　55
Nor e'er will I negotiate for their defense,
Extolling them, though loth to grant their overthrow,
Naught gaining by grudge, since you, my better, prevail.
Yet befits my toil be not idly accomplished.
Since I, like you, exist, a god, selfsame the stock;　　　　60
And crooked-couns'ling Cronus sired me respected
Most of all his daughters, since I both eldest am
And wed to you, commanding the immortals all.

So let us, one and the other, relent the while,
I unto you, you to me; and let the other　　　　65
Gods example take. But bid Athena quickly
Alight on the combat's tumultuous clamor
Of Trojans and Danaans, devising withal
To demonstrate that Trojans first flouted their oaths,
Affronting the triumph-exultant Achaeans."　　　　70

So she spoke, and Zeus omnipotent minded her
And straightway to Athena issued wingèd words:
"To the midst of the Trojans and Argives descend,
To demonstrate that Trojans first flouted their oaths,
Affronting the triumph-exultant Achaeans."　　　　75
So saying, he roused the goddess, by then eager;
And downward she hurtled from Olympus unloosed,
In likeness of a star, a glowing augury
That the wry-witted son of Cronus evinces
To sailors or combatants in their multitudes,　　　　80
And from it glister innum'rable sparks. The like
To it careened Athena earthward, fast joining
The hosts below, and the onlookers stood agog,
Both horse-taming Trojans and well-greaved Achaeans.
And witnessing it, would one address another:　　　　85
"Alas for combative calamitous onset
And brutal battle's din; or Zeus who to mankind

BOOK IV

Allocates dispute now entente ordains somehow."
So one of the Trojans or Achaeans would speak.
But Athena entered the Trojan ranks likened 90
To a man, even to Laodocus, offspring
Of Antēnōr, brave spearman, searching for godlike
Pandarus, were she somehow to encounter him.
And Pandarus she found, Lycaōn's son, a man
Unsurpassed; and attending him a shield-bearing 95
Host, stalwarts all, that followed him whence Aesēpus
Flows. Then standing near, she addressed him wingèd words:
"Should you now attend me, skillful-hearted offspring
Of Lycaōn, you would courageously discharge
A shaft at Menelaus, appreciation 100
And glory procuring from the Trojans and king
Priam especially. From him decidedly
Would you, before others all, bear bounteous gifts
Away, should he witness Menelaus, Atreus'
Warlike son, bronze-slain, on a pyre standing high. 105
But come, let fly, level-aimed, at th' illustrious
Menelaus, and swear to bow-famed Apollo,
Radiant-born, to sacrifice a hecatomb
Of glorious firstling lambs when homeward arrived
To Zeleia's sacrosanct and welcoming hearth." 110
So cajoled Athena, convincing the fool's heart
Within him. And fast deployed he his well-honed bow,
Horn-crafted of ibex that he himself, ensconced
Within a covert, smote, aiming beneath its chest
As it forged from a rocky outcrop. He struck it 115
In the chest, and into a cleft it backward dropped.
The horns atop its head full measured sixteen palms;
These, together fit, a horn-knowing workman honed,
Cannily smoothing them, gilding the top with gold.
Thus stringing his bow did Pandarus position 120
And downward incline it, and his goodly comrades
Concealed him, that the Achaeans o'erwhelm him not
Ere shooting Menelaus, Atreus' warlike son.

He then unlidded his quiver, wresting a shaft,
A feathered stem aforetime unshot, with torments   125
Tinged; and deftly fitted the bitter shaft to string,
Swearing unto Apollo radiant-born, bow-famed,
To sacrifice a celebrated hecatomb
Of firstling lambs when he should homeward come, arrived
At Zeleia's sacred citadel. Next he drew   130
The bow, together catching up the notchèd shaft
And sinewy string of ox; string drawn to his chest
And at the bow the arrow's iron head. And when
The balanced bow was drawn, unto fullness rounded,
Twanged the string, bellowed the bow, and longingly leapt   135
The hurtled shaft irately hast'ning through the ranks.

Then, Menelaus, the blessèd gods immortal
Remembered you, foremost the goddess Athena,
Zeus' daughter, fomenter of plunder who, standing
Afore you, stayed the fervent arrow's wrath, foiling   140
Its flesh-bound flight—as when a mother distant whisks
The willful fly from her child's sweet slumber away—
And herself directed the shaft to where fastens
The gold-buckled belt and overfolds the corselet.
Forward flew the bitter arrow toward the fitted   145
Belt and onward through the fitted fastening sped
Intent—through the artful workmanship careening—
And, lower, through the tasset protecting his thighs,
Foremost defense against arrows to fragile flesh.
And through this withal it whizzed and skimmed the warrior's   150
Topmost flesh, the dark blood suddenly exuding.
As when ivory is dyed to crimson-colored hue
By some Maeonian woman, or Carian,
To be a horse's cheekpiece, and in the household
Lies it deep within, though many a horseman dreams   155
To make it his; yet there as royal trove it lies,
Adornment alike to the horse and horseman's pride.
E'er similar your blood-stained thighs, Menelaus,

BOOK IV

And your muscular shanks and fair ankles beneath.

Then shuddered lord Agamemnon, ruler of men, 160
Seeing sable blood from the wound a'flow. Frighted
Too was daunting Menelaus; but observing
The arrow's barb and thread without his flesh, again
Mustered his deep-settled mettle. But Atreidēs
Agamemnon groaned aloud, by the hand taking 165
Menelaus, and alike groaned their companions:
"Dear brother, for your death, it appears, undertook
I these oaths, casting you alone of the Argives
As combatant to Troy—the Trojans now vilely
Assaulting you, their vows trodden faithlessly down. 170
Yet never are oaths deemed vain and unavailing,
Nor blood of lambs, nor offerings drunk of unmixed
Wine, nor hands tight-gripped wherewith trustingly we pledge.
For even now, though Olympian Zeus begrudge
Fulfillment, yet will fulfillment afforded be 175
And men grievously atone—with their heads, their wives,
Their children. For this my spirit acknowledges:
The day shall come when sacred Troy be reckoned lost,
And Priam, with stout ashen spear, and all his folk;
And aether-thundering Zeus Cronidēs enthroned 180
On high shall afore them grimly wield the aegis,
Wrathful for this deception. Nor will these matters
Lack fulfillment. But, O Menelaus, dread grief
On your account is mine if, dying now, your life's
Allotment stand ordained. Then to arid Argos 185
I return despised, for then would the Danaans
Most desirous be of their belovèd homeland,
And so should we to Priam and the Trojans leave
Their prize—yes, Argive Helen; and yours the moldered
Bones a'mix with Trojan loam, abortive your task. 190
And thus shall some Trojan overweeningly gloat,
Leaping high atop the barrow of glorious
Menelaus: 'Ah, would that thus and evermore

Lord Agamemnon spend his wrath as even now
He Troyward vainly led Achaea's entourage;   195
And Look! Now homeward flies he to his fatherland,
Desolate his vessels, and Menelaus lost.'
When someone thus speaks someday, earth swallow me down!"

And heartening him spoke fair-haired Menelaus:
"Be you comforted, nor the least affright the vast   200
Achaean host. Conveying not death did the shaft
Attach; sooner stayed it my decorate cincture,
The kilt beneath, and the tasset by coppersmiths
Created." Then Agamemnon, speaking, replied:
"Thus be it ever, dear brother, Menelaus.   205
The wound will the physician o'ersee, liniments
Applying, sure remedy to repellent pain."
Then to Talthybius, divine herald, he spoke:
"Talthybius, hasten to summon Machaōn,
Asclepius' offspring, Asclepius most learnèd   210
In liniments, to aid warlike Menelaus
Atreidēs, whom a man expert in archery
Has with arrow assailed, some Trojan or Lycian,
For himself great glory gained, for us agony."
So he spoke, and the herald, hearing, hearkened well.   215
Through the ranks of the bronze-mailed Achaeans he strode,
Intent on finding the warrior Machaōn.
He marked him where he stood, 'round about him seeing
The stalwart host of shield-bearing men that followed
Him from Trica, pastureland of horses. Standing   220
Nearby, he addressed him fleet words as follows: "Up,
Asclepius' son! Lord Agamemnon summons thee
To attend Menelaus, warlike Achaean
Captain, whom someone well practiced in archery
Has with arrow assailed, some Trojan or Lycian,   225
For himself great glory gained, for us agony."
So he spoke, rousing the heart in Machaōn's breast,
And they proceeded through the thronged Achaean host.

BOOK IV

But when arrived where flaxen-haired Menelaus
Was wounded—encompassed 'round by stalwart warriors,   230
As many as gathered—the godlike hero stood
Steadfast among them and quickly dislodged the shaft
From out the tightened belt. And as it was dislodged,
The bitter prongs were broken back; and he loosened
The variegated cincture and, from underneath,   235
The kilt and tasset trim crafted by coppersmiths.
And viewing the wound where the bitter arrow drove,
Outward sucked the blood and ably administered
The mild medicaments which once with kindly thought
The centaur Chirōn on his father had bestowed.   240
While thus they attended war-tempered Atreidēs,
The array of shield-shouldering Trojans advanced
As Danaans donned battle gear, mindful of strife.

Then was goodly Atreidēs industrious seen,
Neither cowering nor bereft of heart for battle   245
But for warcraft awakened, where men covet fame.
Forsook he his horses and bronze-bedecked chariot,
While his squire, Eurymedōn, son of Peiraeus'
Son, Ptolemaeus, kept the snorting steeds apart.
And adamantly did Atreidēs direct him   250
To steady them, should fatigue ever overtire
His limbs, as he lorded through the Danaan ranks.
But further afoot he strode through the Argive ranks,
And whomsoe'er he met of steed-swift Danaans
Submitting to the task aright, these he addressed,   255
Approaching, and emboldened them forcefully thus:
"Argives, relent not from intractable fury,
For e'er stands father Zeus disfavoring falsehood.
As the Trojans first contrived to betray our truce,
Feed vultures, engorged, upon them, body and bone,   260
While homebound on our vessels shall every lovely
Trojan wife and child embark, Troy's glory gutted."
And whomsoe'er he eyed withdrawn from dreadful war

He roundly reprimanded, unsparing his ire:
"Arrow-enamoured Danaans, repugnant all, 265
Have you no shame? Thus stand you fawn-like bewildered,
Immobile, aquiver, verve from breasts absented;
Erst striving a'gambol lush grasslands to traverse?
Now o'erwhelmed, you rashly acquiesce—or perhaps
You await the Trojans' advance on your vessels 270
Stately arrayed aside the sea's hoary expanse,
Perchance to ascertain whether Zeus, extending
His arm, protect you." Thus he sauntered, imparting
Instructions to his soldiers.
      And to the Cretans
He came, moving through the swollen ranks. For battle 275
Were these arming themselves, 'round about wise-hearted
Idomeneus; and Idomeneus stood amid
The foremost fighters, his nerve like a bristling boar's,
While Mērionēs roused the hindmost battalions.
Seeing them, Agamemnon, king of men, rejoiced 280
And forthwith discreetly addressed Idomeneus:
"Idomeneus, you I most esteem of steed-swift
Danaans all, both in warfare and otherwise.
So also at feast, when Greeks within the mixing
Bowl let blend the elders' glinting wine. For other 285
Hair-flown Danaans their allotted share may drink,
But brims your own cup o'er, as overflows my own,
To gladden your spirit. But waken warfare now,
Of value as you erstwhile vaunt yourself to be."
Unto him Idomeneus, Cretan commander, 290
Responded thus: "Lord Agamemnon, to a fault
And evermore will I your sturdy comrade be,
Even as I pledged initially, vouchsafing
My promise; but urge you the other streaming-haired
Danaans that directly be battle our task, 295
Since the Trojans disdained our oaths. Death and distress
Be theirs entire for treacherously transgressing
Our oaths." So he spoke, and Agamemnon, Atreus'

BOOK IV

Son, passed onward glad at heart to the Aiantes,
Traversing the warrior ranks; and these for war 300
Were fitted, formations of footmen attendant.
And even as the goatherd, peering afar, spies
A cloud spread widely o'er the ocean's waste, hurried
By whoosh of West Wind on, and to his distant self
Seems it black unto pitch, surmounting the ruffled 305
Main, and brings it maelstrom and whirlwind, and shudders
He perceiving it and, driving his flock, a cave's
Concealment seeks; just so, aside th' Aiantes twain,
Did the close-packed battalions of Zeus-nurtured youth
Advance dourly to burdensome war, shields and spears 310
A'bristle. And observing them, lord Atreidēs
Delighted, and spoke addressing them wingèd words:
"O you Aiantes twain, bronze-chitoned Achaean
Commanders! From you both—no urging you require—
All orders I withhold; for of yourselves you bid 315
Your battalions engage. I would, O father Zeus,
Athena, and Apollo, that courage alike
To yours within each heart were evident. Then King
Priam's citadel to earth apace would sunder,
By these our hands denuded quite and looted through." 320
Thus emoting moved he past, traversing the ranks,
Next marking Nestor, lucid Pylian orator,
Preparing his comrades—about Bias, shepherd
Of the host, Pleagōn, the mighty Alastōr,
Chromius, and lord Haemōn—and urging them to fight. 325
First amid their cars he arranged the charioteers,
Their horses too, next the plenteous infantry,
Formidable bulwark of battle; but cowards
He herded centerward, that each commit to war,
However much unwilling. To the charioteers 330
First issued he command, directing they restrain
Their steeds nor startle the throng tumultuously:
"Let no man whate'er, trusting in his horsemanship
Or valor, venture apart to engage the foe,

A spectacle thereby to his fellows; nor yet   335
A slacker be found, for thus do you falter all.
But whosoe'er from his own car upend the foe's
Conveyance, thrust he with undeviating spear,
Decidedly, just so. Thus also aforetime
Warriors dismantled intractable city walls,   340
Minds and spirits invested with tenacity."
So rallied them the elder, knowing of battles
Aforetime, at which sight Atreïdēs rejoiced;
And he responded, addressing him wingèd words:
"Dear elder, would the spirit within your breast were   345
In your limbs implanted, and self-assured your strength;
But wretched age constrains you. I would some other
Of these warriors here harbored your years, and yourself
Among the youthful thrived." To him then responded
Horseman Gerēnian Nestor: "Son of Atreus,   350
How greatly would I wish myself again strengthened
With bygone years, aforetime slaying thunderous
Ereuthaliōn. But the gods ne'er grant mankind
Th' entirety at once. I prospered when earlier
Young, but presently dread decline accomp'nies me.   355
Yet nonetheless abide I with the charioteers,
By entreaty and utterance their overseer.
Such the privilege of age. Spears shall young men wield,
More vibrant, more assured their sturdiness than mine."

So he spoke, and Atreidēs passed gladdened at heart,   360
Happening on Menestheus driver of horses,
Peteōs' son, there standing, and the Athenians
Surrounding him, masters of warcry. And wily
Odysseus nearby them stood, and surrounding him
The Cephallēnians well arrayed, industrious   365
Soldiery, the while uncommitted to battle.
No matter that Argives and horse-taming Trojans
Immersed themselves in warcraft, these inactive stood,
Attending the serried advance of some other

BOOK IV

Argive soldiery to importune the Trojans, 370
The clash thus deemed commenced. Viewing this, Atreidēs,
King of men, rebukingly responded, speaking
Wingèd words: "O Zeus-nurtured son of Peteōs
And you as well, in wicked wiles a wonderment,
O deviously minded Odysseus, why stand you 375
Thus cowered, counting on others? Better counseled
You twain, 'mid the foremost assuming positions,
To assay impassioned onslaught; for in feasting
Are you ever first, attending my command, when
We Achaeans lavish dinner on our elders. 380
Then delighting, devour you roasted meat, downing
Honey-cupped and fully aged wine, insatiate.
But now would you uncaring watch were there Argives
Tenfold afore you arrayed, on fighting resolved."
Disdainfully then, askance from beneath his brows, 385
Did crafty Odysseus respond: "Son of Atreus,
What comment this, flown from your teeth unbarriered!
How propose you that we Achaeans have slackened
Whenever we visit keen battle's affliction
On horse-taming Trojans? You will see, if watchful 390
Your regard—or have any regard whatever—
Telemachus' father the foremost merged amid
Horse-commanding Trojans. Rubbish your reprimand!"

Then smilingly lord Agamemnon answered him,
Knowing him indignant, and recanting his words: 395
"Zeus-born Laërtes' son, widely-wiled Odysseus,
I chide you not excessively nor chastise you,
For I know you well disposed and know you willing
As I know myself. But come, such things hereafter
Shall we repair if harshly we have spoken now; 400
And may favoring gods rescind this dissension."

So saying, pressing forward the while, he left them,
Next finding the son of Tydeus, Diomedes,

High-hearted amid his horses and firm-fitted
Chariots positioned; and aside him Sthenelus,   405
Capaneus' son. And observing him, admonished
Lord Agamemnon, addressing him wingèd words:
"Ah me, wise-hearted son of horse-taming Tydeus,
Why cower you thus, why scout you combat's havens?
Tydeus, to be sure, was no such quaking coward   410
But e'er ahead his companions advanced, fighting
The foe amid wasting travail—as witnesses
Attest, for ne'er viewed him I nor met him ever.
Men, however, praise his prowess past others born.
Once came he to Mycenae, not as foe but guest,   415
With godlike Polynicēs to assemble men,
Contesting—as they were—afore Thebes' sacred walls
And entreating stalwart allies for the asking.
And we of Mycenae assented, advancing
Their design; but Zeus impeded them, unveiling   420
Omens of adverse augury. But journeying
Farther on were they next arrived at the river
Asopus, grassy-meadowed, its reeds deep rooted.
Thence as messenger the Danaans sent Tydeus
And, arriving, encountered he the many sons   425
Of Cadmus, boldly banqueting upon th' estate
Of resolute Eteoclēs. Then, though stranger
Among them, horseman Tydeus, not disconcerted,
Though alone, confronted the many Cadmeans,
Challenging them to manly feats, effortlessly   430
Vanquishing them; such his assistant Athena.
But the horse-prodding Cadmeans indignant grew
And set ambush against him homeward journeying,
Surreptitiously, of fifty conscripted youths;
Two their commanders—Maeōn, son of Haemōn, peer   435
Of the immortal gods; and Autophonus' son,
Polyphontēs, constant in combat. But Tydeus
Even on these a distasteful fate inflicted.
He slew them all, allowing the homeward return

Of one alone, namely Maeōn, the gods' portents 440
Obeying. Just so was Tydeus the Aetolian;
Yet to him in combat ill compares his offspring,
Though in assembly conspicuous, outstanding."

So he spoke, and naught said steadfast Diomedes
But accepted his lord Agamemnon's reproof; 445
And in his stead responded the son of acclaimed
Capaneus. "Offspring of Atreus, utter not lies
When aware of the truth. We reckon us of stock
Superior to that whence sprang our ancestors.
We, not they, took seven-gated Thebes, ours lesser 450
The host assembled a'front Thebes' stalwart wall, sure
In heaven's management and Zeus' intercession.
But the Thebans succumbed by blind folly their own,
Wherefore equate not sires and sons in character."

Then looking sharply askance, lord Diomedes 455
Rebuked him aloud: "Good comrade, your silence keep
And consider my words. No shame I regard it
That Atreidēs, shepherd of the host, compel
The well-greaved Achaeans to conflict, since to him
Will great glory redound should Danaans destroy 460
The foe, sacking their sacred city; conversely,
Wrenching pain should the Danaans defeated fall.
But come, give we thought to unwavering valor."
Thus responding, leapt he armored from his chariot
To the plain, and the bronze, as he stirred, resounded 465
Terribly about the prince's breast, such that dread
Might yet discomfit an unfaltering spirit,
As when on echoing seashore, prey to Zephyr's
Agile agency, turgid beats the bursting tide;
Early upon mid-ocean rolls it risen head, 470
But landward crashes thunderously thereafter,
And by headlands uplifted sloshes ever forth,
And the biting brine is spent in piddling foam; thus

On that very day advanced the dread Danaans,
Arrayed their forces for battle's fierce encounter,   475
Each captain ordering his troops aloud, the rest
Marching silently forth. Nor would you have reckoned
That thus abundantly disposed they harbored voice
To spare within their breasts, so mutedly they marched,
Unnerved by their commanders; and on each man gleamed   480
The inlaid gear wherein they advanced appareled.

But the Trojans amassed as ewes, ten thousand-strong
On a prosperous person's property, their milk
Full primed to be expressed; and endlessly they bleat,
Attending the voices of their lambs: even thus   485
Did towering tumult ascend the Trojan host,
For comp'rable speech possessed they none, but muttered
Patois; men mustered and retrieved from sundry climes.
These Ares bestirred; and dazzling-eyed Athena
The Danaans; and Rout and Terror rallied them,   490
And Discord, relentlessly raging, assistant
And sister to slaughtering Ares born. She crests
But little at first then heavenward uprears her
Head; earthbound her footstep fixed, hatred infusing
Throughout the ranks astride their teeming multitudes,   495
Augmenting the groans of men.
                              Now together come,
Congested, erupted their brawn in bucklered blows,
In piercing pikes, and brazen-armored warriors' force;
Nob-naveled shields collided with one another,
And loud the encircling din. Then alike were heard   500
The slayer's exultation and the slaughtered's groan,
And the ground ran blood. As when from teeming wellsprings
Wintry torrents careen through Alpine crevasses,
Their convergence resoundingly quaffed in sunken
Canyon chasms, and the shepherd far remote notes   505
Their commotion; so for these were bedlam and toil
In combat begotten.

BOOK IV

        Antilochus was first
To despatch a Trojan warrior, Echepōlus,
Thalysius' offspring, foremost 'mid the ranks, well armed.
Him he assaulted on his horsehair helmet's crest,   510
Next sinking the spear within his skull. Through the bone
Passed the pointed bronze, darkness encircling his eyes.
Downward listing he dropped as would a parapet
In combat's press. But as he collapsed, stout-hearted
Elephēnōr footwise secured him, Chalcōdōn's   515
Son, the Abantes' stalwart-mannered lord, who dragged
Him away from missiles' range, the more nimbly his
Corselet to despoil; Yet fleetingly managed he.
The proud Agēnōr espied him hauling the corpse,
And where his side aslant his shield uncovered showed   520
The while he stooped, just there impaled him—thrusting deep
With brazen spear—loosened his limbs, and cheated him
Of cherished life. Grievous for Greeks and Trojans grew
The contest for his remains—even as wolves they
Leapt upon the other each, reeling man on man.   525

Then Telamonian Ajax felled the blooming
Anthemiōn's son, Simoeisius, a mere youth—
Alas!—to whom his mother afore had given
Birth beside Simois' banks, passing from Ida,
Companioned by her parents surveying their flocks.   530
For this reason then they called him Simoeisius,
Yet none the rearing's recompense returned he them,
Scant ere then his alotted time, to death consigned
By mighty-spirited Ajax' spear. While foremost
Traversing the ranks, to rightward was he stricken   535
On the chest aside the nipple. And the brazen
Lance unswerving through his shoulder passed, and collapsed
He downward into dust—like a pliant poplar
From bottomland of marshy meadow issuing,
Its branches burgeoning topmost forth. This has some   540
Wainwright with glinting blade despoiled whereby to shape

A charming chariot's rim, and lies the poplar
drying by a river's banks. Thus Zeus-born Ajax
Slaughtered Simoeisius, Anthemiōn's son.

But Antiphōn, Priam's son, his corselet ablaze, 545
Had at Ajax, spear casting from across the throng.
Overpassing Ajax, it punctured Leucus' groin—
Companion to stalwart Odysseus—as he dragged
The corpse of Anthemiōn's son away. Tripped he
Thereon, the corpse outslipping his hands. Acutely 550
Vexed over Leucus' affliction, Odysseus strode
Amid the foremost warrior ranks, his bronze ablaze.
Adjacent the foe he advanced, taking his stand
And, warily glancing about, released his spear;
And the Trojans recoiled aback from Odysseus' 555
Cast. Nor without purpose was his weapon released,
But smote it Priam's bastard son Democoōn,
Sent from Abydus, stud of magnificent mares.
Him Odysseus, indignant for his comrade's sake,
With spear to temple impaled; and out the other 560
Side unsparingly passed the point, and darkness doused
His lids, and thudded his armor to groundward dropped.
Then the foremost fighters and great Hector withdrew;
And the Danaans, bellowing loud, recovered
Their fallen, storming the farther forth. Apollo 565
From Pergamus peered, aggrieved, and to the Trojans
Shouted aloud: "Rise, you horse-taming Trojans, spare
The Danaans no battle's lust, since neither stone
Nor iron-wrought their constitutions to forestall
Flesh-furrowing bronze, and resolute Achilles 570
From fight refrains, anger-engorged aside his ships."

Then was Amarynceus' son Diorēs fettered
By fortune, hard smitten by jagged projectile—
On his right leg by the ankle—by Peirōs cast,
Imbrasus' son, Thracian leader from Aenus come. 575

The devastating stone crushed bone and tendon both,
Pulverizing them; and to the dust he backward
Dropped, extending his hands to his comrades nearby,
His life gasping forth. And he that had smitten him,
Even Peirōs, sped fast alongside and attacked, 580
His spear to mid-navel propelled; and forth o'erflown
Gushed groundward his guts, and darkness enveloped him.
But as Peirōs decamped, Aetolian Thoas
Planted a spear above the nipple in his breast
And the weapon lay lodged in his lung; and Thoas, 585
Swift approaching, from his chest outpulled the weapon,
And, sword drawn, slitted his gut and looted his life.
But his armor he declined, for stood companions
Surrounding him—top-coiffed Thracian men, long lances
Readied. And howsoever lordly, imposing, 590
And haughty Thoas stood, they distanced him backward;
And thus unsettled, he reeled, retreating. The twain,
Extended thus, companioned lay within the dust,
They captains both—a lordly Thracian chieftain one;
Epeian lord the other, bronze-clad his command, 595
And butchered about them the others unnumbered.

Then might no man belittle the turmoil entailed,
Surely not one ranging throughout the ranks unscathed
By razored dart or thrusted bronze, the while untouched,
By Athena herself lead firmly by the hand, 600
From darts in their multitudes defended. For died
Many a Trojan and Danaan on that day,
One aside the other, shrouded headlong in dust.

~ Book V ~

The Battlefield Excellence (or "Aristeia") of Diomedes, His Wounding of Aphrodite and Ares

TAKING HIM BY THE HAND, Athena sequesters Ares from the battle, that Greeks and Trojans might fight, by the will of Zeus, without interference. It is Diomedes' day to shine, and he does so spectacularly, even after initially being wounded in the shoulder by the archer Pandarus. Diomedes' driver, Sthenelus, extracts the arrow while Athena stanches the wound, reviving Diomedes. She further enables him to differentiate gods from mortals, but prohibits his attacking any god but Aphrodite (ally of Troy). Diomedes ferociously engages.

Pandarus, on foot, leaps aboard Aeneas' chariot in a combined attack on Diomedes. Diomedes casts his spear, which breaks through Pandarus' face (the oath breaker dispatched). Diomedes then casts a huge stone at Aeneas, breaking his hip and nearly killing him, but Aeneas is rescued by Apollo and Aphrodite (his mother). Diomedes rushes them, wounding Aphrodite on the hand, Aphrodite dropping Aeneas and leaving him for Apollo to carry off. Finding the earlier sequestered Ares, Aphrodite begs use of his chariot to ascend Olympus, where she bitterly complains to her mother, Dionē. Dionē seeks to comfort her with a catalogue-like recitation of gods who have previously suffered injury at mortal hands. For what comfort it thus provides, Aphrodite is in good company. Zeus reminds Aphrodite that hers are the workings of love not war.

Aeneas, as seen, is destined to survive. He will in fact be the ultimate survivor: escaping Troy with family and entourage to found Rome. Rome will thus be the birth of a majestic new city by a survivor of the old—as related in Virgil's *Aeneid*. Though there is no express mention in Homer of Aeneas' escaping Troy or founding a new city, his semidivine parentage, enduring lineage, and excellent performance against Achilles (Book 20) make him worthy of the destiny Virgil envisions.

Diomedes thrice assaults and thrice fails to injure Apollo as the latter bears off the stricken Aeneas, whereupon Apollo sternly advises him to keep his distance from the gods (Diomedes here oversteps, previously allowed to engage solely with Aphrodite). Aeneas is taken to Apollo's great temple on Pergamus (the citadel of Troy), where Artemis heals him. Apollo creates a phantom likeness of Aeneas to mitigate the sense of his absence from the field and bids Ares rejoin the fight against Diomedes.

Sarpedon, son of Zeus, chastises Hector for the insufficient use of Trojan allies—Hector excessively reliant on his own Trojan contingents. The rebuke spurs Hector to rally the allies and begin a new offensive. As Ares engages and confounds the Greeks, Apollo returns the newly restored Aeneas to the fray. Aeneas immediately joins the slaughter in progress.

In a significant encounter, Sarpedon, son of Zeus (and leader of the Lycian allies), is seriously wounded by Tlepolemus, a son of Heracles. In fact, they are wounded by each other's spears, simultaneously cast. Both men survive through various interventions (including that of Zeus, in the case of Sarpedon). Sarpedon's eventual death (Book 16) begins the sequence leading to the climactic death of Hector (Book 22).

Hera and Athena determine to enter the battle against Ares. Homer provides lavish descriptions of Hera's chariot as she prepares for battle, and of Athena's arming herself. Zeus, upon request, endorses the goddesses' intervention. Finding Diomedes for the moment on the sidelines—airing the wound inflicted by Pandarus—Athena chides him into action against Ares, herself mounting as charioteer. Upon encounter, Ares' spear misses (shunted by Athena), as Diomedes' spear hits Ares in the belly. Ares cries the deafening cry of ten thousand men and goes reeling to Olympus in complaint to his father. Showing no sympathy, Zeus berates him as the most hateful of all his children (war being most hateful). Ares is thus removed from battle (an indication of war's abating fury).

Diomedes has succeeded in wounding both Aphrodite and Ares—love and death respectively, the cause and process of war (the two gods themselves lovers). His wounding of gods is testament to Diomedes' battlefield prowess. The symbolism of the union of Aphrodite/love and Ares/hate is of course profound, finding expression elsewhere in the *Iliad* (Book 21), in the *Odyssey* (Book 8), and especially in the opening Prologue to Lucretius' epic poem, *De Rerum Natura (On the Nature of Things)* (1st century BC). The opposing yet complementary natures of hate and love / male and female are a tenet of Presocratic philosophy (6th and 5th centuries BC) and key to the binary opposition upon which both human existence and civilization itself are predicated.

࿏

Athena now inspired mighty Diomedes,
Tydeus' offspring, that of vigor and grit he make
Display, preeminent amid the Danaans,
Winning wondrous renown. And from off his helmet
And shield Athena wakened unwearying flame,   5
Like to the star of late summer, lustrous its glow
Beyond all other stars once immersing itself
In Ocean's streams; just such a flame from his shoulders
And head did Athena awaken, despatching
Him battle-bound where warriors unwearied contest.   10

Now amid the Trojans was one Darēs, a rich
And blameless man, Hephaestus' priest. Two were his sons,
Phēgeus and Idaeus, both skillful in combat's
Calling and devisings. These two, apart the host,
Against Diomedes drove—they on their chariot;   15
By foot his approach traversing the plain. And fast
Closing in, they lessened the distance between them.
Flung Phēgeus first his far-shadowing spear, and passed
The spearpoint left to the shoulder of Tydeus' son
But smote him not. Then sprinted Diomedes forth,   20
Well leveling and easily casting his lance,
Striking his foe on the breast between the nipples
And wresting him from his car. And Idaeus sprang
Back, abandoning the beauteous chariot; no heart
Had he to bestride his brother's corpse. Nor would he   25
Himself have escaped black fate had not Hephaestus
Defended and saved him, surrounding him in night,
That grief not utterly engulf his agèd priest.

But the offspring of great-souled Tydeus goaded forth
Their team, to his men consigning their conveyance 30
To the hollow ships. But when the great-souled Trojans
Beheld the sons of Darēs—slain the one beside
His car, the other absconding—their hearts were stunned.
Then flashing-eyed Athena, infuriate, took
Great Ares by the hand, the like addressing him: 35
"Ares, O Ares, bane of mortals, O blood-stained
Stormer of citadels, shall we now not allow
The Achaeans and Trojans to clash, on whome'er
Great father Zeus confer renown? But we the twain
From afar shall watch, the wrath of Zeus avoiding." 40

This said, she ushered the impulsive Ares forth,
Apart from the carnage, and sat him on sandy
Scamander's bank. And the Argives vigorously
Pressed the Trojans, each leader despatching his man.
First did lordly Atreïdēs oust great Odius 45
From his car, the Halizonian chief; for even
As he swiveled, Atreïdēs thrust into his back,
Between the shoulders, full forcing the spearpoint through;
And thudding he dropped, his armor 'round him rattling.
And Idomeneus slew Phaestus, son of Bōrus 50
The Maeonian, from Tarnē fertile-soilèd come.
Him, even while ascending his chariot, spear-famed
Idomeneus transfixed, with lengthy spear thrusting
The right shoulder through; and from his chariot he dropped,
And dismal darkness o'erspread him. And his armor 55
Idomeneus' assistants looted and despoiled.
And Atreïdēs Menelaus slew Stophius'
Son, Scamandrius, keen and sagacious huntsman,
With whetted spear, proficient hunter that he was,
For Artemis herself had inskilled him to kill 60
Each manner of beast within mountain forest found.
But little availed him archeress Artemis
Now, nor the archer's skill wherein he once excelled;

BOOK V

But spear-eminent Menelaus Atreidēs
Transpierced the fleeing Trojan, attaching a spear   65
To his back between the shoulders, and out his chest
Hard-forced it through, and crashing full forward he fell,
His armor disjointed. And Mēriones slew
Phereclus, son of Tectōn Harmonidēs, skilled
His hands in exceptional craft of every kind,   70
A likeness to create; and Athena loved him
Exceedingly of men. He it was who fashioned
Steady ships for Alexander, of misfortune
The fount for Trojans all, and for himself, knowing
Naught soe'er of the gods' decrees. After him ran   75
Mēriones and, o'ertaking him, in the right
Buttock transpierced him. The spearpoint bust his bladder
Beneath the bone straight through, and descended he hard
To his knees, demurring; and death enfolded him.

And Megēs slew Pedaeus, of Antēnōr born,   80
Actually bastard born, though kind Theanō
Had caringly reared him as if offspring her own,
Thus indulging her lord. On him advanced spear-famed
Phyleïdēs, his whetted weapon deploying.
A'back his skull it entered, taking tongue and teeth.   85
Earthward he plunged, his palate enclasping cold bronze.
And Eurypylus, Euaemōn's son, slew goodly
Hypsēnōr, son of spirited Dolopiōn,
Made priest of Scamander and honored as a god.
Upon him rushed Eurypylus, Euaemōn's son,   90
With sword raised high—Hypsēnōr fleeing before him—
And o'ertaking him shattered his shoulder, his sword
Sharply low'ring and quickly uncoupling his hand,
Which dropped rolling in bloodied dirt. And on his lids
Dark death descended and obstinate destiny.   95
Thus battled they unceasingly, but naught one knew
For whom Diomedes, offspring of Tydeus, toiled,
Whether he companioned Trojans or Achaeans

For he cascaded the like of winter's torrent
Upon the plain: the teeming outpour overturns 100
Embankments; the embankments keep it not at bay,
Nor do lush vineyard enclosures retard its wrath
When Zeus' downpour releases it; and a'fore it
Topple—perishing aplenty—men's wondrous works;
Even thus a'fore Tydeus' son were Trojan ranks 105
Unnerved nor in their multitudes resisted him.

But when Pandarus recognized him rampaging
Over the plain, battalions in rout before him,
Then against Diomedes, Tydeus' son, drew he
His crescent bow and shot to the corselet's panel 110
A'right of the shoulder as onward he advanced.
Through this sped the bitter shaft, straight bearing its course,
And the corselet was spattered with blood. Over him
Then Pandarus excitedly shouted: "Bestir
Yourselves, you great-spirited Trojans, inciters 115
Of horses. Struck is the best of the Achaeans,
Nor believe I he will long endure the fearsome
Shaft if Apollo, son of Zeus, despatched me true,
Departing emboldened from Lycia's spacious realm."

Thus vauntingly he spoke, but the arrow subdued 120
Not Diomedes who, drawing back, kept chariot
And horses before him constrained, and thus addressed
Sthenelus: "Rouse thee, good offspring of Capaneus;
Descend your chariot and wrest this bitter arrow."
So he spoke, and Sthenelus from his car downleapt 125
And, aside him abiding, withdrew the weapon
From out his shoulder; and from his pliant tunic
Sprang ebon blood, whereat the offspring of Tydeus,
Warcry practiced, prayed. "Hear me, aegis-bearing child
Of Zeus, untiring Athena! If ever stood 130
You in turbulent battle with kindly judgment
Aside my sire, then well disposed be even now

BOOK V

Toward me. Grant, Athena, mine the resolve to slay
This man advanced within my weapon's range, who ere
I was aware of him did wound me and assert—   135
The braggart—how little more I would relish day."
So pronounced he in prayer, and Pallas Athena
Heeded him and lightened his limbs, his feet, and hands
Above; and close approaching him spoke wingèd words:
"Audacious be, Diomedes, son of Tydeus,   140
Battling Trojans all; for your father's might have I
Impressed upon your soul —the dauntless might, his shield
Aloft, that horseman Tydeus aforetime possessed.
And further from your eyes have I dispersed the mist
Once veiling them, that you distinguish and discern   145
Both mortals and gods. Thus, if a god approaches
Making trial of you, abstain you entirely then
From fight with immortals; but if Zeus Cronidēs'
Daughter Aphrodite in the melee be met,
Then upon her bestow the wound of biting bronze."   150

Thus speaking, the goddess Athena departed,
Even the grey-eyed deity; and Tydeus' son
Strode forth 'mid the foremost combatants commingled.
And though his spirit within aforetime focused
On the foe's defeat, thrice the veh'mence enveiling   155
Him now. Even as when a field-dwelling lion
That a shepherd, his woolly sheep policing, wounds
O'erleaping a partition, but it breaks away;
Its rancor enkindled, restricted its recourse,
It feints its way toward the stabled farmstead fleeing,   160
And unsettles the restless flock withal; and cramped
Against the other each, the flock huddles amassed,
Whilst o'er the fence the famished beast bounds furious;
Thus braving the fray mingled bold Diomedes.

Then slew he Astynous and Hypeirōn, shepherd   165
Of the host—the one above the nipple smitten

With cast of bronze-shod spear; and through the collarbone
Beside the shoulder th' other struck with sturdy sword,
Shearing shoulder from neck and back. Abandoned he
Them, but went chasing Polyidus and Abas,　　　　　　　　　　170
Sons of agèd Eurydamas, interpreter
Of dreams—but by their failed return bereft of dreams
To explicate; but them Diomedes despatched.
Continued he next after Xanthus and Thoön
Sons the twain of Phaenops, both much venerated;　　　　　　175
And their father much suffered the hardship of years
And for keep of his possessions no other sons
Begot. There Diomedes slew them both, ending
Their days—from encounter retrieving no transit
Alive, for their father heartache unrelenting.　　　　　　　　180
And remoter kinsmen to th' estate succeeded.

Then slew he two sons of Priam Dardanidēs,
Chromius and Echemmōn, both in a single car.
Even as leaps a lion amid lowing kine
And breaks the neck of a woodland-feeding heifer　　　　　　185
Or cow, so dashed these Diomedes from their car
Most piteously, next despoiling their armor,
The horses shipward to his comrades consigning.
But Anchisēs' son remarked him wreaking havoc
In the ranks and forth sallied through battle's bedlam　　　　190
Hurtling weapons, seeking Pandarus' position,
If he might find him, godlike archer that he was.
Finding him steadfast and bold, he stood before him
Speaking thus: "Pandarus, where now your wingèd shafts,
Your gloried bow wherewith no person hereabouts　　　　　　195
Competes with you, or in Lycia is considered
Your better born? But come, to Zeus your hands uplift
And upon this man unleash a shaft—howsoe'er
O'erpow'ring he be tormenting the Trojans thus.
For of many good men, all worthies, has he loosed　　　　　　200
The limbs—unless he be himself divinely born,

Disfav'ring the Trojans for slighted offerings,
Toward mortals relentless, a disapproving god."

Him then addressed Lycaōn's glorious offspring:
"Aeneas, counselor of the Trojans bronze-attired, 205
To Diomedes all in all I liken him,
By buckler and crested helm and by horses' mien;
But for certain know I not whether god he be.
Sooner be he man, I reckon, even the son 210
Of the sage-minded Tydeus. Not absent the aid
Of some god runs he thus amok; but aside him
Stands stationed a god, mist-enveloped his shoulders,
Who deflects from him my careering weapon's reach.
For already toward him has my shaft sped unleashed, 215
And at the shoulder I smote him, on his corselet
Through, to Hades assuredly despatching him.
Yet I subdued him not. Surely a wrathful god
Is he. But horses have I none, nor chariot have
Whereon to mount; yet in Lycaōn's halls, I think, 220
Are chariots fair equipped, eleven, newly wrought,
O'erspread with cloths, by each its yoke of horses paired,
On spelt and barley feeding. And as I ventured
Troyward, the spearman aged Lycaōn commanded
Me within our well-built halls that chariot-mounted 225
I excel in battle, a leader of Trojans.
But I hearkened not—far better my compliance—
And left the horses lest the maddening melee
See them bereft of fodder, erst surfeited they.
So I forsook them and wayfarer to Ilium 230
Am come, relying on my bow, which bootless bear
I now. Already at two chieftains have I shot—
The son of Tydeus and Atreus' son—and fairly
Have stricken both and fairly the both left bleeding,
Yet only the more provoking them. For the worse, 235
Then, did I my most pliant bow unpeg, coming
That day, a Trojan chieftain, to towering Troy,

Heeding Hector's behest. But should I e'er return,
My glance alighting on my longed-for land, dear wife,
And lofty raftered residence, then allow some   240
Interloper straightway offlop this head of mine
If this very bow I not destroy bare handed,
To dust reduced. The greater use to me be wind."

To him then answered Aeneas, Trojan leader:
"Speak not thus; no better shall it be until we   245
Twain by horse and chariot drawn encounter this man
In mortal strife, matching might to might; now mount you
Upon my car, observing the kind of horses
Tros confers, skilled wherever quickly to career,
Whether routing Achaeans or beating retreat.   250
These twain will witness us safely brought to towering
Troy if Zeus again grant glory to Tydeus' son,
Diomedes. But come, take shining reins and lash
While I engage dismounting; or else abide you
His arrival whilst I oversee the horses."   255
And the splendid son of Lycaōn responded:
"Aeneas, guard the reins yourself and onward spur
Your horses: the better will they draw the crescent
Car when commands their accustomed charioteer
If fated our flight from maddened Diomedes.   260
I would they be not affrighted, distraught, running
Uncontrolled and, lacking your command, forgetful
Be of saving us 'mid battle's confrontation
From great-souled Diomedes who would slay us both,
Driving our whole-hooved team afar. So command you   265
Your vehicle and team, and with sharpened spear
Shall I await this warrior's onrush and assault."
So speaking they mounted the paneled car, rapid
Horses deploying dead-on to Diomedes,
And Sthenelus, glorious son of Capaneus,   270
Saw them and now to Tydeus' son spoke wingèd words:
"Son of Tydeus, Diomedes dear to my heart,

I see two dauntless warriors determined to fight,
Vehement, their fervor ablaze. The one with bow
Accomplished, even Pandarus, offspring avowed 275
Of Lycaōn; whilst Aeneas boasts his birthright
From acclaimed Anchisēs, his mother the very
Aphroditē. But turn and flee; this fury end.
From the forefront withdraw, conserving life and limb."
Then with angered glance beneath darkened brows addressed 280
Him Diomedes: "Recommend me no escape;
Unpersuaded will I persist. Recoils my blood
From tepid flight, nor cower I; e'er resolute
My hardiness. Decline I now to mount the car
But thus—and as I am—will I encounter them, 285
For Athena forbids my fearfulness. And these,
The twain, shall nowise secure their escape by horse,
Though flee the one or th' other. And with this also
Acquaint yourself, storing it fast in your spirit:
If counsel-rich Athena this distinction grant, 290
To despatch them both, here restrain this team of mine,
The reins attached taut to the chariot's rim; and then
Aeneas' coupled horses commandeer, driving
Them from the battle to the well-greaved Argive host.
From those steeds' stock, they assert, loud thundering Zeus 295
Repaid Trōs for his offspring Ganymēdē's theft—
They the best horses e'er beneath daybreak and sun.
Of these Anchisēs, king of men, purloined a breed,
Placing his mares to the steeds, whereof Priam's sire
Knew naught. And from these were offspring six begotten 300
Within his palatial walls; four kept he himself,
At his mangers reared; the remaining two given
Aeneas contriver of rout. Could we but take
These twain, glory's allotment were princely possessed."

On such matters they discoursed. And the other two, 305
Swift-driven, traversed the distance dividing them,
And Lycaōn's glorious son was first to speak:

"O son of sagacious Tydeus hardy of heart,
My shaft and bitter arrow's speed subdued thee not;
Now take the measure of my spear, if it avail." 310
So saying, he brandished and hurled his steadfast spear,
Smiting the very shield of Tydeus' son; and straight
Onward to the corselet traversed the brazen point;
Then boasted aloud Lycaōn's acclaimèd son:
"To the mid-section clean have I wounded thee through, 315
And not long, I conclude, are you like to endure;
And to me have you granted great glory assured."
Then, nothing fearing, addressed him Diomedes:
"A palpable miss, your throw, no hit; but you twain,
I deem, shall not desist 'til one or the other 320
Die—sating the stout-shielded blood-lusting Ares."
So speaking he hurled, and Athena directed
The spear at his nose aside the eye; and through his
Pearly teeth it passed, and the unrelenting bronze
O'erturned his tongue, exiting his chin's lowest point 325
And from within his chariot fast toppled he,
And loudly about him clanged his armor, brightly
Glist'ning; and swerved his swift-footed horses aside,
And there were his strength and spirit spent. But sorely
Dismayed lest the Argives abscond with the body, 330
Aeneas, clenching his shield and far-ranging spear,
Leapt descending, and o'er the foe strode lion-like
With vigor engorged, his javelin held outward thrust,
His shield's perfect circle afore him placed, eager
To slaughter the warrior—whoe'er approached to seize 335
The corpse—whilst shouting deafening loud. But the son
Of Tydeus uplifted a boulder, no small thing,
That today might no two men upraise; yet deftly
Alone high-hoisted it, and therewith struck Aeneas
To the hip, hard at the socket's hold—the cup, 340
As men refer to it, where swivels the hipbone
To socket inset—and crushed the cup, the tendons
Rending; and the jagged stone denuded his skin;

BOOK V

Then dropped the warrior to his knees, thus lingering,
By his stout hand up-propped, and darkness subdued him.　　345

And now would the kingly Aeneas have perished
Had not Aphrodite, daughter of Zeus, even
His mother, quickly marked it; she who conceived him
Neath Anchisēs tending his kine. She enfolded
Her offspring 'round about in alabaster arms,　　350
And upon him spread her resplendent vestiture,
Defense against shafts lest some horse-swift Achaean,
Casting bronze to his breast release life's force within.
Reclaimed she Aeneas from under the fracas;
But the instructions escaped not Capaneus' son,　　355
Those the warcry-deft Tydeus' son had imparted.
His own single-hooved horses he stayed from turmoil's
Ado, taut tensing the reins to his chariot's rim
And, goading the flowing-maned steeds of Aeneas,
Impelled them away to the well-greaved Achaeans—　　360
On his comrade Deïpylus bestowing them
Whom he honored beyond all others of his age
As one like-minded to himself—and bade him drive
The team to the dusky ships. Then he upmounted
His chariot, the bright reins regaining, and again　　365
Quickened his single-hooved horses toward Tydeus' son.
The latter had meanwhile absconded, pursuing
Aphroditē, destructive his bronze, discerning
Her a fragile and battle-weak divinity—
No Athena she nor city-sacking Enyō.　　370
But when happ'ning upon her in his forward press
Amid the host and thronging multitude, Tydeus'
Great-souled son, ever striving to attack, advanced—
His sharp spear readied—skimming the satin-softness
Of her hand. Forthwith through the ambrosial raiment,　　375
By the very Graces woven, the spear entered
Her skin at the wrist above the palm, and outward
Issued the goddess' immortal blood, the ichor

Such as flows in the blessèd gods; for neither bread
Consume they nor partake of flaming wine, wherefore 380
Bloodless they abide, e'er blessèd, undying deemed.
With resounding cry released she her falling son,
And Phoebus Apollo concealed him in a caul
Of dusky cloud lest some Danaan, headlong flown
With bronze upon his person drawn purloin his life. 385

But unto her declaimed Diomedes aloud:
"Daughter of Zeus, from wasting warfare depart you!
Suffices not your fraud on frailest womankind?
But should you play the warrior, you will, I opine,
At war's very name recoil and quake." So he spoke, 390
And withdrew she distraught; and wind-footed Iris
Received her, leading her forth from the throng afar,
Anguished and aggrieved, darkened her ivoried flesh.
And to the battle's left, she found warlord Ares,
Implacable, his spear aside a cloud reposed, 395
Swift his horses the twain nearby. Then to her knees
Downfallen, most earnestly sought she Ares' gold-
Frontleted team: "Spare me, O kinsman, your horses
That in my heavenward retreat I hasten them;
For gravely I fare, by Diomedes wounded, 400
And now would Tydeus' son with Zeus himself contend."
So she spoke, and Ares afforded his horses
Gold-frontleted; and she mounted atop the car,
Her heart distraught, and Iris mounted aside her,
Reins taking to hand; and lightly she lashed the team 405
To start, and the pair unreluctantly hastened.

Straightway to heaven's domiciles arrived, to steep
Olympus, there Iris, swift wind-footed goddess,
Uncoupled the car, loosing the horses, and cast
Ambrosial fodder before them; but the fairmost 410
Cyprian goddess to her mother's knees repaired,
To Dionē, who clasped her daughter to her breast,

BOOK V

Stroking her lovingly and addressing her thus:
"Which child of heaven, dear daughter, so wantonly
Misuses you, arrantly working this outrage?" 415
To her responded the laughter-loving goddess:
"Brash Diomedes, Tydeus' son, has wounded me
As from the fracas I conveyed my treasured son,
Aeneas, dearest to me of all mortal men.
For no longer suffices fierce fighting alone 420
For Trojans and Achaeans, but the Achaeans
Now wreak their attack on the very gods themselves."
To her then responded Dionē fair goddess:
"Take courage, my child, and despite your pains endure.
For many among us, dwellers on Olympus, 425
Have suffered men's affronts, blameworthy sometimes we.
So suffered Ares when mighty Ephialtēs
And Ōtus, Alōeus' sons, restrained him in bonds
Unyielding, and bound he lay in a brazen jar
For thirteen months; and there Ares, insatiate 430
Of battle, had perished had not their stepmother
Beauteous Ēeriboea beseeched Hermēs
Who unfettered Ares—dire his distress—o'ercome
By dreadful bonds. So suffered Hera when wounded
Her breast by the wondrous son of Amphitryōn— 435
Thrice-barbed the dart and dread the pain delivered her.
And towering Hades like the others endured
A grievous dart when this very man, the issue
Of aegis-bearing Zeus, attacked him in Pylos
Amid the dead, consigning him to pain. But he, 440
Olympus bound, came unto the palace of Zeus,
Grieving at heart, transfixed with pain; for lodged the shaft
Within his stalwart shoulder, tormenting his heart.
But Paeēōn applied pain-reprieving unguent,
Restoring him of no mere mortal stock begot. 445
Rash the assailant, who reckoned not his heinous
Impudence, pitching weapons against undying
Deities, their domiciles blessed on Olympus.

163

Now bright-eyed Athena plagues you with this warrior,
Foolish goddess; for the heart of Diomedes 450
Knows not this: that who battles th' immortal gods
Is doomed before his time, nor prattle his children
About his knees once returned from dreaded conflict.
Thus let Diomedes beware, regardless his
Excitement, lest one your better encounter him, 455
That his spouse, Aegialeia, Adrastus' child,
Not awaken her slumbering kin with laments,
Bewailing her husband, best of the Achaeans;
Yes, even she, the stately spouse of Tydeus' son."
Thus speaking, with both hands wiping the ichor, healed 460
She Aphrodite's hand, and the pain subsided.

But Athena and Hera, idly observing,
Sought with mocking words to anger Zeus Cronidēs,
And among them the bright-eyed goddess Athena
Began: "Father Zeus, will you be annoyed with me 465
For this suggestion? Surely now has the goddess
Cyprian Aphrodite urged some Danaan
Maid to escort a Trojan Troyward—her Trojans
Ever so belovèd—and caressing a one
Of the fair-cloaked Argive pretties, has pricked her arm— 470
Daintily displayed—on the garment's golden brooch."
So she spoke, but smiled the father of men and gods
And, summoning golden Aphrodite, rejoined:
"Not to you, my child, is grievous combat given;
Attend you instead the wondrous works of marriage, 475
Whilst elsewise be busied Athena and Ares."
Of such matter conversed they thus among themselves,
But Tydeus' son, crying war, at Aeneas leapt,
Though knowing Phoebus Apollo his protector;
Yet reverence had he none, even of this great god, 480
But e'er desired to despatch Aeneas, stripping
His marvelous armor. Thrice pounced he upon him,
Furiously to slay him, and thrice Apollo

Deflected his glinting shield. But when the fourth time
He attacked like unto a god with ominous 485
Cry, far-darting Apollo addressed him: "Bethink
Yourself, Diomedes, and relent; nor desire
Likeminded with immortals to stand; since ever
Differs the race of deathless gods and mortalkind
Astride the earth." So he spoke, and somewhat aback 490
Relented Diomedes, avoiding the wrath
Of Apollo far-shooting, who next sequestered
Aeneas apart the melee in sacred Troy
Where his temple stood. There Leto and archeress
Artemis, in the sacred haven healing him, 495
Enhanced his renown; but silver-bowed Apollo
Fashioned a wraith in the semblance of Aeneas,
His like in armor too; and about the phantom
Clove the acclaimed Achaeans and Trojans alike,
Their bullhide bucklers and body-encircling shields 500
A'front one another's breasts, with straps aflutter.
Then to maddened Ares spoke Phoebus Apollo:
"Ares, Ares, mortal bane, sanguinary scourge!
Will you not, now entered upon the dreadful fray,
Remove this man therefrom, this offspring of Tydeus 505
Who even now with Zeus Cronidēs dares contend?
Aphrodite's hand at the wrist he abraded
In battle and, godlike, upon me now careens."
So he spoke, sitting high upon Troy's parapet,
And Ares entered the Trojan ranks, malignant, 510
Like to rapid Acamas, Thracian commander,
Calling them forth; and to Priam's offspring, beloved
Of father Zeus, proclaimed: "You issue of Priam,
Zeus-endearèd ruler, how long will you endure
Your men by Achaeans slain? Until they battling 515
Approach our sturdy gates? There falls—alas!—a man
Whom we acclaim the like of belovèd Hector:
Aeneas, scion of great-hearted Anchisēs;
But come now, from struggle save we this goodly man."

So speaking, he enkindled their courage and strength. 520

And Lycian Sarpēdōn goaded godly Hector:
"Hector, whither fled that mettle aforetime thine?
The city's safety you assertively protect
Without allies or hosts but with kinsmen alone;
Yet of these neither mark nor detect I any. 525
But they quake as canines 'round a roaring lion,
Leaving battle to us, sole allies positioned
Among you. For as comrade I come from afar:
Long distant is Lycia by eddying Xanthus,
Whence departed, I left a doting wife and child, 530
Forgoing my belongings abundantly stored,
For which hungers every man having need of them;
And yet I encourage the Lycians nonetheless,
And stalwart stand to engage my man though be there
Nothing of mine for Danaan to commandeer, 535
Bearing it abroad. But skulking here, you nowise
Encourage the fight, waged for your spouses' defense.
Beware ensnarement, the lot of you, in flaxen
Mesh made the spoil and quarry of your enemies
Lest they your high teeming citadel dismantle. 540
Make these by every hour your determined concerns,
Entreating your far-famed commanders allied
To trusted battle, free of what censure ensues."

So spoke Sarpēdōn, and pained was Hector at heart.
Forthwith leapt he groundward from his car, full-armored, 545
Brandishing lances unblunted, ranging broadly
Amid the ranks, urging his men to war throughout
Battle's baneful din. And they, facing about, took
Their stand a'front the Achaeans; and th' Achaeans,
Compactly arranged, stolidly waited attack. 550
And as windy squalls across the sacred threshing
Floor whip the chaff of winnowers when Demeter,
Flaxen-haired, amid th' updriven gale ascending,

BOOK V

Detaches grain from chaff, and high-whitens the husk;
Just so were Danaan heads and shoulders whitened, 555
As contention rekindled amid clouding dust
That wakened neath horses' hooves to fiery aether,
Their chariots wheeling about. Valiantly ventured
Their weaponed hands; and ranging 'round the furious
Fray was rowdy Ares, everywhere extending 560
Night's veil, attentive to the Trojans. Thus discharged
He Apollo's behest, the gold-sworded god who
Enjoined him rouse Trojan might whene'er he noted
Athena, the Danaans' assistant, distant.

And th' archer Phoebus Apollo himself despatched 565
Aeneas forth from out the sumptuous chamber,
With courage imbuing the shepherd of the host;
And amid his comrades Aeneas took his stand,
And they rejoiced seeing him come, whole and alive,
To join them, his courage conspicuously shown. 570

But they questioned him not, for toil disallowed; toil
Of another sort—even that which silver-bowed
Apollo roused; and Ares, torment to mortals;
And Eris, endlessly raging. And opposite,
The Aiantes twain, Tydeus' son and Odysseus 575
Incited the Argives to fight—these fearing not
Before Trojan surge and onslaught, but standing firm—
Like cov'ring cloud, becalmed and blanketed that Zeus
Atop a mountain sets, the cloud unstirred as sleeps
The burr of Boreas and other brutal blasts, 580
Which, wailing, disperse in each direction to whip
The covering mists; even so the Danaans
Withstood the Trojan foe, steadfast and resolute.
And the son of Atreus traversed the ranks, voicing
Directives thus: "Be men, my friends, and heartened be 585
Your valor, and be mindful in the fearsome fight
Of shame in one another's eyes. Of men having

Shame more prevail than perish; for flight profits not
Nor glory confers, be flight your only recourse."

Thus speaking, he swiftly cast his spear, assaulting 590
A foremost fighter, friend to great-souled Aeneas,
Deïcoōn, Pergasus' son, honored of Troy
As Priam's very sons, since with them ever first
And foremost he engaged. Him famed Atreïdēs
Far-ruling struck, casting a spear toward his buckler; 595
But none the resistance the buckler lent—the spear
Passing penetrant through his belt and transpiercing
His nether gut. Groundward he dropped, and about him
Clanged his armor.
          Then slew Aeneas two champions
Of the Argives: the sons of Dioclēs, Crethōn 600
And Orsilochus, whose father dwelt in well-built
Phērē, a man of appreciable means, risen
His line from river Alpheius, its headwaters
Teeming through Pylian terrain. Alpheius had sired
A sovereign over multitudes: Ortilochus, 605
He who had begotten the great-souled Dioclēs,
The self same Dioclēs engendering Crethōn
And Orsilochus, learnèd in warfare's every
Contrivance. And when the two were grown to manhood,
They followed the Argives in dusky ships to horse- 610
Famed Troy, seeking recompense for Menelaus
And Agamemnon, Atreus' sons; but their own selves
Did destiny and death for Trojan soil ordain.
These by their mother were reared, as two young lions
In wooded copses encircling a mountain peak— 615
The twain wresting cattle and hearty sheep, wasting
The steadings of men until prey themselves to men
Wielding whetted weaponry. Even thus they dropped
Neath Aeneas' hand and toppled like tow'ring firs.

But Ares-beloved Menelaus took pity 620

BOOK V

As they fell and strode through the foremost fighting ranks,
Bedecked in dazzling bronze and brandishing his blade;
And Ares awakened his might, portending this:
That by Aeneas' hardihood he be subdued.
But Antilochus, son of great-hearted Nestor, 625
Beheld him and forged through the foremost warrior ranks,
Fearing misadventure follow Menelaus,
And their efforts be for naught. Thus Menelaus
And Aeneas menaced each other, brandishing
Hands and well-sharpened blades, determined for combat, 630
When Antilochus advanced toward Menelaus.
And seeing the pair poised opposite, Aeneas
Awaited them not, keen combatant though he was.
And the pair hauled the fallen to the Argive host,
To expectant arms that upraised the pitied dead, 635
Themselves next wheeling 'round the foremost to engage.

The pair then slew Pylaemenēs peer of Ares,
Commander of the Paphlagonian shieldmen.
Him, positioned still, the son of Atreus transpierced,
Spear-famed Menelaus, hitting his clavicle. 640
But Antilochus struck Mydōn, Pylaemenēs'
Charioteer, Atymnius' resolute son,
Even as he wheeled his uncloven horses 'round,
And by boulder held aloft collapsed his elbow.
And groundward from his hands the white-ivoried reins 645
Slapped the dust. And Antilochus, next leaping, clove
Mydōn's temple with his sword; and snorting he fell,
Catapulting far, from out his well-wrought chariot,
His head and broad shoulders into mud deep driven.
Long languished he there in saturate sand secured 650
Until his trampling horses groundward flattened him.
And the horses Antilochus lashed to the ranks
Of the Achaeans.   But Hector wailing aloud
Hurried toward them, observing them enter the ranks,

And with him battalions of well-armored Trojans,   655
These by Ares and Dame Enyō led—and with her
Deaf'ning Din and Ares wielding a monstrous spear—
A'front Hector berserk; now aft him positioned.
Observing Hector, warcrying Diomedes
Shuddered; and as one who passing an ample plain   660
To a standstill comes, dazed by a rav'nous river
A'rush to the sea and, noting the furious foam,
Stands startled aback; even so did Tydeus' son
Relent, addressing the host: "Comrades, ever awed
Are we by godly Hector, deeming him spearman   665
And warrior resolute, since ever aside him
Adjacent stands doom-distancing divinity,
As stands Ares, even now aside him, likened
To a mortal. But attentive to the Trojans,
Yield slowly back nor mightily contend with gods."   670

So he spoke, the Trojans more nearly approaching.
Then Hector despatched two warriors expert in fight,
Menesthēs and Anchialus, in one car both,
And great Telamonian Ajax took pity
On their demise and approached, standing rooted by,   675
And with cast of his dazzling spear smote Amphius,
Selagus' son who dwelt in Paesus, a man rich
In possessions, rich in cornland; his destiny
An ally to assist king Priam and his sons.
On his belt Telamonian Ajax struck hard,   680
Delivering the far-shadowing spear to his
Abdomen, and thudding o'ertoppled he downward.
Then hastened glorious Ajax despoiling his arms,
And toward him the Trojans delivered their lances,
Glimmering all, whereof many his buckler caught;   685
But planting his heel on the corpse, he extracted
The brazen spear hard outward, the while unable
To plunder the corpse of its marvelous armor;
For by missiles was he beleaguered, and fearful

BOOK V

Of the lordly foe's nimble defense: the many 690
And courageous who beset him, brave spears in hand,
Who despite his height, boldness, and nobility,
Resisted him. And falling back was he stymied.
So in conflict toiled the two, but Tlēpolemus,
Heracles' son, mighty and meet the man, was stirred 695
By insistent fate against godlike Sarpēdōn.
And when to one another narrowed their advance—
The begotten son and grandson of cloud-gath'ring
Zeus—Tlēpolemus was first to address him thus:
"Sarpēdōn, Lycian counselor, why sit you skulking 700
Here, a man unskilled in battle? They lie who claim
You born of aegis-bearing Zeus, since inferior!
Far from Zeus-born fighters aforetime are you born.
Quite other, men say, was Heracles my father,
Battle-constant, lionhearted, who earlier 705
Sacked Troy for Laomedōn's mares with vessels six
And the few outfitting them; yet plundered he Troy
And laid her pavements waste. But yours the craven's heart,
Your men the while depleted. Nor, I surmise, will
Your Lycian arrival assist the Trojan town 710
However bold you be, but sooner defeated
Will you enter, my victim, into Hades' realm."

And Sarpēdōn, Lycian captain, responded thus:
"Tlēpolemus, to that man sacred Troy succumbed
By folly of its witless king Laomedōn, 715
Who surely vexed him over work fairly rendered;
Horses the pay for which he had come from afar.
But for you, I deem, await death and destruction,
That, defeated by my javelin, you afford me
Glory's recompense and steed-famed Hades your soul." 720
Thus Sarpēdōn, as Tlēpolemus uphefted
His ashen spear; and high sped the criss-crossing spears
Released by the pair: struck Sarpēdōn to the neck,
And the point pierced Tlēpolemus through; and nighttime's

Darksome pall, befogging his eyes, enshrouded him.　　　725
And Tlēpolemus punctured Sarpēdōn's left thigh
And rushed the penetrant point, abrading the bone;
But from doom assured did father Zeus redeem him.
Forth from the fight his goodly companions bore him,
Trailing the spear so grievously disabling him.　　　730
But none hastening were there to mark or attend
That Sarpēdōn, were the ashen spear extracted,
Might arise—such the mayhem in assisting him.
And opposite him, the well-greaved Achaeans bore
Tlēpolemus away. And noted it goodly　　　735
Stout-hearted Odysseus, and stirred was his spirit
Within, whether further to follow, pursuing
The son of loud-thundering Zeus, or slay Lycian
Soldiery instead, but not for bold Odysseus
Was it heaven-decreed with burnished bronze to slay　　　740
Preeminent Sarpēdōn; wherefore Athena
Directed his wrath on the Lycian multitude.

Then he massacred Coiranus and Alastōr,
And Chromius, and Alcandrus, and Halius,
And Noēmōn, and Prytanis; and more Lycians　　　745
Yet had Odysseus slain but gleaming-helmed Hector
Observed his doings and foremost amid the ranks
Advanced in blazing bronze high-helmeted, panic
'Mid the Argives inspiring. And in his advance
Sarpēdōn, son of Zeus, rejoiced and addressed him　　　750
A plaintive word: "Son of Priam, suffer me not
To languish here Danaan prey, but assist me;
Then perchance might my life expire within Troy's walls
Since unlikely my homeward repatriation,
There to hearten my loving spouse and infant son."　　　755
So he spoke, but bright-helmed Hector responded not
But speedily darted past, eager to repel
The Achaeans, claiming numerous lives. Then his
Goodly companions settled godlike Sarpēdōn

BOOK V

Beneath a stately oak of aegis-bearing Zeus;　　　　　760
And valiant Pelagōn, his caring attendant,
Pushed the ashen spear to outward past his thighbone,
But his spirit departed him and mist curtained
His eyes. But again he breathed, as a northerly
Gust revived his spirit a'gasp in agony.　　　　　　　765
But the Argives, before Ares' advance and surge
Of bronze-helmeted Hector, neither retreated
To their dusky ships nor gained battle's advantage,
But stepped e'er back as Ares assisted the foe.

Whom first and whom following slew Hector, Priam's　　770
Son, allied with the brazen-hearted Ares? Godlike
Teuthras, and next Orestēs driver of horses;
Trēchus, Aetolian spearman; and Oenomaüs;
And Helenus, Oenops' son; and Oresbius
With glinting tasset who inhabited Hylē　　　　　　　775
By Cēphisis lake, ever mindful of his wealth,
With other landowning Boeotians nearby him.
But when the goddess white-armed Hera viewed Hector,
Wreaking havoc on th' Achaeans in close conflict,
At once addressed she Athena with wingèd words:　　780
"Come now, child of aegis-bearing Zeus, unwearied!
Was our promise to Menelaus for nothing,
That well-fortified Ilium would forfeit be
Ere homeward he returned, if thus be permitted
By ravaging Ares' rage? But advance we twain　　　　785
To combat, quickened by deference to our courage."
So she spoke, and the goddess grey-eyed Athena
Obeyed her command. Then Hera, goddess revered,
Great Cronus' daughter, quickly with radiant Hēbē
Attached the gold-frontleted steeds to the chariot's　　790
Each side, its brazen wheels set—eight-numbered their spokes—
About the iron axle; and solidly wrought
The outermost rims with inlaid gold e'erlasting.
And fitted thereon lay a running tread of bronze,

A marvel to behold; and the naves of silver 795
E'er revolving to the chariot's either side.
The cart itself with tight-fitting straps of silver
And gold stood plaited, and ran two rails around it;
And from the cart protruded a chariot pole
Of silver smelt, and Hera toward its end attached 800
The gold-crafted yolk, and on it the the gold-molded
Halter; and next beneath the yoke led rapid steeds,
A swift-footed team—impatient she for conflict,
Strife, and stridency.
                    And Athena, the daughter
Of aegis-bearing Zeus, let fall to her father's 805
Floor her fairly broidered garment that she herself
Had woven and wrought—craftwork her own—and tunic
Donned of cloud-gathering Zeus, and arrayed herself
In armaments of tearful war, and the next secured
The tasseled aegis about her shoulders, withering, 810
Wreathed 'round with consternation, and therein Conflict,
And therein Valor, and Onslaught stifling the heart,
And therein the Gorgon's visage loathsome with angst,
Harbinger of aegis-bearing Zeus. The helmet
Set she atop her head— twin crested, quadruple 815
Bossed, with men-at-arms from a hundred cities wrought.
Ascended she the flaming cart, her fearsome spear
In hand, heavy and massive, wherewith she depletes
The multitudes of heroes with whom the daughter
Of a mighty sire is wroth. And swiftly Hera 820
Lashed the team a'gallop; and heaven's hingèd gates,
To the Hours entrusted, self-prompted open, groaned,
E'er wakeful their keeping of heaven's empyrean,
That thickest mist be either outed or contained.

From heaven's portals set they their trajectory, 825
And to Zeus Cronidēs, seated aloof, arrived
From th' other gods apart, atop the topmost peak
Of many-ridged Olympus. Then the goddess white-

BOOK V

Armed Hera, staying the horses, inquired of Zeus:
"Father Zeus, no umbrage take you at Ares' deeds, 830
Homicidal all, whereby so goodly a host
of Danaans suffers utterly beaten down,
Merc'lessly, chaotically, sorrow unto me,
While Cypris and Phoebus Apollo silver-bowed
Empower this law-impervious psychopath? 835
Dear father Zeus, will I incur your displeasure
Should I out maniacal Ares from the fray?"
And father, cloud-gathering Zeus, thus responded:
"Rouse you, Athena, driver of spoils, against him
E'er desirous she his discomfort to devise." 840
So he spoke, and the goddess white-armed Hera failed
Not to obey but lashed her horses; and nothing
Loath, they flew between earth and starry firmament—
And as far into distant haze as peers a man
On an outlook perched surveying the wine-dark sea, 845
Such distance leapt the goddess' neighing horses forth.
But when quickly arrived to Troy, where swiftly run
Troy's surging rivers twain—where conjoin Simoïs'
And Scamander's torrents—there the white-armed goddess
Stayed, and from their chariot set her horses free, 850
And 'round about shed ample mist; and Simoïs
Grew grassy ambrosia for them to graze upon.

Then the gods, their footfalls likened to flitting doves',
Impatiently advanced, assisting the Argives,
And when they arrived, where the bravest stood convened 855
Encircling excellent Diomedes, tamer
Of horses—the group like to ravenous lions
Or insat'ate boars, their power no trifling
Matter—there standing, the white-armed goddess shouted,
In semblance the like of great-spirited Stentōr, 860
Whose brazen voice rivals the havoc of fifty
Vigorous men: "Alack, you craven Achaeans,
Daunting but in form alone. So long as dazzling

175

Achilles engaged, wholeheartedly contending,
Never would Trojan legions exit Ilium's 865
Portal, from his pernicious weapon recoiling;
But now emboldened they descend upon our ships."
So saying, roused she the mettle and might of each,
And sprang the goddess to the side of Tydeus' son,
Grey-eyed Athena, finding the prince by his car 870
And team, cooling the wound that Pandarus' arrow
Had dealt, for nettled the sweat beneath th' expansive
Baldric of his rounded shield; therewith was he vexed,
And tired his arm, so that upraising the baldric,
He expunged the blood away. Then grasped the goddess 875
His horse's yoke and said: "Ah, little in likeness
The son to his father Tydeus. Tydeus was slight
Of build but a warrior, even when I forbade
His fighting or his fev'rishly rushing the foe,
That time he arrived apart the Achaean ranks 880
A liaison to Thebes 'mid multitudinous
Cadmeians. I bade him calmly repose and dine
Within their halls; yet he, with his valiant temper
As aforetime, forth challenged the Cadmeian youth
And fully in all things prevailed. Such the helper 885
I to him. But you! Ever am I positioned
Aside you, watching over you, and readily
Exhorting your Trojan offensives. But fatigue
From your strenuous doings infiltrates and slows
Your limbs, or spiritless anxiety perhaps 890
Possesses you. Then were you no begotten son
Of Tydeus, the wise-hearted offspring of Oeneus."

Then answering her spoke mighty Diomedes:
"Discerning you, O child of aegis-bearing Zeus;
I willingly covey my thought, nor conceal it. 895
Nowise does spiritless misgiving possess me
Nor slackness any, but attentive I remain
To those commands that you have deemed appropriate.

BOOK V

Dissension none have you condoned with the other
Blessed gods, excepting Aphrodite, daughter   900
Of Zeus, should she engage; whereupon you bade me
Wound her with burnished bronze. Therefore have I myself
Retreated, ordering the other Danaans
To also gather here, for I notice Ares
Lording himself o'er the battle." And the goddess   905
Grey-eyed Athena answered thus: "Son of Tydeus,
Diomedes, pleasing to my heart, of Ares
Be not fearful, nor of any other god. Thus
Stand I allied; but at Ares directly drive
Your single-hooved horses, at close range smiting him.   910
Nor be bewildered by Ares' furious ravings.
A fully wrought and feckless affliction is he,
Who now conversing with Hera and me, contrived
Objection to both Trojan and Argive support,
But now assists the Trojans and disdains the Greeks."   915

So speaking, and taking hold of Sthenelus, she
Pushed him downward from his chariot, and lightly
He vaulted off; and mounted she upon the car
Aside goodly Diomedes, a god eager
For battle. And loudly creaked the oaken axle   920
Neath its load, for dread the god and peerless warrior
It conveyed. Then Pallas Athena grasped the lash
And reins, toward Ares furiously directing
The single-hooved team as he looted the armor
Of strapping Periphas, among the Aetolians   925
Far the best, the glorious son of Ochesius.
Him was blood-stained Ares looting, but Athena
Donned Hades' helm, that daunting Ares note her not.
Now when Ares, mortal torment, espied goodly
Diomedes, he abandoned huge Periphas   930
A' sprawl—where he had slain and deprived him of life—
And made for Diomedes, tamer of horses.
And when, ever nearing, each a'front the other

Had advanced, Ares thrust high over yoke and reins
With brazen-speared resolve, keen to curtail his life. 935
But the goddess flashing-eyed Athena wrested
The spear in midair, o'er the chariot hefting it,
Its mission sped in vain. Next Diomedes good
At warcry propelled his brazen spear at Ares
And Athena toward his belly sped it onward, 940
Nethermost, where firmly his tassets girded him;
There she assailed and wounded him, piercing his skin,
And at once withdrew the spear. Then bellowed Ares
The like in loudness to nine thousand warriors,
Or ten, conjoined in upheaval's consternation, 945
Whereat trembling and fear unnerved Trojans and Greeks,
Thus raucous the insatiate warlord's alarm.
And as from clouds the darkened air is manifest
When after searing heat a stormy wind ascends;
Exactly so to Diomedes, Tydeus' son, 950
Was brazen Ares manifest amid the clouds,
Broad heaven ascending. Speedily he arrived
At steep Olympus the gods' abode and seated
Himself beside the father Cronus' son, distressed
At heart, the blood immortal profusely flowing 955
From out his wound; and, wailing, spoke wingèd words: "Zeus
Begetter, nurture you no resentment, viewing
These audacities? We gods always dreadfully
Suffer from one another's doings whenever
Favoring mortalkind. Now with you we contend 960
For you have fathered insatiate Athena,
Whose reasoning e'er begets dire machination.
For the other Olympian gods comply with you,
Each to you acceding; but to her you cater,
Whatever her cause, emboldening her instead, 965
Since your own begotten is this pestilent child.
Now lordly Diomedes, Tydeus' son, has she
Unleashed, frenzied he against the immortal gods.
First he wounded Cypris, close thrusting to her hand

BOOK V

Upon the wrist, and next upon myself advanced,   970
Likened in aspect to a god—but quick my flight.
Elsewise had I there long languished in the heinous
Heaps of dead, or helpless remained neath nettling spears."

Then with dour demeanor from under dusky brows
Cloud-gathering Zeus responded: "Sit you nowise   975
Aside me, renegade, whimpering evermore.
Despisèd most to me of all the Olympian
Gods are you; for deem you ever confrontation
Dear, and abhorrent dispute; yours the unswerving
Dauntless strength of your dear mother, even Hera   980
Whom scarce my words control; wherefore by her urgings,
I surmise, you suffer so. However, your pain
I no longer endure, for from my begetting
You descend, and unto me your mother bore you.
But born of another god, baleful as you are,   985
Far the sooner from Olympus were you ousted."
He spoke and bade Paeëōn heal the hurt; and spread
The healer helpful drugs upon it, mending him;
For nowise was he mortal made. And as fig juice
Rapidly thickens pallid milk which, though liquid,   990
Curdles a'stir; thus hellbent Ares hastily
Healed; and Hēbē bathed and enrobed him in gracious
Garb and, exultant in his glory, aside Zeus
Cronidēs seated him. Then returning to Zeus'
Home, departed Argive Hera and protectress   995
Athena, causing accursèd Ares, menace
Of humankind, to still his mortal slaughtering.

~ Book VI ~

Diomedes and the Lycian Glaucus Exchange Armor in a Chivalrous Gesture, the Parting of Hector and Andromache

THE GODS LEAVE THE FIELD, and the Greeks gain the upper hand. Battle melee ensues in which Menelaus is about to spare the Trojan Adrastus in exchange for promised ransom. But Agamemnon intervenes, reproaching his brother for softness, and himself runs Adrastus through. Meanwhile, Helenus, the Trojan seer, urges his brother Hector's return to Troy to convene a solemn procession to the Temple of Athena. Queen Hecuba and the Trojan matrons will lead the procession, its purpose to entreat Athena for Diomedes' removal from battle.

The battle easing during Hector's absence, Diomedes and the Lycian prince Glaucus—the Lycians a principal ally of Troy—meet on the battlefield. Through a detailed and digressive genealogical exchange—"Homeric digression" par excellence—they discover their hereditary friendship. Affirming it, they exchange armor. Glaucus, as Homer wryly notes, gets the worst of it, exchanging gold armor for bronze.

While performing Helenus' bidding, Hector encounters the foot-dragging Paris and entreats his return to battle. True to form, the laggard pretends he was about to do just that. Next rushing to his own residence, Hector inquires into the whereabouts of his wife, Andromache, and is soon at her side. The "Parting of Hector and Andromache" introduces the couple's infant son Astyanax 'ruler of the city'. Frightened by his father's horsehair-plumed helmet, the child shelters in his mother's "fragrant bosom." Fearing for Hector's life—he is the mainstay of Troy— Andromache urges him to fight defensively. He is, as she confesses, "smiling through her tears," her all-in-all. Indeed, Achilles earlier slew her entire family before Andromache's arrival in Troy as Hector's wife. Hector prays for his son's growth and battlefield success. This is the *Iliad*'s only picture of domestic life and concern, one of extreme tenderness, ever relished as such. Its pathos is heightened by Hector's self-professed doom: as Hector goes, so goes Troy. He will yet seek to win glory that future men may know of him (the *Iliad's* perennial concern).

Hector acknowledges, since no man escapes his fate, that he will accept his own when arrived. He dashes back to the battlefield, leaving Andromache at the palace, where the women mourn Hector as if already dead (so strong the premonition). Hector overtakes Paris and again berates his malingering. Paris, true to form, makes excuses. But where has Paris been? Immediately prior to his meeting with Hector, Paris—in a famed Homeric simile—is compared to a well-fed horse, its head held high, accustomed to racing the fields and bathing in bracing river streams. This image of satiety and exhilaration signals the aftermath of sex with Helen. Self-indulged rather than committed, Paris inhabits a world entirely apart from that of his brother Hector.

❦

Now resonated battle's din between Trojans
And Danaans, the battle at random reeling
This way and that throughout the plain, whereon weighted
Weapons, unerringly hurled—evenly meting
Out slaughter—struck home between the streams of Xanthus   5
And Simoïs. First, Telamonian Ajax,
Bulwark of the Argives, forth standing from the host,
Sundered a Trojan phalanx, killing Acamas,
Eussorus' son, best of the Thracian infantry,
Both brave and great of stature. The weapon transpierced   10
His plume-prided helmet's crest. The pointed bronze next
Foraged his forehead, impaling the bone within,
And o'er his lowered lids did leaden death descend.
Then slew Diomedes Axylus, Teuthranus'
Son, a wealthy man whose home was strong Arisbē;   15
Belovèd he of men, to all hospitable
Whom from his roadside domicile he entertained.
But surfaced nary one of these, his guests, to ward
Off woeful ruin. Thus Diomedes smote both him

And the squire Calesius, his charioteer, 20
And passed the pair beneath the earth. Euryalus
Downed Dresus and Opheltius, and next pursued
Pedasus and Aesepus—whom the naiad nymph
Abarbarea bore blameless Bucoliōn,
He Laomedōn's eldest son, a bastard born, 25
Who, tending his flock, with the naiad lay the night;
And she conceiving bore him twins whose sturdy limbs
Euryalus unloosed, offstripping their armor.

And Astyalus slew the staunch Polypoetēs;
And Odysseus brazen-speared despatched Pidytēs 30
Of Percōtē; and Teucer, good Aretaōn.
And Antilochus, Nestor's son of the glinting
Spear, slew Ablerus. Atreidēs Agamemnon,
King of men, despatched Elatus, who in rugged
Pedasus dwelt, by the levees of fair-flowing 35
Satniōeis. And the warrior Lēïtus
Felled the fleeing Phylacus; and Eurypylus
Laid Melanthius low. But Menelaus, great
At warcry, captured Adrastus, his horses twain
Distraught with terror upon the plain; his rounded 40
Chariot, ensnarled in a tamarisk bough, had cracked
At the pole's attachment—the steeds decamping forth
To the town toward which many desp'rately escaped.

But he from out the chariot tumbled headlong
In the dust upon his face. And Atreïdēs 45
Menelaus, far-menacing weapon in hand,
Alongside him stood. Then Adrastus implored him,
Embracing his knees: "Take me alive, you offspring
Of Atreus, a generous ransom accepting.
Many a treasure lies stored in my prosperous 50
Parent's abode, bronze and gold and toil-wrought iron,
Whereof my father would delight you with boundless
Spoils, should he know of me live aside your vessels."

So he spoke, smartly swaying the other's spirit,
And Menelaus had even then consigned him55
To his squire, to be taken to the Argive ships.
But hastily came Agamemnon, reproving
Him thus: "Menelaus, soft-hearted, what care be
This for the likes of these? Has comp'rable kindness
Been vouchsafed you by Trojans in your own abode?60
Let not one of them escape complete destruction,
Nor the might of our hands, even the man-child borne
In his mother's womb; let not even him escape,
But see that the Trojans entirely cease to be,
Unmourned and unnoted." So announced the warrior,65
Counseling aright and swaying his brother's spirit.
Thus Menelaus, great warrior, thrust Adrastus
Away from him, and the warrior Agamemnon
Pierced his flank, and backward he fell; and on his chest
Placed Atreus' son his heel, withdrawing the ashen70
Spear. Then to the Argives shouted Nestor aloud,
Calling: "My comrades, Achaean warriors, squires
Of Ares, let no man now be swayed by plunder,
Thinking shipward to impound sufficient amount.
Sooner let us slay the men; thereafter at ease75
Along the plain shall we plunder the armored dead."

So speaking, he roused the might and resolve of each.
Then had the Trojans, by weakness their own o'ercome,
Again been routed cityward by Argive might,
Argives beloved of Ares, had not Helenus,80
Priam's Son, of augurs best, approached Aeneas
And Hector, remarking: "Aeneas and Hector,
Because in you of Trojans and Lycians beyond
All others resides war's toil—since ever best you
Stand in every undertaking, finest in fight85
And counsel both—maintain your position, the men
Holding firm by the gates, yourselves ranging about,
Lest fleeing to their spouses' embraces they fall,

BOOK VI

To the foe a special satisfaction. But when
Once our battalions are positioned, here standing   90
Shall we engage the Argives steadfastly, distressed
Though we be, necessity weighing upon us.
But you, Hector, to the city returning, there
Plead with your mother and mine: let her assemble
The agèd wives in the temple of flashing-eyed   95
Athena on the citadel, unfastening
The doorway of her precinct. Let her place the robe
That most pleases her—and is amplest in the hall,
The one by herself most regarded—on the knees
Of fair-haired Athena, and vow within her shrine   100
To slay twelve bullocks, yearlings, by the goad untouched,
If Athena upon us confer compassion
And upon Trojan wives and their treasured children;
If she from holy Troy restrain Diomedes,
Tydeus' son, that savage spearman, that confounding   105
Deviser of rout who, I deem, now proves himself
Indomitable throughout the Danaan ranks.
Not even Achilles have we ever thus feared,
That leader of men, reputedly goddess-born.
But Diomedes grows entirely unruly,   110
With none able to countermand his mastery."
So he pronounced, and Hector nowise disobeyed
His kin, and immediately leapt he full armored
Groundward from his chariot and, wielding two sharp
Spears, ranged widely throughout the rout, rousing his men   115
To fight, and waking heinous battle's din. So they,
Rallied and took their stand, opposing the Argives,
And the latter relented, from their slayings stayed.
And reckoned they that one of the gods immortal
Descended starry heaven, aiding the Trojans,   120
That they rallied thus. And Hector shouted aloud
To the host: "Trojans, high-hearted, and you far-famed
Allies, be men, my friends! And with fiery valor
Acquainted be, while I hasten to Troy, bidding

Our spouses and counsel-bearing elders beseech 125
The gods with offerings of sacred hecatombs."
So saying, flashing-helmeted Hector withdrew,
And the blackened leather that rimmed his naveled shield—
Its protective fringe at either extremity—
Touched at his ankles and neck.
                                      But Glaucus, offspring 130
Of Hippolochus, and great Diomedes met
Within space between the ranks, on battle resolved.
And when the pair, approaching each other, stood nigh,
War-crying Diomedes first addressed him thus:
"Who might you be, O most menacing of mortals? 135
For never heretofore afore this time have I,
Thus battling, observed you venture where men win praise.
But now have you stridden forth, ahead all others
In your hardihood, determined to dare my far-
Shadowing spear. Unfortunate they whose issue 140
Face my might. But be you a deity arrived
From heaven, with no heavenly god will I fight.
No, for even Dryas' son, mighty Lycurgus,
Little prevailed once battling with divinities,
He who earlier, down Nysa's numinous slope, 145
Mad Dionysus' nurses chased; and they their wands
To groundward dropped, by the ox-goad cruelly smitten
Of murderous Lycurgus. But Dionysus,
Distraught, descended the billowed brine, and Thetis,
Apprehensively, received him to her bosom, 150
For Lycurgus' bluster had unbalanced him quite.
Then were the gods, reposed at ease, with Lycurgus
Wroth, and the son of Cronus blinded him; and he
But briefly lived, since by all the immortal gods
He lived despised. Thus with the blessèd gods would I 155
Unwillingly fight. But, be yours a warrior's stock
That reaps autumnal yield, approach, and timely test
Upon my whetted blade obliteration's bounds."

Then responded Hippolochus' glorious son:
"Great-souled Diomedes, wherefore interrogate   160
My lineage? Even as the generations
Of leaves, such also those of men. As for the leaves,
Winds earthward scatter some, even as burgeoning
Forests sprout others afresh at springtime's behest.
Even thus a race of men is risen, and thus   165
A race retired. But, attend you this if you will,
That my lineage be perceived, since legion they
That know it. There exists a city, Ephyrē,
In a nook of Argos, pastureland to horses,   170
And there dwelt Sisyphus, most devious of men;
Sisyphus, Aeolus' offspring, who sired Glaucus;
And Glaucus begat the blameless Bellerophōn,
On whom the gods bestowed fine manliness and grace.
But Proetus contrived vile villainy against him,   175
And banished him, seeing him the mightier far;
For Zeus had subjected Argos to his sceptre.
Now Proetus' wife, divine Anteia, lusted for
Bellerophōn, to lie with him clandestinely,   180
But could not upon the steadfast Bellerophōn,
E'er unswerving, the least prevail. So to Proetus,
The king, she fabricated thus: 'Either die you,
Proetus, or slay Bellerophōn, who transgressed my
Inclination, seeking to lie with me in love.'
So she spoke, and the king grew wrathful hearing it.   185
Refrained he from despatching him for reverence' sake,
But sent him with baleful tokens unto Lycia,
Inscribing twin tablets with ominous emblems,
And commanded that his father-in-law see these,
That Bellerophōn be slain. So he departed   190
To Lycia, in the blameless convoy of the gods;
And when to Lycia arrived and to Xanthus' stream,
Broad Lycia's ruler honored him with ready heart.
Full nine days long bestowed he hospitality
And nine oxen slew; but when rosy-fingered Dawn   195

On the tenth appeared, he questioned him, requesting
To see the emblems he had brought; but these received,
The baleful images of his son-in-law, he
First ordered Bellerephōn slay the Chimaera—
Divine her stock, not mortal; frontward a lion, 200
A serpent behind, a she-goat to middle shaped—
Furiously exhaling bane of blazing fire.
And Bellerophōn slew her, trusting the portents
Of heaven. Next he encountered the glorious
Solymi, and this, he said, was the mightiest 205
Famed encounter that ever had befallen him;
And third he despatched the men-measured Amazons.
But the king wove a pestilent plot against him
Returned from these adventures. Choosing from Lycia
The bravest of men, he set an ambush; but not 210
In the least did these prosper homeward returning,
For blameless Bellerophōn entirely slew them.
So, as the tyrant considered him intrepid
Offspring of a god, there he detained him, gave him
His daughter, and fully half his kingly acclaim. 215
And the Lycians allotted him preeminent
Acreage: extensive orchards and arable land
As possessions. And his wife bore Bellerophōn
Three children: Hippolochus, Laodameia,
And Isander. And Laodameia with Zeus 220
Counselor lay and bore him godlike Sarpēdōn,
Crested in bronze, but when Bellerophōn became
Abhorrent to the gods, then widely wandered he
Dispossessed, drifting over the Aelian plain,
His own soul devouring and avoiding the paths 225
Of men; and battle-insatiate Ares slaughtered
His son Isander as he fought the acclaimèd
Solymi; and the angered gold-reined Artemis
Slew his daughter. But Hippolochus begot me,
And of him my lineage I assert; and sending 230
Me Troyward, he firmly admonished thus: that I

E'er bravest be and over all preeminent,
And distance disgrace from the line of my fathers,
Known the noblest in Ephyrē and broad Lycia.
From such bloodline and lineage I claim myself come."   235

So he disclosed, and Diomedes delighted.
Pegging his spear in the plenteous earth, kindly
Addressed he the shepherd of the host: "Verily,
Now aforetime were you visitant within my
Father's house. For goodly Oeneus once entertained   240
The blameless Bellerophōn in his halls and kept
Him twenty days; and one to the other offered
Friendship's genial tokens. Oeneus bestowed a bright-
Scarleted belt, and Bellerophōn a double
Golden cup that I, come Troyward, in my palace   245
Placed. But Tydeus I recollect not, then only
A child when he departed, when Argive power
Expired at Thebes. Thus be I now in mid-Argos
Your guest-friend esteemed; and thus you in Lycia, mine,
Whene'er to that land I sojourn. So avoid we   250
One another's weapons, even amid the fray;
For many there are that I might slay, both Trojans
And lustrous allies, whome'er a god may allow
And my own speed outstrip; and, verily, many
The Argive that you might slay, whomsoe'er you might.   255
And of our armor make we now exchange, that these
Men, too, observe the faith of fatherly rapport."
Having thus discoursed, the two vaulted from their cars,
Clasped each other's hands, and mutually proclaimed
Fidelity's pledge. But Father Zeus Cronidēs   260
Impounded Glaucus' wits, his armor exchanging
Thus with Diomedes, Tydeus' son: for golden
Bronze exchanging, a hundred oxen's worth for nine.

But when hastening Hector reached the Scaean Gates
And mighty oak, converged about him there the wives   265

And daughters of Troy, inquiring after their sons,
After their husbands, brethren, and friends; but he bade
Them, each one, implore the gods instead; yet many
The woman whom worry and heartache encumbered.
But at Priam's magnificent palace arrived, 270
Appointed with polished porticoes—and in it
Were fifty chambers of polished stone, constructed
Aside the other each, where the sons of Priam
Lay aside their wedded wives; and for his daughters,
Over against them within the court, stood twelve roofed 275
Chambers of burnished stone, each aside the other
Built, where lay Priam's sons-in-law, their reverent
Wives beside—there Hector's bounteous mother greeted
Him, leading forth Laodicē, of her daughters
Most commanding in countenance; and clasping his 280
Hand she addressed him saying: "Child, why arriving
Forsake you the furious fight? Surely the sons
Of the Achaeans, villainous their line, pounce hard
Upon you all, the while battling about the town,
And your spirit bids you come, from the citadel 285
Uplifting your hands to Zeus. But remain until
I bring sweet-honeyed wine, libation to outpour,
First to father Zeus and the other deathless gods;
Yourself refreshed next from it, if you will partake.
For a toiling man wine mightily swells the strength, 290
Even as you, defender of your fellows, toil."
Then answering, responded Hector flashing-helmed:
"Honored mother, offer no wine, mind-mellowing,
That you stymie not my craft and I to greatness
Grow indifferent. Moreover, my hands uncleansed, 295
None the outpour of flaming wine do I offer
To Zeus. Nor should Cronidēs, lord of darkened cloud,
Be importuned by one befouled in blood and filth.
No, proceed now to the precinct of plunderer
Athena, with choicest offerings, convening 300
The agèd wives. And the robe that amplest appears

BOOK VI

To you, fairest most within the hall, of all most
Favored, just such a robe upon the knees repose
Of comely-tressed Athena; and at her portaled
Temple offerings pledge of yearling heifers twelve,   305
Unbroken by the goad, if she be pitying
Of Troy, the Trojan matrons, and their progeny,
Entreating she keep Diomedes from sacred
Ilium, that murderous spearman and rampant
Contriver of rout. So, to the driver of spoils   310
Proceed and to her hallowed precinct, and Paris
Will I call, if perchance he comply with my word.
Would that earth immediately open wide for him!
For Olympian Zeus has most grievously reared him
A torment to Troy and stalwart-hearted Priam   315
And Priam's progeny. Upon his entering
Hades' demesne, my affliction were forgotten.

So he admonished; but she retired hallward,
Forth summoning her servants, and they assembled
The agèd wives throughout the town. But she herself   320
Descended the fragrant chamber wherein richly
Broidered robes were stored, by Sidonian women
Designed, whom the godlike Alexander himself
Had from Sidon brought, o'ersailing th' expansive sea
On the quest undertaken for high-born Helen.   325
Of this raiment raised Hecuba one, conferring
It as offering to Athena, the mantle
Most amply and handsomely embroidered, which shone,
A very star, reposing nethermost of all.
Then she left, the aged wives attending after her.   330

When the women had come to Athena's temple,
Atop the citadel, the fair-cheeked Theanō,
Kisseus' daughter, spouse of horse-taming Antēnōr,
Opened the expansive portals, for the Trojans
Had named her priestess of Athena. Then, wailing,   335

Upraised they their hands to Athena, and fair-cheeked
Theanō, taking the robe, on Athena's knees
Reposed it, and praying to the child of mighty
Zeus entreated: "Lady Athena, protectress
Of our city, fairest of goddesses, dash now					340
Diomedes' weapon and provide he plummet
Headlong a'fore the Scaean Gates, that we the while
Our offerings within your temple consummate:
Twelve heifers, yearlings, unaccustomed to the goad,
If compassion you proffer Troy, the Trojan wives,					345
And the tender children theirs." So spoke she praying,
But Pallas Athena o'erpassed the petition.
And so they implored the offspring of mighty Zeus.

But Hector to the palace of Alexander
Advanced, the fair palace he himself had fashioned					350
With men the foremost builders then in fertile Troy;
These a chamber had wrought him, a hallway, and court
Near the residences of Hector and Priam
On the citadel. Thereunto entered Hector,
Beloved of Zeus—his lance eleven cubits' length,					355
And hard blazing a'front it a brazen spearpoint
Firmly fastened about with banded gold. In his
Chamber found he Paris, tending his splendid arms,
His shield and corselet, and handling his crescent bow;
And sat Argive Helen amid her domestics,					360
Delegated glorious handiwork to each.
And observing him, Hector leveled this reproach:
"Strange man, ill becomes you this indisposition.
Your people about the battlements of Troy fight
Perishing, and on your account does contention					365
And caterwaul confound the town about. You would
Yourself with any other be irate, whome'er
You chanced observing in abhorrent war's retreat.
So bestir yourself, lest the town succumb withal."
And to him responded godlike Alexander:					370

BOOK VI

"Hector, since you reprimand me rightly, and not
Exceeding measure, therefore will I speak; and you,
Consider it, reflecting. Not so much irate
Or faulting the Trojans sat I in my chamber,
But sooner seeking to diminish my despair.   375
Even now does Helen, dutifully entreating,
Enspirit me to fight, and thus preferable
I regard it. Victory yet passes from one
Man to another. But come, for a moment stay,
And I will don my battle gear; or proceed you   380
And I will follow, overtaking you perchance."
So he spoke, and bright-helmed Hector responded not.
But beauteous Helen interposed with gentle words:
"Dear brother-in-law of mine, harpy that I am,
Deviser of villainy, detestedly viewed,   385
Would upon that day when first my mother bore me
A whirlwind had hurtled me forth to a distant
Mountain or wave of the boisterous sea, the surge
Asunder wasting me ere befell this wretched
Business. However, since the immortals ordained   390
These ills, would wife I had been to a better man,
One grasping his fellows' reproaches and plenteous
Displeasures. But impervious to revilement
Abides this man, stunted his discernment. Wherefore,
I deem, will he to his due accede. But come, now,   395
Pass within, and upon this chair repose yourself,
Since beyond all others, dear brother mine, does toil
Encompass you e'er for Alexander's folly
And shameless me, to whom Zeus allots a fearsome
Fate, meriting song from men to come hereafter."   400

And to her responded glancing-helmed Hector thus:
"Advise no postponement, dear Helen, your regard
Notwithstanding, for disinclined am I. My heart
E'en now impatient grows to rally the Trojans,
Long pining for my presence. But, no, bestir you   405

This fellow, and let him bestir himself, that yet
Within the city he find and overtake me.
For homeward I proceed to see my cherished wife,
My infant son, and household helpers; for little
I know whether e'er again I shall venture home, 410
Or die even now by immortal decree, slain
By Achaean hands."
      This much relating, Hector
Glittering-helmeted withdrew, and straightway arrived
At his well-built home, discovering not within
The white-armed Andromache. She, with her fair-robed 415
Attendant and child, had positioned herself high
On the battlement, weeping aloud. So Hector,
Not finding his peerless spouse within, drew closer,
Straddling the doorway, and addressed his domestics:
"Come now, you my domestics, directly disclose 420
Where from out the hall the white-armed Andromache
Has gone: to one of my sisters' residences,
Or home of my fair-robed brothers' wives, or temple
Of Athena, where the other fair-tressed women
Of Troy implore the dread offspring of Cronidēs." 425

Then to him responded a bustling attendant:
"Hector, since earnestly you bid the truth revealed,
Neither to any of your sisters or brothers'
Fair-robed wives departed she, nor to the temple
Of Athena, where the other fair-tressed women 430
Of Troy entreat Athena the dreaded warrior,
But sooner Ilium's rampart sought, once learning
Of Trojan misadventure and Danaan might
Ascendant. To the rampart she betakes herself,
Like unto one possessed, the nurse bearing her child." 435
So spoke the attendant, and Hector departed
The doorway, dashing back through the sturdy Trojan
Streets. But when finally arrived at the Scaean Gates—
Once traversing the city, from which he proposed

BOOK VI

To reenter the plain—there came running to meet   440
Him his bounteous wife, Andromache, daughter
Of great-hearted Ëëtion, her sire who had dwelt
Beneath wooded Placus, in Thēbē thereunder,
And had governed the Cilicians; for his daughter
Was she whom bronze-armored Hector had wed. Now they   445
Converged, by a handmaid accompanied bearing
The tender boy, a mere babe, upon her bosom,
Hector's adorèd son, like to a radiant star.
Hector called him Scamandrius, by others styled
Astyanax; for it was Hector alone who   450
Protected Troy. Then, watching his boy in silence,
Hector smiled; but Andromache, weeping, approached,
And clasping fast his hand addressed him thus by name:
"Belovèd! This boldness will prove your undoing.
No pity have you for your infant child, and none   455
For unhappy me, next your widow to become;
For soon the upgathered Danaans will beset
And despatch you. But for me far better it were,
Without you, neath earth to molder, for nevermore
Will consolation endure, when your destiny   460
Dawns—irrevocably set—but sorrow alone,
Lacking sire and queenly mother to comfort me:
My father, alas, the godlike Achilles slew,
For he heartlessly marauded the Cilicians'
Town, well-tenanted, even lofty-gated Thebes.   465
He slew Ëëtion, despoiling him not—reverent
His spirit the while—and burned him richly adorned
In his armor, heaping a barrow upon him.
And 'round about it mountain nymphs, winsome offspring
Of aegis-bearing Zeus, plant elms. And my seven   470
Brothers within our halls, these same, that very day
Descended Hades' house; for all were by godly
Swift-footed Achilles slain amid their shambling-
Gaited oxen and white-fleeced sheep. And my mother,
That was queen neath wooded Placus, here he conveyed   475

Her, amid other possessions, but released her
Thereafter, receiving a ransom unreckoned.
And by Artemis' arrow she perished at home.
Ah, Hector, you are my father, my reverent
Mother, dear kinsman, and most adoring husband.   480
Come, taking pity, on the battlement remain,
Lest follow orphan from child and widow from wife;
And station the host by the fig tree, where the town
May be ably breached, and the battlement o'erwhelmed.
For thrice came the bravest there with th' Aiantes twain,   485
With Tydeus' son, and with glorious Idomeneus,
And with Atreus' sons, there seeking to penetrate,
Either heeding a soothsayer's knowing behest
Or trusting the more on their own intuition."

Then responded great flashing-helmeted Hector: 490
"Woman, I too to these matters attend; indeed,
I were shamed by the Trojans and trailing-mantled
Trojan wives were I to vacillate and cower,
Avoiding war; nor thus does my spirit propose,
As I have learnt ever valiant to be, fighting   495
Foremost among the Trojans, garnering glory
For my acclaimèd ancestry and for myself.
For this to a certainty I conclude: the day
Will come when hallowed Ilium shall leveled lie,
And Priam, and the host of Priam ashen-speared.   500
Yet, the less does Troy's tribulation trouble me—
Neither king Priam's, nor queen Hecuba's, nor my
Brothers', many the gallants they, laid dead in dust
Neath enemy hands—than troubles me yours, when some
Bronze-coated Argive transports you away in tears,   505
Your day of freedom denied. Then to Argos borne,
At another's wroth behest would you work the loom,
Or from springs of Hypereia or Messēis
Draw water, unwilling, by cruel compulsion
Companioned evermore; and someone observing   510

BOOK VI

Your tears will assert: 'So fares the wife of Hector,
Who e'er in war among the Trojans most excelled,
Those tamers of horses, the while they contended
For Troy.' So shall someone assert, and yours the pain
Renewed for want of myself to avert your day   515
Of servitude. But perish I, and upon me
Amply heaped be earth, when I discern your lament
As they lead you dispirited away, enslaved."
So speaking, noble Hector extended his arms
To his child, but back to the bosom of his fair-   520
Girdled nurse he retreated in tears, at his dear
Father's aspect affrighted, and fearing the bronze
And the horsehair plume as he marked it dreadfully
Nodding atop the crested helm. Then laughed aloud
His dear father and reverent mother, and quickly   525
Glorious Hector removed the helm from off his head
And laid it, lustrously bright, to the ground. Next he
Kissed his darling boy close nestled to his embrace
And prayed ardently to Zeus and the other gods:
"Zeus and you other gods, allow this my offspring   530
Also to prove preeminent, even as I
Among the Trojans, and be ever outstanding;
And great be his governance over Ilium,
And may someone someday say of him returning
From battle: 'Far superior than his father he';   535
And may he bear the bloodied spoils of the rival
He has slain, rejoicing the heart of his mother."
So saying, he surrendered his son to his wife's
Embrace, and she to her fragrant breast received him,
Smiling through her tears; and her husband, at the sight   540
Of it, took pity, with his hand caressing her,
And reassured her, saying: "Loving wife of mine,
Be not yourself on my account dispirited;
To Acherōn will none despatch me ere my time;
For his doom, I maintain, has no man e'er escaped   545
Once begotten, whether coward or courageous.

But returning home, yourself consider the tasks
That are yours, the distaff and shuttle; and order
The women to ply their work. Men will tend to war
For those dwelling here, foremost mine the endeavor." 550

So spoke glorious Hector lifting his horsehair-
Crested helm; and speedily homeward departed
His doting wife, ofttimes turning about, shedding
Copious tears. Came she next to the well-fashioned
Palace of man-slaying Hector, and abundant 555
The attendants there busied, and awakened she
Wailing among them, such that in his own abode
Was Hector bemoaned, though yet alive; for they deemed
His fate inexorably decreed, as he fought
Against Argive compulsion. And Alexander 560
Tarried not at his lofty domicile, but donned
His resplendent armor, bedight with bronze, and coursed
Throughout the town, his faith entrusted to fleetness
Of foot. Even as when a stabled horse, sated
Aside the trough, unhinges his halter—headlong 565
Trampling the meadow, accustomed in clement streams
To bathe, exultant, his head held proudly aloft,
And about his shoulders teems the abundant mane;
Delights he in his splendor, and deftly his knees
Convey him to pasturage and equine quarters; 570
Thus even Paris, Priam's son, from summited
Troy forth quickened, his armor agleam, resplendent
As sunlight, laughing for glee. Then on his brother
The godly Hector happened he, the while Hector
Rounded the place where he with his wife had conversed. 575
So, then, did godlike Alexander address him:
"Dear kinsman mine, I doubtless inhibit your haste,
Delaying you thus, nor came I timely, even
As you bade." And Hector flashing-helmed responded,
Answering: "Odd fellow! No one right-minded could 580
Question your prowess in battle, for you are brave;

BOOK VI

But willingly you loiter, always reluctant.
And my spirit within is sorely grieved, whene'er
On your account I hear a Trojan reprimand—
Such sad apportionment of toil have you dispensed.   585
But onward now, these matters later tended to.
Should Zeus allow our stationing within our halls
A bowl for the Olympian gods immortal,
Then were this our deliverance conspicuous,
The Danaans abandoning fortified Troy.   590

~ Book VII ~

The Single Combat Between Hector and Ajax, the Dead Are Buried, the Greeks Build a Wall to Protect Their Encampments and Ships

Upon Hector's return, the battle renews with added force, and Athena is concerned for the Greeks. Seeing her descend from Olympus, the pro-Trojan Apollo joins her near the Scæan Gates. They agree to pause the day's fighting and induce Hector to challenge the Greeks to an outcome-determinative single combat. Nine Greek warriors accept the challenge, lots are drawn, and Ajax is chosen. This is no accident. Notwithstanding Diomedes' earlier show of valor, Ajax is reputed second-best and bravest after the absent Achilles; and the duel between Hector and Ajax anticipates the poem's final single combat between Hector and Achilles (and Hector slain). No slapstick here, as in the earlier duel between Menelaus and Paris. Hector and Ajax fight to a draw, parted by oncoming night. When proposing the duel and its terms—and matters are under his control—Hector speaks rhetorically, in an evenly paced and well-balanced manner. His speech is far less expansive in his final duel with Achilles and his awareness of approaching death (Book 22).

The Trojans meet in council, and Antenor proposes the surrender of Helen as a means of ending the war (this too likely occurring earlier and more than once during the course of the war). Paris objects, though willing to surrender Helen's riches alone. Priam sends a herald to make the offer and demand a truce for burning the dead. Agamemnon agrees only to the latter. When the funerals are concluded, the Greeks, upon Nestor's advice, build an elaborate wall to protect their fleet and campsites. It has a mighty gate, is flanked with towers, and is fronted by a great ditch with sharp up-pointing stakes (i.e., palisades).

The wall provides a focal point for the fighting on the plain, its breach allowing access to the ships and their destruction by fire. The wall, moreover—replete with gate, towers, ditch, and palisades—not only directs attention to this or that specific part of the fortification (versus random encounters on the plain) but also enlarges both the manner of fighting and vicissitudes of death. The wall is thus a structural marvel no less than a narrative expedient. It is another of those devices updating the war's narrative present by way of its past, as such fortifications were doubtless earlier raised. One in fact imagines them as part of the initial "digging in" upon the fleet's arrival at Troy. The fortification curiously focuses the fighting on the makeshift Greek wall rather than on the impenetrable walls of Troy, with the Greeks fighting more to defend themselves and their ships than to breach and capture Troy. Such is the Trojans' advance in Achilles' absence.

That this is not the first such wall is clear from Poseidon's complaint to Zeus of "another wall" the Greeks had built, on that occasion without first offering prayer to the gods. The present wall, he further complains, will surpass the fame of the fortification Poseidon once built for Laomedon, Priam's father and predecessor. Zeus assures Poseidon that when the war is ended he may wash the wall to sea (the event foretold at the start of Book 12).

The two armies pass the night in feasting, but Zeus discourages the Trojans with thunder and other signs of displeasure; *this* even while purporting to fulfill Thetis' request to advantage the Trojans on Achilles' account. Zeus' will, we recall, is fate; and though Troy is ultimately fated to fall, the vicissitudes of fate—including manner and timing—are unforeseeable. Zeus' discouragement of the Trojans is thus consistent with Troy's ultimate doom, even while contrary to the interim promise of Greek adversity.

We pause to note that Book 7 marks the approximate midpoint of Homer's tale. The duel occurs toward the end of the twenty-third day. Remember, in this connection, that the plague in Book 1 lasted nine (non-action) days, and that Thetis, before importuning Zeus on Achilles' behalf, awaits his nine-day stay among the Ethiopians. Also contained in Book 7 are days 24 (truce agreed to), 25 (rites for the slain), and 26 (fortification built).

ஃ

So saying, radiant Hector departed the gates,
With him advancing his brother Alexander
For combat's encounter, both eagerly intent.

BOOK VII

And as a god to longing seamen grants goodly
Gale, when wearied gotten a'battering the brine 5
With timber-burnished oars, and with weariness throb
Their thews; just so to wretched Trojans seemed the twain.
Then each took his man: Paris slew Menesthius,
Who dwelt in Arnē, son of king Areïthous;
Menesthius of mace-bearing Areïthous 10
And ox-eyed Phylomedusa born. And Hector
With sharply pointed spear impaled Eïoneus,
At the tender nape beneath the well-wrought brazen
Helmet's rim, and unloosed his limbs. And Glaucus, son
Of Hippolochus, leader of the Lycians, cast 15
His spear amid battle's disarray at the son
Of Dexius, Iphinous, leaping to his car
Behind swift mares, and smote him upon the shoulder;
And from his chariot dropped he groundward to the dust,
His limbs unloosed. But when Athena dread goddess 20
Gleaming-eyed discerned amid battle's disarray
The Argive ranks destroyed, she descended darting
From Olympus' summit to sacred Ilium;
And quickened was Apollo to encounter her,
Peering from the pinnacle of towering Troy 25
And perceiving her plan for Argive victory.
And so aside the oak god and goddess convened.

Then first to Athena spoke glorious Apollo:
"Why, indeed, from Olympus flown descend you here
Thus avidly, O daughter of thundering Zeus, 30
And wherefore thus enspirited proceeds your way?
Devise and decree you Danaan dominance,
Altering the battle's tack, indifferent become
To Trojan failure? But preferable were it
To convince you, persuading you withal: now let 35
Us daylong discontinue the dreaded battle's
Clash; hereafter will they fight again 'til Troy's high
Citadel be sacked, since thus to you immortals

Stands the outcome decreed: desolate tow'ring Troy."
And answered him bright-eyed Athena as follows: 40
"So be it, far-shooter, performing from afar;
Likeminded am I myself from high Olympus
Come to the tumult of Trojans and Achaeans;
But how think you now to quiet these combatants?"
Then responding spoke the archer lord Apollo: 45
"Let us incite the intrepid spirit of horse-
Taming Hector, if mayhap he dare an Argive,
Whomever and alone, in battle's clash to fight
Him, man to man. So shall the bronze-armored Argives
Proudly urge a rival selected against him." 50

So he spoke, and the goddess bright-eyed Athena
Failed not to attend. And Helenus, the dear son
Of Priam, intuited the tactic wherein
The gods conferred in council; and approaching, stood
Aside Hector, disclosing it him, as follows: 55
"Hector, son of Priam, peer of Zeus in counsel,
Would you somehow abide me, brother that you are?
Command the Trojans and Danaans be seated
And challenge you whoe'er of the Argives ranks best
To contend with you in single-handed combat; 60
Nor predetermined awaits your own demise.
Thus determined is the will of heaven's dwellers
Living blessedly evermore." So he divined,
And hearing his words did Hector gladden greatly;
And amid the host advanced, settled the Trojan 65
Warriors with spear by midsection clasped. And groundward
They reposed themselves. And Agamemnon ordered
The well-greaved Danaans' repose. And Athena
And silver-bowed Phoebus Apollo, both likened
To vultures, sat them—delighting in the warriors— 70
Atop a lofty oak of aegis-bearing Zeus;
And the ranks sat mustered, bristling with helmets, shields,
And weapons. Even as caressing western wind,

BOOK VII

Risen of late, wafts rippling the brine, and darkens
The deep beneath it; so the ordered Danaans 75
And Trojans reposed themselves. And Hector proclaimed
Amid the hosts: "Hear me, you Trojans and well-greaved
Achaeans, that I speak what my spirit commands.
Our pledges has Cronidēs, enthronèd, annulled
And, devising evil, ordains the time whereat, 80
Beneath Argive assault, crumbles towering Troy
Or drop the vanquished Argives aside their vessels.
You comprise the pride of the Panachaean host.
Wherefore volunteer from among you the warrior
Best adjudged whose spirit impels him to grapple 85
With goodly Hector. And this promise I affirm,
Zeus witness it: if that warrior with brazen sword
Despatch me, grant he despoil me of my armor,
To the ships consigning it, but repatriate
My remains that the Trojans and Trojan spouses 90
Confer cremation's recompense upon the dead;
But should I sooner dispose of him, and Phoebus
Apollo grant me praise, his armor will I take,
To sacred Ilium returning it, pendant
Displayed upon Phoebus Apollo's temple wall, 95
The far-striking god; but to the well-benched vessels
Will I send his corpse, that the long-haired Achaeans
Accomplish sacred rites, upheaping a barrow
Upon the spacious Hellespont for him. And some
Day shall someone say, even of later born men 100
A' sail the wine-dark sea in his well-crafted ship:
'Abides there the barrow of a man days agone
Despatched whom, upon a time in his prowess pleased,
The glorious Hector slew.' So shall someone say,
And ne'er shall my glory perish."
                              So he proclaimed, 105
And resolutely hushed were they, highly chagrined
For their reluctance, but fearful for the doing.
Finally arose Menelaus among them,

Apportioning censure, his words disparaging,
His grievance bruited aloud: "Ah me, you braggarts—   110
Achaean women, no longer Achaean men!
Consternation unthinkable this; a disgrace-
Begotten shock should none of the Achaeans arise
To challenge Hector. May you sooner one and all
To the elements be restored—cowardly, you,   115
Crouching, contemptible, ignominious all.
Against this warrior I arm myself, and above
Be victory by the gods immortal assigned."

Thus having spoken, he donned his wondrous armor.
And now, Menelaus, were forfeit of your life   120
Foreseen—by Hector overcome, since mightier far
Was he—had not the Achaean kings arisen
Taking hold of you; and lordly Agamemnon,
King Atreïdēs, not detained you by the hand,
Straightway addressing you and calling you by name: 125
"Deranged you stand Menelaus, nurtured of Zeus,
And this your derangement becomes you least of all.
Forbear you for all you are abused, and refrain
From battling your better—even battling Hector,
Son of Priam, by many another abhorred.   130
Quakes even Achilles to encounter this man,
He superior far to you. Sooner withdraw
And aside your companions be seated apart.
Against this man shall the Danaans designate
An alternate. However fearless Hector be,   135
However insatiate of war, gladly I say
Will his limbs unloose once fleeing furious clash
And contention's dread." So spoke the warrior, turning
His brother's mind, for well he urged; and the other
Obeyed. Then gladly from off his shoulders his aids   140
Removed his gear; and Nestor arising, declared
Amid the Danaans:
          "O, for shame! In truth, great

BOOK VII

Sadness now engulfs Danaan land. Verily,
Aloud would old Peleus lament, good counselor,
Myrmidon orator, chariot commander who, 145
Once probing me at home, exceedingly rejoiced,
Exultantly proud, when hearing the pedigree
And lineage of the Panachaeans. Were he now
To learn that these a'fore Hector affrighted stood,
He would his hands uplift, imploring th' immortal 150
Gods aright, that the soul depart from out his limbs,
Descending Hades' domain. I would, O father
Zeus and Athena and Apollo, that I were
Young, as when aside the swift-flowing Celadōn
Pylians and Arcadians, their spears unsparing, 155
Assembled, contending beneath the battlements
Of Pheia, about Iardanus' rivulets.
As their champion stood stalwart Ereuthaliōn
A godlike warrior, about his shoulders wearing
The armor of King Areithous, a king beloved, 160
Whom men and comely-waisted women Maceman called,
For he fought with neither shadowing spear nor bow,
But mace-armed ravaged brave battalions rank by rank.
Him Lycurgus slew by guile, not the least by might,
At a narrows where availed him not his iron 165
Mace to save him from destruction, for Lycurgus
Sooner despatched him through the belly, unawares,
With spear's thrust piercing him; and staggered he backward
Upon the ground, there denuded by Lycurgus
Of the armor which the brazen warlord Ares 170
Had bestowed, the which he amid Ares' maelstrom
Thereafter wore. But Lycurgus, senescent grown
Within his halls, gifted the arms to his faithful
Squire Ereuthaliōn to wear. And wearing them,
Ereuthaliōn assembled the hardiest, 175
But they, affrighted, quaked, nor challenged him any;
But me my much-persisting heart compelled to fight
With what hardihood I might summon despite my

207

Fill of years. So I contended, and Athena
Gave me glory. Tallest was he and tenacious   180
Most of any other man I'd slain—a sprawling
Hulk laid every which way aground. Would now that I
Were as sturdy, my strength again as resolute;
Then would flashing-helmeted Hector find his match
The while you Panachaean chiefs—yes, you—are loath   185
To challenge Hector resolutely face to face!"

So scolded the elder as nine in all uprose:
Risen foremost was Agamemnon, king of men;
And Tydeus' offspring next, dauntless Diomedes;
Following them th' Aiantes, clothed in furious   190
Valor; and next Idomeneus and his comrade
Mērionēs, fast peer of Enyalius
Slayer of men; and, following, Eurypylus,
Glorious offspring of Euaemōn; arose then
Thoas, Andraemōn's son, and goodly Odysseus—   195
These each intent to contend with mighty Hector.
Then among them again spoke Gerēnian Nestor,
Accomplished horseman: "Cast you now lots, inclusive
To the last of you, for one to be selected.
For truly shall he credit the well-greaved Argives,   200
And gladden his own soul if emerging alive,
Defying th' engagement and death in dire combat."
So he declaimed, and each designated his lot,
Casting it into the helm of Atreïdēs
Agamemnon amid prayer, hands uplifted   205
To the immortal gods. And thus would one say, eyes
Uplifted to broad heaven: "Father Zeus, bestow
The lot on Ajax, or on Tydeus' son, or else
On the very king of Mycenae rich in gold."
So they spoke, and horseman Gerēnian Nestor   210
Firmly shook the helm, and outleapt the lot therefrom
That they coveted each, even that of Ajax;
And everywhere the herald showed it, left to right

BOOK VII

Amid the throng, to the chiefs of the Achaeans—
But they knew it not, each man disavowing it. 215
But displaying it here and there amid the group,
He accosted him whose name it designated,
Who cast it into the helmet: even wondrous
Ajax. Ajax held forth his hand, and the herald
Coming closer, laid the lot therein. And looking 220
On it, Ajax, elated, acknowledged as his
The marking. He next tossed the lot upon the ground,
Aside his foot, and spoke: "My friends, surely the lot
Is mine, and my heart rejoices, for I propose
To vanquish valorous Hector. But come you now, 225
Even as I accouter myself, proffer prayer
To almighty Zeus Cronidēs, secretively
Among yourselves, that the Trojans discern it not;
Or openly if you will, since before no man
Whomsoever tremble we. For no one by force 230
Or by stated intent shall rout me once engaged,
Nor yet by expertise since, begotten and reared
In Salamis, I deem myself expert enough."
So he averred, and proffered they prayer to Zeus
Cronidēs; and thus would one speak, peering upward 235
To broad heaven: "Father Zeus who from Ida rules,
Greatest, most glorious, grant Ajax victory
And grant he garner glorious acclaim; but should you
Also love Hector, and share he in your concern,
May glory and grit be equally given both." 240
So they conversed, and Ajax appareled himself
In gleaming bronze. But when about his flesh entire
He stood full arrayed in armor, then Ares-huge
He rushed. As when battle-prompted Ares embarks
Amid combatants conjoined by Zeus Cronidēs 245
To soul-consuming malignity committed;
Just so huge hastened Ajax forth, the Danaan
Defender, a smile upon his ferocious face,
The feet that conveyed him implacably pacing,

The while he shook his far-shadowing lance. Then glad 250
Grew the Argives viewing him. As for the Trojans,
Dread fearfulness buckled their limbs, each one of them,
And pounded Hector's heart within his chest; and yet
He endured foreclosed from reentering the ranks,
Himself having issued the duel's invitation. 255

So Ajax approached, his shield like a city wall,
A brazen shield with bullhide sevenfold, the which
Had Tychius wrought with toil, one preeminent
Among artists crafting hide, hailing from Hylē,
Who had fashioned for Ajax a shimmering shield, 260
Heptalayer-hided from fatted bulls, and wrought
Thereon a layer, eighth, of bronze. This bore Ajax
Telamon's son afore his breast, advancing forth;
And positioned proximate Hector threatened thus:
"Hector, beyond peradventure will you now find 265
In man-to-man combat the kind of commanders
That amid the Argives accosted stand, even
After Achilles, to lion's choler kindled,
Who keeps to the keels of his curvèd ships, angered
Past measure at Agamemnon Atreïdēs. 270
Yet such in our numbers are we to engage you;
Thus, accepting this grim challenge, stand firm and fight."
And flashing-helmeted Hector responded thus:
"Ajax sprung of Zeus, offspring of Telamon, chief
Of the host, do not assume, addressing me thus, 275
To make assay of me as if I were maiden
Or child unmindful of warlike deeds. Fully
Knowing am I of strife and slaughterings of men,
Knowing my buckler of seasoned hide both leftward
And rightward to set, which I defiantly wield 280
In warcraft; know I the inroad to battle's bruit
Amid chariots swiftly drawn and know, close-quartered,
To mark the measure of maddening war. Yet ill
Content am I to smite you, being who you are,

BOOK VII

Catching you unprepared; but openly instead 285
If perchance I strike home." So he spoke, releasing
His shadowing spear, and struck the shield of Ajax,
Its bullhide sevenfold, upon its topmost bronze,
The eighth layer thereon. Through six folds driven flew
The untiring bronze, halting at the seventh fold. 290

Then, in turn, threw Zeus-begotten Ajax his own
Far-shadowing spear and struck the son of Priam's
Shield, to each side balanced well. The unsparing point
Transpierced the buckler through, and through the decorate
Corselet sped it a'sunder, and nigh to his ribs 295
Through the tunic tore; but sideways poised, escaped he
Darkness and death. Then the twain in tandem deployed
Their Lances like lions rapaciously driven
Or bristling boars, whose might not mildly reckoned stands.
Squarely then, his spear released struck Priam's son bold 300
Hector's shield, where the bronze stood arrested, backward
Bent its point; but Ajax, bounding, pierced Hector's shield.
Clean through clove the spear, staggering Hector's assault.
Unto his neck came it cutting and black the blood
That burst therefrom. Yet Hector flashing-helmed endured 305
Unfazed and, giving ground, with sturdy hand upgrasped
A stone positioned on the plain—large, dark, and barbed—
And therewith struck the dread bullhided heptafold
Of Ajax dead to center on the boss, the bronze
Loud-pealing in reply. Then Ajax uphefted 310
An outsize stone and, whirling, released it with brawn
Unbounded; and Hector's buckler to inward burst
Undone by the millstone's might; and faltered Hector's
Stricken knees; and backward beaten lay his body's
Length by his buckler blanketed. But Apollo 315
Leto's son balanced him aright. And now by sword
Had they their blows exchanged inflicted hand to hand,
Had not the heralds, messengers of Zeus and men,
Emerged: one from the Trojans, and one from the bronze-

Mailed Achaeans—Talthybius and Idaeus, 320
Men prudent both—and between the pair their sceptres
Placed. And the messenger Idaeus, well-practiced
In counsel, proclaimed: "No longer contest, dear sons,
Nor battle. You are both of Zeus cloud-gathering
Beloved, and as spearmen both respected, as well 325
We are aware. Moreover, nighttime nears apace,
And e'er's the benefit of yielding unto night."
Telamonian Ajax responding declared:
"Idaeus, bid Hector relate the same, for he
It was who summoned our best to encounter. Take 330
He the lead, and his lead will I follow aright."
Then great flashing-helmeted Hector responded:
"Ajax, since a god has granted you eminence
And wisdom too, and rendered you spear-distinguished
Amid the Danaan rank, let us presently 335
Refrain from dreaded strife and war; hereafter then
Shall we engage anew 'til gods between us judge,
Victory granting to this or the other host;
But now is nighttime nigh, and fitting our repose
And nighttime's rest: that you gladden the Danaans, 340
Your companions and kinsfolk, settled by their ships—
Such kin as you claim—even as I encourage
Through Priam's high-towering town the Trojan men
And trailing-attirèd women who shall enter
The gods' assembly, giving thanks on my account. 345
But come, gifts let us bestow, each on the other,
Marvelous their renown, that someone someday say,
Whether Trojan or Argive, that we strove in soul-
Consuming strife, in amity yet departing."
Thus having spoken, entrusted he his silver- 350
Studded sword, to Ajax handing it, its scabbard
And broad-belted strap well trimmed; and Ajax on him
His scarlet-tinctured belt conferred. Thus they decamped:
One 'mid the congregated Argives; the other
To the Trojan throng. And these delighted seeing 355

BOOK VII

Hector as he approached, spirited and intact,
Clear of Ajax' might and hands indomitable;
And to Troy they conveyed him, scarce believing him
Secure. And the well-greaved Achaeans brought Ajax
To Atreidēs Agamemnon, celebrating 360
Greatly in his victory.
                And when they at length
At Atreidēs' huts arrived, lord Agamemnon,
Commander of men, slaughtered before them a bull
Of five years' age, for Cronidēs Zeus selected.
This they flayed and dressed and capably divided 365
Limb by limb, and spitted the pieces and roasted
Them through, and carefully drew them from steaming spits;
Next—done their toil, the repast prepared—they feasted;
Nor of adequate portion was palate deprived.
And wide-ruling Agamemnon Atreïdēs 370
Unto Ajax allotted the backbone and chine.
But having set aside the desire for viand
And refreshment, commenced the elder straightaway
Wise counsel's web to weave, even agèd Nestor 375
Whose plan aforetime best appeared. With good intent
To the Argives declared he, addressing them thus:
"Son of Atreus and you other Panachaean
Lords, many the Danaan dead, their hair a'flow,
Whose dusky blood about Scamander's eddied tide 380
The war god has dispersed, their spirits descended
To Hades' house. Befits it thus that daybreak end
This combat of Achaeans; and we, together
Come, the ox- and mule-drawn carts of corpses hither
For cremation drive, distant somewhat from the ships, 385
That each man's bones be homeward to his children borne
Whene'er again returned we see our native land.
And a single all-honoring barrow construct
We at the pyre, uprisen from the plain, and thence
A lofty rampart raise, protecting our vessels 390
And ourselves; and within it fit we portals fast,

A passage provided for chariots driven through,
And hard by without imbed we a harrowed ditch,
A restraint against infantry and chariots
When transpires the trial of tested Trojan onslaught." 395
So he spoke, and alike did every king concur.

And thus amid the Trojans was conference held,
Tumultuous and fierce, upon Troy's citadel
Aside King Priam's doors. Among them first to speak
Was wise Antēnōr, thus: "Hear me now you Trojans, 400
Dardanians, and allies all, that I may speak
What commands the heart within me. Now rally you,
And Argive Helen surrender we, her treasures
Too, unto lord Agamemnon to carry off.
False proven to our faithful pledges fight we now, 405
Thus gone our expectation, barring this advice."

Thus having spoken, he retired; and prince Paris
Among them uprose, husband of fair-haired Helen,
Who called him aloud, in wingèd words inveighing:
"Antēnōr, no longer pleasingly speak you thus, 410
Knowing better suited words of consultation,
But if thus earnestly you propose, truly have
The gods unto your wits laid waste. Thus plainly I
Assert, affirming it afore these Trojans here:
Helen, my wife, will I not renounce. But her store 415
Of treasure from Sparta to Troy transported, that
Will I return, augmenting it with wealth my own."
Thus speaking he withdrew, and amid them arose
Dardanian Priam, in deliberation the gods' own peer.
Well disposed toward them, he addressed 420
The assembly, speaking forth: "Hearken unto me,
You Trojans and Dardanians and allies all,
That I might speak what commands the heart within me:
Enjoy you your repast for now throughout the town,
Even as aforetime, and careful watch maintain, 425

Heedful every man; and at dawn let Idaeus,
To the shadowy vessels descending, declare
To the offspring of Atreus, lords Agamemnon
And Menelaus, the word of Alexander,
On whose account this commotion accrues, and grant 430
He further convey this our deliberation:
That they consider relenting from heinous war
Until the dead be burned. Thereafter shall we fight
Anew until the gods decree our fates, granting
One side victory or granting it the other." 435
So he declared, and readily hearkened they all
And obeyed, and by companies took their supper
Throughout the camp; and Idaeus, come dawning, sped
Onward to the curvèd ships. There he discovered
The Danaans, Ares' attendants, assembled 440
Beside cable and stern of Atreïdēs' ship;
And amid them took the reverberant herald
His position, pronouncing: "Offspring of Atreus,
And you other princes Panachaean, Priam
And the other Trojan commanders bid me state— 445
Be you gladdened and contented to attend it—
The word of Alexander, from whose deeds persists
Contention. The trove entire to Ilium conveyed
Within his hollow hulls—would he had perished first!—
The lot of it would he restore, augmenting it 450
From gain his own; but the wedded wife of mighty
Menelaus will he nowise e'er surrender
Though the Trojans entreat her returned. Moreover,
Commend they this message as well conveyed, whether
Readied you stand to end this unsparing dispute 455
'Til war's fallen be burned. Thereafter shall we fight
'Til grant the gods glory to one or th' other side."
So he spoke, and remained they entirely silent;
But at length spoke warcry-adept Diomedes:
"Now take no man his treasure from Alexander 460
Nor anywise Helen, for even the witless

Conclude that Troy stands fated, and the Trojans folk
To destruction decreed." So he spoke, and shouted
Aloud the sons of the Achaeans, acclaiming
The tidings of Tydeus' son, tamer of horses. 465
Then unto Idaeus spoke lord Agamemnon:
"Idaeus, you have now yourself adjudged the word
Of the Danaans, how it is they make reply;
Thus be their counsel confirmed, with which I concur.
As concerns the corpses, their cremation deem I 470
Warranted; nor be withheld from the wasting dead
Placation's speed of flame and pyre. As for our oaths,
Let Zeus our witness be, Hera's thundering lord."
So saying, he uplifted his staff to the gods,
And Idaeus drove returning to sacred Troy. 475

Now sat they in assembly, Dardanian lords
And Trojans alike in one body collected,
Awaiting Idaeus' return; and arrived, spoke
He his report, taking position among them.
Then fast prepared they for their designated tasks, 480
Some high-hoisting the dead and others scouting wood.
And th' Achaeans also roused themselves, exiting
Their crescented vessels, some hefting the wasted
And others seeking wood.
                      The sun anew reclaimed
Her rounds, rising heavenward from limpid-gliding 485
Deep-flown Oceanus, when the hosts together
Reconvened. Then was it hellish, recognizing
The fallen dead however much their comrades laved
The clotted blood away and, with copious tears
The more, corpses to litters high hoisted and heaped. 490
But from weeping aloud restrained Priam his folk.
And quietly were corpses upon pyres amassed,
And with aching hearts consigned they the dead to flame,
Next reentering inviolate Ilium.
And likewise, for their part, the well-greaved Achaeans 495

BOOK VII

Amassed the fallen high upon pyres, unsettled
At heart and, to fire committing them, departed
To their hollow ships. Now, with dawn barely a'light
And from darkness but little distinguished, chosen
Argive men, from among those present at the pyre, 500
Upraised a single barrow 'round about, rearing
It upward aloft the plain; and nearby a wall
Uplifted and lofty barricade—a bastion
To persons and prows. Fast-fitted were the portals
There positioned, a gateway for chariot assault. 505
And harrowed they without a ditch hard by, immense
And gaping wide, planting pickets and stakes therein.
Thus labored the long-haired Achaeans; and the gods
Alongside lightning-wielding Zeus arrayed, surveyed
The brazen-armed Danaan toil; and among them 510
Earth-shaking Poseidon spoke first: "Zeus Cronidēs,
Be there anywhere on boundless earth a mortal
Man whoe'er that will speak unto divinity
The nature of his thought? Observe you not withal
That the flowing-haired Achaeans construct a wall 515
O'ertow'ring their ships and about it drive a ditch,
But to the gods no sacred hecatomb ordain?
To a certainty as widens dawn will the wall's
Great fame decline, and men no longer recollect
The wall which I and lord Apollo toiling built 520
For warrior Laomedōn." Then, very much
Troubled, addressed him cloud-gathering Zeus: "Ah me,
You most powerful shaker of earth, what protest
Now? Exceedingly might other gods regard such
Incidence—their hold and heft far feebler than yours; 525
But as broadly as Dawn disseminates shall your
Own fame expand. But be daring! When the hair-flown
Danaans, heaving-to, have homeward drawn their ships,
Seeking fatherlands and kin, then asunder raze
The wall, and outward be it swept to sea; the great 530
Beach as aforetime blanketed with spreading sand,

The Danaans decamped, scant consequence to you."
On such matter they discoursed, the sun declining,
And stood the Achaean exertion accomplished;
And taking supper, they slaughtered oxen throughout   535
Their huts. And many ships wine-laden from Lemnos
Set anchor by, through Euneus' largesse, Jason's son,
Whom Hypsipylē had borne to him. Refreshment
For Agamemnon and Menelaus apart
Meted he of vintage wine, a thousand measures   540
Bodied-full. And the flowing-haired Achaeans thence
Procured them wine: for bronze some buying it, others
For glinting iron; some for hides, for cattle some,
And some for slaves; and full the food they furnished them.
And the night through the fair haired Achaeans feasted;   545
So too in the town the Trojans and their allies.

And the night through counselor Zeus devised for them
Adversity proclaimed in thund'rous eruption;
And sallow fear enfolded them, and flowed their wine
From out their beakers to the ground; nor to drink dared   550
Any one ere oblation made to Cronidēs.
And finally surrendered each warrior to sleep.

~ Book VIII ~

The Trojans Advance to the Wall and Encamp, the Greeks Beleaguered, the Second Day of Battle

Zeus assembles the gods, threatening Hades' pains if they assist either side; though Athena, at her own request, is allowed to aid the Greeks by counsel alone. The armies engage, and Zeus from Mount Ida weighs in his balances the fates of either side, frightening the Greeks with thunder and lightning. Showing his essential impartiality, Zeus had similarly frightened the Trojans at the close of Book 7. Though Troy's fate is foregone, the Greeks will yet suffer adversity.

Encircled while fighting alone on the plain, Nestor is rescued by Diomedes—chivalrous youth coming to the rescue of old age. Such is Diomedes' nature (see Book 5). Diomedes had called to Odysseus for assistance; but Odysseus, also true to nature, pretends not to hear, being too smart to risk his life on elderly Nestor's account. For the rest, Book 8 focuses—again—on Diomedes' exploits and those of Hector. Though Ajax is designated best after Achilles, it is Diomedes who again "picks up the slack" in Achilles' absence.

The rescued Nestor mounts Diomedes' car, serving as charioteer. Diomedes hurls at Hector and misses, striking his charioteer instead. Hector, though pained, continues on, enlisting a different charioteer and hurling a near-fatal blow at Diomedes. Nestor urges retreat and Diomedes acquiesces, regretting the ill repute his retreat might one day occasion. Hector taunts Diomedes for the retreat, vowing Troy will never be taken. He continues in pursuit of Diomedes and Nestor.

Hera seeks to incite Poseidon to aid the Greeks, but to no avail, Poseidon reminding her that Zeus had forbidden the gods' intervention. So Hera stirs Agamemnon to rally the troops, which he does, standing at the midpoint of the ships drawn along the shore, chastising Greek ineffectiveness and praying for flight from destruction. Moved by the entreaty, Zeus inspirits the Greeks, and the battle turns in their favor. Telamonian Ajax and the archer, Teucer, work effectively in tandem (Ajax shielding Teucer between bow shots); and Agamemnon, noting it, commends the archer's skill. Teucer shoots at Hector but misses, hitting his charioteer instead. With yet another charioteer onboard, Hector dismounts his car, uplifts a boulder, and hurls it at Teucer, even as the latter prepares to shoot. The boulder strikes Teucer at the shoulder, snapping his drawn bowstring. His half-brother, Ajax, bestrides and protects him while companions carry him off. Hector and the Trojans rally, repelling the Greeks to their wall and as far as the ships.

Hera and Athena converse, preparing to aid the Greeks, but are restrained by Iris at Zeus' command. Returning to Olympus, the two are disdainful of Zeus, vowing at the very least to counsel the Greeks, as they had earlier proposed. Zeus dismisses Athena's anger, foretelling Hector's continued rampage until Achilles reenters the fray in defense of the fallen Patroclus.

As night descends, Hector orders a Trojan watch throughout the plain to assure the Greeks do not embark and sail off (likely for want of the absent Achilles). He orders innumerable fires lit the length of the Trojan encampment, and also within and about Troy to protect against ambush. Food and supplies are brought from Troy, Hector vowing to reengage Diomedes the next day. The campfires are lavishly described in what is known as the "Watchfire Scene," and so concludes Book 8 with heightened visual and imagistic effect. Storyline and poetic enterprise merge, as the Trojans would not be lighting watchfires on the plain but for Achilles' absence.

※

O'erspread the dawn her saffron robe around the world,
And lord Zeus Cronidēs in thunder delighting
Convened the throng of Olympian gods immortal,
Cloud-resident on craggy-crested Olympus.
Exhorted he the gath'ring, and the gods gave ear: 5
"Hearken unto me, you gods and goddesses all,
That I speak what the spirit within me commands.
Let not any goddess nor any god, for that,

BOOK VIII

Attempt to contravene my word, but assent you
Alike thereto, that I straightaway accomplish 10
My purpose: whomever I distinguish ranging
Wayward from the gods to hearten either Trojans
Or Danaans, dearly and deservedly drubbed
Shall he return Olympus-bound; or captured hurled
Headlong to hateful Tartarus, remotest off, 15
Its portals iron pounded wrought, its threshold bronze,
Where gapes neath earth the pit profound, hewn as distant
Neath Hades as starrèd heaven o'erheightens earth.
Then shall you acknowledge me of gods mightiest
E'ermore. But approach and assay me now, you gods, 20
And ascertain: from heaven sling a golden cord
And, tautly gripping it, you heaven-dwellers all,
You would not dislodge me earthward from Olympus
However much endeavoring to dethrone me;
But were I with gladdened heart to attempt the same, 25
Then would you all midst earth and oceans be deposed,
And the rope next secured about a pinnacle
Of snowbound Olympus, that you all pendant be.
So much superior to men and gods am I."

Thus he spoke, and utterly silenced they remained, 30
Astonished at his words, for imperiously
Had he admonished their ranks. But finally spoke
The goddess among them, Zeus' daughter Athena:
"Communal father, Cronus' offspring evermore,
Preeminent in majesty, know we fully 35
Well your might endures unyielding; but pity we
The Argive spearmen perishing, their destiny
Determined. Yet will we assuredly desist
From battle as you bid, though conferring counsel
On the Danaan host, advantaging them thus, 40
That they by your recalcitrance not wasted be."
Then smiling, cloud-accumulating Zeus replied:
"Take heart, dear offspring of Tritōnis begotten,

I presently conceal my spirit's full intent
Though wishing well disposed and favored to abide."   45
So saying, he harnessed his chariot to bronze-hooved
Horses, fleet-paced their flight, their manes of flowing gold,
His godly countenance gold-attired about him;
And grasped to hand the gold-wrought whip, and from his car,
Hand raised, the lash laid leniently upon his steeds   50
To hasten them along, and onward they hurtled,
Nothing loath, from starry heaven's middle passage
Unto earth. To Ida he fared, fountain-fabled
Mount of feral beasts, even to Gargarus
Where stand his redolent altar and demesne. There   55
Zeus Cronidēs stayed his steeds, disengaging them,
Mantling the pair in a plenteous mist, himself
On the lofty-pinnacled summit triumphant,
Descrying all Troy and the beached Danaan hulls.

But the Achaean host, its hair long-flown, throughout   60
The encampment steadfastly feasted on supper,
And arisen therefrom arrayed itself in arms.
And from their side the Trojans likewise armed themselves
Throughout the town; fewer they were, but nonetheless
Stood firm, of necessity, fervently fighting   65
For their spouses' and offspring's protection. The gates
Scraped open wide, and the host hastened forth, footmen
And charioteers alike, and the tumult towered.
But when together come within constricted space,
Slammed they shield upon shield, weapon upon weapon,   70
Breathing bronze-breasted combatants' rage; and fastened
Each within the other, their bossed shields locked—and great
The resultant tumult. Then alike were the groans
And triumphant hollers of slain and slayer heard,
And garnet the ground with gore. For as long as dawn   75
And the hallowed day enlarged, thus long the missiles
Of either side landed felling the folk. But when
Helios to mid-heaven had arrived, lord Zeus

BOOK VIII

Cronidēs uplifted his golden scales aloft
And therein set two fates of grievous death: a fate   80
For the horse-taming Trojans, a fate for th' Argives.
Then upward by its midpoint he gripped the balance,
And Danaan fortunes foundered—resolution
Disfav'ring the Greeks descending toward plent'ous earth,
And fav'ring the Trojans ascending high heaven.   85
And from Ida Zeus thundered aloud, a fiery
Flash amid the Danaans deliv'ring, whereof
The sight o'erwhelmed them, pale terror suffusing them.
Then neither Idomeneus nor Atreïdēs
Dared abide, nor dared abide the Aiantes twain,   90
Attendants of Ares. Stayed only Gerēnian
Nestor, Achaean protector; not of his own
Accord, but his steed was sorely wounded, since lord
Paris, husband of fair-haired Helen, had smitten
It with an arrow topmost to the pate, foremost   95
From the skull where sprout the hairs of horses and where
Deadliest delves the spot. Thus panicked with pain, leapt
The horse, uprearing, the shaft confounding its brain,
And writhing on the brazen frame, the horse upset
The team-drawn chariot. And as the elder, springing   100
Forth with sword swung at the traces, the swift horses
Of Hector approached, coursing through the rout, bearing
A dauntless charioteer, even Hector. And now
Were forfeit the elder's life had not Tydeus' son,
Exceeding in warcry, acutely taken note   105
And with horrific cry exhorted Odysseus:
"Zeus-engendered seed of Laërtes, Odysseus
Many-minded, where flee you running cowardly?
Wouldst have a spearman's weapon planted in your back?
But abide, that Nestor from this beast be rescued."   110
So he spoke; but the wily, steadfast, and dextrous
Odysseus ignored him and accelerated
Toward the Danaan vessels. But Diomedes,
Though solitary amid the foremost fighters,

Stood afore the horses of elderly Nestor, 115
Offspring of Nēleus, addressing him wingèd words:
"Old sir, younger fighters o'errun you; and, alas,
Your force is failed and grievous age companions you,
And wounded is your squire and sluggish your horses.
But come now, ascend my car and yourself behold 120
Such steeds, well skilled, as Trojans relish: quick to course
In each direction whether in pursuit or flight
Across the plain, the very steeds I once purloined
From Aeneas, contriver of rout. Your horses,
The twain, shall our squires attend henceforth, but with these 125
Shall you and I through the horse-taming Trojans tear,
That Hector comprehend the spear's rage of my hand."

So he spoke, and horseman Gerēnian Nestor
Failed not to attend, and the horses of Nestor
Were by two attendants taken, staunch Sthenelus 130
And manly Eurymēdōn. And the other two
Ascended Diomedes' car, Nestor taking
The lustrous reins and hurrying the horses on,
And nigh unto Hector they speedily advanced.
In his forward-rushing rage the son of Tydeus 135
Cast at him without striking, but sooner wounded
The commander of his chariot—Eniopeus,
Son of stalwart Thebaeus, controlling the reins—
Him upon the breast he smote aside the nipple.
As he pitched from the car, the rapid-pounding steeds 140
Reared sideward and recoiled, and perished there his life.
And dread dolor for his driver's sake enshrouded
Hector's soul; yet there he left him strewn, lamenting
Even so, and another dauntless driver sought.
Nor long of master was his team deprived, but found 145
He canny Archeptolemus, Iphitus' son,
Whom he installed behind his fleet-flying team, reins
Supplying to his hands.
     Then were misfortunes wrought

And ruin past remedy, and Trojans hemmed like lambs
In Ilium, had not the father, begetter 150
Of men and gods perceived. Terribly thundering,
He launched his glistering lightning bolt, hard driven
To groundward afore the horses of Tydeus' son,
And foul the sulfurous flame arisen therefrom;
And aside the chariot cowered the steeds, dismayed. 155
Then from Nestor's grip the polished reins unraveled;
And, disheartened most, addressed he Diomedes:
"Son of Tydeus, come, turn your single-hooved horses
To flight. Discern you not that Zeus-assured success
Eludes you? Presently Zeus Cronidēs bestows 160
Glory on Hector; to us hereafter will he
Also provide it, be he inclined; but a man
Shall ne'er impede Zeus' plan, howe'er resolved he be,
For Cronidēs stands far the more formidable."
To him responding, Diomedes excelling 165
In warcry exclaimed: "Yes, verily, old Nestor,
Such matter all do you unerringly relate,
But dreadful grief on this account o'erwhelms my heart,
That Hector someday say among the Trojan host:
'Tydeus' son, afore me retreating, sought safety 170
Amid the vessels.' So someday shall he boast; then
Wide gape the ground for me."
      And to him responding,
Retorted the horseman Gerēnian Nestor:
"Ah me, Diomedes wise-hearted, what drivel.
Though Hector deem you weakling and coward, yet will 175
Trojans and Dardanians be impervious,
Also the wives of the great-hearted Trojans, bearers
Of shields, whose courageous husbands you have slaughtered."
So he spoke, directing his single-hooved horses
About-faced to the fray, and with glorious clamor 180
And groan-begetting shafts the Trojans and Hector
Assaulted the host; and blaze-helmeted Hector
Shouted aloud: "Son of Tydeus, past others all

Were the swift-horsed Danaans wont to honor you
With deferential seating, meats, and brimming cups.   185
But seeming womanly will you now court disdain.
Go, timorous tool; since by no retreat of mine
Shall you ascend atop our battlements, herding
Our women to your ships—ere then decreed your doom."
So he spoke, and Diomedes paused, pondering   190
Whether to wheel his horses, fighting face to face.
Thrice wavered he in spirit, and thrice Cronidēs
Counselor from summited Ida thundered aloud—
For Trojans the token of battle's turning tide.
And shouting, called Hector aloud to the Trojans: 195
"You Trojans, you Dardanians, and you Lycians
Clashing at close quarters; be you manly, my friends,
And be you dauntlessly resolved. Zeus Cronidēs
With willing disposition grants me victory,
Exultation too; and to the Argives distress,   200
Cretins they that contrived these fortifications,
Ineffective these against my might, and trifling;
And lightly shall our horses overleap the trench.
But when at length I attain the vessels, let fire
Consumptive recollected be, that I ignite   205
The ships aflame, the men aside them slaughtering,
These very Achaeans neath the smoke confounded."
So pronouncing, to his horses declared he thus:
"Xanthus, Aethōn, Lampus, and goodly Podagrus,
Recompense you now the care that Andromache,   210
Eëtiōn's great-spirited daughter, meted you
Thus unstintingly—honeyed spirit-enhancing
Wheat and blended wine chomped heartily whenever
Your hearts required it—sooner for you than for me,
Who first by right her stalwart wedded husband is.   215
But gallop in pursuit, that we of Nestor's shield
Lay hold, the fame of which now heavenward ascends—
Gold unalloyed its making, arm-grips included,
And also from off his shoulders seize the breastplate

Of horse-taming Diomedes, lavishly dight, 220
Which Hephaestus fashioned, laboring. Ah, could we
But possess the twain, certainly this night might I
Expect the Danaans ship by ship departed."
So spoke he self-assured, and reverèd Hera
Indignant grew; and shuddered she upon her throne, 225
Making heaven heave, and unto Poseidon earth-
Shaking god spoke, saying: "Alas, earthshaking god,
Far-famed your sway; bears not the spirit within you
Some pity's mite for these expiring Achaeans?
Yet, honoring you, to Helicē and Aegae 230
Bring they offerings, favoring and full; so now
Fashion you their victory. For were we resolved
To assist the Achaeans in routing the foe,
Thus obstructing broad-browed Zeus, infuriated
Would he fret, secluded in Ida's solitude. 235
Then greatly wroth earthshaking Poseidon replied:
"Hera, intemp'rate of tongue, what utterance this!
I would sooner forbear confrontation with Zeus,
Son of Cronus, by far the more powerful he."

On such matters they discoursed, one with the other. 240
But for the Argives all the sector by the wall's
Moat lay congested with a huddling of horses
And of fighting men; congested all by Hector
Priam's son, peer of rapacious Ares the while
Zeus granted him glory. And now would he have torched 245
The ships had Hera not roused Agamemnon,
Quick'ning the Achaeans thereby. So hurried he
His step alongside the Argive vessels and huts,
In his sinewed grip clenching his violet cloak,
And stood by the dark-shadowed ship of Odysseus, 250
Huge its hull, to the seashore's midpoint positioned,
Whence a shout might reach to either end—to the huts
Of Telamonian Ajax and Achilles;
For the two had thus stationed their vessels afloat

At the outermost points, trusting in their courage 255
And strength of hands. There uttered he a piercing cry,
Appealing to the Achaeans: "O, you Argives,
Shamelessly vile, solely in semblance fair. Whither
Wasted that swagger now, when we declared ourselves
The bravest; those boasts which aforetime on Lemnos 260
You idly spewed, surfeiting on flesh of straight-horned
Kine and quaffing bowls of ruddy wine, bragging each
Of you one hundred Trojans—no, twice the number—
Would slaughter, fighting face to face, but unable
To battle Hector alone, calmly positioned 265
To make bonfire of our vessels? O father Zeus,
Lived there e'er aforetime so steadfast a king whom
With folly you infatuated, great glory
Begrudging him? Yet verily now I aver
That never—here voyaging in my curvèd ship, 270
This perilous passage assaying—refused I
Fair altar of yours but thereon burned the fatted
Thighs of bulls, desiring the doom of well-walled Troy.
But, Zeus, this favor now fulfill: to us safe flight,
At least, and refuge grant; and grant you disallow 275
Danaans by the foe altogether destroyed."

So he spoke, and the Father pitied his weeping,
And consented that his men be saved not savaged;
Whereupon appeared an eagle, most consummate
Auspice, swift of wing, clasping a fawn in its claws, 280
The kid of a sprightly hind. By Zeus' elegant
Altar the eagle dropped the fawn, where verily
The Argives had accustomed grown to render Zeus—
The source of omens all—their offerings. And they,
Knowing the bird from Zeus arrived, more vehemently 285
Against the Trojans moved, mindful of battle's joy.
Then might no man of the Argives vaunt—for all they
Stood well numbered—that he ahead Diomedes
Drove swift of steed to overleap the trench, fighting

BOOK VIII

Man to man; rather, very first was he to fell   290
A warrior Trojan-armed, even Agelaus,
Son of Phradmōn. Verily had he turned his steeds
Retreating but, while wheeling 'round, Diomedes'
Spearcast skewered him from behind, between the shoulders
Impaling him; so plummeted he from his car,   295
His armor pealing loudly. And after him came
Agamemnon and Menelaus Atreidai;
And thereafter the Aiantes twain appareled
In valor's vehemence; and next Idomeneus,
And Idomeneus' companion Mērionēs,   300
The like of Enyalius slayer of men;
And Eurypylus next, Euaemōn's splendid son;
And Teucer last, tense taut his backward curving bow.
And behind the shield of Ajax, Telamon's son,
Stood Teucer, Ajax lifting the shield to sideward;   305
And Teucer, sighting occasion and shooting forth,
Would strike a man amid the throng who, now outstretched,
Lay life-curtailed where earlier he stood, while Teucer
Recoiled aback—as a child behind its mother—
Neath Ajax' refulgent shield, its refuge secure.   310

Whom first, then, of Trojans did faultless Teucer take?
Orsilochus first, Ophelestēs, and Daetōr,
Godlike Lycophontēs; and Amopaōn, son
Of Polaemōn; and Ormenus, Melanippus,
And Chromius: these he successively despatched   315
Unto bounteous earth. And thus beholding him
Did Agamemnon, king of men, rejoice, that he
With merciless bow so staggered the Trojan host.
And striding aside him he stood, thus calling him:
"Teucer, son of Telamon, dear soul, true leader   320
Of legions, shoot on, and endure you a beacon
Of Danaan deliverance and testament
To Telamon your sire, who reared and relished you,
A bastard lad abiding within his dwellings.

On him, from the living absented, bring honor. 325
This too I declare, consider it accomplished:
If aegis-bearing Cronidēs and his offspring
Athena grant Ilium's battlement demolished,
Following mine shall your own booty richest be,
Whether tripod, or horses to chariot teamed, 330
Or a woman ascending astride your bedstead."
To him responding replied the peerless Teucer:
"Most glorious issue of Atreus, why induce
Me thus to what I have coveted heretofore?
I never forbear so far as strength sustain me, 335
But from the time we Troyward incited their rout,
Even from that moment have I stayed, awaiting
Bow in hand to stagger them. Eight long-barbed arrows
Have I even now discharged, their tally fully
Lodged in flesh of brazen-battled youth; but this dog 340
Accursed eludes me." He spoke, and from his string let
Fly another dart at Hector straight, his spirit
Compelled to shoot. But Hector he missed, skewering
With his shaft the groin of goodly Gorgythiōn,
Glorious son of Priam, who was consort to his 345
Mother, even exquisite Castianeira,
From Aesymē brought, in beauty a goddess born.
And as bends a garden poppy by bulk its own
And by vernal-showered droplets, drooping its head;
So sideward slouched the helmet-laden warrior's head. 350

And Teucer from his string shot another arrow
Against Hector straight, his heart constrained to smite him,
But again missed his mark—for Phoebus caused the dart
To swerve aside; but smote he Archeptolemus,
Hector's charioteer, on the breast by the nipple 355
As forward he bolted to battle and discord.
As he pitched from the car, the rapid-pounding steeds
Reared sideward, recoiling, and languished there his life.
And dread sorrow for his driver's sake enshrouded

BOOK VIII

Hector's heart; yet there he forsook him, embittered 360
For his companion's demise. And Cebrionēs,
His sibling, happening nearby, he commanded
Assume the horses' reins; and, hearing, he failed not
To obey. And Hector, from his radiant car
Dismounted groundward, dreadfully shouting aloud; 365
And stone taking to hand, rushed on Teucer, hellbent
On attacking him. And now from out his quiver
Had Teucer drawn a bitter shaft, to his bowstring
Nocking it firm, yet even as he drew it back,
Bright-helmeted Hector dashed the raging archer 370
With jagged stone where collarbone and shoulder met,
Twixt neck and breast—mortal the spot—and palsied grew
His hand about the wrist, and sank he to his knees,
And weakened thus, released the bow from out his grip.
But observing his brother's collapse, ran Ajax 375
And bestrode him sure, with buckler concealing him
Completely. Then stooped his companions beneath him,
Even Echius, Mecisteus' son and goodly
Alastōr, and shipward conveyed him groaning loud.

Then again in Trojan hearts the Olympian 380
Marshaled might, and to the gaping ditch repulsed they
The Danaans; and amid the foremost Hector
Drove, exultant in might. And as the hunter hound
Swift-footed stalks its prey, lion or feral swine,
Biting at it buttock and flank from close behind, 385
Waiting that it wheel about; no less did Hector
Restrict the flowing-haired Achaeans, the hindmost
Ever cutting down; and they to rout were driven.
But from their rout past picket and trench retreating,
Butchered the while beneath Trojan hands, they halted, 390
Gath'ring by their ships, each to the other calling,
And heavenward extended their hands, offering
Impassioned multitudinous supplication.
But Hector wheeled his fair-maned horses fully 'round,

His eyes the Gorgon's or war god's, waster of men; 395
And observing them, the goddess white-armed Hera
Took pity and forthwith in wingèd words addressed
Athena: "Alas, child of aegis-bearing Zeus,
Shall we inattentive remain to this slaughter
Of Danaans, shriveled their wretched destinies, 400
As this warrior, this Hector, pounces—Priam's son,
Whose rampage eclipses all patience? And alas
For the ills he inflicts." And to her responded
The goddess flashing-eyed Athena: "Sooner might
This fellow forfeit life and limb in his native 405
Land, by Argives slain; but rages dire-minded Zeus
My father—the reprobate—obstacle ever
To my purpose; nor recollects he how often
To Heracles' rescue I arrived, his lineage
Beleaguered by labors imposed by Eurystheus. 410
For ever to heaven Heracles cried, and thence
Would Zeus send me, Heracles' helper. Had I Zeus'
Present plan foreseen, then when Eurystheus ordered
Heracles to the warden Hades' domicile
To wrest from Erebus the loathsome hellish hound, 415
Never from dizzying eddy of river Styx
Had Heracles returned. But Zeus now detests me,
Bringing Thetis' design to fruition, she who
Kissed his knees and stroked his chin, exhorting kudos
For Achilles sacker of cities. But the day 420
Shall doubtless come when again he designates me
Darling flashing-eyed. But as for us, now ready
You our single-hoovèd horses the while I visit
Aegis-bearing Zeus' high-roofed abode and, for fight
Appareled, ascertain whether Priam's offspring, 425
Even Hector flashing-helmed, rejoices when we
The twain our stations take astride the battlement.
Sooner will dismembered Trojan multitudes glut
Bird and canine with fatted flesh, slain by the ships
Of the Achaeans."

BOOK VIII

So she spoke, and the goddess 430
White-armed Hera failed not to attend; and nearing
The gold-frontleted horses harnessed them—even
Hera venerate goddess, great Cronus' daughter.
But Athena, daughter of aegis-bearing Zeus,
To her father's floor let fall her richly broidered 435
Robe, limpid silken apparel that she herself
Had labored making, product of her handiwork,
And 'round her wrapped the tunic of Zeus, convener
Of clouds, and decked her in armor for dreadful war.
Then mounted she the flaming car and seized her spear, 440
Sturdy, massive, and huge, wherewith she vanquishes
The ranks of men, of heroes with whom she is wroth,
A puissant father's child. And Hera hastening,
Set the horses on, promptly applying the lash.
And on their hinges groaned of their own accord broad 445
Heaven's gates—by heaven's lofty dwellers assigned
The Hours to guard, whether wide dispersing the night
Or fast hemming it in. There through the gates they drove
Their goaded steeds. But when father Zeus from Ida
Discerned them, full indignant he grew, despatching 450
Golden-winged Iris his messenger: "Depart you,
Swiftest Iris, repel them, permit you not their
Entry to provoke me thus, for to failed effect
Between us shall such conflict come. For thus I speak,
And truly shall it transpire: beneath their chariots 455
Will their crazèd horses hobbled be and themselves
From out their chariot thrown, the cars a ruin wrought.
Nor for a decade's course of circling years shall they
Be comforted from wounds, wherewith the thunderbolt
Consume them, that my daughter flashing-eyed discern 460
The father whom she challenges; whilst for Hera
The slighter my wrath and disfavor, given she
Is ever wont to thwart whatever I ordain."

So he spoke and, bearing the tidings, rose Iris

Storm-footed, forth faring from pinnacled Ida 465
To lofty Olympus; and there—gaining the gate
Of abundant-ridged Olympus—arrested them,
Speaking Zeus' command: "Whither hasten you, and whence
Your driven dispositions? The son of Cronus
Forbids the Danaans this assistance, and thus 470
Threatens the repercussion: beneath your chariots
Will your crazèd horses hobbled be and yourselves
From out your chariots thrown, the cars a ruin wrought.
Nor for a decade's course of circling years shall you
Be comforted from wounds, wherewith the thunderbolt 475
Consumes you; that you, his flashing-eyed girl, discern
The father whom you challenge; whilst against Hera
The slighter his wrath and disfavor, given she
Is ever wont to thwart whatever he ordains.
But a bold and barefaced bitch are you, proposing 480
To flaunt afore your father's face your heinous spear."

Thus threatening, swift-footed Iris departed.
But addressing Athena, spoke Hera: "Alas,
You child of aegis-bearing Zeus, truly now, will
I abstain from seeking to battle Cronidēs 485
For mortalkind. Of mortalkind let fail the one,
Succeed the other, as may befall. As for Zeus,
By his heart's own counsel be he guided, and judge
Alike for Trojans and Danaans as befits."
So speaking, she turned the uncloven horses back, 490
And the Hours, unfastening the flowing-maned teams,
To stalls ambrosial tethered them, the chariots
Settling atilt to the shimmering inner wall.
And the goddesses sat themselves on gilded thrones
In spirit sore dismayed amid the other gods. 495
But Cronidēs from Ida drove his well-wheeled car
And team to th' immortals' gathering, and for him
Th' acclaimed earthshaking Poseidon unyoked the team,
The chariot setting on a stand, a coverlet

BOOK VIII

Thereover cast; and stentorian Zeus ascended 500
His gilded throne, and beneath his feet great heaven
Quaked. Alone sat Hera and Athena, from Zeus
Apart, neither questioning nor attending him.
But he intuited all, speaking thus: "Why grieve
You, Hera and Athena? Surely you tire not 505
Of posting Trojans to battle where men win praise,
Thus feeding the hate you nurture them. Nonetheless,
Because my hands and might are irrepressible,
As many the gods on Olympus lodged could not
Deter me. Recollect how tremors, possessing 510
Your pliant limbs, once seized you ere ever you had
Tested battle and warfare's waste. For thus I speak,
And truly were it done: not in your chariot, when
Blasted by my thunderbolt, would you have entered
This demesne where deities keep their domiciles." 515
So he proclaimed, and Athena and Hera groused
The while, sitting aside him, contriving troubles
For Trojans. And Athena, keeping silent, said
Nothing, because distempered by her father Zeus
And fiercely vexed withal.
                   But lady Hera's breast 520
O'erboiled with bile and she belabored him, saying:
"Dreadest son of Cronus, what word declare you thus!
Well know we ourselves your insup'rable power,
Yet we pity the Achaeans, those perishing,
By hateful fate confounded. Yet from fight shall we 525
Forbear as you command, while providing guidance
To the Argives, to their advantage best suited
That, to your wrath abandoned, they not perish all."
Answering her, cloud-gathering Zeus responded:
"At sunrise will you sooner see, ox-eyed queenly 530
Hera mine, the son of Cronus, most mightily
Preeminent, rain grievous havoc on the host
Of Argive spearmen; for o'erpowering Hector
Shall not from battle cease 'til swift-footed Peleus'

Son be revealed, from his Argive vessel ventured, 535
That day when bow to stern they ferociously fight
Over fallen Patroclus, for thus of heaven
Is it ordained. And your dudgeon I deem as naught
Though descend you the bottommost extremes of earth
And ocean's realm, where Titans Iapetus endure, 540
And Cronus, wanting the warmth of Hyperion's
Beams and benevolent breezes, and harrowing
Hell encloses them about. Though hellbound reckoned
Your destination, yet consider I your wrath
A will-o'-the-wisp, bitch unbettered that you are." 545
So he spoke, and white-armed Hera responded not.

To Ocean retreated the lustrous sun, veiling
The visage of grain-giving earth. For the Trojans
Then ended the glistering day despondently;
But for the Achaeans, thrice-sought and pleasing came 550
Gloomy night. And glorious Hector convened his host
Apart the ships, forth summoning them on vacant
Ground aside an eddied stream where most the terrain
Showed clear of corpses. Forth stepped they from their chariots,
Attending unto Hector belovèd of Zeus, 555
Who rallied them. In his hand he wielded a spear
Of eleven cubits' length, whereupon the point
Shone bright with bronze, 'round it running a ring of gold.
Leaning thereon, spoke he thus among the Trojans:
"Attentive be, you Trojans and Dardanians 560
And allies all: I had reckoned to wreak havoc
Upon the Argives and their vessels, thereafter
Returning to windswept Troy; but darkness approached,
Allowing respite to the Argives and their ships
Aside the breakered sea. For now, at least, we yield 565
To dark'ning night, our supper preparing. Loosen
Your fair-maned horses and set fodder before them
And from Ilium straightway convey you oxen
And fatted sheep, and bring you honey-hearted wine

BOOK VIII

And bread from out your homes, and further gather you 570
Plenteous wood, and the nighttime through ignite we
Bountiful fires a'front the dawn, their radiance
Heaven-reaching, lest the flowing-haired Greeks by night
Escape, absconding on spacious ocean's passage.
No, let not a man of them unanguished embark, 575
Nor easily; but let their ranks be homeward come
With wounds to worry for, from arrow or sharpened
Weapon as vesselward they veer, that others fret
To mete war's dolorous trials upon horse-taming
Trojans. And let heralds dear to Zeus throughout Troy 580
Proclaim that stripling youth and hoary-templed men
Convene about the town upon the battlement;
And let the womenfolk, and each of them, kindle
Bonfires at their doors; and let studious watch
Be kept lest the city fall ambushed and captured 585
While absent the men. So be it, great-spirited
Trojans, even as I state; and shrewd my counsel
Prove and sufficient for now. But this at daybreak
Shall I speak to attentive horse-taming Trojans:
Zeus and the other gods I ardently implore 590
To cast these curs away, to their own fates forfeit
Whom their fates here ferried on warring ships. Tonight,
However, shall we of our own selves mindful be;
But early, ere dawn, in our battle gear arrayed,
Awaken we sharp combat by the hollow ships. 595
Then shall I perceive whether Diomedes, great
Tydeus' son, thrust me against the Argive rampart
Away from the Argive ships or—if slaying him
With brazen spear—I decamp with his bloody spoils.
Tomorrow shall he value his own manliness, 600
Assuming he withstand my spearpoint's swift approach.
Sooner, I surmise, amid the foremost shall he
Stricken lie at the rising of tomorrow's sun
With many the comrade looking on. Ah, would I
Were undying, even ageless, throughout my days 605

237

And, as Athena and Apollo, exalted
As this day now visits evil on the Argives."
So Hector addressed them, and the Trojans shouted
Approval. And from under their yokes they released
Their sweaty steeds, tethering them with thongs, each man   610
Fast by his chariot; and quickly from out the town
Brought they oxen and fat sheep, supplying themselves;
And from home storage bread and honey-hearted wine
And wood as well, sufficiently cut, offering
Sacrificial fats whereof the coiled scent wafted   615
Heavenward from the plain below high spiraling.

These then, puissant at heart throughout the tiring war,
Deferred to night, their fires aflame in multitudes.
Even as when in heaven 'round the radiant moon
The stars shine stately forth as windless wanes the air,   620
And to view revealed rise mountain peaks, and headlands
High, and wooded vales—and infinite the aether
Neath from heaven cleft—and discretely stand the stars,
And rejoices the shepherd at heart; thus the fires
In their fabled multitudes between the vessels   625
And Xanthus refulgent that the Trojans kindled
A'front the face of Ilium; a thousand fires
Each upon the plain, by each sitting fifty men
In the glinting incandescence; and their horses,
On barley whites and rice-wheat sated, stood erect   630
Aside their cars awaiting rosy-fingered Dawn.

~ Book IX ~

The Embassy to Achilles: Agamemnon Seeks to Reconcile Achilles with Gifts

After the preceeding day's defeat, Agamemnon proposes quitting the war and returning home. Diomedes opposes the idea, challenging Agamemnon to leave if he wishes but insisting that he and the others will stay and fight. Nestor praises Diomedes for his wisdom and resolve but without necessarily endorsing his proposal. Nestor urges a strengthening of the guard and the convening of a dinner-council at Agamemnon's tent to consider the deteriorating situation. Agamemnon follows this advice.

After dinner, Nestor raises the issue of Brisēïs, and of Achilles' slighted honor, urging that Agamemnon make amends. Agamemnon in turn admits to his *atē* 'madness' and willingness to be reconciled. He enumerates, in catalogue fashion, the many gifts he will offer. Among them is Brisēïs herself, on account of whose theft Achilles has withdrawn (Agamemnon swearing never to have slept with her). Nestor convinces Agamemnon to send three envoys, chosen by Nestor himself: Telamonian Ajax, Odysseus, and the elderly Phoenix (Phoenix appearing only here in the *Iliad*, though elsewhere mentioned). The choices, though unexplained, are nonetheless apparent: Ajax' appeal will be soldierly; Odysseus', subtly persuasive; and Phoenix', both paradigmatic (relying on mythological precedent) and emotional (Phoenix once Achilles' mentor and father figure).

As the envoys approach, they find the most epic of epic heroes playing the bard: Achilles, to lyre self-accompaniment, singing *klea andrōn* 'the glories of men'. These, more specifically, are *klea andrōn/(h)ērōōn* 'the glories of men who were heroes/warriors'. We marvel as the greatest epic hero of all, semidivine of a goddess born, seeks the consolations of epic poetry. The words no less than the subject of Achilles' song are strategically withheld, though the fact alone of his resort to epic poetry says much for the genre's development and its principal theme of transcendent glory. Achilles is the only Iliadic hero who sings epic poetry. Through him we enter a mirrored vestibule where the ancient hero reflects on heroes more ancient yet; the epic genre reflecting on itself.

It is tempting to think that Achilles sings of Meleager, the protagonist of the famed Calydonian Boar Hunt. The hunt was an earlier Greek-hero unifying expedition (like the *Iliad* itself), and the parallels between Meleager's and Achilles' situations are instructive. We are thus not surprised to find this the subject of Phoenix' exhortation, even as Phoenix tenderly recalls his days as Achilles' "nursemaid"—burping him at the supper table. It is noted that the Greek of the Meleager story in Phoenix' exhortation (*Il.* 9.624-643) is disjointed, to say the least—likely drawn from different but here unsynthesized versions of the tale. We assume the original audience, knowing the essentials of the story in full, made sense enough of the *Iliad*'s telling. To minimize confusion, I have replaced certain pronouns with proper names.

Cordially receiving the envoys, Achilles rejects each of their entreaties. He does so passionately and at length because he sees through Agamemnon's self-serving hypocrisy, loathes it, and will not be had for the buying. It is Achilles' singularly impassioned moment and, as Homer portrays it, the apex of Achilles' insight into the heroic code to which he has committed his life. It is also Achilles' *challenge* to the heroic code, insofar as he now appreciates that valor and personal integrity—in a word, *merit*—lack just reward.

Ajax and Odysseus return to the Greek camp, but Phoenix (at Achilles' request) stays the night—from a sense of Achilles' affection for him, as we may assume, or as a small "moral victory," showing Achilles' influence over one of the envoys.

Note that Achilles is here variously referred to as "Achilles," "Pēlēïdēs," "Aeacus' son," or "Aeacus' offspring" (see p. 59), usages dictated by meter or preferred for poetic affect.

❧

Thus watched the Trojans, but Consternation, comrade
Of gruesome Rout, had commandeered the Achaeans,
And beset past forbearance were their commanders,
Of mettle bereft; and endured they one and all

BOOK IX

Dismayed. As when twin blasts bestir the teeming main,   5
The Zephyr and Northerly angered grown from Thrace
Of a sudden coming on, and crest the darkling
Swells together ascendant; the wrack and tangle
Strewn upon the sea; even so lay Argive hearts
Within their breasts asunder rent. But Atreus' son,   10
With misgiving past suff'rance suffused, labored this
Way and that, instructing the resonant heralds
To summon each Argive to meeting, naming him,
But not shouting aloud; and amid the foremost
Struggled he. And thus gathered they, sitting aggrieved,   15
And stood Agamemnon shedding a tear, even
As a dark-watered fountain over precipice
Spilling its dusky stream; even so, deep groaning,
Addressed he the Argives, announcing: "My brethren,
Argive leaders and rulers: Cronus' son, great Zeus,   20
Has embroiled me in piteous blindness of heart,
Cruel god, that aforetime did promise and assent
That, after sacking well-walled Troy, I would homeward
Return, but now has crafted a callous deceit
And orders me Argos-bound, ingloriously,   25
The while so many have perished. Thus, I surmise,
It pleases Zeus, his sway supreme, who has toppled
The fortresses of many towns, and will topple
Others yet, for unalloyed his might. But come now,
Even as I bid, obey you: flee we away   30
On our curvèd ships to our native land; vanished
Our hope that Troy's vast avenues be overturned."
So he proclaimed, and to silence were they tempered.

Long quiet the Achaeans sat, and sorrowing,
But at length Diomedes battle-cry acclaimed   35
Declared among them: "Son of Atreus, first with you,
As well befits among these mustered, will I deal,
For your folly of heart, O King, and thus nowise
Be you wroth with me. Earlier among the Argives

You belittled my bravery, calling me weak 40
And unwarlike, and this the Achaeans observed,
Young and old. But for you, dividedly, the son
Of crooked-minded Cronus disposition made:
By sceptre he granted you honor surpassing
But denied you valor, where greatest power lies. 45
Strange king, thus think you the sons of the Achaeans
Weaklings and unwarlike, as you claim? No! Be your
Own heart ready to return, then hasten you now;
Before you lies the way, your ships to seaward set,
Which followed you in multitudes from Mycenae. 50
But remain we other flowing-haired Achaeans
'Til Trojan towers be shattered. Or, let them also
Reembark, returned to their longed-for native land;
Yet Sthenelus and I, we twain, will battle on,
'Til Troy be taken, for with heaven's help we come." 55

So he proclaimed, and the sons of the Achaeans
Shouted their assent, applauding Diomedes,
Tamer of horses. Uprising, then, spoke horseman
Nestor among them: "Son of Tydeus, surpassing
In battle's craft are you; and in council, of those 60
Your own age best. None of the Danaans in their
Multitudes would deride or contradict your word.
Yet idly you speak; in truth, you are young, and could
Be son my own, my youngest born. Yet, prudently
Counsel you Argive kings, holding forth as befits. 65
Yet, In truth, your elder affirmed, will I respond,
My word to accomplishment come; nor shall comment
Of mine be scorned, not even by Agamemnon.
A kinless, lawless, hearthless man is he who loves
Harrowing strife among his very own. But now, 70
At present, to night's descent be we surrendered,
Anticipating supper; and at intervals
Let guards stand watch along the ditch without the wall.
To the young men thus I command; but thereafter,

BOOK IX

Agamemnon, take you control, for most kingly   75
You stand. Fix you a feast for the elders. Fitting
And rightly done were this. From out your huts o'erflows
The Thracian wine Danaan vessels bring each day,
Delivered you the wide sea o'er; divertissements
Have you at hand, ruling lordly over many,   80
And 'midst the many here assembled shall you heed
The wisest considered plan; since desperate the need
Of the Danaans for measures well considered.
Adjacent our ships stands the foe arrayed, watchfires
Flaunted. What warrior in the prospect takes comfort?   85
This night shall either ruin our host or save it."

So he spoke, and swiftly they hearkened and obeyed.
Forth rushed the armored sentinels 'round Nestor's son,
Thrasymēdēs, shepherd of the host, and around
Ascalaphus and Ialmenus, Ares' sons,   90
And around Mēriones and famed Aphareus
And Deïpyrus, and Creon's offspring, goodly
Lycomedes. Seven captains governed the guards,
And with each went a hundred youths, long spears to hand,
And sat they coming midway trench and wall between,   95
And set fires a'light, their meals making ready each.
But Atreus' son led the assembled Achaean
Counselors to his hut, and laid banquet before them,
To their desire, abundantly. Then cast they hands
On the victuals set before them. But when they had   100
Satisfied desire of food and drink, directly
Nestor the elder commenced weaving counsel's web,
Even Nestor, whose plan appeared best aforetime.
He with true intent addressed them, counseling thus:
"Gloried Atreus' son, Agamemnon, king of men,   105
With you I start, no less than with you concluding.
You are ruler over multitudes, and sceptre
Has Zeus vouchsafed you, and acumen, that for your
Folk you rule clear-sighted. Thus befits it that you

Beyond all others not only speak but hearken, 110
Accepting counsel for the common betterment,
When hearts bid others speak; for any proposal
Will by you determined be. So will I declare
What to me seems fitting, and no person other
Shall readily devise a better plan than that 115
Which I propose, now and aforetime, since the day,
O Zeus-nurtured King, whereon you seized Brisēïs
From wroth Achilles, fast leaving his hut—flouting
Our judgment, for all I ventured to dissuade you;
But to your lordly mettle you succumbed, scorning 120
A surpassing man, by the immortals themselves
Distinguished, for you took—and keep—his honor's meed.
However, let us quickly contemplate amends,
Persuading him with kindly gifts and gentle words."

To him responded Agamemnon, king of men: 125
"Old sir, not falsely recounted stands my folly;
Purblind was I and deny it not. The value
Of many men is he whom Zeus to heart receives,
As he even now honors this man, dismantling
The Argive ranks. Yet, given I was blind, yielding 130
To my lamented passion, desire I to make
Amends, offering ample recompense. The gifts
Then, distinguished all, shall I among you number:
Seven tripods by flame untouched, and ten talents
Of gold, and twenty copper cauldrons, and horses 135
A dozen, race-enlaureled, fabled their fleetness;
Nor lacking gain nor unpossessed of precious gold
Whoe'er won riches equaling those awarded
Agamemnon for his steeds. And further seven
Women will I gift, skilled in goodly handiwork, 140
Women of famed Lesbos whom when he took Lesbos
Upon a time, I selected from the pillage,
Those far surpassing all women in grace. The like
Shall I give, and among them her whom I purloined,

BOOK IX

The dear daughter of Briseus, and swear evermore 145
A mighty oath, to have never mounted her bed
Nor dalliance indulged with her, as custom allows
Alike for man and womankind. And should the gods
The taking grant of Priam's high-towering town,
Then enter he therein as we Danaans split 150
The spoils, and heap his hulls with gold and bronze enough,
Himself taking twenty Trojan women, fairest
After Argive Helen. And if to Achaean
Argos and its verdant lands returned, son-in-law
Shall he become to me, and I will honor him 155
Even as Orestes, in prosperity reared,
Belovèd son of mine. In my porticos three
Daughters have I: Chrysothemis, Laodicē,
And Iphianassa. Of these let him escort
To Peleus' house, lord of th' ashen-spear, the maiden 160
He adores, from bridal gifts exempt. And further
Redress I propose: a splendid dowry displayed,
The like unto has daughter ne'er afforded been,
And seven populated cities will I give,
Cardamylē, Enopē, and grassy Hīrē, 165
And hallowed Pherae, and deep-meadowed Antheia,
Fair Aepeia, and vineyarded Pedasus, all
On sandy Pylos' promontories nigh the sea.
And within dwell men in flocks and kine afflúent,
Men whose generous gifts shall acclaim him a god 170
And neath his sceptre steer his laws to flourishing
Fulfillment. This for him will I effectuate,
If he but renounce his wrath. Let him relent—Death
Alone is neither mollified nor overcome,
Wherefore stands he by humankind detested most 175
Of deities. So, let that man defer to me
The more kingly being and elder begotten."

Then responded horseman Gerēnian Nestor:
"Atreus' son acclaimed, Agamemnon, king of men,

Nowise paltry the gifts you offer Pēleidēs; 180
But come, let us quickly despatch selected men
To the tent of Pēleidēs Achilles; nay, those
Whom I select, and let them comply. First of all
Let Phoenix, Zeus-beloved, command the way; and next
Great Ajax and goodly Odysseus, the heralds 185
Eurybatēs and Odius attending them.
But now pour water for our hands, and reverent
Silence be maintained, while we confer devotions
On Zeus Cronidēs for compassion on us all."

So he spoke, and pleasing to them was his saying. 190
And the heralds poured water o'er their hands, and youths
To overflowing filled the mixing bowls, offpouring
Next, to every cup, first droplets for libation.
So, pouring libations and consuming all they
Desired, they departed Agamemnon's tent; 195
And horseman Gerēnian Nestor commanded
Them, with piercing glances each, and especially
Odysseus, to determine how best to prevail
Upon peerless Achilles. So they proceeded,
Traversing spacious ocean's reverberant strain, 200
With ample petition to kingly Poseidon,
Encircler of Earth, that they readily persuade
The stalwart heart of Aeacus' son. And came they
To the tents and ships of Achilles' men, finding
Him with lissome lyre—richly wrought, silver the bridge 205
Upon it—delighting his soul; the lyre a spoil
From Ēëtion's citadel plundered aforetime.
Therewith gladdened he his spirit, the gloried deeds
Of warriors recounting, with Patroclus seated
Quietly alone across from him, awaiting 210
That Aeacus' offspring make pause of his singing.
Escorted by goodly Odysseus advanced they,
Standing squarely before him, and Pēleïdēs,
Lyre in hand, leapt in amazement forth, forsaking

BOOK IX

The seat whereon he sat. And beholding the men,
Stood Patroclus too. Then swift-footed Achilles   215
Delivered this greeting: "Welcome be unto you
And your arrival—sore must be the need—you that
Despite my temper are dearest of Danaans."
So saying did godly Achilles show them in,   220
On purple carpets and couches reposing them,
And straightway summoned Patroclus standing nearby:
"Son of Menoetius, a larger crater bring you,
Stronger beverage mix, and drinking cups dispense,
For cherished beneath my roof be these men arrived." 225

So he spoke, and Patroclus attended his friend's
Command. Then lowered he a grill, a sturdy one,
To the gleaming fire, with chine of goat and fatted
Sheep, with hog's back greased and plump. And Automēdōn
Steadied them all while the godlike Achilles carved. 230
Then sectioned he the meat with care and spitted it
On skewers, and the son of Menoetius, godlike
His aspect, set the fire ablaze. But when the fire
Was waste, and lessening waned the flame, he dampened
The embers and overlaid the spits, and sprinkled   235
With sacred salt the viands on spit-racks arranged.
And when the meat was roasted through, and on platters
Placed, Patroclus took the bread, apportioning it
In decorate baskets upon the board; and dealt
Achilles the meat, sitting across exalted   240
Odysseus, by the opposite wall, and ordered
His companion Patroclus to make offering;
And to the flame cast he sacrificial portions.
They extended their hands to the fare positioned
Before them; but when the desire of food and drink   245
Was satisfied, then nodded Ajax to Phoenix,
And goodly Odysseus noted it and, filling
A cup with wine, thus offered a salutation:

"Hail, Achilles! Lack we no feasting's allotment
Either in Agamemnon Atreïdēs' hut, 250
Or presently here; for here be feast best suited
To spirit and resolve. However, rich repast
Is presently trifling, given our reversal!
No, Zeus-begotten prince, pernicious the outcome
We see approaching—our vessels' predicament, 255
Whether safely they abide or perish—unless,
Appareled in might, you return. The high-hearted
Trojans, their glorious allies too, at the ships
And by the parapet raise encampments, bonfires
Kindling throughout their host, no longer intending 260
Deferral, but sooner our vessels' destruction.

And Zeus, son of Cronus, his omens to rightward,
Hurls lightning; and Hector, greatly exhilarate,
Rages frenziedly on, in Cronidēs trusting,
Reckoning not of any man or deity, 265
His choler in command. He prays that sacred Dawn
Will hastening, come; claims that he from the topmost
Stern of every ship its ensign will detach, full
Flame to every vessel furnish, and havoc loose
Upon the Greeks afflictedly inhaling smoke. 270
And dreadfully fear I this as well, that the gods
His boasts fulfill, and we be fated to perish
In Troyland here, far from horse-pasturing Argos.
But up, if determined you stand, however late,
To rescue your Argive companions, exhausted 275
From tumult of hostility. Later will grief
Attend you, wanting remedy to mitigate
The hurt once wrought. Rather, good friend, as advances
The hour, ponder the thwarting of doomsday's decree.
For surely Peleus, your father, admonished you, 280
That day despatching you from Phthia to follow
Agamemnon: 'Son of mine, strength shall Athena
And Hera bestow, so be their intent, but tame

BOOK IX

You that prideful impulse lodged within, kindliness
Being better. Be done with rancor ill-contrived, 285
That the Argives, young and old alike, more highly
Honor you.' So the elder directed, but naught
Do you recall. Yet, forbear even now; from heart-
Rending anger refrain. Confers Agamemnon
Largesse if you but relinquish your rage. But come, 290
Attend you well the riches I enumerate,
Those hoarded in his tents, that Atreus' son affirms:

Seven tripods by flame untouched, and ten talents
Of gold, and twenty copper cauldrons, and horses
A dozen, race-enlaureled, fabled their fleetness; 295
Nor lacking gain nor unpossessed of precious gold
Whoe'er won riches equaling those awarded
Agamemnon for his steeds. And further seven
Women will he give, skilled in goodly handiwork,
Women of Lesbos, whom when you took Lesbos 300
Upon a time, he selected from the pillage,
Those far surpassing all women in grace. The like
Shall he give, and among them her whom he purloined,
The dear daughter of Briseus, and swear evermore
A mighty oath: never to have mounted her bed 305
Nor dalliance indulged with her, as custom allows
Alike for man and womankind. And should the gods
Grant the taking of Priam's high-towering town,
Then enter you within as we Danaans split
The spoils, and heap your hulls with gold and bronze enough, 310
Yourself taking twenty Trojan women, fairest
After Argive Helen. And if to Achaean
Argos and its verdant lands returned, son-in-law
Shall you become to him, and he will honor you
Even as Orestes, in prosperity reared, 315
His well-belovèd son. In his porticos three
Daughters has he: Chrysothemis, Laodicē,
And Iphianassa; of these may you escort

249

To Peleus' house, lord of th' ashen-spear, the maiden
You adore, from bridal gifts exempt. And further   320
Redress he presents: a splendid dowry displayed,
The like unto has daughter ne'er afforded been;
And seven populated cities will he give,
Cardamylē, Enopē, and grassy Hirē,
And sacred Pherae and deep-meadowed Antheia,   325
Fair Aepeia, and vineyarded Pedasus. All
On sandy Pylos' promontories nigh the sea,
And within dwell men in flocks and kine affluent,
Men whose generous gifts shall acclaim you a god,
And neath your sceptre steer your laws to flourishing   330
Fulfillment. This for you will he effectuate,
If you but renounce your wrath. But if Atreidēs
Agamemnon be detested to your heart—he
And his gifts—take pity, then, on the other Pan-
Achaeans anguished throughout the host; for godlike   335
Will these regard you, and verily shall you gain
Great glory in their eyes. Now might you slay Hector
Who in woeful despite would brazenly approach,
Boasting no Argive his equal revealed of those
To Priam's city arrived on the teeming main."   340

Answering him swift-footed Achilles replied:
"Zeus-born son of Laërtes', mindful Odysseus,
I speak my response of necessity outright,
Even as I think it and determine it done,
That seated in my presence you from prattle cease;   345
For hateful to me as th' entrance to Hell itself
Is that person concealing one thing in his mind
Yet speaking another. Rather, speak I what best
Appears to me. Not in the least shall Atreus' son
Agamemnon persuade me, nor any Argive,   350
Since this battle by all accounts has bootless been,
And against a hostile foe unending. Equal
The outcome of evasion or of hardihood,

BOOK IX

And like station the hero and coward command,
While diligent and idle alike a common 355
Death consumes. Nor enjoy I anything for trials
Of heart, for life hazarded at war. So the bird
Brings morsels to her chicks, whatever she may find,
But herself fares far the worse; even thus have I
Through sleepless nights and blood-bespattered days endured 360
Contesting with Achaeans on their wive's account.
Twelve the demesnes of men I demolished by fleet,
To these by land eleven added, Troy's fertile
Fields throughout. From all of them I impounded spoils,
Prized and plentiful, the lot of which to Atreus' 365
Son, Agamemnon here, I e'er deposited,
Which he, at leisure by his ships malingering,
Took, allotting some—a piddling part—the better
Part retaining. Some he apportioned as prizes
To princes and kings, which for them remain intact; 370
But from me alone, of the Danaans all, does
He appropriate my wife, my delectation.
Let him beside her bedded pleasure take. But why
Must Trojans and Danaans thus contend? And why
Has he Troyward mustered and brought his host, this son 375
Of Atreus? Was it not for fair-haired Helen's sake?
Do these sons of Atreus twain alone of mortal
Men adore their wives? No, whoe'er is consort true
And sound of mind his own adores and dotes upon;
Thus I adored her with all my heart, though spear-bride 380
By pedigree. But now that he appropriates
My honor's prize, purloined from my embrace, swindling
Me evermore, desist he from this trial of me
Who knows him well; not the least shall he persuade me.
But with you, Odysseus, and the Danaans all, 385
Safeguard he from ravenous flame the ships well kept.
Verily, much in my absence has he achieved:
A wall has he built and driven a ditch hard by—
Wide and great it stands—and positioned stakes therein,

Their employment against Hector, slayer of men, 390
Unavailing. But while amid the Argives I
Contended, never would Hector foment the fight
Beyond the Trojan rampart, but would dare advance
To the Scaean Gates alone, and oak tree. There once
In combat, man to man, he withstood me, barely 395
Surviving my onset. But now, since with goodly
Hector I decline to be engaged, tomorrow
Will I sacrifice to heaven's dwellers, stocking
My vessels full, when seaward they embark. Then note
You, if you will, and if you any interest take, 400
My dawn-resplendent vessels astride the teeming
Hellespont, my men eagerly plying the oar.
And should earthshaking Poseidon fair passage grant,
The third day my coming to fertile Phthia home,
My possessions, plenteously warehoused, awaiting 405
My return, from the time I first ventured to Troy.
With even more shall I return: with ample gold,
Grey iron, burnished bronze, and fair-cinctured women:
All that I by lot obtained. Yet, repossessed is
My prize by him who first provided it—scornful 410
His pride—high-handed Atreidēs Agamemnon.
To him announce you this, even as I enjoin:
Let the Danaans e'ermore discontented be
Should he thus endeavor another to oppose,
Appareled his might in impudence. Yet from me 415
He concealeth his gaze, steeped in depravity.
Not in strategy nor deed will I assist him
Who, by impudent transgression, inveigles me
Surpassingly. Never again his knavery!
But be he ruined at his ease, since counselor 420
Zeus Cronidēs sequesters his judgment away.
Abhorrent his gifts, a whittle's worth regarded.
Not should he ten and twenty times the sum bestow
Of his possessions all, and yet more, deriving
I care not whence: not the treasure accumulate 425

BOOK IX

In Orchomenus or Egyptian Thebes, where wealth
In handsome store lies heaped in men's abodes—yes, Thebes,
Where hurtling forth from each a hundred gates soldiers
Twice a hundred with horses and chariots alight;
Nor should he gifts confer, their aggregate the sum   430
Of sand and dust; not even thus shall Atreidēs
Disjoin me from my pain, 'til ousted the offense
That rankles me past reckoning. Agamemnon's
Daughter as wife of mine to be I disavow,
Though equal in mien to golden Aphrodite,   435
And in handiwork to gleaming-eyed Athena,
Zeus' daughter. Despite such riches I refuse her.
Some other Argive let him choose, like in station
To himself, the more regal than I. For, preserve
Me heaven and bring me home, then Peleus, I think,   440
Will acceptably marry me off. Danaan
Maidens throughout Phthia and broad Hellas abound,
Daughters of town-protecting potentates; of these
Whomever I select will my belovèd be.
Thus oftentimes my stately spirit prodded me   445
A wooed and wedded wife to take, a fitting mate,
And from Peleus' possessions my pleasures acquire,
As plenteous as the elder had procured; for not
Equal life's worth the wealth entire that Ilium
Tallied aforetime, they say—that well-occupied   450
Citadel, when peace prevailed before e'er arrived
The sons of Achaeans—nor all the marble
On rocky Pytho's portal laid, shrine of th' archer
God Apollo. For cattle may full plundered be
And goodly sheep, and tripods for the lifting had,   455
And dappled steeds withal; but not as captured spoil
May breath of man be repossessed once exited
The barrier of his teeth. For my goddess mother
Silver-footed Thetis declares that matching fates
Attend my doom of death: that, should I here remain,   460
Combatant at Troy, then lost my homecoming day,

253

Though perdure my distinction imperishably;
But if homeward to my belovèd land returned,
Then forfeit I fabled renown while attaining
Life in full abundance, absent sudden demise. 465
And you others, since Ilium's goal evades you,
Be you hastily homeward fled, for mightily
Thundering Zeus, from afar his force afforded,
Extends his hand o'er Troy, and her folk stand resolved
Withal. But quickly go, my word to the Argive 470
Chieftains convey—such being your elder duty—
That they measure the means of a different plan,
One to this superior, to rescue their ships
And the numerous Danaan ranks alongside them,
For nowise at present avails their proposal, 475
As my indignation implacably abides.
However, let old Phoenix here with us remain
And slumber sound, that on the morrow he embark
Aboard my ships to my dear native land returned,
If thus he intend; but by no constraint of mine." 480

So he spoke, and all were to silence quieted,
Astounded at his words; for fearsome was the force
Wherewith he refused them. But at length old horseman
Phoenix, a'burst in tears, replied on their behalf,
Because greatly distressed for the Danaan ships: 485
"If truly you ponder a homeward departure,
Indifferent, O wondrous one, to our rapid ships
Aflame, because anger encompasses your heart,
How then, dear child, can I alone, without you here
Remain? It was to you the old horseman Peleus 490
Assigned me when despatching you from Phthia forth,
A mere child, to Agamemnon, yet unknowing
Of wretched war and empowering assembly
Whence eminence emerges; thus he empowered me
Apace, paramount precept imparting, that you 495
Be a speaker of words and a doer of deeds.

BOOK IX

Wherefore, dear child, no intention have I ever
Distant from you to endure, even should a god
Himself to dispossess me of my dotage pledge,
Endowing me with youthful brawn as on the day   500
I departed Hellas, home of winsome women,
Avoiding discord with Amyntōr, my father,
Ormenus' scion. For greatly angered he grew
On account of his fair-haired concubine, on whom
He ever doted, his wedded wife disdaining,   505
My mother. So e'er she importuned me, clasping
My knees, that I couple with her, that Amyntōr
Find her contemptuous. And thus did I hearken
And acquiesce; but my father, immediately
Cognizant, rained curses upon me, invoking   510
The loathsome Erinyes, that he might never seat
Upon his knees an offspring of me begotten;
And the gods fulfilled his curse, even Lord Hadēs
And dreaded Persephonē. Then I determined
To slay him with sharp-whetted weapon; however,   515
One of the immortals allayed my vexation,
Infusing my spirit with public opinion
And with the stigma of the multitude, that I
Amid the Argives be not parricide proclaimed.
Then was my heart content to tarry no longer   520
Within, there in the halls of my incensèd sire;
And many the fellow and kinsman implored me
Throughout, plenteous their prayers, attempting to stay
Me there within the halls; and many the goodly
Sheep they slaughtered for me, and shamble-gaited kine,   525
With many a fat-swollen swine singeing a'stretch
O'er Hephaestus' flame; and frothy the vintage flown
From the old man's amphorae. For nine nights entire
Kept they watch about my person, their sentinels
In rotation; nor was torch extinguished—one guard   530
Placed below by the well-fenced courtyard portico;
The other on the porch by my bedchamber door.

255

But when settled upon me the tenth ebon night,
Then verily I dashed my crafted chamber doors
And nimbly leapt the courtyard fence, undetected   535
By guards or any household domestic within.
Through spacious Hellas afar I fled, arriving
Next to cultivated Phthia, mother of flocks,
To King Peleus, who received me with ready heart,
And loved me as loves a father his cherished son,   540
His sole begotten and heir to great possessions.
Prosp'rous he made me, providing numerous folk,
And dwelt I at the farthest Phthian boundary,
O'er the Dolopians ruling; and I reared you
The warrior that you are, O godlike Pēleidēs,   545
In my own heart dearest me; for with no other
Would you to banquet go or dinner take until,
Settling you on my knees, I tendered savory
Bits of food, cutting the pieces and providing
You wine; and oft with spittle was my tunic stained, 550
The wine gurgled forth in your infancy's travail.
So have I toiled and suffered much for you, yielding
To heaven's interdiction of offspring of my
Body born. But you have I e'er aspired to make
My son, O Achilles, that you, in time's passage,   555
Redeem me from decrepitude. Thus, Achilles,
Master you your zealousness, for a pitiless
Heart becomes you not. No, even the immortals
Submit, and theirs the greater glory, worth, and might.
Their hearts by petition may from wrath be redeemed, 560
By gifts, earnest prayer, and sacrificial savor
Whene'er a man overreaches in transgression.

For Amends are daughters of mighty Zeus, shriveled,
Squinty-eyed and stumbling; and follow they ever
On foible. But dread is foible and fleet of foot,   565
Wherefore out from under Amends and far forward
Outruns she their ranks, resolutely prevailing

Wherever implanted throughout the earth, harming
Humankind; and then administer the Amends
Their healing powers. Now, whosoe'er respects Zeus' 570
Daughters as he arrives, him they favor, heeding
His appeal; but if one reject them, obstinate,
Gainsaying their power, implore they Cronus' son,
That bewilderment attend him, that he stagger
Until his amends be made. But you, Achilles, 575
Observant be that honor attend Zeus' daughters,
Resolute honor, as minds nobly begotten
Confer. For were Atreus' son not tendering gifts
And promising more hereafter, but persisting
Angrily minded, no warrant then to manage 580
Your wrathful disposition, nor aid the Argives,
Grievous though their need. But gifts innumerable
Proposes he, the more promising hereafter,
And stalwart warriors has he sent, entreating you,
The best selecting from out the Achaean ranks, 585
Those unto yourself deemed dearest and most favored.
Spurn not their proposals nor purpose hither come,
Though your resentment were earlier lacking fault.
So gather we from the glory of men bygone,
Men who were heroes, when wasting wrath consumed them, 590
Appeased were they by off'rings and supplications.

"An occurrence from aforetime I remember,
Its outcome resolute, to you, friends, recounted.
Once the Curētes, with the battle-contentious
Aetolians, fought 'round the town of Calydōn, 595
Slaughtering one another—the Aetolians
Defending lovely Calydōn; the Curētes
Desirous to destroy it. For on Calydōn
Had gold-enthronèd Artemis sent pestilence,
Indignant that Oeneus had withheld the firstlings 600
Of his harvest, the fruits of fertile orchard lands;
While reaped the other gods repast of hecatombs,

And nothing provided he Artemis alone.
Unmindful being or merely inattentive,
Injudicious was Oeneus' mind by all accounts. 605
Wherefore incensed grew the archeress, Zeus' daughter,
Directing against him a calamitous boar,
Wild and white of tusk, wreaking withering damage,
Wasting Oeneus' orchardland, many the massive
Tree uprooting, and heedlessly displanting them 610
Upward from root to apple blossom. But the boar
Did Meleager quell, Oeneus' son, mustering
Huntsmen aplenty and hounds from numerous towns,
For nowise could the burly boar by few be slain,
And to dolorous barrow consigned it huntsmen 615
Aplenty. But for its carcass kindled the god
A din and raucous cry, for the head and shaggy
Hide, between Curētes and great-souled Aetolians.
Now, the while warred Meleager, dear to Ares,
The while beleaguered were the Curētes, nor might 620
They convene outside their walls, though superior
In number. But when wrath beset Meleager,
Wrath augmenting even the spirits of others,
Wise though they be; then, indignant with his mother,
Althaea, lay he consoled alongside his fair 625
Wedded wife, Cleopatra, child of fair-ankled
Marpessa and Idas, she born of Euēnus;
It was Idas, bred strongest of men aforetime,
Who fronted his bow against Phoebus Apollo
For Marpessa's sake, whom the god had abducted. 630
In their halls, Idas and reverent Marpessa
Named Cleopatra Halcyonē thereafter,
Since Marpessa, having once intoned the mournful
Halcyon's cry, wept for far-working Apollo's
Earlier theft of her.
               Thus by Cleopatra 635
Meleager lay, nursing his soul-draining rage,
Angered at Althaea, for she implored the gods,

Ever aggrieved by the death of her dear brother.
And beating bountiful earth, implored she Hades
And dread Persephonē, tearfully staining her 640
Plaited garb, that Meleager her son be slain.
And th' Erinys, goddesses in darkness ensconced,
Implacably disposed, from Erebus heard her.
Then th' enemy's din descended about their gates,
And raged the disruption of battlements besieged, 645
And th' Aetolian elders implored Meleager,
Sending prominent priests and promising fine gifts,
That he bestir himself, defender to the town.
Where Calydōn's fields extended, fully fertile,
There they bade him a fifty-acre tract select, 650
Vineyard the half, arable land the remainder,
To be sectioned from the plain. And Oeneus, the old
Horseman, firmly implored him, astride the entry
To his high-vaulted chamber, pounding the fitted
Doorway and beseeching his son; and his sisters 655
Earnestly entreated him, and honored mother,
But he disavowed them the more, and earnestly
His comrades, to him dearest and truest of all;
Yet they nowise assuaged his disconsolate heart,
Until his own quarters at length were buffeted, 660
And Curētes atop towering turrets torched
The well-walled town. Then truly his fair-girdled wife
With weeping beseeched Meleager, relating
The plenteous travails of men whose town is taken:
The men are slain, and burnt the town to ashen waste, 665
And foes take their children and fair women captive.
Then, hearing the heinous report, was his spirit
Restored, and he left, donning his glittering arms.
Thus from th' Aetolians repelled he the dreadful
Day, to his own heart yielding; but thereafter they 670
Reneged on the promised gifts, plenteous and pleasing,
Notwithstanding he had shielded them. But yourself
Be otherwise disposed nor let heaven turn you,

Dear comrade. Hard it were to salvage ships aflame.
But come, have for the taking these gifts, and godlike   675
Shall the Greeks consider you. But if forfeiting
Gifts you embark upon man-wasting war, the bane
Of men, then forego you the requisite honor,
Though You thwart the foe."
                            Then answering, swift-footed
Achilles responded: "Old Phoenix, my father,   680
Fostered of Zeus, such honor I decline: honored
Instead by Cronidēs' ordinance I abide
Here stationed at my sturdy ships the while life's breath
Remains within my breast and forward my supple
Knees convey me. And this I say; observe it well: 685
Seek not to confound my heart with lamentation
And sorrow, doing the pleasure of that warrior
Agamemnon; no call have you to favor him,
Lest loathsome you become to me that cherish you.
The better fare you vexing him who vexes me.   690
Be you king as I am, sharing my honor's half.
These, then, my message shall convey, but abide you
On comfortable cushions reposed, and come morn
Shall we determine whether to return or not."

He spoke, and to Patroclus signaled silently,   695
Brows raising, to spread a spacious couch for Phoenix,
That th' others take the cue and speedily depart
His lodging. But among them the godlike Ajax,
Telamon's son, spoke, saying: "Son of Laërtes,
Zeus-born Odysseus of many wiles, be we gone!   700
For static stands the purpose of our embassy,
Purposeless, and in this manner ended. Befits
It quickly to convey to the Danaan host
These tidings, saddening though keenly awaited.
But obdurate Achilles has a prideful heart   705
Of fury wrought within his breast nor considers
His comrades' affection—pitiless one!—which e'er

BOOK IX

By the ships, beyond others all, we have shown him!
For recompense is had from a brother's slayer,
Or for murdered son; the murderer remaining 710
In the realm, the indemnity distributed;
And the kinsman's haughty soul, by quittance paid, is
Quieted. But the gods have presently suffused
Your heart with obdurate and dismal disregard,
Seeing that you rage for a solitary girl, 715
Whereas now are seven offered, the fairest far,
And in profusion other gifts surpassing these.
So, be you propitious in spirit and mindful
Of your dwelling place; for we stand beneath your roof,
We who from the Danaan multitude desire 720
Beyond others all to stand well in your regard."

Then answering swift-footed Achilles replied:
"Zeus-begotten Ajax, Telamon's son, captain
Of the host, you somehow seem to voice these concerns
Even as I would speak them; yet enraged I stand 725
Whenever I consider this: how Atreidēs
Has degraded me amid the Danaan host,
As if a reviled vagabond. Nonetheless,
Depart you now and my tidings speak, that nowise
Will I consider drawing battle's blood, 'til grim 730
Priam's son, even goodly Hector, be arrived
At the huts and ships of the Myrmidons, slaying
The Danaans and torching my vessels to ash.
But reaching my hut and dark vessel, then, I deem,
Will Hector desist, fervent for fight though he be." 735

So he spoke, but took they each a cup twin-handled,
Poured offerings, thence proceeding along the line
Of ships, Odysseus leading them. But Patroclus
Ordered his handmaids and companions to straightway
Spread thick bedding for old Phoenix; and they obeyed 740
Spreading the couch, as enjoined, with fleecy mantles

And layers of lustrous linen. There Phoenix slept,
Biding dawn of day. But Achilles slept inside,
Secluded innermost within the well-built hut,
And aside him a woman from Lesbos procured,   745
Even Phorbas' daughter, fair-faced Diomēdē.
And Patroclus slept opposite him, slumbering
By him the slender-waisted Iphis, whom godlike
Achilles had granted him, taking steep Scyrus,
Enyeus' city.
              But when the others arrived   750
At the huts of Agamemnon, the Danaans,
To each side arrayed, received them with golden cups
And questioned them, and Agamemnon, king of men,
Was first to enquire: "Come, Odysseus, and declare,
You, most admirable, most wondrously acclaimed,   755
Whether he intends to protect our ships from flame,
Or instead by anger yet possessed denies us."
Then replied the goodly much travailed Odysseus:
"Most glorious Atreïdēs Agamemnon,
King of men, he declines to abandon his rage   760
But with indignation swells the more, renouncing
You and your gifts. On your own counsel reliant
He enjoins you enlighten the Argives, to wit,
How together both vessels and host be rescued.
For himself, he threatens, come daybreak, to embark   765
Upon his broad-benched curvèd ships; moreover, he
Proposes the like command be given others,
Sheer Ilium's goal an impossibility.
For Zeus to a certainty, his voice audible
Afar, extends his hand above Troy, and the folk   770
Are filled with hardihood. Thus Achilles. And these,
Even they that attended me, confirm it so—
Ajax and the heralds twain, circumspect the two.
But the elder Phoenix reposed him there the night,
Achilles enjoining that Phoenix follow him   775
Tomorrow, shipboard to his longed-for native land—

If he will—but not taking him perforce embarked."

So announced Odysseus, and silenced they became,
Amazed greatly at his tidings, for skillfully
Had he spoken. In sorrow long silent remained   780
The Danaans, but at length Tydeus' son, practiced
In warcry, addressed them this word: "Most glorious
Atreidēs Agamemnon, commander of men,
Would you had never petitioned the peerless son
Of Peleus nor proffered such inducements! Scornful   785
He in any event, and unavailingly
Have you encouraged him. But now shall we truly
Grant him rein, to depart or tarry as he will.
Later will he battle, when bids his heart within,
Or bids a god. Meanwhile, follow as I advise: 790
Endeavor you to sleep, your spirits satisfied
With meat and wine wherein might resides, and manhood;
But when beauteous rosy-fingered Dawn appears,
Marshal the chariots and soldiers before the ships,
Straightaway inciting them, and yourselves amid   795
The foremost fight."
                So he declared, and assented
The chieftains thereto, admiring the words of horse-
Taming Tydeus' son. And pouring libation, went
Each to his hut, reposing him in gifted sleep.

~ Book X ~

The Night Raid, Diomedes and Odysseus Capture and Kill the Trojan Spy Dolon

Agamemnon is livid at Achilles' refusal. Little sleeping the night, he wakens select Greek leaders to plan new strategy. Menelaus, Nestor, Odysseus, and Diomedes are in turn enlisted to rouse yet other leaders. Homer here evokes the sluggishness and malaise of night as the Greeks try fitfully to sleep, and as those sent to rouse them are neither sure-footed nor recognized proceeding from hut to hut. It is a fitting mise-en-scène for the night raid that follows. The ensuing council determines to send spies into the Trojan camp for reconnaissance. Undertaking the hazardous assignment, Diomedes selects Odysseus as companion. They arm themselves in particularly dread armor—its pedigree described—and both pray to Athena, who sends a shrieking heron as auspicious omen.

On the Trojan side, Hector has convened a council for spying on the Greeks, promising horses and chariot—once supposedly Peleus'—to whoever volunteers. The ill-favored Dolon volunteers (the name meaning "deceit") on condition that Hector swear to the promise made (which Hector does). It is a cynical exercise—Hector's inducement and Dolon's motivation speaking poorly for the enterprise, to say nothing of Dolon's lowly status. Dolon attires himself in unconventional gear (wolf- and ferret-skin cloak and hat) and proceeds toward the ships, intercepted en route by Diomedes and Odysseus. Affrighted by Odysseus' spearcast (an intentional miss, but landing nearby), Dolon immediately capitulates, offering both information and ransom for his life. Odysseus chastises Dolon for his greed and credulity (thinking he could ride, let alone possess, Peleus' horses, which are not, in any event, Hector's to give). From Dolon they learn of the Trojan and auxiliary forces, especially those of the lately arrived Rhesus, leader of the Thracians.

After again begging for his life, Dolon is beheaded and stripped of his apparel and armor, the latter hidden in nearby bushes—and the bushes marked—to be retrieved upon return. Following Dolon's directions, they first proceed to Rhesus' encampment. Diomedes there brutally slays twelve Thracians in their sleep, Rhesus last among them, while Odysseus secures Rhesus' fabled horses. Retrieving Dolon's armor, they triumphantly return with Rhesus' horses. Odysseus and Diomedes bathe away the night's exertions and prepare for offerings to Athena.

Long viewed as extraneous to the *Iliad*'s plot, the *Doloneia* (as it is called) enjoys a decided pride of place. It follows thematically, as noted, because the Trojans are encamped *outside* the walls of Troy, allowing them and the Greeks alike the excursions here described. It shows Diomedes and Odysseus discharging a mission unique from the standpoint of Iliadic narrative. And it is successful: combining "edge-of-your-seat" suspense with grisly detail.

※

Slumbered the other chieftains aside their ships,
Those of the Argive soldiery throughout the night,
By bountiful sleep subdued; but Agamemnon,
Son of Atreus, the people's shepherd, resisted
Sweet repose, for a restlessness encumbered him.　　　　5
Even as when the husband of fair-haired Hera
Unlooses the lightning's bolt in rains torrential
And unspeakable, or hail or snow—when blizzard
Blasts the tilth—or yet amply opes the mordant maw
Of wasting war; even so groaned Agamemnon　　　　10
From deep within his breast, unsettled, past repose.
As often as he scrutinized the Trojan plain,
So gasped he at the fires in blazing flame a'burst
Before the face of Troy and at the dissonance
Of pipes and flutes and passionate warrior ferment.　　　　15
But whenever viewing the dark vessels and mass
Of the Achaean warriors, then, fast extracting
The hair from out his scalp, implored he Cronidēs;

BOOK X

And from his noble heart groaned forth, exasperate.
And to his spirit seemed this plan superior: 20
To confer with Nestor, Nēleus' son, if perchance
He might devise some cunning stratagem, warding
Doom from off the Danaan host. So he arose,
Secured his tunic about his breast, donning fair
Sandals beneath his shining feet, and next clad him   25
In skin of tawny lion, fiery and great, full
Down to his ankles flown, and firmly grasped his spear.
Nor the less uneasy was Menelaus found
Nor settled slumbers upon his lids—dreading aught
Befall the Danaans who on his account sailed   30
Troyward o'er the expansive main for battle's sake.
With dappled leopard's skin adorned he first his back
And, hoisting it, positioned a brazen helmet
Atop his head, and stalwart weapon took to hand.
Then advanced he rousing his brother who nobly   35
Ruled o'er the Danaans, by them venerated
Like to a god. Him descried he sternward of his
Ships, fair armor attaching about his shoulders,
And welcome was Menelaus striding forth. First
Spoke Menelaus skilled at warcry: "Why, my lord,   40
Do you thus arm yourself? Will you now a comrade
Select from Argive ranks to spy upon the foe?
No, sorely I regret that none might exercise
This undertaking, informing on the Trojans
Throughout th' immortal night. Right hardy of spirit   45
Must that person be." To him responding, ruler
Agamemnon spoke: "Necessity have we both,
O Zeus-begotten Menelaus, of cunning
Counsel that shall deliver and save the Argives
And their ships, since altered is Zeus' heart. To Hector's   50
Off'rings, as now appears, his mind inclines rather
Than to ours. For never have I seen, nor gathered
From another, that one within a single day
Confer such devastation as now does Hector,

Zeus-beloved, confer upon the Greeks, such doings 55
Mortally done—no divinity's offspring he.
But swiftly traverse the ships and hither summon
Ajax and Idomeneus, and I'll to goodly
Nestor, wakening him, and bidding he direct
The guards amid their vital duties, his presence 60
Decisive; his person respected. To his son,
The guards' captain, together with Mērionēs,
Aide to Idomeneus, have we especially
Delegated this matter."
               Then to him replied
Menelaus good at warcry: "To what purpose 65
Do you, then, enjoin me? Go I there to abide
With them, awaiting your arrival, or hasten
In return, having stated your particulars?"
To him did Agamemnon, king of men, reply:
"Remain you there lest somehow we miss each other 70
Moving forth, for ample the paths throughout the camp.
But wherever you go, upraise your voice and bid
The men be wakeful, each by lineage summoning,
And by his father's name due honor giving each;
And tread not overproud, but busied let us be. 75
Even thus, I deem, does father Zeus as birthright
Distress us with heaviness of woe." So he spoke
And sent his brother well instructed, but himself
Proceeded forth toward Nestor, shepherd of the host,
Finding him beside his hut and dusky vessel, 80
Upon a cushioned bed, and there beside him lay
His armor high adorned, his buckler and twin spears,
And gleaming headgear; and by his side the flashing
Warrior's belt wherewith the elder was accustomed
To be protected when for battle, bane of men, 85
He armed himself, leading his people forth, yielding
Not to grievous age. Rising upon his elbow
He lifted his head, addressing Agamemnon,
And questioned him thus: "Who come you solitary

BOOK X

To the ships, traversing the camp in darkened night 90
While other mortals sleep? Seek you one of your mules,
Or some comrade? Speak, advancing not silently
Forth, and your business state." Then responded Atreus
Agamemnon, king of men: "Nestor, Nēleus' son,
Great glory of th' Achaeans, 'tis I, Atreus' son 95
Agamemnon, whom Zeus past others distresses
With turmoil ever so long as endureth breath
Within my breast and sturdily bear me my knees.
I wander thus because languid sleep eludes me,
Sooner disquiet me war and Argive despair, 100
The likes of which excessively unsettle me.
My spirit o'er-vaults my breast, and neath me tremble
My stately limbs. But if aught you would do, seeing
Slumber escapes your lids as well, then come! Proceed
We to the sentinels, inspecting them up-close 105
Lest, fatigued and toil-beset, they slumbering lie
Oblivious to their duty. The enemy
Bivouacs nearby, nor know we the least whether
Even in dead of night they intend engagement."

Then answered him horseman Gerēnian Nestor: 110
"Most glorious offspring of Atreus, Agamemnon,
King of men, surely will Cronidēs for Hector's
Sake but partially conclude his counsels, for all
That Hector nurtures them; rather, as I surmise,
With troubles far exceeding ours will Hector deal, 115
Should Achilles from crushing ire reclaim himself.
So gladly will I follow, but rouse we others
Too, both spear-famed Tydeus' son and wise Odysseus,
Swift Ajax, and Phyleus' valiant son. And these too
Should summoned be, the godlike Ajax and lordly 120
Idomeneus, for farthest off repose their ships.
But Menelaus will I reprove, though valued
And revered he be, even if it anger you;
Nor from plaint will I forbear the while he slumbers,

That thus to your toil he abandons you. Better 125
That he range among the chieftains, exhorting them
Because of the need unending they now endure."
And Agamemnon, king of men, responded thus:
"Old sir, censure him some other time, for often
Is he slack and from effort aloof, yielding nor 130
To sloth nor inattention but ever looking
To me, awaiting my lead. But wakening now
Before I did, he attended, and I myself
Despatched him to summon those you enumerate.
But onward now. We shall find them a'fore the gates 135
Amid the sentinels, where I bade them gather."
Then responded horseman Gerēnian Nestor:
"So will none of the Achaeans either rebuke
Or disobey him whene'er he calls to any
Or gives command." So stating, he donned his tunic 140
About the breast, and beneath his shining feet fair
Sandals bound, and around him buckled a purple
Double-folded cloak whereon the pile abounded.
Then seized he his spear, brazen-sharp, far-shadowing,
And to the bronze-armored Achaean ships advanced. 145

First then, the horseman Gerēnian Nestor wakened
Odysseus, calling aloud, he the gods' equal
In counsel; and quickly the summons encircled
Him about; and exiting his hut, he addressed
Them, saying: "How is it you wander thus alone 150
Amid the ships and camp throughout th' immortal night?
What need be this?" Then responded Gerēnian
Horseman Nestor: "Zeus-born Laërtes' son, many-
Minded Odysseus, be not wroth, for great sorrow
O'ermasters the Argives. But come, that another 155
Be wakened—whome'er it befits—to consider
Aright, whether to flee or fight." So he stated,
And many-minded Odysseus strode to his hut
And about his shoulders a shield cast dazzling dight

BOOK X

And followed after them. And to Diomedes 160
They came, Tydeus' son, finding him outside his hut,
His armor near; and around him slept his comrades,
Their shields beneath their heads, groundward driven their spears
On butt spikes, figured erect; the bronze effulgent
Far, like the lightning of Zeus Cronidēs. But slept 165
The warrior, hide of field-dwelling ox neath him strewn,
And lustrous most the carpet beneath his shoulders.
And aside him came horseman Gerēnian Nestor,
With his heel's touch prodding and prompting him awake,
Rebuking him face to face: "Up now, Tydeus' son, 170
Why slumber you the nighttime through? Perceive you not
The Trojans even now encamped on th' upper plain
Hard by the ships, and scant the space constraining them?"
So he spoke, but swiftly from sleep the other sprang
And, addressing him, spoke wingèd words: "Untiring 175
Are you, old man, no surcease of toil conceding.
Are there no younger sons of the Achaeans who
Might waken each king, making rounds throughout the host?
But you, old horseman, are quite beyond endurance."
Then horseman Gerēnian Nestor responded: 180
"Indeed, dear friend, you have spoken this correctly.
Peerless sons I possess, and there are sundry men
Who might readily summon the others. But now
Overmastering emergency encumbers
The Achaeans, for balances our survival 185
On the razor's edge: be it Argive slaughter
Or survival. But go now, waken swift Ajax
And Phyleus' son, for you are younger, if perchance
You pity me." So he spoke, and Diomedes
Appareled him about in lion pelt, tawny 190
And prodigious, extending to his feet, and grasped
His weapon and proceeded, rousing the fighters
From their quarters to escort them. When next they joined
The gathered assembly of sentinels, they found
Their leaders unslumbering, but waiting awake 195

And well weaponed. Even as canines watch keenly
Over the pent-up sheep when th' intrepid lion
Marauders woodlands and verdurous mountain slopes,
And hasten the huntsmen and their hounds closing in,
And perishes canine slumber; just so perished   200
Sweet sleep from their lids away, as through the toxic
Night they stood vigilant, for ever attentive
They remained, anticipating Trojan approach.

Once arrived, the old man, heartening them, rejoiced
And spoke, addressing them wingèd words: "Precisely   205
To your watches attend, dear children, nor slumber
Anyone, lest Troy be malignantly merry
At our expense." This said, he hastened through the trench,
By his Achaean commanders accompanied,
As many as to council had been called. With them   210
Withal went Mērionēs and Nestor's glorious
Son, as participants enlisted to the plan.
Thus progressing through and from out the channeled trench,
They settled the while in passable space where ground
Showed clear of fallen dead, even where tenacious   215
Hector had again retreated from the slaughter
Of Danaans once darkness had descended. There
Sitting, they conferred among themselves, and horseman
Gerēnian Nestor first enquired among them:
"My friends, exists there no man who, assured of his   220
Fortitude, would amid the obdurate Trojans
Go, slaughtering an enemy straggler, perhaps,
Or, better, garnering some Trojan-spun report
Of strategy among themselves devised, whether
Eager they be to retain the vessels in view   225
Or once again betake themselves to Ilium,
Seeing they have now much worsted the Achaeans?
All this ascertaining, be he returned unscathed,
Great among men beneath heaven's reach his glory,
And glorious the gifts given him; for by princes,   230

BOOK X

Commanders of their vessels, from these shall warriors
All a darkling ewe present him, with suckling lamb—
Possession past compare—and ever to banquets
And solemn feasts shall he congenial partner be."
So he affirmed, and all fell fast to silence hushed. 235

Then spoke among them Tydeus' son, at warcry deft:
"Nestor, inspires me my heart and manly spirit
To enter the enemy camp nearby, even
The Trojan camp; but were another to join me,
Greater the confidence and assurance acquired. 240
When two go paired together, balanced is their sense
Of judgment, however formed; but if one alone
Decides, plodding is his thought and paltry the plan."
So he spoke, and ardent were many to follow
Diomedes. Keen were th' Aintes, Ares' squires; 245
Keen was Mērionēs and keenest Nestor's son;
Keen was spear famous Atreidēs Menelaus;
And also minded to steal upon the Trojans
Was steadfast Odysseus, for e'er intrepid beat
The heart within his breast. Then among them proclaimed 250
Lord Agamemnon, king of men: "Diomedes,
Son of Tydeus, dearest to me—select that man
Whome'er you will as companion, the best of those
Tendering allegiance; for many are eager.
And from deference shown to kingliness and lineage 255
Do not disdain the man of abler merit shown,
The worse choosing as colleague." So he spoke, fearing
For fair-haired Menelaus. But again addressed
Them Diomedes deft at warcry, holding forth:
"Should you bid me a comrade select, how should I 260
Omit Odysseus, like unto a god, whose heart
And spirited hardihood are inspiration,
Belovèd of Athena for his fortitude?
Were he to attend me, e'er exiting blazing
Flame would we, the two, return—for circumspectly 265

Shrewd is he exceeding others." Then addressed him
Godlike enduring Odysseus: "Son of Tydeus,
Praise me not excessively nor reprove me aught,
For the Argives already know whereof you speak.
But be we sooner departed, for wanes the night   270
And advances dawn, the stars a'fore us fading.
Two watches have transpired, night's third alone remains."
This said, the twain appareled them in dreadful gear:
On Tydeus' son did battle-staunch Thrasymēdēs
A twin-edged sword bestow—his own left by his ship—   275
Also a shield, and upon his head a bullhide
Helm lacking horn and crest, the helm a skullcap called
That guards the heads of strapping youths. Mērionēs
Next with quiver, bow, and sword supplied Odysseus
And firmly on his head a hide-wrought helmet set,   280
Fast stiffened within by many a taut-stretched thong;
While without, to this side and that, close fitted ranged
The ivory teeth of a white-tusked boar, cunningly
Well arranged, and the helm was felt-padded within.
This cap Autolycus stole out of Eleōn,   285
Having earlier burgled the well-built abode
Of Amyntōr, Ormenus' son; and he gave it
Cytherean Amphidamas at Scandeia,
And Amphidamas gave it Molus as guest gift,
But he on his son Mērionēs conferred it,   290
And now, securely it covered Odysseus' head.
So when in dreaded arms the twain accoutred stood,
Onward they progressed, the chieftains abandoning.
And rightward unto them sent Pallas Athena
A close-swooping heron; and though by murky night   295
It flew obscure, they heard its cry. And Odysseus
By the presage pleased proffered prayer to Athena:
"Hear me, offspring of aegis-bearing Zeus, who e'er
Reigns aside me through adversity—no movement
Of mine evades you—now again especially   300
Confer your care and consent we shipward return

BOOK X

With good renown, having accomplished mighty deeds,
For Trojans a cause for concern." And Tydeus' son,
At warcry skilled, offered further prayer: "Child of Zeus,
Unwearied one, to me as well now hearken you;   305
Protect you me as you protected my father,
Goodly Tydeus, in Thebes when forth as Danaan
Envoy he decamped. The bronze-chitoned Achaeans
He left by th' Asopus, there to the Cadmeians
Bearing kindly mien; but devised he returning   310
A baneful enterprise with you, divine goddess,
His kindly disposed assistant. So stand you now
Aside me concordant, affording protection,
And to you as recompense be my sacrifice
A yearling heifer broad of brow, unbroken she,   315
Which no person yet beneath toil's yoke has tethered;
Her will I sacrifice, gilded her horns with gold."
Thus they prayed, and Pallas Athena attended.
Their prayers delivered to mighty Zeus' daughter,
The twain like lions moved amid the murky night,   320
Amid the slaughter, amid the corpses, past arms
And blackened blood.
                    Nor allowed Hector the lordly
Trojans' slumber but assembled them together,
The noblest, as many as were Trojan leaders
And chiefs; and when together he had gathered them,   325
Contrived a cunning plan and said: "Who presently
Would promise me, and to completion bring, this feat
For bounteous gift, and guaranteed the gift withal?
A chariot will I give and arch-necked horses twain,
Yes, those by the Danaan ships determined best,   330
To the man whoe'er shall venture—and for himself
Great glory acquire—to approach the rapid ships,
Learning whether guarded they stand as formerly
Or whether the foe, beneath our hands subdued, plans
Flight among themselves throughout the uncaring night,   335
Fordone by dread fatigue." So he spoke, and grew they

To silence quieted.
                Now among the Trojans
There lived a certain Dolon, son of the herald
Eumēdēs, abounding in gold and bronze, ill graced
To behold but swift-footed nonetheless; brother   340
Alone amid sisters five. Spoke he then a word
To Hector and the Trojan host: "Hector, my heart
And manly aspect impel me approach the swift-
Coursing ships, spying them out. But come, I implore,
Lifting your sceptre, promise truly to confer   345
The harnessed chariot finely outfitted in bronze,
And the horses conveying Peleus' peerless son.
Then to you no negligent agent shall I prove,
Nor one to disappoint, as I enter the campsite
To the very vessel of Agamemnon come   350
Where, I surmise, the chieftains hold council whether
To flee or fight." So he spoke, and Hector, his staff
Upraised, thus pledged and said: "Now be my witness Zeus
Himself, loud-thundering lord of Hera. The steeds
No other Trojan man shall mount; but you alone,   355
I deem, shall they evermore delight." So he spoke,
An empty oath proclaimed, persuading Dolon's heart.
Expediently then o'er his shoulders he cast
His curvèd bow, a wolf's skin throwing over him,
And o'er his head a casing fit with ferret pelt,   360
And grasped a sharpened javelin, and from the host
Proceeded to the ships. Undestined, however,
His returning therefrom with the tidings Hector
Hoped for. But once Dolon quit the gathered horses
And men, Zeus-sprung Odysseus descried his advance,   365
And addressed Diomedes: "Some or another
Man from the campsite approaches—whether as spy
Upon our ships or spoiler of dead men's corpses
Know I not; but let us embolden his advance,
Nearing as he approaches, thereafter rushing   370
And quickly seizing him; and should he outrun us

BOOK X

In fleetness of foot, hem him inward toward the ships
Away from the camp, ever brandishing your spear
Lest cityward he scape." This said, the two settled
Down 'mid the motionless dead, apart the passage,   375
While witless Dolon whizzed by. But when between them
Lay the furrowed length of a ploughing mule—for mule
The better is than ox at pulling fitted plough
Through depth of fallow land—the two pursued after;
And Dolon stopped when hearing them, hoping at heart   380
To view the arrival of Trojan companions
Alerting him to Hector's altered directive.
But when a spearcast's distance off he perceived their
Grim aspect, hastened he his limbs to flight—and fast
Followed they after. As when in wooded places   385
Sharp-toothed hunting hounds, have relentlessly driven
Hind or hare, and bawling e'er runs it a'fore them;
Just so did Tydeus' son and Odysseus sacker
Of cities draw Dolon away, pursuing him.
But as he approached the sentinels, fast fleeing   390
Toward the vessels, Athena strengthened Tydeus' son
That no bronze-armored Argive, second arriving,
Might by imposture claim he wasted Dolon ere
Diomedes. And unswerving Diomedes
Closed upon him, spear in hand, shouting, "Stand or die!"   395
For I shall reach you with this weapon and, I think,
With this my hand guaranteeing your destruction."

He spoke and cast his spear, purposefully missing
The man, and rightward o'er his shoulder the polished
Spearpoint passed, gripping the ground beneath; and Dolon   400
Staggered in amazement, stammering, paralyzed,
Faint with fear; teeth unsettled with dental distress;
And the two overtook him hard panting for breath
And seized his hands, and tearfully he addressed them:
"Take me alive, and ransom my own shall I give,   405
For endowed with gold, with bronze, and toil-wrought iron

I bide, whereof my father unbound riches
Would dispense, knowing me safe at the Argive ships."
Then answering him spoke many-wiled Odysseus:
"Courageous be, dismissing suggestions of death; 410
But come, this declare and truly speak: Where go you
Thus alone, shipward from the host, in murkiness
Of night when other mortals repose. Devise you
The plunder of corpses here along the way? Did
Hector to the hollow ships release you—a spy 415
To our planning—or did your spirit compel you?"
To him responded Dolon, unnerved his shaken
Limbs: "Hector with many delusions has addled
My wits, who promised me the single-hooved horses
Of lordly Achilles and his chariot with bronze 420
Well dight, and bade me through the dusky night advance
On the Danaans, determining if the ships
As aforetime stood defended or if the Greeks
By now o'erpowered by our might, among themselves
Abandon watch, plan flight, by dread fatigue undone." 425
Then bemused replied many-minded Odysseus:
"Truly then your spirit craves regal recompense,
Even the steeds of tempestuous Peleus' son.
But for mortals be they tiring to tame or drive,
Save for Achilles to a goddess mother born. 430
But this now relate and tell it true: where, coming
Here, did you leave Hector, shepherd of the host? Where
Bides his battle gear, where stand his horses? And where
Range the Trojan sentries, and where their bivouacs;
And what their plans and planning's covert contrivance: 435
To bide securely at a distance from the ships
Or, once trouncing the enemy, townward return."

To him then answered Dolon, Eumēdēs' offspring:
"Now will I aright relate everything. Hector
With his advisors convenes council by the tomb 440
Of godlike Ilus, apart from the commotion;

BOOK X

But concerning the sentinels whereof you ask,
Not a single one secures or protects the host;
And as concerns the Trojan watchfires, men remain
Alert who must, one another's caution urging;   445
But the allies, from many lands assembled, sleep,
And on Trojans the vigil confer, as neither
Child nor spouse of theirs resides nearby." Then to him
Odysseus many-minded spoke: "How stands it then?
Sleep they apart or with horse-taming Trojans mixed?   450
Precisely confide, that I may know." Then answered
Dolon, Eumēdēs' son: "Now plainly will I tell
This too. Toward the seashore lie the Paeonians
With curvèd bows, the Carians, the Leleges,
Caucōnes, and goodly Pelasgi. And by lot   455
Toward Thymbrē the Mysians and lordly Lycians lie,
And horsebacked-fighting Phrygians and Maeonians,
Chariot masters. But why of all such point by point
Debrief me? For if access to the Trojan host
Compel you, then here by themselves the Thracians lie,   460
Most recently arrived and outermost encamped;
And with them Rhesus, Eïoneus' son, their king,
Whose resplendent horses my own eyes have beheld,
Steeds whiter than snow, whirlwinded fleetness their flight;
And cleverly crafted his chariot, with silver   465
And gold inlaid. And bearing armor he arrived—
Gold unalloyed, huge its heft, wondrous to behold;
Such armor as befits no mortal man to bear
But th' immortal gods alone. But consign me now
To the swift-borne ships or here in pitiless bond   470
Abandon me and leave, ascertaining whether
Truly and aright I have reported, or not."
Thus dour his demeanor, Diomedes replied:
"No, dear Dolon, devise not flight within your heart,
Truthful your tidings or not, since detained you now   475
Endure. For should we release or discharge you, straight
To the Danaan vessels will you persevere,

Either as spy or combatant in open fray;
But if chastened beneath my hands you forfeit life,
No longer will you linger, a Danaan bane." 480
Thus he rebuked, and Dolon with muscular hand
Prepared to take hold his chin and entreaty make,
But Diomedes leapt upon him, sword in hand,
Straight driving it through his neck, both sinews slashing;
And mingled his mouth with dust, the while discoursing. 485
Off-stripped they from his head the cap of ferret pelt,
Took the wolf's skin, bending bow, and shadowing spear;
And these divine Odysseus hoisted high in hand
To Athena dispenser of spoils, and praying
Spoke: "Goddess, in these rejoice, for greatly to you 490
Of dwellers on Olympus we show our respect;
But now to the horses and Thracian bivouacs
Conduct us." So he proclaimed, and uplifted high
The spoils, from a tamarisk bush suspending them,
There setting a marker plain to see, gathering 495
Thickets of reed and luxuriant tamarisk
Lest the locale elude their sighting on return.
Thus journeyed they through murky night, onward forging
Midst the fallen, o'er armor splotched with clotted blood,
And quickly arrived at the Thracian encampment. 500

Now these beset with weariness lay slumbering,
And on the ground alongside them lay well arranged
Their strapping battle gear in rows numbering three,
And hard by each a yoke of horses. And Rhesus
Slept among them, his headlong horses near him tied— 505
Slackened the reins—to the upper chariot's rim. Him
Odysseus first saw, who signaled to Tydeus' son:
"In truth, Diomedes, here stands the man and here
The horses that Dolon now Hades-bound described.
But come now, make display of might and mien; nowise 510
Does standing otiose become you, sword to side.
Rather, untie the steeds. Or slaughter the soldiers,

BOOK X

And I'll attend the steeds." So ordered he, and Zeus'
Daughter grey-eyed Athena kindled his courage.
And fast pivoting fore to aft, he ruthlessly 515
Butchered them, and among them rose gruesome the groans
As they by sword were slaughtered, reddening the earth.
And even as a lion pounces unperceived
With murderous hunger upon sheepfold or goats;
So Diomedes Tydeus' son applied himself, 520
Expunging Thracian warriors, twelve strong together.
But whomsoever Tydeus' son approached and slew,
Of him from behind would shrewd Odysseus take hold
Dragging him by foot aside, and on this reflecting
That the handsome-maned horses pass effortlessly, 525
Unaffrighted at heart as o'er corpses they trod,
Unused to such as they were. But Diomedes,
Having come upon the king, the thirteenth Thracian,
Stole his honey-sweet life as heavily he breathed;
For like unto nighttime malevolence towered 530
Diomedes Tydeus' son above his visage,
By contrivance of Athena. Meanwhile steadfast
Odysseus loosed the uncloven horses, by their
Reins together guiding them, and drove them forward
From the throng, prodding them with his bow, his bright whip 535
Left behind within his richly decked conveyance;
And he whistled, signaling to Diomedes.
But tarried Tydeus' son, reflecting what greater
Audacity to dare: whether the chariot
To commandeer, wherein the splendid armor lay, 540
And thence remove it by the pole; or upward hoist
The arms and bear them forth; or whether sooner yet
More Thracian lives to take. The while he pondered thus,
Approached him the goddess brilliant-eyed Athena,
Addressing the goodly Diomedes: "Think now 545
Of return to the hollow ships, O spirited
Diomedes, lest frustrated stand your return
And some other god bearing Trojan aid advance."

So she spoke; and knowing the voice of the goddess
Thus advising, he mounted the steeds—Odysseus 550
Prodding them with his bow—and onward they careened
To the swift Achaean ships.
                            But attentive watch
Kept Apollo silver-bowed, seeing Athena's
Support of Tydeus' son; and wrathful he entered
The Trojan commotion, opposing her, spurring 555
Hippocoön, Thracian counselor, good kinsman
To Rhesus, who leapt awake and—seeing the place
Deserted where earlier the horses had pastured,
And the soldiers perished in ghastly massacre—
Emitted a groan, summoning his companions 560
By name; and from the Trojans uprose a clamor
And unspeakable confusion as they quickened
together. And surveyed they the horrid doings
By Achaeans condoned, departing thereafter
Away to their hollow ships.
                            But when regaining 565
The place where the Trojan spy lay executed,
Zeus-beloved Odysseus restrained the rapid steeds,
And groundward leapt Tydeus' son, conveying the spoils
A'drip in blood to Odysseus, and remounted
Lashing the horses lightly; and compliantly 570
Sped the pair onward to the ships, for wonted were
They to be there. And Nestor, first hearing the sound,
Announced: "Dear friends, Argive commanders and rulers,
Shall I falsehood speak or truly state what commands
The heart within me? The sound of swift-footed steeds 575
Rings thundering in my ears. Would that Odysseus
And valiant Diomedes have thus speedily
Commandeered their horses from the Trojans away.
But misgives my spirit unspeakably, that those
Bravest of Argives amid mayhem of Trojan 580
Encounter managed ill."
                            Not fully yet spoken

BOOK X

The word, and they themselves appeared. And as they leapt
To earth, the others took delight, welcoming them
With arms' embrace and gentle words. And the horseman
Gerēnian Nestor was first to inquire of them: 585
"Come, tell me now, Odysseus, amply to be praised,
Great glory of the Argives, how the pair of you
These horses took: by stealth amid the Trojan host,
Or by profit of gift from some divinity?
Wondrous their likeness to glimmering sun. Ever 590
Battle I with the Trojans, nowise delaying
By the vessels, methinks, old warrior that I am;
But never yet such horses have I seen, neither
Imagined. But some divinity I surmise
Conferred them, encountering you; for thunderous 595
Zeus embraces the twain of you as does brilliant-
Eyed Athena, offspring of aegis-bearing Zeus."
Then answering him spoke many-wiled Odysseus:
"Nestor, Nēleus' son, great glory of the Argives,
Surely might a god, willing it, bestow horses 600
Far better than these, for mightier far are gods.
But these horses, concerning which you ask, dear sir,
Are from Thrace arrived; and their lord with his comrades
Twelve beside him the glorious son of Tydeus,
Diomedes, slew; and thirteenth slain was Dolon 605
Nearing our ships, by Hector and the Trojans sent
For reconnaissance of our encampments." So spoke
He, parading the steeds triumphant through the trench,
And followed the other Achaeans, rejoicing.
But arrived at the well built hut of Tydeus' son, 610
They secured the steeds at the manger with leather
Thongs well crafted, where stood the swift-footed horses
Of Diomedes, champing honey-sweet fodder.
And a'stern his ship Odysseus set the bloody
Spoils of Dolon 'til sacred offerings be made 615
To grey-eyed Athena. But they within the sea
Immersed themselves and were cleansed of abundant sweat

From thighs, shoulders, and shins. And when the teeming tide
Had from their dirtied skin dissolved the ample grime,
Replenishing their spirits, they bathed in smooth-glossed   620
Tubs and, with purified bodies, bounteously
Anointed them with blended oil and sat for feast,
And from foaming mixing bowls o'erflown drew honey-
Sweetened wine, oblation befitting Athena.

~ Book XI ~

*The Savagery and Wounding of Agamemnon,
Patroclus Seeks to Identify a Wounded Greek and
(at Nestor's Urging) Will Seek to Impersonate
Achilles, the Third Day of Battle*

As dawn breaks, goddess Strife incites the Greeks to renewed battle. Elaborately arming himself, Agamemnon prepares to command the Greeks, the fearsome description of his armor—the "Arming of Agamemnon"—prelude to his imminent savagery. Hector prepares the Trojans, equally fervent for battle, while Strife alone rejoices. The other gods stand apart, disfavoring Zeus' plan to aid the Trojans. But Zeus indifferently surveys the battlefield.

Agamemnon's slaughterous rampage drives the Trojans to the Scaean Gates, whereupon Iris (at Zeus' command) bids Hector refrain from combat until he sees Agamemnon wounded and retiring from battle. Hector reorganizes the Trojans for continued confrontation, and the sides engage. There follows a catalogue of Trojans who continue falling to Agamemnon until he suffers a spear wound beneath the elbow. Agamemnon yet continues to rampage until growing pain requires his retreat, whereupon Hector inspires the Trojans with renewed confidence.

The tide so turns that Trojan victory seems assured, but Odysseus and Diomedes stabilize the situation. Hector seeks to attack them, but Diomedes strikes a blow to Hector's helmet, causing him to stagger in a deathlike swoon. But he revives and escapes, followed by the threatening Diomedes.

Diomedes is struck to the foot by Paris' arrow, the occasion serving for an exchange of taunts. Odysseus provides Diomedes cover as the latter extracts the arrow, remounts his chariot, and returns to the ships. But Odysseus now finds himself alone, surrounded and fearful of death. He yet perseveres against seemingly insuperable odds. Menelaus and Ajax hear his call and succeed in extracting him from near-certain death. Ajax then briefly rampages, picking up the slack.

But all this goes unheeded by Hector, who is fighting across the plain in the vicinity of Nestor and Idomeneus. Paris there wounds Machaon the physician-fighter (son of Asclepius), who had earlier treated Menelaus' wound (Book 4). Given Machaon's value as a physician, Nestor hurries him off to his (Nestor's) tent. The Trojan Cebrionēs next directs Hector's attention across the plain, where Ajax continues the slaughter. Ajax, for his part, is dazed and exhausted from the day's efforts and reluctantly retreats to safety, helped by Eurypylus and other Greeks who see him fatigued.

Achilles, from the stern of his ship, notes Nestor's and Machaon's retreat. He calls to his companion Patroclus—"and this to him was evil's beginning"—to inquire at Nestor's tent into the man's identity. Meanwhile, Nestor and Machaon have retired to the seashore to bathe and be refreshed, Machaon's wound apparently needing little more. Returned to his tent, Nestor has his serving woman/concubine Hecamēdē prepare a heartening potion, served in a most specially crafted—and historically attested—style of cup that Nestor had brought from home (see pp. 23–24).

Patroclus enters Nestor's tent, declining to be seated. He confirms Machaon's identity and seeks quickly to depart, conveying the news to Achilles. But the long-winded Nestor detains him with an enumeration of the day's wounded, followed by a lengthy excursus on his own prowess as a young warrior. The recitation segues into Nestor's recollection of a meeting at Peleus' abode during the pre-war muster throughout Greece. Impressively present were Achilles, Patroclus, Menoetius (Patroclus' father), Odysseus, and Nestor.

Nestor's tireless harangue concludes with the entreaty that Patroclus seek to feign the presence of Achilles by appearing in Achilles' armor, if Achilles will allow it. This, as Nestor believes, will cause Trojan fear and setback. It is singularly bad counsel from the oldest, wisest and most respected of the Greek counselors. Making his now long-delayed return to Achilles, Patroclus is further detained encountering the wounded Eurypylus, to whom he attends.

Book 11 opens on day 28 of the *Iliad*. The same day variously extends through Books 12–17 and part of 18.

BOOK XI

Now was Dawn from lord Tithonus' couch arisen,
Lending light to Olympian gods and mortal men,
And Zeus sent appalling Strife to the Argive ships,
Conveying belligerent tidings manifest.
Fast stood she by Odysseus' dusky ship, huge hulled;   5
Midway stationed the ship, a shout's reach either way
Whether to the tents of Ajax Telamon's son
Or of Achilles—for to remotest reaches
Had they anchored their sculpted keels, in their valor
Trusting and in their sinews' strength. There stood goddess   10
Strife, spine-chilling, sounding clamor and disquiet.
Fomented she passion in every Argive heart
For combat and for battling on incessantly;
And for them engagement was sweeter grown by far
Than homeward e'er returning in their hollow ships.   15
But shouted Agamemnon aloud, ordering
The Danaans to ready themselves for battle,
And himself amid them donned irradiant bronze.
First attached he greaves about his legs; splendorous
They were, with ankle-safeties of silver fitted.   20
Next a corselet secured he across his chest
Which Cinyras once gave him, a guest-gift, hearing
The great report to Cyprus borne of th' Achaean
Ship-bound trial to Troy. A breastplate he thus bestowed,
Delighting the king. Set thereon were fillets ten   25
Of dusky cobalt, a dozen gold, and twenty
Of tin; and cobalt the snakes that upward slithered
Toward the neck, three to either side, like to rainbows
On cloud by Cronus' son inlaid, for mortalkind
A portent. And 'round his shoulders he set a sword   30
Glistering with studs of gold, silver the scabbard
About it, fitted with golden straps. And seized he
His dauntless shield effulgent, protecting a man
From side to side, a handsome shield encompassed 'round

With circles ten of bronze, and upon it twenty 35
Spurs of coruscating tin, atop them a knob
Cobalt-tempered; and crowning it the Gorgon's glare,
Ghastly, grim countenanced, above her towering
Terror and Rout. From the shield was strap of silver
Slung whereon writhed a triple-headed cobalt asp, 40
Each direction turned but to single neck affixed.
Upraised he to his head a helmet, double-horned
With bosses four, with horsehair crest—and from above
The plume swayed dreadfully. And two hefty brazen-
Tipped lances he took, keen pointed; and to heaven 45
The bronze glistened distantly afar; and thundered
Athena and Hera withal, honor paying
The potentate of gold-resplendent Mycenae.

Then to his charioteer issued each man command
To stay his horses smartly ordered at the trench; 50
But they on foot, majestic their armor, swiftly
Forward surged—unquenchable the cry arising
A'fore the face of Dawn—and ahead the chariots
Reached the trench, taking their places; and thereafter
Followed straightway the chariots. And among them 55
Cronidēs wakened deadly din, and from heaven
Showered dewdrops dark with blood; for intended he
A dauntless multitude to Hades downward hurled.
And o'er against them, on the incline of the plain,
The Trojans gathered 'round sturdy Hector, peerless 60
Polydamas, and Aeneas, by the Trojans
Throughout the realm as gods admired; and the three sons
Of Antēnōr—Polybus, and bold Agēnōr,
And youthful Acamas, like to the immortals.
And amid the foremost bore Hector his buckler 65
Well balanced side to side. And as from crowding clouds
Peers a glittering star malevolent, which next
Behind the shadowy mass retreats; even so
Would Hector now amid the foremost be revealed,

BOOK XI

And now 'mid the hindmost stand concealèd, looming, 70
Emblazoned in bronze, like to the bolt of father
Aegis-bearing Zeus. And as reapers positioned
O'er against each other set the stocks to tumbling
In a prosp'rous person's burgeoning barley field,
And abundantly fall the handfuls; even so 75
Leapt each upon the other, Argives and Trojans
Wreaking Cain, nor would either side of fatal flight
Take thought, but confrontation bound them everywise.
And wolf-like they careened, and Strife with frantic groans
Rejoicing looked upon it; for Strife alone was 80
Party to the fracas, whereas the other gods
Indifferent stood apart—at peace in their abodes
Where constructed stood, high within Olympus' folds,
Palatial residence for each. And disparaged
They Zeus Cronidēs, cloud-enveloped, for granting 85
Trojan acclaim. But Cronidēs Zeus considered
Naught of the gods, but reposèd apart from them,
Exultant in glory, surveyed the Trojan town,
Th' Argive ships, the brazen glint, the slayers and slain.

The while Aurora reigned and rose the sacred day, 90
So long in weaponry did either camp prevail,
And fell the folk. But arrived the hour when woodsman
On mountain glade prepares his meal, and weary his
Arms of felling trees, and fatigue besets his soul,
And falters his sustenance-famished energy; 95
Even then did the valorous Argives invade
The ranks, through them summoning their companions all.
And foremost among them hastened Agamemnon,
Slaying his man Bienōr, shepherd of the host,
Both him and following him Oileus his comrade, 100
Inciter of steeds. Deftly descending his car,
Oileus revealed resolute and steadfast bearing,
But even as he hurtled forth, Agamemnon
To his forehead straight despatched his spear unsparing;

289

And little served his brazen-weighted helmet's brim, 105
But sped the spear through bronze and bone alike, spattered
About his brain within, his ferocity foiled.
The two did Agamemnon, king of men, discard,
Their chests laid bare, and of their armor dispossessed.
And moving thence, he slew Isus and Antiphus, 110
Sons of Priam, one a bastard, one in wedlock
Born, the twain by single car conveyed, the bastard
Commanding the reins; but acclaimèd Antiphus
Stood fast in fight aside him. The twain Achilles
Had with willow tendrils bound on Ida's mountain 115
Spur, seizing them while herding sheep, and for ransom
Had redeemed them; but now wide-ruling Atreus' son
With hard cast spear struck Isus' chest above the gut,
And attacked Antiphus with sword aside the ear
And hurled him from his steeds. Then sped he gathering 120
Their battle gear, well recognizing Priam's sons;
For he had earlier descried them by the ships,
When Achilles had delivered them from Ida.
And as a lion easily mangles the cub
Of the fleetest doe, with frantic teeth engulfing 125
It and, to its lair arrived, purloins its pulsing
Life; and its stricken mother, though happening near,
Assistance none provides—for equally quakes she
And recoils, and through tangled thicket and woodland
Hurtles wildly, hard-hastening a'sweat to scape 130
The beast's unnerving onset; even so, not one
Among the Trojans could avert the twain's demise,
Being themselves against the Danaans deployed.

Then slew he Hippolochus and the unswerving
Peisander, sons of wise-hearted Antimachus, 135
Who longing beyond others all to garner gold
From Alexander—goodly gifts—would suffer not
Fair Helen's return to warlike Menelaus.
The two sons lord Agamemnon despatched—the twain,

BOOK XI

In one chariot borne, together drove the steeds—   140
For the shining reins from out their hands had fallen
And the horses were confounded; but a'front them
Lion-like leapt Agamemnon; and from their car
The twain on knees entreated him: "Take us alive,
You son of Atreus, and a worthy ransom take.   145
Many the treasure lies stored in Antimachus'
Palace—bronze and gold and toil-wrought iron—wherefrom
Our father would confer fine payment past surmise
Were we aside the ships among the living found."
Thus weeping, they implored the king, pathetically,   150
But wholly heartless the speaker that responded:
"If truly you be issue of Antimachus
Wise-minded who, among the assembled Trojans,
When godlike Odysseus and Menelaus came
As envoys, would have then had Menelaus slain,   155
Foreclosing his release and return to the Greeks,
Repay now the price of your father's proud offense."
He spoke, and groundward pulled Peisander from his car,
Driving a spear through his chest, and back he stumbled,
Staggering. But Hippolochus leapt down and where   160
He stood was slain—both arms by sword offshorn; his head,
Offstruck, amid the ranks a roller trundling through.

These two he ignored, but where the ranks were routed
Most, there hastened he, and attended him other
Achaeans. Footmen slew footmen fleeing perforce,   165
And horsemen horsemen slew—and high from beneath them
The dust ascendant of thunderous horses' hooves,
As horsemen with bronze dispensed havoc. And rampaged
Agamemnon the more, summoning the Argives.
As when devouring flame on timbered woodland falls,   170
By currents whipped everywhere awhirl, and crackle
The thickets, root and branch, by lashing flame assailed;
Even so, neath merciless Agamemnon fell
The heads of Trojans as they fled. And the arch-necked

Horses rattled past, their emptied chariots in tow 175
O'er the battle's lifeless leavings, for their peerless
Drivers longing—these fallen groundward, dearer far
To rav'ning birds than to their wives. But Cronus' son
Extracted Hector from the melee, from the dust,
From the flattening of men, from bloodshed and din. 180
But quickly followed Atreus' son, to the Argives
Roaring rabidly; and past the tomb of ancient
Ilus, Dardanus' son, sped the Trojans across
The plain, past the fig tree freely flourishing, e'er
To gain the town; and fast followed Agamemnon, 185
Bellowing, his invincible hands with carnage
Spattered. But having once attained the Scaean Gates
And oak tree, there stopped the forces, one another
To confront. But some there remained, stampeded yet
On the open plain, like lion-beleaguered kine— 190
Stealthy the lion at nighttime stalks, directing
Its kill at one alone whose neck its vise-like maw,
Ere breaking, encloses, its innards thereafter
Devouring blood and all; just so did Atreus' son
Lord Agamemnon alight upon the Trojans, 195
The hindmost ever scattering and killing off.
And many from their cars upon their faces fell
Or tumbled beneath blows of Atreus' son a'back,
For raged he 'round and all about, his weapon gripped.
But once approaching the steep-walled Trojan city, 200
Then from the firmament shown the father of gods
And mortals, on Ida's splendidly watered peaks
Reposed, retaining close to hand the thunder's bolt,
And thus ordered Iris gold-wingèd messenger:
"Speed thee, swift Iris, and unto Hector announce: 205
So long as he observe Agamemnon, shepherd
Of the host, maniacal amid the foremost
Fighters, the warrior ranks annihilating all,
So long bid him forbear but order the Trojans'
Continued contention untamed against the foe; 210

BOOK XI

But when buffeted either by arrow or spear
Agamemnon mounts his car, then murderous brawn
Shall I bestow on Hector, that to the well-benched
Ships he be arrived, the sun setting, the sacred
Darkness coming on."
      So he spoke, and wind-footed   215
Iris resolutely complied, from Ida's heights
To sacred Troy arrived. There she found Priam's son
Goodly Hector atop his smartly fitted car
And, advancing, delivered the goddess these words:
"Hector, son of Priam, peer of Zeus in counsel,   220
Sends me Zeus Cronidēs this counsel to convey:
So long as you observe Agamemnon, shepherd
Of the host, maniacal amid the foremost
Fighters, the warrior ranks annihilating all,
So long constrain yourself, but order the Trojans'   225
Continued contention untamed against the foe;
But when buffeted either by arrow or spear,
Agamemnon mounts his car, then murderous brawn
Shall he bestow on you, that to the well-benched ships
You be quickly arrived, sun sinking and sacred   230
Darkness coming on." Thus speaking, the swift-footed
Iris departed; and Hector full-armored leapt
Groundward from his chariot and, brandishing lances
Well whetted, ranged wide throughout the ranks, heartening
Them to fight and arousing dreaded battle's din.   235
So they pivoted 'round, against the Achaeans
Arrayed; and the Achaeans, opposite, strengthened
Their battalions, the panoply spectacular;
And persisted they facing each other, and sped
Agamemnon foremost forth, keenest for combat.   240
Tell me now, you Muses, dwellers on Olympus,
Who foremost it was encountered Agamemnon,
Either of Trojan host or its illustrious
Allies. Iphidimas it was, Antēnor's son,
A man valiant and tall, nurtured in deep-soiled Thrace,   245

Mother of flocks; and Cisseus his grandfather reared
Him, yet a child, in his house, father to fair-cheeked
Theanō. But the child, come the laureled measure
Of maturity, Cisseus assayed to detain,
His granddaughter giving, Theanō. Thereafter— 250
A bridegroom newly wed from his bridal chamber
Departing—sought he glory in Achaean clash
With hollow vessels twelve that followed him. Now these,
The shapely ships, he moored at Percōtē, himself
To Ilium wayfaring come—but currently 255
Face to face with Atreus' son Agamemnon come.
And when each had confronting the other approached,
Missed Atreus' son, his spear to no avail released,
But Iphidamas stabbed him neath the corselet's belt,
Weighting the thrust with force of his trustworthy hand; 260
But fast the glinting girdle held: long beforehand
Was the spearpoint, assaulting silver, bent like lead.
Then wide-ruling Agamemnon, taking the spear
To his grip, extracted it forth like a lion,
From Iphidamas' hand dislodging it, and smote 265
Him with his sword, uncoupling his limbs. So dropped he
There, stilled in brazen sleep, a piteous youth, far
From his wedded wife, once boon to his townsfolk, far
From the bride whose charms he but lately had secured.
Yet much had he given for her—a hundred kine, 270
A thousand thereafter promising, goats and sheep
Defying count, in tandem from his herded flocks;
Then did Agamemnon, Atreus' son, despoil him,
Displaying his armor amid the Danaans.

But when Coön among warriors preeminent, 275
Antenōr's eldest son, observed this, great anguish
Enveiled his eyes for his lamented brother's sake;
And by Agamemnon unperceived, approached he
Sideways, spear in hand, stabbing him on the forearm
Beneath the elbow, and the glimmering spearpoint 280

BOOK XI

Sped directly through, whereat Atreus' son, shepherd
Of the host, recoiled but continued even so
In combat to cavort and, with wind-tempered spear
In hand, came crashing on Coön as he staunchly
Dragged Iphidamas by foot, his very brother,   285
Of same sire begotten, whilst he hollered aloud
To the boldest all. But even as he hauled him
Through the throng, Agamemnon, with bronze-fitted spear
Thrusting hard neath his decorated shield, smote him
And unloosed his limbs and, come near Iphidamas,   290
Severed his head. There was Antēnōr's progeny,
By might of Agamemnon, Atreus' son, consigned—
Their weighted fortunes descending unto Hades.

But Agamemnon sweeping past o'ertook the ranks,
Armed with spear, sword, and mighty stones, even as blood   295
From his wound welled warm. But the laceration dried
And, when ceased the blood to flow, excruciate pain
Enveloped Agamemnon. Even as the pang
That overtakes a woman in travail, the pain
Th' Eileithyiae, assistants in childbirth, impart—   300
Even Hera's daughters, guardians of contractions;
Just so did glorious Agamemnon agonize.
Then leapt he to his chariot, bidding his driver
Advance to the hollow ships, for grievously ached
His heart, and to the Argives hollered he aloud: 305
"My friends, Achaean captains and commanders all,
Straightway from the ships let us rav'ning battle's din
Repel, for impious Cronidēs detains my stride
The daylong against the Trojans." So declaring,
He bade his driver lash the steeds, cascading-maned,   310
To the hollow ships; and willingly sped the pair,
Full flecked a'foam their fronts, dust-smudged their undersides,
The while delivering their injured king from war.
But when Hector observed Agamemnon's retreat,
Loud he called, alerting the Trojans and Lycians: 315

"You Trojan hosts, you Lycians, and Dardanians
That closely quartered clash, be you men and bethink
You of valored fury. Gone is the best of men,
And to me has Cronidēs great glory consigned.
Against the Argives goad your horses single-hooved, 320
The greater glory to attain." So proclaiming
Aroused he every warrior's spirit and resolve.
And even as when a huntsman his white-toothed hounds
Unleashes upon a lion or bristling boar;
So Hector, Priam's son, Ares' peer, mortal bane, 325
Unleashed the tenacious Trojans upon the Greeks,
Himself, with soaring heart midst the foremost striding,
Falling in on the fray—like an infuriate
Deafening deluge flogging the violet deep.

Whom first, whom finally, did Hector Priam's son 330
Despatch when Zeus vouchsafed him glory? Asaeus
First, and Autonous, and Opitēs and Dolops,
Clytius' son, Opheltius, and Agelaus,
And Aesymnus, and Orus, and Hipponous, hard-
Fighting. These Argive leaders slew he, thereafter 335
Trouncing on the throng. And as when the West Wind whips
The clouds, by South Wind borne aloft, its violent
Squalls assailing them, and many the ocean wave
Forth undulates, the upblasted foam high scattered
By reel of riotous wind; just so the many 340
Danaan heads by Hector hewn. Then done were deeds
And ruin past retrieval, and the Danaans
Flung in flight upon their ships, had not Odysseus
Called to Diomedes Tydeus' son: "Tydeus' son,
What keeps us? Be our furied valor forgotten? 345
But come, good companion, here firm beside me stand,
For shameful the result should Hector flashing-helmed
Attain the ships." Answering him, spoke powerful
Diomedes: "Full enduring do I persist,
However passing the advantage, for Zeus cloud- 350

BOOK XI

Gathering wills Trojan triumph; his trifle we."
He spoke and groundward cast Thymbraeus from his car
With spear thrust leftward to the breast, and Odysseus
Smote Molion, that prince's godlike squire. These then
They thwarted, midst the havoc having halted them. 355
But ranged the two tumultuously through the throng.
As when twin high-hearted boars fall on hunting hounds;
Spirited even so, on Trojans dealt they doom,
And the encircled Danaans reaped heartening
Repose—escaped from Hector, Priam's progeny. 360
Then derailed they a car by the puissant issue
Of Percosian Merops commanded, a man
Above others in soothsaying skilled, who nowise
Allowed his sons' enlistment in man-wasting war;
But not in the least did they obey him, odious 365
Doom of death encountering. These Diomedes,
Tydeus' son, renowned of spear, divested of life
And spirit, dispossessing them of battle gear.

Then Zeus, from Ida observant, evenly set
The mark between them, and they with reciprocal 370
Slaughter resumed. And Diomedes, Tydeus' son,
Wounded the warrior Agastrophus, Paeōn's son,
Upon the hip with hoven spear, and nowhere stood
His horses near to rescue him; and stupefied
He reeled, his driver having elsewhere stood the steeds, 375
And on foot 'mid the foremost thundered he and died.
But Hector sharply noted them across the ranks
And shouting darted fervent forth, and followed him
The Trojan soldiery. And seeing it, warcry-
Practiced Diomedes shuddered and next addressed 380
Odysseus nearby: "Destruction overwhelms us,
Even mighty Hector here; but come now, endure,
From our positions repelling his thrust." He spoke
And poising his spear far-shadowing released it;
Nor departing his hand sped the weapon in vain 385

But battered him at helmet's height where bronze by bronze
Was buffeted, his fair skin unscathèd, for failed
The spear 'gainst the threefold-crested helm that Phoebus
Apollo had furnished him. But Hector sprang back
To a distance and mixed within the ranks, dropping 390
To his knee, thus steadied; and sinewy the hand
That supported him, and stifling the darknesses
Descending. But Diomedes 'mid the foremost
Fighting men kept his spear's trajectory in view,
Reclaiming it earthward implanted. Then Hector 395
Once again revived and, leaping to his chariot,
Reentered the ranks, fleeing fate. But Tydeus' son,
Fast following with fearsome spear, addressed him thus:
"Once again, you dog, escape you predestined death,
Although nearly forced to confront it; but again 400
Has Phoebus Apollo saved you, whom you surely
Pacify whene'er among hurtled spears you stride.
Death will I doubtless dispense upon some other
Occasion met, a god perhaps my helper then.
But to the others now, whome'er I encounter." 405
So he spoke, despoiling the armor from spear-famed
Paeōn's son. But Paris, fair Helen's paramour,
Advanced on Tydeus' son, defender of the host—
Paris, poised aside the pillar aforetime built
By laborers near to the barrow of Ilus, 410
Dardanus' son, advisor to men long expired.

Now was Diomedes despoiling from his chest
The bright corselet of glorious Agastrophus
And from his shoulder the shield and ponderous helm,
When Paris, extending his bow from the handgrip— 415
Deftly from the crescent flew the shaft—assailed him
At the metatarsal, the arrow traversing
Fully through and firmly to the ground implanted.
And merrily amused leapt Paris from his lair
Vaunting haughtily: "Got you! Nor the least vainly 420

BOOK XI

Has my arrow sped. Would I had gotten your gut
Lowermost and wrested your life away; so would
The Trojans with griefs overwhelmed have found repose,
Who now like bleating goats before the lion blench."
Unfazed did Diomedes, Tydeus' son, respond: 425
"Arrogant ranting bowman, coiffed ogler of girls!
Were you suited in armor to contend with me,
Your effort resolute, then profitless your bow,
And arrows pouring forth. And now, but abrading
My lower foot, you boast and make ado whereof 430
I fathom not—no more than if a witless child
Or woman had assaulted me, for blunt the dart
Of a weak and worthless wight. But otherwise, when
From my forearm flying—though slight the contact made—
My spearpoint proves its spite, then fated falls the man 435
Forthwith, his spouse's cheeks in caterwauling spent.
His offspring go fatherless, while neath him reddens
The ground, in guts and gore awash—more plenteous
Than womenfolk the scavengers surveying him."
So he spoke, and spear-famed Odysseus approaching 440
Stood stalwart a'fore Tydeus' son who, positioned
Behind him, disengaged the dart, the vexation
Suffusing his flesh throughout. Then to his chariot
Leapt Tydeus' son, shipward commanding his driver,
For sorrowed he at heart.
                        Now spear-famed Odysseus 445
Solitary stood, nor did any Danaan
Aside him abide, for panic had subdued them.
Angered then, he addressed his great-spirited soul:
"Woe alas, what now befalls? Shocking is craven
Escape, but worse yet my vulnerability 450
Here, by myself, since Zeus Cronidēs disperses
The other Achaeans. But wherefore considers
The spirit within me thus? Weaklings I reckon
Those cowering from combat, whereas it becomes
The brave to hold their ground heroically, whether 455

Stricken they or striking forth."
                              While thus he pondered
In spirit and mind, the shield-bearing Trojan ranks—
Their own pain enduring—advanced and closed on him.
And even as hounds and hearty youths drive a boar
From side to side 'til it venture from the thicket,   460
Whetted its ivory tusks within its curving jaws,
And from either side they goad him, and grind his tusks,
But stay they its onslaught dreadfully delivered;
Just so, about Odysseus dear to Zeus, converged
The Trojan throng. Stupendous Deïopitēs   465
Smote he forthwith in the shoulder with razored spear,
Descending from atop him; the next despatched he
Thōon and Eunomus, and Chersidamas next
As he vaulted from his chariot; him he punctured
At the belly with his spear, beneath his bossèd   470
Buckler, and downward he dropped, hands clutching the dust.
From these, then, he retired, skewering Charops through,
Hippasus' son, to wealthy Socus brother born;
And assisting him came Socus, a godlike man.

Drawing close to Odysseus, stood he and declaimed: 475
"Odysseus, ever praised, of toil and trickery
Insatiate, upon this day will you either
Boast o'er both Hippasus' sons—having slain and stripped
The siblings of their armor—else forfeit your life,
By my weapon wasted through." So saying, he cast   480
At his buckler well balanced side to side. Straight through
The shining shield sped the daunting spear, puncturing
His ornamental corselet, uplifting the skin
From his ribs; but Pallas Athena prevented
Its entry to his viscera. And Odysseus,   485
Knowing his spear had spared a mortal spot, recoiled,
Thus speaking to Socus: "Ah wretch, assuredly
Now lights upon you death incontrovertible
Whilst you delay my slaughtering Trojans; but here,

I say, will this day your undoing bring, and death, 490
And soon succumbing to my spear will you provide
Me glory—hastened your soul to horse-famed Hades."
He spoke, and Socus, pivoting to flee, made off;
But even as he turned, matched Odysseus his spear
To Socus' back, between the blades, through to his breast, 495
And he fell with a thud. And divine Odysseus
Exulted over him: "Ah, Socus, son of wise-
Spirited Hippasus, tamer of horses, death's
Bind of a sudden has upended you; nor have
You avoided it. Wretch that you are, nor father 500
Nor queenly mother will lower your viscid lids,
But flesh-devouring vultures, their pinioned expanse
Intermittently brisk o'erhead, will finish you.
But, should I die, Argive interment awaits me."
So speaking, he wrenched the spear of high-spirited 505
Socus from both flesh and bossèd shield, and the blood
Freed by the spear spewed forth, sickening his senses.
But the great-souled Trojans, seeing Odysseus bleed,
Hollered forth throughout the ranks, one to the other,
And together converged. But he recoiled, calling 510
To his comrades. Thrice shouted he aloud, as loud
As shouts any man; and thrice heard Menelaus,
Ares-belovèd, his call and addressed Ajax
Nearby: "Zeus-sprung Ajax, Telamon's son, captain
Of the host, the cry of stout-hearted Odysseus 515
Resounds like that of a man apart, by Trojans
Overpowered, standing secluded on the plain.
But hasten, our course advancing through the throng,
For such is the wiser way. I worry some ill
Will befall him alone among the Trojans, though 520
Stalwart he engage and ever commands he high
Argive regard."
                So saying he wrested the lead
And Ajax followed, a godlike man. And they found
Odysseus dear to Zeus, Trojans besetting him

'Round about like mountain-bred jackals, tawny skinned, 525
Around an afflicted long-horned stag by huntsman
Struck with bow and racing arrow. From him a'flight
The stag breaks in escape, the blood yet flowing warm,
And quick the knees conveying him; but when at length
The weapon overpowers him, the starving beasts 530
In umbrous gullies dissever the stag. But leads
Some deity a deadly lion a'front them,
And the jackals in every direction disperse,
And the famished lion feeds; just so the Trojans,
Proliferant, beset the wise and sly-minded 535
Odysseus, encircling him. But the man, darting
Forth with spear, his pitiless day of doom postponed.
Then fast approached Ajax, his shield a city wall,
And positioned himself nearby, and the Trojans
Helter-skelter fled, and warlike Menelaus 540
Led Odysseus forth, clasping him fast by the hand
'Til with chariot and horses his driver arrived.

Then Ajax, leaping on the foe, slew Doryclus,
Priam's bastard son, and with a thrust thereafter
Pandocus, and also Lysander, Pyrasus, 545
And Pylartēs. And as when a flooding river
Chastises the flatlands, a wintry mountain spate
Propelled by rain of Zeus—brittle oaks aplenty
And plenteous the pine entangled in its deluge,
And vast the detritus to seaward offloaded— 550
Even so warred wondrous Ajax, tumultuous
O'er the battle that day, hewing human and horse.
Nor was Hector yet alert to it, elsewhere held
To the battle's left near the flowing Scamander
Where heads by the score were successively severed, 555
And lamentation's unslakable register
Rose around Nestor and warlike Idomeneus.
With these did Hector contend, effectuating
Deadly offensive with horsemanship and weapon,

Lev'ling battalions and felling the fighting young. 560

Yet would the goodly Danaans have stayed the course
Had not the fair-haired Helen's lord Alexander
Slowed excellent Machaōn amid his dauntless
Doings and to rightward struck his shoulder with dart
Of triple barb. Then the fury-breathing Argives 565
Feared, with the battle's turn, that somehow the Trojans
Might detain him. And promptly spoke Idomeneus
To goodly Nestor: "Nestor, Nēleus' son, great pride
Of the Danaans, come, ascend you your chariot,
And let Machaōn mount beside you, and quickly 570
Command your uncloven steeds to the rapid ships;
For most valued of men, the physician, abides
Who extracts war's weapons and fit poultice applies."
So he spoke, and the horseman Gerēnian Nestor
Failed not to obey. Quickly mounted he his car, 575
And beside him ascended Machaōn, offspring
Of Asclepius, the peerless camp physician;
And the horses, lightly lashed, surpassingly flew
To the vessels, for there most preferred they to be.
But Cebrionēs, noting well the Trojan rout, 580
Drew his chariot alongside Hector's, proclaiming:
"Hector, while the two of us here with the Argives
Vie on the outskirts afar of clamorous war,
Routed are the other Trojans, horses and men,
And it is Ajax, progeny of Telamon, 585
Who panics them pell-mell. This I plainly perceive,
For expansive the shield about his shoulders set.
But come, drive we there also our horses and cars
Where horsemen and footmen uncommonly contest,
Mutual the slaughter, unquenchable the cry." 590
So saying he lashed his fair-maned horses, and they
To the whistling whip responded, the car atilt
Past Achaeans and Trojans careening, trampling
Dead and shields; and bloodied the axle shaft entire,

Splattered from beneath; and the vehicle to aft 595
Dispersed the spray from its horses' hooves and wheel rims.
And Hector craved to penetrate the ranks of men
Leaping therein to shatter them; and dire his din
Of battle raised against the Argives, and little
The rest afforded his spear. But ranged he with spear 600
And sword and boulders hurled among the ranks of men,
While avoiding mighty Ajax, Telamon's son.

Now father Zeus Olympian-born roused Ajax
Who, overwhelmed though he was—on his back o'erslung
His buckler of bullhide sevenfold—anxiously 605
Retreated, looking throngward—like a feral beast
Wheeling 'round, ever striding backward step by step.
And just as from the mead a tawny lioness
Is driven by hound and countryfolk that suffer
Her not—she alert throughout the night the fattest 610
Of the herd to seize—then for relish of flesh she
Lunges forth, yet accomplishes nothing thereby,
For dense the lances by brawny hands delivered
And fiery the faggots afore which she retreats,
And although biding undeterred, her spirit gnarled, 615
Departs with dawning day; so Ajax departed
Unwillingly, by the Trojans disquieted,
By the imminent threat to the vessels dismayed.
And as when a mule, slipped past the boys, impinges
On the maize, a sluggish mule about whose ribs stand 620
Many a cudgel cracked, yet e'er it encroaches
Laying waste the luscious corn, and thwack it the boys
About, though meagre their might withal and little
From its fodder's fill do they dislodge it; just so
Did the high-hearted Trojans, aside their allies 625
From many lands assembled, smite Ajax, offspring
Of Telamon, assailing his shield with lances
To its middle point, and upon him ever press.
And now, summ'ning insatiate strength, would Ajax

BOOK XI

Deter the Trojans, tamers of horses, wheeling 630
Wide upon them, and now again pivot in flight.
But he kept them from reaching the vessels, himself
Between Trojans and Argives fighting unrestrained.
And of spears by burly hands commanded did some
Assail him, within his fearsome buckler lodging, 635
While greater numbers ere gaining his person failed,
Their fury grounded, fain to be glutted with flesh.
But when Euaemōn's glorious son Eurypylus
Detected him by thick-flying missiles beset,
Aside him with javelin striking he arrived 640
And smote Apisaōn, Phausius' son, host's shepherd,
Neath the midriff to the liver, efficiently
Loosing his limbs; and Eurypylus sprung forward
To strip his armored plate. But when godlike Paris
Observed the plunder of Apisaōn's armor, 645
Against Eurypylus drew he straightway his bow
And with dart to rightward of his thigh detained him;
And though the arrow broke, yet throbbed the thigh within,
And to the throng of his companions he withdrew,
Avoiding fate, and let forth with a frantic cry 650
Alerting the Achaeans: "My friends, commanders
And Danaan lords, turn 'round and hold position,
Keeping pitiless doom from great Telamon's son,
Beset by missiles as he is; nor discern I
His exit from dolorous fight. So attend you 655
The foemen about great Ajax, Telamon's son."
So spoke the injured Eurypylus, and ran they
And rallied by Ajax, their shields to shoulders pressed,
Their spears high-hoisted; and meeting them came Ajax,
Turning 'round to take his stand, having reached the host 660
Of his brethren. So contended they in semblance
Of blazing fire; but Nēleus' mares, awash in sweat,
Bore Nestor from the fray, and with him Machaōn,
Host's shepherd.
    And goodly swift-footed Achilles

Beheld and marked him, Achilles standing sternward 665
Of his vessel hugely hulled, surveying the toil
Of vertiginous battle and tearful retreat.
And forthwith he spoke to his comrade Patroclus,
From beside his vessel calling; and issued he
In likeness of Ares from his tent—and for him 670
Was this disaster's onset. First spoke Menoetius'
Valiant son, saying: "Why, pray, do you summon me,
Achilles, what need have you of me?" And answ'ring
Him swift-footed Achilles replied: "Goodly son
Of Menoetius, my own spirit's delectation, 675
Now will the Achaeans, I think, enfold my knees
In prayer, for unbearable hardship o'erwhelms them;
Yet go, Patroclus, beloved of Zeus. Have Nestor
Identify that man, now wounded and taken
From war. From behind, in truth, seems he everywise 680
Machaōn's like, Asclepius' son, but his features
Discern I not, for his raging steeds hurtled by.

So he spoke, and his comrade Patroclus obeyed,
Traversing the length of the Argive ships and tents;
But when the others to Nestor's tent arrived, they 685
Dismounted to bounteous earth, and Eurymedōn
The squire unhinged the horses from the elder's car,
And the twain from their tunics dried the sweat, fronting
The seashore's salty breeze; thereafter they entered
The tent, settling themselves, and for them the fair-haired 690
Hecamēdē decanted drink, she whom Nestor
The agèd one had delivered from Tenedos
When Achilles laid it waste, the daughter of great-
Hearted Arsinoös, whom th' Argives had chosen
For Nestor since ever excelling in counsel. 695

First she set for them a smoothly burnished table
Crafted with cobalt feet, and thereon a brazen
Basket set, with an onion to season the drink,

And pale honey and cakes of sacred barley meal,
And aside them stationed a comely cup studded   700
With rivets of gold, from home by the elder brought.
Four were its handles, twin the doves feeding at each,
While from under, and twin to the handles upraised,
Ran buttressing. Scarce might another man avail
To lift the cup from off the counter fully brimmed,   705
But th' elder Nestor heartily hefted it high.
Therein the woman, goddess-like, mixed a potion
Of Pramnian wine, grating goat's-milk cheese therein
With a brazen utensil, then scattered it through
With white barley meal and, blending the potion,   710
Bade them imbibe. Then, when the twain had partaken,
Sitting purged of parching thirst, they took their pleasure
In conversation, quickened the discourse throughout,
When at the door Patroclus stood, a godlike man.
And seeing him, uprose the elder from his chair,   715
Grasped his hand and escorted him inside, bidding
Him be seated. But Patroclus, standing apart,
Declined and spoke, saying: "No chair for me, old sir
Nurtured of Zeus, for nowise will you persuade me.
Revered and dreaded most is he despatching me,   720
Inquiring whom you convey thus wounded. But see
I with my very eyes the stalwart Machaōn;
And now as go-between will I return, bearing
Word to Achilles. Well know you, Zeus-nurtured sir,
How dreadfully determined Achilles can be,   725
Pleased ever as he is the blameless to indict."

Then responded horseman Gerēnian Nestor:
"Wherefore abides Achilles thus dispirited,
Observing the missile-tormented Danaans
But nowise observing the anguish pervasive   730
Throughout the camp? For waste the finest by their ships,
Smitten by dart or by thrust of lance afflicted.
Smitten is Tydeus' son, mighty Diomedes;

Wounded is spear-famed Odysseus, and Atreus' son;
And wasted is Eurypylus, the arrow sped 735
Unto his thigh. And this man, by arrow stricken,
Have I recently conveyed from the fight away.
Yet the dauntless Achilles nowise considers
The Argive host nor commiserates whatever.
Awaits he, pray, the ships a'waste aside the sea, 740
Destroyed in conflagration, despite Danaan
Endeavor, and we ourselves to slaughter assigned?
For not as erst unwavering thrives the vigor
Of my supple limbs.
     Would I were young, and my pith
As taut as when the looting of kine kindled strife 745
Between our people and the Eleans, that time
I slew stout Itymoneus, th' unflinching offspring
Of Hypeirochus, a man settled in Elis,
When I was herding the kine of our reprisal
While he, intent on the same, was wounded and fell 750
Amid the foremost by spear from my hand released;
And in terror fled the countryfolk about him.
And greater than great the pillage we assembled
Throughout the plain: fifty herd of kine, as many
Flocks of sheep, as many droves of swine, as many 755
Grazing herds of goats, and fifty tawny horses,
And a hundred mares to boot, most of them nursing;
These we hastened to Nēlēian Pylos by night
Into the citadel, and Nēleus delighted
At heart for the copious spoils allotted me 760
Upon my stripling's achievement in war. At day's
Arrival, the heralds made loud proclamation
That all to whom debts undischarged were due convene
At goodly Elis. And those aright assembled
As the Pylians directed, and made division; 765
For to ample folk were th' Epeians indebted,
Seeing we Pylian few had been sorely misused.

BOOK XI

For mighty Heracles had come exploiting us
In the years aforetime, and slain were the bravest
Among us. Twelve were we, sons of peerless Nēleus,   770
And of that count I alone survived, th' others all
Succumbing, and thus the Epeians, bronze-tunicked
And proud of heart withal, wantonly proceeded
Egregiously against us.
                    And from out the spoil
Selected Nēleus a herd of cattle and flock   775
Of teeming sheep, three hundred counting, and with them
Their herdsmen; for to him in fair Elis was owed
Great obligation: even four horses, winners
Of prizes, their chariot too, slated to enter
The games, for a tripod intently competing.   780
But Augeias ruler of men there detained them,
Discharging the driver despondent for his team.
On this account, by actions spurred and words alike,
Was Nēleus infuriate, taking recompense
Past count, and the rest gave to the folk, apportioned,   785
That they divide it, and no man of equal share
Be defrauded. Thus with such matters we troubled
And about the town to the gods made offerings;
And on the third day came the Epeians en masse
Descending, many men and horses single-hooved;   790
And among them the two Moliones arrayed,
Accoutred in battle gear, striplings aforetime
In rav'ning valor unproven.
                    Now sits a town,
Thryoessa, steeply mounded, on the Alpheius
Far off, of sandy Pylos lowest situate.   795
This they besieged, planning utterly to raze it.
But once having completed their sweep of the plain,
Pallas dashing by night from Olympus appeared,
Directing that for warfare we array ourselves;
And nowise reluctant were those she assembled   800
In Pylos but for battle already provoked.

309

Now Nēleus forbad me from outfitting myself
But hid my horses away, deeming I knew yet
Naught of martial doings. But amid our horsemen
I excelled, albeit on foot, for Athena   805
Thus ordained it.
     There runs a river hard seaward
Descending, Minyēïus, by Arēnē,
Where we awaited dazzling Dawn—we the Pylian
Horsemen—and footman formations were next arrived.
Thence diligently at noontime we came in arms   810
Accoutred to Alpheius' sacred stream. To Zeus
Supremest we worthy offerings sacrificed,
And to Alpheius a bull, and to Poseidon
A bull, but to grey-eyed Athena a heifer
Of the herd; and next throughout the host our supper   815
Took by companies, next yielding to sleep, each man
In his battle gear about the stream's embankment.
But the great-souled Epeians around the city
Had amassed, determined to raze it utterly;
But ere that might transpire, there appeared a direful   820
Deed of war; for when shone the sun above the earth,
Prayed we Athena and Zeus, and in battle joined.

And when the strife of Pylians and Epeians
Commenced, first was I to slay my man, absconding
With his single-hooved steeds, yes, even the spearman   825
Mulius, Augeias' son-in-law, who held as wife
The fair-haired Agamēdē, Augeias' eldest
Daughter, in all drugs skilled upon bountiful earth.
Him fast approaching me I smote with my bronze-tipped
Spear, and dropped he to the dust; but I ascended   830
His car and 'mid the stoutest fighters stood prepared.
But this way and that fled the great-souled Epeians
When they saw the man fallen, even he who led
The horsemen and fought surpassing others. But sprang
I, a darkling gale upon them, taking fifty   835

BOOK XI

Chariots, and amid the fleeing a warrior pair
Befriended the dust, beset by my spear. And next
The Moliones had I slain, twin progeny
Of Actōr's line, had not Poseidon, their father,
Wide-ruling shaker of earth, from battle saved them, 840
Enshrouding them in thickened mist. Zeus then granted
Great power to the Pylians: for so long did we
Rampage through the plain, felling foes and collecting
Their goodly battle gear, even until we drove
Our horses to wheat-opulent Bouprasium 845
And to Olen's rock, and to that location called
Alesium Hill, whence Athena again repelled
The throng. Then, leaving him, I felled my final man.
But from Buprasium the Argives drove their horses
Back to Pylos. And all, among gods, asserted 850
Themselves for Zeus; and among mortals, for Nestor.
Such was I, a warrior, if such I ever was.

But of valor's measure seeks Achilles alone
The benefit, for I reckon he will later
Lament the folk hereafter perishing. Ah, friend 855
Patroclus, Menoetius, your father, thus enjoined
When despatching you from Phthia to Atreus' son;
And present were we twain, lord Odysseus and I,
And all things heard within the halls, even the charge
As he enjoined it. For, assembling many men 860
Throughout the abundant Achaean land, came we
To the well-constructed house of Achilles' sire;
There in the house we found Menoetius the warrior
And you and, with you, Achilles. And the old man
Peleus, chariot-lord, was burning a fattened 865
Thigh of bull within the court's enclosure to Zeus,
In thunderbolt rejoicing, clasping a golden
Goblet whence flowed as fellow to the offering
A fiery wine. The two of you were diligent
About the roast, we standing by; and Achilles, 870

Leaping up, with wonder amazed us, ushering
Us forward, bidding us be seated, and setting
Recreations full a'fore us, a stranger's due.
But once with aliment and spirits satisfied,
First was I to speak, bidding you both attend us; 875
And sat you most attentive, and the two enjoined
You well: old Peleus bade Achilles, his offspring,
Ever to excel and all others to surpass;
But to you, Patroclus, Actōr's son Menoetius
Issued this command: 'More nobly born than you stands 880
Achilles, my child; and though you elder be, far
Better his might. Yet furnish him advice, wisdom's
Word provide, and counsel him; and benefiting
Will he heed you.' So old Peleus admonished you,
And so have you forgotten. Yet, even now speak 885
Suitably to wise-hearted Peleus' son, be he
Moved to obey. Mayhap with heaven's assistance
You might convince him, awakening his spirit.
Good is friendship's persuasion. But if he eschew
Some prophecy and his mother some word from Zeus 890
Confides, then let him send you forth and mobilize
Aside you the rest of the Myrmidons—if thus
To the Danaans you afford deliverance.
And thus upon you be conferred his equipment
In warfare worn, that the foe perchance mistake you 895
For him and in the fray fight less aggressively,
And the fearsome Danaans recapture their breath,
Fatigued though they be. For fleeting the breathing space
In battle; and deftly might you, the unwearied,
The wearied townward hasten with clamor of war, 900
From the ships and tents away."
                              So speaking he roused
Patroclus' spirit, and sprinted he the distance
Of the ships to Achilles, Aeacus' offspring.
But when in his running Patroclus gained the ships
Of godlike Odysseus, where convened assemblies 905

BOOK XI

And adjudications, and where altars stood built
To the gods, there Eurypylus met him, Zeus-born
Euaemōn's son, to the mid-thigh arrow-smitten,
From out the battle limping, the dampening sweat
Upon his head and shoulders shed; alarming his   910
Wound—a black burble of blood—his spirit the while
Unyielding. Seeing him, the stalwart Patroclus
Took pity and uttered wingèd words, lamenting:
"Ah, you dismal men, Danaan lords and leaders,
Thus were you destined, from estates and friends far-off   915
With whitish fat to fête Troy's canine coterie!
But come, this tell me, Eurypylus, Zeus-fostered
Warrior, will the Argives avert brave Hector's might
Or presently perish beaten beneath his spear?"
And to him replied the wounded Eurypylus: 920
"No longer, Zeus-nurtured Patroclus, will th' Argives
Collapsed upon their vessels consider defense.
For truly, all those who aforetime were bravest
Repose now by the ships, hapless and handicapped
By Trojan hands increasingly hardy become.   925
But provide you assistance and to my vessel
Convey me, and from my thigh extract the weapon.
Cleanse and warmly lave the blood away, applying
Healing elixirs to the wound; unguents, as men
Will announce, learned from Achilles whom Cheirōn taught,   930
That most righteous of centaurs. For of the doctors
Podaleirius and Machaōn, the one lies
Lame, I believe, amid the huts, himself needing
Healing, and the other on the plain sates Ares."
And to him again spoke valiant Menoetius' son: 935
"What portend these things, and what recourse, O warrior
Eurypylus? I go to apprise wise-hearted
Achilles of the word Gerēnian Nestor
Has disclosed, staunch Argive mainstay. But even so
Will I assist in allaying your affliction."   940

313

He spoke, and clasping the warrior beneath his arms
Conveyed him to his hut. And seeing them, his squire
Spread oxen hides upon the ground. There Patroclus,
Leaning over him, with knife extracted the dart
From his thigh, and with limpid waters laved black blood   945
Away, applying an acrid pain-deadening
Root, having ground it to powder within his hands,
And the blood, clotting, abated, and dried the wound.

~ Book XII ~

Hector Storms the Barricade and Enters the Greek Camp, the Fourth Day of Battle

THE BOOK BEGINS WITH a quasi-editorial comment: the Greek wall, while helpful for as long as it stood, would not long endure. Poseidon and Apollo would see to its destruction by natural forces, the plain restored to the status quo ante. *This* because the Greeks had failed to offer the requisite prayers and sacrifices before building it. While the *Iliad* abounds in retrospection, this is a rare *pro*spective, i.e., post-Iliadic, reckoning—a stride from the war never-ending to a time when it has passed from sight and mind (but not from storytelling).

As Zeus continues to press the Greeks, they are huddled in fear aside their ships. Hector attempts to penetrate the wall, but without success in negotiating the trench and palisades. Polydamas advises attacking on foot, instead of by chariot, and Hector agrees, dividing his men into five contingents for the assault. The Trojan Asius, with a contingent of his own, disdains a frontal attack but seeks leftward to end-run the trench, through a gate used by the Greeks for their own comings and goings. Asius there encounters fierce opposition, conceding the folly of his plan. Indeed, it was for Hector, not Asius, that Zeus intended glory.

Amid the melee, an ill-omened eagle, in its talons a serpent, appears to the left of the Trojans. In response, Polydamas seeks to end the Trojan onslaught. But Hector opposes retreat and successfully presses on, inflicting great damage on the Greek fortification. The Lycian Sarpedon now takes the lead, substantially advancing the assault. He addresses his comrade Glaucus (see Book 6), owning that their preferential treatment among Lycia's warrior elite requires utmost valor. In one of the poem's most poignant insights, Sarpedon opines that were he and Glaucus immortal, living forever, they would have no need of glory-conferring battle. In other words, glory is as close as a mortal comes to immortality. The gods, themselves immortal, have no need of glory. It is from Sarpedon's utterance that emanate the spokes (as it were) of the poem's glory wheel. Everything (to continue the analogy) turns on and returns to *kleos*–its substance, acquisition, or failed attainment.

The force of the Lycian attack catches the wall's defenders unprepared as they scurry to call up reinforcements, including the Aiantes and the archer Teucer. Ajax slays Epicles, a comrade of Sarpedon, and Teucer seriously wounds Glaucus. Enraged at the wounding of Glaucus, Sarpedon kills a Greek and manages to severely compromise the wall, facilitating access. Sarpedon is then beset by both Ajax and Teucer, but to no avail, for Zeus would prevent the death of his son in proximity to the Greek ships. Sarpedon rallies his men, and the Lycians and Greeks fight fiercely to a stalemate. Zeus then confirms that glory will be Hector's. With a huge stone retrieved from the ground—but made light by Zeus—Hector smashes the gates open, penetrates the barricade, and routs the Greeks to their ships.

※

So amid the huts Menoetius' glorious son
Attended Eurypylus' wound, but the others,
Trojans and Argives, fought amassed. Nor was the ditch,
By the Danaans dug with tow'ring wall above,
Protection long secure—the rampart preserving   5
The ships, the trench encircling it—since the Argives
Had slighted the gods their hecatombs, that the wall
Protect their ample plunder and vesseled storeholds.
But against the will of the deathless gods the wall
Endured; by consequently biding but briefly   10
The while Hector persisted, and Pēleïdēs
Raged, and Priam's citadel unruined remained.
Thus long the great Danaan barricade endured
Steadfast. But once the Trojans' mightiest succumbed,
And many an Argive too—some slain, some surviving—   15
And Priam's town after ten years lay demolished,
And the Greeks shipboard decamped to their native land,

BOOK XII

Then archer Apollo and lordly Poseidon
Bethought them of the barricade, to topple it,
Against it releasing the ragings of rivers   20
In seaward cascade descending Ida's summits:
The Rhēsus and Heptaporus and Carēsus,
Rhodius, Grēnicus, Aesēpus, and goodly
Scamander and Simoïs, by the banks whereof
Lay helmets aplenty, and bullhide shields by dust   25
O'erlaid, and the race of heroes semidivine.
On these of a sudden loosed Phoebus Apollo
Full-rivered founts and torrents that nine days battered
The fortification, and Zeus-engendered rains
Without rest, that tides speedily topple the wall.   30
And the trident-armed shaker of earth himself now
Governed supreme, in tides depositing boulders,
Beams, and braces—once by the Argives tiringly
Raised—and overwashed the Hellespontic spoilage,
Furnishing the acclaimèd shore with sand anew,   35
Having ruined the rampart and redirected
The torrents to their narrows, where they earlier
Were wont in clement-coursing rivulets to surge.

Thus, later, Apollo and Poseidon; but then
About the rampart echoed clash and battle's wail   40
And resounded the balanced tower struts, battered
And beset; and the Greeks, by vengeful Zeus o'erwhelmed,
Languished captive and subdued, clustered by their ships,
There stayed by the rioting Hector, contriver
Of route, while he as aforetime fought, likened to   45
A whirlwind. And as when amid huntsmen and hounds
A lion or savage boar wheels 'round, palpable
Its temper; and towering folk array themselves
And, in their stand against it, from mighty hands hurl
Javelins forth, thick flown their multitudes; yet its   50
Dauntless heart neither cowers nor recoils—its might
Its own undoing—and oft pivots it about,

Assaying the columns of men, and wheresoe'er
It assail there buckle the ranks; even so hied
Hector through the throng, seeking his comrades, spurring 55
Them on to traverse the trench, even as his own
Swift-footed horses insistently neighed and balked,
Peering o'er the brink; for the wide-gaping chasm
Affrighted them, nor was it easily o'erleapt
At a single bound nor by chariot traversed, 60
For beetling banks to every side surrounded it,
And o'ershrouded it stood with sharpened palisades,
A Danaan deterrent implanted for foes;
Not lightly might a horse a'front its chariot
There enter, though strove the footmen to traverse it. 65

Then Polydamas approaching Hector advised:
"Hector and you other Trojan chiefs and allies,
Folly it is to drive swift horses through the trench.
Punishing the expanse to span, and fit the stakes
Within, close abutting the barricade itself. 70
For nowise can charioteers, descending, engage
Confined—thus treacherous the enclosure, I vouch,
Wherein calamity lurks. For if thund'ring Zeus
In his maleficence annihilate the Greeks,
Then let the like betide, and the Danaans here 75
Molder, far from Mycenae by no fame acclaimed;
But should they, turning, rout us from the ships, and we
Labor in the ditch entangled, then shall not one
Of us, I think, a'front the Argive offensive
Flee, if but to recount the disaster in Troy. 80
But follow as I bid; behooves it to obey.
Suffer attendants check the horses channelside,
While we fully armored in concert march afoot
With Hector, that the Danaans withstand us not,
Since destruction's bond is firmly fixed about them." 85
So Polydamas urged, and of his prudent plan
Did Hector greatly approve, leaping straightway armed

From his car to the ground. Nor idly abided
The other Trojans in their cars but leapt they too,
Noting Hector afoot. Then by his charioteer						90
Did every warrior bid his horses unharnessed
There at the channel; but the men, fully marshaled
Deployed In five divisions the better to tend
Their leaders. Some to Hector attached and peerless
Polydamas—the bravest and most numerous—						95
Specially raging to topple the wall and fight
By the hollow ships. And followed Cebriones,
Third in their ranks, and by his chariot had Hector
Left another, less warlike than Cebriones.
Others did Paris, Alcathous, and Agēnōr							100
Lead; and others yet led Helenus and godlike
Deïphobus, progeny of Priam; and next
Among them in command was martial Asius,
From Hyrtacus descended, whom from Arisbē
His regal steeds a'fire transported from river						105
Selleïs. And of others yet was Anchises'
Valiant scion commander, even Aeneas,
And with him both Antēnōr's sons, Archelochus
And Acamas, accomplished in sundry combats.
And Sarpēdōn led the illustrious allies,							110
Choosing Glaucus and warlike Asteropaeus
As comrades, for decidedly best and boldest
Apart himself adjudged he them; since he of all
Remained preeminent. And they, with tough bullhide
Enshielding their ranks from one man to another,					115
Set straight against the Danaans, declining thought
Of delay incurred in laying waste the vessels.

Then the other Trojans and their far-famed allies
Heeded the counsel of blameless Polydamas.
But Asius, son of Hyrtacus, leader of men,						120
Resolved not to entrust his steeds to his squire
And charioteer but charged th' Achaean ships, chariot

And all, the fool, for little fated his escape
Or safe retreat, or glory with horse and chariot
From the vessels to windy Troy returned. Ere that,　　　125
Disastrous misfortune detained him by spearcast
Of Idomeneus, Deucalion's lordly son;
For leftward of the vessels he drove where th' Argives
Earlier entered, sped chariot-drawn from the plain.
There, hard lashing his horses, he infiltrated,　　　130
Finding the gates by neither door nor bolt secured,
But by the choicest men wide-open held, if thus
To war-weary companions vesselward returned
They salvation afford. Eyeing that very site,
He directed his team, and followed him his men　　　135
With shouts aloud, imagining scant Achaean
Resistance and Argives seeking security;
Such fools they were! For greeted them the warriors twain
At the entrance, valiant haughty sons of Lapith
Spearmen bred, Polypoetēs, Peirithous' offspring,　　　140
And Leonteus, equal to Ares, bane of men,
The pair positioned afore the tow'ring portal.
Even as on mountaintops the lofty-crested
Oak, day in and out, abides the driven deluge,
Firm from aforetime its roots; so trusting in arms　　　145
These twain abode the nearing Asius and stood fast.
But rose the Trojans hard against the hulking wall,
Shouting aloud and hefting their bullhides aloft,
By Asius led, by Iamenus, Orestes,
Oenomäus, and Adamas, Asius' son.　　　150
And Polypoetēs and Leonteus, Lapiths both,
From behind the wall roused the well-greaved Achaeans
To fight in defense of the ships; but observing
The Trojan assault on the wall—the Danaans
Responding with uproar and dread—the twain pressed forth　　　155
Before the gates, the like of feral boars biding
In some mountain dale the deafening surge of dogs
And disquieted throng; the boars tearing slantwise

BOOK XII

Decimate the trees, extracting them root and limb,
Whence bursts a clattering of tusks 'til one, lastly 160
Striking forth subtracts a life away; so clattered
The bronze about the Argives' breasts, smitten the twain,
Their faces toward the foe; for hardily they fought,
Trusting the host above and in valor their own,
The host from towered vantage points discharging stones, 165
Defending their lives, their huts, their swift-faring ships;
And earthward to snowflakes likened plummeted stones,
Snow that implacable wind and shadowing clouds
Bounteously shower in flight o'er fertile earth;
No less the missiles distributed from the hands 170
Of Argives and Trojans alike, and raucous rang
The helms and bossèd shields by brunt of weapons struck.
Then Asius, Hyrtacus' son, groaned mightily
Smiting his thighs, and thus indignantly proclaimed:
"Father Zeus, familiar with lies unremitting 175
Are you, for I wagered the Danaan warriors
Would ne'er withstand our might and unwithering hands,
But they, as bees or trimly tapered wasps construct
A home by the rugged road, forsaking it not,
Abiding there to bar the huntsman from their young; 180
Even so these Argives, though standing two alone,
Intend to stand their ground afore the gate, slay they
Or be slain." So he spoke, but speaking thus moved not
The purpose of Zeus, intending Hector's glory.

But others by other gates hard battled, and hard 185
Were it for me to tell, godlike, the tale complete,
For conflagration 'round the stone-set rampart raged
As the Greeks, beset and destitute, defended
Their ships perforce, and the gods to the Greeks allied
Lamented, and fought the Lapiths untiringly. 190
Then Polypoetēs, Peirithous' excellent son,
Hard casting, smote Damasus through his bronze-cheeked cap,
Nor aided the cap—the brazen point destroying

The bone straight through, the brain spattered within. Faltered
He thus in his fury. And the next he slaughtered   195
Oremnus and Pylōn. And Leonteus, scion
Of Ares, slew Hippomachus, Antimachus'
Son, to the midpoint with spearcast transpiercing him.
Thereafter, drawn the weapon from its sheath, he smote
Antíphatēs, darting upon him through the throng—   200
The first at close quarters killed, and backward he reeled
Upon the ground. And next he despatched Orestes,
Iamenus, and Memōn, with bounteous earth
Acquainting one and all.
                    While these of armor lay
Despoiled, the youths attendant on Polydamas   205
And Hector—these the bravest and most numerous
To penetrate the wall and set the ships afire—
Yet hesitant delayed, attentive at the trench,
For a bird had fast descended as they readied
Their assault, a lofty-wingèd eagle, leftward   210
Flown the host that in its talons bore a bestial
Snake, blood-red, alive the while and writhing, nor yet
Of fight forgetful; but backwardly it twisted
And on the breast aside the neck its captor stung
'Til the agonized eagle groundward dropped the snake,   215
Which fell 'mid the throng; the eagle loudly shrieking
Aloft the tumultuous squalls. And the Trojans
Shuddered seeing the writhing snake amid them sprawled,
A portent of aegis-bearing Zeus.
                            Then approached
Polydamas addressing Hector thus: "Hector,   220
Bear I ever your reproach in the assembly
Despite my good advice, since unseemly it were
That a disputatious rank and file address you
In assembly or combat; but ever should they
Glorify your might. But now I discourse as best   225
Befits the need. Let us not continue vying
With the Argives for their vessels, for this result

BOOK XII

I presage: as o'er the Trojans this bird was flown,
Those ardently endeavoring to cross the ditch—
A lofty-wingèd eagle leftward flown the host, 230
In its talons bearing a bestial blood-red snake,
Writhing the while alive, but dropping it groundward
Ere to its nestled roost returned, on its fledgling
Young conferring naught of the fare thus labored for—
Thus we, dismantling the Danaan gates and wall, 235
The Argives put to rout, shall find in that very
Route our own retreat in manifest disarray,
For wholly abandoned shall the Trojans be whom
The Danaans, aside their ships defending them,
With bronze shall have leveled. Thus would an augur bode, 240
With omens familiar, by the folk well esteemed."
Then Hector of the flashing helm from beneath his
Brows glanced angrily and said: "Polydamas, what
You speak no longer pleases me; more decorous,
And other, the counsel you ken. But if truly 245
You assert, the very gods, undoubtedly, do
Waste your wits away, that you enjoin me ignore
Loud-thundering Zeus' directives, who has plainly
Reassured me and nodded in like-mindedness.
To birds aloft you sooner offer fealty, 250
The like of which I reckon not and disavow,
Traverse they rightward toward dawning sun or leftward
Toward murky dusk. But rather let us mindful be
Of counsel come from Zeus, king of both mortalkind
And everlasting gods. One mandate be assured: 255
To fight for one's country. Wherefore fear you battle?
For if the rest of us perish by the vessels,
None's the anxiety over your well-being,
For your spirit shirks the fight, unmartial your heart;
However, if aloof from fighting or battle 260
You remain, or repel others with like prattle,
Then prompt your death by my spear's adjudication."

323

Thus having spoken he proceeded, and followed
They with wondrous din; whereat did Zeus, delighting
In the thunderbolt, a blustery gale upraise 265
From Ida's peak, directing dust against the ships
And bewildering Danaan wits, but brilliance
Vouchsafing Hector and the Trojans. Thus trusting
In both Zeus' portents and prowess their own, they sought
To topple the towering wall, downward dragging 270
The turrets, o'erthrowing the rampart, forth prying
The Argive cantilevers built from the outset
To fortify the towers. These they uprooted
Pulling hard, seeking to flatten the Argive wall.
But they, bracing the battlements with oxen hides, 275
Hurled from the wall at the Trojans ent'ring beneath.
And about the towers traversed th' Aiantes twain,
Instilling Danaan hard-mindedness—one man
With mild, another with strident, words berating,
Whomever they witnessed withdrawing from the fray: 280
"Friends, those dauntless 'mid the Danaans, the middling
Too, and those doubtless dismayed—for not equally
Weighed are warriors—now looms there sufficient travail
For all, and to this I believe you sensible.
Let no man be shipward encouraged, regardless 285
The commotion there occurring, but onward press,
Exhorting one another, that Olympian Zeus
Rejoicing in thunder permit us to repulse
This rampage, forcing the foe's reentry to Troy."
So exclaimed the twain, kindling Achaean courage. 290
And as snowflakes falling thick on a wintry day
When lord Zeus counselor bestirs himself to snow,
Displaying his powers to mankind: dampening
The winds and dispersing the flakes unflaggingly
'Til blanketed be high-pinnacled mountain peaks, 295
The lotused lowlands, the looming promontories,
And fertile tillage of men; and o'er frosted cliff
And foam-quickened harbor hurries the whitened hoar,

BOOK XII

The port, by furied surf upon it falling, cleansed,
While all else beckons blanketed, when reigns tempest 300
Torrent of Zeus; even so from either side flew
Thick the stones, some upon the Trojans, others yet
Upon the Argives, the volley unrelenting,
The lofty wall by deafening din surrounded.
Not even then might the Trojans and glorious 305
Hector past gated wall and transom penetrate,
Had not counselor Zeus encouraged his offspring,
Sarpēdōn, against the Achaeans, a lion
Against curve-hornèd kine. Instantly a'front him
He hoisted his buckler, nimbly balanced from side 310
To side, a beauteous buckler of battered bronze
By the smithy hammered hard, its many-layered
Bullhide steadfastly riveted 'round and about
With gold. Holding this before him and brandishing
Lances twain, he moved—a mountain-nurtured lion 315
Long lacking for meat, and instructs him his haughty
Spirit, assaying the sheep, to enter their pent-
In domain. For though sure to encounter herdsmen
Within, readied their spears, their dogs deployed, guardians
Among the sheep, he yet ne'er foresees him ousted 320
From the woolen steading; thus, either hurtles he,
Seizing one from amid the flock, or is himself,
Heroically miened, by swift-handled spear undone;
Just so did his mettle drive godlike Sarpēdōn
Hastening in onslaught against the barricade. 325

And now addressed he Glaucus, Hippolochus' son:
"Glaucus, whence the source of our high estimation,
Surpassing all others with seating, ample cups,
And apportioned meats in Lycia, whilst everyone
Like unto gods adjudges us? And great demesnes 330
By river Xanthus we possess, fair orchard tracts
And expanses of wheat-bearing ploughland; wherefore
Upright need we stand, foremost amid the Lycians,

Hard accosting calamitous war, that many
A man of our bravely armed companions conclude: 335
'No sluggards they that in Lycia rule, even these
Our kings that consume fat sheep and honey-sweetened
Wine, the choicest; but laudable too their valor,
Seeing they be soldiers midst the Lycians esteemed.'
Ah, friend, if once from this contention fled, our lot   340
Were ever agelessness and immortality,
Neither would I myself amid the foremost fight
Nor to contention quicken you for glory's sake.
But now discerning everywhere death's destiny
Apparent, from which no one secures avoidance,   345
Go we, either granting or garnering glory."

So he proclaimed, and Glaucus neither disobeyed
Nor turned aside, but the twain moved forward ahead
The mighty Lycian host. Seeing them, Menestheus,
Son of Peteōs, quaked, for came they bearing bane   350
As they converged upon his enclave; and dread-filled,
Observed he the fortification's length, but failed
To find from among the commanders a warder
Of woe for his comrades. And marked he th' Aiantes
Insatiate of war positioned there, and Teucer,   355
Nearby, now emerged from his hut. But in nowise
Might his shout attain their hearing, so deafening
The din; and rose heavenward the crash of smitten
Shields, and of horsehair-crested helms, and of the gates—
The bolts fastened, the foe before them positioned   360
Forcefully seeking to penetrate and enter.

To Ajax then he quickly despatched the herald
Thoötēs: "Run you, goodly Thoötēs, and call
Ajax; or rather the Aiantes, both of them,
Since herein prudence lies; elsewise follows ruin,   365
Utter and swift. Upon us press the Lycian chiefs,
Who locked in furious fight ever fearsome fare.

BOOK XII

But if heartache and battle's strife the twain of them
Torment, at least let dauntless Ajax, Telamon's
Son, attend, and Teucer too, with bow proficient,   370
To follow him." So he spoke, and the aide failed not
To hearken and obey but ran, undertaking
The wall's full breadth amid the bronze-clad Achaeans,
And arrived standing proximate the Aiantes,
And immediately spoke: "You Aiantes, chiefs   375
Of the bronze-coated Achaeans, seeks Peteōs'
Son, Zeus-nurtured, your assistance, if but briefly,
To lessen war's toil—both of you, if possible,
Since preferrèd far, for here will utter slaughter
Be accomplished. Upon us press the Lycian chiefs,   380
Who fierce in ardent fight formidable remain;
But if here too rages the encounter, at least
Let dauntless Ajax, son of Telemon, attend,
And Teucer, arrow-proficient, alongside him."

So he spoke, and mighty Ajax, Telemon's son,   385
Disappointed him not, and immediately
In wingèd words addressed Oïleus' son: "Ajax,
Remain you now with stalwart Lycomēdēs here
And rouse the Argives to engage, but there go I,
To brutal conflict called; yet mark you my return   390
When once I have assisted them." So left Ajax
Telemon's son; and fast attended him Teucer
His brother, they of the same parent begotten,
And with them bore Pandiōn Teucer's curvèd bow.
Now when passing along the inward wall, they reached   395
The mighty-hearted Menestheus' post, arriving
To men hard-pressed, the foe was crowding the rampart,
To whirlwind akin, even the dauntless rulers
And leaders of the Lycians.
                        Next, fighting they clashed
And the battle cry uprose. First Telamon's son,   400
The mighty Ajax, despatched his adversary,

Even great-souled Epiclēs, Sarpēdōn's comrade;
For he finished him off with a jagged stone, huge
Where it lay, uppermost amid the weaponry;
Nor deftly in both hands today might a warrior 405
Midst mortal men enduring now take hold of it,
Even one palpably primed, but aloft Ajax
Hoisted and hurled it. Shattered was the four-horned helm,
And bashed the bones in Epiclēs' head; and plunged he,
A diver from the board, and breath abjured his bones. 410
And Teucer atop the rampart wounded Glaucus,
Hippolochus' son, by arrow, as forth he rushed,
Where his forearm was exposed, disengaging him
From the fray. Escaping notice he vaulted down,
That no Danaan take credit for the wounding. 415
But Sarpēdōn was pained upon Glaucus' retreat
When, turning 'round, he noted it, yet nonetheless
Remembered battle's rage and with spear smote Thestōr's
Son, Alcmaōn, the point expertly extracting;
And headlong spearward he fell, about him clanging 420
His bronze-embellished armor. But Sarpēdōn strong-
Handed wrenched the battlement, laying hold of it,
And throughout its length it foundered—the wall above
Defenseless and spent—and cleared a path for many.
And at once came Ajax and Teucer against him. 425
And smote him Teucer with a barb on his brilliant
Breast-encircled strap, brace to his sheltering shield;
But Zeus kept death from Sarpēdōn, that destiny
By the vessels be debarred; and Ajax, leaping
Upon him, thrust against his shield, but the spearpoint 430
Penetrated not for all that Sarpēdōn lurched
Beneath Ajax' onslaught. So from the parapet
He withdrew somewhat, but sparingly to be sure,
For yet yearned his heart for the getting of glory,
And, wheeling about, addressed he the Lycian host: 435
"Lycians, why slackens now your wrathful enterprise?
Hard were it for me alone, though driven my might,

BOOK XII

To breach the wall, providing passage to the ships;
But with me advance, our count securing the cause."
So he said, and they much fearing their king's rebuke   440
'Round their counseling leader increasingly pressed;
And the Greeks, opposing, formed their own battalions
Within the wall; and mammoth the work before them,
For neither could the Lycians breach th' Achaean wall,
Their pathway pressing to the ships; nor th' Achaean   445
Spearmen e'er repel them quite from the rampart back,
Whenever converged in approach. But as contend
Two men with measuring rods at the boundary
Mark where fields converge and in the slender clearance
Go head to head for parcels fairly sized; just so   450
Were the warring sides by the battlements disjoined.

And above the rampart breast to breast they battered
One another's bullhide bucklers and rounded shields—
Shield fastenings aflutter—to the quick many
Cutting via access of intemperate bronze   455
Both those wheeling about as they battled, their backs
To bronze exposed, and those through their bucklers transfixed.
Extensively with blood of men from either side
Were the daunting Danaan defenses bedewed,
And of Trojans too, yet the Trojans even thus   460
Could little rout the foe, but both held evenly,
As a kind-hearted widow in wool-wearied hand
Maintains the scale: to one side stationing the weight,
To the other the daylong's woolen allotment,
Making them equal, a paltry support for her   465
Offspring providing. Thus evenly weighed the war
'Til Zeus granted victory's glory to Hector,
Priam's son, who first o'erleapt the Achaean wall,
With strident shout to the Trojans, calling aloud:
"Rouse you, horse-taming Trojans, break th' Achaean wall,   470
And cast god-kindled flame to catch the ships ablaze."
So he spoke, spurring them on, and heeded they well,

With menacing weapons assailing the ramparts,
Intent on dislodging their sturdy defenses.
And Hector grasped and uplifted a stone, lying   475
Before the gate, thick at the base but deadly sharp.
Not readily might any two, the best about,
Have hefted it—a wagon's load—from off the ground,
As men are nowadays, but blithely he handled
It quite alone; and crooked-counseling Cronus'   480
Offspring disburdened it—as when a shepherd takes
A fleece, effortlessly in one hand bearing it,
And little enough does the burden annoy him;
Even so hoisted Hector the stone, directly
Bearing it toward the slats securing the stoutly   485
Fitted gates. Doubly reinforced were they, and high
And doubled within the crossbars that constrained them,
And solitary set the clasp that fastened them.
Approaching, he stood hard by and, firmly planting
Himself, demolished the portals dead-on, his stance   490
Squarely set that the cast be fully successful.
And the pivots broke asunder, and fell the stone
By its own weight within; and the gates groaned grinding
To either side, the grapplings undone, and the slats
By th' inbursting boulder were dashed ev'ry which way   495
Open, and in leapt mighty Hector, his visage
The semblance of sullen night, as fearsomely flared
The bronze about him; and brandishing double spears
He strode, imposing to whoe'er took his measure
(Except to the gods); unstoppable when within   500
O'ervaulting; his forehead with fire forth a'blazon.
And wheeling 'round within the throng he commanded
The host ascend the rampart; and hearing him, they
Heeded well. Some scaled the wall forthwith, and others
Through the well-wrought gateway poured, and amid the din   505
The Danaans withdrew to their ships in retreat.

~ Book XIII ~

Battle is Waged for the Greek Ships, Poseidon Aids the Greeks, Mayhem Reigns, Idomeneus Deters the Trojan Advance

Zeus looks away from the war, anticipating the gods' neutrality. Poseidon takes the occasion to intervene on the Greeks' behalf, descending to his wetlands palace nearby, and from there by chariot to Troy.

Assuming the guise of the Greek soothsayer Kalchas, Poseidon first encourages the Aiantes. From there he encourages the Greeks, who remain by their ships in despair of Achilles' absence. The Greeks succeed in repulsing Hector, turning the battle's tide, with heavy fighting and valorous deeds to every side.

Poseidon, taking the form of the warrior Thoas, encounters the Cretan leader Idomeneus and rallies him to fight, proposing the two fight side by side. Idomeneus proceeds to his tent to arm himself (Poseidon disappearing into the ranks). Idomeneus encounters his squire Mēriones, who has forfeited his spear and come to get another. The two converse, Idomeneus colorfully holding forth on the difference between valor and cowardice. Finding a replacement spear, Mēriones catches up with Idomeneus, entering the fray where help seems most needed. Poseidon, remaining mortal in appearance, continues to motivate Idomeneus and the Greeks. The battle accelerates, the combatants gaining narrative prominence by either defending wounded comrades or angrily emerging when seeing one fall. The descriptions of injury and death are many and brutal, a vivid canvas of slaughterous melee. So many ways to die!

Idomeneus slays the Trojan ally Othryoneus, boasting over his fallen corpse in some of the finest sarcasm the *Iliad* has to offer. As he drags the corpse away, Asius seeks to intervene but is also slain by Idomeneus. Deïphobus, rushing forth to avenge Asius, casts at Idomeneus, hitting Hypsenor instead. In another bout of fine Homeric sarcasm, Deïphobus boasts that, though hitting the wrong man, he has nonetheless provided Asius a companion to the underworld. Deïphobus then rallies Aeneas to confront Idomeneus, and the slaughter resumes: Mērionēs (squire to Idomeneus) slays Adamas, son of Asius; Menelaus slays Peisander, using the occasion to repeat his grievance over the theft of Helen and the resultant war.

Elsewhere on the plain, Hector presses the Trojan assault. The Trojans might yet have been repulsed but for the strategic thinking of Polydamas, who urges removal to a safe location and a breathing space. Hector agrees, but when seeking to gather his chieftains finds most of them either dead or wounded (the wounded having returned to Troy). Hector, however, finds Paris and, as usual, upbraids his cowardice. Paris protests that he is "trying his best." The exchange is characteristic of Hector's disdain of Paris (Books 3 and 6).

Hector and Paris now join the thick of battle. Ajax and Hector exchange taunts (the two having dueled in Book 7). An eagle appears to the right—a favorable omen—and the Greeks take heart. Hector responds with a renewed challenge, and the sides untiringly engage.

Now when Zeus had driven Hector and the Trojans
To the ships, consigning the hosts to toil and tears
unrelenting, he turned his godly gaze away,
Focused afar toward the Thracian horsemen's dwelling,
And domains of the Mysians, fighters hand to hand;   5
And of the Hippomolgoi, delighting in mares'
Milk; and of the Abii, upstanding of men.
No longer turned he his vision Troyward, deeming
Not within his heart that the gods immortal would
Favor either Trojans or Danaans. But lord   10
Poseidon, shaker of earth, kept attentive watch,
Marveling at the battle's bearing from his vantage
Atop the highest peak of sylvan Samothrace,
Whence visible all Ida lay, whence Priam's town,
And the Danaan ships. There he sat, emerging   15

BOOK XIII

From the sea and, pitying the Argives, viewed them
Thus bested by the Trojans; and at Zeus enraged,
Abided. Fast descending the rugged mount, forth
Strode he on steadfast step, the lofty mountain tops
And woodlands apprehensive neath th' immortal foot 20
And Poseidon's o'erpow'ring pace.
                                   Thrice he advanced,
Fast arriving with his fourth step unto Aegae,
Where deep within a wetland rose his palace: famed,
Gilded, glowing, imperishable evermore.
There he advanced and harnessed close beneath his car 25
Two brazen-hoovèd steeds, fleet-flighted, their manes flecked
With gold; and in gold appareled, proceeded he
Wielding his well-wrought whip of gold, and ascended
His car, catapulting headlong o'er the billows,
And beneath him capered sea beasts to either side 30
From out the boundless brine, acknowledging their lord;
And widely cleft the ocean in gleeful greeting.
Quickly sped the steeds—nor wetted was the brazen
Undercarriage—and unto the Argive vessels
Snorting they gamboled and deposited their lord. 35

An expansive cavern in marshland depths exists
Between Tenedos and blustery Imbros. There
Earthshaker Poseidon paused his steeds, freeing them
From their car, providing ambrosial provender
On which to feed; and at their feet affixed fetters 40
Of unbreakable gold, not to be unfastened,
That the horses there settled remain, awaiting
Return of their sovereign. And lord Poseidon
Approached the Argive host; but the Trojans, teeming
In swarms like to tempest blast, attended Hector, 45
Priam's son, implacably, their shouts resounding,
Thinking to decimate the Danaan vessels,
And therewithal the bravest. But lord Poseidon,
Enfolder and shaker of earth, once surfacing

The ocean depths, sooner rallied the Danaans, 50
Like unto Kalchas in mien and untiring voice.
First he addressed th' Aiantes twain, that were themselves
Already ardent: "Aiantes, will you secure
The Achaean host, mindful of your fortitude
And shunning ignominious rout? Nowhere else 55
Fear I the Trojan advance indomitable,
Multitudinous, ascending the parapet
And o'ertoppling it, yet the well-greaved Achaeans
Will forestall them. No, disaster rather threatens
Closer by, where maniacal Hector commands 60
With flame and conflagration—yes, hellbent Hector
Who hails himself a rightful son of mighty Zeus.
But may some god inspire you twain, resolved firmly
Here to root yourselves, likewise inspiring others;
So might you wrest him from the rapid-running ships, 65
His persistence notwithstanding, though urge him Zeus."
Then with staff did the earthshaking god Poseidon
Smite them, steadfastly instilling tenacity,
Lightening their limbs, their tendons, and hands above.
And himself, even as a supple-wingèd hawk 70
Prepares its flight, from altitude prescribed atop
A rocky pinnacle, and alights it fiercely
Plainward, whatever prey pursuing; even so
Dartlike departed Poseidon.
                              And of the pair
Swift Ajax, Oïleus' offspring, first recognized 75
The god and immed'ately addressed Telamon's
Son: "Ajax, given that an Olympian god
In soothsayer's guise entreats us protect the ships,
Not Kalchas the seer, reader of omens, is he.
For fully apparent the telltale tracks behind 80
Him imprinted as he departs; thus clearly
Recognizable are gods. And now does greater
Passion impel me exceedingly battleward
To fight—my every limb from head to foot intent."

BOOK XIII

Then responding Telamonian Ajax replied: 85
"Even so my own invincible hands would fain
Collect my spear, and wakened is my might, and swift
Stand both my feet beneath me, and eager I bide
To encounter Hector, Priam's son, in combat
One on one—Hector, incessantly infuriate." 90
Thus conversed they one with the other, their spirits
Rejoicing in combative wrath within, infused
By Poseidon; whilst the shaker of earth rallied
The shipbound Achaeans, their spirits reviving.
For oppressive travail had exhausted their limbs 95
And immense their pain within, viewing the Trojans
Mounted en masse o'er th' enormous wall. There looking
Shed they bounteous tears from beneath their brows, fearing
Retreat from ruin nevermore. But Poseidon,
Lightly passing through, bestirred their strong battalions. 100
By Teucer first alighting and by Leïtus,
He encouraged them on, and by Pēneleōs,
The warrior, and by Thoas and Deïpyrus,
Mērionēs and Antilochus, both wonders
Of warcry—these he addressed, admonishing them 105
With wingèd words:

       "For shame, you Argive juveniles!
In your labor had I trusted for our vessels'
Well-being; but if to dread warfare you demur,
Then openly appears our day of punishment
At Trojan hands. For very shame! Assuredly 110
Great this marvel, the which I view, and dreadful most,
The likes of which I ne'er supposed conceivable:
The Trojans on our ships unloosed—they earlier
Resembling panicked woodland hinds, the straying prey
Of leopards, wolves, and jackals, by their cowardice 115
Discernible; nor does fight infuse them; just so
The foe aforetime, absent the faintest courage,
Lacked mettle against Argive strength and stamina.

But now, behold! Engages the foe far from Troy
By the hollow ships, our leader of no account 120
And our ranks remiss. Thus enraged at him, their hearts
Lack gallantry, and slain among the ships they lie.
But if in truth the warrior son of Atreus,
Wide-ruling Agamemnon, be responsible,
Dishonoring the swift-footed son of Peleus, 125
No basis this for slackness in our enterprise.
Rather, let us rapidly repair the affront;
A large-hearted hero can admit atonement.
This slacking no longer befits us, this absence
Of rage and might, this cessation of manliness. 130
I would myself not fault one lax in war, howe'er
Pitiful he be, but with you am I angered
Exceedingly, you weaklings. The greater carnage
By your sloth will you occasion. Rather, summoned
Be your spirits—each of you—to full commitment 135
And shamefulness; for great remains the melee now
Developing. Hector, excelling at warcry,
Battles by the ships, shattered both long bolt and gate."

Thus did Poseidon awaken the Achaeans,
Ordering them. And encircling th' Aiantes twain, 140
Their battalions arranged themselves, so fierce their force
That Ares himself were averse to dismiss them,
Likewise Athena inciter of hosts. For stood
The bravest full readied for valorous Hector
And the onset of Troy—contending lance on lance, 145
Shield with serried shield, buckler with clustered buckler,
Helm on helm, and man on man; and the helmeted
Horsehair crests collided, the combatants lurching
In alignment—wide shouldered, compressed, proficient
With spears, crisscrossed the upper shafts in hefty hands; 150
And fully focused their goal, assembled to fight.

Then drove the Trojans forward in close formation,

BOOK XIII

And Hector guided them, pitching ever onward
Like a boulder descending—the tumid rain-swept
Winter's tide uprooting it away, when the flood 155
With staggering surge dislodges the steadfast stone;
Upward leaping sails the stone aloft, and headlong
It lunges, disconcerting wooded pathways below.
Leveled at length to even grade, it rolls no more,
For all its former hurriedness; Just so threatened 160
Hector, e'er pitching forward toward the water's edge,
To imperil Danaan tents and ships, slaying
As he sped. But when the stalwart Greek battalions
Stood opposite, then, by all their approach was he stayed.
And the sons of the Achaeans confronted him, 165
Stabbing with swords and twin-edged spears, repulsing him,
So that reeling he retired. Then he emitted
A piercing shout, howling aloud to the Trojans:
"You Trojans, you Lycians, you Dardanians, all
At close quarters engaged, manage your ground. Not long 170
Shall the Danaans delay me though rampart-like
Arrayed; sooner, I aver, will they encounter
My spear, if the mightiest of gods has uplifted
My heart, the loud-thundering husband of Hera."

So saying, he roused the morale of every man. 175
Then strode among them Deïphobus, high-hearted
Son of Priam, holding before him his buckler
Well balanced to every side, lightly advancing
Beneath bold buckler's cover. And Mērionēs,
Taking aim with trusted spear a'gleam, cast and struck, 180
Smiting the symmetrically sided bullhide shield,
Yet little drove therethrough, for sooner broke the spear-
Shaft in its socket; and Deïphobus, distraught
At the hostile hurl of heart-wise Mērionēs,
Thrust his buckler forth, but Mērionēs sooner 185
Reentered his comrades' ranks, exceedingly wroth
For the victory lost and shaft that had shattered.

Off to the Argive vessels and huts he ventured
To lay hold the spear standing upright in his tent.
But contended the others, and a cry arose   190
Unslakable, and Telamonian Teucer
Stood first to slay his man, the spearman Imbrius,
Son of Mentōr, rich in horses. Pedaeus was
His dwelling ere came the sons of the Achaeans;
And helpmate had he, Mēdesicastē, daughter   195
Of Priam out of wedlock born; but when th' Argives'
Curvèd ships arrived, ventured Imbrius to Troy,
Esteemed among Trojans, dwelling in Priam's halls,
And of Priam deemed honored offspring. Teucer smote
Him, hard lunging with his weapon, neath the earlobe,   200
And next withdrew the spear, and Imbrius toppled
Like a mountain-risen ash tree, viewed from afar,
From all sides observed, felled by the unfeeling bronze,
Which groundward disperses leaf and limb; even so
He dropped, his bronze-adornèd armor resounding,   205
and approached Teucer wanting to despoil him.
But Hector at the onrushing champion cast,
And Teucer, looking dead-on upon him, barely
Escaped the impudent spear; but Hector despatched
Amphimachus, son of Cteatus, Actōr's son,   210
Spearing him through as he entered the fray, and down
He toppled, his armor collapsing about him.
Then drove Hector forth, poised to despoil the helmet
From the illustrious head of Amphimachus.
But Ajax sprung with resplendent spear, forth rushing   215
Toward Hector, yet transpierced him not, for the dreaded
Bronze protecting him, but battered his buckler's boss
And back from the corpses repelled him, assuring
His retreat—corpses by the Greeks from battle drawn.
Then did Stichius and valiant Menestheus,   220
Athenian commanders, bear Amphimachus
To Achaean safety, and Imbrius the twain
Aiantes reclaimed, their spirits fury infused.

BOOK XIII

And as when lions twain have commandeered a goat
From tooth-honed hounds, in their muzzles conveying it   225
Through thicket and brush, clearing the ground beneath them;
Just so the twain-helmed Aiantes held Imbrius,
Lifting him to loot his armor. And Oileus' son
Severed Imbrius' head from its tender neck, wroth
O'er Amphimachus' slaying and, with a swing sent   230
It rolling orb-like amid the rout, discarded
In the dust at Hector's feet.
                              Then was Poseidon
Grievously enraged at heart when his grandson fell
In the ghastly fray, and along the huts and ships
Of the Danaans proceeded, encouraging   235
The hosts; and for the Trojans was he planning pains.
And spear-famed Idomeneus encountered him there,
Idomeneus come from a comrade earlier found
Returning from battle, knee torn by trenchant bronze.
Him his comrades carried off, but Idomeneus   240
Had charged the healers and was headed to his hut,
For yet was he impatient to confront the foe;
And the shaker of earth addressed him, likening
His voice to that of Andraemōn's offspring, Thoas,
Who throughout Pleurōn and steep Calydōn governed   245
The Aetolians and stood revered by the folk,
A veritable god: "Idomeneus, Cretan
Counselor, whither departed, tell, the taunts wherewith
The Argives once threatened the Trojans?" And answered
Him the dauntless Cretan leader Idomeneus: 250
"Thoas, insofar as I observe no one is
Worth the blame, for able in battle be we all.
Nor governs faint-hearted cowardice anyone,
Nor to sluggishness succumbing does anyone
Evade disastrous clash; even so, I surmise   255
That Zeus Cronidēs, his might supreme, is mindful
Of the Argives namelessly perished here distant
From Argos. But, Thoas, since aforetime in fight

You proved stalwart and prompt to inspire another
Wherever you encountered avoidance of war, 260
Continue so, to every warrior summoning."
And Poseidon, shaker of earth, responded thus:
"Idomeneus, may one homeward never again
Return from Troy but distraction sooner provide
For dogs, whoever readily decides this day 265
To shun the fight. But rouse yourself, taking weapons,
And hasten we the cause though being two alone,
If usefulness be our calling. Comes fortitude
From fellowship, even of those in misery;
For known are we even with the valiant to fight." 270
So speaking he retired, a god into the toil
Of men. And Idomeneus, as soon as arrived
To his well-hewn hut, ensconced him in casted bronze,
And seizing two spears flew forward—like to lightning
That Zeus Cronidēs takes to hand and brandishes 275
From Olympus' peak, a sign displayed to mortals,
Ablaze its dazzling radiance; and as thus he flew,
Beamed the bronze from Idomeneus' breast refulgent.

And his comrade Mērionēs encountered him
Near his hut positioned; for proposed he to fetch 280
Himself a spear, and Idomeneus addressed him:
"Mēriones, Molus' son, swift-footed, closest
Of my companions, why hither now come, quitting
Torturous encounter? Be you perchance stricken,
Undone by some martial affliction? Or mean you 285
Some message to impart? Myself do I prefer
No delay at the huts, but to fight." And to him
The judicious Mēriones next responded:
"Idomeneus, counselor of the brazen-coated
Cretans, I seek to secure a spear if perchance 290
One lie available in your huts; for the spear
I earlier brandished now fragmented stands, dashed
On the buckler of o'erweening Deïphobus."

BOOK XIII

And answered the Cretan leader Idomeneus:
"Spears for the taking will you chance upon, be they   295
One or twenty, against the hut's bright entrance wall
Arrayed, spears of Trojan warriors which I often
Despoil from off the fallen. For I reckon not
To fight the adversary from afar; wherefore
Have I helms, spears, bucklers, and corselets aplenty."   300
Then to him responded prudent Mērionēs:
"In my own hut surely and dusky ship as well
Are Trojan spoils in abundance for the taking,
But yonder somewhat; for not unmindful of might,
No, not unmindful I of standing in battle   305
Amidst the bravest where men win glory whene'er
The struggle of war ascends. Others of the bronze-
Coated Achaeans might perhaps unknowing be
Of my warcraft; but you, I gather, know it well."
And to him the Cretan Idomeneus answered: 310
"Well know I your valor; why speak the tale thereof?
For were our bravest for ambush now assembled
By the vessels where the best vaunt their bravery,
There revealed stand both the valorous and craven,
For constantly the craven's color changes cast,   315
Nor steadfast settles the spirit within his breast,
But falters he from foot to foot, often shifting
To either side, and throbs aloud his heart within
As he reckons death, teeth clattering; but valor's
Complexion altering not endures; nor worries   320
The brave exceedingly when posted for warriors'
Ambuscade but prays forthwith for inundation
Of woeful war. Not even there would one disdain
Your courage or strength of hand.
                              For were you stricken
By dart in battle's toil or howsoever harmed,   325
Not from behind to your neck would the weapon strike
Nor to your back, but would about your breast alight
Or find your underbelly as you forward strode

Amid the frolic of foremost fighters. But come,
No longer let us tarry here, of such matters 330
Prattling like children, lest the supercilious
Find fault; but proceed to your hut for the weapon."

So he spoke, and Mērionēs resembling swift
Ares quickly from the hut procured a brazen
Spear, and with battle's exalted thought attended 335
Idomeneus. And as man-punishing Ares
Proceeds to war attended by his offspring, Rout—
At once tireless and doggèd, dismantling bravest
Fighters' dispositions—the two full-armed advance
From Thrace amid the Ephyri or Fiery Folk, 340
Great-hearted, but disavow them of either side,
Randomly glorifying one or the other;
Just so did Idomeneus and Mēriones,
Commanders of men, emblazoned in bronze advance.
And Mēriones spoke to Idomeneus thus: 345
"Son of Deucalion, where precisely prefer you
Within the throng to fight: to rightward of the host,
Or through its midst, or perhaps leftward to engage?
For leftward seem the Argives poorest to perform."
And even thus to him replied Idomeneus: 350
"Amid the ships at their midpoint stand there others
For defense: the two Aiantes, and Teucer, best
Of the Argive archers and quick at close quarters.
From these shall Hector, Priam's son, have combat's fill,
Be he e'er emboldened—the difficulty his, 355
However much raging for war—to overcome
Their force and fists unfailing, and to fire the ships,
Unless Cronidēs himself set the blazing brand
Upon them. But great Telamonian Ajax
Would to no man submit, no man that be mortal 360
And on Demeter's increase reared, that might by bronze
Be cleaved or crushed by mighty stone. No, not even
To Achilles keen router of warrior ranks

BOOK XIII

Would Ajax yield in close-pitched fight; but in fleetness
Of foot may no man with Achilles vie. But do   365
You, even as you urge, to leftward storm the host,
That we may know whether fame be found or forfeit."

So he proclaimed, and Mērionēs, swift equal
Of Ares, led the way, reaching the host whither
Idomeneus commanded him proceed. Now when   370
The Trojans discerned Idomeneus, in fierceness
Likened to flame, he and his companion richly
Armor-adorned, a shout arose throughout the throng
And toward him hurtled all, and by the ships arose
A clash of all combined. And as career the squalls   375
When shrilly blows the wind on the day dust thickest
Throngs a passage, and the surge confoundedly lifts
A daunting cloud of dust; just so their combat clashed,
And zealous in the throng they fought with sharpened bronze
To slaughter one another. And the broil, bearing   380
Death unto mortals, bristled with pointed spears poised
For disseverance of flesh, and blinded was sight
By blazing gleam of helmeted bronze, and freshly
Burnished corselets, and dazzling shields as men advanced
Bewilderedly. Beyond stalwart of spirit   385
Would the warrior be exulting in such struggle
And moaning not. Thus were Zeus' two mighty scions,
Divergent in device, designing grim ordeals
For mortal heroes. But Zeus assigned victory
To Hector and the Trojans, thus honoring   390
Achilles fleet of foot, though nowise intending
To annihilate the Danaan multitude
A'front the face of Troy, but would bestow glory
On Thetis alone and her stalwart-hearted son.

But amid the Danaan host Poseidon ranged,   395
Rousing it, from the slate sea stealthily rising,
For vexed was he to see the Achaeans o'ercome

By Trojan cohorts; and exceptionally wroth
With father Zeus was he, the two decidedly
Of selfsame stock and parentage, but elder born   400
Cronidēs Zeus and wiser, wherefore Poseidon
Avoided open confrontation but ventured
Throughout the host in mortal likeness e'er disguised
Exhorting the Argives. Thus knotted the outcome
Of grievous strife and wretched war, thus tautly drawn   405
The doom unbreakable one side to the other
That e'er the footing of multitudes unfastened.
Then, greying though he was, Idomeneus convoked
The Achaeans and routed the foe, among them
Leaping. For he despatched Othryoneus, native   410
Of Cabesus—Trojan sojourner now—newly
Come seeking battle's renown; and he petitioned
The hand of Priam's comeliest daughter, even
Cassandra, without courting gifts, but promising
An awesome deed: that he would drive perforce from Troy   415
Th' entire Argive host. And Priam the elder
Promised her betrothal and nodded his accord,
And Othryoneus fought, trustful of the promise.
But Idomeneus with resplendent spear took aim
And, casting, stopped the other's approach; nor availed   420
Him his brazen corselet; but the spear sped fully
Through his gut, dropping him with a thud, and boasted
Idomeneus over him, saying: "Verily,
I count you, Othryoneus, blessed beyond mortals
If truly you accomplish all you undertook   425
For Dardanian Priam, who promised you his child.
Right! We the like would promise too, accomplishing
It whole, and would to the pick of Agamemnon's
Daughters acquiesce, forth fetching her from Argos
For your betrothal fully allied with us   430
You vanquish Troy, that well-populated city.
Now follow us, do, that we deliberate those
Nuptials of yours by the seafaring ships, for rest

BOOK XIII

Assured we are amply bounteous betrothers."
So saying, the hero Idomeneus hauled him 435
Foot-wise through the dismaying fray. But Asius
To Othryoneus' rescue came on foot, standing
A'front his steeds, the which his henchman charioteer
Held reigned, the horses breathing upon his shoulders.
And Asius yearned to strike Idomeneus; but he, 440
Anticipating him, hit home, casting quickly
To the throat beneath the chin; the bronze directly
Driven through. And he toppled as topples an oak
Or poplar or tow'ring pine that among mountain
Shipwrights drops, a ship's timber to sharpened axes. 445
Thus afore his chariot and horses lay Asius
Outstretched, lamenting loud and clenching bloodied dust.
And the charioteer sat stupefied, nor retained
The wits once his, nor ventured turning his horses
Around to salvage his life; but the battle-staunch 450
Antilochus took aim, cleaving him to the gut,
Nor availed him his brazen corselet—to the gut
By the spear incised—and from his well-built chariot
He toppled, heaving, and great-souled Antilochus
Nestor's son drove the horses from the Trojans forth, 455
Gracing the ranks of the fitly greaved Achaeans.

Then Deïphobus, sorrowing for Asius,
Drew nigh Idomeneus, propelling his weapon,
But Idomeneus, close eyeing him, avoided
The brazen shaft, for neath his well balanced buckler 460
He concealed himself—cunningly devised the shield
He bore, of bullhide made, molded with dazzling bronze,
Rods crisscrossing bolstering it. Beneath the same
He hunkered down, and sped the brazen spear o'erhead,
And his buckler rang hollow as the spear glanced off. 465
Yet nowise idly did Deïphobus despatch
The weapon from his ample hand, but leveled he
Hypsenōr, Hippasus' son, shepherd of the folk,

Beneath the midriff at the liver and forthwith
Loosed his limbs. And Deïphobus exceedingly   470
Exulted, heartily above him declaiming:
"Verily, I surmise, lies Asius avenged
Somewhat, and spiritedly heartened, descending
To Odious Hades, obdurate detainer,
For behold, an escort have I provided him!"   475
So he spoke, and the boast dearly grieved the Argives.
Distressed it most the sagacious Antilochus;
And yet, mindful remaining despite desolation
O'er his comrade's plight, he ran and bestrode him,
And with buckler well protected him. Then knelt two   480
Steadfast companions, even Mecisteus, Echius'
Son, and goodly Alastōr, and bore Hypsenōr,
Heavily groaning to the hollow Argive ships.

Nor did Idomeneus' might abate, but sought he
To e'er blanket some foeman in bleakness of night;   485
Or himself, heaving heavily, to ward havoc
From the Greeks. Then the dear son of Aesyetēs,
Nurtured of Cronidēs, the warrior Alcathous—
Son-in-law to Anchisēs he, having married
The eldest of his daughters, Hippodameia,   490
In whom her sire and reverent mother delighted
Within their halls, for she surpassed in comeliness,
In wisdom, and splendid handiwork the maidens
Of her age, thus the finest man in spacious Troy
Had wed her—this Alcathous, Poseidon subdued   495
Neath Idomeneus, lord Poseidon bewitching
His shining eyes and arresting his glorious limbs,
Foreclosing him aback from flight and all escape;
Yet firmly set he stood, even as a pillar
Or leafy high-towering tree, and the warrior   500
Idomeneus transfixed him with full-frontal thrust
To his breast and cleft the bronze chiton about him
That from his person aforetime had warded death;

But now anguished he aloud, split about the spear,
And thudding he dropped, his heart by the lance transpierced,   505
Its beating then causing the weapon to quiver—
But Ares the war god at last stilled its fury.
But o'er him Idomeneus immoderately
Delighted, announcing aloud: "Deïphobus,
Shall we now perhaps suppose the outcome settled—   510
Three for one man slain—since thus haughtily you vaunt?
But abide, good sir, and accost me that you know
The caliber of Zeus' begotten here standing
Before you. For Zeus first Minōs begat, keeper
Of Crete, and Minos thereafter a son begat,   515
Even the singular Deucaliōn, the last
Begetting me, lord over many in broad Crete.
And now have the vessels borne me Troyward, a scourge
To you, your father Priam, and the Trojans all."
So he spoke, and conflicted was Deïphobus: 520
Whether to cede, siding with a great-souled Trojan,
Or encounter him alone. And as he pondered,
Appeared it preferable to near Aeneas;
And hindmost aback the throng he glimpsed him, secure,
For Aeneas was e'er with goodly Priam vexed,   525
That, supreme amid warriors, Priam considered
Him triflingly. Then drew Deïphobus closer,
Speaking wingèd words: "Aeneas, Trojan counselor,
Now truly befits it that you aid your kinsman,
If anywise a kinsman's grief dishearten you.   530
But come you with me to Alcathous' assistance,
Avuncular your brother-in-law, who loved you,
A mere stripling within his home; him, I report,
Has spear-famed Idomeneus despatched." So he spoke,
And awakened the emotions in Aeneas' breast,   535
And against Idomeneus he went, intending
Warlike exploit; but Idomeneus nowise balked,
No coddled infant he, but like a boar endured
Atop a mountain that stays—confidently strong

In some lone locale—the commitedness of men 540
Amassed against him; whetted his teeth, upbristled
His backside, and ignited his glistening eyes,
Preparing to trample determined men and hounds.
But spear-famed Idomeneus tenaciously faced
Aeneas' offensive, hollering and looking 545
Emphatically toward Ascalaphus, Aphareus,
And Mērionēs and Antilochus, masters
Of warcry. And addressing them wingèd words, he
Exhorted them thus: "Hither, friends, advance me aid,
Who am alone, dreading swift-footed Aeneas. 550
He triumphs, accomplished in battle's butchery,
And in flow'r of youth and fullness of force excels.
Were we of similar age and disposition,
Swiftly would he assert himself, or maybe I."

Thus he spoke, and all stood unified beside him, 555
Shouldering shields. Aeneas, facing opposite,
Assembled his companions, toward Deïphobus
Looking, toward Paris and Agēnōr, commanders
Of the Trojans sharing power; and followed them
The folk as follow sheep the ram when drinking deep 560
At feeding time, and right gleeful the shepherd's heart;
Even so did Aeneas exult, perceiving
His people follow him. Then fought they ragingly
At close quarters o'er Alcathous' corpse, brandishing
Mighty lances; and dreadfully 'round their bodies 565
Resounded brazen armor as in the melee
One toward the other they rushed; meanwhile Aeneas
And Idomeneus, both stalwart peers of Ares,
Excelled, in his eagerness each, with sword and spear
To lacerate the other. First Aeneas cast, 570
But watchful Idomeneus dodged the bladed edge
Hurled vainly from Aeneas' hand, groundward dashing,
Whereupon Idomeneus smote Oenomaüs
Directly to the gut, cracking his corselet's plate,

BOOK XIII

His intestines erupting 'round the bloody bronze, 575
As dust-engulfed he despondently groped the ground.
Idomeneus from the body withdrew his spear
But succeeded not—hard pressed within the melee—
To plunder it of armor, even as his strength
Began to flag—dispossessed of stamina he 580
To reclaim his weapon or weapon's cast avoid.
Thus, though circumventing contention's day of doom,
His feet from battle no longer firmly bore him,
And at him slowly retreating Deïphobus
Cast vehemently, fierce as aforetime, but afresh 585
Flung wide, striking Ascalaphus, Ares' offspring,
And pierced the spear his shoulder through, and by fistfuls,
Headlong in the dust he rummaged, accosting earth.

Ares, berserk and bellowing loud, knew not yet
Of his fallen offspring, for he sat recumbent 590
On the summit of Olympus under golden
Clouds, by Cronidēs' writ, where sat the other gods
As well, their following in the fray forbidden.
Meanwhile, furiously clashed the men about the corpse.
Deïphobus wrenched the helm from off his temples, 595
But Mērionēs, lunging the like of quickened
Ares, struck—inflicting a blow to his forearm,
Such that the visored helm dropped from his hand, dashing
Loudly to the ground. Then Mērionēs vaulted
Over, vulture-like, snatching at its shoulder's gash 600
The weapon from his arm, neath cover of his men
Concealed. Then Deïphobus' brother Politēs
Hoisted Ascalaphus 'round the waist, bearing him
From the frenzied fracas 'til reaching his rapid
Horses, positioned they toward the rear with driver 605
And daedal cart. These delivered him cityward
Groaning deeply, the blood bilging from his shoulder.
But the rest continued on, and unquenchable
Rose the cry.

    Then Aeneas assailed Aphareus
Calētōr's son who turned to face him, striking him   610
On the throat with his sharpened spear, and to leftward
Sank his head, his buckler, and helm; and soul-slaying
Death enfolded him about. Then Antilochus,
Perceiving opportunity, at Thoōn leapt,
Fully penetrating him as he wheeled away,   615
Dissevering the vein that traverses the back
Upreaching to the nape, the vein severing clean.
And Thoōn foundered in the dust, extending both
Hands to his comrades nearby; but Antilochus
Leapt to despoil him, cautiously looking about,   620
For the Trojans, from side to side encircling him,
Rained weapons on his brilliant buckler, succeeding
Not to penetrate Antilochus' tender flesh,
For lord Poseidon, shaker of earth, protected
Nestor's son, no matter th' innumerable blows,   625
For ever advanced Antilochus 'mid the foe,
A venturer among them, spear never at rest,
Weapon high flourished and threatening; steadily
He poised to release it or thrust at close quarters.

But sweeping through the multitude escaped he not   630
Adamas, Asius' progeny, who squarely smote
Him on the buckler, hard thrusting with sharpened bronze,
From close at hand besetting him. But Poseidon
Dark-haired god reduced the spearpoint's rage, grudging it
Antilochus' life. And half the spear stood rigid,   635
Like a fire-scorched stake in his adversary's shield;
Half grafted to the ground; and Adamas 'mid his
Peers withdrew, defrauding fate. But Mērionēs,
Firmly casting withal, disabled him midway
Between navel and privates, where the war god is   640
Especially unforgiving. Even there fixed
He his spear, and the other, falling toward the shaft,
Endured like a bull that mountain-dwelling herdsmen

BOOK XIII

With thick-twisted strappings secure and drag perforce;
Even so, did he when smitten convulse the while, 645
But briefly, until the warrior Mērionēs
Approached and extracted the spearpoint from his flesh,
And shadowy nighttime o'ermantled his eyelids.
Then Helenus, nearby him, struck Deïpyrus
To the temple straight with a mighty Thracian sword 650
And tore his helmet off; and, escaping his head,
The helm fell groundward, and one of the Achaeans
Collected it toppled forth, and tenebrous night
Descended on Deïpyrus, devouring him.

But Atreus' son Menelaus was pained thereat 655
And strode onward menacing the prince, the warrior
Helenus, flaunting his razored spear while th' other
Nocked his bow. So the twain concomitantly cast,
The one with lethal lance, the other with arrow
From his archer's string. Then to Menelaus' breast 660
Did Priam's son with dart hit home on the hollow
Of his corselet, and glanced the bitter blow therefrom.
And as when from a generous winnowing plate
The dark-skinned beans or chickpeas, by the winnower
Thrown aloft, bounce high on the risen blast, shedding 665
Chaff about the threshing flood, so from the corselet
Of noble Menelaus glanced the arrow off,
Careering wide. But Atreus' son Menelaus
Excelling in warcry cast and smote Helenus
To the hand wherein he grasped his burnished weapon, 670
And through bow and hand alike the brazen spearpoint
Cleanly drove; and unto the ranks of his comrades
He retreated, eschewing fate, hand downward hung,
Trailing the ashen spear which mighty Agēnōr
Extracted, binding the hand in a fleecen sling 675
From his stewart secured for the people's shepherd.

But Peisander, though courting dreary destiny

At Hades' door, assailed lordly Menelaus;
But you, Menelaus, subdued him in battle.
Now when they close approached, the one toward the other   680
Nearing, Menelaus threw wide, his spear released
In vain; but Peisander, thrusting, smote glorious
Menelaus' shield, though in nowise succeeded
Driving the metal through, for the ample buckler
Obstructed it, snapping the spear at the socket;   685
Yet joyed he stood with victory's expectation.
But Atreus' son, his silver-studded sword withdrawn,
Leapt upon Peisander; whilst he from neath his shield
Commanded a battle-axe, bronzed and well mounted
Upon hardened grip of olivewood long-polished;   690
And the adversaries straight engaged. Peisander
Struck Menelaus on his helmet horn-embossed,
The horsehaired helmet battered topmost to the plume.
But as he hurried headlong, fastened Atreidēs
On his forehead o'er the nose's ridge; and rattled
The bones within, his eyeballs bloodied full, and fell   695
He dustward at Menelaus' feet o'erdoubled
On the ground, and of his armor Atreïdēs
Rapidly despoiled him, foot set upon his chest,
And boasted aloud:
                "Thus surely depart you hence
From the vessels of the horse-striding Danaans,   700
You haughty Trojans, of war's din insatiate
And in plenteous lechery and dissolution
E'er intentive, confounded curs, exhibiting
Contempt for the wrath of Cronidēs thunderer,
The god of hospitality, bringing to naught   705
Your towered town someday; you in Hellas looting
My wedded wife and unstinting treasure therewith
For what dalliance she provided. Now propose you
With ruinous fire to waste the seafaring ships,
Destroying Danaan battalions. But bereft   710
Of the bedlam shall you be, though belligerent.

BOOK XIII

Father Zeus, your prudence, men aver, eclipses
Others' all—men's and gods'—yet from you this havoc
Emanates, advantaging Trojan impudence,
E'er headstrong and intensifying combat's din.   715
Satiety all o'erwhelms: slumber, love, and song,
Whate'er their sweetness be, no less the winsome dance.
With these instead of war would any be content,
But of battling are the Trojans insatiate."
This said, Menelaus stripped the bloodied armor   720
From off the corpse, providing it his companions,
And himself returned commingling with the foremost.

Then leapt at him king Pylaemenēs' son, even
Harpaliōn that Troyward followed his dear sire,
Seeking Trojan fame, though denied return to his   725
Native land; and soundly battered he the buckler
Of Atreidēs from close nearby, yet managed not
To drive the metal through, and among his comrades
Shrank, avoiding fate, warily glancing about
Lest bronze the least betide him. But Mēriones,   730
As he retreated, discharged a bronze-tipped arrow,
Striking to the right-sided buttock, and traversed
The arrow through, to the bladder beneath the bone.
And there among his beloved companions seated
Relinquished his life, wormlike outstrung on the plain,   735
His black blood outpouring, deep dampening the ground.
And the great-hearted Paphlagonians busied
Themselves about him, and to chariot bearing him
Bolted to sacred Ilium, sorrowing the while,
And with them his father, shedding tears; but no blood-   740
Price for his fallen son was paid.
                              And grew Paris
Overwroth at his slaying, for 'mid the many
Paphlagonians had Harpaliōn been his host
And, raging for his sake, released a bronze-tipped shaft.
A certain Euchēnōr there was, born of a seer   745

Named Polyïdus, valiant he and affluent,
Corinth his abode. On the briny he embarked,
Aware of the ominous fate awaiting him,
For oft proclaimed his goodly sire Polyïdus
That he must either atrophy of dire disease   750
Within his halls or midst Danaan ships be slain
A casualty of Troy; so evaded he
Alike the strenuous scourge of the Achaeans
And abhorrent pestilence, less the pain to bear.
At the jawbone neath the ear did Paris smite him,   755
And departed his spirit immediately,
And detestable darkness devoured him about.
Thus likened to blazing flame they fought, but Hector
Beloved of Zeus had little heard or ascertained
That Trojans leftward the vessels were falling   760
To the Argives; and soon manifest were Argive
Renown—thus busied the enfolder and shaker
Of earth, incessantly goading the Argive host.

But Hector pressed onward within where first he leapt
The gate and wall, bursting the Argive entrenchment, 765
Even where the vessels of Protesilaüs
And Ajax cumbered the breakers and hoary brine
Where, beside them the rampart had been lowest built,
There unabated both men and horses battled:
There the Boeotians and Ionians—their tunics   770
Trailing—the Locrians, and Phthians, and glorious
Epeians labored greatly to bridle his rush
To the ships but failed to discountenance Hector—
His likeness like to flame itself. Also labored
The elect of the Athenians. Among them   775
Peteōs' scion, Menestheus, was commander,
And followed him Pheidas, and Stichius, and valiant
Bias; but th' Epeians were led by Megēs, son
Of Phyleus, and by Araphiōn and Dracius,
And 'mid the Phthians, by Medōn and Podarcēs,   780

Staunch in fight. The one, even Mēdōn—a bastard
Born to godlike Oïleus, kinsman of Ajax—
Who dwelt in Phylacē, distant his native land,
For Mēdōn had despatched his stepmother's brother,
She Oïleus' consort; and th' other, Podarcēs, 785
Was son of Iphiclus, scion of Phylacus.
These in their armor outfitted at the forefront
Of the Phthians fought alongside the Boeotians,
Defending the ships. And Ajax, Oïleus' son,
Would nowise abandon—no, not for an instant— 790
The side of Ajax, son of Telamon; rather,
As wine-colored oxen concordantly coupled
Fallow-wise apply themselves to the fitted plough,
And from behind their horns trickles sweat descending;
Parts them the polished yoke alone, as from furrow 795
To furrow they labor 'til the plough traverse
The tillage all; just so th' Aïantes twain secured
Their stand, the first at the second's side positioned.
Many valiant companions attended Ajax,
They relieving him steadily of his buckler 800
When fatigue o'erpowered him, and perspiration.
But the Locrians attended not Oïleus'
Great-hearted son, for they cowered at close quarters,
Lacking brazen helmets with horsehair-thickened plumes,
And lacking bucklers and ashen spears. But trusting 805
In bows and woolen slings well plaited, they followed
Him to Troy and with such weapons ever battled,
Intending to trounce the foe. So some in war gear
Richly furnished fought the foe and bronze-clad Hector
While others behind them let fly from their cover; 810
And arrow-beset were the Trojans confounded.

Then had the Trojans retreated, disconsolate,
From vessels and huts unto wind-encompassed Troy
Had not Polydamas neared Hector, exclaiming:
"Hector, how persuasion eludes you, leaving you 815

Resourceless. For all a god has bestowed on you
And you alone, in works of war and counsel too,
You suppose yourself superior to others.
But with no such facility are you favored:
God-given to one man are works of war; the dance   820
To another, and to another yet the lyre
And song, and to another's breast far-seeing Zeus
Firm heedfulness affords, advantaging many;
And many that man saves, of his own gifts mindful.
So I impart what to me appears yet soundest: 825
Behold, this consumption of battle increases
And the great-hearted Trojans, having now traversed
The wall, stand some apart in arms whilst others fight—
Fewer fighting more—scattered among the vessels.
But falling back, convene you all the fiercest here.   830
Then might we consider the outcome of each plan,
Whether to fall on the well-crafted ships if some
God so warrant it or simply retreat unscathed,
Abandoning the ships. But for myself, I fear
Argive requital for our yesterday's doings,   835
Seeing that a man insatiate of strife retains
Himself apart and little longer, I surmise,
Will linger aloof the contention." Thus proposed
Polydamas, prudent his plan by Hector deemed
Who leapt well armored immediately groundward   840
From his car, and thus addressed him in wingèd words:
"Polydamas, hold you the bravest here while there
I venture toward the foe, but quickly to return
When once communicated stand my directives."
Thus determined he spoke, austere as a snowbound   845
Peak, and hurried shouting aloud to the Trojans
And allies. And hastened they all toward the goodly
Polydamas, Panthous' son, upon hearing him.
And ranged he 'mid the best seeking Deïphobus;
Helenus, stalwart lord; and Adamas, Asius'   850
Son; and Asius, son of Hyrtacus—if perchance

He might encounter them. But them he discovered
Little uninjured or alive, but some sternward
Of the Argive ships were strewn, by the Argives slain;
And some by the wall were wounded or hard stricken.   855
But one he encountered leftward of the slaughter,
The goodly Alexander, fair-haired Helen's lord,
Encouraging his comrades and urging them on.
Him he approached and addressed with scandalous words:
"Evil Paris, fairest to behold, woman-crazed,   860
Deceiver: where, I ask you, is Deïphobus;
Helenus, stalwart lord; and Adamas, Asius'
Son; and Asius, son of Hyrtacus? Where tell me
Is Othryoneus? Now is towering Ilium
To ruin consigned, its destruction assurèd."   865

Then answered godlike Paris: "Hector, since your mind
Devises blameless indictment, earlier in truth
Did I abandon the battle; yet my mother
Bore me not an utter weakling. And from the time
You sparked your comrades' fortitude aside the ships,   870
From such moment have we engaged the Argives here
Unceasingly; but dead are the comrades of whom
You ask. But Deïphobus and lord Helenus
Have alone escaped, to the arm spear-smitten both;
Yet Cronidēs kept death aside. But wheresoe'er   875
Incline your heart and spirit, lead; and there will we
Readily attend you; nor, I surmise, shall we
In fortitude default whilst abides our resolve.
Beyond this no man fights however eager to."

So the hero spoke, his brother's mind o'erwinning,   880
And speedily they advanced where confrontation
And clamor keenest ranked—about Cebrionēs,
Peerless Polydamas, Phalcēs, and Orthaeus,
Godlike Polyphētēs, Palmys, and Ascanius,
And Morys, Hippotiōn's son, who the morn before   885

Had from deep-soiled Ascania come, reinforcements
To their peers. And to battle Zeus incited them.
And forward they strode like eddies of dreadful wind
Ravaging earth beneath Cronidēs' thunderbolt,
And with wondrous din upturn the main, and many 890
The wave upon the thunder-sounding sea uprears,
High-arching and flecked with foam—men in the forefront
And those close following; even thus the Trojans
Rank by rank, some in the forefront, others behind,
Brazen their armor, fell in with their commanders. 895
And led them Hector, Priam's offspring, Ares' peer,
Bane of mortalkind, holding before him his shield—
To every side well balanced, full thickened with hides,
Whereon was welded bounteous bronze—and about
His temples rattled the crest of his dazzling helm, 900
And strode he everywhere from side to side, making
Assay of battalions and testing their resolve
As beneath cover of shield he incited them;
But there was no disheartened Achaean resolve.
And came Ajax on mighty stride and in challenge 905
First addressed him. "Goodly sir, approach. Why seek you
Vainly to affront the Argives thus? In no way,
Rest you assured, are we in contention unschooled,
But by Zeus' disdain the Danaans stand undone.
You doubtless seek, think I, the wreckage of our keels; 910
But rest assured our hands in their defense avail.
Ere that transpire will Troy's well-populated town
Most likely taken be, wasted beneath our hands.
As for yourself, the day approaches close, I say,
When, fleeing, will you Zeus implore and the other 915
Gods immortal, that your fair-maned steeds fly swifter
Than falcons—Troyward headed, trailing clouds of dust."
As thus he presaged, flew a bird upon his right
And loud hollered the Argive host, on the omen
Reliant. But Hector replied, "Ajax, braggart 920
And idle-tongued, would to a certainty I knew

That I were son e'ermore of aegis-bearing Zeus,
That queen Hera mothered me the like in honor
To Athena and Apollo as sure I know
This moment summons Danaan decimation, 925
And within it shall you perish, dare you abide
My spear that will rend your lilied flesh, jettisoned
To satiate with vein and viscera the dogs
And birds of Troy, once fallen by the Argive ships."

Thus speaking he led on, and the others followed 930
Amid clamor supernal, and clamored the host
Behind them. And th' Argives, opposite, raised a shout
Its equal, not forgetting their prowess, but stood
Firmly opposing the onrush of Trojan chiefs.
And hollers from either side uprose, ascending 935
The firmament and visage of splendorous Zeus.

~ Book XIV ~

The Deception of Zeus: Aphrodite and the God Sleep Assist Hera in Seducing Zeus Who Then Slumbers as Hera Aids the Greeks

ATTENDING TO THE WOUNDED Machaon (brought to his tent in Book 11), Nestor is alarmed at the battle's increasing severity. Leaving his tent, he surveys with dismay the Greeks' rout and their broken fortifications. Thinking he might rejoin the fray, he instead determines to find and confer with Agamemnon. He meets Agamemnon, Diomedes, and Odysseus, and apprises them of the situation. Agamemnon proposes escape by night and return to Greece, to which Odysseus strenuously objects. Diomedes, apologizing for what might be deemed youthful impertinence (so also in Book 5), boasts of his lineage, urging that he, Odysseus, and Agamemnon (though wounded) rally the troops with their presence. As Agamemnon thus proceeds, Poseidon appears to him in the guise of an old man and encourages him with prospects of repelling the Trojans and claiming victory.

Seeing Zeus' partiality toward the Trojans, Hera undertakes to foil him. She goes to her chamber on Mt. Ida where she attires herself in finery—lotions, jewelry, tasseled cincture, fine clothing, and veil—planning to seduce Zeus and divert his attention through sleep. She obtains further attractions from Aphrodite and, seeking sleep from Hypnos, prevails on him with the bribe of a nymph to take as wife (the nymph he has always wanted). Hypnos humorously requires Hera to swear an oath by the river Styx—the gods' mightiest oath—that she will deliver on her bribe. He subsequently accompanies Hera to Mt. Ida, where he ascends a tree. Thus positioned above Zeus, he will induce the promised slumbers. (His position on high suggests sleep's descent.) Upon Zeus' inquiry, Hera makes excuses for her presence: she has stopped to see him while en route to another matter, her horses and chariot (Zeus notes their absence) left at the foot of Mt. Ida.

Increasingly overtaken by Hera's allure, Zeus proposes she immediately come to bed and, in one of the poem's most comical episodes, avows his passion by protesting he has never wanted any of his former lovers (cataloguing them) as he now wants Hera. Their union is consummated. Beyond its narrative function, as explained, the union recapitulates (judging from its fruitful effect on earth, below) a *hierogamy* 'divine marriage' or fertilizing ritual. Zeus sinks into post-coital slumber as Hypnos/Sleep hastens to Poseidon, urging him to continue assisting the Greeks. Poseidon continues as chief aid to the Greeks, Hector assuming the like role for the Trojans.

Seriously disabled by a huge stone thrown by Ajax, Hector is borne from the plain. Dizzied and spitting blood, he finally revives in Troy. Hector's disablement by Ajax, second mightiest of the Greeks after Achilles, foreshadows Hector's death by Achilles (the duel between Hector and Ajax in Book 7 the first forecast of that event). Hector's absence from the plain energizes the Greeks, who force a Trojan retreat.

Nor was Nestor incognizant of warcraft's cry,
Albeit at his wine, but to Asclepius' son
Addressed he wingèd words: "Reflect, good Machaōn,
How these matters fall. Louder by the ships resounds
The cry of stalwart youths, yet sit you now reposed 5
Imbibing flaming wine until Hecamēdē
Fair-haired make balmy your bath and cleanse your clotted
Wounds, but go I quickly, sound vantage to secure."
So speaking, he lifted his son's well-crafted shield,
The buckler of Thrasymēdēs, beaming brazen 10
In the hut, but the latter his father's now bore.
And grasped he a sturdy spear edged with sharpened bronze
And, standing outside, beheld impious doings:
The Argives routed; and the high-hearted Trojans
Driving them; and the Danaan wall demolished. 15
And as when swells the roiling sea with pregnant wave,
The supple gusts of whistling winds foretokening
Release, nor forward rolls the surf nor side to side

BOOK XIV

Until Zeus-directed gale descend; even so
The elder pondered, mind divided 'twixt the twain: 20
Whether to haste swift-steeded to the Danaans
Or to lord Agamemnon, shepherd of the host.
And as he pondered, this the prudent course appeared,
To seek out Atreus' son.
      But the others fought on,
Felling one another, and about their bodies 25
E'er clashed th' unyielding bronze as they parried with swords
And two-edged spears. And Nestor was met by the Zeus-
Nurtured kings as they approached him from the vessels,
Even all that had been wounded in war—Tydeus'
Son, Odysseus, and Atreidēs Agamemnon. 30
Distant from the fight on the shore of the hoary
Sea had they updrawn and positioned their vessels,
And a'front their bows had fashioned their defenses.
For the strand, however immense, nowise contained
The entire fleet, and the host was close constricted; 35
Thus had they drawn the vessels bow to stern, filling
As much of the wide-mouthed shoreline as the headlands
Between them allowed. And the kings approached, moving
In a group, each leaning on his spear to survey
The combat and toil, and grieved were their hearts within. 40

And the elder, Nestor, accosting them, startled
Their spirits all. Then wide-ruling Agamemnon
Uplifted his voice, addressing him: "O Nestor,
Son of Nēleus, most acclaimed of the Achaeans,
Why abandon you the encounter, bane of men, 45
Arriving here? I fear that resolute Hector
His word and threat accomplishes with which once he
Menaced us, proclaiming amid the Trojan host
That he would not return from our vessels to Troy,
Absent the vessels afire and our fighters slain. 50
Just so he proposed, and thus is it accomplished.
Alas! The other well greaved Achaeans surely

Swell with anger against me—as does Achilles,
Not least intending to save the ships." Then answered
The horseman Gerēnian Nestor: "Yes, verily, 55
Thus determined transpire these matters, nor could Zeus
Thunderer otherwise contrive them. For toppled
Is the wall unbreakable in which we trusted
As protection for the curvèd ships and ourselves.
And the Trojans untiring by the vessels fight, 60
Relenting not; nor might one resolve, however
Fully observant, whence routed are the Argives;
Thus crumble they confusedly, and the battle
Cry ascends high heaven. But now consider we,
Should thought avail, how present matters be resolved: 65
From fighting we refrain; battle fails the wounded."

Then responded the king of men, Agamemnon:
"Nestor, since proximate the vessels they engage,
And the sturdy parapet has availed us naught
Nor anywise the trench whereat the Achaeans 70
Labored grievously, hoping at heart it would serve
As stalwart hindrance for the vessels and ourselves,
Thus be it somehow mighty Zeus Cronidēs' wish
That the Achaeans here perish, far from Argos
Forgotten. This I perceived when with ample heart 75
He assisted the Danaans, and perceive it
Equally now when he glorifies the Trojans—
As though gods invincible—and constricts our might
And hands. So come as I bid, and obey we all.
From the vessels most adjacent the shore, draw we 80
Our ships away, these to the bright sea conveying,
And secure them afloat with anchor stones, biding
Immortal night if by night's behest the Trojans
Desist from war—and next hauling the fleet entire;
For none is the shame in retreating from ruin, 85
Yes, even neath night's concealment. Better our flight
Afar from bane than captive taken hereabouts."

BOOK XIV

Then crossly peering from neath his brows responded
Devious Odysseus: "Son of Atreus, what word
Escapes the barrier of your teeth, ill-omened   90
That you are? Would you commanded some different
cowardly host, no kingship claiming over us
To whom Zeus has allotted from youth to old age
The commission of wasting war, until perish
Every one of us. Do you truly consider   95
Abandonment of Troy, that thoroughfaring town,
On which account a torment untold besets us?
Be silent lest other Achaean ascertain
What should escape the lips of no person whate'er—
No sensible person possessing perception—   100
And especially a sovereign revered by men,
To wit, these Argives here. But I repudiate
Your resolution, this balderdash, commanding
Us, though contending and engaged, to draw seaward
Our vessels even-keeled, that more than heretofore   105
The Trojans be rejoiced—be victors even now—
And slaughter befall our feckless selves. For with ships
In retreat, the Argives forsake their enterprise
With ne'er a backward glance, gladsome their getaway.
Then, king of hosts, be your counsel our undoing."   110

To him responded Agamemnon, king of men:
"Odysseus, my heart beats sorely disconcerted
O'er this your harsh reproof; yet never would I urge
That Achaeans flee unwillingly, ships well-benched
Drawn downward to the billowed brine. But now would I   115
Prefer one better counseled for advice; whate'er
The measure of his years, right welcome would that be."
Then amid them Tydeus' son, Diomedes, spoke:
"Stands the man nearby, inquire of him no longer
If persuaded you will be. And begrudge me not,   120
Any of you, that I stand the least experienced.

But of fearless father and lineage am I come,
Of Tydeus, in Thebes interred beneath ample earth.
For Portheus three excellent sons begat, who dwelt
In Pleurōn and towering Calydōn—Melas, 125
Agrius, and third the horseman Oeneus, father
To my father and in valor preeminent.
There dwelt my forefather, Oeneus, but my father,
Far wandering, made Argos his home, even thus
The Olympians and Zeus desired it somehow. 130
And wedded he a daughter of lord Adrastus,
And flourishing in substance resided—bounty
Of wheat-bearing acreage his, and orchard plantings
'Round about, and plentiful cattle; and excelled
He with spear among the Achaeans—and of such 135
Have you likely heard, since true. Wherefore imagine you
Not that I languish in lineage or am cowardly,
And thus belittle my speaking, whate'er I speak
Aright. Return we of necessity to fight,
Though sorely wounded, but in battle past the range 140
Of missiles deployed, lest suffering wound on wound.
But to combat will we motivate the others,
Even those aloof in high dudgeon enduring,
From battle withdrawn." Thus he spoke, and readily
They attended and obeyed. So they proceeded, 145
And led them Agamemnon, overlord of men.

But far-famed Poseidon kept no uncaring watch
But attended them in semblance of an elder.
And taking Atreïdēs Agamemnon's hand,
Addressed him, declaring wingèd words as follows: 150
"Son of Atreus, now, I surmise, does Achilles'
Deadly heart within his breast delight, beholding
The Argive rout and slaughter, lacking such insight
As he altogether lacks; sooner perish he
Stricken by the immortals. But the blessèd gods 155
Begrudge you nothing. Even yet will the leaders

BOOK XIV

And chieftains of Troy lift dust aloft, stampeding
The expansive Trojan plain, yourself viewing them
Headed from the Greek encampment toward tow'ring Troy."
So saying, he shouted, shatteringly, rushing   160
Across the plain, as nine or even ten thousand
Warriors in battle shout, joining in Ares' strife;
Even thus thunderously shouted the shaker
Of earth, instilling great strength in Argive spirits
Each, to clash in battle and unrelenting war.   165

Now Hera golden-throned atop Olympus' peak
Observed Poseidon, recognizing him straightway
As he careered about in fame-conferring fight,
Her own brother and brother-in-law; and buoyed
Rose her spirit. And she espied Zeus, reposed high   170
On the topmost ridge of fountain-runneled Ida,
And exceedingly she loathed him. Then queenly ox-
Eyed Hera considered how best to inveigle
The mind of aegis-bearing Zeus. And this plan apt
To her appeared: to visit Ida fittingly   175
Adorned, that Cronidēs delight in taking her
Clasped closely aside him in love's caress whilst she
His lids and machinations all suffused with warm
And gentle slumber. So went she to her chamber,
By Hephaestus fashioned, her dear son, who fit it   180
With sturdy doors, to posts secured by hidden hinge,
That no other god might open. Entering therein,
She closed the shimmering doors.
                              With ambrosia first
She removed each stain from her heavenly body,
Anointing herself amply with oil. Ambrosial   185
And redolent its scent such that if decanted
In Cronidēs' residence, with threshold of bronze,
The aura would permeate all heaven and earth.
With this she anointed her beauteous self, combed
Her hair, and plaited the fair plentiful tresses   190

That streamed ambrosial from off her immortal head.
Next, in ambrosial garment wrapped she clothed herself,
A robe with consummate skill by Athena made,
Bountifully broidered about. And fastening it
With golden clasps, girded Hera her lower waist   195
With a hundred-tasseled sash, and through piercèd ears
Placed earrings hung with droplet-clustered ornaments,
The grace whereof glowed greatly. And with veil above,
Newly made and glistening, the goddess divine
Concealed herself, and white streamed the veil as sunshine;   200
And neath her dazzling feet, fair the sandals fastened.
And having thus adorned herself, she exited
Her chamber and summoned Aphrodite, speaking
Apart from the other gods as follows: "Would you
Now, dear child, by my petition be persuaded,   205
Or begrudge me, aggrieved that the Argives receive
My support while yours are the Trojan directives?"

Then rendered Zeus-born Aphrodite this response:
"Hera, daughter of Cronidēs, goddess revered,
Speak your mind since to its fulfillment I aspire,   210
If fulfill it I can and fulfilled it may be."
Then resplendent Hera deftly devising spoke:
"Bestow now love and desire, wherewith you subdue
Both immortals and mortalkind. For I journey,
Visiting the bounds of all-nurturing Gaia   215
And Oceanus who have engendered the gods,
And mother Tethys—the two that nursed and cherished
Me within their halls, receiving me from Rhea
When far-seeing Zeus Cronidēs entombed Cronus
Under earth and unharvested sea. Them will I   220
Visit, ending, I hope, their enduring dispute,
Since now continually abstain they aloof
From each other and from conjugal bed and love,
Since anger distempers them both. If I with words
Their sprits might induce, rejoining them in love,   225

To them ever reverenced and cherished would I be."
Then responded laughter-loving Aphrodite:
"Becomes it not your bidding to decline, for sleep
You the night in Cronidēs' encircling caress."
She spoke and from her breast unbound the decorate   230
Belt, with all manner of allurement embroidered:
Therein love, therein desire, and dalliance therein,
Beguilements unsettling the steadfast of spirit.
This she consigned to her hands, addressing her thus:
"Take, attaching to your breasts, this belt with every   235
Blandishment adorned. For not, I aver, will you
Depart, the doing undone, whate'er your spirit
Might wish accomplished." So she declared, and ox-eyed
Queenly Hera smiled and smiling arranged the belt
About her breasts. Then homeward went Aphrodite,   240
Daughter of Zeus. But the lady Hera darted
Leaving Olympus, to Pieria and charmed
Emathia arrived, o'er-ranging the powdered peaks
Of Thracian horsemen, but little making contact
With the topmost pinnacles, and from Athos trod   245
The swelling sea, entering Lemnos the city
Of godlike Thoas. There she accosted Sleep, Death's
Brother and, clasping him by the hand, addressed him:
"Sleep, lord of all gods and humankind, if ever
You heeded word of mine, so acquiesce you now,   250
And ever grateful will I be. Lull Zeus asleep,
His eyes becalmed beneath his brows when once in love
Aside him I have lain. And gifts will I lavish,
A handsome throne, gold-crafted, imperishable,
That goodly Hephaestus, my son, strong-sinewed god,   255
Shall labor, fashioning, a stool beneath it set
To ease your feet while frolicking your time away."
And elated Sleep replied responding: "Hera,
Honored of goddesses, mighty Cronus' sister,
Some other of the immortals would I lightly   260
Lull to sleep, even the rivulets of river

Oceanus, from whom they issue engendered;
But from Zeus Cronidēs will I distance myself,
Soothing him not to slumber unless he himself
Command it. For aforetime did behest of yours 265
Ensnare me—that time when high-hearted Heracles,
Scion of Zeus, departed from Ilium, having
Wasted the Trojan town. Then beguiled I the mind
Of aegis-bearing Zeus, shedding me about him
While you within your heart concocted villainy 270
Against his son, rousing billows of savage wind
O'er the foaming deep, delivering him to Cos,
That well-tenanted isle, from his kinsmen afar.
But Zeus, awakening, grew wroth and flung the gods
Throughout the palace in every which direction; 275
And me especially he sought and had propelled
From firmament to flinty-fathomed depths, submerged
Entire, had not Night intervened, subduer
Of gods and men. To her in my flight I arrived
Secure, and Zeus relented, albeit enraged, 280
For reluctant was he to afford displeasure
To hurried Night. Nonetheless, you now command me
Undertake this doing, nowise dischargeable."

To him the ox-eyed queenly Hera responded:
"Sleep, why thus obsess at heart? Think you Cronidēs 285
Far-seeing will aid the Trojans, even as waxed
He aforetime wroth for Heracles' sake, his son?
This grant, and a girlish grace will I award you
To wed and call your wife; even Pasithea."
So she spoke and rejoiceant Sleep responded thus: 290
"Come, by th' inviolable waters of Styx attest,
With one hand set to bounteous earth, the other
To boundless sea, that all before us witness be,
Even the nethergods with Cronus, that truly
You will give me of the girlish graces one, yes, 295
Dearest Pasithea for whom for all my days

Aforetime I have pined." Thus he spoke, and Hera
White-armed goddess with alacrity complied, swore
As he commanded, and entreated all the gods
Called Titans, resident in Hades. But after 300
She had sworn and concluded the oath, the goddess
And Sleep decamped, leaving Lemnos and Imbros, robed
Around in mist, and journeyed rapidly away,
En route to many-fountained Ida sped, the mother
Of feral beasts, even unto Lectum, where first 305
They left the sea, making landfall; and the topmost
Forest bristled neath their feet. And there Sleep halted
Ere Cronidēs noted him, ascending a fir
Tree, supremely thrusting upward from Mt. Ida,
Invading the vaporous heavens. Thereupon 310
Alighted he on fir bough densely blanketed,
Like to a clear-voiced mountain bird that immortals
Call Chalcis, and men Cymindis.
                              But the goddess
Flew swiftly upward to Gargarus peak, the top
Of towering Ida; and cloud-gathering Zeus 315
Beheld her, whereupon delirium dismantled
His wits, even as when in dalliance and love they
First copulated, their parents none the wiser.
And standing before her spoke Zeus, to this effect:
"Hera, what call from Olympus compels you here, 320
For absent the chariot and horses bearing you?"
Then craftily the Olympian queen responded:
"I travel to visit the boundary of earth
All-nurturing, and Oceanus, fountainhead
Of gods begotten, and mother Tethys, the twain 325
Having loved and reared me in their halls. Them will I
Visit, wanting to end their enduring dispute,
Since now persistently aloof have they remained
From one another and from marriage-bed and love,
For vexation discomfits them. And my horses, 330
At the foot of fountainous Ida fastened, stand,

Whence they will bear me o'er a treacherous terrain
And untiring main alike. But on your account
Have I now come from Olympus lest hereafter
You resent my departure, surreptitiously 335
Made, to Oceanus' full fathomless abode."

Then addressing her, cloud-gathering Zeus replied:
"Hera, travel you there some other time. But now,
We two, convene we neath quilts and ecstatic sheets,
For never yet has love of goddess or woman 340
Of mortal born commanded me thus or mastered
The heart within my breast—no, not when overcome
With love of Ixion's wife who begot Peirithous,
The peer of gods in counsel; or of fair-ankled
Danaë, daughter of Acrisius, who bore 345
Perseus, above warriors all preeminent;
Or of far-famed Phoenix' child who begot Minōs
And godlike Rhadamanthys; or of Semelē;
Or Theban Alcmēnē begetting Heracles,
A son resolutely bold, Semelē begetting 350
Dionysus, source to mortals of vineyard joy;
Or of Demeter, fair-tressed queen; or of splendid
Leto; and now of your very self, as even
Now I love you, and sweet longing envelopes me."
Then crafty-minded queenly Hera responded: 355
"Dreaded Cronidēs, what doings declare you thus?
If you desire on Ida's peaks in passionate
Embrace to be bedded, all clear will be observed:
How will it appear if by the gods immortal
We be espied abed, we two, the other gods 360
Apprised of it? Then never could I, from our sleep
Awakening, innocently bask in your house—
Shameful the appearance! But if thus your desire
And steadfast your intention, you have a chamber
Fashioned by Hephaestus, dear son of yours, fitted 365
Firmly its doors upon their posts. There venturing,

BOOK XIV

Bedded shall we be if bed be your obsession."
Then Cronidēs cloud-gathering Zeus responded:
"Hera, fret not that god or mortalkind observe,
In gold-thickened cloud thus concealed shall I hide us,   370
That Helios, the sun himself, will want for sight,
Whose penchant for observances e'ermore prevails."

Therewith did Cronidēs clasp Hera to his chest
And beneath them sacred earth made gladsome grasses
Grow, flow'r of dewey lotus, crocus, and teeming   375
Hyacinth to blanket the surface beneath them.
Therein the two reposed, in cloudiness attired,
In golden billow whence dewy drops descended.
On Gargarus summit thus slumbered Zeus, by love
And sleep subdued, enfolding the lady Hera.   380
But Sleep to the Argive ships decamped with tidings
To the circler and shaker of earth, and approached,
Speaking wingèd words: "Alacrity, Poseidon!
Encourage the Achaeans and furnish them fame,
If but briefly the while, since Zeus yet slumbers fast;   385
Sleepiness quite suffuses him, since coaxed abed
By Hera's deft allure." So he spoke, departing
To the fabled tribes of men, prompting Poseidon
To assist the Danaans the more. Quickly then
To the forefront sped, he shouted aloud: "Argives,   390
Shall we yet again cede victory to Hector,
Priam's son, that he capture the vessels, winning
Glory? For Hector himself commands the outcome
Whilst Achilles loiters by the hollow ships, his
heart filled with hate. But without him might we manage,   395
Ourselves bestirrèd and bearing each other aid.
So come, even as I enjoin, obey we all:
Donning our bucklers, the largest and best we have,
Protecting our heads with refulgent helmets' fire,
Taking our stoutest spears—proceed we by my lead.   400
Nor will Hector the longer withstand us, I vow,

However desirous. And whoe'er be valiant,
Bearing small buckler before him, let him confer
It on a henchman, a larger buckler claiming."
Thus he proposed, and well they listened and obeyed. 405
Diomedes, Odysseus, and Agamemnon
Atreidēs, wounded though they were, set the others
In array, and proceeded exchanging armor—
The ablest fighters the best outfitted; the flawed
Furnished the worst. Their brazen armor donned, they stepped 410
To Poseidon's pace. In his mighty hand he grasped
His grievous sword, keenly edged, with lightning a'flash;
Which encountered in battle were harrowing quite,
A'fore it quaking mortalkind, keeping apart.

Hector opposite them assembled the Trojans. 415
Brave Hector and dark-haired Poseidon thus fiercely
Contended—Hector for Troy, and for the Argives
Poseidon, and plangent the tumult the armies
Unleashed by the Argive vessels and encampment,
As the sea insistently sounded about them 420
And to shoreward hurtled reverberant surges
More raucously than when tempest-driven from the north;
Nor more forcefully roars a blaze than when feeding
On desiccate woodlands across the forest floor;
Nor bellows more boldly the hellbent wind a'howl 425
Through treetops than the howl horrific by Trojans
And Argives raised against each other contending.
First cast Hector at Ajax, fully fronting him,
Nor faulty his aim. The weapon struck where the twin
Bands crossed his chest—those of his buckler and silver- 430
Studded sword sustaining his undefended flesh.
And furious was Hector, his spear wastefully spent,
And avoiding death he retreated neath cover
Of his men. And as he withdrew, Telamonian
Ajax smote him with a stone lying thereabouts 435
Of those there brought to steady the vessels ashore.

BOOK XIV

Of those seized Ajax one, striking above the rim
Of Hector's shield, by the neck, which spun him top-like
Around as he dithered in divers direction.
As headlong falls an oak uprooted by lightning 440
Released by omnipotent Zeus—sulf'rous the reek—
Leaving none undismayed who chance standing nearby,
For dreaded stands the thunderbolt of father Zeus;
Even so toppled Hector downward tasting dust,
His spear, dislodged, departed his hand, and his helm 445
And shield buckled inward, his decorate armor
Resounding about him.
                And came the Achaeans,
Clamoring loud as they rushed, intending to drag
Him away, on the Trojans discharging their darts;
But none could injure or strike the people's shepherd, 450
By Trojan princes e'er securely surrounded—
Polydamas, Aeneas, Agēnōr, noble
Glaucus, and Sarpēdōn, Lycian spearmen's leader.
Of the others too remained no one unmindful
Of Hector, shields interlocking to protect him. 455
And his companions uplifted him, bearing him
From battle and toil to his fleet-footed horses,
Aback the formations of fighting men stationed,
The driver with decorate car awaiting him.
These then cityward conveyed him anguished with pain. 460
But arrived at the tide of fair-flowing Xanthus,
Of immortal Zeus begotten, they dismounted him from the chariot,
Laid him upon the ground, and doused him with water;
And regaining sentience, opened Hector his eyes;
Then forward kneeling he vomited dark blood—next 465
Crashing groundward prone—and again did inky night
Enveil his vision, reeling yet from the upset.

When the Argives 'spied Hector departing the plain
They were heartened, more incitedly assailing
The Trojans. Ajax, Oïleus' fleet son, first sprang 470

Upon Satnius, Ēnops' son, with bladed tool
To run him through—beauteous the naiad that bore him
To Ēnops tending cattle by the riverbanks
Of Satnioeis. Oileus' son, approaching, smote
Him to the flank, felling him cold; and crazed the row   475
Between Trojans and Achaeans for his remains.
Approached Polydamas, son of Panthous, as spear-
Wielding avenger and wounded Prothoēnōr,
Areilykus' offspring, rightward to the shoulder;
And savage the spearpoint there passing; and fell he   480
Earthward dropping dead to the dust. Polydamas
Vaunted over him, gloating: "Again, I attest,
Not vainly exits the spear the vigorous grip
Of Polydamas; but some Argive bears it off—
A steadying staff—to guide his gait to Hades."   485
Grieving, groaned the Argives on account of the vaunt.

And most did it pique Telamonian Ajax,
For the companion closest him had there collapsed.
So aimed he well at Polydamas in retreat,
But Polydamas leaping sideways avoided   490
Dismal death, and the spear lodged in Archelochus,
Antēnōr's son, for his death had the gods decreed.
It struck where head and neck conjoin atop the spine,
Slicing the sinews aback the skull; and visage
And head, clean severed, more quickly encountered dirt   495
Than the corpse that followed after. And Ajax called
Thus to Polydamas: "Think you, Polydamas,
And truly relate whether this man doth merit
The killing, he an equal to Prothoēnōr:
Worthy he seems—neither vile nor of lineage vile—   500
A brother, perhaps, or son of the horse-táming
Antēnōr, yes, and to him most bearing semblance."

Thus spoke he knowingly, and despondence beset
Trojan dispositions. And Acamas astride

BOOK XIV

His brother wounded the Boeotian Promachus 505
Who by the feet assayed to extricate the corpse
From under Acamas. And Acamas swaggered,
Boldly announcing: "You Argives, raging archers,
Insatiate of boast; not solely o'er us, observe,
Shall hardship and toil prevail, but in like degree 510
Shall Achaeans recoil. Note how your Promachus
Sleeps, defeated by my spear, that my brother's blood
Be not long unavenged. Truly for such reason
Wants a warrior his kinsman as warder of ruin."
So he spoke, and grief gripped the Argives adjudging 515
The boast, and stirred it especially the spirit
Of prudent Pēneleōs who rushed Acamas,
But Acamas withstood the onslaught of princely
Pēneleōs. But the latter, thrusting, slaughtered
Ilioneus, Phorbas' son, a holder of herds 520
Whom, specially loved of Trojans, Hermes endowed.
And to Phorbas bore his mother, Ilioneus,
A solitary child. Him Pēneleōs struck
Beneath the brow, penetrating the eye, the orb
Outrooting, the shaft traversing the socket through 525
And outing the tendons of his neck; and sat he
Extending both his hands. But Pēneleōs, sword
Aloft, forcefully drove upon his neck, groundward
Lopping head and helmet hewn. But the ample spear
Transfixed the socket yet; and uphoisting the spear— 530
A stalk topped by a poppy's head—Pēneleōs
Proudly proclaimed: "Trojans, instruct on my behalf
That Ilioneus' father and lady mother
Weep within their halls; for the wife of Promachus,
Alegēnōr's son, will not relish the return 535
Of her beloved spouse when we Danaan lads
Decamp aboard our ships, evacuating Troy.
So he spoke, and trembling beset their limbs straight through,
And sought each man to distance his own destruction.
Tell me now, you Muses dwelling on Olympus, 540

Who of the Argives early absconded with blood-
Stained spoils once the illustrious shaker of earth
Had intervened. First truly was Telamonian
Ajax, who smote Hyrtius, Gyrtius' son, commander
Of the stalwart Mysians. And Antilochus stripped 545
The spoils of Phalcēs off, and Mērionēs slew
Morys and Hippotiōn, and Teucer slaughtered
Periphētēs and Prothoōn. And Atreus' son,
Thrusting to his flank, pierced Hyperēnōr, people's
Shepherd, and the cleaving bronze disemboweled him, 550
And hastened his soul, escaped through the stricken wound,
And darkness descended his sight. But fighters most
Despatched Ajax swift son of Oïleus, for none
Like unto him pursued 'mid the routing of men—
Fleet-footed he—when Zeus Cronidēs sanctioned flight. 555

~ Book XV ~

Zeus Awakens and Chastises Hera,
The Greeks are Repulsed to Their Ships,
the Doings of Ajax, the Fifth Day of Battle

Zeus wakes from sleep on Mt. Ida, surveys the extent of what has transpired—the Trojan rout, Hector wounded—and scolds and threatens Hera for her treachery, reminding her of past retributions he has visited on her and on other sometime recalcitrant gods. Hera makes excuses, all accepted by Zeus, who will relent if she promises to cooperate by removing Poseidon from the plain and inspiriting the recovered Hector to lead the fighting on.

Bringing renewed focus to the storyline and fatedness of events, Zeus recollects his promise to Thetis, that he would distress the Greeks (Book 1) for the dishonored Achilles' sake—this his renewed priority. He further prophesies his son Sarpedon's death at the hand of Patroclus; Patroclus' death (in revenge) at the hand of Hector; and Hector's death (in revenge) at the hands of Achilles. Only then will fate be fulfilled, the Trojans ultimately repulsed and Troy taken.

Hera leaves Ida for Mt. Olympus, where she is cordially received by the feasting gods. She intends to bruit her dissatisfaction with Zeus but is considerate not to spoil their feasting (this also Hephaestus' concern, end of Book 1). She eventually holds forth against Zeus' innate sense of superiority (against which nothing can be done). She gains the gods' sympathy by pointing to the death of Ascalaphus, son of the war god Ares. Infuriated by this reminder, Ares arms himself, intending to reenter the fray, but is stopped and disarmed by Athena, who fears the outcome of Ares' renewed participation.

Hera bids Apollo and Iris visit Zeus on Olympus and do whatever he commands, to wit, force Poseidon's withdrawal. Iris delivers the message to

Poseidon, reminding him of Zeus' superiority. An indignant Poseidon avers that Zeus rules only heaven and earth and that—following the primordial tripartite division—he, Poseidon, rules the seas, and Hades the underworld. Poseidon, in brief, will not obey. However, and with Iris' importuning, he reconsiders—i.e., the hierarchy cannot be disavowed—but swears eternal enmity against Zeus if the latter allow Troy's survival.

Affirming his own superiority, Zeus approves Poseidon's withdrawal. He then dispatches Apollo, aegis in hand, to rally Hector and the Trojans, while the Greeks, lacking Poseidon, retreat. The Greek Thoas, dismayed at Hector's revival, harangues the Greeks to engage the foe, and the Greeks rearm themselves with fresh resolve. Apollo takes the lead, brandishing the aegis; and the Greeks, though fighting hard, are routed amid the continuing mayhem—impaled as they fall into their own protective trench. But Apollo levels enough of the fortification to create a walkway for the Trojans. His action forces the Greeks even farther back to the ships, where the battle feverishly continues. No longer content to fight in the melee, Ajax boards the ships, repelling the Trojans with a pike intended for battle at sea (no such battle actually recounted in Homer).

Hearing the uproar, Patroclus—still tending the wounded Eurypylus—emphasizes his need to reach Achilles, completing the mission on which he was sent, namely, to identify the wounded Machaon (Book 11). Meanwhile, the two sides battle to a stalemate, and a Trojan effort to burn the ships proves unsuccessful. There ensues an archery assault by the Greek Teucer who, depleting his supply of arrows, dons traditional battle gear and takes a stand aside Telamonian Ajax. Noticing this, Hector rallies his troops, as does Ajax the Greeks, and general melee ensues. The pike-armed Ajax, onboard the ships, heroically defends them deck to deck, killing off no fewer than twelve assailants.

※

But when the Trojans in their rout had traversed both
Trench and palisade, many vanquished by Argive
Hands, restrained they remained aside their chariots,
Abashed and ashen with fear; and Zeus Cronidēs
On Ida awoke, aside him white-armed Hera.   5

BOOK XV

Vaulting forth, observed he the Trojans and Argives:
Routed the Trojans, Argives driving from behind,
And among them lord Poseidon, and Hector prone
Upon the plain, his companions gathered 'round him,
Faint he with labored breath, forth spewing blood, for not   10
The feeblest of the Argives had engaged with him.
And Zeus lord ruler of gods and men took pity
And with fearsome regard rebuked Hera, saying:
"Wearisome Hera, this scurrilous scheme of yours
Removes intrepid Hector from the fight and routs   15
The Trojan host. For such contrivances as these
Will you especially ache, stripped and flogged to stripes.
Recall you not when by your ankles you were strung
Aloft, by suspended anvils counterweighted,
A golden band unbreakable restraining both   20
Your wrists? And dangled you there, thrashing middle air,
Cloud-encased, and the Olympian deities
Indignant grew, succeeding not as they assayed
To loosen you. No, whomsoe'er I caught I snatched
And from the threshold hurled until he tasted earth,   25
His strength unstrung. And yet my spirit even so
Was unrelieved of endless pain for Heracles
The godlike, whom you—with the North Wind's contrivance,
Releasing his gusts o'er the tireless sea—bore off
Maliciously to well-populated Cos. Thence   30
I rescued and restored him, laboring sorely
Between times, to Argos pasture of horses. Such
Recollect I again for you, that you desist
From deception, learning how little it avail—
To wit, that dalliance wherewith you bedded me when,   35
Absent the immortals, you crafted trickery."

So he proclaimed, and ox-eyed queenly Hera quaked
And with wingèd words addressed him: "Now be Gaia
My witness, and Heaven above, and the ebbing
Styx aflow, the greatest and most harrowing oath   40

Wherewith gods pledge; be witness your own countenance
And the marriage bed we keep, by which ne'er would I
Be forsworn: by no wish of mine does Poseidon,
Shaker of earth, afflict Hector and the Trojans,
Assisting these others. Sooner I surmise his 45
Own spirit impels him, seeing the Danaans
By their vessels constrained, wherefore he pities them.
But devoutly would I have him forbear withal,
O dark hurler of thunder, howso you command."

So she spoke, and smiled the father of men and gods 50
And, answering her in wingèd words, responded thus:
"If truly, ox-eyed queenly Hera, your counsel
Concurred with mine hereafter when among the gods
You sit, lord Poseidon, however impassioned
His purpose, would quickly defer to our wishes. 55
But if true your declaration, decamp you now
Amid the tribes of gods and here summon Iris
And bow-famed Apollo, that she, amid the host
Of bronze-mailed Achaeans sped, instruct Poseidon
To cease from fight, returning home. But let Phoebus 60
Apollo wake Hector, inspiring him with fight,
That he forget the grief that now torments his heart
And annihilate the Argive host, bestirring
Within them unsettling disorder that, tumbling
Back amid the umbrous vessels of Achilles, 65
They fall, and Achilles enlist his companion
Patroclus—though falling to glorious Hector's spear
Afore the face of Troy—after Hector despatches
Other youths aplenty, among them my offspring,
Divine Sarpēdōn. And incensed for Patroclus 70
Shall godly Achilles slay Hector, whereafter
Shall I from the ships unleash a Trojan retreat
Unending, uninterrupted, 'til the Argives
Take towering Troy through counsel of Athena.
But continues my wrath unabated 'til then, 75

BOOK XV

Nor allow I any other immortal god
To reinforce the Argives 'til accomplished be
The longing of Achilles, Peleus' son, even
As I first agreed when nodding my assurance,
The goddess Thetis clasping my knees and craving   80
Acclaim for Achilles, ransacker of cities."

So he proclaimed, and the goddess white-armed Hera
Failed not to obey but thence retired from Ida's
Ridge to Olympus' peak. And even as deftly
Courses the mind of one traversing distant space,   85
And ponders he within his breast, "Would I were here
Or yon," and limitless range his imaginings;
Just so, and thus eagerly, advanced queen Hera,
Atop steep-pinnacled Olympus appearing
Where convened the immortals at Cronidēs' house,   90
Assembled all. And they arose observing her
And toasted her coming. But ignored she the lot
And from fair-cheeked Themis, running first to greet her,
Took the cup, and Themis addressed her wingèd words:
"Why come you, Hera, likened unto one distraught;   95
In truth has Zeus your royal spouse unsettled you?"
Then did the goddess white-armed Hera make reply:
"Ask not, dear Themis, of this delicate matter.
His humor know you well: how supercilious,
How resolute. But let the gods commence their well-   100
Apportioned feast within the halls, as I relate
Amid the immortals the wretched villainy
Proposed by Zeus. No heart, I aver, will it please
Whether mortal or divine if pleasant repast
Be proposèd."
             Having thus advised, the lady   105
Hera assumed her seat, and the gods grew angered
Throughout Cronidēs' house. And her lips signaled mirth,
But above sullen brows her forehead slackened not,
And indignant the while she berated them thus:

"Fools, to be witless wroth with Zeus! Truly would we, 110
Approaching, draw near and subvert his will by deed
Or interdiction, but distant he sits, deeming
This matter unworthy of consideration.
For amid the gods immortal he deems himself
Unequaled, in muscle and might. Be contented, 115
Just so, to suffer his villainy, whatever
He propose. Even now, I surmise, has sorrow
O'erwhelmed Ares, that his offspring, of mortals all
The dearest him, to combat has succumbed, even
Ascalaphus whom Ares designates his own." 120
So she proclaimed, but Ares struck his sturdy thighs
With palms downturned and thus plaintively responded:
"Dwellers on Olympus, hold me not to account
If at the Argive ships I avenge my offspring's
Demise, guaranteed though I be by Zeus' lightning 125
To lie prostrate in the bloodied dust of the dead."
So he spoke, bidding Rout and Terror his horses
Yoke, and himself donned dazzling armor. Far greater
The choler and outrage then risen, and graver,
Twixt Zeus and the immortals had not Athena, 130
Fearful for the gods, sped exiting the portal—
The throne abandoned where she sat—and seized the helm
From Ares' head and the buckler from his shoulders,
And snatched from out his mighty hand the brazen spear,
Now placed aside, rebuking maddened Ares thus: 135
"Deranged that you are, distraught, and wizened of wit!
Unavailing your ears to listen, and truant
Your measure of meet and proper comprehension.
Harken you not to what white-armed Hera proclaims,
Consort of lordly Cronidēs, just now arrived. 140
Would you yourself, this vengeance to fruition brought,
Return perforce to Olympus despite your pangs,
For us other gods sowing seeds of misfortune?
For fast will Zeus forsake the great-hearted Trojans
And Achaeans and himself to Olympus fly, 145

There to unleash consternation, on each laying
Hands in turn, both the guilty and the innocent.
Wherefore I encourage you for your offspring's sake
To put fury by. Ere now have fallen many
Superior to your son in sturdiness and hand, 150
Or will yet be felled; thus difficult to rescue
The lineage and offspring of man." So she spoke,
Relegating furious Ares to his throne.

But Hera summoned Apollo from out the hall,
And Iris, messenger of the immortal gods, 155
And speaking, addressed them wingèd words: "Summons Zeus
The pair of you to Ida, and hasten, please do;
And once arrived afore Zeus' commanding presence,
See you to that which he imposes and commands."
Thus instructing, queenly Hera returned anew, 160
Installed upon her throne; but forward sprang the twain
Posthaste, arriving to many-fountained Ida,
Mother of feral beasts, and found far-seeing Zeus
Upon Gargarus' topmost summit, circleted
With radiant cloud. And they entered the presence 165
Of cloud-gathering Zeus; and his heart angered not
Beholding them, for Hera's order had they fast
Obeyed. And first to Iris spoke he wingèd words:
"Speed you your way, swift Iris, to lord Poseidon,
Bearing this message and trusty messenger be: 170
Command him, quitting war's mangling maw, to rejoin
The immortal gods or beneath the briny plunge.
And if, dismissive of heed, he refuse, bethink
He himself, in spirit and heart, that however
Hardy he be, he will ill endure my onslaught, 175
For far abler in might am I, and elder born.
Yet recks he not, affirming himself my equal,
That afore my godhead stand all gods confounded."
So he spoke, and failed not the wind-footed Iris
To attend, but Troyward from Ida descended. 180

And as when glistening frost or hail escapes the clouds,
Aether-borne by blustering winds disseminate;
Even so, fleetly hastened Iris forth and nigh
Poseidon encircler of earth approached and said:
"A word for you, O dark-haired encircler of earth, 185
Have I come conveying from aegis-bearing Zeus.
He bids your withdrawal from battle, rejoining
The gods' assembly or submerged within the brine;
And if ignoring his bidding you disobey,
He threatens himself to approach, besetting you 190
In combat, and bids you avoid his valiant hand,
Averring his superiority of force
And generation. Yet parade you his equal
Afore whom every other god confounded stands."

Wrathful then responded the glorious encircler: 195
"For heaven's sake, though great his might, egregiously
Has he spoken, if by force and despite my will
He would restrain me, like in honor to himself.
For three brothers are we, of Cronus and Rhea
Begotten: Zeus and myself, and Hades the third, 200
Lord of the lifeless below. And parceled by thirds
Exists the portion allotted each. I indeed
When lots were drawn the hoary sea apportioned took,
My habitation evermore; and claimed Hades
Nether night; and Zeus the expansive firmament, 205
By aether and cloud augmented. But shared remain
The precincts of Olympus and broad-breasted earth,
Wherefore to Zeus will I in nowise acquiesce,
But sooner rule he quietly his one-third realm,
Whatever his power. And seek he not by force 210
Imposed to disquiet me as though craven born.
His sons and daughters, issue of his proper flesh,
Let him sooner bully and bellow at, they who
Perforce will accede to whatever he command."
And windy-footed Iris in turn responded: 215

"Is this, O encircler of earth, you dark-haired god,
Your tiding for transmittal to Zeus, adamant
And harsh, or might you reconsider? For good hearts
Are ever pliant. You know how the Erinyes
Doggedly follow, assisting the eldest born." 220
Then again responded the earth-encircling lord:
"Goddess Iris, this word have you rightly spoken,
And befits it when a messenger gets the gist.
But by this am I unsettled, spirit and soul,
Whene'er with unmindful talk one thinks to berate 225
Another in allotment alike to himself,
To whom fate has affirmed a commensurate part.
But now I yield, indignation notwithstanding.
And the more will I recount, attend you my threat:
If despite Athena driver of spoils and me, 230
And despite lord Hephaestus, Hermes, and Hera,
He spare steep Troy, insistently preserving it,
And accelerate Argive atrophy, then know
He this, that betwixt us twain persists this choler
Unabated." So counseling, the earth shaker, 235
Seaward bound decamped the Danaan multitude
And plummeted deep, by the Argives sorely missed.

Then lord cloud-collecting Zeus to Apollo spoke:
"Dear Apollo, to Hector brazen-armored go,
For now the enfolder and shaker of earth has 240
Returned to the deep, averting our utter wrath;
Else were our dispute apparent to others, too,
Even to gods in the netherworld with Cronus.
But thus preferable far for Poseidon and me
That he yielded, ere then though enraged, avoiding 245
My hands, for replete with toil the result. But take
The tasseled aegis and, savagely shaking it,
Affright the Argive warriors. As for yourself,
Far-shooting archer, be glorious Hector your care,
The while bestirring his mettle, until such time 250

As the Argives decamping, gain the Hellespont
And their ships. Thence will I myself both word and deed
Contrive, providing respite to Argive travail."
So he spoke, nor slighted Apollo his father's
Command but descended Ida's slopes—a falcon, 255
Swiftest slayer of doves, the fleetest bird a'flight.
Goodly Hector he found, wise-hearted Priam's son,
Upseated, no longer prone, newly gathering
Grit, and of his comrades around him cognizant.
And his heaving and sweating had ceased, for the will 260
Of aegis-bearing Zeus revived him. And Phoebus
The far-working archer god approached and proclaimed:
"Hector, Priam's son, why sit you faint and aloof
From the others? What concern this that constrains you?"
Then, though exhausted, proclaimed Hector brazen-helmed: 265
"What god are you, O mighty one, that questions me
Directly? Know you not that by the Argive ships,
As I slaughtered his comrades, war-crying Ajax
Cast stones assailing me, a stone staying my strength?
And seemed I that moment to enter Hades' house, 270
Passing on, as I reposed wheezing forth my life."
Then the far-shooting god Apollo addressed him:
"Be of courage, so awesome a helper has Zeus
Despatched from Ida to your aid, even myself,
Apollo of the golden sword, who time ago 275
E'er protected tow'ring Ilium and yourself.
But come now, command the ranks of charioteers
To incite their steeds, charging the hollow vessels;
And hastening ahead will I, routing the Greeks,
Ready all." So speaking, he wakened Hector's might. 280
Even as when a stabled horse, at the manger
Fully sated, his halter bursts, and headlong runs
O'er the plain, accustomed in fair-flowing waters
To bathe, exultant, his head on high uplifted,
And about his shoulders surges his streaming mane, 285
And delights him his splendor as quickly his knees

BOOK XV

Convey him to equine retreats and pasturage;
Thus sprightly plied Hector his knees and rapid step,
Inciting his charioteers at the god's command.
And as dogs and rustic rabble rout a hornèd 290
Stag or feral goat, but sheer the cliff or shading
Shrub protecting it, nor manage they to find it,
And their clamor summons a well-maned lion forth,
And quickly they flee though earlier determined;
Even so the Argives thrusted in throngs with swords 295
And two-edged spears, but when glimpsing Hector ranging
About the warrior ranks, panic unnerved them quite,
And their hardihood at their very feet collapsed.

Then among them spoke Thoas, son of Andraemōn,
Of the Aetolians far the finest—javelin-skilled 300
In throwing, but equally resolute in close
Encounter—by few of the Achaeans surpassed
In council whene'er young men compete in debate.
Intending them well, he addressed them as follows:
"Truly great the marvel I behold, that Hector 305
Now has risen, cozening fate. In truth, our hearts
Had one and all fancied him dead by Ajax, son
Of Telamon, but now has some god delivered
And defended him, he who has undone the knees
Of Argive multitudes; this, I deem, will endure 310
Even now, since by mandate of thundering Zeus
He strides, advancing, an ardent champion. But come,
Let us comply as I command. As for the host,
They shelter by their vessels; but we, declaring
Ourselves best within the host, take we position, 315
Being first to face Hector, spearpoints forward poised
Provoking his retreat; then, I aver, will he
Seek, however keen, to avoid the Argive host."
So he spoke and, hearing, they readily obeyed.
Those with Ajax and Idomeneus, with Teucer, 320
With Mēriones, and Meges, peer of Ares,

Signaled the chieftains and mustered for fight, fronting
Hector and the Trojans, but fared the multitude
To the Argive fleet away. Then forward advanced
The foe in close array, and Hector commanded, 325
Dauntlessly advancing, as Phoebus Apollo
Afore them advanced, his shoulders be-shawled in mist,
Fronting the dread ferocious aegis—radiantly
Fringed about—that the smithy Hephaestus conferred
Upon Zeus as ensign in the rout of warriors; 330
This ahead the host held Apollo in his grip.
And the gathered Argives awaited their advance,
And sounded the warcry, deafening all around,
And arrows leapt from bowstrings, and hurtled weapons
From forceful hands discharged; some finding young warriors 335
Speedy to battle, while others, finding nothing,
Fell midway gripped to ground with deficit of flesh
On which to feed. Now, so long as Apollo held
The aegis steadfastly to hand, even so long
Did the weapons of both sides batter their targets, 340
And warriors fell; but when, brandishing the aegis,
He frontally faced the swift-driving Danaans,
Imparting a deafening shout, then rendered he
Faint the fortitude within their breasts, and forgot
They their ruinous might. Even as when wild beasts twain 345
With consternation fill the herded kine or flock
Of sheep, coming in deadly darkness upon them,
And want they for their herdsman; thus the Danaans
Were defenseless driven in rout, for Apollo,
Exalting the Trojans and Hector, unnerved them. 350

Then amid augment of mayhem took man his man.
Slew Hector Stichius and Arcesilaüs,
Brazen-coated they: one a Boeotian captain;
The other, trusted companion of unstinting
Menestheus. And Aeneas despatched Iasus 355
And Medōn, he a bastard son of the godlike

Oïleus, and brother of Ajax, but dwelt he
In Phylacē far from his native land, having
Slain the kin of his stepmother Eriopis,
To Oïleus wed; and Iasus the Athenians   360
Led, son of Sphelus, son of Bucolus. And slew
Polydamas Mecisteus; Politēs, Echius
In the forefront of the fight, and felled was Clonius
By goodly Agēnōr; and Paris from behind
Struck Deïochus, amid the foremost fleeing,   365
In the shoulder, the bronze neatly burrowing through.
The foe despoiling these of armor, the Argives
Sought safety, faltering about the tunneled trench
And whetted stakes, fleeing this way and that perforce
Behind their wall. And Hector, shouting to his men,   370
Proclaimed: "Hasten to the vessels, abandoning
The blood-stained spoils. Whome'er from the vessels I mark
Aloof on the farther side, there shall I devise
His death, nor shall his kinsfolk, men and women both,
For the lifeless corpse kindle a funeral pyre,   375
But dogs afore the town devour him." So saying
With hand upraised, lashed he inciting his horses,
And called aloud to the Trojans along the ranks;
And they in unison returned the shout, fast sped
Their chariot-drawing steeds amid wondrous tumult.   380
And afore them with facile foot did Apollo
Collapse the trench's banks and with fullness thereof
A pathway long and broad create for the men,
Of spearcast's length when casts a man making trial
Of his strength. Thereover traversed they rank on rank,   385
And afore them Apollo, bearing the hallowed
Aegis displayed aloft. And deftly he leveled
The Danaan battlement, even as surfside
A youngster scatters sand, one in his childishness
Sculpting a plaything, and then again confounding   390
It with hands and feet, mere sport; thus lightly did you,
O archer Apollo, confound the Danaan

Effort and exertion, fast routing the Argives.

Thus aside their vessels were the Argives halted
And pent, palms holding uplifted and hailing one 395
Another, the throng fervidly praying the gods,
As did Nestor—the Argives' fair-favoring wind—
To starry-studded heaven outstretching his hands:
"O father Zeus, if e'er a single one of us
In corn-yielding Argos tendered you offering 400
Of fatted thigh of bull or ram, praying for home,
And you so promised, assenting with head inclined,
Be mindful now, Olympian god, and redeem us
From the pitiless doom of this day, nor afford
The Trojans defeat the Danaans." So he prayed, 405
And Zeus counselor thundered aloud, hearing the plea
Of the agèd son of Nēleus. But the Trojans,
Perceiving the thunder of aegis-bearing Zeus,
Advanced the more fiercely, intent on encounter.
And as th' unbridled briny with prodigious surge 410
O'erclashes a vessel to starboard, incited
By wasting winds high-roiling the mountainous wave;
Even so were the Trojans, descending the wall,
With warcry inciting a chariot incursion
Alongside the grounded ships, some at close quarters, 415
Twin-barbed their spearheads, others from horseback busied.
But the Argives, having ascended their dusky
Vessels ashore, retrieved lances across them lain—
Brazen-soldered their tips—for encounters at sea,
And from their crafts with these engaged.
                                        And Patroclus, 420
The while the Danaans and Trojans contended
About the rampart, from the rapid ships removed,
Thus long attended the hut of Eurypylus,
Heartening him with conversation and spreading
Unguents on his grievous wound, assuaging its pangs. 425
But seeing Trojans a'rush the wall and Argives

BOOK XV

Fled crying aloud, he mightily lamented
And, smiting his thighs with the flats of opened hands,
Exclaimed: "Eurypylus, no longer can I stay,
However driven your need, for bitter the broil   430
Now abounding. But be solaced by your steward,
And I to Achilles will quicken, exhorting
Him to battle, perchance with heaven's assistance
Enlivening him—for good is a comrade's call.
Thus speaking, he hastened forth; but the Achaeans,   435
Although firmly resisting the Trojan advance,
Availed not in dislodging them from the vessels,
Though fewer they; nor e'er could the Trojans, gaining
Upon the huts and ships, o'ercome the Achaeans.
But as the carpenter's line aligns a vessel's   440
Timbers, the workman precisely extending it,
Athena imparting his expert's precision.
Thus evenly extended their combativeness.
So contended they, battling about the vessels,
But Hector stormed straight upon glorious Ajax,   445
Their travail now centered about a single ship;
Nor might one repulse the other seeking to torch
The ship, nor the other beat him back, since a god
Had impelled him. Then glorious Ajax released
His spear, smiting Calētōr's breast, son of Clytius,   450
As he sped with torchflame toward the ship; and toppled
He hard thudding, the flare disengaging his grip.
But Hector, attentive to his cousin, dustward
Descending aside the darkened vessel, loud called
The Trojans and Lycians unstintingly: "Trojans,   455
Lycians, and Dardanians, in combat close-quartered
Engaged, within this narrow surrender no ground;
Sooner save Clytius' son lest of arms he be
Despoiled, the Danaans in fight having downed him
At the ships." So speaking he hurled against Ajax,   460
Missing him; but Lycophrōn, Mastōr's son, Ajax'
Attendant from Cythera residing nearby—

393

Having slain a man in Cythera—him, standing
Alongside Ajax, Hector struck with bladed bronze
At the skull above the ear, and to dust aside   465
The ship he dropped, formidable his undoing.
And Ajax quaked, addressing his brother these words:
"Dear Teucer, a companion trusted by the two
Of us is dead: Mastōr's son whom, whilst abiding
With us—from Cythera come—we honored at home   470
Like unto our parents. Him has great-souled Hector
Slain. Where now those arrows, rapid flown and fatal,
And the bow once gifted by Phoebus Apollo?"
So he spoke, and Teucer obeyed and ran, taking
Position aside him, carrying curvèd bow   475
And arrow-containing quiver; a projectile
Straight 'gainst the Trojans releasing, smiting Cleitus,
Famed Peisēnōr's son, compeer of Polydamas,
The lordly son of Panthous, even as Cleitus
Held the reins, controlling his steeds, driving them hard   480
Where the Argive battalions were largely in rout,
Thus gratifying Hector and the Trojan host.
So, calamity quickly laid claim to Cleitus
That none might avert however much wanting to,
For pierced a groan-begotten dart a'rear his neck,   485
And he toppled from his chariot, whereat his horse
Recoiled sideward, o'erturning the empty car.
And lord Polydamas noted it first, striding
Toward the horses. These he bestowed on Astynous,
Protiaōn's son, enjoining him retain them   490
Nearby, keeping watch the while on Polydamas;
But Polydamas amid the foremost returned.

Teucer from his quiver took a dart, for brazen-
Armored Hector marked, which had concluded Hector's
Escapades aside the Argive vessels and huts,   495
Had the arrow but struck, endeavor though it did
To vanquish Hector's life. But not unseen by Zeus

BOOK XV

Was Hector nor to chance consigned; Zeus guarded him,
Denying glory to Teucer, Telamon's son.
For Zeus snapped the bowstring, sturdily intercoiled,   500
Even as Teucer on Hector drew, and sideward
Diverged the deeply bronzed weapon and dropped the bow,
Whereat Teucer shuddered, addressing his brother:
"Alas, truly has a god revoked our counsels,
Having wrested the bow from my hand and broken   505
The newly woven string that I entwined today,
That it succeed in delivering teeming darts
Fast flown and sure." And Ajax, son of Telamon,
Responded: "Alack, good friend! Abandon the bow
And leave the fast-flown arrows be, since confounds them   510
A god to spite the Danaans; but your weapon
Take to hand and a buckler upon your shoulder,
And fight the Trojans, and so enjoin the others.
Indeed, not without sweat, for all their ascendance,
Might they consider possession of our vessels.   515
So, be we attentive of battle."
                             So he spoke,
And Teucer, returning the bow to his hut, donned
A buckler about his shoulder, four-layered strong,
And on his stalwart head a well-wrought helmet set
With horsehair crested high, and frightfully the plume   520
Swayed from its crest; and took he a lusty javelin
Sharp-tipped with bronze and, running apace, proceeded
Aside Ajax, standing aright. But when Hector
Noticed Teucer's arrows unavailingly spent,
He called yelling loud to the Trojans and Lycians: 525
"You Trojans, Lycians, and close-quartered Dardanians,
Be men, my friends, and amid the hollow vessels
Be mindful of fervent valor, for verily
I observe how Zeus repudiates Teucer's shafts,
Valiant though Teucer be. Readily distinguished   530
Is Cronidēs' might to mortals delivered—whom
He affords unfettered fame and whom he forestalls,

Withholding help, even as now he forestalleth
Argive might, conferring it on us. So, clash you
Close-quartered by the vessels, and if anyone 535
Assaulted or by weapon struck death-destined be,
Dead let him abide. No shame is it to perish
Defending one's country. Sooner secured one's spouse
And children thereafter, both lands and home unharmed,
If only decamp the Danaans and their ships 540
Unto their native land." So saying, he aroused
The resolve of every man.
                    And Ajax again
Hollered from opposite them to his companions:
"What cowardice, Achaeans, surely must we now
All perish grievously or deliverance gain, 545
Thrusting threat from the vessels away. Believe you
That if flash-helmeted Hector lay hold the ships,
Each one of you afoot will homeward bear himself
Unto his native land? Hear you not how howling
Hector impels his men to set the ships aflame? 550
For not to dance but to battle bestirs he them.
And for us remains no counsel, no stratagem
Superior to this: to engage them close-quartered
Hand to hand. For preferred withal to live or die
Than be bound e'ermore in deadly confrontation, 555
Bootlessly thus, with meaner men aside the ships."
So saying, he roused the mettle and might of each.
Then Hector slew Schedius, son of Perimēdēs,
A Phōcian leader; and Ajax, Laodamas,
Leader of footmen, brilliant son of Antēnōr; 560
And Polydamas slew Otus of Cyllēnē,
Companion of Phyleus' son, captain of the great-
Souled Epeians. And Megēs, observing it, surged
Upon him, but Polydamas crouched, avoiding
Him, and Megēs missed his mark, for lord Apollo 565
Impeded Polydamas' death 'mid the foremost
Combatants; but Megēs hard wielding smote Croesmus

Squarely to the breast, and he toppled with a thud,
And Megēs from his shoulders stripped the armor off.
Meanwhile, spear-skilled Dolops emerged, Lampus' offspring, 570
Whom Lampus, Laomedōn's son, begat, even
Lampus' bravest son, well schooled in furious fight.
Thrust Dolops with spear at the shield of Phyleus' son,
From close range moving upon him. But protected
Him his well fashioned corselet, the very armor 575
Metal-fitted afore and aft in which he fought.
This from Ephyrē and the river Seleïs
Had Phyleus brought in guest friendship for Euphētēs,
Granting it him as battle attire, deterrent
To weapons all; and now it saved his very son. 580
Then smote Megēs upon the topmost brazen crown
Of the helmet horsehair-plumed which Dolops displayed,
Severing the plume, newly scarlet dyed, which dropped
Desecrate in dust. Now, while Megēs continued
Fighting with Dolops and longing for victory, 585
Arrived warlike Menelaus to Megēs' aid,
And by Dolops unseen stood weaponed aside him
And cast, assailing Dolops' shoulder from behind;
And straight sped the spear, darting dastardly onward,
Savaging his chest and toppling him face forward; 590
And advanced the pair despoiling the brazen plate
From off his corpse. But Hector to his kinsmen called,
First chiding Melanippus, Hicetaōn's son.
Ere then had he pastured his shambling-gaited kine
In Percōtē, the Danaans yet distant far; 595
But soon as the curvèd Danaan ships arrived,
He circled back to Troy, with preeminent place
Among the Trojans, dwelling in Priam's palace
And loved by Priam like unto his offspring born.
Him Hector admonished, addressing wingèd words: 600
"Shall we then slacken, Melanippus? Has your heart
So little concern for kinsman slain? Observe you
Not their struggle for Dolops' armor? But approach,

For no longer abroad be the foe but at hand
Until it either be destroyed or lofty Troy 605
Be taken entire, beaten its inhabitants."

So saying, he advanced, a godlike man, others
Hard following him; and great Ajax, Telamon's
Son, thus heartened the Achaeans: "Be men, my friends,
Having shame in your hearts, and be attentive each 610
To the other's disdain in dread battle. Such men
Emerge more often alive. But from the routed
Comes neither glory nor grit." So he spoke, but they
Themselves endeavored to prevail, taking his word
To heart, and arrayed themselves in brazen defense 615
About the ships, and Zeus incited the Trojans
Against them. And Menelaus good at warcry
Enjoined Antilochus: "Antilochus, youngest
Achaean, swiftest of foot, and fiercest in fight,
Would you vaulted forth, afflicting some man of Troy!" 620
Thus speaking he hastened off, spurring the other,
And Antilochus from amid the foremost leapt
And, scanning clear about, deployed his deadly spear,
And shrank the Trojans from the warrior as he cast.
Nor vainly did he cast, but struck Melanippus, 625
High-hearted, Hicetaōn's son, upon the breast
Aside the nipple as he tangled in battle;
And thudding he fell, darkness enfolding his eyes.
And upon him sprung Antilochus like a hound
Leaping upon a stricken fawn that a huntsman, 630
Loosing its limbs, assaults upvaulting from its lair.
Thus, poor Melanippus, leapt staunch Antilochus
Upon you in your might, his purpose to despoil,
Though by goodly Hector not unseen, who charged him
'Mid the fracas; whereat Antilochus recoiled, 635
Swift warrior that he was, and like a feral
Beast, somehow mischievous, fled—one that a herdsman
Or hound has savaged aside the kine, escaping

BOOK XV

Ere together assembles a muster of men;
Even so fled Nestor's son, and mighty Hector, 640
And the Trojans with wondrous cry rained groan-laden
Darts upon him. But turning he stood, once arrived
At the host of his companions.
                          But the Trojans
Like ravening lions assailed the ships, doing
Zeus' behest who—ever increasing their courage— 645
Dazed Danaan hearts, denied them glory, and drove
The others on. For Zeus determined addition
Of fame for Hector Priamidēs, that he set
The hollow ships to wondrous unrelenting flame,
Thus accomplished Thetis' imperious prayer. 650
Just so bided counselor Zeus, that his eyes espy
The glare of ship-borne flame, whereupon he would force
A Trojans retreat from the vessels, conferring
Argive glory. Thus devising roused he Hector,
Priam's son, against the hollow ships, already 655
Driven he and looking, like spear-wielding Ares,
Enraged, as when ravening flame on mountain flares,
From deep-wooded thicket fanned. And at Hector's mouth
Formed foam, and horrid his eyes beneath harrowed brows,
And about his temples shook Hector's prodigious 660
Helmet as he strode; for Olympian Cronidēs
Defended him from heaven, granting him alone
Amid the many his honor's due and glory.
But passing would this prove, since Pallas Athena
His doomsday even then appraised neath the power 665
Of Peleus' son.
                  But Hector yearned to break the ranks
Of men, assaying them wherever he discerned
The choicest arms amid the greatest warrior throng.
Yet even so availed he not to shatter them,
Though eager to; for tower-like maintained they ground, 670
Looming precipice-like aside the hoary sea,
Braving shrill-winded onslaught and the assailant

Swell of waters; even so did the Danaans
Relentlessly resist and remain, firm rooted.
But luminous Hector, as though fanned unto flame, 675
Forth bounded amid the throng, pouncing upon it,
Even as when from under clouds a wasting wind
Incites the waves o'er a vessel washed, and in foam
Enfolds her hull, and bellows the storm-blasted wind
Against the sail, and quake the sailors' hearts within 680
That from death were their spirits but barely preserved;
Thus keenly was Achaean constancy dispelled.
But on them he pounced like a menacing lion
Encountering cattle innumerably ranged
That feed on marshy bottomland; and among them, 685
Unskilled in fighting feral beasts, a herdsman tends
The slaughter of a horn-curved ox. Ever prowling,
Stocks the beast aside them—now favored the foremost,
Now favored the furthest kine—then midmost leaping
Trounces his prey, panic-stricken repelling them; 690
Just so were the Argives desperately dispersed
By Hector and father Zeus, though Hector slaughtered
But one, Periphētēs of Mycenae, Copreus'
Offspring—Copreus who once transmitted his labors
To valiant Heracles from lordly Eurystheus. 695
And to Copreus—abhorrent sire—was born that son,
In excellences unbettered, both in fleetness
Of foot and in fight, and foremost in perception
Among the Mycenaeans. Thus greater glory
To Hector delivered, for while wheeling about, 700
Periphētēs stumbled on his armor, a shield
Fashioned down to his feet, a defense against darts;
Thereon he faltered falling back, and wondrously
Around his temples as he staggered rang the helm.
And Hector quickly noticing it, ran standing 705
Aside the man, skewering his breast with a spear,
Slaying him in the presence of his companions.
But no assistance offered they, though suffering

BOOK XV

For their fellow, themselves by Hector affrighted.

Stood they now facing the ships, the endmost vessels 710
Encircling them, even the ships first shoreward hauled;
But the Trojans advanced. And the Argives, yielding
Perforce from the farthermost ships, abided fast,
Assembled by their huts, nor scattered they, constrained
By shame and dread about the camp, but constantly 715
Called each to the other summoning. And Nestor
Of Gerēnia, Argive guardsman, especially
Implored the men, invoking their parents' repute:
"My comrades, be men, and in your hearts consider
The shame of others and be mindful each of you 720
Of offspring and spouse, of parents and possessions,
Whether be they alive or dead, as may befall.
For the sake of those absent I now beseech you
Staunchly stand holding your ground." Thus he incited
The fortitude of every man, and from their eyes 725
Athena thrust the wondrous mist, and mightily
From either side light entered, alike from the ships
And fighting. And all saw Hector apt at warcry
By his comrades joined, those to rearward abstaining
And those by the vessels engaged.
                            Now great-hearted 730
Ajax, no longer satisfied to stand aloof
Where the other Argives retiring stood, bestrode
The vessels plank to plank with powered stride, wielding
A ring-fitted pike, on hand for sea engagements,
Extending the length of two and twenty cubits. 735
And as a seasoned horseman harnesses a team
Of four from many horses chosen, and hastens,
Impelling them along a thronging thoroughfare
From the steppe to a towering town—a marvel
To the multitude observing it—and hurtles 740
He, firm-footed ever and steadfast as they fly,
From one horse to another bounding; even so

Did Ajax range, transversely bestraddling the decks
Of countless ships, his voice ascending heavenward,
As e'er with deaf'ning cries he bade the Danaans 745
Secure their huts and vessels. Nor remained Hector
With the armored Trojan host, but as a tawny
Eagle bestirs a drove of feathered fowl a'wing
The river's gradient, congregating geese, or cranes,
Or long-necked swans; even so barreled Hector forth 750
Against a dark-prowed ship, rushing frenzied thereon;
And from behind with mighty hand Cronidēs Zeus
Incited him, rousing the throng alongside him.
Then again was ferocious fighting underway
Aside the vessels, creating the impression 755
That they unfatigued and unflagging contended,
Thus savage their assaults. And fighting thought they thus:
The Argives imagined they should never escape
Disaster but should perish, while each Trojan heart
Sought conflagration for the vessels and demise 760
Of Danaan warriors. Such were their thoughts, standing
Each host across the other. But grappled Hector
The stern of a ocean-faring ship, a fine ship,
Swift on the brine, that had borne Protesilaüs
To Troy, but lacked the return to his native land. 765
About this ship slaughtered Trojans and Achaeans
One another closely ranged, nor longer aloof
Endured they mere arrows and darts, but positioned
Man against man in unity of heart, they fought
With hatchet and lethal battle-axe, with great swords 770
And twin-edged spears. And scattered many blades, dark thonged
And heavy hilted, to the ground, some from the hands,
Others from the shoulders of combatant warriors;
And the black earth ran with blood. But Hector, grasping
A vessel by its stern, would not loosen his hold, 775
But kept the stern post in hand, calling the Trojans:
"Bring fire, and together deliver the warcry!
Now has Zeus a day provided as recompense

To destroy the ships here come despite the gods' will,
Bringing woes aplenty by dint of counselors'   780
Cowardice who restrained me and withheld the host
When most I wanted to fight by the vessels' sterns.
But if distance-sounding Zeus then dampened our wits,
He now incites us onward, providing command."

So he spoke, and assaulted they the Argives more,   785
But Ajax no longer abode, sorely beset
By arrows with foreboding of death, but gave ground
Some seven feet along the deck-connecting bridge,
Abandoning the shapely ship. There poised, astute
With spear he stood, staunchly deterring from the ship   790
Whichever Trojans would ignite untiring flame;
And called e'er with dreadful cries to the Danaans:
"Friends, Danaan warriors, attendants of Ares,
Be men, my friends, and bethink you of furious might.
Imagine we some other helpers behind us,   795
Or perhaps some stronger wall preventing ruin?
Nowise possess we a city enclosed with walls
Wherein to fashion defenses with host to turn
The battle's tide. No, upon the plain of armored
Trojans wage we war, distant from our native land,   800
The seashore our sole assistance. Thus, strength of hand
Holds salvation's glow, not our sluggishness in fight."
He spoke, and at the Trojans continued driving
Fiercely with deadly implement. And whichever   805
Trojan with blazing flame attacked the hollow ships,
Favoring Hector's disposition, Telemon's
Son awaited him, hard thrusting with his weapon,
And twelve the men he rent in battling for the ships.   810

~ Book XVI ~

Deeds and Deaths of Sarpedon, Cebrionēs, and Patroclus, the Sixth Day of Battle

FURTHER TO NESTOR'S REQUEST (Book 11), Patroclus entreats Achilles to allow his assisting the Greeks, wearing Achilles' armor and fighting with his troops (the Myrmidons): Thinking Achilles has reentered the fray, the Trojans will retreat, affording the Greeks relief. Achilles agrees but limits Patroclus to defensive action alone, i.e., securing the ships, but nothing more. The situation is dire. Homer describes the beleaguered Ajax, then invokes the Muse to relate how the ships were first set afire, despite Ajax' effort.

Patroclus dons Achilles' armor—but leaves the Pelian ashen spear (p. xxxiv) which Achilles alone can wield—while Achilles' immortal horses, here described, are yoked to their car. The warriors Achilles brought to Troy are next described in their five divisions. These Achilles marshals for battle, to be led by the disguised Patroclus. From a special cup brought from home, Achilles pours libation to Zeus for the success and safekeeping of Patroclus. The prayer, as Homer relates, is granted in part but otherwise denied. Patroclus will succeed in driving the Trojans from the ships but will not return alive. Seeing Patroclus in Achilles' armor, the panicked Trojans take him for Achilles. In the ensuing melee, Patroclus exacts slaughter for comrades slain in Achilles' absence.

Patroclus engages and kills Sarpedon, son of Zeus and leader of the Lycian host. Seeing Sarpedon's fate approach, Zeus ponders saving him, a move to which the other gods—Hera warns him—would strongly object as being contrary to fate. Indeed, following Zeus' example, every god would intervene to save a mortal offspring (frustrating the war's subtextual purpose of eliminating the race of demigods and thus conclusively separating gods from men; see p. 59). The dying Sarpedon calls to Glaucus, seeking to have him rally the Trojans to protect his corpse. Glaucus does so, appealing to Hector's regard for Sarpedon, one of Troy's most committed allies. Patroclus dismounts and pulls his spear from Sarpedon's body, the latter's entire midriff yielding with it. An extended battle ensues over Sarpedon's corpse, in which Sarpedon himself cannot be seen for all the men and dust that swirl about him. Zeus considers having Hector slay Patroclus then and there, deciding instead to allow Patroclus' approach to the walls of Troy (essentially nullifying Achilles' prohibition). The Greeks finally succeed in stripping Sarpedon's armor and sending it off to the ships. Zeus enjoins Apollo to cleanse and anoint Sarpedon's body, which Sleep and Death convey to Lycia for eternal repose. The "Death of Sarpedon" as described in the *Iliad*, is famously depicted on the Euphronius Vase aka the Sarpedon Krater (6th century BC).

Patroclus rampages toward the walls of Troy and three times assails them. He is then warned by Apollo to stand down, for it will not be Patroclus' fate to take Troy. Three failed attempts always—and ominously—signal overreach.

Apollo urges Hector in pursuit of Patroclus. Patroclus kills Hector's charioteer, Cebrionēs, who falls from his chariot. Hector dismounts and engages Patroclus over the corpse. Yet another extended, though shorter, battle ensues over the corpse of Cebrionēs, the Greeks finally prevailing to take it as Patroclus slaughters onward.

The battles over the corpses of Sarpedon and Cebrionēs, for all their length and exhaustive detail, are but dress rehearsals for what will be the battle over the corpse of Patroclus, once slain by Hector. And Patroclus, slain in Achilles' armor, is poignant dress rehearsal for Achilles' own death (not occurring in the *Iliad*). Patroclus' death, thus anticipating Achilles', is Achilles' death by proxy—for which Hector will pay with his own life and spoliation.

Apollo, before the walls of Troy, dazes and disarms Patroclus with a hand's blow to the back. Euphorbus next wounds him, and Hector administers the fatal blow. In his life-and-death duel with Achilles (Book 22), Hector will plead that he did not himself kill Patroclus but was only third in the line of assailants.

BOOK XVI

Thus they fought by the well-benched ship. But Patroclus
Approached Achilles, shepherd of the host, weeping
Bitterly, even as a dark-watered fountain
That spills its dusky stream o'er a desolate cliff;
And divine swift-footed Achilles took pity 5
And responded, addressing him wingèd reply:
"Why, Patroclus, weepest thou like a witless child
That runs by its mother, wishing to be lifted,
Grabs her gown, and hinders her haste, and tearfully
Insists 'til the mother uplift it? Even so, 10
Patroclus, shed you tender tears. Have you something
To impart unto the Myrmidons or myself,
Or are there Phthian tidings to which you alone
Are privy? Menoetius, Actor's son, they tell us,
Yet abides, and yet breathes Peleus, Aeacus' son, 15
Amid the Myrmidons. For them especially,
Were they departed, would we grieve. Or lament you
The Argives, now perishing for their presumption
Aside the hollow ships? Speak out, conceal it not,
That we both may know."
                     Then, O gallant Patroclus, 20
You answered groaning heavily: "O Achilles,
Peleus' son, far mightiest of the Achaeans,
Be not irate. So dire the sorrow inflicted
On the Argives, for those aforetime the bravest
Lie stricken or wounded aside the ships. Stricken 25
Is mighty Diomedes, Tydeus' son; wounded
Is spear-famed Odysseus and Agamemnon too;
And with thigh-striking dart is Eurypylus stung.
These the healers deft in many medicines tend,
Seeking to assuage the wounds; but you, Achilles, 30
Are impossible! Wrath never so possess me
As that possessing you, however valorous.
What benefit will anyone to come e'er have

Of your rejecting the Danaan's redemption
And deathly ruin? Your father, O heartless one,   35
No knightly Peleus was; nor Thetis your mother,
But bitter salted brine and beetling cliffs your kin,
Thus unbending your mind. But if harbors your heart
Prophetic voice and speaks your reverent mother
Knowingly from Cronidēs, then at least send me   40
Speedily onward, along with the Myrmidons
Despatched, to the Danaans as deliverance.
And allow I attire myself in that armor
Of yours, that the Trojans by our likeness deceived
Retreat from fight, allowing Danaan repose.   45
Scant is combat's breathing-space, and the unwearied
That we be may surely repulse the wearied back
And away from the vessels and huts to the town."
Thus praying he spoke, fool that he was, since truly
He prayed for his own dreadful destiny and death.   50

Angered then, swift-footed Achilles responded:
"Zeus-born Patroclus, what, alas, affirm you thus?
No oracle within my ken consider I,
Nor confers my mother aught from Zeus Cronidēs,
But unforgiving grief enfolds my heart within   55
Whenever a person appearing to surpass
His equal in power purloins and claims his prize.
Grief unforgiving is this to my heart, given
All I have suffered. The girl the Argives gave me,
Selected as my prize, that I by spear acquired,   60
To a well-walled city laying waste, her has lord
Agamemnon, this offspring of Atreus, reclaimed
From my arms as though from a sojourning stranger.
However, let all such matters go, for nowise
Be it my goal this wrath forever to augment;   65
And yet I intended a choler uncontained
Until such time as warcry ensnared my vessels.
But come, shoulder you my glorious arms aright

408

BOOK XVI

And to battle bring the war-loving Myrmidons
If thus dreaded the Trojan cloud now encircling 70
The ships, and the Argives stand vexed without defense,
But for sorry sand between seashore and themselves;
Yes, even the Greeks on whom tireless Troy descends,
Sorely in need of my radiant helmèd gleam.
But the Trojans repulsed in rout would fast upfill 75
The waterways with dead were lord Atreïdēs
Thus inclined. Yet fight the Trojans about the ships.
For Diomedes, Tydeus' son, does not with spear
To riot rage, defending the Danaan host;
Nor yet have I heard Atreïdēs' call, howling 80
From his hated head; but sooner the man-slaying
Hector's call, breaking to every side as he wakes
The Trojan host, its tumult uptearing the plain
As it routs the Greeks in battle. Yet even so,
Patroclus, save the ships from disaster, falling 85
Ruthlessly upon them lest fleet and all be torched
With towering flame, depriving the Danaans
Of their homeward return. But closely attend you
And grant I provide the sum of valued counsel,
Seeking my glory's guarantee and recompense 90
For their slighting inattention, that they return
The beguiling girl with glorious gifts besides.
From the ships having driven them, return you here
And, if Hera's loud-thundering lord grant glory,
Desire you not thus distant from my side to fight 95
The war-enamored foe, lessening my glory;
Nor yet, though delighting in bloodletting carnage,
Lead onward into Troy lest descend some heaven
Dwelling divinity engaging you in fight,
For archer Apollo especially loves them. 100
But return you instead, deliverance granting
To the ships, letting th' others overrun the plain.
For I would, O father Zeus—so help Athena
And Apollo—that no Trojan escape his death

Of all Trojans that be, nor any Danaan, 105
But that we alone escape ruin, and alone
Raze Ilium's sacred diadem."
                    Thus they spoke;
But Ajax no longer endured, sorely beset
By missiles. For the will of Zeus o'erpowered him
And the Trojans by their weapons, and forcefully 110
Sounded the helm that glistened 'round his temples,
Smitten as it was about its well-wrought bosses;
And faltered his left shoulder as he firmly clenched
His gleaming shield, nor might they dent it about him
For all they assailed it with darts. And with increase 115
Of labored breath was he beset, and from his limbs
Throughout abundant streamed the sweat, nor easily
Breathed he howsoe'er, but evil with evil joined.

Now tell me you Muses, dwellers on Olympus,
How fire was first fomented at the Argive ships. 120
Hector, closing on Ajax, severed his ashen
Spear at the socket by the point's firm base, shearing
The point away so that Ajax, Telamon's son,
Vainly brandished a lopped-off weapon, and the head
Of bronze fell clunking to the ground. And Ajax knew 125
In his blameless soul, shuddering at the godly
Doings, how thundering Zeus had discredited
His battle's might, intending Trojan victory.
Then out from under missiles he escaped, as flame
Ablaze from Trojan hands burst forth atop a ship, 130
Unquenchable flame ascending wide above her.
Thus was the stern by flame engulfed. But Achilles
Smote hard his thighs, addressing Patroclus: "Up now,
Zeus-born Patroclus, master of horsemen. Behold,
I view by the vessels a crackling orange scourge. 135
No vessels shall they take, impeding our escape!
Quickly don my armor whilst I gather the host."
So he spoke, and Patroclus arrayed him in bronze

BOOK XVI

Agleam, the greaves about his shins first fastening,
Exquisite greaves with silver ankle-pieces set,   140
And next uplifting about his chest the corselet
Of swift-footed Aeacus' son. Most richly wrought
It was, bedight with stars. And about his shoulders
Placed the brazen silver-studded sword, thereafter
Uplifting protective buckler and well-wrought helm,   145
Its horsehair crest fast set atop his sturdy head,
The plume fretfully gesturing from high above,
And in his hands secured two unrelenting spears
But declined the spear of Aeacus' consummate
Offspring, that weapon ponderous and persuasive.   150
This could no other Achaean command; Peleus'
Son alone comprehended it—the Pelian
Ashen spear that old Cheirōn from Pelion's peak
Had given Aeacus, for heroes' doom designed.
And he commanded Automedōn the horses   155
Quickly couple; for after Achilles breaker
Of men Patroclus most honored him, e'er faithful
To attend his battle call. At his bidding, then,
Automedōn coupled the horses, Balius
And Xanthus outflying the wind, that the Harpy   160
Podargē to Zephyrus bore as she meadow-
Grazed aside Oceanus' stream, and third to these
Placed he peerless Pedasus—taken aforetime
By Achilles when he plundered Eëtion's town—
That, being mortal, with immortal steeds kept pace.   165

But Achilles, striding amid the huts, prepared
The Myrmidons, and they like to ravening wolves
Rushed forth, their hearts filled with hardihood unbridled—
Like devouring wolves that have mangled a great horned
Mountain stag, spattered their snouts with gore; together   170
They pant with darting tongues to lap the frosty flow
Of rivulets, upbelching blood and gore the while,
Intrepid the hearts within their breasts, their bellies

Protuberant; just so the Myrmidon leaders
And chieftains sped forward circling Achilles' squire. 175
But among them stood Achilles himself, urging
Both horses and shield-bearing men. Fifty swift ships
Had Zeus-cherished Achilles led Troyward; in each
At the oarlocks sat fifty companions, and five
The leaders most trusted to issue directives, 180
Himself standing king, over all preeminent.
Menesthius one rank led, flashing-corseleted,
Son of Spercheius, the rain-swollen river. Him
Did the lovely Polydōra, Peleus' daughter,
To tireless Spercheius bear, a maiden bedded 185
With a god, though actually to Perieres'
Offspring Bōris born, who publicly espoused her,
Providing courting gifts uncounted. And warlike
Eudōrus captained the next contingent, the son
Whom dance-delighting Polymēlē, fair daughter 190
Of Phylas, out of wedlock begat. Enamored
Had she aforetime been of Argeïphontēs
When among songful maidens he first discerned her
On Artemis' dancing floor, gold-arrowed huntress
Of the echoing chase. Forthwith made he trial 195
Of her chamber, lying with her clandestinely,
Even the guileless Hermes; and a goodly son
She bore him, Eudōrus, spectacular his speed
Of foot and warcraft. But when the birthing goddess,
Eileithyia, at length to light delivered him 200
Imbibing sunlight's pageantry, then did stalwart
Echeclēs, Actōr's son, convey her to his home,
Having courted her with countless gifts; but Phylas
The elder exceedingly cherished Eudōrus,
Equal unto cherished offspring his very own. 205
And captained the third rank the warlike Peisander,
Maemalus' son, a man among the Myrmidons
Preeminent after Patroclus in spearfight.
And the fourth contingent the old knight Phoenix led,

BOOK XVI

And Alcimēdōn the fifth, an unrivaled son   210
To Laërtēs born. But when at length Achilles
Had set them in array, well dividing their ranks—
Commanders included—he conveyed this command:
"Myrmidons, allow none, I enjoin, to forget
The threats aside the vessels wherewith you threatened   215
The Trojans whilst I indulged my disposition,
Upbraiding me withal, every one asserting:
'Cruel Achilles, surely on bile your mother
Nurtured you, O ruthless one, your comrades subdued
By the vessels, thoroughly thwarted. No, let us   220
Now homeward return in our seafaring vessels,
Since peevish your temper and insufferable.'
Oft with such words complaining you upbraided me,
But now reawakened is combat's endeavor,
Your fervor aforetime. Wherefore, with stalwart heart   225
Let each man fatigue his foe." Thus speaking, he roused
The vigor and zeal of each, and increasingly
The battalions compressed upon hearing their king.
And as a man with close-set stones constructs the wall
Of a towering house, mindful of monstrous winds;   230
Thus stood their helms and shielded panoply displayed.
Converged buckler on buckler, helmet on helmet;
And as the men nodded their heads, the horsehair crests
Upclustered, from helmeted ridges arisen.
Thus their formations, one by the other disposed;   235
And a'front them all, two warriors readied to fight,
Even Patroclus and Automēdōn, single-
Minded each, commander each of the Myrmidons.

But Achilles went to his hut, and fair adorned
The chest he opened that silver-footed Thetis   240
Placed for his comfort onboard, filling it richly
With tunics, wind-sheltering cloaks, and woolen rugs.
Therein lay buried an opulent cup from which
Others all were forbidden from drinking flaming

Wine. And he himself poured offerings exclusive 245
To father Zeus. Removing the cup from the chest,
He laved it with sulfur, and in clear-currented
Water cleansed his own hands clean, and the claret blend
Decanted, and at a distance aside made prayer.
And as he poured libation, high upward peering, 250
The thunder-bolting father marked and noticed him:
"Pelasgian Zeus, O king far-off residing,
Of wintry Dōdōna overlord—about it
Dwell the Selli, interpreting your oracles,
Crouching upon the ground, their feet ever begrimed, 255
Aforetime hearing my prayer you regarded me,
And decisively smote the Danaans; now too
My entreaty grant: myself will I continue
Among the vessels but despatch my companion
To fight among the Myrmidons. Augment his fame, 260
O far-seeing Zeus, and bolster his heart within,
That Hector ascertain Patroclus' competence
To fight alone or, if unyielding rage his hands,
Solely when fighting aside me. But when battle's
Disturbances have from the vessels abated, 265
Then safely return he to the ships, his armor
Intact and his comrades fighting at close quarters."
So praying he spoke, and Zeus counselor heard him,
And the father ceded part, and part rescinded:
That Patroclus deter the attack at the ships 270
He permitted; that he safely exit the fray
He forbad. Achilles, reciting devotions
And pouring libations to father Zeus, returned
To his tent, storing the cup in the chest away,
And lingered, emerging beside the entryway, 275
For resolved he the dread contention of Trojans
And Danaans to survey. But those with stalwart
Patroclus arrayed forged untiringly onward,
Rushing the Trojans, straight streaming like wayside wasps
That boys delight to antagonize, tormenting 280

BOOK XVI

Their nestings alongside the way—bothersome boys,
On the waspish swarm a single woe dispensing.
And the wasps, if perchance some passer-by provoke
Them, forth issue en masse, stoutheartedly surging,
Each preserving its young; with just such vehemence   285
And vexation spilled the Myrmidons from their ships,
And rose a cry implacable. But Patroclus,
To his comrades loudly shouting, called: "Myrmidons,
You comrades of Achilles Pēleidēs, be men,
My friends, ever mindful of furious valor,   290
That we glorify Achilles, finest by far
Of the Achaeans, he and his fiery Comrades
Fighting closely quartered, that lord Agamemnon
Wide-ruling his blindness know, that he dishonored
The best of the Achaeans." So saying, he roused   295
Vehemence and vexation in each to the last,
And descended they in hordes upon the Trojans,
And harshly resounded the ships at the outcry.
But when the Trojans saw Menoetius' valiant son,
Himself and the Myrmidons blazing in armor,   300
Unsettled was each man's heart and rattled their ranks,
Thinking swift-footed Achilles had discarded
His rancor, now seeking reconciliation;
And each peered 'round in pursuit of deliverance.

Then first Patroclus released his splendorous spear,   305
Direct to the midpoint where thickest thronged the men,
Even by the vessel of Protesilaüs
Great-spirited, and smote Pyraechmēs their commander,
Marshaling the Paeonian chariot commanders;
From fair Amydōn he, by the wide-flown Axius.   310
Him shoulder-wise he wounded, and backward to dust
Dropped he groaning, and his comrades scattered, routed,
Even the Paeonians, for Patroclus had
Panicked them all, having slain their preeminent
Leader. Away from the vessels he scattered them,   315

415

Slaking the flame and abandoning the wreckage.
And the Trojans with wondrous din were outdriven,
And the Danaans o'er the hollow ships poured forth,
The uproar unabated. As when the father
Upgath'ring lightning from a mountain's lofty crest   320
Removes dense cloud away, and clear to view uprear
The mountain peaks, the headlands high, and sylvan vales,
And from heaven forth ineffable aether breaks;
Just so the Danaans, having driven greedy
Flame from the vessels away, briefly took their rest   325
Though no finish to fighting found. For the Trojans,
By the Ares-favored Danaans undeterred,
Remained by the hollow ships, ever attempting
Direct confrontation, yielding perforce alone.

Then each through the melee his adversary slew.   330
First Menoetius' valiant son smote Areilycus'
Thigh, hurling his piercing spear as the latter turned,
Fleeing, forth driving the bronze clear through. The weapon
Fractured the bone, and grinning he greeted the ground.
And stalwart Menelaus, thrusting, smote Thoas   335
Upon the breast where left uncovered by his shield,
Unstringing his limbs. And Phyleus' son as he tracked
The onrushing Amphiclus, the quicker became
Than his rival, smiting him lowest to the leg
Where thickest bulks the muscle; and on the spearpoint   340
The tendons tore apart, and darkness coated him.
Then of Nestor's offspring did one, Antilochus,
At Atymnius thrust with deadly spear, and pressed
The fractious weapon through his flank, and prone he fell.
But Maris lunged from a'near at Antilochus,   345
Weapon in hand, for his dear brother's sake incensed,
Positioning himself before the corpse. Godlike
Thrasymēdēs, however, the speedier proved
And before his foe could counter, at the shoulder
First assailed him, missing not—the spearpoint shearing   350

BOOK XVI

The base of the arm from the musculus away
And asunder decidedly breaking the bone.
Thudding he fell, and darkness enfolded his eyes.
So these twain by brethren twain o'ercome descended
To Hades domain, good comrades of Sarpēdōn, 355
Spearmen sons of Araisodarus who nurtured
The raging Chimaera, a curse to mortalkind.
And Ajax, Oïleus' son, rushed Cleobulus
And captured him live in the turmoil entangled,
And even there undid his might, smiting him hard 360
To the neck with hilted weapon drawn. And with blood
Warmed the blade, and o'er his eyes descended fearsome
Fate and porphyrous death. Then rushed Peneleōs
And Lycōn together, for with spears had they missed
The other each, both having vainly cast; but rushed 365
They with swords close-to. Then Lycōn on the hornèd
Helm high crested with horsehair drove, and his weapon
Fell shattered at the hilt. But struck Peneleōs
At his neck beneath the ear, and there resided
His Weapon; the head, from skin alone suspended 370
To sideward hung, and earthward toppled he, a corpse.
And Mērionēs quickly o'ertook Acamas,
Catching his right shoulder, even as Acamas
Mounted his chariot, from which he careened, and mist
Dropped gently o'er his lids. Then Idomeneus smote 375
Erymas' mouth, ruthlessly rending it with bronze,
And clean through the cranium cut the brazen blade,
Breaking the bones asunder. His teeth flew dislodged,
And his eyes suffused with blood which mouth and nostrils
Spurted whilst he gaped—in death's black billow absorbed. 380

These leaders of the Argives then slew each his man.
And as rav'nous wolves attack lambs or kids, choosing
Them from out the flock, by shepherd's inattention
Scattered wide about the mountaintop, and swiftly
Observing it, waste the wolves the wavering young, 385

Thus the Trojans by Danaans ravaged, minded
Of discordant flight and forgetting their fiery
Fierceness. And mighty Ajax strove ever to cast
At bronze-fitted Hector; but battle-savvy—vast
His broad shoulders enshielded by bullhide buckler— 390
He ever viewed the arrow's whir and thudding spear;
And though apprehending victory's turning tide,
He stood firm, protecting his trusty companions.
And as a cloud from Olympus whisked heavenward
From radiant air when Zeus disperses the storm; 395
Thus from out the ships rose Trojan rout and shouting,
Nor traversed they the trench well ordered as before.
His swift-footed horses bore Hector gear and all;
But he abandoned the Trojans, whom the hollowed
Ditch inhospitably detained. And through the ditch 400
Did chariot-drawing steeds relinquish readily
Their lords' conveyances, pole-impaired. But followed
Patroclus, commandingly calling the Argives,
Intending the Trojans vexation, whilst they streamed
Shouting, everywhere retreating, soundly dispersed. 405
And neath the clouds spread a dusty whirlwind, and back
From the vessels townward strained the uncloven steeds.

And Patroclus, where discerning the crowd gathered
Densest in retreat, there he pressed shouting aloud;
And neath his chariot axles the Trojans tumbled 410
Headlong in succession from their cars, upended
Every chariot. And o'er the trench the horses
Nimbly leapt in their forward flight, the immortal
Steeds by the gods given Peleus, a glorious gift;
And Patroclus drove at Hector, much desiring 415
To cast and strike, but Hector's steeds outdistanced him.
And even as all the earth beneath a tempest
Lies darkened at harvest, when Zeus Cronidēs rains
Unrelentingly, whensoe'er indignant grown
With scoundrels in assembly congregate, crooked 420

BOOK XVI

And unconcerned their justice whene'er they convene,
And of requital reck they naught, so their rivers
Flood and overflow, and fail their furrowed hillsides
Neath mountainous cataracts careering headlong
In tumult to the russet sea, husbandry's tilth   425
Upturned; even thus heaved the horses retreating.
But when Patroclus had broken the foremost ranks,
Grimly he detained them at the ships, permitting
Nary a footstep townward; but between the ships
And river, just where the rampart reared, he bolted   430
Brave to slay them, vengeance exacting for many
A dead companion. There he cast first at Pronous
With glinting spear to the breast where it lay exposed
Beside the buckler, and loosed his limbs; and thudding
He toppled. Next on Thestōr, Enops' son, he rushed.   435
Petrified he sat, witless in his polished car,
The reins slipped from his hands; but Patroclus approached
Jolting him on the jaw and pushing with spear straight
Through the teeth. And retaining the spear, wrested him
Over the chariot, as when a fisherman perched   440
On a jutting cliff reels in from out the briny
An awesome fish with line and splendent brazen hook;
Just so extracted him the weapon from his car,
Agape, face greeting the ground, and forfeiting life
As he fell. Then the onrushing Erylaüs   445
Smote he squarely with a stone atop the forehead,
And shattered the skull within its helmet's casing,
Whereupon he toppled headlong toward earth, and life-
Devastating demise confined him fast. Thereafter
Erymas and Epaltēs and Amphoterus;   450
And Tlēpolemus, Damastor's son; and Echius,
Enippus, Pyris, Ipheus, and Polymēlus,
Argeas' offspring—all these in quick succession
Patroclus propelled to earth. But when Sarpēdōn
Saw his loosely tunicked comrades thus cascaded   455
Afore the hands of Patroclus, Menoetius' son,

419

He called berating the godlike Lycians: "For shame,
You Lycians, whither abscond you? Be swift instead
To fight; for I myself will face this man, learning
Who it be that thus commands—the cause of Trojan 460
Casualties—weakening the knees of warriors
Many and good." He spoke, and from his chariot
Leapt fully armored to the ground. And Patroclus,
Eyeing him from the oppugnant side, leapt downward.
And as crescent-beaked and crooked-taloned vultures 465
Bestride a lofty rock, rowdily contending;
Just so with shrieks against the other rushed the two,
And Zeus, forkèd-couns'ling Cronus' son, took pity
Seeing them and addressed Hera, sister and wife:
"Ah, woe am I, that Sarpēdōn dearest of men 470
To me is fated by Menoetius' son to die!
And my counsel's aim against itself is sundered,
Whether to snatch him yet alive and set him far
From tearful war in fertile Lycia or despatch
Him now beneath Patroclus' mastery and might." 475

Then to him responded queenly ox-eyed Hera:
"Dreaded son of Cronus, what word have you spoken!
A mortal man aforetime doomed to fate wouldst now
Again from dol'rous death redeem? Do as thou willst;
But be apprised we other gods do disapprove. 480
And this, moreover, I impart; attentive be:
If Sarpēdōn be homeward delivered alive,
Consider even hereafter that other gods
May desirous be to remit their own afar
From homicidal war, for legion the offspring 485
Of deities fighting about great Priam's town,
And grim the ire you instill among immortals.
But if beloved he be and anguishes your heart,
Suffer his combatant's death at Patroclus' hands,
Menoetius' son, and when his soul and life depart, 490
Command you Death and Sleep to convey him away

BOOK XVI

Until to Lycia's broad domain arrived; and there
Will his brethren and kinsfolk inter him aright
With pillar and barrow befitting the fallen."
Thus she spoke. Nor spurned the father of gods and men 495
Her counsel but released bloodied raindrops to earth,
Honoring his belovèd son—proper issue
Whom Patroclus in deep-soiled Troy would shortly slay,
From his fatherland afar.
       Now, when they approached
In their advance, each against the other, then smote 500
Patroclus glorious Thrasymēlus, the stalwart
Squire of princely Sarpēdōn, low to the belly,
Crippling his limbs. But Sarpēdōn missed Patroclus
With brazen spear as Patroclus swirled about him,
Sarpēdōn smiting Pedasus the horse instead; 505
And the neighing beast, choking forth its life, convulsed
And collapsed to the ground with a groan, and dwindled
His life away. But th' other two horses upreared
To left and right, and creaked the yoke, and atop them
Lay the reins a'tangle, the trace-horse overthrown. 510
But for this Automēdōn, renowned of spear, found
Remedy. Gath'ring the sword from aside his thigh,
Sprung he forth and detached the trace-horse, not idling,
And righted the other two, tautening the reins;
And together anew the two warriors emerged 515
In soul-devouring strife. But again Sarpēdōn
With dazzling spear fell short, and o'er the left shoulder
Of Patroclus the spearpoint soared, smiting him not.
But Patroclus in turn rushed onward with his bronze,
And issued the spearshaft not vainly from his hand 520
But struck where midriff embraces the thumping heart,
And he fell as falls an oak or poplar or pine
That mountain-ranging shipwrights fell with whetted axe
To be a vessel's timber; even so outstretched
Before his team he lay, loud groaning and clutching 525
The bloodied dust. Even as the guileful lion

Penetrates a herd, killing a high-hearted bull,
Tawny amid the gait-trailing stock and, groaning,
Perishes the bull in the lion's maw; just so
Struggled Sarpēdōn, the Lycian shieldmen's leader, 530
As Patroclus finished him, and to his comrades
Hollered, addressing them: "Dear Glaucus, warrior born
Among warriors, now needs prevail your spearman's
Power, your constancy in clash; now welcome be
Detested war if swift you be. First make the rounds 535
And urge the Lycian leaders for Sarpēdōn fight;
And you yourself on my behalf, unstinting, fight
Lest in time hereafter I stir your compunction
And memorialize your reproach whilst living,
Should the Danaans despoil me of my armor, 540
Low fallen that I am contending by the ships.
Sooner steadfast be and encourage all the host."

As thus he spoke, death's certainty encircled him,
His eyes and nostrils both; and Patroclus set foot
Upon his breast, spear withdrawing, midriff and all, 545
And together extracted both spearpoint and soul
Of Sarpēdōn, and Myrmidons braced the snorting
Steeds—the beasts terrified—eager to flee their car.
But dolor descended on Glaucus when hearing
Sarpēdōn's plea, and stirred the spirit within him 550
For the succor he failed provide; and with his hand
He gripped his wounded arm, the wound torturing him,
Inflicted by Teucer's arrow while he warded
Off slaughter protecting his comrades, even while
Mounting the palisade. Then prayed he Apollo, 555
Far-shooting, and called: "Hear me, O king, abiding
Perchance in fertile Lycia or haply in Troy,
But who everywhere assistance readily grants
Unto sorrowing men, in sorrow as even
Now besets me; for grievous my wound, and my arm 560
To either side abounds with agony, nor breaks

BOOK XVI

The bloodied flow, and weighs heavily my shoulder
On the wound's account, and I nowise persevere
Amid the foe, unable to wield my weapon,
For a man far the noblest has perished, even 565
Sarpēdōn, son of Zeus, whom Zeus has abandoned,
His own child born. But you, O king, of this grievous
Hurt now heal me, allaying my pain, and provide
The mettle whereby to summon my Lycian friends,
Urging them to forward fight, and myself contend 570
For the corpse of a man having met his demise."
So he pleaded, and Phoebus Apollo heard him.
And he immediately caused the torment to cease
And stanched the blackened blood from his agonized wound,
Emboldening his heart; and Glaucus perceived it, 575
Thus joyed by Apollo so quickly responsive.
He first made the rounds, urging the Lycian leaders
For glorious Sarpēdōn fight, and then, long striding,
Entered the Trojan ranks, seeking Polydamas,
Panthous' son, and goodly Agēnōr, and sought he 580
Aeneas and bronze-fitted Hector thereafter.
And approached he with wingèd words upbraiding him:
"Hector, now for our allies display you utter
Disregard, that far from their friends and native land
Here waste their lives away. And yet indifferently 585
You treat them. Dead lies Sarpēdōn, Lycian leader,
By brazen Ares butchered neath Patroclus' spear.
So, friends, your stand beside him take, and resentment
Rile your spirits lest Myrmidons despoil his bronze—
Doing him disgrace—wroth for the Danaan dead 590
Whom by spearpoint we slew aside the rapid ships."

So he spoke, infusing the Trojans with anguish
O'erpowering and ungoverned, deep sorrowing
For Sarpēdōn who e'er upright stood for Ilium,
Though stranger from afar regarded. Abundant 595
The folk who followed him, and in fight he towered

Preeminent among them. And toward the Argives
Sped they straight, and Hector led them, for Sarpēdōn's
Sake distraught. But th' Argives charged, by Patroclus roused,
The son of shaggy-chested Menoetius, who first   600
Addressed the Aiantes, already zealous they:
"You Aiantes twain, tenaciously persist you
Holding the foe at bay, such valor displaying
As once you owned amid fighting men aforetime—
Or bolder yet. Lies low the man, the first to leap   605
The Danaan wall within, even Sarpēdōn.
So let us now remove and desecrate his corpse,
Despoiling his chest of its bronze. And his divers
Companions, now gathered to safeguard the body,
Let us pitilessly with brazen spear destroy."   610

So he proclaimed, rendering them tenacious most
To rout the foe. Then, when the squadrons had bolstered
Their forces—the Trojans and Lycians, the Argives
And Myrmidons—contended they hard for the corpse
Of Sarpēdōn, their holler heavenward released,   615
And loudly the men's armor resounded. But Zeus
On the unended fight set baleful night, that war
With midnight's toil being waged for his chosen son.
And the Trojans forced a keen-eyed Argive retreat,
For struck they a Myrmidon, one nowise the worst,   620
Even Epeigeus, Agacles' great-hearted son,
Erst ruler in Boudeium well-inhabited;
He, having slain a worthy kinsman, to Peleus
Prostrate arrived and to silver-footed Thetis,
And with Achilles, breaker of warrior ranks,   625
They despatched him to battle in horse-famous Troy.
Famed Hector smote Epeigeus grasping Sarpēdōn,
With a boulder to the skull, riven asunder
The heavy helm and collapsed within, and headlong
Fell he o'er Sarpēdōn, and spirit-slaying death   630
Spilled forth about him. And pain beset Patroclus

BOOK XVI

For his comrade slain, and amid the foremost ranks
He descended, a falcon, attacking starlings
And jackdaws; even so, straight against the Lycians
And Trojans, O Patroclus, master of horsemen, 635
You swooped, your heart bile-blackened for your companion.
And Sthenelus he smote, Ithaemenēs' dear son,
With a stone to the neck, severing the sinews.
Then yielded the Trojans 'round glorious Hector
As far as the flight of a well-balanced javelin 640
That a man casts testing his muscle in contest
Perchance or beneath punishing combat's constraint.
Thus aback the Trojans drew, and the Danaans
Drove them. And Glaucus commander of the Lycian
Shieldmen wheeled about, slaying great-souled Bathyclēs, 645
Belovèd scion of Chalcōn, who resided
In Hellas and stood preeminent in substance
And wealth amid the Myrmidons. Him, turning back,
Of a sudden did Glaucus hard-thrusting transfix
High upon the breast, in pursuit o'ertaking him. 650
And thudding he dropped, the Argives steeped in despair
That perished so goodly a man; but the Trojans,
Heartily triumphant, gathered closely thronging.
And nowise remained the Danaans unmindful
Of their daring, but focused their might on the foe. 655
And slew Mēriōnēs a Trojan warrior
Full armed, Laogonus, Onētōr's dauntless son,
A priest of Idaean Zeus, revered of the folk—
A veritable god. Riven was he 'twixt jaw
And ear, and speedily the spirit departed 660
His limbs, and baneful the darkness blanketing him.
And Aeneas at Mēriōnēs cast, hoping
Beneath cover of shield to retard his advance;
But, unerringly viewing him, Mēriōnēs
Avoided the brazen spear, forward stooping low, 665
The weapon firmly grounded earthward behind him,
Its feathers aquiver 'til death-dealing Ares

At length dampened its fury. Then Aeneas wroth
At heart spoke thus to Mēriones: "Deft dancer
That you be, forever done were those foot-free days   670
Had I succeeded, striking." And Mēriones
Spear-famed answered: "Aeneas, not simple were it
For you, however bold, to quench each defender's
Fortitude, come his turn to test you. Even you
Are mortal made. Should I but swing with lethal sword   675
And sunder you down, then quickly—for all your triumphs
And might's assurance—would you glory yield to me,
And your spirit to horseman Hades."
                         So he spoke,
But Menoetius' fearless son rebuked him, saying:
"Mēriones, why speaks a daring warrior thus,   680
One like yourself? Good friend, nowise by revilements
Will Trojans surrender the corpse; ere then will earth
Cover their multitudes. The objects of combat
Reside in strength of hand; those of words, in council;
Wherefore to increment of war, not words, aspire."   685
So stating he advanced, and the other followed,
A godlike man. And even as woodcutters' din
Disperses afar, from mountain dales resounding;
So from men on capacious earth arose the thud
Of brazen spears, of hides, and of well wrought bucklers,   690
Each on th' other with lances and swords descending;
Nor could a man, though knowing him well, the stalwart
Sarpēdōn have recognized—for altogether
Lay he blanketed face to feet in bloodied dust
And weaponry. And thronged they yet about the corpse   695
Like farmstead flies abuzz buckets of brimming milk
In winsome spring when milk o'ertops the runny rim;
Just so 'round the wretched cadaver they clustered.

Nor to the contention was Zeus inattentive
But debated ever observant in spirit,   700
Meditating on Patroclus' approaching death,

BOOK XVI

Whether even there, o'er the goodly Sarpēdōn,
Glorious Hector, Priam's offspring, should slay him,
Stripping the armor from off his corpse, or augment
War's industry for many more. And as he mulled, 705
This best suited appeared: that Achilles' bold squire
Again drive the Trojans and bronze-armored Hector
Toward Troy, dismantling numerous lives. In Hector
Foremost roused he cowardly rout—and he vaulted
Hurtling to his car, bidding his comrades escape, 710
And of Zeus' sacred balances recking the weight.
Nor stood the valiant Lycians firm but disbanded
En masse, seeing Sarpēdōn mortally stricken
And lying prone 'mid the aggregate dead; for many
Had toppled upon him when Zeus had tautened fast 715
The ligature of conflict; but stripped they the bronze
From Sarpēdōn's chest and shoulders, and the valiant
Patroclus to his comrades conveyed it to take
To the curvèd ships. And then cloud-gathering Zeus
To Apollo spoke: "Up now, dear Phoebus, and purge 720
From Sarpēdōn the sable blood, from ravages
Removing him; and bear him next away, laving
Him in the river's rush and with ambrosial oil
Anointing him, swathing him 'round in immortal
Apparel. And consign him to swift conveyers, 725
Even to Sleep and Death, twin brethren, who hasting
Shall bear him to Lycia's broad domain. There beneath
Barrow and pillar shall his kinfolk inter him,
For such be the due of the dead." So he enjoined,
Nor disobeyed Phoebus his father's directive 730
But descended Ida's slopes to the battle's broil,
And forthwith uplifted the fallen Sarpēdōn,
From weapons' range removed; and bearing him away,
In river's rush immersed him and with ambrosial
Oils anointed him, in apparel immortal 735
Clothing him, and to rapid conveyers consigned
The corpse, even to Sleep and Death, those brethren twain,

Who promptly reposed him in Lycia's wide domain.

But Patroclus, calling aloud to his horses,
To Automēdōn too, upon the Trojans pressed— 740
Infatuated mightily, fool that he was;
For, had he heeded the orders of Peleus' son,
He would in truth have overcome the fiendish fate
Of horrid death. But e'er prevails the plan of Zeus
O'er that of men, for even the dauntless he drives 745
To retreat, from him the victory readily
Seizing, and otherwise emboldening warriors
To fight, and infusing Patroclus with fury.
Then whom first despatched you, and whom last, Patroclus,
When the gods summoned you deathward? Adrastus first, 750
Then Autonoös, Echeclus, and Perimus—
Megas' son—and Epistōr, and Melanippus,
And next Elasus, Mulius, and Pylartes:
These he slew while th' others were mindful each of flight.
Then would the sons of the Achaeans have sacked high- 755
Towering Troy by Patroclus' fearsome doings
As upward, spear to hand, and everywhere he raged,
Had lord Apollo not bestrid the sturdy wall,
Death for him devising, but boon unto the foe.
Patroclus thrice approached the high wall's pediment, 760
And Apollo thrice rebuffed him, pushing with hands
Immortal against his shield. But when a fourth time
He godlike advanced, then with redoubtable cry
Did Apollo address him wingèd words: "Stand down,
O Zeus-fostered Patroclus; fate has not decreed 765
That the lordly Trojan town by your exertions
Be taken, nor by Achilles', far your better."
So he declared, and Patroclus soundly withdrew,
Avoiding the wrath of far-shooting Apollo.

But Hector at the Scaean Gates delayed his steeds, 770
Considering whether to rejoin the turmoil,

BOOK XVI

Again doing battle or call and upgather
The host to the wall. The while thus considering,
Approached him Phoebus Apollo, most resembling
The warrior Asius, a young and strapping youth, 775
Uncle to horse-taming Hector and thus brother
To Hecabē, and Dymas' son that in Phrygia
Abode by Sangarius' streams. In such likeness
Apollo, son of Zeus, proclaimed: "Hector, wherefore
From battle forbear you, unbecomingly so? 780
Would I were as much the stronger than you as now
I am weaker; then shamefully would you retreat.
But against Patroclus sooner propel your steeds
If, honored by Apollo, you slay him perchance."
So speaking he withdrew, a god into the toil 785
Of men. Then to the wise-hearted Cebrionēs
Gave glorious Hector command to lash his horses
Battleward. But entered Apollo approaching
The throng, instilling deadly panic midst the Greeks,
Providing glory for Hector and the Trojans. 790
But Hector let the other Argives be, nor sought
To stay them, but directly drove his sturdy-hooved
Steeds at Patroclus; and Patroclus, spear in hand,
Vaulted groundward from his chariot to confront him
While grasping with his other hand a stone, jagged 795
And crystalline, fast encompassed within his grip.
Firmly leaning to, he released it, nor lacked it
Purpose or target, smiting Hector's charioteer
To the forehead, even Cebrionēs, bastard
Son of glorious Priam, grasping the horses' reins. 800
And instantly the stone dislodged his brows, the bone
Collapsing, and to the dust before him footward
Dropped his eyeballs and, acrobatically deft,
He catapulted forth, breath-departed his corpse.
Then, mocking, you addressed him, O knight Patroclus: 805
"Observe how nimble the man, how lightly he jumps!
Were he, in truth, on the gusty main, this plunger

Would gratify many, deep diving for oysters,
Leaping, despite the stormy swell, from off his ship
As plainward now he plummets headlong from his car;   810
Thus diving men amid the Trojans too exist."

So saying, rushed he the corpse of the warrior
Cebrionēs, like a lion that despoiling
The farmstead is wounded on the breast, his very
Daring his undoing; thus on Cebrionēs   815
Raveningly you leapt, Patroclus. And Hector,
Opposite him, leapt groundward from his chariot.
So the twain engaged in strife for Cebrionēs
Like unto lions that on mountain peaks contend,
Both hung'ring for a slaughtered hind, high-hearted both;   820
Thus also for Cebrionēs, the masters twain
Of warcry—even Patroclus, Menoetius' son,
And glorious Hector—hard battled one another,
With barbarous bronze desirous of rending flesh.
Hector, grasping the corpse by the head, persevered;   825
And Patroclus, opposing him, grasped at the foot;
And about them the others, Trojans and Argives,
Joined the frenetic fray. Even as the East Wind
And South, assaulting forests in mountainous glades,
Strive each the other to outdo, forests of smooth-   830
Barkèd cornel, beech, and ash which together pitch
Their lengthy limbs with wondrous din 'mid the cracking
Of broken boughs; just so the Argives and Trojans
Sprang one on the other in clash, nor considered
They crippling flight. And surrounding Cebrionēs   835
Stood many embedded spears, and many wingèd
Arrows from bowstrings sped, and great buckler-smiting
Stones, as men about him fought. But in eddied dust
Stretched he mightily in his might, to horsemanship
Oblivious.
        Now as long as Phoebus bestrode   840
Midheaven, so long the weaponry of either

Side contused the other, felling the folk; but set
The midday star at the hour of oxen-grazing,
The Achaeans proved superior past measure.
From the darts' descent they disengaged the warrior 845
Cebrionēs, and from the Trojan battle din,
Divested his chest of armor; and Patroclus
Upon the Trojans leapt maliciously. Thrice then
He pounced upon them, the peer of rapid Ares,
Horrendously shouting, and slew he thrice nine men. 850
But when the fourth time he advanced, godlike his gait,
Then for you, Patroclus, impended life's demise,
For contentious Apollo next encountered you,
A dreadful god. But Patroclus discerned him not
Traversing the tumult through, for in teeming mist 855
He approached, behind Patroclus situated,
And with flattened hand assailed his broad-shouldered back,
Setting Patroclus' eyes a'spin. And smote Phoebus
The helmet from his head, that rang rolling beneath
His horses' hooves—the horn-helmeted feathers dust- 860
And blood-befouled. The casque had aforetime escaped
Corruption, since protecting evermore the head
And magnificent brow of a godlike hero,
Even Achilles, but now had Zeus determined
That Hector have the helmet for his head, though death 865
Nearby him stood. And in Patroclus' hand the far-
Shadowing spear fragmented whole—the spear massive,
Strong, and brazen-tipped. And from his arm the tasseled
Shield and baldric groundward dropped, and lord Apollo,
Cronidēs' resplendent scion, loosed his corselet. 870
Then dimmed his addled mind and beneath him failed his
Lustrous limbs, and stood he dazed; and from behind him
Nearby a Dardanian assailed him on the back
'Twixt the shoulders, casting his spear, even Panthous'
Son, Euphorbus—those of his own years surpassing 875
In spearcast, and in horsemanship, and in fleetness
Of foot; and, to a certainty, fighters a'score

Had he ousted from their cars since charioted
In warfare's employment arrived. And he it was
That first at you, O knight Patroclus, cast his spear, 880
Subduing you not; but dashing back reentered
The host, the ashen spear extracting from your flesh,
Enduring not to face Patroclus, though shaken
In battle and unarmed. But Patroclus, o'ercome
By stroke of god and spear, withdrew into the host 885
Of his companions, deflecting fate. But Hector,
Beholding the great-souled Patroclus in retreat,
Wounded by whetted bronze, approached him through the ranks
And to the belly jabbed, boring the bronze on through;
And down he thudded to the Argives disbelief. 890
As when a lion o'erwhelms an unrelenting
Boar, great-hearted contestants they for a paltry
Rivulet concealed upon a mountain peak, whence
Intend they both to drink, and the lion perforce
Rebuffs the panting boar; just so did Hector, son 895
Of Priam, slay Patroclus—who in his turn had
Many slain—from nearby with spear transpiercing him,
And over him gloating delivered wingèd words:

"Patroclus, somehow you thought to despoil our town
And, seizing its women's freedom-day, to bear them 900
Away in your ships, to your beloved native land,
You fool. Instead, my horses advance before them,
And with spear wage I battle preeminently
Amid the war-loving Trojans, for whom I stay
Their day of ruin; but as concerns you, vultures 905
Shall here ingest you. Poor wretch, even Achilles
Despite his valor availed you not, who, I think,
Though remaining apart, explicitly affirmed
Your aggression: 'I admonish you, return not,
O horse-borne Patroclus, unto these hollow ships, 910
'Til you have cloven the tunic about the breast
Of man-slaying Hector and reddened it with blood.

So, I think, he addressed you, persuading your wits
In your witlessness."
                    Then, expiring, you replied,
O knight Patroclus: "Relish your boasting, Hector, 915
Evermore, for Zeus Cronidēs and Apollo
Granted you victory, they that deftly subdued
And despoiled me. But assailed me a score your ilk,
Here then beneath my weapon had they perished all.
No, harsh Fate it was and Leto's son that slew me; 920
And, of men, Euphorbus, while you but third availed.
And this also I disclose, remember it well:
Not long will you remain alive; your death even
Now approaches, and mighty fate, that you be slain
Neath hands of Achilles, Aeacus' peerless son." 925

And even holding forth death's fog enfolded him
And swiftly his spirit retired, to Hades fled,
Lamenting its fate, leaving manliness and youth.
And Hector undaunted addressed him though perished:
"Patroclus, why thus prophesy my destruction? 930
Who can know if Achilles, fair-tressed Thetis' son,
Be sooner smitten by my spear, forfeit his life?"
So saying, from the wound he pulled the brazen spear,
Setting his foot on the corpse and thrusting it back
From the spear. And immediately, spear in hand, 935
Pursued he Automēdōn, godlike assistant
To Aeacus' swift-footed son, wanting to strike;
And headlong conveyed him the horses immortal,
Glorious gift of heaven's dwellers unto Peleus.

~ Book XVII ~

Fight for the Body of Patroclus, Deeds of Ajax and Menelaus, the Seventh Day of Battle

Rushing to defend Patroclus' body, Menelaus slays Euphorbus, the first Trojan to have struck Patroclus. Seeing Menelaus strip Euphorbus' armor, Hector advances to oppose him, giving Menelaus pause whether to stay the course. Briefly retreating, Menelaus returns with Telamonian Ajax, and the two repulse Hector as he prepares to behead Patroclus. Having killed Patroclus, Hector strips him of Achilles' armor and sends it back to Troy, "providing him[self] great glory."

His Lycian allies berate Hector for the Trojans' failure to have kept their leader Sarpedon's body from Greek hands. They wonder, after such ineffectiveness, how the Trojans expect to take Patroclus. Indeed, the taking of Patroclus would enable an exchange for Sarpedon. Hector spurns the rebuke. (The allies are unaware that Sarpedon's armor alone was taken, his corpse divinely returned to Lycia.)

Intercepting the chariot bearing Achilles' armor to Troy, Hector doffs his own in exchange for Achilles'. Zeus fits the armor to Hector's size while prophesying the doom that awaits him. More than that, when Achilles next slays Hector in Achilles' own armor, it will be a suicide in effigy, with Achilles' death fated to follow Hector's.

The Greeks giving way, Ajax assumes the primary defense of Patroclus' body. Hector rallies the countless allies who have joined the Trojan cause, reminding them that he generously compensates their service and expects them to perform accordingly. Though Ajax manages to hold the line, Menelaus doubts the outcome, summoning the Greek leaders and all nearby to join the defense. Thus reinforced, the Greeks hold the line.

Rallied by Apollo, Aeneas leads the Trojans as the battle intensifies, a battle seeming like no other: the vicious and costly tug of war for a corpse.

Meanwhile, Achilles knows neither of Patroclus' death nor of Patroclus' having advanced, alone, on the walls of Troy.

In one of the poem's most touching scenes—prelude to the surreal to come—Achilles' immortal horses stand pillar-like, weeping, muddy-maned, missing their driver Automedon and thinking him slain. Zeus observes the scene and laments that immortal horses, gifted to the mortal Peleus, should suffer human emotion. Zeus will yet inspire them to retrieve Automedon and return him to the ships (which the horses do). Alcimedon espies the abandoned chariot and mounts it, urging Automedon onboard. Alcimedon will drive, while Auomedon dismounts to fight when necessary. The pair is seen by Hector and Aeneas, who again hope to capture the horses. Noting them, Automedon calls for reinforcements (from those protecting Patroclus' corpse) to keep the horses from being taken. Hector's and Aeneas' design on the horses thus fails as the "Battle over Patroclus' Body" continues inexorably on.

Concerned that Achilles does not yet know of Patroclus' death, Ajax sends Menelaus to dispatch Antilochus with the news. Shocked by Menelaus' account of events, Antilochus removes his armor—the more quickly to run to Achilles. Amid fearsome resistance led by Hector and Aeneas, the Greeks manage to hoist Patroclus and advance him toward the ships. It is the evening of day 28.

Homer's extended similes provide relief from gruesome descriptions of battlefield slaughter. As the fighting in Book 17 is the most intense of any book in the *Iliad*, Book 17, with thirteen extended similes, contains more than any other book (see Index of Extended Similes at www.poemoftroy.com).

※

And Menelaus beloved of Ares failed not
To note Patroclus, by the Trojans slain in war,
But fared he in bronze aflame amid the foremost
Fighters, straddling Patroclus, as over a calf
Its mourning mother stands lowing that delivered   5
Her calf first-born, parturition ere then unknown;
Even so, bestrode Menelaus the fair-haired

BOOK XVII

Patroclus, afore him placing his spear and well-
Balanced shield, eager to slay the man whoever,
Approaching, should seize the corpse. Then was Euphorbus, 10
With ashen spear equipped, himself also mindful
Of peerless Patroclus, taking his stand nearby
And addressing Atreïdēs, Ares belovèd:
"Menelaus, son of Atreus, nurtured of Zeus,
Commander of hosts, retreat you leaving the corpse, 15
Forgoing the bloody spoils? For other than I
No Trojan nor Troy ally acclaimed by spear's
Ferocious point despatched Patroclus; wherefore grant
That I garner a goodly renown, lest casting
I destroy you, despoiling your honey-sweet life." 20
Then sorely incited, fair-haired Menelaus
Addressed him: "O father Zeus, to no one's credit
Are overweening boasts. Not such is the leopard's
Confidence, nor lion's, nor wild boar's of baneful
Disposition, in whose breasts the greatest fury 25
Lies, defying measure all, as is the spirit
Of Panthous' son of goodly ashen spear. Even
Hyperēnōr, that mighty tamer of horses,
Profited not of his manhood when triflingly
Underestimating my mettle, he resolved 30
That of the Argives all was I the greatest rogue.
Not on his feet, I aver, did he homeward fare,
His longing kin and belovèd wife to gladden.
No less do I intend your fame to diminish
Should against me you stand; but sooner I command 35
You gone, unto the throng returned, and cross me not
Ere ill befall; knows it even a fool when done."

So he spoke, in nowise dissuading the other,
Who answered him saying: "Truly, Menelaus,
Nurtured of Zeus, now for my brother whom you slew, 40
And over whom you boasted, will you make amends,
For you widowed his wife in her bridal chamber

437

Newly built, giving his parents unspeakable
Pain and despair. Truly for them and their heartache
Would I now this relief from their sorrow bestow: 45
Conveying and offering your armor and head
At the feet of both Panthous and loving Phrontis.
Yet not overlong shall our labor lie idle
Or ill decided, be it for triumph or flight."
So saying, he struck at his buckler, well balanced 50
To every side, but failed the bronze to penetrate;
And the point angled back in the unyielding shield.
Then with his spear did Menelaus, Atreus' son,
Assail him, first petitioning Zeus Cronidēs.
Of his heavy hand assured, hard-weighting the thrust, 55
He gored him conceding ground at the gullet's base,
And promptly through his tender neck the point traversed.
He fell with a thud, and the armor about him
Clanged, and his tresses alike to the Graces' own,
Tight plaited with silver and gold, lay drenched in blood. 60
And as a man rears an olive-tree sapling, far
Distantly planted, where abundantly bubbles
The water, a lovely flourishing shoot, and gusts
Of rambunctious wind disquiet its burgeoning
Bloom and allure, and suddenly a full raging 65
Wind erupts, from its trench uprooting the sapling
And laying it prostrate to ground; no less did you,
O Atreus' son, Menelaus, Euphorbus slay,
Ashen his spear, and begin despoiling his arms.
And as when a mountain-bred lion, unflagging 70
Its fortitude, has grabbed from out a grazing herd
The heifer most delectable, first grasping her
Neck with muscly maw, then breaking it, thereafter
Enragedly gorging upon entrails and blood,
And 'round about the hounds and hollering herdsmen 75
Their distance keep, not wanting to encounter him,
For sallow the fear that seizes them; so dared not
A soul to encounter acclaimed Menelaus.

BOOK XVII

Immediately had Menelaus despoiled
Euphorbus' armor but that Phoebus Apollo 80
Begrudged it him and, assuming mortal likeness,
Even of Mentēs, Ciconian commander,
Roused Hector, peer of fleet Ares, to oppose him,
And wingèd were the words he uttered, thus speaking:
"Hector, now haste you vainly to possess what ne'er 85
You may attain, even the steeds of Aeacus'
Wise-hearted son, but onerous for mortal men
Their mastery, save for Achilles swift of foot
Whom a mother immortal bore. Meanwhile, warring
Menelaus, Atreus' son, bestrides Patroclus, 90
And has the choicest of the Trojans finished off,
Even Panthous' son, Euphorbus, arresting his
Furious spirit."
            So pronouncing, returned he,
A god, to human toil. But clouded Hector's soul
With darkling doubt, sorrowing as he considered 95
The ranks, and immediately observed the one
Despoiling the glorious armor; the other
Prostrate on the ground, lifeless from his wound, his blood
Spewed forth. Then 'mid the foremost fighters hastened he
In fiery bronze accoutred, and a piercing cry 100
Discharged, like to Hephaestus' unquenchable flame.
Nor by Atreus' son Menelaus went the cry
Unheard, but worriedly addressed he his great-
Hearted spirit: "Woe and alas! If I renounce
The glorious arms and abandon Patroclus 105
For vengeance' sake, I worry that some Danaan,
Beholding it, be wroth with me. But if alone,
For honor's sake, I meet Hector and the Trojans,
I fear to be outnumbered, one against many,
For flashing-helmèd Hector leads them here en masse. 110
But why debates my spirit thus? When a warrior
Ventures against heaven's will to fight one honored

By a god, significant is the affliction.
Thus, let none of the Danaans resentful be,
Whosoever observe me surrendering ground 115
Before Hector, who fights with heaven's assistance.
But if I might somewhere find Ajax, at warcry
Renowned, then might we battle-minded turn to fight,
Though defying heaven's will, to rescue the dead
For Achilles, Peleus' son. Best were that of ills." 120
While thus he pondered in mind and heart, the Trojan
Ranks forth hastened led by Hector. Menelaus
Then surrendered ground, leaving the corpse, e'er turning
About like a well-maned lion that dogs and men
From its lair expel with spears and shouts, and congeals 125
The heart in its once-proud breast and from the farmstead
Slinks it grudgingly; even so from Patroclus
Parted fair-haired Menelaus, turning to take
His stand once gaining the throng of his companions
And glancing about for Ajax, Telamon's son. 130
Him he aptly noted leftward of the melee,
Exhorting and heart'ning his comrades to battle,
For marvelous the fear by Apollo instilled.
And running, quickly he encountered him and spoke:
"Ajax, hither come, good friend, so shall we hasten 135
Defending the fallen Patroclus, that somehow
We convey the denuded corpse to Pēleidēs,
But the flashing-helmeted armor keep Hector."

So spoke he rousing prudent Ajax' heart who strode
Amid the foremost fighters with Menelaus 140
Flowing-haired aside him. And when Hector had stripped
The glorious arms of Patroclus, ventured he
To remove and behead him with razored weapon,
Discarding the corpse as canine fodder for Troy.
But Ajax, with shield the heft of a city wall, 145
Approached, and back to the throng of his companions
Hector ceded ground, and ascending his chariot,

BOOK XVII

To the Trojans presented the glorious arms
For transport to Troy, assuring him great glory.
But Ajax with buckler protected Patroclus   150
Like a lioness straddling her whelps 'round about,
The while piloting her pups met by foresting
Huntsmen; then exulting in her power, lowers
She her brow, obscuring her eyes; just so bestrode
Ajax the fallen Patroclus and aside him   155
Atreus' son, Menelaus, beloved of Ares,
Nursing great sorrow within his breast. And Glaucus,
Hippolochus' offspring and Lycian commander,
With glaring glance from beneath his brow, chid Hector
Disapprovingly: "Hector, fairest to behold,   160
But wanting warfare's wherewithal. You idly boast
Unparalleled renown though coward to the core.
Bethink you now how you alone, with Ilium's
Native born, might disenthrall your dwellings and town.
For of the Lycians, at least, will no man battle 165
For the city's sake in thwarting the Danaans,
Since profitless against the foe and unending
Appears this war. How might a meaner man assist
Among the embattled, you wretch, when Sarpēdōn,
Comrade and guest alike, is left to the Argives, 170
A sorry spoil and quarry, one who most often
While yet alive and vibrant, advantaged both you
And Ilium. But now evince you no resolve
To redeem him from ravening dogs, such that were
Any Lycian to obey my word, then homeward   175
Were we gone, and Troytown relinquished and ransacked
Entire. But were the Trojans intrepidly brave,
Unaccustomed to concern, as men demonstrate
Who labor defending their fatherland, ah, then
Should Patroclus be quickly redeemed and returned 180
Unto Troy. For if this man, a corpse, to Priam's
Town were come, we from the fracas extracting him,
Straightway would the Argives return the grand armor

Of lordly Sarpēdōn, restoring his person
To Troy. For despatched is Achilles' surrogate— 185
Achilles shipbound, far best of the Achaeans—
Together with comrades close-quartered when clashing.
But failed your fortitude face to face with Ajax
Great-Hearted, to confront him as a challenger,
Immersed in the melee's clamor, fully engaged, 190
Since he, a paradigm of pow'r, surpasses you."
Then angrily glancing from neath his brow, answered
Hector flashing-helmeted: "Glaucus, how speak you,
Being as you are, a word thus overweening?
Truly, my friend, I gauged you in sagacity 195
Far greater than others in fertile Lycia's land,
But your counsel entirely disregard I now
As vilifying, averring my avoidance
Of Ajax face to face. I balk at no battle,
Rest assured, nor at the clamor of chariots. 200
But e'er the intention of aegis-bearing Zeus
Prevails, since he hastens the valiant man to rout
And roundly revokes his victory when haply
He rouses men to fight. But standing aside me,
My friend, note closely and contemplate my labor: 205
Whether the day's advance will proclaim me coward
As you propose, or hinder many an Argive—
However perfervid their valor—from fighting
For dead Patroclus." So speaking, he called loudly,
Addressing the Trojans: "You Trojans, and Lycians, 210
And Dardanians all, at close quarters combatant,
Be men, my friends, unforgetful of fervid might,
Whilst I assume the arms of peerless Achilles,
The arms resplendent that I despoiled from the corpse
Of the dauntless Patroclus, purloining his life." 215

Thus speaking, Hector flashing-helmeted withdrew
From the fighting's roar, and running on hastened foot
Caught up with his companions—they not distant yet—

BOOK XVII

Pursuing those cityward bearing the armor
Of Peleus' son. Abstaining the while, and at rest 220
From tearful toil, he doffed his fighting gear. His own
He conveyed to the war-loving Trojans to take
To sacred Ilium, himself appareling
In the armor immortal of famed Achilles,
By the gods immortal to his father given 225
And which he, become older, had gifted his son;
Yet the son in his father's armor grew not old.
But when cloud-gath'ring Zeus espied Hector afar,
Attiring in armor of godlike Achilles,
He nodded his head and addressed himself these words: 230
"Alas, poor wretch, truly lodges death in no part
Of your spirit albeit nearby its approach,
But into the panoply immortal you step
Of a princely man afore whom countless others
Quake, whose kind and courageous comrade you have slain, 235
The arms despoiling, indecorously, from off
His head and shoulders. But for now I endow you
With mettle, considering that Andromache
Will nevermore greet you returning from battle
Nor the glorious arms of Achilles acquire." 240
Thus spoke Zeus, with clouded eyebrows affirming all,
And configured the armor to Hector's physique.
And Enyalius and Ares, gods of war,
Permeating Hector, imbued him with boldness.
Then entered he the ranks of his splendid allies, 245
Standing, crying aloud, manifestly agleam
In the arms of Achilles, great-souled Peleus' son.
And through the ranks he strode, heartening every man,
Mesthlēs, Glaucus, Medōn and Asteropaeus,
Deisēnōr, Thersilochus and Hippothoüs, 250
Phorcys, Chrōraius, and Ennomus, the augur—
These did he hearten, addressing them wingèd words:
"Hear me, you thousand-folded allied tribes, dwelling
Hereabouts. With forces in nowise deficient

I assembled you each from your cities and towns,   255
That with alacrity you rescue the Trojan
Wives, their children too, from the war-frenzied Argives.
Thus minded, the riches of my folk I lavish
To sustain you, and furnish gifts, lifting the strength
Of your numbers. So, steadied now in turn, let each   260
Man fight unquestioning, whether he live or die;
For such is the dalliance of war. And whosoe'er
Shall deliver the perished Patroclus, to lie
'Mid the horse-taming Trojans, to himself making
Ajax yield, one-half the plunder provide I him,   265
Half keeping myself as though equal our glory."

So he proclaimed, and upon the Argives they rushed
En masse, spears brandishing, and their spirits within
Ever hoped from goodly Ajax, Telamon's son,
To extricate Patroclus—naïfs that they were!   270
For numberless the lives he purloined contesting
For the corpse. Then Ajax, well versed in warcry he,
To Menelaus spoke: "My dear Menelaus,
Nurtured of Zeus, no longer entertain I hope
That we, a lonely pair, will manage by ourselves,   275
For less I fear Patroclus' feeding dogs and birds
Of prey than fear I for myself, befall what may,
And fret alike for you since combat's fog descends,
Enwrapping all about, even Priam's offspring,
And for us is decided destruction assured.   280
But assemble the chieftains if it benefit."
So he spoke, and Menelaus warcry-adept
Hearkened willingly, emitting a strident shout,
Entreating the Danaans: "Dear friends and Argive
Leaders, you that quaff at public cost at the board   285
Of Atreidēs Agamemnon and give orders
Each to his people, you whom honor and glory
Of Zeus attend—it is difficult to observe
Each combatant 'mid the commanders, so boundless

BOOK XVII

Battle's discord ablaze. Rather, let each man fight 290
Unprompted and be put to shame that Patroclus
Lies a plaything to Trojan curs." So he declared,
And swift Ajax, Oïleus' son, embraced his words,
And quickly running arrayed himself aside him,
And followed Idomeneus and Idomeneus' 295
Comrade, Mērionēs, peer of Enyalius,
Slayer of men, and others. Who of wits possessed
Could tally the names of the many that followed
Upon these arousing the Argives to warfare?

Then forward forged the Trojans, their formation fit, 300
By Hector led. And as when at a river's mouth
A heaven-nurtured riptide unsettles the surge,
And shoreward to either side resound the headlands
As bellows the breaking brine; even with such din
Of voices clamored the foe. But the Achaeans 305
Squarely commanded the ground about Patroclus
With resolve unstinting, in brazen shields ensconced.
And o'er their gleaming helms shed Zeus a thickened mist,
For even aforetime was stalwart Patroclus
Never resented by Zeus the while he excelled 310
As Aeacidēs' squire; and Zeus now disapproved
Patroclus' enduring as sport of fiendish dogs,
Even those of Troy, and hastened his protection.
The Trojans first routed the glancing-eyed Argives
Who, quitting the corpse, to a distance retreated; 315
Yet the high-hearted Trojans slew nary a soul
Among them, though trying, and the Argives returned
To recapture the corpse, given the modest space
That divided them, for Ajax enspirited
Them effectively, he in mien and martial feats 320
Superior to all save Peleus' peerless offspring.
Strong through the foremost fighters he strode, a feral
Boar amid mountains easily scattering hounds
And lusty youth, wheeling upon them through the glades;

Even so did lordly Telamon's son, glorious 325
Ajax, within their numbers entering, lightly
Disperse the enemy battalions positioned
Around Patroclus, desperately desiring
To draw him forth, unto the town remanding him,
Glory begetting for themselves.
                        Now Hippothous, 330
Conspicuous son of Pelasgian Lēthus,
His baldric about either ankle securing,
Was footwise through the fray extracting Patroclus,
Obliging Hector and the Trojans. But evil
Swiftly visited him, such as none might avert, 335
Though wanting to, for Telamon's son, emerging
From the tumult, assaulted him on his brazen
Cheek-shielding helmet, and the horsehair-crested helm
Was punctured by the spearpoint and riven by spear
And mighty hand; and outward the gash seeped the brain 340
Dripping blood, lengthwise staining the resolute shaft;
And there faltered his force, and falling from his grip
Where they lay on the ground were the feet of manly
Patroclus, and hard thereby he toppled, headlong
On Patroclus' corpse—his loamy Larissa now 345
Distant—nor in the least requited his parents'
Nurture, but brief his life, purloined by the great-souled
Ajax' weapon. And Hector cast hard at Ajax,
And the latter, intently eyeing him, barely
Avoided the brazen point; yet Hector leveled 350
Schedius, son of great-souled Iphitus, surpassing
He 'mid the Phocian folk inhabiting lustrous
Panopeus, being sovereign over multitudes.
Him smote Hector below the sturdy collarbone,
And tidily through passed the rigid point, outing 355
At the shoulder's base, and thuddingly he tumbled,
His armor banging about him. But Ajax next
Smote wise-hearted Phorcys, Phaenops' son, to the gut
As he straddled Hippothous, and broke his corselet's

BOOK XVII

Plate, and the bronze delivered his bowels therethrough 360
As groundward he fell, clutching the earth in his palms,
Whereat the foremost fighters and glorious Hector
Retreated, and the Danaans shouted aloud,
Dragging the dead Hippothous and Phorcys away
And commencing to plunder their shoulders of arms. 365

Then had the Trojan ranks been again driven back
Unto Troy by the Argives, Ares-advantaged,
Trojans fleet in cowardice—the Argives gaining
Eminence, unstinting allotment of Zeus, their
Puissance unparalleled—except lord Apollo 370
Roused Aeneas in form assumed of Periphas
The herald, Epytus' son, in his heraldship
Agèd grown aside his agèd father, with whom
In kindly disposition abided he e'er.
In Periphas' person spoke Phoebus Apollo: 375
"Aeneas, how might you ever defend steep Troy,
Heaven disallowing it? Others have I known
That trusted in their strength and might, in their valor
And numbers, protecting their folk though grim the odds;
But Zeus Cronidēs, his preference our own, supports 380
Our mastery over the Greeks; yet harbor you
Unbounded fear, refraining from fight." So he spoke,
And Aeneas, gauging his aspect, knew Phoebus
Apollo far-shooting and summoned to Hector:
"Hector, and you other allies and Trojan chiefs, 385
Shame surely were ours if before the Danaans,
Ares-beloved, we were driven back to Ilium,
Trounced in our timidity; yet, staunch beside me
Stands a god declaring Zeus, advisor supreme,
Endures as our battle's adjutant. So, make we 390
Straight for the Danaans lest fallen Patroclus
Be readily drawn to their vessels." So he spoke,
And leapt far to the fore of the foremost fighters.
There positioned erect and deftly pivoting,

He opposed the Greeks directly. Then Aeneas 395
With spearcast wounded Leiōcritus, Arisbas'
Son, valiant comrade of Lycomēdēs, Ares-
Beloved who, pitying his fallen companion,
Close approached him, taking his stand. And casting
His spear, smote he Apisaōn, son of Hippasus, 400
Host's shepherd, below the midriff to the liver,
And instantly hobbled his knees—Apisaōn,
That from lush Paeonia had come, exceptional
He, and bested in fight by Asteropaeus
Alone. But as he fell, brash Asteropaeus 405
Greatly pitied him, hastening forth desirous
To fight the Danaans, but in the effort failed,
For by bucklers encompassed stood they stoically
Shelt'ring Patroclus, gripping their razor-edged spears
A'front them. And Ajax ranged the ranks, commanding 410
Each man to encircle the corpse but to move not
Forward ahead the others, as one excelling,
Besting all, but to staunchly stand aside the corpse,
Doing battle hand to hand. Thus towering Ajax
Commanded; the earth besodden with blood discharged 415
And the dead dropped fallen in droves—of the Trojans
And their confederates and of the Danaans;
For they too contended with bloodshed unmeasured
Though proved their companies fated by fewer far,
For thronged they ever to prevent full destruction 420
Among themselves within the host.
       And thus they fought,
In likeness of blazing flame, nor would you have thought
That sun or moon remained, for nighted in darkness
The chieftains battled, fighting about the body
Of slain Menoetius' son. But the other Trojans 425
And well-greaved Danaans did battle, contented
Beneath the aether's calm, and o'er them extended
Effulgence of luminous sun, and exited
Blanketing cloud from mountainous earth. And they fought

BOOK XVII

At times resting themselves and regrouping apart, 430
Avoiding one another's groan-begetting darts.
But those at center endured hardship unsparing—
Continuous combat in darkness—most sorely
Beleaguered beneath merciless bronze, even those
That were chieftains. And still a famed warrior pair, 435
Thrasymēdēs and Antilochus, knew not yet
Of peerless Patroclus' death, but accounted him
Still alive—heroes they, resisting the Trojans
Throughout the throng—and the twain, fending the demise
And rout of their companions, fought standing apart 440
Complying with Nestor's command, who had spurred them
To battle away from the hollow ships. The fury
Flamed fully throughout the day, and with the sweat
Of their labors were the feet, knees, and legs of each
Warrior defiled, and sullied too his arms and eyes 445
As battled the hosts o'er the goodly attendant
Of swift-footed Peleus' son. And as when a man
On his folk bestows the hide of a mighty bull,
Oil-soaked for stretching, and they, taking hold,
In a circle stand and stretch it, and downward drips 450
The greasiness from the tug of multiple hands,
And to its uttermost expands the hide throughout;
Even so from every quarter they haled the corpse,
This way and that in restrictive space. And their hearts
Brimmed hopeful—for the Trojans, that they convey it 455
To Troy; but for the Argives, to the hollow ships.
And fiercely flared the fight for Patroclus, nor could
Ares rouser of hosts nor Athena make light
Of the carnage, such was the rage it engendered.

Such burden of men and steed did Zeus Cronidēs 460
That day distribute and o'er Patroclus require.
Nor yet cognizant was the godlike Achilles
Of Patroclus' demise, for distant from the ships
Contended they beneath the walls of Troy. Wherefore

449

Achilles thought not of Patroclus' misfortune 465
But, instead, of his return once gaining the gates;
Nor yet whatever imagined that Patroclus
Without him would capture the town—or even with—
For such from his mother had he often confirmed,
Privately attending her whene'er she conveyed 470
Significant tidings from eminent Zeus. And yet
Never mentioned his mother the catastrophe
Befallen: that his companion far the dearest
Had been slain. But those about the corpse, their whetted
Spears in hand, unwaveringly thrusted onward, 475
Slaying one another. And thus would a brazen-
Coated Achaean relate: "Friends, no glory ours
In returning to the vessels; no, even here
Let darkened earth devour us, that better by far
Than relinquishing Patroclus to the Trojans, 480
Tamers of horses, Troyward for Troy's glory gone."
So also a great-hearted Trojan would declare:
"My comrades, though fated together to perish
Aside this man, let no one from the fray retreat."
Thus would one recount, courage awaking in each. 485
So they clashed, and the clamor of iron uprose
Through desolate aether unto deafened heaven.
But wept the two steeds of Achilles, Peleus' son,
Where they stood from the battle apart, presuming
Automēdōn, their charioteer, reposed in dust, 490
Stricken by man-slaying Hector. For the valiant
Son of Diōrēs often plied them with his lash,
And many times provided them encouragement
And other times threats; yet neither steed was minded
To return to the vessels or vast Hellespont 495
Nor yet to resume confrontation with the foe;
But as a pillar steadfast abides, positioned
At the barrow of the dead, advantaged just so,
Afore their resplendent chariot they abode, heads
To earth extended. And torrid the tears teeming 500

BOOK XVII

Groundward from their eyes as they deeply lamented
Their absent charioteer; muddied now their stunning
Manes beneath their yokes, flaring wind-flown aforetime.
And Cronidēs Zeus attended their affliction
And pitied them, shaking his head and reflecting: 505
"Ah, gloom-ridden pair, why ever gifted we you
To king Peleus, a mortal, you being ageless
And immortal? Was it to have you sorrow too
Among miserable man? For naught more miserable
Exists, I think, amid all that crawls or catches 510
Breath on earth than man. Yet truly, not upon you
Nor upon your magnificent car shall Hector,
Priam's son, ascend; to that will I not consent.
Suffice it not he retains the armor, vaunting
Its possession? No, within your knees and spirit 515
Will I strength instill, that you opportunely save
Automēdōn from death, bearing him to the ships.
But to the Trojans shall I yet the glory grant
Of their protracted butchery, until night nears
The curvèd vessels, the sun sinking, and sacred 520
Darkness come." So saying, breathed he a rarefied force
Into the steeds that downward from their manes dislodged
The dust and fleetly bore the car amid the fray
Of Trojans and Achaeans. And behind them fought
Automēdōn, though mourning for his companion, 525
And pounced upon the Trojans, a vulture on geese,
For lightly would he evade the furious fight
And lightly charge, beleaguering the gathered foe.

But no warrior in pursuit did he despatch,
Since unable in the headlong melee alone 530
To steady his spear and control the racing steeds
While assailing warriors. But at length espied him
A companion, even Alcimēdōn, son
Of Laërcēs, Haemon's son, who approached behind
The chariot, addressing Automēdōn: "What god, 535

Automēdōn, has thus so meanly valued you
And swept your wits away that in the headmost ranks
You fight alone, foolhardy and unassisted?
For your comrade is slain, and Hector bears his arms,
Even the arms of Aeacidēs, and glories 540
Therein." And to him responded Automēdōn,
Son of Diōrēs: "Alcimēdōn, what Argive
Warrior avails the like to rein immortal steeds,
Their exuberance and stride, except Patroclus,
The gods' own equal in counsel while yet alive? 545
But death and fate have now subdued him. However,
Take you the lash and the glittering reins, while I
Dismount and fight." Thus he spoke, and Alcimēdōn
Ascended the battle-swift car and artfully
Grasped the reins and lash, and Automēdōn leapt down, 550
And glorious Hector noted them and straightway spoke
To Aeneas nearby: "Aeneas, sound counselor
Of the Trojans brazen-armed, see I before me
The twain horses of swift-footed Aeacus' son
Advancing into battle's view with cowardly 555
Charioteers. This pair would I fast apprehend,
Should you thus agree, seeing that the charioteers
Would little withstand our assault and battle's might."
So he spoke, and Aeneas attended him well,
And forward pressed the pair, their shoulders protected 560
By bullhide bucklers toughened and dry, and ample
The welded bronze thereon. And trod alongside them
Chromius and godlike Arētus, who eagerly
Wanted to slaughter the men and abduct the high-
Necked horses. Dullards they, for not without bloodshed 565
Would they finish their dealings with Automēdōn
Who praying to Cronidēs Zeus was filled about
His darkening heart with hardihood and courage,
Addressing his comrade thus: "Alcimēdōn, keep
The horses in proximity and let their breath 570
Fall squarely on my neck; for truly I expect

BOOK XVII

That Hector, Priam's son, will be unsatisfied
Until mounting behind Achilles' fair-maned steeds,
Despatching us and scattering the Argive ranks,
Or himself being haply 'mid the frontmost slain."   575
So he spoke, the Aiantes and Menelaus
Summoning: "You Aiantes twain and Danaan
Chiefs, and you Menelaus, commit now the corpse
To the care of those bravest about you, to stand
Firmly about it, repulsing the warrior ranks,   580
But from the two of us, still living, repel you
The pitiless day of our doom, for here pressing
Hard in the tear-ridden conflict come Priam's son
And stewart Aeneas, choicest of Trojans all.
Yet remains the result for gods to determine.   585
I too will cast, Cronidēs the outcome condone."
He spoke taking aim and cast his far-shadowing
Spear, smiting the shield of Arētus, well balanced
To each side, but the buckler contained not the cast
Which quickly pierced the bronze and settled to his gut.   590
And as when a man, with hefty keen-cutting axe,
Neatly severs the horns of a farmsteaded ox,
Cutting the keratin through, and the ox heaves forth
And falls; thus hove Arētus lighting on his back;
And the axe, surpassingly sharp, fixed aquiver   595
In his gut, and slackened sank his limbs. But Hector
Released his marvelous lance at Automēdōn
But he, unerringly eyeing him, averted
The brazen spearpoint, stooping forward, and the lance
Attached behind him to the ground, and the lance butt   600
Quivered until Ares at length checked its choler.

And now to one another near had they battled
With sword had not the twain Aiantes from their rage
Uncoupled them, for they traversed the throng when their
Comrade called; and, fearful, Hector and Aeneas   605
And godlike Chromius retreated anew, leaving

453

Arētus there to lie, stricken with affliction;
And Automēdōn, swift Ares' peer, of his arms
Despoiled him and boasted, saying: "In truth, I gain
From Patroclus' death grief's transitory respite,   610
Though slaying an inferior fighter." This said,
He seized the bloody spoils, placing them in his car,
And himself strode thereon, bloodied his feet and hands,
As a lion having gutted a bull. Again
The melee recommenced, merciless, tear infused   615
O'er fallen Patroclus; and Pallas Athena
Descending from heaven incited the struggle,
For Cronidēs far-seeing ordained that she drive
The Danaans, for now was Zeus' spirit altered.
As Cronidēs for mortals a rainbow extends   620
From heaven forth—ill fortuned—a portent for strife
Or frigid storm that halts men's works upon the earth,
Unnerving the flocks; so Athena, in fateful
Cloud enfolded, entered the Argive soldiery,
Enspiriting each man. First urging Atreus' son,   625
The valiant Menelaus—for he stood nearby—
She spoke, likened to Phoenix in form and tireless
Voice: "For you, Menelaus, disgrace shall surely
Await, recrimination too, if Achilles'
Trusted comrade by rabid dogs neath towering   630
Troy be torn; but hold and exhort the others fight."
Then responded warcry-seasoned Menelaus:
"Phoenix, old sire, belovèd father aforetime,
Would that Athena sanction my vigor, from rush
Of weapons shielding me! So should I willingly   635
Stand by Patroclus, assisting him; thus sorely
In spirit disheartens me his death. Yet Hector
Possesses the dread fury of fire, his onslaught
Relenting not, to wreak havoc, for Cronidēs
Accords him acclaim." So he spoke, and the goddess   640
Grey-eyed Athena was foremost gladdened to be
Of deities to whom prayer was offered. And she

BOOK XVII

Strengthened his shoulders and knees, and in his spirit
Stirred the fly's relentless mettle that e'er driven
From the skin of man yet pertinaciously bites,　　　　　　645
Sweetly imbibing the savorèd blood; just so
With comp'rable courage buoyed she his spirit
And, straddling Patroclus, staved he the foeman off.

Now among the Trojans dwelt a certain Podēs,
Eëtion's son, a man both wealthy and stalwart,　　　　　　650
And Hector respected him conspicuously
For friendship at feast and especial comradeship.
Him, upon his belt, as he attempted to flee,
Fair-haired Menelaus assailed, his blade boring
Through; and he toppled, thudding; but Menelaus,　　　　　655
Atreus' son, hauled the corpse from amid the Trojans
To the throng of his companions. Apollo then
Accosted Hector, provoking him, in likeness
Of Phaenops, Asius' son, dearest of his guest-friends,
Who abode in Abydus; and in his likeness　　　　　　　　660
Far-working Apollo spoke: "Hector, what Argive
Will ever respect you, given your surrender
A'face Menelaus, aforetime a weakling
Warrior? Now, needing no assistance, he purloins
The corpse from under the Trojans and disappears.　　　　665
He has murdered your trusted companion, worthy
Among the best, even Podēs, Eëtion's son."
So he spoke, and dolorous grief beset Hector
As he moved amid the frontmost fighters, bedecked
In flaming bronze. And Zeus took his tasseled aegis,　　　670
Far dazzling, and upon cloud-blanketed Ida
Greatly thundered amid lightning's flash, the aegis
Wielding, victory on the Trojans conferring
But putting the Argives to rout. Peneleōs
Of Boeotia initiated the retreat　　　　　　　　　　　　　675
And, where standing, eyes on the foe unfailingly
Fastened, sustained a grazing wound to the shoulder;

But a spearpoint, close propelled by Polydamas,
Bore inmost to the bone. And Hector, close fighting,
Wounded Leitus, great-souled Alectryōn's offspring, 680
Upon the hand at the wrist, marking his exit
From battle; and distressedly he eyed the scene,
Recoiling, his spear held firm, abandoning hope
Of battling the Trojans. And as Hector followed
After Leitus, Idomeneus struck him to the 685
Corselet, on the breast beside the nipple, the long
Spearshaft in its socket snapping; and the Trojans
Shouted loud. And Hector cast at Idomeneus,
Deucalion's son, standing in his chariot,
Closely missing him but smiting Coëranus, 690
Mēriones' companion and charioteer,
Who had accompanied him from well-built Lyctus.
For on foot had Idomeneus initially
Come from the ships, and would have provided goodly
Glory to Troy, had Coëranus not happened 695
By driving swift-footed horses. So he arrived,
Light and deliverance bearing Idomeneus,
Repelling his ruthless day of doom, but himself
Unto man-slaying Hector succumbing. This man,
Coëranus, Hector assailed at the juncture 700
Of jaw and ear; and quickly exited the spear
From neath his nether teeth, and at midpoint severed
His tongue asunder, and he toppled from his car,
Groundward dropping the reins; and stooped Mēriones
To gather them up, addressing Idomeneus: 705
"Apply now the lash until reaching the vessels.
Know you that victory even now outruns us."
So he spoke, and Idomeneus drove the horses
Fair-maned to the vessels, for desolation had
Savaged his soul. Nor was great-spirited Ajax 710
Nor Atreus' son unaware that Zeus supported
The Trojans, turning battle's tide to favor them;
And first of them spoke Telamonian Ajax:

BOOK XVII

"For shame, now might anyone, however witless,
Understand that Cronidēs Zeus advantages   715
The Trojans. For whoever casts strikes home. Be he
Craven or courageous, Zeus directs his weapon.
But for us our weapons plummet vainly groundward.
But let us consider the optimal measure
For rescuing the corpse and ourselves returning   720
Unhampered to euphoric comrades—unsettled
They in viewing Argive failure and believing
The fury and undaunted hands of man-slaying
Hector persist unstopped 'til the vessels be torched.
But I wish some companion, with quickness suffused,   725
Would inform Achilles who nowise, I gather,
Intuits the woeful tiding of his dearest
Companion's demise. But the like see I nowhere
Among the Achaeans, for behazed are they cloaked,
Both they and their horses. O father Zeus, uncloak   730
The Argives, haze with aether replacing, and grant
Our sight clear viewing, for they slaughter us by day
For their amusement's sake." Thus he spoke, and father
Zeus took pity as he wept, and straightway dispelled
The darkness, driving the mist away. And the sun   735
Illumined them, revealing the battle to view.

Then to Menelaus spoke Ajax: "Look about,
Menelaus, Zeus-nurtured, if so you perceive
Antilochus alive, great-hearted Nestor's son,
And hasten him unto Achilles, wise-hearted,   740
Announcing his comrade is fallen." So he spoke,
And Menelaus, warcry-practiced, minded him
And made off, as a much wearied lion departs
A steading, by dogs and vexèd kin unsettled,
That prevent his taking the fattest of the herd,   745
Vigilant they the nighttime through; but persists he,
Lusting for flesh though achieving nothing thereby,
For thick fly the weapons that mark him, from hardy

Hands discharged, the torches afore his visage lit,
From which, despite himself, he falters and, come dawn,   750
Disgruntled disengages; thus from Patroclus
Decamped warcry-practiced Menelaus sadly
Against his will, apprehensive that the Argives
In wretched rout forsake him, quarry to the foe.
And he generously enjoined the Aiantes   755
And Mērionēs, saying: "You Aiantes twain,
Danaan leaders, and you, O Mēriones,
Grant each man remember the kindness of hapless
Patroclus, ever gentle to all whilst alive;
But fate and death have now undone him." So saying,   760
Blonde Menelaus departed with chary eye
To every side, as an eagle which, men attest,
Sees keenest of all things wingèd under heaven,
To which, however high aloft, appears the hare
Swift-footed neath a bramble bush, low cowering,   765
But plunges the eagle upon him, swooping down
And purloining his life; just so, Menelaus,
Zeus-nurtured, did your vision, everywhere ranging
Amid the cluster of your companions, discern
Antilochus yet alive. Him full readily   770
He marked to the fighting's leftward flank, quickening
His comrades and prodding their might. And drawing close,
The fair-haired Menelaus spoke, saying: "Up now,
Antilochus, nurtured of Zeus, be acquainted
With catastrophe; may it never have occurred.   775
Even now, I surmise, you behold it complete,
How a god predestines anguish for the Argives,
To the foe allotting victory; while slaughtered
Lies the best of Achaeans, even Patroclus,
And despair untold on his account is suffered   780
By Argives one and all. But straightway hasten you
To the ships, conveying this word to Achilles,
If he be prepared to accept the pillaged corpse
On board, though Hector holds the flash-helmeted arms."

BOOK XVII

So the report, and Antilochus grew anguished   785
Hearing it. Long he stood, speechless and stunned, his eyes
Welling with tears and subverted his vocal force.
Obeyed he Menelaus' mandate nonetheless
And set himself running, entrusting his armor
To Laodocus his dear companion wheeling   790
Aside him with single-hoovèd horses. Weeping
The while, his feet then furthered him from the battle,
The dire tidings to Peleus' son delivering.
Nor was your heart, Zeus-nurtured Menelaus, apt
To help the Pylian men, hard pressed by their champion's   795
Absence, for great their longing for Antilochus;
But Menelaus for them sent Thrasymēdēs,
Himself returning to protect Patroclus' corpse,
His stand taking quickly aside th' Aiantes twain
And promptly telling them: "Antilochus have I   800
Sent to the vessels of fleet-footed Achilles
But believe the latter, howe'er with Hector wroth,
Will from battle abstain, bereft of armor all.
But ourselves, let us make the most propitious plan
Whereby to extricate the body and escape   805
Demise and fate amid the fighting's din." And him
Did great Telamonian Ajax answer thus:
"All this, Menelaus, have you rightly spoken,
But now speedily stoop, you and Mērionēs,
Beneath the corpse, upraising and conveying it   810
From battle's toil away; but behind you will we
Twain contend against goodly Hector and the foe,
One in spirit as in name, even we that are
Wont to stand stoutly erect in dreaded assault,
Each to the other's side entrusted."
                              So he spoke,   815
And the others, lifting Patroclus' corpse aloft,
On mighty shoulders hoisted it; and behind them
The onlooking foe did boisterously protest

459

The corpse's conveyance, by Achaeans reclaimed.
And they leapt upon them, like hounds rushing a grim- 820
Visaged boar in the forest, wounded a'front youths
At the hunt. And now attacking had they rent it
Apart; but whensoever it careered their way,
Displaying its force, they ceded ground, recoiling
In divers direction; even so the Trojans 825
Ever followed the while in throngs, thrusting their swords
And double-edged spears, but whene'er the Aiantes
Circled 'round to repel them, their complexions paled
And dread conflict for the dead none dared to endure.
Thus hastened they from out the fracas to the ships, 830
Intending rescue for the corpse, the conflict wild
As fire about them set, that falling on a town
Of men o'erspreads and consigns it to flame, gutting
Everything in conflagration altogether,
And tempestuous winds upstir it teeming forth; 835
Even so, upon their undaunted advance did
The din of warring men and charioteers intrude.
But as donkeys lurching side to side a great ship's
Beam or timber tow from atop a mountain path,
And struggle their laboring lungs neath toil and sweat 840
Alike; so quickened these to recover the corpse.

And behind them th' Aiantes resisted the foe
As a forested headland positioned perchance
Athwart a plain, restraining the furious flow
Of churning river tides and e'er rechanneling 845
Them placidly o'er the plain, and powerless they,
For all their might, to overwhelm it; even so
The Aiantes retarded the Trojan advance,
But these ever followed after, two above all:
Great Hector and Aeneas, son of Anchises. 850
And as scatters a cloud of jackdaws or starlings,
Frantically screeching when marking the falcon come,
Death to small birds delivering; so neath Hector

And Aeneas the youths of the Argives dispersed,
Ever shrieking, e'er of their prowess unmindful,   855
And many the wasted arms that fell, detritus
Of the Danaan flight, unwearying the war.

~ Book XVIII ~

Achilles' Anguish for Patroclus,
Thetis and the Nereids Mourn,
Hephaestus Forges New Armor for Achilles

Antilochus reaches Achilles with news of Patroclus' death. Even as Antilochus approaches, Achilles is filled with foreboding. Seeing the Greeks again driven toward the ships, he surmises Patroclus has suffered ill, and Antilochus confirms the worst. Overwhelmed with grief, Achilles and his camp commence the rituals of mourning. Antilochus, in a telling gesture, holds Achilles hands for fear of his suicide.

Thetis from the sea depths hears Achilles' sorrow and begins her own lament amid the Nereids, essentially lamenting Achilles, though he is yet alive. Thus scripted are the events leading to Achilles' death. Thetis and the Nereids ascend the brine to mourn with and comfort Achilles. Better he had never been born, laments Achilles, to which Thetis responds that he will exact vengeance against Hector but himself be slain thereafter. Achilles vows to produce many a Trojan widow before then but not, his mother advises, until she has secured him new armor from Hephaestus.

As Thetis proceeds to Olympus and Hephaestus, the Greeks have not yet managed to extricate Patroclus from the fray, Hector thrice grabbing Patroclus' feet and trying to drag him off. Hector is close to succeeding when Iris appears to Achilles, instructing him to make his presence known despite his lack of armor and inability to engage. This he will do by showing himself at the trench and shouting aloud. Athena drapes the aegis about his shoulders, enhancing his appearance. Shouting thrice superhumanly loud, Achilles infuses the Trojans with consternation, causing the death of a dozen of their best. Amid the mayhem, the Greeks finally extricate Patroclus.

As the day's hostilities end, the Trojans hold a strategy session. Polydamas vigorously argues retreat behind the city walls, now that Achilles has reemerged. Hector argues for presence on the plain and the continuation of his drive against the ships. Foolishly, remarks Homer, the Trojans side with Hector.

The mourning continues in the Greek camp as the corpse of Patroclus is cleansed and anointed. Achilles, as he vows, will not administer funeral rites until he avenges Patroclus' death by slaying and decapitating Hector (he does not do the latter) and until he captures twelve Trojan youths whom he will slaughter and add to Patroclus' funeral pyre—an indication of barbarity past and yet to come.

Arrived at Hephaestus' palace, Thetis is greeted first by his wife, Charis (Favor), and then by the smithy himself, who recalls an earlier time when Thetis "saved" him in difficult straits. Her wish, then, is his command. Thetis provides a summary of events occurring to date—starting with her own sorry marriage to the mortal Peleus, and ending with Achilles' need for new armor. Hephaestus activates a legion of bellows, readies both melting pots and precious materials, and sets to work.

The "Shield of Achilles," occupying 130 lines, is the locus classicus of artistic ekphrasis (Gr. *ek* 'out/out of' + *phrazo/phraso* 'speak/will speak'): that which is related in detail and for its own sake, outside the principal narrative, i.e., a set piece. The shield is cosmos-inclusive, centered by earth, ocean, sun, moon, and stars. It radiates outward toward its triple rim with the fullness of human activity in war and in peace, namely, marriage; siege and warfare; sacrifice; judicial proceedings; pasturage and its perils; agricultural activity, festivity, and produce. Indeed, the shield's cosmic inclusiveness is emblematic of Achilles' Homeric characterization. As painter and critic Henry Fuseli (1741–1825), speaking of the "unison of homogeneous powers," submits,

> each individual of Homer forms a class, expresses and is circumscribed by one quality of heroic power; Achilles alone unites their various but congenial energies. The grace of Nireus, the dignity of Agamemnon, the impetuosity of Hector, the magnitude, the steady prowess of the great[er], the velocity of the lesser Ajax, the perseverance of Ulysses, the intrepidity of Diomede[s], are emanations of energy that reunite in one splendid centre fixed in Achilles (Fuseli, "Ancient Art," 38–39).

BOOK XVIII

Like the Iliadic narrative itself, description of the shield contains digression of its own. The craftsmanship, with its precious metals and uncanny fashionings, is a marvel of *trompe l'oeil*. It is the description not of a static object but of an object emerging before our eyes as Hephaestus works on it figure by figure, grouping by grouping, scene by scene—the depictions seeming possessed of motion, voice, and breath beneath Hephaestus' workmanship. As the German dramatist Gotthold Ephraim Lessing (1729–1781) observes, "Homer does not paint the shield finished, but in the process of creation. Here again he has made use of the happy device of substituting progression for coexistence, and thus converted the tiresome description of an object into a graphic picture of an action." Lessing, LAOCOON: *An Essay upon the Limits of Painting and Poetry* (Farrar, Straus and Giroux, 1969), 114. With its triple rim depicting Oceanus roundabout, the shield portrays an ordered whole, far removed from battlefield chaos. The shield inevitably reflects parts of the *Iliad*'s own storyline, even as it anticipates its recipient's return to the fold and ordered society.

We bear in mind that Achilles never needed armor to begin with, being vulnerable only at the heel. However, this mythic element ill suits Homer's narrative. Indeed, one can little imagine Achilles' fighting unarmored—a picture bordering on the supernatural (if not ridiculous) and quite out of sync with the *Iliad*'s everywhere-armored combat and armor-stripping. Moreover, the epic tradition can little forgo the bravura description of the most magnificent armor ever for the epic's most magnificent hero. Mythologies differing as they do, Homer chooses those elements best suited to his story. It is yet—outside of the *Iliad*—with an arrow to the heel that Paris (of all people) slays Achilles.

❧

So contended they ablaze, and Antilochus,
Swift-footed messenger, came unto Achilles.
Him he found a'front his stern- and bow-horned vessels,
Considering matters even now transpiring,
In anger addressing his towering spirit: 5
"Woe and alas, how are the long-haired Achaeans
Again o'er the plain driven shipward? May the gods

Have not presently fulfilled—woe unto my soul—
The words which my goddess mother erstwhile foretold:
That whilst yet I lived the finest of Myrmidons						10
Should by Trojan hands out-shutter the light of day?
In truth, Menoetius' valiant son must now be dead,
The stubborn soul! Verily, I bade him return
To the ships once putting harmful flame to flight,
And not engage with Hector." While considering						15
Thus in mind and heart, the son of illustrious
Nestor, awash in tears, approached and delivered
The grievous word: "Woe am I, dear son of prudent
Peleus, inconsolably dire are the tidings
I convey. Would they had never been! Lifeless lies					20
Patroclus, with contention 'round his naked corpse,
But his armor the flashing-helmèd Hector holds."

So he spoke, and grief's dark cloud consumed Achilles;
And by the fistful seizing sooty dust he strewed
It about his head, spoiling his comely aspect,						25
And on his fragrant tunic settled ebon ash,
And outstretched in dust lay he himself, most mighty
In his mightiness, and with hands his very own
Tore at his hair, uprooting it. And the slave girls
That Achilles and Patroclus arrogated							30
In battle, shrieked aloud, afflicted in spirit,
And hastened surrounding wise-hearted Achilles.
And they pounded their breasts, and their brittle knees shook
Weakened beneath them; and Antilochus nearby
Them wailed, abundant his tears, holding Achilles'					35
Hands firmly in his own, for grimly his noble
Heart groaned forth, and Antilochus feared that, cutting,
Achilles slit his throat. Then vastly and aloud
Achilles groaned, and his reverent mother heard him,
Seated in ocean's brine aside her agèd sire,						40
Whereat she convulsed and keened, and the goddesses
Thronged 'round, even the Nērēïdes, as many

BOOK XVIII

As inhabited ocean's depths.
                        There were Glaucē
And Thaleia and Cymodocē, Nēsaeē,
And Speiō and Thoē, and ox-eyed Haliē,   45
Cymothoē, Limnōreia, and Actaeē,
And Melitē, Iaera, and Amphithoē,
And Agavē, and Dōtō, Prōtō and Nauē,
Pherousa and Dynamenē, Dexamenē,
Amphinonē and Callianeira, Dōris   50
And Panopē, and glorious Galatea,
Nēmertēs, Apseudēs and Callianassa;
And there were Clymenē, Ianeira, Maera
And Ianassa, Ōrithyia and fair-tressed
Amatheia, and other the Nēreids as dwelt   55
In ocean's recesses. From within their grotto
They beat their breasts in unison, and Thetis led
The lament: "Now listen, you daughters of Nēreus,
Listen and lament my ineffable sorrow.
Ah, alas disconsolate me, and anguish mine,   60
That to my grief engendered I the best of men;
For once an incomparable son had I borne,
Among warriors preeminent, and sapling-like
He rose as a tree in an orchard richly sown.
In curvèd vessels I directed him to Troy   65
To do battle with the Trojans; but ne'er again
Shall I welcome him returning to Peleus' home.
And while yet he abides looking out on the sun,
Knows he seclusion's woe, nor soothes him my presence.
Still will I visit him, beholding my dearest,   70
Most cherished boy, to fathom the grief he endures
While disengaged his spirit and conflict averse.

So saying, she quit the cave, and tearful the nymphs
That followed her, and 'round them was parted the tide,
And when they were come unto richly planted Troy,   75
They ascended the shore, each trailing the other,

Where the Myrmidon ships lay anchored close arrayed
About swift Achilles. Then beside him groaning
Aloud appeared his queenly mother, plangently
Weeping, embracing his head, and speaking wingèd   80
Words in tears: "Dear child of mine, why sorrow you so?
What anguish aggrieves you? Disclose it, speaking true.
Cronidēs has fulfilled your wish, whom earlier
You exhorted, your arms outstretched, that the Argives,
Missing you, aside their vessels be constricted,   85
And intermittently suffer grief." Then deeply
Lamenting, swift-footed Achilles responded:
"My mother, Olympian Zeus has accomplished
These petitions outright, but woefully for me:
I behold my perished companion Patroclus   90
Whom foremost I honored of all my companions
No less than honoring myself. Him I forfeit,
And Hector, slaying him, possesses his armor,
Plundering it outright; resplendent its proportions,
Wondrous to behold, that the gods tendered Peleus,   95
A most glorious gift, that day they bedded you
To mortalkind. Better your having abided
The brine, undying, the naiads attending you,
And that Peleus' nuptials had been mortal assigned.
But thus it is, that you encounter misfortune   100
Unrelieved, unbounded, for your too mortal son
Whom you never again shall greet when homeward come.
And now my spirit urges me no longer live,
Amid mankind abiding, except that Hector
First waste beneath my weapon, repaying the debt   105
He incurred for ruin of Patroclus, offspring
Of Menoetius." Then Thetis again addressed him,
Shedding abundant tears: "Doomed to a speedy end
Shall you be, speaking thus, dearest scion of mine,
For after Hector's death is your own death decreed."   110
Greatly moved, responded swift-footed Achilles:
"Might I die then immediately, since remiss

In assisting my companion as he perished.
From his native land far distant has he fallen,
Lacking my assistance when requiring it most. 115
Now will I ne'er again to my homeland return,
Since failed in my deliverance of Patroclus
And of my other comrades—the many forfeit
To goodly Hector—but here haunt the ships instead,
Profitless burden to earth, I that in combat 120
Eclipse the bronze-coated Achaeans, however
Much others surpass me in council. So pass strife
From gods and mortalkind alike, and wrath, goading
A man to grow infuriate, however wise;
That choler which sweeter far than trickling honey 125
Upsurges like smoke in a man's disposition,
As now Agamemnon, king of men, has provoked
Me to wrath. Yet for all this anguish consider
We these matters done—the rein of necessity
Curbing our spirits—that I move as avenger 130
Of the man I loved, slaying Hector, accepting
Fate and death whenever Zeus and the other gods
Determine it. For not even great Heracles
Evaded death though dearest to Zeus Cronidēs,
But o'erpowered him fate and Hera's dread pronouncement. 135
So too will I, when comparable fate befalls,
Lie buried and dead. But now glorious renown
Will I secure, causing many a deep-bosomed
Spouse, Dardanian and Trojan, to wipe from tender
Cheeks their tears with both their hands away, unmeasured 140
Their misfortune; and know they I have overlong
Recused myself from combat. Nowise attempt you
To stay me therefrom because you so adore me;
I shall never be dissuaded."
                    Then answered him
His mother the goddess silver-footed Thetis: 145
"Truth you speak, my child; indeed, no idle matter
Your warding from everywhere-beleaguered comrades

Their day of destruction. But your goodly armor
The Trojans hold, that armor full-brazen agleam.
This on his shoulders bears flashing-helmèd Hector, 150
Exulting therein. Yet not much longer, I deem,
Will he thus delight, his own demise impending.
But from the war god's toil abstain, until seeing
Me here returned. For with the morrow's rising sun
Will I return, bearing armor from Hephaestus." 155
So saying, she readied herself for departure,
To her sea sisters speaking this imperative:
"Plunge you below within the deep's broad-bosomed brine,
Seeking the elder of the sea, our father's home,
Reporting all. To high Olympus go I now 160
To Hephaestus' house, famed artisan, for my son
Entreating shining arms, that he might furnish them."
So she spoke, and beneath the surge they plummeted.
And the sea goddess, slim silver-footed Thetis,
Leapt Olympus-bound, seeking armor for her son; 165
But the while she soared, toward high heaven spirited,
The Danaans fled with wondrous shout before man-
Slaying Hector, pressed shipward to the Hellespont.
But the Argives had failed to remove Patroclus,
Achilles squire, from where he weapon-pierced reposed. 170
For now and anew approached him the chariot host
Of Troy, and Hector, Priam's son, like unto flame.
Thrice from behind by the feet seized glorious Hector
Patroclus' corpse, to the Trojans calling aloud,
Thus determined to dislodge him; and thrice the twain 175
Aiantes, in fury's valor veiled, repelled him
From Patroclus back. But Hector, in his power
Ever confident, now charged, and securely stood
Commanding his forces and nowise yielding ground.
And as utterly founder the farmstead shepherds 180
To repel a tawny lion from the carcass
It would plunder, thus salivates the lion; so
Th' Aiantes failed, twain warriors, to dishearten

BOOK XVIII

Hector, Priam's son, from Patroclus' corpse away.
And now had he secured the corpse, earning acclaim 185
Everlasting, had not windy-footed Iris
Hurried her downward from Olympus with tidings
For Achilles that he arm himself for battle—
Iris, concealed from Zeus and th' others as Hera's
Emissary. And neared she speaking wingèd words: 190
"Bestir thee, son of Peleus, dreadest most of men.
Provide assistance aside the ships by fighting
For Patroclus where warriors one another slay,
These seeking to protect the corpse while the Trojans
Would sooner retire it to windy Troy; for most 195
Unwavering is Hector to carry it off.
And his spirit exhorts him to sever the head
From off its tender neck, to Ilium's rampart
Appending it. So, linger no more, Achilles!
Let dread devour your soul that Patroclus be spared 200
Spoliation, plaything to Trojan dogs, since yours
The dishonor for whatever shame befalls him."

Then swift-footed goodly Achilles responded:
"Goddess Iris, who sent you here as messenger?"
And to him again spoke windy-footed Iris: 205
"Lady Hera sent me, Cronidēs' glorious wife,
And Cronidēs high-enthroned knows nothing of it,
Nor any other immortal inhabiting
Snow-bound Olympian heights." Then answering,
Swift-footed Achilles replied: "But, how ever 210
Shall I enter the fray? The Trojans hold my gear,
And my goddess mother enjoins me from battle
'Til welcoming her return, for from Hephaestus
Entreats she the making of glorious armor;
No other man exists whose metal I might wear, 215
Excepting the shield of Ajax, Telamon's son.
But he, I gather, fights fully engaged, wreaking
Havoc, spear in hand, defending dead Patroclus."

And to him again spoke windy-footed Iris:
"Well gather we that in Trojan hands your splendid 220
Armor lies; but repair you, even armorless,
Aside the trench and stand, showing yourself to Troy,
That by your presence overwhelmed, the town forbear
From fight, and repose the Achaeans' warlike sons,
Exhausted as they are; for sparse the breathing space 225
In war." Thus having bidden, swift-footed Iris
Departed; but Achilles belovèd of Zeus
Bestirred himself, and about his stately shoulders
Wise Athena tossed the tassel-trailing aegis,
With glorious golden mist enhaloing his head, 230
And emanated out the mist a lambent glow.
And as when to exalted aether smoke unfurls
From a parapet, ascending on an island
By the foe besieged, and the men within contend
Throughout the day in hateful war atop their walls, 235
And with eventide upblazon the beacon fires
In quick array, each sequentially following,
And aloft to neighboring townsfolk the display
compellingly calls, dire summons for ship-sped aid
Averting doom; even so from Achilles' head 240
Rose heavenward the glow. Then, from the wall removed,
Achilles reached the trench, there stationing himself,
Of his mother's mandate mindful. There stationed, he
Shouted, and shouted Pallas Athena as well,
An ineffable wonder heard throughout the foe, 245
Clear as clarion trumpeter afar sounding
His call, urging the rush of a murderous host
Intent on a city's capture; thus clear the call
Of Aeacus' son; and sank Trojan hearts dismayed,
Hearing the brazen voice, and their fair-maned horses 250
Backward stepped their chariots, their hearts boding ill.
And the charioteers stood petrified, observing
Th' unfaltering flame, sinister over the head
Of Peleus' great-spirited son, by the goddess

BOOK XVIII

Grey-eyed Athena awakened. Thrice o'er the trench 255
Hollered goodly Achilles, and thrice confounded
Stood the Trojans and their confederates. And there
And then, amid their cars and weaponry, perished
Twelve their best; and the Danaans readily drew
Patroclus out, placing him on a bier. And thronged 260
His comrades circling him in tears; and among them
Swift-footed Achilles—in tears, beholding his
Trusted companion reposed on the bier, mangled
By merciless bronze, aforetime well panoplied
His person but nevermore welcomed returning. 265
Then ox-eyed Hera enjoined the untiring sun
To journey on, unwillingly, to Ocean's streams.
So retired the sun and th' Argives refrained from fight.

And on the other side the Trojans, enjoying
Night's reprieve, from beneath their chariots unfastened 270
Their swift-flying steeds, and mustered in assembly,
Thinking the while of supper and drink. Full upright
They stood as the muster assembled, nor motioned
Any man sit—cowered all in consternation
By aspect of Achilles who had long refrained 275
From fractious fight. Then first among them speaking
Rose Polydamas, highly circumspect, Panthous'
Sagacious son, comrade of Hector, same night born,
He in oratory outstanding; the other
In spearcast. And well intending, he addressed them: 280
"My friends, consider you well and judiciously:
I enjoin your retreat unto towering Troy
Nor aside the vessels slumber, awaiting dawn,
Here encamped on the plain and distanced from the town.
For so long as Achilles' rancor persisted 285
Against Agamemnon, so long the Achaeans
Were easily fought; yes, even I delighted
When alongside the vessels we bided the night,
Hoping at some point to vanquish the foe. But fear

I, now despondent, that swift-footed Peleus' son, 290
O'erweening his heart, be disinclined to visit
The plain whereon we Trojans and Achaeans e'er
Encounter Ares' wrath but will force us contend
For dear spouses and town. So, townward our retreat—
My word observe—for truly thus shall it transpire. 295
For presently persistent night impedes the foot
Of Peleus' rapid son, but if tomorrow he
Appear, in person panoplied, here finding us,
Then shall we sufficiently his acquaintance make;
And happily shall some in flight reach sacred Troy, 300
With many the Trojan by curs and vultures torn—
May I never hear the tale thereof. But if my
Counsel be observed, however beleaguered we,
Keep we tonight our forces in Troy's meeting place,
Guarded the town throughout its walls and lofty gates, 305
Bolted from within their tall well-polished portals.
But come the risen dawn, in our armor arrayed,
Marshall we upon the battlements, and fully
The worse for him, thus from the ships undertaking
His incursion, we on the rampart palpable. 310
To his ships shall he then repair, having sated
His arch-necked horses with running amok, vainly
Driving neath the town. But futile his intention
To enter the city and groundward destroy it.
Ere then shall Trojan strays and curs consume him whole." 315

Then with angry glance from beneath his brows, flashing-
Helmeted Hector addressed him: "Polydamas,
What you say no longer pleases me, for you bid
Us retreat and stand constricted within the town.
Have you not yet savored your fill of containment 320
Within the walls? Lauded once was Ilium by men
Aforetime for gold and bronze, but now the riches
Depart their households, and vanish valuables
Untold, to Phrygia gone, and lovely Maeonia,

BOOK XVIII

Since mighty Zeus is angry grown. But now that Zeus, 325
Forkèd-couns'ling Cronus' son, vouchsafes me acclaim
By the ships, penning the Argives against the sea,
Expatiate no more, you simpleton, the like
Wisdom among the folk, for nary a Trojan
Will attend you, nor I condone it. So come you, 330
And as I propose, so be it promptly done: take
Now your repast throughout the host by companies;
And carefully watch, being wakeful every man.
And whoever in Troy be thus disconcerted
About his goods, gather and gift he them the folk, 335
In common for them to consume. Preferable
The Trojan consummation of such benefit.
But come morning and the dawn, in arms accoutred
Let us vessel-bound commence the dire encounter.
But if Achilles awaken irascible 340
By the ships, angrily be he subdued, if thus
disposed, for never afore him will I recoil,
Evading dreaded war, but willingly greet him,
If he it be that garner great glory, or I.
Alike are all to Ares who slays the slayer." 345
Thus Hector addressed their gathering, and shouted
The Trojans forth, the fools, for Pallas Athena
Had pillaged their wits that they favored the purpose
Of Hector, Polydamas' sounder advisement
Disdained, and happily supped they throughout their huts. 350

But the Achaeans the nighttime through lamented
Patroclus. And among them commenced Peleus' son
The lament and yowl, laying his man-slaying hands
Upon his comrade's breast, keening vehemently;
Even as the bearded lion whose whelps some deer- 355
Hunting man abducts from a closely wooded dale,
And the lion to his lair returned grieves greatly,
Stalking afar through many a hollow and gorge,
Tracking the man's footstep and gait, if anywhere

He fathom him, for implacable his anger; 360
Thus enraged, Achilles addressed the Myrmidons:
"O, for shame! Vain the word uttered that occasion,
When I sought to hearten the warrior Menoetius
In our halls, relating that, once capturing Troy,
I would restore him his offspring, to his homeland 365
Opoeis come with glorious spoils allotted him.
But Cronidēs accomplishes no man's intent,
For by destiny's decree shall we two redden
This selfsame soil of Troy, since I shall not return,
Welcomed by agèd horseman Peleus to his halls, 370
Nor by my mother, but deep the earth hereunder
Shall contain me. But now, Patroclus, following
You to Hades, no interment will I provide
'Til head and armor of Hector be here conveyed,
Your great-souled slayer, and before your pyre, enraged 375
For your slaying, I cut the throats of twelve stalwart
Sons of Troy. Meanwhile will you lie aside the ships,
Even as you are, and surrounding you shall deep-
Bosomed women lament, Trojan and Dardanian,
Unendingly weeping, even those that we two 380
Captured by longspears, labor, and might, waylaying
Their proudly populous cities." So proclaiming,
Dread Achilles ordered his comrades swiftly set
A three-leggèd kettle afire wherewith to lave
The crusted bloodiness of Patroclus away; 385
And they placed the kettle on a vigorous flame,
Bathwater-brimmed, with timber to burn beneath it,
And the warming flame played 'round the kettle's belly.
The water in the burnished cauldron having boiled,
With rich elixir cleansed they and anointed him, 390
Deadening his wounds with ancient embrocation
And, reposing him on a bed, blanketed him
From crown to sole with linen swath, a white mantle
Settling over it. And the Myrmidons throughout
The night aside Achilles bewailed Patroclus. 395

BOOK XVIII

But Zeus addressed Hera his sister and his spouse:
"You have succeeded, O ox-eyed queenly Hera,
In waking swift-footed Achilles. Verily,
Are these long-haired Achaeans children of your own."
Then answered ox-eyed queenly Hera: "Dreaded Zeus, 400
What assertion this? A mortal, being mortal,
Will likely for another do whate'er he can,
Untutored in my instruction. How then was I,
Proclaiming myself greatest among goddesses—
Both in pedigree and as your reverent wife, 405
Since your sovereignty over immortals extends—
No vexation against the Trojans to contrive?"

Thus the two conversed, but silver-footed Thetis
Approached Hephaestus' house, imperishable,
Brazen-crafted, glinting as though with stars adorned, 410
Of all immortal domiciles preeminent,
That the club-footed god had himself constructed.
Him toiling a'sweat she espied, even bustling
Busily about his bellows crafting tripods,
Twenty in all, interior wall adornments 415
To the feet of which were golden wheels appended,
That they instantaneously enter the gods'
Assemblies whene'er he wished, and homeward return,
A marvel to behold. Thus far were they fashioned,
But wanting crafted ears, which he labored making, 420
Forging the rivets to fit. And while occupied,
Thus refining his design, the goddess silver-
Footed Thetis approached. And Charis, of radiant
Headband, whom the glorious god of body-hardened
Forearms had wed, observed her arrival. And she 430
Clasped her hand, directly inquiring: "Wherefore, tell,
Enter you our house, welcome and venerated
Guest, dear Thetis, goddess flowing-gowned? Aforetime
You rarely called. But follow upon my welcome."
So saying, the luminous goddess guided her, 435

Tendering a silver-studded settle, rich wrought
And wondrous, and placing a footstool neath her feet;
And she called to Hephaestus, famed craftsman, and spoke:
"Hephaestus, do come; dear Thetis requests your help."
And the famed god of the body-hardened forearms   440
Responded: "Indeed, a dread and honored goddess
Visits my abode, she that extricated me,
Tormented and reduced by my dog-faced mother's
Betrayal, she that because of my affliction
Hid me in lameness away. Then had I languished   445
Desolate, had not Thetis and Eurynomē,
Daughter of backflowing Ocean, delivered me.
With them fully nine years long, I crafted cunning
Handiwork within their cavernous vaults: brooches,
Spiraled armbands, necklaces, and rosettes, and great   450
Ocean circling me about, murmuring with foam,
A surge unspeakable. Nor knew any thereof,
Whether god or mortal man. But Eurynomē
Knew, and Thetis, even they that delivered me.
And now is Thetis to my home arrived, wherefore   455
Befits her renumeration for having saved
My life. But see you to Thetis' entertainment
Whilst I settle my bellows and appliances."

Thus expounding, he uprose—an awesome hobbling
Hulk—from his anvil block, but beneath him sprightly   460
Moved his legs. He set his bellows apart the flame
And rested the collected tools with which he toiled
Within a silver case, and wiped his visage clean,
His hands, his sturdy neck, and wooly chest, and clad
Him in a tunic, seizing a hefty sceptre   465
As he lumbered forth. But steadying their master's
Balance stepped swift-moving maidens, fashioned the like
Of young women but cast of gold. In their spirits
Understanding dwells, and discourse too, and artful
Handiworks, a gift by the immortals given.   470

BOOK XVIII

And these busily bustled, assisting their lord,
And he, approaching haltingly aside Thetis,
Set himself on a splendorous chair, clasping her
By the hand, thus speaking and naming her: "Why now
Visit you our dwelling, an honored and welcome   475
Guest, belovèd Thetis, gown-trailing goddess? Erst
Came you rarely. What need you? My heart is inclined
To grant it, if at all the need be grantable."
And the goddess tearfully answered him, saying:
"Hephaestus, has any Olympian goddess   480
Sustained such strictures, such woes unnumberable
As those that Zeus Cronidēs has apportioned me
Beyond others? Only me amid the daughters
Of the sea did he subdue beneath mortal man,
Even Peleus, Aeacus' son, and I suffered   485
His bed albeit entirely against my will.
But now he lies immobile, by odious age
Undone; and he provided me a son to bear
And rear, among warriors preeminent; and up
He shot, a sapling. However, uprearing him   490
As a tree within an orchard plot, I sent him
Troyward in hollow ships to battle with Trojans;
But never again shall I greet him, to Peleus
Returned. And yet draws he breath, beholding the sun
In agony, and no comfort have I rendered him.   495
The girl the Danaans awarded him as prize
Has lord Agamemnon reclaimed from Achilles'
Very arms, and wastes his spirit for want of her.
But the Trojans confined the Danaans aside
Their ships, egress denying, and to Achilles   500
The Danaan elders prayed, enumerating
Glorious gifts. But he, declining to avert
Their rout, provided his armor to Patroclus,
Delivering him to battle with many men
Aside him. They battled about the Scaean Gates,   505

And that same day had the city been marauded
But that once Menoetius' courageous son contrived
Destruction, Phoebus slew him amid the foremost
Fighters, granting Hector glory. Thus to your knees
Arrived, I implore you be genially disposed, 510
That you furnish my son—his future foreshortened—
Helmet, shield, and corselet, and greaves finely fitted
With ankle attachments. For the armor once his
Has Patroclus to Hector surrendered in death,
By Hector slain, leaving my offspring to anguish." 515

Then the famed mighty-muscled god responded:
"Take heart, nor disconsolate be your spirit.
From dreaded demise would I sooner save him
When descends that doomful day as, verily,
Shall I see him armored well—such as many 520
A one of men shall marvel at, whoever
Shall behold it." So saying he left her there,
Proceeding to his bellows and, toward the fire
Directing them, exacted their performance.
And the twenty bellows, beneath melting-pots 525
Exhaling, a fearsome blast of every force
Emitted, now to aid his laboring gait,
And now howe'er Hephaestus wished his labors
Managed. And consigned he the obdurate bronze
To the flame, and supple tin, and precious gold, 530
And silver too, thereafter on the anvil
Block a mighty anvil setting; and in one
Hand his massive hammer, tongs in the other.
And first he fashioned a shield, fitly crafted
And great, cunningly in every part contrived, 535
And fastened around it a marvelous rim
Thrice-layered aglitter, and thereto attached
A strap. Five the layers comprising the shield;
And on it, exquisitely wrought, was many
A singular figure fixed.

BOOK XVIII

      Therein he wrought   540
The earth, therein heaven's canopy, and there
The sea, the tireless sun, and moon to fullness
Formed; therein the constellations all wherewith
Be Heaven decorate—mighty Orion,
The Pleiades, Hyades, and Bear which men   545
The Dipper call, e'er in its place revolving
To Orion's view and alone setting not,
Declining broad Ocean's ablutions.
         Therein
Also he affixed two cities of mortal
Men, fine cities unsurpassed: the one managed   550
Marriages and banqueting, and with torches
Ablaze from their bowers escorted young brides
Amid public approbation, the nuptial
Song ascendant. Young men whirled dancing about,
Around them resounding th' accompaniment   555
Of lyre and flute; and the women all marveled,
Positioned afore their doorways.
           But the folk
Assembled at the gathering place wherein
Rancor had risen as two men contested
The blood award of a person slain. The one,   560
Affirming adequate payment, presented
His case to the folk; but declined the other
To accept it, and each to arbitration
Deferred decision. And the folk prodded both,
Hailing the one and the other, and heralds   565
Restrained them. And sat the elders in sacred
Enclosure on burnished stone, holding clear-voiced
Heralds' sceptres with which they signaled response
And next announced their considered decisions.
And two talents of gold were to center set: 570
The parties' compensation for the elder
Among them soundest in judgment determined.
But hemming the other city lay warriors

Entrenched, dazzlingly armored, twin-divisioned;
And twin the tactics condoned: whether to waste 575
The town or divvy twixt townsfolk and themselves
The trove retained by the lovely town within.
Yet the entrapped disclaimed capitulation,
Arming themselves for ambush against the foe;
Their spouses and infant offspring securing 580
The wall, and aside them the city's elders.
And forth sallied the besieged, by Ares led
And Pallas Athena, both gold-encrafted;
And gold the garb wherein they were configured,
Fastidiously fabricated the two, 585
As suited their divinity, outsizing
The others all; the men about them smaller.
But once come to a locale fit for ambush,
Where ran a riverbed and watering place
For all manner of beast, there they awaited 590
In resplendent armor panoplied about.
Two lookouts, apart the others configured,
Prepared for the sighting of crumple-hornèd
Kine and sheep, the herd presently detected;
And a pair of herdsmen pleasantly piping 595
Accompanied them, remarking naught amiss.
But the ambuscade, viewing their arrival,
Advanced resisting them, quickly corralling
The cattle and comely flocks of fleecy sheep,
And killing the herdsmen.
      And the besiegers, 600
Calculating their attack, heard much ado
Amid the kine, and a'mount their high-stepping
Horses quickened them apace, the ambuscade
Accosting straightway and, deploying themselves
At large, engaged at the riverbank, sharpened 605
Their brazen spears, one with another grappling.
And entered amid them Dissension and Din
And Fate the destroyer—taking their man

BOOK XVIII

Be he hale, or alive but newly wounded,
Be he expired while dragged away by the feet 610
Through the fracas. And flowing from Fate's shoulders
Was the battle-bloodied apparel she bore.
The parties like unto mortal men engaged
And fought, each side hauling the corpses away
Of the other's slain.
                Therein he also set 615
Ploughland a'crumble, spacious and fecund, thrice
Ploughed, and numerous quite the ploughmen therein,
Their oxen trundling straight, then wheeling about.
And whene'er one turned, attaining the limit
Of the bound, then came a comrade, a goblet 620
Of honeyed wine into his hands providing,
Whilst each, returning back along the tilth, strove
Keenly to reach the opposing deep-soiled bound,
And blackened the tilth behind them, appearing
Positively ploughed although of purest gold— 625
The prodigious marvel this of craftsmanship.
There also designed he a royal demesne,
The reapers gathering crops, sharp scythes gripped fast.
Groundward fell some handfuls loosely clenched, disposed
Along the swath, but binders trussed the bounty 630
With pliable plaits of straw. Sheaf binders three
Aside each reaper, and boys behind them scooped
The residue, duly upgatheing it
For conveyance to the binders; and the king,
Sceptre in hand, bestrode the swath in silence, 635
Rejoicing at heart. And heralds, by an oak
Apart, prepared a feast, expertly dressing
A stolid ox for sacrifice selected;
And the women sprinkled white barley enough
For the workers' midday meal.
                    Therein he set 640
A vineyard too with clusters fully laden,
A fair vineyard wrought of gold; but pendant black

The grapes therein, plumping on silver supports;
And 'round it he fashioned a cobalt trench, fenced
About in tin; and solitary the path 645
The vintagers trod, upgathering the yield;
And dreamy-eyed girls and boys bore the honeyed
Fruit in plaited canisters; and among them
A youngster beguilingly bowed the viol—
Tempered its timbre—intoning a cadence 650
Sublime of the enraptured Linos refrain;
And his companions in unison stomping
Amid roisterous dance skipped following him.
And modeled he therein a herd of hornèd
Kine fashioned of gold with infusion of tin; 655
And the lowing kine from cowshed to pasture
Shuffled forth along the resounding stream, reeds
Lightly rustling. And gold the herdsmen, numbered
Four, that strode aside the kine, and nine the dogs
Swift-footed in their retinue. But lions 660
Twain, dread beasts, had seized amid the foremost kine
A lowing bull bruiting its torment abroad
As the young men and yelping canines followed.
The lions, guzzling blood-clotted viscera,
Had rent the bull's great hide; the flustered herdsmen 665
Wanting to release the canines upon them;
But they demurred, fastening not on the beasts,
But stood hard by, yelping from their distances.
And there, moreover, the brawny-armèd smith
A great pasturage engraved, woodland-bound—home 670
To fleecy sheep—roofed canopies, pens, and folds.
The musclebound smith thereon also contrived
A cunningly crafted dancing floor, like that
Old Daedalus made in commodious Crete
For comely Ariadne. Thereon danced youths 675
And charming girls the worth of many cattle,
Coupled one to the other by hands and wrists—
The maidens in fine linen attired; the youths

In glimmering oil-lustered tunics bedecked.
And the maidens moved winsomely chapleted, 680
And the youths with golden blades on silver straps.
And effortlessly now and anew they sped
Upon trusting feet, as when sits a potter
At his wheel, the wheel fitted his frame, and makes
Assay of it, whether it will work; and now 685
Again they ran in rows, one toward the other,
And flawless the frolic o'er the dancing floor,
And fine the fellowship, and two the tumblers
Twirling about, leaders becoming the dance.
About the buckler he cunningly inscribed 690
Oceanus, the shield's roundness enclosing.

But when thus contrived the shield completed stood,
Wrought he a corselet outflaming flame itself,
And heavy the helm he handily hammered,
To Achilles' head high fitted, a helmet 695
Richly wrought, admired, top-crested with gold,
And of pliant tin he wrought him sturdy greaves.
But when the glorious god had to perfection
Fashioned all, he gathered and presented it
To Thetis, Pēleïdēs' mother, and hawk- 700
Like from snowy Olympus she descended,
Hephaestus' radiant armature in hand.

~ Book XIX ~

Achilles and Agamemnon Reconciled, Briseis Restored

THETIS BRINGS ACHILLES the marvel of Hephaestus' newly made armor. It fills the Myrmidons with amazement, and Achilles with increased desire for revenge. Thetis preserves Patroclus' body from corruption, commanding Achilles assemble the Greeks and reconcile with Agamemnon. Assembling the Greeks, Achilles renounces his wrath. Agamemnon does likewise—in a roundabout and thus self-exculpatory manner—via a lengthy digression concerning *Atē* 'Madness, Deception, Delusion' in the timing of Heracles' birth. Yes, he too, Agamemnon, has been led astray by *Atē* when divesting Achilles of prize and pride.

In an ostensible show of good faith, Agamemnon makes an offer of gifts, which he will immediately have brought to Achilles' presence. But Achilles can wait on gifts, he wants immediate battle and revenge. The practical Odysseus urges dinner and restraint, for there is no fighting on an empty stomach; moreover, the dead require burial. The gifts, says Odysseus, may be displayed at dinner, when Agamemnon can also swear to having never violated Briseis. Agamemnon approves the plan, bidding Odysseus have three men convey the gifts (and Briseis) from his hut. He further commands that the herald Talthybius bring a boar for supper. The gifts are displayed and described, and Agamemnon slaughters the boar, using it as occasion for his oath. Achilles, however, will continue to abstain from food and drink until vengeance is had.

The assembly dissolved, the chieftains return to their huts, the gifts conveyed to Achilles' tent. Seeing the dead Patroclus, Briseis bitterly laments, recalling that he was ever kind and considerate toward her. Achilles steadfastly abstains from food, recollecting, as he laments, how Patroclus was wont to prepare dinner in his tent. Returning from Troy, moreover, Patroclus would have collected Achilles' son (Neoptolemus) on the Island of Scyrus, where Achilles had fathered him en route to Troy. Patroclus would have brought Neoptolemus back to Phthia, though finding upon arrival that Achilles' own father, Peleus, was either dead or enfeebled.

Zeus directs Athena to fortify Achilles with ambrosia the while he abstains from food. The next day, Achilles arrays himself in Hephaestus' armor, the scene described at length. His immortal horses are yoked to their car, and Achilles implores they return their driver safely, as they failed to do in the case of Patroclus. Endowed with the power of speech by Hera, the horse Xanthus disavows blame for Patroclus' death, attributing it to fate and Apollo. He further prophecies Achilles' death. Acknowledging his fate, Achilles drives onward.

Achilles' horse endowed with speech exemplifies Homer's occasional recourse to the unnatural or surreal (as when the horses earlier stood pillar-like and wept or when Achilles shouted from the trench). Achilles' battle with the two personified rivers of Troy—Scamander and Simoïs—will constitute another instance of the surreal, as will ultimately the death of Hector, Hector's perception of its approach, and Troy's portrayal after its occurrence. Homer now depicts the divinely armored Achilles as both unreal and uncontainable. So too will be the rampage that ends in Hector's death. It is day 30 of the story.

༄

Now saffron-robèd Dawn arose from Ocean's flow,
Light restoring to Olympus and mortal men,
And came Thetis to the ships, bringing gifts divine,
Where she found her darling boy, lying prone, clasping
Patroclus and wailing aloud; and his comrades,   5
Collected 'round about him wept. Then the goddess
Sublime, standing aside him, to their midst arrived,
Enfolded his hand and spoke, thus addressing him:

"We suffer, my Achilles, greatly afflicted
That this man lies insensate, since fated his death,   10
By the gods' volition irrevocably fixed.

BOOK XIX

But take you now from Hephaestus' toil this armor,
Imposing, surpassingly fine, such as warrior
On his shoulders has never displayed." So speaking,
She set the suit a'front Achilles, and deeply   15
Resounded its splendor. And consternation seized
The Myrmidon host, nor ventured a one of them
To look thereon, recoiling back instead. But when
Achilles surveyed the armor, a greater wrath
Engulfed him, and his eyes glinted grimly like flame;   20
And gladdened he gathering the glorious gifts
Of Hephaestus. And gratified in surveying
Their boundless distinction, straightway to his mother
Addressed he wingèd words: "My mother, the armor
Gifted by the god reflects what craft immortal   25
Should rightly be: past mortal manufacture all.
So now for confrontation I prepare myself,
While fearful remaining for the deluge of flies
Upon the bronze-inflicted wounds about the corpse
Of Menoetius' valiant son, breeding worms therein   30
And profaning his flesh—for life has disclaimed him
And putrefies his element." Then answered him
The goddess silver-footed Thetis: "My offspring,
Recount not the occurrence. From him will I stave
Excessive affliction, that no insect pollute   35
The battle-fallen. For though twelve months' duration
He repose, yet ever firm shall his flesh remain,
Surpassing even its present state. But amass
To their meeting place the warriors of Achaea,
Your rage renouncing against Atreidēs, shepherd   40
Of the host, and then, mantled in might, for battle
Outfit yourself." So saying, generous mettle
She meted him, and in Patroclus' nostrils dropped
Ambrosia and ruddy nectar that steadfastly
Stymied putrefaction.
                    But splendid Achilles   45
Bestrode the shore, unleashing a harrowing cry,

Arousing the Argive warriors. And even those
'Mid the ships that aforetime had bided aboard—
The helmsmen, the pilots, the supper dispensers—
Congregated, even those, assembling, aghast,   50
That Achilles stood manifest who long had kept
Aloof from heinous war. And haltingly came two
Attendants of Ares, even Diomedes
Stalwart in fight and divine Odysseus, leaning
On their lances, their lacerations smarting yet.   55
And they a'front the gathering seated themselves;
And after them, last, Agamemnon, king of men,
Diminished by wasting war, the wound inflicted
By Coön, Antēnōr's son, thrusting with brazen
Spearpoint. But when the Achaeans had gathered all,   60
Swift-footed Achilles arose, proclaiming thus:

"Son of Atreus, proved this the better for us both,
For you and me, who in sorry circumstances
Quarreled for a girl, soul-devouring our dispute?
Would that arrow-armèd Artemis had shipside   65
Slain her the day I designated her my spoil,
When once having captured Lyrnessus. Then fewer
The Danaans—unyielding my wrath—that had fed
Beneath combatant hands on dust and boundless earth.
Far the better that for Hector and the Trojans.   70
But long, I surmise, shall the Argives remember
The strife that has sundered us. And yet, concluded
Let us deem such matter, despite our pain, bridling
Our spirits as we must. Now verily ended
Declare I my wrath, nor does anger unending   75
Behoove me. But up now, incite you to battle
The long-haired Achaeans, that I might encounter
The Trojans, again assaying their mettle's might
If they think to bivouac by our ships; for many,
I think, would sooner find themselves alive, whoe'er   80
Escapes the ire of war and this my lethal spear."

BOOK XIX

So he spoke, and glad were the well-greaved Achaeans
That great-souled Achilles had thus renounced his wrath.
And among them spoke the wounded Agamemnon
From where he was sitting, nor stood he among them: 85
"Friends, Argive warriors, squires of Ares, right it is
To grant the speaker's prerogative unhampered.
Labors even the skilled amid interruptions,
For how might a speaker, amid clamor and crowd
Impeded, attend or propound, however well 90
He converse? To Peleus' son I address myself,
But attentively listen you other Argives,
Heedful everyone. Too often have the Argives
Rehashed my infraction, inveighing against me.
However, account me in no way culpable; 95
But blame Zeus, Fate, and dark-treading Retribution,
That within the assembly that day implanted
Grim delusion when I plundered Achilles' prize.

"But what might I do? A god accomplishes all.
Eldest daughter of Zeus is Delusion, accursed, 100
Deceiving everyone. Delicate her footstep,
For absent her advance by land; but o'er the heads
Of man her stride, to mankind meting misery,
Now one man, now another in turn entangling.
And aforetime deluded she Zeus Cronidēs, 105
Of prerogative unsurpassedly possessed.
Yet Hera, even of womankind, beguiled him
With artifice that day when labored Alcmēnē
In fair-walled Thebes deliv'ring warrior Heracles.
Then, boasting, divulged Cronidēs among the gods: 110
'Hearken unto me, you gods and goddesses all,
That I declare what commands my spirit within.
Today shall Eileithyia, midwifing goddess,
Disclose unto light a mortal blood-descended
From my own generation, holding mastery 115
O'er those amidst whom he dwells.' But devisingly

Responded queen Hera: 'Perjured be you proven,
And your statement unattained. But come, Olympian,
And by oath assert that the man from your bloodline
And ancestry descended shall administer   120
Those dwelling 'round him, whosoe'er this day shall drop
At woman's knees.' So she spoke, and Zeus Cronidēs,
Unmindful of her devisings swore mightily,
Whereby was he wholly deluded. And downward,
Abandoning Olympus dashed Hera, and quick   125
To Achaean Argos came, where the comely wife,
She knew, of Sthenelus, son of Perseus, was found,
Pregnant seven months with her belovèd child which
Hera ordained untimely born; but Alcmēnē's
Birthing Eileithyia delayed. And queen Hera,   130
To Cronidēs announcing it, this word divulged:
'Father Zeus, in lightning's dread delighting, convey
I this word for your consideration. Even
Now is born a glorious man, lord o'er the Argives,
Eurystheus, offspring of Sthenelus, Perseus' son,   135
Descended of your line; and suited his lordship
O'er the Danaans.'"
                    So she spoke, and repellent
The pain possessing Zeus and, provoked, fast gripped he
The Lustrous-tressèd Atē and somberly swore
That Atē of Olympus and spangled heaven   140
Be dispossessed, Atē the confounder of men.
So he proclaimed and, whirling her above his head,
Heaved her from aethered heaven; and quick she arrived
To the tilth of men. At thought of her Zeus ever
Groaned, most when beholding his offspring, Heracles,   145
In drudgerous service to Eurystheus' command.
And even I, when mighty Hector flashing-helmed
Wreaked havoc on the Argives by their ships, could not
Disremember Atē, who erst deluded me.
Yet because deluded and of my wits deprived   150
By Zeus, would I now make amends with recompense

BOOK XIX

Past reckoning. But stir you to battle, rousing
The rest of the Myrmidons. Gifts now prepare I
To provide, even those intrepid Odysseus
Promised yesterday when first to your hut arrived. 155
Or, should you prefer, remain though eager for war,
And the gifts shall my attendants bring assembled
From my vessel, for your sufficiency assured."
Then swift-footed Achilles responded and said:
"Glor'ous Agamemnon, Atreus' son, king of men, 160
Bestow your gifts as may befit, or retain them
As you will, but bethink us speedily of war
Since this splitting of hairs and dithering impedes,
For weighty the work unrealized: that the folk
Again behold Achilles at the forefront poised 165
With brazen spearpoint decimating Trojan hosts.
Let everyone, fighting the foe, reflect on this."

Then many-wiled Odysseus responded, saying:
"Courageous though you be, O godlike Achilles,
Urge not the Argives into battle sans repast, 170
Since not of brief degree be conflict's interchange
When once the warrior ranks engage and into them
The gods breathe matching might. But bid the Danaans
Victuals and vintage take aside their hollow ships,
Since strength and courage lie therein. For there is not 175
A man who battles throughout the day 'til sunset,
The while fasting from food. For though fervent in fight,
Yet, unexpectedly, a weariness of limbs,
And hunger, and thirst beleaguer him, and buckle
His knees beneath. But whoever with ample food 180
And drink the daylong battles on undaunted, his
Spirit within abides, and his limbs, unweighted
'Til all from warring cease, endure. So disperse you
The Danaans and bid them prepare their dinner,
And bid lordly Agamemnon produce the gifts 185
Afore the assembly place, that every Argive

Survey them, and delighted be your heart. And pledge
He, standing amid the Argives, that ne'er straddled
He the woman's bed nor dalliance with her indulged
As custom bids, O king, between women and men; 190
And the spirit inspiring you propitious be.
Thereafter, let him make amends within his hut,
A sumptuous feast, that nothing elude your due;
And toward others hereafter, Atreus' son, shalt thou
Propitious be, since nowise culpable a king 195
Who makes amends with others if anger without
Cause encompass him about."
      And Agamemnon
Atreïdēs, king of men, again responded:
"Pleased am I, O Laërtes' son, to hear your words,
For you address the matter most fittingly through, 200
Recounting all. This oath am I prepared to swear,
My spirit commanding me, nor shall I forswear
Myself before the god. But let Achilles here
Remain the while, although craving confrontation,
And you others too remain 'til gifts be conveyed 205
From my hut, and we swear fidelity of oaths
With sacrifice. And you, Odysseus, I command
Select three princes from the Panachaean host
To bear the offerings from my vessel, those we
Yesterday promised Achilles; escort the woman Brisēís too. 210
And let Talthybius forthwith prepare a boar
Within the Danaan encampment—sacrifice
To Zeus and Helios."
      But answered swift-footed
Achilles and said: "Most glorious Atreïdēs, king
Of men, Agamemnon, be these matters better 215
Managed othertimes, whene'er battle offers pause
And abates my wrath withal. Now sprawl they slaughtered
Whom Hector, son of Priam, slew when Zeus vouchsafed
Him glory—and the twain of you command us dine!
Sooner would I see the sons of the Achaeans 220

BOOK XIX

Fight fasting and unfed and at sunset prepare
Banqueting enough, the butchery requited.
'Til such time neither liquid nor solid traverse
My throat whilst my companion lies lifeless by bronze,
Doorward his feet, compatriots keening about;   225
Wherefore, suffice nor victuals nor valuables,
But butchery, bloodshed, and the groanings of men."

Then many-wiled Odysseus responded, saying:
"O Achilles, son of Peleus, far mightiest
Of the Achaeans, fitter are you and finer   230
Far in arms; yet superior I in counsel,
Being elder-born and more discerning; wherefore
Resignedly bear you the precept I propose:
Quick is battle's surfeit when monstrous the slaughter
But paltry the gain, when Zeus, assigning battle,   235
Tips the scale. But let no man empty-bellied mourn
A corpse. Countless the casualties day to day—
And what respite from travail? Sooner becomes it
Inter the dead, hearts numbed, making solitary
Dirge the salve. But those enduring battle's travail   240
Must ever mindful be of nourishment, the more
Staunchly, unyieldingly, to greet the foe in bronze.
And allow none, awaiting another's summons,
To skulk amid his friends, for be the summons this:
'Ill prospers he who loiters amid the vessels;   245
Sooner united against the Trojans our drive.'"

He spoke, and bade follow him the sons of glor'ous
Nestor, and Megēs, son of Phyleus, and Thoas,
And Lycomēdēs, Creiōn's son, Mērionēs,
And Melanippus too; and to Atrēidēs   250
Agamemnon's hut they proceeded, and forthwith
Allied were utterance and deed. Seven tripods
From the hut they produced, even as promised him,
And twenty the gleaming cauldrons, and horses twelve;

And speedily the women appeared, accomplished 255
In goodly handiworks; seven were they, the eighth
Fair-cheeked Brisēïs. Then sequestered Odysseus
The impressive weight of ten talents' gold, leading
The way, and assisted sundry Danaan youths.
These they exhibited at the gathering place, 260
And arose Agamemnon; and Talthybius,
Godlike his voice, aside the people's shepherd stood
Grasping a boar, and Atreidēs withdrew the blade,
E'er within his sword's great sheath suspended, and cut
From the boar its firstling hairs, and lifted his hands, 265
And prayed to Zeus; and th' Argives sat silently by,
Attentive to their king, as was fitting. And he
Spoke in prayer, eyes ascendant to heaven upraised:
"So witness me Zeus, supremest and best of gods,
And Earth and Sun, and forces of retribution 270
That under earth avenge whoever falsely swears,
That ne'er upon the girl Brisēïs placed I hand,
Neither seeking to lie with her nor otherwise,
But steadfast in my huts abided she untouched;
And if this pledge be proven false, exact the gods 275
Th' unsparing penalty with which they discipline
Whoever, swearing oaths, transgresses against them."
He spoke, the boar's throat slitting with pitiless bronze,
And, whirling it, cast the carcass afar as food
For fish in the roiled expanse of the hoary sea. 280
But Achilles uprose, and among the Argive
Warriors spoke: "Father Zeus, far-reaching the folly
You fashion for men. Never had Agamemnon
Thus fully wakened my fury nor seized the girl,
Defying my will, had Zeus not perchance decreed 285
Danaan deaths untold. But to sustenance now,
That we may battle on." So he spoke, and quickly
The gathering cleared. And scattered they each to his
Ship. But the great-hearted Myrmidons busily
Continued preparing the gifts, bearing them off 290

BOOK XIX

To the godlike Achilles' ship, stationing them
Within his huts, and settling the women therein,
And noble stewards swiftly sequestered the steeds.

But Brisēïs, like to golden Aphrodite,
Viewing the mercilessly mangled Patroclus, 295
Melted 'round him in a pool, lamenting aloud,
Tearing her breasts, comely visage, and tender neck.
And lamenting she spoke, the like of a goddess:
"Patroclus, of my hapless bosom beloved, quick
I quitted you when departing this hut, and now 300
Light on you lifeless—you, the convener of hosts—
Whilst returning hereto. Thus with me does evil
E'er with evil abide. My husband, unto whom
My father and reverent mother gave me, viewed I
Butchered by bronze before our town, and my brothers 305
Three, beloved, of my mother born—these very three
One day of doom despatched. But you, when Achilles
Slew my husband, demolishing godlike Mynēs'
Town, did disallow my sorrowing, determined
To wed me to Peleus' son, taken to Phthia 310
Aboard his ship and fêted in marriage amid
The Myrmidons. Wherefore endlessly I lament
Your loss, bemoaning the gentleness that was yours."
So spoke she wailing, and sorrowed the women all,
Patroclus the pretext but each for pain her own. 315
And 'round Achilles pressed the Danaan elders
Pleading that he eat, but declined he to partake,
Groaning the more: "I beseech you if friends you be,
Enjoin me not hastily thus toward sustenance,
Since dismal my dolorous heart. Until sunset 320
Will I abide, enduring even as I am."
So he stated, dismissing the other chieftains,
But the two sons of Atreus remained, and goodly
Odysseus, Nestor, Idomeneus, and th' elder
Phoenix, chariot lord, seeking to alleviate 325

His steadfast desolation; but nowise consoled
Would he be 'til entering battle's bloody maw.
And so pondering, sighed he heavily and spoke:
"So aforetime were you, O hapless one, alas,
Most precious of my friends, accustomed dext'rously   330
To ready in our hut a savory repast
Whensoever the Danaans hastened themselves
To tearful strife against the horse-taming Trojans.
But now you lie mangled, and naught will my spirit
Of supper partake, albeit fully at hand,   335
Because of urging on your account. Naught the more
Horrid might I encounter, even should I learn
Of my dear father's decease, who now doubtless sheds
Plenteous tears in Phthia, wanting for a son
Like me, who withers amid unfamiliar folk,   340
Fighting Trojans on abhorrèd Helen's behalf;
Or be informed of his decease who on Scyrus
Is reared for me, my belovèd son—should godlike
Neoptolemus yet survive. For earlier
Had I hoped at heart that I alone might perish   345
Far from horse-pasturing Argos, here upon earth
Of Troy, whereas you would return unto Phthia,
From Scyrus reclaiming my son in your rapid-
Plying ships and showing him all: my possessions,
My slaves, and my fine high-raftered roof. For by now,   350
As it appears, has Peleus drawn his last; elsewise
Endures he, by hateful age aggrieved, expecting
The most woeful intelligence, that I am dead."

So spoke he weeping, and th' elders joined the lament,
Each longing for home and happiness left behind.   355
And as they lamented, observed them father Zeus,
To mercy moved, and forthwith addressed Athena:
"Child of mine, now utterly forsake you your man!
Come now, does Achilles so little concern you,
There sitting before his vast twin-beakèd vessel,   360

BOOK XIX

Mourning his dear companion, while th' others retire
To dinner, and he all drink and food refuses?
But go you, shedding ambrosia within his breast
And honeyed nectar, that hunger's torment shun him."
So saying he enjoined Athena, already 365
Impatient; and she like a full-wingèd falcon
Screeching, vaulted, cleaving the godly firmament.
Then as the Achaeans about the camp attired
Them for battle, she shed within Achilles' breast
Ambrosia and ruddy nectar, that grievous pangs 370
Of hunger forebear from his being; and she
To the sturdy abode of Cronidēs, her sire,
Decamped, the Danaans departing their vessels.
As when teeming snowfall flitters from high Heaven,
Chill neath northerly blast of brightest aether born; 375
Flitted just so th' efflugence of helms from the ships
Ashore: the studded bucklers, the sturdy-plated
Corselets, and ashen spears. And the glist'ning thereof
Did heavenward ascend, and everywhere did earth
Beneath the lustrous gleam delight, and din uprose 380
From beneath the feet of men.
                                    And among them stood
Famed Achilles attired for war. Grated his teeth,
And flamelike flared his eyes, and insuff'rable grief
Suffused his heart. Against the Trojans thus enraged,
He accoutred him in the gifts of Hephaestus, 385
Which the muscly smithy had labored creating.
The greaves unto his shins affixed he first; gorgeous
They shone, with silver ankle-pieces fitting firm,
And next the corselet placed about his chest, and o'er
His shoulders slung the brazen silver-studded sword, 390
And next assumed th' incomparable shield from which
Resplendence rose as of the incandescent moon.
And as when o'er the waters glint of gleaming flame
To seamen manifest ascends, and swells it 'top
A mountain in some lonely place, and uneasy 395

499

The seamen whom tempest across the teeming deep
Has borne from friends away; just so from Achilles'
Shield rose splendor heavenward, the shield decorate,
Incomp'rable. And lifting the mighty helmet,
He positioned it atop his head; and starlike   400
Shone the horsehair-crested helm, around it swaying
The golden plumes Hephaestus set about the crest
Abundantly. And Achilles of himself made
Trial within the armor, to assure its fit
And flexibility about his brilliant limbs.   405
And winglike to him the armor, enspiriting
The people's shepherd. And from its casing drew he
His father's spear, huge, heavy, and rugged, that none
Of the Danaans excepting he might handle—
Achilles thus alone adept at wielding it—   410
Even the ashen Pelian spear the centaur
Cheirōn had given his sire from Pelion's peak
For the slaughter of heroes.
                            And Automedōn
And Alcimus, busied everywhere, yoked the steeds;
'Round their bellies fixed they straps and fitted their jaws   415
With bits, and drew the reins behind the jointed car.
And Automedōn took hold the luminous lash
Well fitted to his hand and leapt upon the car;
And followed him Achilles well furnished for war,
In his armored effulgence Hyperion's like.   420
Then to his father's horses called he terribly
Aloud: "Xanthus and Balius, you far-famed offspring
Of Podargē, in some better way devise you
The safety of your charioteer's returning
To the Argive host once battle's toll is taken,   425
And forsake him not then, as you did Patroclus."
And from beneath his yoke the well-hoofed Xanthus spoke,
Addressing him, at once bowing his head—his mane
From beneath the yoke-strap cascading aside him
Downward to earth; and the goddess white-armed Hera   430

Imparted him speech: "Yes, truly now for the while
Will we save you, heroic Achilles, though your
Appointed doom ensue; nor ours the blame therefore
But the gods' and o'erwhelming Fate's. For by no sloth
Or sluggishness of ours are Trojans triumphant,   435
Stripping the armor from off Patroclus' shoulders;
But Apollo alone, whom fair-haired Leto bore,
He, by far best of immortals, slew Patroclus
'Mid the foremost ranks, granting glory to Hector.
But we the twain could outdistance westerly gusts,   440
Which people affirm are, of all gusts, fleetest far.
But yours is death by a god and mortal fated."
When thus he had spoken, the Erinyes ended
His speech. Then, his spirit deeply stirred, Achilles
Swift-footed responded: "Xanthus, why prophesy   445
My death? What need of that? Know I fully myself
That destined doom awaits me here, from my father
And rev'rent mother removed; yet ne'er will I quit
The least until glutting the Trojans with battle."
He spoke, and battle-crying onward drove the steeds.   450

~ Book XX ~

The Gods Prepare for Battle, Achilles Returns to the Plain

Upon Achilles' return to battle, Zeus convenes a council, permitting the gods to assist whomever they will. The gods convoke the hosts, Zeus thunders from Olympus with unprecedented force, and the gods pair up one against the other. As Achilles rages to find Hector, Apollo urges Aeneas to battle him. Aeneas is reluctant, reminding Apollo of a prior occasion when he (Aeneas) barely escaped Achilles. Apollo repeats the directive, instructing Aeneas to enlist his mother Aphrodite's aid, since he, Aeneas, is goddess-born while Achilles is merely the offspring of a sea nymph. While both are immortal, the goddess is of higher rank, and Aeneas thus more likely to prevail against Achilles (shaky reasoning, to be sure). As Aeneas proceeds in search of Achilles, Hera contrives with the gods for Achilles' protection. Poseidon now essentially disapproves of the gods' involvement in human affairs. However, he believes that if Apollo or Ares hinder Achilles, the gods should freely intervene. Meantime, the gods content themselves as observers though Zeus had consented to their engaging. The scene underscores the undecidedness of divine intervention, i.e., its hiddenness from human awareness.

In the combat that follows, Achilles and Aeneas inevitably confront each other. Achilles accuses Aeneas of mercenary motives: surely Priam has somehow bribed him—either with land or the promise of succession—to confront Achilles. He then reminds Aeneas how he (Achilles) had early routed Aeneas (as Aeneas had previously informed Apollo). Aeneas holds forth with an extended recitation of lineage, boasting its advantage but concluding that all talk is idle where deeds alone determine outcome.

Casting his spear, Aeneas strikes with such force that Achilles staggers, momentarily doubting the protective value of Hephaestus' shield. Achilles, too, strikes credibly. The two then rush each other—Achilles with sword, Aeneas with stone—an encounter preempted by Poseidon, who prophesies the ordained status of Aeneas and his progeny as *survivors*. Poseidon intervenes to whisk Aeneas away (i.e., Aeneas somehow manages to escape), scolding him for thinking to engage Achilles, the only Greek with power enough to kill him. Fate's mandate is such that the pro-Greek Poseidon saves the Trojan Aeneas. Achilles and Hector encourage their respective forces, Apollo urging Hector to maintain a low profile as Achilles rages in search of him.

There follows a catalogue of those slain by the rampaging Achilles. Grieving to see his brother Polydorus slain, Hector confronts Achilles. The two exchange boasts before engaging but are separated by Athena and Apollo, frustrating both the engagement and Achilles' revenge (while building anticipation for the approaching final encounter). There will be another occasion, ponders Achilles, as he continues his maniacal assault. It is the continuation of day 30.

Prominent throughout the *Iliad*, both on his own and paired with Hector, Aeneas is shown to best effect in Book 20, boasting a long and distinguished pedigree, followed by a palpable blow to Achilles' divinely made shield. It is Aeneas, when Troy is taken—the event not recounted in Homer—who escapes with family, followers, and effigies of household gods. The group voyages amid adventurous landfalls—Aeneas' love affair with Queen Dido of Carthage the most illustrious and tragic of them all. Ultimately arrived at Latium, the future site of Rome, they defeat the indigenous populations (with allied help), thereby initiating the preeminent course of Rome and its history (events recounted in Virgil's *Aeneid*). By his performance in the *Iliad* and the *Iliad*'s prophecy concerning his and his line's survival, Aeneas is Virgil's perfect survivor—founding what will be the greatest city of Rome from the ruins of the once greatest city of Troy. The process—historically known as *translatio imperii* 'transference of rule'—has since had prominent iterations, e.g., Spenser's configuration of Britain's imperium as legacy and continuance of Rome's; Manifest Destiny for the fledgling United States analogous to Britain's global reach.

BOOK XX

❧

Thus aside you by the curvèd ships, Achilles,
Insatiate of war, the Argives readied them
To fight; so also opposite them the Trojans
Upon the ascending plain. But Zeus from the peak
Of many-ridged Olympus bade Thetis summon 5
The gods to assembly and, everywhere hast'ning,
She directed them come to the palace of Zeus.
No river that flowed, save Ocean, shunned the appeal
Nor nymph of those inhabiting the beauteous glades,
The river-gladdened rivulets, and grassy meads. 10
And come to Cronidēs house, they seated themselves
Within the polished colonnades which Hephaestus
With artful craft had wrought for Cronidēs. Within
Zeus' palace they appeared; nor did lord Poseidon,
Shaker of earth, disregard the goddess' summons 15
But from the sea ascended to the gathering,
And seated among them queried the plan of Zeus:
"Wherefore, O lightning wielder, have you called the gods
To this gathering place? Perhaps you contemplate
Some measure affecting the Trojans and Argives, 20
Their contention at present most intractable."
Then responding, cloud-assembling Zeus made answer:
"Certain you know, Earth Shaker that you are, the plan
Within my breast, wherefore my summons to you here.
Mankind, though doomed to die, affects me. Nonetheless, 25
Will I for my part here on Olympus repose,
Vantaged to gaze and gladden my heart; but proceed,
You others, amid the Trojans and Achaeans,
Assisting this or th' other side as may befit.
For if Achilles alone affrayed the Trojans, 30
Nowise might they menace swift-footed Peleus' son.
In truth, earlier they trembled at the sight of him,
Taking note; but today his spirit runs amok
Intemperately for his comrade, and I fear

His rush upon the wall, defying Fate's decree."   35

So spoke Cronidēs, waking unrelenting war,
And the gods, their minds discordant, ranged for combat.
To the gathered ships moved Hera and Athena,
Poseidon, shaker of earth, and helper Hermes,
He surpassing all others in cunning of mind;   40
And with these Hephaestus, limping but exultant
In vigor, his slender legs nimble beneath him.
But to the Trojans flew flashing-helmèd Ares,
And with him Phoebus Apollo, his locks unshorn,
And arch'ress Artemis, and Leto, and Xanthus,   45
And laughter-loving Aphrodite. Now, so long
As stood the gods removed from mortal kind, even
So long the Argives most exultantly triumphed,
Seeing Achilles near, although earlier aloof
And distant from dismal bloodshed. But dread dismay   50
Descended on the Trojans each, when discerning
Swift-footed Achilles ablaze in arms, equal
To baneful Ares. But when Olympian gods
Upon the fray had entered, appeared then sturdy
Strife, inciter of hosts; and shouted Athena   55
Aside the harrowed channel parallel the wall,
And bellowed she now aside the reverberant
Shore, shrill and strident her cry. And over against
Her, Ares, daunting as darkened whirlwind, shouted
To the Trojans, calling aloud from the topmost   60
Parapet and thence speeding zealously the length
Of Simoïs' bank over Callicolōnē.
Thus to combat's clash the immortal gods convoked
The merging hosts, creating accursèd havoc.
Then roundly thundered the father of gods and men   65
From high Olympus, and from below Poseidon
Caused monumental earth and mountain crests to quake.
Shaken were the fundaments of divers-fountained
Ida, her towering peaks, the Trojan city,

BOOK XX

And ships of the Achaeans. And Hades below, 70
Lord of shades, recoiling in dread, leapt fearfully
From his throne, remonstrating openly lest earth
Be cloven wide by the earth-shaking god, and Hell,
His abode, lie exposed to gods and mortalkind,
That dire and dreaded abode by the gods despised. 75

Deafening the din as gods discordant battled,
For against Poseidon stood Phoebus Apollo
With wingèd darts; and against Enyalius
The goddess bright-eyed Athena; and the huntress—
Golden-arrowed and reverberant in pursuit— 80
Even archeress Artemis, sister to him
That fires from afar, opposed Hera. And Hermes
The helper uprose against Leto. And against
Hephaestus surged the vast deep-eddying river
The gods call Xanthus, but men Scamander. Thus gods 85
Challenged gods. But, exceeding others, Achilles
Coveted conflict with Hector, son of Priam,
For indefatigably drawn was Achilles
To sate Ares, bloody his hide-layered buckler.
But Apollo, spurring the host, urged Aeneas 90
To meet Achilles in encounter, infusing
Him with hardihood, and the god likened his voice
To that of Lycaōn, Priam's son. Thus likened,
Lord archer Apollo accosted Aeneas:
"Aeneas, Troy's counselor, where now reside those threats 95
Wherewith, raising your cup, you were wont to convince
The coronate Trojan chiefs of confrontation
With Achilles, face to face, Peleus' godlike son?"
And to him Aeneas replied: "Son of Priam,
Why command you my encounter with spirited 100
Achilles, against my wish and inclination?
No fledgling encounter is this with Achilles
Swift of foot; no, he threateningly repelled me
Once aforetime from Mount Ida, having happened

Upon our kine, and ravaged Lyrnessus, wasting 105
Pedasus as well; but Zeus promptly intervened,
Hastening my knees and enspiriting my soul;
Elsewise had I succumbed to Achilles' choler,
And Athena's—she ever going before him,
His deliverance, bidding him slay the Trojans 110
And neighboring Leleges with unblunted blade.
Wherefore, may no man e'er with Achilles contend,
For ever hovers over him some misfortune-
Staving god. Of volition its own flies his spear
Without pause until piercing the entrails of man. 115
And yet, were the gods evenhandedly to gauge
The outcome of our conflict, not casually
Would he vanquish me though vaunting himself of bronze."

Then responding spoke lord Apollo, son of Zeus:
"Warrior that you are, petition the gods ever- 120
Lasting, for of Aphrodite, daughter of Zeus,
Are you deemed begotten, whilst issues Achilles
From a lesser divine—offspring of Zeus versus
Daughter of Nēreus, old man of the sea. But stand
With bronze inexorable facing him, nor let 125
Him rout you with ultimatums and taunting words."
So saying, breathed he great strength into Aeneas,
People's shepherd, who then moved amid the foremost,
Outfitted in flaming bronze. Nor strode Aeneas
Unnoted by white-armed Hera as he ventured, 130
Questing for Achilles amid the warrior throng,
But convening the immortals, she counseled thus:
"Consider you both, Poseidon and Athena,
The most expected outcome. Aeneas proceeds
Accoutred in brazen bronze to face Achilles, 135
And Phoebus Apollo hastens him. However,
Let us now divert Aeneas, or otherwise
Stand as well, one of us, aside swift Achilles
And, increasing his spirit, prevent his mettle's

Failure, that he be strengthened by a god's support— 140
The Trojan gods unworth the wind that formerly
Pervaded Troy amid conflict and strife. But come we
From Olympus firmly resolved that Achilles
Today from the Trojans incur no impairment,
Though he suffer yet whate'er the Fates have fashioned 145
Since first by the depth-dwelling Thetis begotten.
And should Achilles not discern this from a god,
Malevolent will he deem the gods hereafter,
For gods revealed are difficult to gaze upon."

Then Poseidon: "Hera, be not overangered, 150
Ill it becomes you. Preferable any means
To that of gods confronting other gods, for such
Becomes us ill as well. But sooner retire we
Apart the fray, aptly taking our vantage point,
And war shall be for humankind. But should Ares 155
Or Apollo choose to fight, checking Achilles,
Restraining him from fight, then immediately
Shall we combative be as well—and directly,
I think, will they the contest quit, to Olympus
And the gods' assemblies returned, and by our hands 160
And conviction o'erpowered perforce." So saying,
Dark-haired Poseidon proceeded to the lofty
Wall of godlike Heracles, the tow'ring structure
The Trojans and Pallas Athena had designed,
Deterring the demon of the deep whenever 165
It resolved to coerce him from seashore to plain.
There sat Poseidon and the other immortals,
Their shoulders in impregnable cloud enshrouded;
And they of the other side sat opposite them,
On the crest of Callicolōnē, close by you, 170
O lord Apollo and city-sacking Ares.
Maneuvering thus, they settled to either side,
But reluctant either side to commence the clash
Though Olympus-enthronèd Zeus had consented.

Yet copiously o'er the plain ran men and steeds, 175
Awesomely brazen—and loud the earth resounded
Neath their rushing feet—advancing for contention.
And a pair, superior past others, stood opposed
In confrontation in the swath between the hosts,
Ardent for combat: Aeneas, Anchises' son, 180
And goodly Achilles. Aeneas first approached
With menacing mien, helmet nodding heavily,
Undaunted with shield afore his breast, a brazen
Spear aside him. And from the other side emerged
Achilles, a ravenous lion that herdsmen 185
Strive desperately to slay, even as gathered
Townsfolk look on. The lion, at first dismissive,
Goes his way; but when some daring youth affronts him,
Wounding him with spear—his mouth agape and foaming
At the teeth—he upgathers himself; his gallant 190
Spirit grumbles low, and to either side his tail
Larrups ribs and flanks, and smolders he for conflict
And, refulgent his eyes, infuriately prowls,
If he slay some man or himself be taken down,
His onrush thwarted; just so, his ferocity 195
And manly might awakened, Achilles advanced
To encounter great-hearted Aeneas in fight.
And when the pair approached, one against the other,
Pēleidēs Achilles spoke first to Aeneas:

"Aeneas, wherefore in confrontation have you 200
Exited the throng? Bids your spirit battle me,
Expecting to inherit Priam's sovereignty
Amid the horse-taming Trojans? But no, despatch
Me as you will—nor then shall lordly Priam yield
His sovereignty to your control, for his offspring 205
Be many, and firm his soul. Or have the Trojans
Apportioned you some piece of preeminent land,
An appealing tract of orchards and prime tillage,
That, vanquishing me, you might possess? Difficult

I deem the doing, for aforetime with my spear   210
Did I affright you, as I recall. Remember
You not the instance when quite alone, on quickened
Foot descending Mt. Ida, you forsook your kine
When I had routed you? Never turned you looking
Back that day. Thence you escaped unto Lyrnessus,   215
But I marauded it, assistance receiving
From Athena and father Zeus, and the women
Led I captive, rescinding their day of freedom;
But saved you Zeus and the other gods. However,
Not today, as I surmise, shall he assist you   220
As you think. Rather, I myself encourage you,
Returning to the throng, all challenge to renounce
Lest bad befall. Even a fool might discern it."
Then Aeneas answering him proclaimed: "Caution
Me not, Pēleïdēs, as though a child, for know   225
I as well the handling of mockery and taunt.
Comprehend we each other's lineage and line,
Having garnered the glories related of old,
But never have our eyes each other's parents viewed.
Men designate you offspring of dauntless Peleus   230
And regard your mother sea-born fair-tressed Thetis.
But from doughty Anchises derives my descent,
And from my mother Aphrodite. Of the two
Shall the one pair or other mourn a son today;
For not with childish prattle think I to depart   235
The fray, leaving your vaunted company. And yet
Please you acknowledge my lineage, for legion
Those acclaiming it. First did Zeus cloud-gatherer
Beget Dardanus, and founded he Dardania,
For sacred Ilium thrived not yet upon the plain,   240
A habitat for men, but on Ida's many-
Fountained slopes abode the folk. And Dardanus sired
A son in turn, lord Erichthonius, richest
Deemed of mortalkind, of three thousand steeds possessed
Which he pastured upon the marshes; mares they were,   245

Rejoicing in their yearlings. By these a' grazing
Was the North Wind entranced and likening himself
To a stallion dusky-maned bestrode them; and they,
Conceiving, bore fillies twelve. These, when traversing
The bounteous grain-giving earth, would skirt the topmost 250
Stalks of ripening corn, leaving them undamaged,
And traversing the ocean's liquid breadth, would skim
The topmost-cresting breakers of the blenchèd brine.
And begot Erichthonius Tros, for kingship
O'er the Trojans; and from Tros in turn three noble 255
Sons were sired: Ilus, Assaracus, and godlike
Ganymēdēs, most arresting of mortals born—
And for his beauty Zeus sequestered him aloft,
In his comeliness Zeus' cup to carry, lodging
Among the immortals. Ilus in turn begot 260
A peerless son, Laomedōn—Laomedōn
Begetting Tithonus, Priam, and Clytius,
And Hiketaōn, scion of Ares. Capys
Was son to Assaracus, and Capys begot
Anchises. Anchises begot me; and Priam, 265
Goodly Hector. Thus the lineage, descent, and blood
Whereof I stand avowed. But as for dauntlessness,
Zeus increases or diminishes it for men,
However he please, his power unstoppable.
But come, converse we no longer as children do, 270
The two of us standing mid combat's clash and broil.
Abuses enough exist for us to bandy—
In their abundance a hundred-benchèd hull would
Ill sustain the load. Twisted is mortal discourse,
And many the word emitted, and manifold, 275
And whate'er the need does utterance e'er fulfill,
And whate'er the word you speak will you spoken hear.
But why squabble and contend we thus, like women
That, waxing wroth in soul-devouring strife, descend
The street contending endlessly, now true their words, 280
Now false? For wrath enjoins them argue even thus.

BOOK XX

But from battle, ardent as I am, will you not
By words deter me ere the matter man to man
Be settled with bronze-tipped spears; but come, more quickly
Assay we one another."
                    Thus speaking he drove   285
His unswerving spear at the other's wondrous shield,
And 'round its point the shield echoed deafeningly;
And Achilles distanced the shield away from him,
His forearm firm, unflagging his fear, for he deemed
The far-shadowing spear of mighty Aeneas   290
Perforce would transpierce it, but vain the perception,
Nor apprehended he that magnificent gifts
By gods to mortals given are not readily
Overmastered, nor falter they. Nor was the shield
Pierced by Aeneas' spear, for the gold detained it,   295
Hephaestus' doing. But through double folds it drove.
Yet thee there were, for five had the feeble-footed
Smithy fashioned—two bronze and two within of tin,
And of gold between, arresting the ashen spear.
Then in turn Achilles hurled his own shadowing   300
Spear, smiting Aeneas' shield, well balanced throughout,
Beneath the rim, outermost, where the bronze ran thin
And thinnest the bullhide behind it; and through it,
At that spot, sped the Pelian spear; and resounded
The battered buckler, and Aeneas, recoiling   305
In consternation, forward extended the shield,
And the spear, passing over behind him, stood pegged
To the ground, expending its vehemence, beshorn
The sheltering shield of two protective layers.

And escaping the spear he arose, eyes misting   310
With immeasurable grief that seized him entire
For the spear's near implantation. But Achilles,
Incensed, drew his deadly sword and assaulted him,
Crying exceedingly loud, and Aeneas took
To hand a boulder's bulk—daunting the endeavor—   315

Stone no two mortal men might manage as mortals
Are today; yet lightly aloft he wielded it.
Then Aeneas with bolder would have have battered him,
As forward he rushed, approaching, on either helm
Or shield, his defense against woeful destruction; 320
And Achilles in quickened combat had with sword
Purloined Aeneas' life had not lord Poseidon,
Shaker of earth, been wary. And straightway he spoke,
Admonishing the immortals: "Observe you now,
I grieve for great-hearted Aeneas who anon, 325
Having honored far-working Apollo's command,
Will enter Hades' house, by Achilles despatched,
Fool that he was! Nor in the least will Apollo
Reclaim him from bloodletting's dread? And yet, why should
An innocent vainly suffer for transgression 330
Not his own, since ever pleasing his offerings
To the immortals o'er heaven ruling? But come,
Deliver we him from death lest Zeus Cronidēs
Somehow be provoked, should Achilles despatch him;
His demise for avoidance decreed, that the race 335
Of Dardanus neither seedless recede nor end—
Dardanus, beloved of Zeus above all children
Delivered him of womankind. For father Zeus
Patently despises Priam's descent, and now
Shall bold Aeneas be king among the Trojans, 340
His bloodline throughout posterity perdurant."
And to him responded ox-eyed queenly Hera:
"Poseidon, amid measures that you devise,
Contemplate the end and outcome for Aeneas,
If you will protect or see him lying butchered, 345
For all his valor, by Achilles Peleus' son.
We two, Pallas Athena and I, have sworn oaths
Beyond number among the immortals to cease
From actions averting Troy's fated extinction,
Not even if Troy in fatal conflagration 350
Burn, to ash consigned by the warlike Achaeans."

BOOK XX

Mindful of this, earth shaker Poseidon decamped
To the battle and hurtling of weapons, reaching
The point where Aeneas and famed Achilles stood.
O'er Pēleidēs' visage placed he vaporous mist   355
And extracted the ashen bronze-encompassed spear
From out the buckler of great-hearted Aeneas,
Stationing it afore the feet of Achilles.
But grasped he Aeneas, lifting him off the ground,
And o'er many the rank of warrior and chariot   360
Aeneas sprang, forth hastened by the god's own hand,
And reached he the periphery of the fiercesome
Fray, for which the Caucōnes were accoutring them.
Then Poseidon, shaker of earth, approached and spoke,
Reproving with wingèd words: "Aeneas, what god   365
Enjoins you fight, foolhardy and closely quartered,
The high-spirited offspring of Peleus, knowing
He stands loftier and more dearly loved of gods
Than you? But sooner give ground whenever chancing
To encounter him, lest before your fated day   370
You encounter Hades' domain. But when, dying,
Peleus' son fulfills his fate, then emboldened be
To fight among the foremost; for of the Argives,
Achilles—and Achilles alone—will slay you."
So saying he left him there, having told him all,   375
Next did the miraculous mist quit Achilles
And with prescient perception labored he withal,
And, angered, addressed his own great-spirited self:
"Startling wonderment my vision, alas, surveys:
Here lies my weapon on the ground, yet the warrior   380
At whom I hurled it, longing to slay, is elsewhere.
Thus, Aeneas as well seems favored of the gods,
Though I reckoned his ranting of little account.
To Hell with him. No heart shall he again possess
To battle me, since now elates him his escape.   385
But come, gathering the war-enamored Argives

Will I engage the remaining Trojans, setting
My gall against them." He spoke, and bounding the ranks,
To each man called aloud: "From the Trojans keep you
Your distance no longer, you goodly Danaans,   390
But come, advance every Argive, fevered for fray,
Upon the foe. Burdensome for myself, despite
My strength, alone such numbers to engage, fighting
Them all. Nor the war god, albeit immortal,
Nor Athena could plummet the trough of such toil,   395
Slogging therein. Indeed, as I avail with force
Of hands and feet, I will nowise prove the laggard;
No, not the least, but will shatter their defenses,
My threatening weapon a blight on Trojan cheer."

So spoke he urging them, but glorious Hector   400
To the Trojans shouted aloud, announcing he
Would forward forge to face Achilles: "You Trojans,
Full hearted, fear not Peleus' son. I too with words
Could fight the very immortals, but onerous
It were with spear, for gods be the greater challenge.   405
Nor shall Achilles witness his boasting fulfilled;
But part will he effect and part leave incomplete.
Afore him shall I fare though furnace-like his hands
And his fury an inferno." So he proclaimed,
Exhorting them; and the Trojans, fronting the foe,   410
High hefted their weaponry, and confounding were
The clamor and clash ascendant. Then Apollo
To Hector appearing spoke: "Hector, no longer
The champion play against Peleus' son Achilles,
But bide him in the melee and amid the din,   415
Lest somehow distant he attack or strike nearby."
So pronounced the god, and Hector again melded
With the throng, by fear of the utt'rance overcome.

But Achilles assaulted the Trojans, his heart
In might attired, a horrific cry emitting.   420

First Iphitiōn he slew, Otrynteus' offspring,
Leader of a mighty host whom a naiad nymph
Had unto Otrynteus, taker of cities, borne
Beneath snowbound Tīmolus in the bounteous
Hydē's demesne. Him, as he catapulted forth, 425
Did spear-releasing Achilles smite on the head,
And cloven asunder it hung, and he tumbled
With a thud, and exulted godlike Achilles,
Declaring: "There you lie, Iphitiōn, dreadful
Most of men. Here your demise, though your begetting 430
Gygaea's waters witnessed, where lie the holdings
Of your ancestors, by Hyllus heaving with fish
And by whirling Hermus." So spoke he vauntingly,
But darkness took the other, and the running rims
Of Argive chariots dismembered him, outward strewn 435
To the forefront of the fracas. And after him,
Achilles speared Dēmoleōn, Antēnōr's son,
A stalwart lord defender, to the temple struck,
His helmet fitted with brazen cheek protectors;
Nor stayed the brazen helm the spear, but passing sped 440
The point and battered the bone asunder, the brain
Besplatt'ring about within. Thus did Achilles
Arrest his force. And Hippodamas, next, leaping
From his chariot in flight before him, assailed he
Skewering his back, and bellowing breathed he his last; 445
Even as bellows a bull when by young men hauled
About the altar of Poseidon, for in such
Delighteth lord Poseidon. Bellowed even so
Hippodamas while languishing for want of breath. 450
But Achilles, spear to hand, pursued the godlike
Polydōrus, Priam's son, whom Priam nowise
Permitted to engage, the youngest of all his
Progeny and most the belovèd of his eye,
And in fleetness of foot exceeding quite. But now 455
Of his fleetness making foolish display, he forged
Through the foremost fighters and forfeited his life,

For swift-footed Achilles, his better, smote him
Squarely on the back—straight casting his spear as past
He sped—even where the golden clasps shone fastened 460
On his belt and the doubled corselet met. Therethrough
En route to his navel passed the point. And groaning
He fell to his knees, and bleak the cloud that covered
Him recoiling, bowels in his hands clasped toward him
As he sank.
          But when Hector beheld his brother 465
Polydōrus clutching his entrails as earthward
He collapsed, a mist o'erhazed his eyes, nor endured
He the longer to range apart but proceeded
Toward Peleus' son, brandishing his spear, in aspect
Like unto flame. But when Achilles beheld him, 470
Even then he vaulted forth conveying in vaunt:
"Ah, stands the man nearby who surpassing others
Has stricken the spirit within me, having slain
The companion I honored. Not the longer then
Shall caution the encounter mark." Thus he pronounced, 475
And with angered glance from beneath knit brows, addressed
Goodly Hector thus: "Closer come, and more quickly
Attend death's calling." And by him nowise cowered,
Did Hector, coruscating-helmed, make this reply:
"Son of Peleus, think not with words to frighten me 480
As if a child, since well enough I comprehend
Contemptuousness and demeaning utterance.
Know I, the lesser, your superiority.
Yet the outcome within the gods' discretion lies,
Whether, such as I am, I deprive you of life, 485
Since keen aforetime stands my weapon credited."

He spoke, and hurled his readied weapon, but Pallas
Athena imperceptibly deflected it
From Achilles, restoring it unto Hector,
There before his feet. But Achilles savagely 490
Assaulted, eager to slay and crying aloud,

BOOK XX

But Apollo snatched Hector apart—easily,
As might a god—and shrouded him in heavy mist.
Thrice then, weapon in hand, swift-footed Achilles
Assaulted him, and thrice thrashed he abundant mist; 495
But when for the fourth time assailing him, tearing
Like a god, then with excruciate cry addressed
He wingèd words: "Cur, once again have you cozened
Death though close approached its duress, but Apollo
Saved you, whom surely you must supplicate whene'er 500
Entering the hurtling of spears. Yet, verily,
In encounter will I mangle you hereafter
If likewise my assistance be divine. But now
Onward to others, whomsoe'er I chance upon."
So saying, with spearthrust smote he Dryops squarely 505
On the neck, and down he tumbled a'front his feet.
But disregarding him, he vanquished Dēmouchus,
Philētōr's son, valiant the man and tall, striking
With heft directed at the knee and, thrusting next
With unerring sword, purloining his life away. 510
Then rushing on Dardanus and Laogonus,
Twain offspring of Bias, he ousted them groundward
From their car, smiting one by spear and the other
By sword at close quarters. Then Tros, Alastōr's son,
He slew—Tros who came clasping his knees, desiring 515
Thereby to be saved, should Achilles render him
Captive, releasing him alive, slaying him not,
Pitying one of kindred years—fool that he was
Thus benighted, since persuasion was beyond him,
And neither movable nor well inclined was he 520
But exceedingly severe. Sought he nonetheless
To grasp Achilles' knees, seeking to assuage him,
But Achilles to his liver smote, and the liver slithered downward,
And black the upswollen blood suffusing his breast,
The darkness devouring his vision as he dropped. 525
Achilles next assaulted Mulius, piercing him
At the ear, and steadfast through the opposite ear

The brazen point emerged. Then smote he Echeclus,
Agēnōr's son, to the head with his hilted sword,
Warming the reddened blade along its hardened length; 530
And dismal his death and fierce the fate descending.
Next he smote Deucaliōn where join the elbow's
Tendons. Just there the brazen blade traversed him through
As with weighted arm he bore Achilles' attack,
Awaiting death's destined approach; but Achilles, 535
Severing his head at the neck, sent it trundling,
Clanging helm and all, and upspurted the marrow
From his spine, and reposed he outstretched o'er the plain.
Then pursued he Rhigmus, Peirēs' peerless offspring,
Come from fertile Thrace. Him to the innards he smote, 540
Bronze within belly lodged, and bounded he flying,
Quitting his car. And Areithous his companion,
As he swung his horses 'round, Achilles impaled
Through the back, and he catapulted from his car
And the horses ran amok.
      As uprises flame 545
Through the gaping gorges of tindered mountainsides,
And the fathomless forest relentlessly flares,
And whips the goading wind the lambent flame aswirl;
Even so he raged a'rush like conflagration,
Resembling a god, descending ever on those 550
He selected for death—and the moldering earth
O'erflooded with blood. And as a man yokes broad-browed
Oxen, loud their bellowing, to trample barley
On a fashioned threshing floor, and beneath their feet
The grain is briskly husked and sorted; even so 555
Beneath great-hearted Achilles' single-hoovèd
Steeds lay corpses and shields, together all compiled,
And with blood beneath was his axle rod spattered,
And the rims 'round his chariot smitten with drops
From off the horses' hooves and off the whirling wheels; 560
But Achilles juggernauted, gaining glory,
Hands insup'rable splendidly stippled with blood.

~ Book XXI ~

Achilles Battles the River Scamander, Hephaestus Checks the River's Advance

THE TROJANS FLEE ACHILLES, some toward the town, others falling into river Scamander, where they either drown or are butchered by Achilles. Achilles takes twelve alive from the river to sacrifice (as he said he would) on the pyre of Patroclus.

Returning to the plain, Achilles encounters Lycaon, a son of Priam, whom he had earlier captured at Troy and ransomed on Lesbos, only to confront him anew as combatant at Troy. Achilles appreciates the irony. Lycaon begs for mercy but to no avail. Achilles slaughters and throws him into the increasingly abused and irate Scamander. Achilles next confronts the ambidextrous Asteropaeus, newly arrived leader of the Paeonian allies. Asteropaeus lets fly with two spears at once: one hitting Achilles' shield; the other visiting a flesh wound on Achilles' arm (and drawing blood). Achilles hurls and misses, the spear becoming firmly lodged in the river bank. Asteropaeus vainly attempts to extricate it, but not before Achilles slays him with his sword, boasting over the fallen corpse. Reclaiming his spear, Achilles turns on the Paeonians, panicked over their leader's demise.

The river Scamander, given human voice, upbraids Achilles' treatment of his waters. Achilles, however, continues his water-bound attack, even as the river disgorges its many dead. As Scamander gains the upper hand, Achilles exits the waters, attempting escape on the plain. But Scamander pursues him in a tidal surge. Fearing watery death, Achilles beseeches the gods, wishing he had sooner perished at Hector's hands. Athena and Poseidon take note, assuring Achilles that Scamander will soon relent. They bid Achilles refrain from further combat until all Trojan fighters have escaped into the city, whereupon he will confront Hector.

Scamander and the newly heartened Achilles continue, indecisively, to do battle. Scamander seeks the aid of nearby river Simoïs, disclosing a strategy for jointly overcoming Achilles. Hera enlists Hephaestus to combat Scamander with flame which, as an ancillary benefit, she will accelerate to burn the accumulated dead. Hephaestus all but reduces Scamander to steam, everything within him scorched and burning. Scamander implores Hephaestus to relent (and Hera to restrain her son, which she does). Scamander replenishes his waters, only too happy to retire from human antagonisms.

The gods, who had earlier amassed one against the other, now partake in a mock theomachy (battle of the gods), incited by both their preferences for mortal favorites and their jealousies and senses of offended prerogative. The battle humorously mimics the *Iliad*'s own fighting. It further spoofs the theomachy related in Hesiod's *Theogony (Birth of the Gods)*: the battle in which the Zeus-led Olympians defeat the earlier generation of Titan gods, banishing them to the underworld. Milton's Hesiod-inspired theomachy in *Paradise Lost* pits God's angels against Lucifer's, the "fallen" with their leader consigned to Hell.

Achilles continues his rampage, driving the Trojans toward Troy. Priam orders the Scaean Gates opened to receive them, as Apollo distances Achilles. All remaining Trojans escape into Troy but for Agenor—at the forefront of those attacking the Greek fortification (Book 12)—who stands to oppose Achilles. Agenor debates flight versus standing firm in much the way Hector will do when soon confronting Achilles. Agenor taunts and then casts at Achilles, hitting him to no effect on his newly wrought greave. Apollo wrests Agenor from the fight, assuming his likeness, and leads Achilles on the proverbial wild goose chase, thus contriving to distance Achilles from the remainder of Trojans seeking escape into the city. It is still day 30.

❧

But when arrived at the ford of the fair-flowing
River, even swirling Xanthus that immortal
Zeus begot, there Achilles severed the Trojans,
And drove one part o'er the plain to the city,
Even where the Greeks had fled the preceding day   5

BOOK XXI

Whilst rampaged glorious Hector; in that direction
Routed, some took flight, and Hera dispensed a dense
Detaining mist. But the others became ensnared
In the deep-flowing silver-eddied surge. Therein
With fearsome din they fell, and the catapulting 10
Surge resounded, and loud echoed the banks throughout;
And wailed the men flailing in every direction,
Foundering in the eddies.
      And as when beneath
A licking flame refuge-taking locusts escape
Into a river, and flame, relentless, sears them, 15
Indefatigable its advance, and crave they
The water's sanctum; just so before Achilles
Lay fathomless Xanthus with chariots and warriors
Confoundedly filled and aflow. But Zeus-nurtured
Achilles upon Xanthus' bank there left his spear, 20
Leaning against the tamarisks, and himself leapt
Godlike in, with solitary sword—and dreadful
The deed he intended to do—and pivoting
Each way 'round and about, he persistently pounced;
And hideous the howling of warriors harrowed 25
By his sword, and the water reddened rife with blood.
And as a'front a large-mawed dolphin fly other
Fish affrighted, a fair-shelt'ring inlet filling,
And devours the dolphin whate'er of them he will;
Even so toppled Trojans from o'er Xanthus' bank 30
Into the river's fathomless gaping eddies.
And with hands fatigued from slaughter, selected he
Twelve youths alive from out the current, as blood-price
Of perished Patroclus, Menoetius' son. These dazed
As deer he positioned, binding their hands behind 35
Them with well-cut thongs which they themselves about their
Pliant tunics wore, and to comrades conveyed them
For escort to the hollow ships.
      Then sprang he back
Again, raging to rive and hew, and encountered

523

A son of Dardanian Priam, Lycaōn,   40
Fleeing from out the river, even Lycaōn
Whom aforetime he had apprehended, leading
Him coercively from out his father's orchard,
Whence by moonlight he had exited, having hacked
With brazen blade some tender shoots of native fig   45
To fashion chariot rails. But upon him stole brave
Achilles, an unlooked-for affliction. Earlier
Had he sold him on well-built Lemnos, there taking
Him on his vessels, and Jason's son had purchased
Him for gold. Thereafter a guest-friend gave ransom,   50
And steep the expense incurred—even Eëtion
Of Imbros who sent him to goodly Arisbē
Whence he escaped unto his father's house returned.
For fully eleven days, from Lemnos arrived,
His comrades fêted him, but on the twelfth, a god   55
Again unto Achilles' hands delivered him,
Who unto Hades' house would this time hasten him,
However unamenable. Thus swift-footed
Achilles noticed him unarmed and lacking helm,
Nor possessed of spear, having jettisoned them all;   60
For a sweat oppressed him in retreat from the tide,
And a languor enveloped his faltering limbs.
Then incredulous Achilles addressed his heart:
"Behold, quite the marvel is this before mine eyes.
Truly will the great-hearted Trojans I have slain   65
Be resurrected from all-enveloping shade,
Even as this man surfaces, circumventing
Inflexible fortune since formerly trafficked
To sacrosanct Lemnos. But the sea's grizzled grey,
Detaining grudging multitudes, arrests him not.   70
But further encounter he our spearpoint, that I
Observe and confirm whether likewise he return
From Hades' house or remitted be to fruitful
Earth which detaineth even a mightier man.
So pondered he waiting, but the other approached,   75

BOOK XXI

Delirious, eager to clasp his knees, fully
Desperate to escape dark destiny and death.
Then godlike Achilles high-hefted his weapon,
Yearning to smite him; but Lycaōn crouched, running
Beneath it, clasping his knees; and the spear o'erpassed　　80
His back, landing firm in the ground though preferring
On human flesh to gorge. Then begged him Lycaōn,
One hand enfolding his knees, th' other his whetted
Weapon arresting nor at all releasing it,
And thus implored him, conversing in wingèd words:　　85
"By your knees I entreat you, dreadest Achilles,
And you, adjudge me true and be compassionate,
You nurtured of Zeus, for as sacred suppliant
I come, having initially at your table
Partaken of sustenance when you captured me　　90
In the well-furrowed orchard, taking me afar
From sire and friends. You sold me in sacred Lemnos,
Where I procured you a hundred oxen, thrice that
Next expending in purchase of my liberty.
And this my twelfth day is since arriving to Troy　　95
After plenteous pain, where unfeeling fate once
Again redelivers me into your hands; yes,
Of father Zeus am I detested, since again
Into your hands conveyed and to lifetime abridged.
The mother that bore me was called Laothoē,　　100
Child of the elder Altēs, lord of the martial
Leleges, tending steep Pedasus by the stream
Satnioeis. This daughter, one among several,
Wedded Priam as wife, twain offspring begetting,
Polydorus and me, whom alike you now slay.　　105
Amid the foremost footmen Polydorus lies,
The godlike, prostrate, struck by your unsparing spear,
And even now does calamity reclaim me,
For I imagine no escaping you, a god
Deliv'ring me into your hands. Yet another　　110
Thing will I reveal, and enclose it in your heart:

525

Slay me not, since not from the selfsame womb begot
As Hector, who slew your kind and courageous friend."

So addressed him Priam's glorious son, imploring;
But he responded ruthlessly: "Wretch, propose not 115
Ransom nor speechify. Until Patroclus met
His fated day, even 'til that day I inclined
To spare the Trojans, taking them alive to sell
O'erseas; but now nary a one shall be redeemed
From Death, whome'er along the walls of Troy a god 120
Unto my hands consigns—not one of the gaggle
Of Trojans and, specially, none of Priam's sons.
So perish you as well, my friend, and why complain?
So perished Patroclus, by much superior.
And perceive you not the trappings of my manhood, 125
How splendid and how tall, of goodly father sired,
And of goddess mother begotten? Yet no less
On me weigh death and steadfast doom. Some dawn, midday,
Or eventide a warrior will do me in,
Whether with leveled arrow or fast-flighted spear." 130
Thus he asserted, and weakened Lycaōn's knees,
And melted his heart. And crouching low, he released
Achilles' spear, raising his hands. But Achilles,
Keen drawn his sword, attacked him at the collarbone
Aside the neck, and sank the twin-edged sword within, 135
And lay he flattened to earth outstretched, and the blood
Spurted dark to the dampened ground. Achilles then
Gripped him by the foot, riverward removing him,
Plaything to the tide, and vaunted in wingèd words:
"With fishes now slumber you, that casually 140
Lick your lacerations; nor shall your dear mother
Lay you out lamenting your death, but eddying
Xanthus to the broad-bosomed billow shall bear you,
And fishy tribes, upsurging from tumescent depths,
Shall feasting find in Lycaōn's glistening fat. 145
So perish all, 'til Troy's tow'ring heights be taken,

BOOK XXI

All in panic, as I despoil you from behind.
Nor shall the fair-flowing silver-eddied vortex
Avail you—though to him, I think, you have ever
Tendered multitudes of bulls, and deep within its 150
Maelstrom alive submerged your single-hoovèd steeds.
Yet, even so, pitilessly perish you all
Until paid be the damage for Patroclus' death
And Danaan despair, whom shipside you slaughtered
Whilst I my distance kept." So he inveighed, and grew 155
The river increasingly wroth, gauging the means
Wherewith to hinder Achilles' despicable
Doings and keep ruin from Troy. But Peleus' son,
Raising his shadow-casting spear, upleapt upon
Asteropaeus, Pēlegōn's offspring, eager 160
To slay him, of the wide-flowing Axius born
And of Periboea, eldest of the daughters
Of Acessamenus, for with her lay the deep-
Eddying Axius. Achilles hurtled toward him,
And th' other stood forth from the river to face him, 165
Spears in hand. And Scamander emboldened him, wroth
O'er the youths slain in battle whom Achilles cleft
Brutally aside his streams.
                          But when near the two
Approached, one toward the other advancing, Peleus'
Swift-footed son first addressed Asteropaeus: 170
"Who be you among men, and whence come, daring thus
To confront me? Unfortunate they whose offspring
Defy me." Then responded the glorious son
Of Pēlegōn: "Great-souled son of Peleus, wherefore
Question you my line? From deep-soiled Paeonia, 175
A land far-off, I hail, commanding the long-speared
Paeonians, and this be my eleventh morn
Since arrival to Troy. Descends my lineage
From wide-flown Axius—whose fairest waters o'erspread
Earth's visage— who fostered spear-famous Pēlegōn, 180
My father professed. And now fight we, Achilles."

So he spoke, forebodingly. But goodly Peleus'
Son upraised his spear of Pelian ash; howe'er,
The ambidextrous warrior Asteropaeus
Simultaneously spent two weapons. With one   185
He smote the shield, in nowise penetrating it,
For the inlaid gold, Hephaestus' gift, repelled it.
With the second dealt he Achilles' right forearm
A glancing blow, and readily ran the black blood;
But the spearpoint overpassed him, fixing itself   190
In the ground, though hungry with flesh to be glutted.
Achilles in turn with preparedness released
His spear, set for foeman's slaughter, but the ashen
Lance beyond its target flew, lodged to half its length
In Scamander's bank, there firmly fixed. But Peleus'   195
Son, the blade from aside his thigh extracting,
Forcefully leapt upon him, the other vainly
Attempting with stoutness of hand to extricate
Achilles' spear embedded in Scamander's bank.
Thrice he set it quivering in his eagerness   200
Outward to wrest it, and thrice forsook the effort.
But on the fourth might he have twisted and splintered
Achilles' invincible spear except sooner
Approached Achilles, with blade purloining his life.
To the abdomen aside the navel he bore,   205
And to earth piled Asteropaeus' intestines,
And night, as gasping he lay, enshrouded his eyes."

And Achilles, leaping upon his chest, despoiled
The armor from his corpse, in these words exulting:
"Thus repose! Hard it is to contend with children   210
Of Cronidēs, though of a river begotten.
From broad-flowing Axius you boast yourself born,
Whilst I descend from the bloodline of Cronus' son.
The father that begot me is among many
Myrmidons ruler, even Peleus, Aeacus'   215
Son, and Aeacus of Zeus was begot. Wherefore,

BOOK XXI

As Zeus is mightier than seaward-spilling streams,
So mightier, too, Zeus' race above rivers all.
For aside you swirls a forceful flow, avail you
As it may; but o'erpow'ring be issue of Zeus;   220
Nor with him does kingly Achelōus vie nor
Tempestuous forces of deep-flowing Ocean
Whence all rivers flow, whence all springs, and every sea,
And unfathomed well; even Ocean stands dismayed
Afore Zeus Cronidēs' bolt and thunderous peal,   225
Whene'er aloud from heaven's dome they detonate."
He spoke, from the bank extracting his brazen spear,
Leaving Asteropaeus supine in the sand
Where he lay submerged in sable flow, exhausted
His life—the delectation of aquatic swarms   230
From about his kidneys fast masticating fat.

But Achilles advanced upon the Paeonians,
Chariot lords, paralytic by the river bank,
Having viewed the foremost among them forcibly
Subdued beneath the hands and sword of Peleus' son.   235
There despatched he Thersilochus, Astypylus,
Mydōn, Mnēsus, Thrasius, and Ophelestēs,
Also Aenius. And yet more of the Paeonians
Had Achilles submerged had not the deep-eddied
River defiantly reproached him, its features   240
Resembling a man's, its recessed voice upwelling:
"Achilles, exceeding mankind for the better,
Exceeding it in evil too, since the gods grant
You ready assistance. If Cronidēs sanction
Your slaying of Trojans, from out my flow at least   245
Dislodge them, your work to the doleful plain confined.
Crushed are my currents with casualties, no use
At all seeking to exit myself to the sea,
Choked with corpses as I am whilst you ruthlessly
Butcher away. But yield; I am sorely amazed,   250
You lord of hosts." Spoke then swift-footed Achilles:

"Thus shall it be, Zeus-nurtured Scamander, even
As you bid; but my slaughter of Trojans proceeds,
Troyward gathering them until making assay
Of Hector man to man to slay him or be slain."   255
So saying, leapt he godlike upon the Trojans.
Then to Apollo the eddying river spoke:
"Come now, lord of the silver bow, issue of Zeus,
Keep you nowise the command of Zeus Cronidēs
Who steadfast enjoined you encourage the Trojans,   260
Protecting them 'til descending dusk has darkened
The rich-soiled earth."
                    He spoke, and spear-famed Achilles
Cascaded from the scarp, submitting to the flow;
But against him swelled the river, its force incensed,
Its stream roist'rously stirred whilst propelling apace   265
Accumulated corpses compacting its bed,
Men slain by Achilles. These he dislodged to land,
Bellowing like a bull, and the living he drew
Beneath his winning waves, in generous whirlpools
Sheltering them. Turbulently towered the tide   270
Atop Achilles' head, battering his buckler
And forcing him back, nor profited his foothold.
Then clenching an ample teeming elm, he downed it
Roots and all, rupturing the bank, over-spanning
The thrashing stream with leafage and branch and, fallen   275
Within it, impeding the flow; but Achilles
Ascended, cresting the maelstrom on quickened foot
A'flight o'er the plain, beset with apprehension.
But the turgid river persisted, denying
Achilles his devastations and distancing   280
Downfall from the Trojans; but Achilles yielded,
The length of a spearcast, swooping like an eagle
That towering predator, alike the strongest
And speediest-pinioned. Eagle-like he bounded,
And upon his breast rang the bronze reverberant   285
As he distanced from the flood, headlong advancing;

BOOK XXI

And the river followed, its onslaught relentless,
And like to a farmer drawing a stream down course
From a dusky spring to his plants and garden plots,
Rake in hand, and from the sluice clears branches away,   290
And the pebbles beneath are upswept in the flow,
And accelerant the run with murmuring sound
As it descends, rapidly o'ertaking the one
Himself directing it; thus ever the torrent
O'ertook Achilles albeit fleetest of foot,   295
Since mightier immortals than men. For as oft
As swift-footed Achilles fled the water's force,
Pondering if the immortal gods that hold broad
Heaven had endless flight decreed, so oft pounded
The turgid spate of river's rage, outpoured upon   300
His shoulders from above; and high would he hurtle,
His spirit vexed, and e'er the flow fatigued his knees,
Careening enraged about them, snatching the ground
From beneath his feet.
                Then did Achilles unloose
A bitter cry, peering upward to broad heaven: 305
"Father Zeus, how happens it that not a single
God approaches and, in this my predicament,
Extracts me from the tide, come what may thereafter?
No deity I inculpate as much as my
Dear mother, whose deception has deluded me,   310
That beneath the high fortifications of Troy
I should promptly die by mandate of Apollo.
Would that Hector had despatched me, foremost of men
Here fashioned! Then, intrepid the slayer had been
And intrepid the slain. But now to wretched death   315
This destiny ordains me, doomed in the deluge
Of Scamander like a swinekeep in a current
Entrapped, attempting in winter to traverse it."

So he spoke, and Athena and Poseidon drew
Aside him, likened in aspect to mortalkind   320

And, clasping his hand within theirs, reassured him,
And among them lord Poseidon, shaker of earth,
Spoke first: "Son of Peleus, tremble you not o'ermuch
Nor fearful be, since we arrive, helpers divine,
With Zeus' consent, the goddess Athena and I. 325
Accordingly, consider neither fate nor death
In the tidewater's surge, for soon shall it relent,
Of which you yourself shall know. But this assessment
We confer, if perchance you find it persuasive:
"Continue your onslaught combatively until 330
The Trojan host sequestered be in the vaunted
Towering citadel, whoever flees within.
But for yourself, when you have taken Hector's life,
Return you to the ships, for we grant you glory."

Thus having spoken, to Olympus departed 335
The pair away, but advanced Achilles plainward
For the gods' pronouncement had enspirited him.
And decidedly over-flooded was the plain,
And countless the costly arms and youthful corpses
Battle-slain and bloated there. But he, straight surging 340
Against the flood leapt sprightly on his feet, nor might
The wide-flowing river restrain him, for amply
Had Pallas Athena empowered him. Nor yet
From Achilles would godly Scamander withdraw,
But, ascended and crested aloft with rage, called 345
Aloud to Simoïs: "Dear brother, constrain we
This man's pace, plying our coupled proficiencies
Since soon will he demolish Priam's town. Nor will
Trojans withstand his onslaught.
                                But help you quickly.
From your cisterns and wells with water fill your streams 350
And all your torrents rouse. Raise you a hearty wave
And waken thunderous din of tree trunk and stone,
That we discourage this predominant warrior
Who vows with gods themselves to strive; for, I surmise,

BOOK XXI

His power will not least avail, nor anywise 355
His magnificence, nor yet that goodly armor,
Somehow determined deep beneath our waters laid
In mud. And him will I ensepulcher in silt,
Past recollection opulently overlaid;
Nor will his upgathered remains be notable, 360
Farthest beneath bottomless sediment buried,
Within the graveyard I become, his own barrow
Unobserved when companions offer obsequies."
He spoke, tumultuously charging Achilles,
High roiling on with foam, blood, and dead men aswirl, 365
And doleful the flood of the heaven-fed river
Upward ascending and arched to envelop him.
But in fear for Achilles queen Hera declaimed—
Lest the driving undulate river destroy him—
Directly addressing Hephaestus her offspring: 370
"Up now, dear limping-footed son of mine, for deem
We the eddying river your match to oppose.
But inflict now a blistering brilliance of flame,
And hast'ning will I gather a sea-born typhoon
Of westerly wind and brightened south to consume 375
Trojan corpses and battle gear, the tempest e'er
Driving your flame along; and by Scamander's banks
With scourge of fire complete, provoke conflagration.
Nor grant he deter you by wheedling words or threat,
But rage you unstopped until hearing me holler. 380
Then, and only then, rescind your unstinting flame."

She spoke, and Hephaestus awakened wondrous flame
Ablaze. First on the plain was it enkindled quick,
Consuming the dead, the multitudinous dead
By Achilles slain, lying strewn thereon; and parched 385
Was the plain throughout and stayed the teeming waters.
And as when at harvest time, the North Wind anon
Dries a freshly watered orchard, and pleased is he
Who tends the plot; thus desiccated lay the plain,

Of its dead depleted. And next he encircled 390
Scamander with gleaming flame. Aflame was the elm,
The willow, and tamarisk; aflame the lotus;
And gone the generous galingale and rushes
'Round the river rooted. Reeled the eels recoiling,
And dashed the eddied fish, descending to every 395
Streamlet of the river's deepnesses, destitute
Amid the havoc of Hephaestus dealing death.
Parched through was the puissant river; and thus speaking
Addressed the god: "Hephaestus, no god seconds you,
Myself included, O lord of conflagration. 400
Discontinue this dispute, and as concerns
The Trojans, hasten Achilles their disarray.
What part have I in dispute or dispensing aid?"
So he spoke, fully flaming the while, and his fair
Streams seethed. And as a cauldron boils within, alight 405
Its glimmer, rendering lard from a fatted hog,
And blisters it from every side, dry the kindling
Beneath it; so in conflagration burned his streams,
And the water steamed nor further essayed pursuit
But stood detained, the assault of many-minded 410
Hephaestus undoing him. And Scamander prayed
Straightaway in wingèd words: "Wherefore, O Hera,
Has your son thus assailed me beyond others all?
In the matter of fault the less blameworthy I
Than those who encourage the Trojans. However, 415
Quit I now if you command, so let Hephaestus
Quit as well. And accept you this my solemn oath:
Never again shall I from Trojans counter doom
And defeat, not even as Troy incinerates,
The daylong consumed, and let craven Achaeans 420
Be those who destroy it."
                       But the goddess white-armed
Hera, faced with this avowal, straightway addressed
Her dear son Hephaestus: "Forbear you, Hephaestus
My gloried son, nowise befits it to combat

BOOK XXI

An immortal on mortals' account." So she spoke, 425
And Hephaestus quenched his divinely blazing flame,
And yet again within its banks Scamander coursed,
And its flow relinquished rage, and halted the twain,
For Hera stayed them. But her spirit yet smarted,
For the gods sustained their strife, grievous and grating, 430
Their inclinations most martially contentious.
And entirely cacophonous their contending,
And reverberated Earth, and all Olympus
Pealed as with a trumpet. And Zeus heaven-enthroned
Allowed it, indulging his laughter, finding it 435
Comical that gods immortal cavorted so.
Then forbore they no longer, for Ares, breaker
Of bucklers, began the broil, first toward Athena
Bounding, brazen his spearpoint, rebuking her thus:
"Wherefore again, dog-fly goddess, elicit you 440
Gods with gods to fight, uncontrolled your recklessness?
Have you forgotten exhorting Diomedes,
Tydeus' son, to wound me; and yourself openly
With spear to attacked me, rending my handsome flesh?
Thus now, it appears, shall you provide recompense 445
For your transgression." So saying, he assaulted
Her aegis, frightful, tassel-flown, against which Zeus'
Own lightning little prevails; thereon murderous
Ares stormed, launching his spear. But ceded she ground,
Taking to her stout hand a stone reposed upon 450
The plain—great, jagged, and black—that men aforetime
Reckoned a bound'ry marker. With this she stymied
Ares' rage, thwacking his neck, unnerving his limbs.
Across a quarter acre staggered he crashing,
Befouling his features with ash, and rattled his 455
Armor about him. But Pallas Athena laughed,
Proclaiming aloud and addressing wingèd words:
"Fool, perceive you not, to this day, how much mightier
Than you, who dare oppose me, I profess myself?
Accordingly shall you effect your mother's curse, 460

Who in anger against you concocted this ill,
For abandoning the Argives and assisting
The overweening Trojans." Thus speaking her piece,
She averted from Ares her radiant eyes.
Him then laughter-loving Aphrodite guided   465
By the hand, and was removing him a'mutter
Much and groaning hard, his breathing barely resumed;
But when the goddess white-armed Hera beheld her,
Spoke she unto Athena disapprovingly:
"For goodness' sake, you aegis-bearing child of Zeus,   470
Unwearied one, behold! There again that dog-fly
Amid the warriors escorts Ares, bane of men,
Away from warfare's fury; but have you at her."

So she spoke, and Athena well-heartened pursued
And, rushing Aphrodite, smote her sturdily   475
On the bosom, enfeebling her knees where she stood;
And her heart dissolved. So upon plenteous earth
Lay the two outspread and, parading about them,
Athena admonished in wingèd words: "Just so
In the maelstrom be those who bolster the Trojans   480
Against the breastplated Argives, and so be they
Stalwart and steadfast even as Aphrodite—
Testing my might—has to Ares' assistance come;
Then long before now were this discord determined,
And the well-peopled city of Ilium sacked."   485
Thuswise she pronounced, humoring white-armed Hera.
But earthshaking Poseidon to Apollo spoke:
"Phoebus, wherefore stand we apart, we two? Befits
It not, given others have engaged. More shameful
It were shunning fight to return to Olympus,   490
To the brazen threshold afore the house of Zeus.
Begin then, because you are younger begotten;
Suits it not that one earlier born and wiser
Commence. Dullard, how witless your spirit within!
Remember you not the travails we twain alone   495

BOOK XXI

Withstood among the Olympians at Troy, that time
We came at Zeus' command in service to lordly
Laomedōn, a year's duration, fixed our wage,
Our taskmaster he, his command set upon us?
Constructed I a wall about the Trojan town, 500
Exceedingly fair, expansive, that the city
Ne'er demolished be; and you, Apollo, herded
His sleek shambling-gaited kine amid sylvan spurs
Of many-ridgèd Ida. But when expended
Were the gladsome seasons ending our indenture, 505
Laomedōn defrauded us, releasing us
With impudent report, stating he would tether
Our feet and hands above and sell us to islands
In distant locations; indeed he intended,
Gripping battled bronze, to detach our very ears; 510
Thus, aggrieved we departed, angered for the gain
Agreed to but given not. Now on his people
Confer you your favor, no effort devoting
To punish the impudent Trojans—destroying
Their offspring completely, their doting spouses too." 515
Then Phoebus Apollo, far working, responded:
"Shaker of earth, deranged would you consider me,
For quarreling against you on mortals' account.
Forlornèd they that flourish like foliage afire,
Fleetingly feeding on fruits of the field, only 520
To falter and fail. But, forthwith discontinue
We this strife, to their own devices leaving them."
So stating he retreated, shamed for contention
With his uncle. But his sister railed against him,
Even Artemis queen of feral beast and wood, 525
This admonitory word addressing: "Flee you,
O far-toiling god, to Poseidon providing
Dominion? Bear you his idle boast, O petty
Godhead apparent, impotent your marksmanship,
Aimless as wind? Nevermore will I welcome you 530
As once aforetime in our father's halls, boasting

537

Amidst heaven's dwellers that you would openly
Fight with Poseidon." Thus she spoke, but Apollo,
Who from a distance toils, answered not. However,
The reverèd wife of Zeus waxed wroth, reviling   535
The archer queen: "How now resolve you, irreverent
Rogue, to gather yourself against me? No facile
Foe am I considered that you engage me thus,
Bow-bearing though you be; since Zeus against women
Fashioned you a lion, that you slay whomever   540
You might of them. Far better your slaughtering beasts
And deer throughout the wood than contending amain
With your superiors. Continue nonetheless
To assay the fray that you ascertain how much
The sturdier I be should you encounter me."   545
Therewith in her left hand snared she the other's hands
By the wrists and, deploying her right, unshouldered
Artemis' gear, and grasping her very weapons—
Much smiling the while—contused her about the ears,
Writhing every which way; and poured the rapid darts   550
From out her quiver forth. Then Artemis decamped,
From queen Hera flown in tears, even as a dove
Cowering from the falcon in a clefted rock,
Unreachable nor likely to be caught; so fled
Artemis in tears, weapons wasted where they lay.   555

But to Leto spoke Hermes, slayer of Argus:
"Leto, in nowise shall we fight; hard to bandy
Blows were it with a spouse of cloud-summoning Zeus,
For among the immortals vaunt you openly
To have vanquished me once in battle." So he spoke,   560
And Leto gathered the arrows and curvèd bow
Scattered randomly amid the smoke-thickened swirl,
And reclaiming her daughter's equipment returned.
But the maiden, arrived at the palace and bronze
Threshold of Zeus, sat weeping at her father's knees,   565
While fluttered about her her fragrant apparel,

BOOK XXI

And her father, Zeus Cronidēs, embracing her,
Made inquiry, gently and cheerfully laughing:
"Who now of heaven's sons, dear child, has wantonly
Molested you, open transgression committing?"   570
And replied the chapleted pretty one, huntress
Of the resonant chase: "Your own wife attacked me,
Father, even white-armed Hera from whom quarrel
And dissension impend o'er humankind." Such their
Exchange to the other each. But lord Apollo   575
Entered holy Troy, troubled o'er the city's well-
Fashioned fortifications, lest the Achaeans
That day demolish them past destiny's decree.
But the other immortals heavenward returned,
Some furious, others exultant, and reposed   580
Them aside their cumulus-gathering sovereign.

But Achilles continued to butcher alike
Both the Trojan host and its sturdy-hoovèd steeds.
And as when smoke upcurling ascends Olympus,
Emitted from a burnt and taken town, and wrath   585
Of Zeus impels it, travail and ruin alike;
Thus cast Achilles privation and reversal
On Troy. And the elder, lord Priam, positioned
Atop the imposing parapet saw monstrous
Achilles and afore him in dread disarray   590
The Trojan host retreating, and assistance none.
Groaning then, and from the wall descending groundward,
He rallied the gates' glorious guardians all:
"Gatekeepers, part you and open set the portals
'Til the city receive those dispersed in retreat,   595
For here labors Achilles, master of tumult,
Harbinger of tragedy. But whensoever
They repose, behind the wall ingathered, fasten
The double doors, denying Danaan warriors
Entry within." So he proclaimed, and they unlatched 600
The gates, unbarring the bolts; and the gates, yawning

Wide and unlocked, brought deliverance, as bounding
Toward Achilles, Apollo parried Trojan doom.

Meanwhile, escaped the Trojans within the city
And towering walls, with dust from the plain begrimed 605
And sere with thirst, while Achilles insensately
Assaulted them; for most fearsomely had fury
O'ertaken his heart, and lusted he for glory.
Then had fallen towering Troy to Argive force
Had Phoebus not prodded the goodly Agēnōr, 610
Antēnōr's son, a warrior steadfast and stalwart.
Taking his stand aside him, he granted him grit,
Providing protection from havoc's heavy hand.
Then leant he on the oak, self-enveloped in mist.
So Agēnōr, now noting Achilles, sacker 615
Of cities, stood still; and apprehensive at heart
And immesnsely dismayed, addressed his spirit thus:
"Alas, if I flee ahead fearsome Achilles,
There where the others confoundedly are driven,
In disgrace thus o'ertaken shall I butchered be. 620
But should I quit them, incited by Achilles,
Son of Peleus, and flee elsewhere from the city
To the plain, relying on Ida's glens and spurs
To shelter me in thickets, then, at eventide,
Having laved me in the river and cooled myself 625
Of sweat, to towering Troy might I yet return.
But wherefore within me communes my spirit thus?
What if he ignore me from city plainward gone
Only to bolt and capture me on quickened foot?
Then were there no avoiding unyielding demise, 630
For beyond pertinacious is his reckoning.
And what if I encounter him a'front the town?
His flesh, I gather, also yields fully to bronze,
And his is but a single life and men regard
Him mortal, though Cronidēs allot him glory." 635
So saying, he collected himself, awaiting

Achilles; and the spirit, worthy within him,
Prepared for violence and warcraft. And even
As the pard proceeds from out the copse and thicket,
Confronting the huntsman opposed her, nor fearful 640
Nor fain to flee when hearing the howling of hounds,
And anticipating her, the huntsman smites first
With dart or thrust, yet even thus impaired, the pard
Persists in scathing savagery, whether gouging
Him or gored; so stalwart Antēnōr's offspring, 645
Goodly Agēnōr, stood to assay Achilles,
His buckler before him to all sides well balanced,
Hefting his spear and shouting loud to Achilles:
"Indeed, glorious Achilles, you would fain expect
This day to take the lordly Trojan town, you fool! 650
Rather, abundant yet the heartache awaiting
On Troy's account. Within her we stand, numerous
Our folk and valiant, that on account of parents,
Spouses, and sons protect Troy; rather, be it you
Who here encounter ruin, however dreaded 655
And daring a warrior." He spoke, hurling the spear
From his hand, and neath the knee hit Achilles' shin,
Missing him not; and the greave of newly smithied
Tin terrific rang; but back from the stricken tin
The bronze rebounded, nor skewered, for the bounty 660
Of Hephaestus obstructed it. And Peleus' son,
Next upon godlike Agēnōr turned; but glory
None did Apollo grant, but wrested Agēnōr,
Enshrouded in mist away, despatching him forth
From the fray, unseen, to peaceful evanescence. 665

But contrived Apollo to distance Achilles
Away from the folk; thus, likened to Agēnōr
Throughout, did Apollo far-working approach him.
And Achilles hastened forward to o'ertake him
And pursued him the length of the wheat-bearing plain 670
Toward deep-eddied Scamander, sequestering him—

Achilles by shrewdest devising of Phoebus
Apollo e'er nearing to close on Agēnōr,
But e'er failing just slightly his effort. Meanwhile
The remaining Trojans were routed in flight, glad   675
To be standing within the walls, the town a'throng;
Nor dared they the while to await one another
Outside th' assaulted town, ascertaining perchance
Who had persisted and who in melee perished;
But impetuously poured they within the walls,   680
Whomever his footing and knees might enable.

~ Book XXII ~

The Death of Hector:
Hector Dragged by the Heels Behind Achilles' Chariot Around the Barrow of Patroclus

THE TROJANS SAFE WITHIN their walls, Hector alone remains to oppose Achilles. Meanwhile, at the plain's far corner, Agenor halts Achilles' pursuit by revealing himself as Apollo in disguise. An indignant Achilles denounces the ruse, claiming he could have killed many more had he not been thus misled. As Achilles rushes toward the city, Priam and Hecuba, alarmed at his approach, separately plead that Hector retreat.

Hector ponders a course of action, concerned for what others will say if he flees—especially Polydamas, whose advice to withdraw into the city Hector had previously spurned. Hector is also concerned for the reproach of the women of Troy, who will deem Hector's demise—affecting them all—a matter of his own doing. He considers laying aside his weapons and begging for mercy, promising a return of Helen and her possessions; no, promising half the wealth of Troy itself. Hector, however, wakens from this reverie, fearful that playing the suppliant, he will be slain "like a woman." With Achilles' quickening approach—perceived in a kind of slow motion as Hector considers and rejects alternatives—Hector's resolution fails, and he flees, with all Troy watching from the battlements.

Hector's life "passes before him" as he traverses familiar peacetime locales, the twin sources of river Scamander and the washing basins earlier visited by the mothers and daughters of Troy "when there was peace, before the Greeks arrived." No prize footrace *this*, but the contest for Hector's life! Achilles pursues Hector three times around the walls of Troy—Achilles ever on the verge of overtaking Hector; Hector ever on the verge of escaping Achilles—but neither quite succeeding. Thus, the slow-motion quality, as in a dream—capture ever imminent, escape all but succeeding—a spooled-out-like-toffee effect. As noted, even before the pursuit itself, Achilles' onrush and approach are narratively "slowed," each "phase" punctuated, as it were, by Hector's thought processes: Achilles drawing near, Achilles drawing nearer yet, Hector "noticing" Achilles' approach, Hector actually "aware" of it, etc. All slowed and segmented to wring from this excruciating finale the maximum emotional and psychological effect. The depiction, dare we say, is entirely "modern."

Zeus harbors misgivings about Hector's approaching demise. He is disabused of them by Athena, who descends to the plain. Achilles continues his pursuit, ever driving Hector from the walls of Troy, from which Hector hopes for a downpour of weapons in his defense. Achilles would have then overtaken Hector had not Apollo furnished Hector one last surge of energy. Achilles signals the Greeks refrain from participation, which can only diminish Achilles' glory. Zeus weighs the protagonists' fates in his scales. Hector's sinks downward, and Apollo abandons him.

Athena encourages Achilles, proposing for the greater glory that the two join in slaying Hector (Achilles offering no objection). Disguised as Hector's brother Deïphobus, Athena then goes to Hector, proposing the two of them join in slaying Achilles. After an exchange of taunts, in which Achilles rejects Hector's plea for respectful treatment should he fall, the two exchange ineffective spearcasts. Hector calls to Deïphobus for another spear, but Deïphobus is no longer present. This, Hector now realizes, signals his doom. Wanting to secure a glorious death—a delusional thought; no one "dies well" in Homer—the sword-wielding Hector rushes the charging Achilles. However, Achilles lands his weapon in Hector's unprotected neck, rebuking Hector's foolish belief that Patroclus' death go unavenged. Dying in Achilles' armor (looted from Patroclus), Hector pleads that his body be returned to Troy for proper rites. Achilles categorically rejects the request, saying he (Achilles) would sooner devour Hector than see him properly interred. Nor will Achilles entertain an offer of ransom (a position he ultimately abandons). The Greeks gather around the dying Hector, marveling at his might and size, jabbing him with their own spears even so.

Achilles' desire to attend the corpse of Patroclus, lying by the ships, will wait. Piercing Hector's ankles and attaching his corpse to the back of his chariot, Achilles singularly defiles Hector's body, dragging it three times around the barrow of Patroclus, all Troy looking on, Priam and Hecuba

BOOK XXII

included. Achilles has been drained of all humanity. Knowing his own death ordained and approaching, he is now the dead dragging the dead. Slaying Hector in Achilles' own armor, Achilles has effectively slain himself in effigy.

Hecuba's and Priam's laments are recounted, and Priam restrained from exiting the city to plead for Hector's body. The laments reach the ears of Andromache, sequestered at her handiwork within the palace. She mounts the wall and beholds her fallen husband, swoons at the loathsome spectacle, and bitterly laments, focusing on the fate now to befall the fatherless Astyanax—soon to become a social pariah amid peers and adults alike. It is still day 30.

Troy, synaesthetically imagined—and as dictionally supported in the Greek—is an eye aflame in tears [*Il.* 410-411 (433-44)], the miniaturization, as it were, of Scamander aflame in the fight at the river. This is the masterstroke and capstone of a surrealistically conceived and developed narrative, including the stand, pursuit, and death of Hector—his death (no less than Achilles') from the outset affirmed, feared, and anticipated; Hector's death the death of Troy itself.

⁂

So huddled they throughout the town, routed like deer,
Shedding their sweat, drinking deep and quenching their thirst,
At rest on the heartening ramparts while the Greeks
Earnestly approached the wall, shields against shoulders.
But Hector, bound by intractable fate, endured   5
Where positioned a'front the city's Scaean Gates.
Then unto Achilles spoke Phoebus Apollo:
"Wherefore pursue me, swift-footed Achilles, you
Of mortal lineage, I a god immortal born?
Not the least ascertain you my divinity   10
For all you incessantly rage. Concerns you not
The energy now exerted, routing Trojans
To the town whilst you challenge me here in battle?
Unknowing death am I, and never to be slain."
Then a' burst with spite answered godlike Achilles: 15
"You have deceived me, far-working god that you are,

Cruelest of divinities, diverting me here
From the wall; else had warriors enough yet tasted
The dust ere entering the town. Now of ready
Fame have you deprived me, easily saving them 20
Since deities no fear of deterrence admit.
Revenge would I exact of you were power mine."

So he spoke, hurtling sturdy-hearted toward the town,
Speeding like a prize-capturing chariot horse
That lightly passes o'er a full expanse of plain; 25
Just so swiftly plied Peleus' son his feet and knees.
Him old Priam first beheld, speeding brilliantly
Across the plain, likened to the star appearing
At harvest time—and brightly gleam its beams amid
The starry host of nighttime's darkened gallery— 30
The star men call Orion's Dog, shining brightest
Of all, and yet a dire harbinger, visiting
Toilsome fatigue on disconsolate mortalkind;
Even so hard glittered the bronze upon the breast
Of careening Achilles. And old Priam moaned, 35
Beating his head and uplifting his hands, calling
Aloud as he groaned, entreating his dear Hector,
Who, furious afore the gates, awaited combat
With swift Achilles. Outstretching his arms to him
Old Priam implored and spoke:

                    "Hector, dear offspring, 40
I entreat, await not that man alone, with none
To hearten you, lest quickly you encounter doom,
Slain by Peleus' son, since mightier far is he,
And ruthless. Would the gods as I do valued him,
Then would vultures and dogs devour him uninterred 45
As would heartache's affliction renounce my being,
For he has bereft me of offspring, well numbered
And brave, slaying or selling them off on islands
Outlying. For even today I nowhere note
Those offspring twain, Polydorus and Lycaōn, 50

Among the Trojans here mustered within, the two
By Laothoë begotten, among women
A princess. But if yet alive amid the foe,
Then rightly shall we ransom them with bronze and gold
From stores thereof, for many the gifts that name-famed 55
Atlēs bequeathed to his daughter; but if they now
Be dead, to Hades' house descended, then shall grief
Engraft my heart, their mother's too by whom begot;
But briefer the grief to the host entire should you
Escape encounter with Achilles. But enter 60
The walls, my child, a savior to the Trojan men
And women. Deny Peleus' offspring great glory,
Protecting your own life. And for miserable me,
Past the doorstep of senescence, compassion show—
For yet I feel—whom father Zeus will ruthlessly 65
Despatch, enduring numerous ills: my offspring
All perishing, my dear daughters abducted, my
Treasure chambers chastened, my caring children cast
In horrific clash aside, my daughters-in-law
By base Danaan hands dragged off; and my own self 70
Last of all to carrion-eating curs consigned
As I enter my door, when someone by weapon
Propelled or thrust appropriates my life. Even
The dogs that tableside I bred within my doors,
Guardians of my gates, having once gulped my blood 75
Shall lie there, unsettled their hearts in the gateway.
All for the young is decorous when in combat
They fall by bronze defeated and in death reposed;
And though perished, pellucid the beauty about.
But when dogs devour a mortal elder's remains, 80
Tearing his timeworn head, his beard, and nakedness—
Most contemptible among mournful mortals this."

Thus implored King Priam, pulling his hoary hair
Asunder from his scalp, desperate to dissuade him.
And opposite Priam his mother wailed the next, 85

Tearfully unloosing the gathers of her robe
And revealing her breasts, and amid teeming tears
Addressed Hector wingèd words: "Hector, my offspring,
Respect and pity me if breast of mine e'er stilled
Your discomfort to clement forgetfulness lulled. 90
Of this be you mindful, dear child, and fend the foe
From within the walls nor oppose him face to face.
Merciless is he. For should he slaughter you, ne'er
O'er your bier, dear boy begotten of my own self,
Shall I wail nor shall your bounteous wife, but far 95
From us, to the Danaans ships removed, shall dogs
Dispose of you." Thus sobbing his parents addressed
Their belovèd son and offspring, beseeching him.
But they dissuaded him not, abiding the might
Of Achilles' advance.
     Even as a serpent 100
Lies expectant in its lair, having ingested
Deadly toxins, and dread the temper gripping it,
And ghastly its glow'r as it coils aside its den;
Thus even Hector with hardened resolution
Gave not ground, his shield against the wall propped upward. 105
Then, mightily perturbed, he addressed his own great-
Hearted spirit: "Woe and alas! If I enter
The gates, preeminent will Polydamas be
In reprimand since he bade me lead the Trojans
Townward that malignant night when swift Achilles 110
Stirred himself, yet I disregarded him. Better
Far had I listened! But seeing I have ruined
The host, unthinking in my folly, shamed am I
Before Trojans and Trojan wives with trailing robes
Lest another one, worse than I, this tale intone: 115
'Self-confident Hector wreaked havoc on the host.'
So will they say; but for me far preferable
To confront Achilles man to man, slaying him,
And so retire or gloriously perish here.
Or, what if I lay aside my bossèd buckler 120

And heavy helm, propping my spear against the wall,
And myself approach the peerless son of Peleus
And promise him that Helen and all the plunder
With which Alexander loaded Troy-faring ships—
The impetus of this dispute—will we confer 125
On the Atreïdae to carry off; and more,
And in addition, adjudge deserved division
Of everything the town possess, and thereafter
An oath from the Trojans take, by its elders sworn,
That they will naught conceal, by halves dividing all— 130
Yes, the weal complete of the teeming town possessed.
But why considers my spirit such incidents?
May it not befall that proximate I approach,
And he no pity allot me, or otherwise
Compunction show, but slaughter me outright, unarmed, 135
As a woman, once setting my armor aside.
Now is it impossible from oak or boulder
In whatever dalliance to indulge, as maiden
And youth, even as youth and maiden dallying
With the other each. Better the contest forthwith, 140
And by heaven determined allotted the boast."
So he pondered waiting, as Achilles closed in—
Equal to Enyalius, lord of battles,
Shining-helmed warrior—brandishing the Pelian ash,
His fearsome spear; his bronze circumradiant blazing 145
Like glint of incandescent fire or rising sun.

But trembling befell Hector when aware of him,
Nor presumed he longer to remain where standing
But forsook the gate and wall and affrighted fled;
And rushed the son of Peleus after him, in his 150
Fleetness of foot assured. And as a hawk atop
Mountains, quickest of wingèd kind, serenely swoops
O'er trembling dove, it dashing deftly a'fore him,
And he hard a'wing ever after her pursues,
Piercing his cry and his spirit impels him pounce; 155

Just so Achilles, infuriated, followed
As Hector absconded neath the ramparts of Troy,
Plying nimble knees.
                   Past the watch place and swaying
Fig they sped, ever farther from the battlement
Along the wagon track, and traversed the double   160
Fair-flown fountains whence eddy the supply and source
Of swirling Scamander. Warm the water of one,
Venting vaporous fumes as if from glowing fire;
The other, even in summer, frigid as hail,
Or ice, or sleeting snow, all water-formed. And there   165
By the very sources stand the washing-troughs, broad,
Stone-wrought, and lustrous where the wives and fair daughters
Of Troy in days bygone their radiant garments washed,
In peacetime, before the Danaan arrival.
Past these they ran, one fleeing, and one in pursuit: 170
Fled a good man a'fore and ran one mightier far
In pursuit; and wagered they not for hide of bull
Or sacrificial beast—fair prizes apportioned
For fleetness of foot—but for the life of Hector,
Tamer of horses, they vied. And as when single-   175
Hooved horses, prizewinners all, press swiftly about
The turning posts, and ample the prize assigned them,
A tripod perhaps, or fallen warrior's widow;
Just so circled thrice the twain about Priam's town,
The gods themselves looking on.
                            Then among them Zeus,   180
Of gods and mortalkind the patriarch, spoke first:
"Alas, my eyes behold a belovèd person
Pursued around the walls, wherefore sorrows my heart
For Hector who e'er provided me, on highest
Ida's crests and elsewhere atop the citadel,   185
The thighs of unnumbered oxen, and nonetheless
Does Peleus' goodly son pursue him 'round the walls
Of Troy. So come, you gods, bethink you and reflect
If from death he be redeemed or finally slain,

BOOK XXII

Fine though he be, by implacable Achilles." 190
Then answered the goddess flashing-eyed Athena:
"O Father, lightning empowered, dark-cloud ensconced,
What protestation this? Will you again redeem
From grievous death a man long since summoned by fate?
Do it, then. But understand, we other gods all 195
Disapprove." And responded cloud-gathering Zeus:
"Take you courage, dear daughter Tritogeneia,
Rarely ever disclose I my full intention
Though toward you remaining ever kindly disposed,
So take counsel as you will, discarding constraint." 200

So saying, he stirred Athena, already keen,
And the goddess darted down from high Olympus.
But rapid Peleus' son, unceasing his pursuit,
Beleaguered Hector. And as high on mountain peaks
A hound from its hiding extracts a doe, chasing 205
It through hollows and vale, and momentarily
Takes it refuge, thicket bound, yet tracks it the hound
Undeterred 'til the doe be found; even so failed
Hector to escape unrelenting Achilles.
And, for as often as in lunging toward the gates 210
Of Troy he sought protection by the battlement,
That his companions, releasing spears, assist him;
So oft, anticipating him, would Achilles
Toward the plain reroute him, preempting his safety.
As in a dream profits not the man pursuing 215
Another fled before him—profits not the one
To overtake nor the other to flee; just so
Foundered Peleus' son to o'ertake rapid Hector
And Hector to outrun him. But now had Hector
Escaped Death's decree had not Apollo plainly 220
Approached him one last time, inciting his courage
And quickening his knees. And goodly Achilles
Signaled to his companions, tolerating no
Interference, lest another smite him, winning

Acclaim, himself adjudged second.
                                But when four times full   225
They had reached the springs, then the Father extended
His golden scale, setting two lots of grievous death
Thereon—one for Achilles, the other for horse-
Taming Hector—then lifted it by its middle,
And down sank Hector's lot, to Hades descendent,   230
And Phoebus abandoned him. But to Peleus' son
Was bright-eyed Athena manifest and, sidling
Next him, addressed Achilles this wingèd account:
"Now truly I reckon, most glorious Achilles,
Zeus-beloved, that the two of us, slaying Hector,   235
Shall for Argives greater glory gain, and acclaim,
Though insatiate of battle he; for no more
Is his escape allowed, though Phoebus Apollo
Far-working seek to save him, demeaning himself
Before aegis-bearing Cronidēs. But abide   240
You now, taking breath; and I myself will effect
Hector's engagement face to face." So she announced,
And obeyed he, buoyed at heart, and stood settled
Aside his bronze-barbed ashen spear.
                                    But she left him,
To undaunted Hector going, her demeanor   245
Like to Deïphobus in form and forcefulness;
And, approaching nigh, she addressed him wingèd words:
"Dear brother, verily constrains you Achilles,
Herding you headlong around the town; but approach,
Remain we in anticipation, repulsing   250
His attack." Then responded great Hector, flashing-
Helmed: "Deïphobus, truly aforetime were you
Best of all my brothers, of Hecuba begot
And lordly Priam, but the larger my regard,
Seeing you for my sake venture without the wall,   255
Observing my plight whilst the others bide within."
To him again the goddess flashing-eyed rejoined:
"Rest assured, dear brother, that my queenly mother

BOOK XXII

And father, and acquaintances all, earnestly
Entreated my staying in Troy, so tremble they   260
Before that man. But greater grown within my heart
The grief on your account. But now for warfare's sake
We unify, nor be our spears ungenerous,
That we discern if Achilles vanquish us both,
To the hollow vessels bearing the bloodied spoils,   265
Or if perchance by your hand o'erpowered he be."
Thus with dulcet voice and guile deceived the goddess.

And when they approached yet closer to each other,
Then to Achilles glancing-helmeted Hector,
Standing firm, first spoke: "No longer, son of Peleus,   270
Will I flee as thrice before I fled 'round Priam's
Towering town, lacking mettle to encounter
You man to man; but now commands me my spirit
To confront you, slay or be slain. But approach you,
And summon we gods to witness—let them peerless   275
Guardians be to these our understandings: no ill
Shall I commit thee if Zeus vouchsafe me prevail,
But sequestering your armor, will I return
Your remains to the Argives, and likewise do you.
Then, with infuriate glance from beneath his brows   280
Spoke Achilles: "Unbearable Hector, lecture
Me not of understandings, as understandings
None exist between lions and men. Thus also
Oaths between lambs and wolves that coupled bide poorly
Evermore. Even so is it impossible   285
That we two e'er reconciled be. Neither shall we
Broker guarantees until one or the other
Fail, sating the bullhide-shielded Ares with blood;
So bethink you of valor's devices. And now
May your warrior's unswerving arm and spearmanship   290
Sustain you, likelihood of flight relinquishing,
Since Pallas shall presently prepare my weapon.
Now this moment remunerate my comrades' pains,

Whom you slew run amok with your spear." So he spoke
And poised his far-shadowing spear, releasing it; 295
But valiant Hector, seeing it approaching nigh,
Evaded it, crouching low, conscious of the cast.
And the brazen spear, o'erflying him, passed firmly
To the ground; but the goddess Athena grasped it,
Delivering it to Achilles, by Hector, 300
Shepherd of the host, unseen. And Hector addressed
Peleus' peerless son: "You have missed, nor appear you,
O godlike Achilles, to augur my demise,
Though thinking so—but that was mere glibness of tongue
And knavery to effect my forgetfulness 305
Of grit and fortitude. Not fleeing shall I fall,
Spear planted in my back, but passing through my chest
Should heaven permit. Now, in turn, my brazen spear
Evade. Might you but welcome it whole to your flesh
And, with your decease, abate battle for Trojans, 310
Trojan misadventure that you are." So speaking,
He poised his far-shadowing spear and hurled, fully
Striking Achilles' shield nor missing it the least;
But distantly it ricocheted. And indignant
Hector fumed for the faltered shaft's trajectory, 315
And he stood despondent, wanting some other spear.
Then loud he called to white-shielded Deïphobus,
Seeking a second spear, but he had disappeared.
And Hector intuited his fate, thus speaking:

"Woe and alas, the gods now summon me to death 320
For I deemed the warrior Deïphobus nearby,
But bides he within the city, and Athena
Has deceived me. Verily, my death approaches,
Its coming expected and ineluctable.
Thus aforetime did it gratify Cronidēs 325
And his offspring, far-working Apollo, they who
Full-heartedly earlier rendered assistance.
But here also hastens destiny, unhindered.

BOOK XXII

Yet I perish nor worthless nor wanting glory,
But working feats that future ages recollect." 330
So pronouncing, he withdrew his whetted weapon,
Pendent aside his flank, a hefty, fearsome sword,
And upgath'ring himself leapt like an eagle down
That high through the darkened overcloud darts dashing
To the plain, seizing a tremulous lamb or hare; 335
Just so descended Hector brandishing his sword.
And Achilles rushed upon him, his heart o'erflown
With fury—afore him his shield, fair and richly
Dight, assurance fixed; his four-horned helmet nodding.
And heavy set about its crest gestured feathers 340
Of gold, handiwork of artisan Hephaestus.
As stands a star distinct, conspicuous aloft,
Starry Hesp'rus, fairest to heaven afforded;
Even so upflared Achilles' blade refulgent,
Poised atop his sturdy hand as he determined 345
Good Hector's demise, closely eyeing his body,
Its yielding point to find; for everywhere his skin
Protected stood by Patroclus' brazen armor,
The protection he had plundered from Patroclus
Once piercing him through. But an opening appeared 350
Where collarbone divides shoulders and neck, even
The throat granting readiest entry to ruin;
Even there, as Hector rushed upon him, goodly
Achilles unleashed his weapon straight, and athwart
His Neck the shaft directly passed, but the weighted 355
Spear dissevered not the jugular, permitting
Him answer Achilles. Collapsed he then in dirt,
And over him goodly Achilles exulted:

"Hector, somehow you imagined while despoiling
Patroclus that you would endure, encountering 360
Not my measure since I loitered afar, you fool.
Though no helper to him, much mightier the one who
Loitered by the ships to loose your limbs thereafter.

555

Ignobly shall mongrels and vultures devour you,
Whilst for him the Argives fit funeral afford." 365

Then feebly answered flashing-helmeted Hector:
"By your life, your knees, and parents I implore you!
Suffer not that dogs devour me by the Argive
Ships, but of bronze and gold be given abundance,
Gifts my father and dear mother shall afford you, 370
And unto them restore my corpse that the Trojans
And Trojan wives confer the meed of fire in death."
Then, with angry glance from neath his brows, swift-footed
Achilles responded: "Beg me never, you dog,
By parents or by knees. Would that fury and spleen 375
Compelled me partition your remains, and myself
Down them raw, venging your villainy, as surely
As none now respire to deliver you from curs;
Not should your parents bring and apportion ransom
Ten- and twentyfold while promising tenfold more! 380
No, not though Dardanian Priam bid your weight
In gold be paid, not even then shall your queenly
Mother bemoan the bier whereon she placed the son
Of herself begotten; but scavengers ingest
You evermore." And even while dying, uttered 385
Flashing-helmeted Hector: "Well do I know you
And expect nothing more, nor would importuning
The outcome remake. Truly iron-made the heart
Within your breast. But deliberate, lest I mete
The measure of heaven's revulsion against you, 390
When Apollo and Paris subdue you, for all
That you are valorous a'fore the Scaean Gates."

Even as Hector spoke, death's veil enveloped him
And departed his soul away, to Hades flown,
Deploring its doom, abandoning fortitude 395
And fire. And Achilles addressed him though perished:
"Lie thou dead. My destiny will I accept when

BOOK XXII

Zeus ordains it, and the other immortal gods."
So he proclaimed, from the corpse extracting his spear,
Placing it apart, and from shoulders down started 400
Stripping the blood-stained armor. And thronged the other
Argives near, admiring the physique and wondrous
Splendor of Priam's son, nor spared they piercing his
Corpse in their approach. And thus might someone, peering
At his comrade, say: "More facilely is Priam's 405
Son now managed than when earlier he torched the ships."
Thus would one speak and, nearing, pierce him yet again.
But once swift-footed Achilles had despoiled him,
Among the Danaans declared he wingèd words:
"Dear comrades, Achaean leaders and commanders, 410
Since the gods vouchsafe the slaying of this warrior
Who greater damage wrought than all other Trojans
Combined, come, assay we now the town, divining
Dardanian intent—whether they abandon it,
Now that this man defeated lies, or endeavor 415
In his absence to endure." But wherefore detains
Me such discourse? Lies there a corpse aside the ships,
Unlamented, uninterred, even Patroclus,
Whom, whilst yet alive and quick my knees, I never
Shall forget. Yes, though Hades' souls forgotten be, 420
Yet recollects my spirit dear Patroclus' own.
But come, singing a paean, you Achaean sons,
Return we to the hollow ships, this corpse in tow.
With Hector's demise have we garnered great glory—
A very god revered by the foe throughout Troy." 425

So he spoke, crafting depravity for valiant
Hector. A'rear both his feet he pierced the tendons,
Heel to ankle, connecting oxhide thongs therethrough,
Next attaching feet to car, the head left dragging;
Then, having mounted, hoisting the glorious arms 430
Within, he smartly whipped his horses, speeding them
On, and willingly they flew. And ascended dust

From under Hector thus conveyed, and dark the hair
To either side outflown, and polluted with filth
The head so fair aforetime. But now had Cronus' 435
Son surrendered Hector, savagely assaulted
By the foe in his native land—thus was his head
With dust defiled.
     And his mother, tearing her hair,
Flung far her glimmering veil, lamenting aloud
As she looked on her son. And Priam emitted 440
A pitiful groan, and o'erwhelmed the populace
Throughout the town by gnashing and lamentation.
And likest resembling this was it: as though all
Beetling Troy were a'simmer in flame. And labored
The people to master maddened Priam, anxious 445
To pass the Scaean Gates and so entreating them,
Rolling in refuse the while, each person calling
By name: "Refrain you, dear subjects, and acquiesce,
For all your concern, to my quitting the city
Alone, to th' Achaean vessels gone, imploring 450
Achilles, that worker of outrage, that perhaps
He pity my condition and advancing years.
A father has he too, I deem, like unto me,
Even Peleus, that begat and raised him, a bane
To Troy, but torments inflicting, past others all, 455
On me, rampantly slaying my sons in their prime.
Yet lament I not as much for them, however
Great my grief, as for one alone, whose hapless loss
To Hades' house delivers me—yes, for Hector.
Ah, would he had perished in my embrace, our fill 460
Of heartache granting to the mother that sadly
Begot him, no less than to me!"
        Thus he bewailed,
And the townsfolk their threnody added thereto,
And 'mid the Trojan women commenced Hecuba
Unnerving lamentation: "My dearest offspring, 465
Alas! how shall I harbor the harrowing grief

Of your death, you who throughout the town were ever
Vaunted every hour, benison and protection
To the Trojan folk, who greeted you god-likened?
Whilst yet alive you exulted being lauded, 470
But now you repose, by death and fate confounded."
So she spoke weeping.
                        But Andromache knew naught
Of Hector's demise—for tarried faithful report
Apprising her that he beyond the gates remained.
But wove she a pattern, purple and double-plied, 475
In the tow'ring palace's women's apartments,
Broidering flowers of various hue thereon.
And summoned she her fair-tressed attendants throughout
The house, to place a tripod within the fireplace,
That hot bathing be readied for Hector whene'er 480
He returned from battle—unwitting she, knowing
Not that radiant-eyed Athena had reposed him
Far from bathing neath Achilles' hands. But hearing
The lament and wailing from the wall she staggered,
Dropping the shuttle from out her hand, and hailing 485
Her fair-haired attendants, spoke: "Attend and follow,
Two of you, that I ascertain what deeds betide.
Heard I the voice of my husband's reverent mother,
And heaves the heart within my breast unto my mouth,
And benumbed the knees beneath me, for verily 490
Some evil approaches Priam's sons—be distant
Its tidings from my ear—and dolefully I fear
That intrepid Achilles has isolated
Valiant Hector, severed apart from the city,
Compelling him onto the plain, that he forget 495
The fearlessness aforetime possessing him;
For tarried he not 'mid the multitude but ran
In a rush, to none surrendering primacy."

So saying, hastened she heart-stricken through the hall,
Like a maenad, by attendants accompanied. 500

But when arrived to the wall and assembled throng,
There by the turret she stopped, glancing murkiness,
And afore the city saw Hector dragged about,
And headlong ran the steeds, untiring, trailing him
Toward the Argive vessels. Then midnight's murkiness 505
Descended on her visage, enveloping her,
And backward toppling, she panted forth her spirit,
From off her head dismantling the fair apparel—
The headscarf, the diadem, and entwinèd band,
And veil that golden Aphrodite erstwhile had 510
Conferred, when coruscating-helmeted Hector
Had escorted her, his bride, from Eëtion's house,
Lavishing limitless nuptial gifts. And around
Stood her sisters-in-law and other kin, who propped
Her up among them, distraught unto death itself. 515
But when again respiring, her spirit reclaimed,
Addressed she the women, yet heaving as she wailed:
"Ah Hector, alas, to a single fate seem we
To have been begotten, you in Priam's palace,
And I in Thebes 'neath wooded Placus, Eëtion's 520
Abode, father to my childhood and uprearing,
Father and daughter ill-fated, cruelly decreed.
Would he had never begotten me! Now go you,
Departing to Hades' domain beneath the depths
Of earth, but me you abandon to wasting woe, 525
A widow in your halls, a mere infant your son
Of our haplessness born. Nor will you profit him,
Hector, nor he you, seeing you are gone. Escape
This Achaean war as he may, labor and grief
Shall yet be his fortune hereafter as others 530
Purloin his lands. His day of orphanhood deprives
A child of playmates, his demeanor despondent,
Ever tearful his eyes, and needful his effort.
He attaches to his father's friends, one tugging
By the tunic, another by the cloak; and those, 535
Briefly commiserating, tender him a cup,

Moist'ning his mouth but staying not his thirst. A child
Twin-parented repels him from the feast, smiting
Him hard, and with words of revilement reproves him:
'Be ruined, you! No father of yours enhances   540
This companionship.' Then comes the child returning,
Tearful, to his widowed mother—Astyanax,
Who, on his father's knees, aforetime fed solely
On marrow and heartening meats; and when slumber
Intruded, ceased he from his childishness, asleep   545
In a downy bed or on his nurse's bosom,
Encompassed by bounteous fortune. But having
Lost his doting father, torments will attend him,
My "Astyanax"—a Trojan designation—
Since you, Hector, alone "commanded the city,"   550
Protecting its turrets and stately entrances.
But now by the bekèd ships from kin sequestered
Shall slithering worms consume you, once mongrel dogs
Make provender of your repose, hapless your corpse.
Yet raiment lies within the halls, finely woven   555
And fair, women's handiwork. The same to blazing
Flame will I consign, of no enjoyment to you
Since perished be their benefit, but a tribute
To your glory from the women and men of Troy."
So spoke she weeping, and wailed the women withal.   560

~ Book XXIII ~

The Immolation of Patroclus, the Games in His Honor

ACHILLES AND THE MYRMIDONS do honor to Patroclus' body. Achilles prepares a funeral feast, slaughtering and spitting beasts for dinner. Achilles is "taken" to the quarters of Agamemnon, where a heated cauldron awaits, that he bathe himself of blood and gore before dinner; but he refuses until the completion of Patroclus' rites.

After all have dined, Achilles retires to the seashore. There, as he falls asleep, the ghost of Patroclus appears, demanding the rites of burial. Patroclus wishes, among other things, his remains placed aside Achilles', since Achilles—should he need reminding—will himself shortly die. Their attempted parting embrace is frustrated by Patroclus' ghostly state.

Agamemnon the next morning sends men, mules, and wagons to cut and gather wood. The pyre is supplied, a funeral procession held, and offerings of shorn hair made to the dead. Achilles slaughters additional animals, including two of his own dogs and, lastly, the twelve Trojan youths he had earlier taken captive—piling all atop the pyre, crowned by Patroclus' corpse. Achilles' actions are here the excessive counterpart of his earlier wrath and resolve: Achilles an absolute, everything done to excess. Meanwhile, Apollo preserves Hector's body from further decay.

The pyre will not ignite, whereupon Achilles beseeches the winds while Iris visits them to secure their cooperation. A charming scene ensues (call it comic relief). Iris finds the winds dining chez Zephyr. When they see her, each desires she sit beside him. Messenger that she is—and always headed somewhere—she declines the invitation, delivers Achilles' message, and speeds off. The winds dramatically undertake Iris' bidding. The pyre ignites, and Achilles and the Greeks spend the night in offerings of libation and lamentation. Pyre and vigil endure the night through.

Patroclus' remains are gathered into a golden urn, a tomb is raised, and the ritual concluded.

Achilles then hosts funeral games, the doings extended over the better part of Book 23. These include chariot and foot races, boxing, wrestling, spear-casting, discus, archery, and more. The occasion, over which Achilles magnanimously presides and for which he provides lavish prizes, signals his societal reintegration. The games also mimic thematic concerns and battlefield doings to droll effect. Thus, in the first competition, Achilles intends to award the first-place prize to the second-place finisher, only to be reminded of the impropriety of taking another's prize (as his was taken at the start of the poem). In the final contest, with Agamemnon a contestant, Achilles acknowledges the king's superiority to all and, without contest, urges him cede first prize to the younger contestant, Agamemnon taking second prize. The king magnanimously agrees. Thus the prize taker at the poem's start becomes the prize giver at its conclusion. For the rest, the games are largely played amid derring-do, advantage taking, mishap, guffaws, and foolish talk—the battlefield's bravura boasts, gruesome wounds, and slaughterings turned to cuts, scrapes, bruises, and petty argument over cheating and unfairness. How different and appropriately tailored these games vis-à-vis the foreboding reference in Achilles' pursuit of Hector:

> Fled a good man afore and one mightier far
> In pursuit; and wagered they not for hide of bull
> Nor sacrificial beast—fair prizes apportioned
> For swiftness of foot—but for the life of Hector
> Tamer of horses they vied... (22.171-175)

At one point an argument develops between Idomeneus and Oïlean Ajax concerning who has taken the lead in the chariot race, as the contestants are still somewhat far distant. As if the argument were itself one of the funeral games, the suggestion is made, amid wager, that Agamemnon declare the "winner."

The book spans days 30–33. The ghost of Patroclus appears the night of day 30. The wood is cut and the pyre ignited on day 31. The pyre burns throughout day 32. The games occur on day 33.

BOOK XXIII

Thus prevailed wailing throughout the town; but the Greeks,
To their vessels and vast Hellespont arriving,
Scattered each to vessel his own; yet Achilles
Disallowed the Myrmidons be thus disbanded
And 'mid his battle-loving companions declared: 5
"You swift-steeded Myrmidons, trusted comrades all,
Release not your single-hooved horses from their cars,
But with horses and chariots approach, lamenting
Patroclus; for of such are the dead deserving.
Then, discharging morbid-measured lamentation, 10
Our steeds shall we unfasten and together sup."

So he directed, and commenced they their keening,
And Achilles led. Then, lamenting, prompted they
Their fair-maned horses thrice to encircle the corpse,
And Thetis first among them wakened wailing's want. 15
Wetted the sand, and wetted the warriors' armor
With tears—so mightily the inciter of rout
They lamented. And Achilles, again leading
The wretched threnody, laid his man-slaying hands
On his comrade's chest: "Hail, dear Patroclus, even 20
In Hades, for now I fulfill what aforetime
I promised: that I would deliver Hector, here
Dragged for the dining of dogs, and sever the throats
At your pyre of twelve preeminent Trojan youths.
Such my rage at your slaying." Thus he spoke, dealings 25
Most horrid for Hector devising, lying prone,
Bereaved, in the dust at the bier of Patroclus.
And from every horse unfastened they its harness
Of gleaming bronze, and the neighing horses reposed,
And themselves were num'rous seated aside the ship 30
Of swift-footed Pēleïdēs, who next prepared
For them a bounteous funeral feast. Many
The silken bull there buckled beneath the razor,

And multitudinous ewes and muttering goats,
And amply fatted white-tusked swine to lengthwise stretched   35
Upon Hephaestus' spitted flame, and everywhere
'Bout the carcasses blood, by flask retrievable.

But lordly swift-footed Achilles was hastened
Unto goodly Agamemnon, the Argive chiefs
Travailing greatly in their doings, so irate   40
For his companion he. But when finally arrived
At Atreïdēs' quarters, the clear-voiced heralds
Bade a hefty cauldron on the fire positioned,
Thinking thus to convince Achilles cleanse himself
Of blood and gore. But he refused them quite, an oath   45
Adding thereto: "No! By Zeus who is loftiest
And best of gods, to no bathing will I submit
Before lifting Patroclus on high to his pyre,
Heaping a barrow about him, and shearing off
My hair, since ne'er again shall torment similar   50
This transpierce my spirit while lingering among
Mortalkind. But consent we the while to banquet,
However meaningless. But morningtide entreat
You the folk, lord Agamemnon, to upgather
Kindling and promptly hasten as befits the dead—   55
When descending, consigned unto nether darkness—
That obdurate flame discharge them from sight away,
And the host in its affairs find reaffirmance.

So he ordered, and attentively they complied.
And supped they, each warrior readying his repast,   60
Nor did any spirit encounter deficient
Bounty of feasting. But having sated desire
For viands and drink, proceeded each to his hut,
Reposed. But Peleus' son 'mid the Myrmidons lay,
Deep groaning, by the strand of the thunderous sea   65
In an alcove where battered the breakers ashore;
And when slumber's languid descent had taken hold,

BOOK XXIII

Dissolving his disquiet, for vastly wearied
His marvelous limbs with hurtling after Hector
Unto stormy Troy, there lit on him the spirit 70
Of woebegone Patroclus—the semblance his own
In stature, aspect, and pleasing voice, and attired
The like withal—which, pendent o'er Achilles' head,
Addressed him thus: "So sleep you, having forgotten
Me, Achilles: to me whilst living dutiful, 75
Indifferent in death. But burial bestow,
Assuring my deliverance unto Hades.
The souls, the semblances of those once laboring,
Detain me, at a distance removed, forbidding
Alliance with the departed beyond Styx' bound, 80
That I aimlessly amble the broad-gated house
Of Hell. But I earnestly implore: extend me
Your hand, for never again from Hades returned
Shall I forge once offered to flame's reclamation.
Nor again shall we, alive, apart from our dear 85
Companions, sit conversing. But abhorrent fate
Has gaped for me, the fate appointed me even
At birth; and you yourself, O godlike Achilles,
Destined also to die beneath Troy's prosperous
Parapet. And this too I implore, provide it 90
Accomplished if persuasion accomplishment grant:
Repose my remains adjacent yours, Achilles,
That they together rest, even as together
We were reared in Peleus' house that time Menoetius
Brought me, a lad, unto your land from Opoeis 95
Because of manslaughtering rage, when in arrant
Folly I slew Amphidamus' son, intending
It not, in disdain over dice. Then knight Peleus
Accepted me into his home, nurtured me,
And e'er your attendant denominated me. 100
Thus contain us a single cinerary urn,
The amphora of gold, by your mother furnished."

567

Then answering, inquired swift-footed Achilles:
"Wherefore, O belovèd head, are you hither come
Charging me in each respect? For in each respect, 105
Shall I accomplish all and, as you enjoin me
Shall obey. But approach yet closer though it be
But briefly, that we embrace withal, discharging
Lamentation's fill." Thus uttering, outstretched he
Loving arms, enveloping naught as the vision 110
Vanished, vapor-like, beneath the earth, gibbering
Gently. And Achilles, with wonderment o'erwhelmed,
Arose and drove his hands together, declaiming
A word in lament: "Behold, even in Hades'
House remains there something, a phantom, a spirit; 115
Though mind be absent from it, for throughout the night
Has Patroclus' spirit loomed hapless over me,
Tirelessly repining, and in particulars
Instructing me, so wondrously like to himself."
So he declared, prompting tearful want within each. 120

And rosy-fingered Dawn illumined them the while
They wailed about the wretched corpse. But Atreidēs
Despatched men and mules from every hut and quarter,
Gathering wood; and staunch the one who bestirred them,
Mēriones, the manly Idomeneus' squire. 125
And forward they pressed, wood-cleaving axes in hand
And tautly woven ropes, and before them the mules;
And ever uphill, downhill, sideward, and aslant
They advanced. But when to spurs of many-fountained
Ida come, immediately they set themselves 130
To cutting high-crested oaks, sharp-edged their bronze;
And ever o'er-keeled the oaks amid crack and crash.
Next the Argives rived the trunks apart, binding them
Behind mules; and the mules uptore the earth as they
Labored plainward hard trampling through the underbrush. 135
And the woodcutters too carried logs, for so bade
Them Mēriones, manly Idomeneus' squire.

BOOK XXIII

Then were they offloaded, recumbent by the shore,
Where Achilles planned a barrow for Patroclus
And himself. But when the limitless panoply   140
Of cloven wood had been offloaded, reposed they
Together, thronged and waiting.
                              Then Achilles bid
The bellicose Myrmidons begird them with bronze
And attach, each man, his horses to his chariot.
And they arose, assuming their arms and mounting   145
Their chariots, charioteers and warriors alike.
In front advanced the charioteers and, following,
A footman's contingent, a host eclipsing count,
And in the middle bore his comrades Patroclus.
And garb-like they covered the corpse with strands of hair   150
Dispersed thereon; and behind them, grieving, Peleus'
Son took hold the head, for peerless the companion
Whom he hasted on his harrowed path to Hades.
But come to Achilles' appointed location,
Reposed they Patroclus' corpse, skyward upheaping   155
Bounteous wood about him.
                         Then, again, swift-footed
Achilles bethought himself. Positioned apart
The fire, he cut and detached a golden lock, rich
Outcrop, erstwhile preserved for river Spercheius,
And vexingly spoke, surveying the wine-dark sea: 160
"O Spercheius, in vain my father promised you
That, homeward finally coming to my native land,
I would shear my hair to you and offer holy
Hecatomb—betokening manhood's arrival—
And, furthermore, make offering of fifty rams   165
Without blemish unto your circulant waters,
Where stand your altar and redolent sanctum. So
Vowed Peleus, fulfillment denied of his promise.
But now, deprived of return to my fatherland,
I tender this lock to Patroclus' possession."   170
Thus speaking, he lodged the lock within his comrade's

Hands, and within them all awakened keen lament;
And radiance of day had descended on their tears
Had not Achilles approached lord Agamemnon,
Saying: "Atreidēs, since to you especially 175
Defers the Danaan host, with sadness be they
Sated, and presently disbanded from the pyre,
And bid them their supper prepare; and we who hold
The deceased most dear will attend to the balance,
The chiefs helping.
                  And Agamemnon, king of men, 180
Upon this notice straightway disbanded the folk
Amid the balanced ships, but those attentive most
Abided there about the corpse, upheaping wood
To fit the pyre, five-score cubits long extended,
And topmost upon the pyre positioned the corpse, 185
Disconsolate. And flayed they many goodly sheep
And sleek shambling-footed cattle, assembling them
Before the pyre. And great-souled Achilles gathered
The fat from about them and therein enfolded
The corpse from crown to foot; and the flayed carcasses 190
Heaped thereon; and positioned he twain amphorae
Of honey and oil, leaning them aslant the bier;
And straightway hefted horses four, towering-necked,
Upon the heap and, doing so, groaned hopelessly.
Nine were the hounds beneath his table hankering, 195
And of a twain Achilles slashed the jugular,
Casting the dogs thereon. And twelve valorous sons
Of the great-hearted Trojans despatched he with bronze,
Thus perpetrating odious deeds against them.
And thereupon incited he the ferrous rage 200
Of fire, to fan throughout, and lamented aloud,
Calling on his comrade, addressing him by name:
"Hail, my dear Patroclus, even in Hades' house,
For now fulfill I all aforetime promised you.
The flame fully envelops twelve valorous sons 205
Of the great-hearted Trojans, these aside you set;

BOOK XXIII

But Hector, Priam's son, no flame but dogs shall feed."
Thus threatening, he spoke, but no dog would devour
Hector, for Aphrodite, Zeus' daughter, kept dogs
From Hector day and night and oil-anointed him—   210
The scent ambrosial, rosy sweet—that Achilles,
Dragging Hector's body 'round, not compromise it,
And o'er him poured Phoebus Apollo from heaven
To plain a dolorous cloud, protecting the place
Whereon the corpse reposed lest the sun, untimely   215
Penetrant, despoil members, muscle, and marrow.

But Patroclus' pyre ignited not. Then again
Divine swift-footed Achilles bethought himself.
Positioned apart the pyre, presented he prayer
To the Zephyr winds and Boreas, West and North,   220
Fair offerings setting apart, and fervently—
The while pouring libation from beaker of gold—
Prayed winds descend, that conflagration claim the corpse
And that quickened to kindling be timber and beam.
Next Iris intervened, to the winds transmitting   225
Achilles' petition. With temperate Zephyr
Were they all together found for feast. And Iris
Halted from her haste upon the stone-hewn threshold;
And beholding her, uprose the winds and beckoned
Her each to himself. But Iris, speaking, declined: 230
"Unseated I remain, for to Oceanus'
Streams I hasten—where the Ethiopians burn
Hecatombs unto the gods—that I fitly see
My share of sacred feasting; but prays Achilles
Temperate Zephyr and North Wind arrive, and vows   235
Offerings fit to awaken the pyre to flame
Whereon Patroclus lies for whom the Argives grieve."
Thus speaking, she departed. And with wondrous din
They ascended, deafeningly driving the clouds
Before them. And swiftly blown, they attained the sea,   240
And bulked the billow beneath their assailant blast;

And on amply soilèd Troy they swooped, descending
On the pyre, and plentifully plumed the wondrous
Wasting flame. And contentedly the livelong night
The flame persisted on the pyre; and through the night,   245
Dipping his two-handled cup, Achilles drew wine
From a golden bowl, outpouring it and soaking
The ground, e'er summoning the spirit of hapless
Patroclus. And as father bewails his offspring,
The while burning his bones, a son newly betrothed   250
Whose death to his blighted kin is catastrophe;
So wailed Achilles for his comrade while burning
His remains, circling the pyre in crippling lament.

But when the morning star emerged, courier of light
To the wakening world and herald of saffron-   255
Robèd Dawn o'er oceans suffusing—even then
The pyre subsided, its dim embers abating.
And homeward turned the winds across the Thracian tide,
Inciting teeming turbulence. Then Peleus' son
Repaired apart the embered glow and laid him down,   260
Expended; and sweet sleep o'erpowered him. But those
With Atreidēs approached him together, their rush
And ruckus awakening sleeping Achilles,
And upright arising, proffered he this response:
"Son of Atreus, and you other Panachaean   265
Lords, quench you first the smoking pyre with sparkling wine,
Even that o'er which force of fire held mastery.
Next collect we Patroclus' bones, Menoetius' son,
Distinguishing their residue; for readily
Apparent they, midmost to the pyre positioned,   270
While th' other objects smoldered at the burning bounds,
Men and horses mingled. Then place we the remains
Within a golden urn double-layered in fat
'Til I myself to Hades summoned be. But none
Need you labor erecting a plenteous barrow   275
But such solely as befits. But in aftertime

Do you Danaans build it broad and towering,
You by the benched vessels abiding when I die."
Thus he, and obeyed they swift-footed Achilles.
First dampened they the site with darkling wine, wherefrom 280
Th' inferno had risen and soft settled the ash,
And tearfully resettled the ashen remains
Of their gentle companion in a golden urn,
Enfolding it in double-layered fat, storing
The urn, and with soft lawnèd cloth o'erlaying it. 285
Then patterned they a tomb about the pyre, setting
Foundation, and nimbly substructured a barrow,
Preparing to retire.
           But stayed them Achilles
Thus assembled, seating them in an arena,
And from his ships he paraded prizes: tripods, 290
Oxen, horses, cauldrons, and comely-accoutred
Women, spirited mules, in order setting them:
A woman for the winner, deft her decorate
Handiwork, and an ear-handled tripod holding
Measures two and twenty for him finishing first. 295
And as second prize a mare apportioned he, six
Years old, unbroken, with a mule foal in her womb;
And as third prize a cauldron by fire unbefouled,
A fair cauldron, four measures its depth, yet glossy;
And as fourth place he tallied two talents of gold; 300
And as fifth a double-handled urn by flame yet
Untouched. Then arose he addressing the Argives:
"Son of Atreus, and you other well-greaved Argives,
Such the prizes awaiting the charioteers.
If we Achaeans in some other's honor now 305
Contested, surely would I take the foremost prize
To store within my hut, for you know my horses
Outperform by far all equine excellence,
For immortal they stand and Poseidon bestowed
Them on Peleus, my father, whence they passed to me. 310
But naught will I compete; neither will my horses,

For they have forfeited the glory of so kind
A charioteer, who oft did liquid unguents pour
Upon their manes when laving them in glinting rills.
For him they stand mourning, manes upsweeping the ground,   315
Hearts gripped by grief. But you others, prepare yourselves
Throughout the host, whosoe'er of the Achaeans
In his horses and finely fitted chariot trusts."
So spoke Peleus' son, and the swift-paced charioteers
Bestirred themselves.
                 And first risen was Eumēlus,   320
King of men, dear son to Admētus, consummate
In horsemanship. And next arose Diomedes,
Leading Tros' horses beneath the yoke, even those
Of which he had prior dispossessed Aeneas
Though Apollo had Aeneas himself preserved;   325
And next rose Atreus' son, fair-haired Menelaus,
Zeus-sprung, and rapid the steeds tethered neath their yoke:
Agamemnon's Aethē and his own Podargus.
Mare Aethē had Echepolus Anchises' son
Unto Agamemnon Atreïdēs gifted,   330
Thereby evading conscription to windswept Troy,
Preferring his homestead in spacious Sicyōn,
Abundant his riches by Cronidēs conferred.
Menelaus led her neath the yoke, and eager
She, exceedingly, to race. Next, Antilochus   335
Prepared his fair-maned horses, he the peerless son
Of kingly Gerēnian Nestor, Neleus' son,
Who nurtured in Pylos the swift-footed horses
Attached to his car. And approached his sire, for his
Edification holding forth—amiably   340
Toward one so prudent:
                 "Antilochus, although young
Yourself, yet have Zeus and Poseidon favored you
And with every means of horsemanship endued you,
Wherefore no special need see I for lecturing,
For you relish the turning post's wheeling and whirl.   345

And yet, your horses slowest in the race appear,
And thus I deem them your undoing. Others' steeds
Are speedier far, but the drivers deficient
In cunning the likeness of yours. Accordingly,
Dear son, consider you each ilk of cleverness, 350
That no accolade, circumventing you, escape.
The woodsman by cunning more than power prevails;
The helmsman, by cunning upon the wine-dark sea,
Securely calms his prow afore buffeting winds;
And by cunning outstrips his foe the charioteer. 355
The one man, on his chariot and steeds reliant,
Wheels heedlessly past, wide to every rail; hurtle
His steeds o'er the raceway, wanting restraint and rein.
The other, with wily wits but substandard steeds,
Focuses on the turning post and flies close by, 360
Consistently well applying the oxhide reins,
Gripping them tight and watching the man in the lead.
The marker I now describe—remember it well—
Standing near a fathom's level above the ground,
A withered stump of oak or pine which plaguing rain 365
Decayeth not, and two white stones to either side
Are firmly fixed against it at the course's crux,
And 'round about it propitious the racing plain—
A monument perhaps to someone long since passed,
Or made the turning post of races long ago, 370
And now has dread Achilles designated it
His turning post. Upon it pressing hard, close drive
Your steeds and car; and yourself, leaning slightly left
Within your fitted car, to rightward set the goad
And, shouting, free your grip and grant your horses rein, 375
And let the near horse edge the marker close, the wheel's
Well-crafted nave grazing lightly the marker's side—
With regard for avoiding the stone—lest perchance
You disable your horses, destroying your car,
Delighting others but disparaging yourself. 380
No, dear boy, be highly circumspect; for if there

You outmaneuver your competitors, no one
Shall outrun or overtake you, though pursuing
On goodly Arion, swift steed of Adrastus,
Descended of bloodline divine, nor upon steeds   385
Of Laomedōn, laudably indigenous."

So saying, Nestor, son of Neleus, sat him down,
To his offspring the sum of it all imparting.
And last readied were Mēriones' fair-maned steeds.
Mounting their cars, they next cast lots for position,   390
Achilles scrambling the lots; and outleapt the lot
Of Antilochus, Nestor's son; and following
Him had lord Eumēlus place; and Menelaus,
Spear-famed son of Atreus, aside him; and the next
Mēriones; and finally Diomedes   395
Who, far the best, the outermost position drew.
Stood they arrayed, and Achilles identified
The turning post, far distant on the level plain,
And stationed he Phoenix, his father's follower,
As umpire thereby, to parse and unerringly   400
Reckon the race. And the contestants together
Uplifted the lash, each over his horses' yoke
And, applying the reins, commanded them aloud.
And swiftly they traversed the plain, and neath their breasts
Uprose the dust, lingering like whirlwind or cloud,   405
And streamed their manes upon the coursing gusts. And now
Adhered the cars to bountiful earth, and in turn
Bounded aloft. And the drivers maneuvered well,
Each handler's heart for victory hammering hard,
As hoarsely they hollered to their steeds through the dust   410
Hovering over the plain. But when the steeds neared
The final course, to the hoary sea returning,
Then palpable the worth of each competitor,
His paces decidedly proven. And the fleet-
Footed mares of Eumēlus, Pherēs' son, hurtled   415
Straightway to win; and steady behind came the steeds

BOOK XXIII

Of Diomedes, bred by Tros—not far behind
But near to heel, ever seeming to mount upon
Eumēlus' car, his back and ample shoulders warmed
By heavy breath, for directly overhead strained   420
The snouts of the hastened steeds.
                              And now had Tydeus'
Son outstripped him straightway or driven to a draw,
Had not Apollo grown rankled and swatted forth
From out his grip the lissome lash. Then, angered, shed
He tears, seeing the mare streaming swiftlier still   425
While his own steeds dithered, stymied for want of whip.
But not unaware was Athena of Phoebus'
Duplicity and, swiftly come to Tydeus' son,
Restored him his lash and revitalized his steeds;
Then, incensed, assaulted Eumēlus and shivered   430
His horses' yoke. And swerved his mares to every side,
The pole rolling groundward released. And Eumēlus
Himself was cast from the chariot aside the wheel,
Abrading his elbows, skinning his chin and nose
And battering the brow above his eyes; his eyes   435
Welling up, and subdued was the the drift of his speech.
Then Tydeus' son, tilting his steeds to the side, drove
On, outdistancing the others, for Athena
Bestowed great glory and galvanized his horses.
And fair-haired Menelaus, Atreus' son, pursued,   440
But Antilochus addressed his father's horses:
"Forward now, you two, display your utmost speed!
With the horses yonder I bid you now contend,
Those of Tydeus' son, wise-hearted Diomedes,
Which presently grey-eyed Athena empowers,   445
Vouchsafing their driver renown. But the horses
Of Menelaus quickly o'ertake, and be not
By them outdistanced, lest be you discredited
By Aethē, mare that she is. But why falter you,
Good steeds? For this much is absolutely certain: 450
Nestor, shepherd of the people, shall take no note

577

Of you hereafter but sooner with razored bronze
Dispose of you, should our dereliction result
In a meaner prize. With utter speed have at them,
And this will I myself contrive and implement, 455
That at the narrows they be stymied, rest assured."

So he spoke, and they, affrighted by their master's
Reprimand, more swiftly onward ran; then straightway
Stalwart Antilochus espied a narrowing
In the road ahead. On the surface lay a rift 460
Where gathered winter waters, having partly gouged
The raceway; the ground recessed and furrowed about.
There drove Menelaus anticipating none
To pass abreast of him. But Antilochus turned
His single-hoovèd horses, driving them outside 465
The track, and followed after him, tilting somewhat
To sideward. And Atreïdēs stood terrified
And shouted to Antilochus: "Antilochus,
Recklessly you drive; sooner rein your horses in!
Here the way narrows but widens further ahead; 470
Thus wasteful of my chariot will you wreck us both."
So he spoke, but Antilochus the more grimly
Exerted the goad as one gone deaf. And as far
As a young man flings a discus from his shoulder,
Released in assay of his strength; thus the distance 475
They kept. However, the mares of Menelaus
Recoiled, for strenuously back he jolted them
Lest the single-hooved horses collide on the track,
The well-plaited chariots o'erturning, and themselves,
In their fervency for victory, heaved dustward. 480

Then fair-haired Menelaus reprovingly spoke:
"Antilochus, lives no mortal more malicious;
Be damned, since we Danaans falsely deemed you wise.
And yet, not oathless will you bear this prize away."
So he pronounced and, calling to his horses, said: 485

BOOK XXIII

"Abstain you not, I command, nor grief-stricken stand.
Fatigued before yours will their feet and knees weaken,
Lacking resilience." So he spoke and they, fearing
Their master's rebuke, the faster ran, more briskly
Abreast the others drawing. But the Danaans,   490
Settled in the gathering place, looked on, viewing
The horses traversing the plain through the dust. First
To discern was Idomeneus, Cretan leader,
Positioned apart from the throng, highest of all
As outlook installed. And hearing Diomedes   495
Shouting, regarded it readily from afar;
And he sighted the horse to the fore hard heaving,
A bay entire but for the marking white upon
Its forehead imprinted, curvatured like the moon.
He rose, and among the Achaeans spoke, saying: 500
"Friends, Argive commanders and lords, do I alone
Discern the steeds or do you besides? Others take
The lead, it now appears, and other the driver;
For Eumēlus' mares, from the outset in the lead,
Now traverse the plain, apparently impeded,   505
They that excelled on the outward course. Verily
I first surveilled them approaching the turning post,
But now have they wholly vanished from my eyesight
In each direction. Did the reins perchance escape
The charioteer, powerless he to properly   510
Pilot the post, scanting the turn whereat he crashed
To earth, his car undoubtedly destroyed, frighted
The failing mares, and falt'ring, by terror beset?
But standing, observe you for yourselves, for little
See I clearly; yet still that man seems Aetolian   515
To me, a commander among the Achaeans,
Even Diomedes, horse-taming Tydeus' son."

Then spoke Oilean Ajax ill favoredly:
"O Idomeneus, aforetime yet fatuous!
Yet from a distance the high-stepping horses pound;   520

Nor youngest appear you among the Achaeans,
Nor keenest your vision, yet constant your yammer.
Among his superiors falters the braggart's boast.
The same mares that earlier led lead yet, even
Those of Eumēlus, and he himself stands erect, 525
Securely controlling the reins." Then the Cretan
Commander cantankerously retorted thus:
"Ajax, insuff'rable fool, clueless in counsel,
In all things deficient among the Danaans,
And dense! Come, a tripod or cauldron let us stake, 530
Calling upon Agamemnon, son of Atreus,
To determine the leaders—which mares crediting—
Schooling acquired at a cost." So he responded
And straightaway did lesser Ajax, much angered,
Arise in reply, their strife exacerbated, 535
But for Achilles' sound-minded intervention.
"None the longer, lords Ajax and Idomeneus,
With recriminations assail you each other,
For that were unseemly. With others contend you,
Otherwise and elsewhere. But now be seated both, 540
Here in the gathering place, and follow the steeds,
As here for victory's prize are they soon arrived;
And then know all, each for himself ascertaining,
The stature of Argive steeds: which straggle behind,
Which capture the lead." Thus he spoke, and Tydeus' son 545
Hurtled hard as he drove and, lashing, applied stripe
Upon stripe from his uplifted arm, and his steeds
In their gallop e'er thundered traversing the track,
And smitten with dust was the charioteer—his
Car o'erlaid with gold and tin—accelerative 550
Behind his horses' hooves, the wheel-rim impressions
On the low rising dust indistinguishable.
Toward the finish line he lunged, unstinting the sweat
That groundward dripped from the horses' torsos and necks.
And from his dazzling car Diomedes himself 555
Vaulted down, the goad inclining against the yoke.

BOOK XXIII

Nor the least loitered Sthenelus but speedily
Claimed the prize on his spirited comrade's behalf,
The woman and twin-eared tripod to take away,
And himself loosed the horses from under their yoke. 560

In second place drove Antilochus of Neleus'
Line, more shiftily than swiftly guiding his steeds
And passing Menelaus. The latter, howe'er,
Maneuvered his steeds at a quick-closing distance.
And by space maintained by horse behind a chariot, 565
One drawing its master forward—and strains the horse
Toward the hindmost section of the car ahead it,
For hugs it extremely close behind, and barely
Breathes the distance between them pummeling the plain—
Even by play thus minimal Menelaus 570
Trailed Antilochus though at first the former lagged
The distance of a discus toss. Nevertheless,
Had Menelaus pulled ahead—for the mettle
Of fair-maned Aethē, Agamemnon's mare, increased
Apace—and had the contest been further prolonged, 575
Menelaus had surpassed him to the finish,
Nor doubtful left the issue.
                                But Mērionēs,
Idomeneus' stalwart squire, flew forth, a spear's cast
Behind Menelaus, for his fair-maned horses
Slowest stepped of all, least expert of drivers he; 580
And last behind the others trailed Admētus' son—
His chariot careening, his steeds hard driven.
And swift-footed Achilles at the very sight
Of him took pity, and amid the Danaans
Stood speaking wingèd words: "By far the superior 585
Man with his single-hoovèd horses lags last, but now
Let us allocate him second place, as befits,
With Diomedes assured first place to relish."
So he spoke and all agreed, even as he bade.
And now had he awarded the mare—the Argives 590

Affording approval—but that Antilochus
Great-hearted Nestor's offspring uprose and replied,
Claiming his due of Achilles, son of Peleus:
"Achilles, great my agitation to follow
If thus you handle me, for you plan to pilfer 595
My prize, well knowing that Eumēlus' car and steeds
And himself as well suffered harm, upstanding though
He be. Had he only beseeched the immortals,
Sooner than last had he completed the contest.
But should you pity and adjudge him deserving, 600
Your hut bears a surfeit of cattle, bronze and gold,
And with domestics and single-hoovèd horses.
Choose you therefrom, a finer prize awarding him,
Doing so this moment, that the Argives applaud.
But the mare will I not forgo. On her account 605
Come all who may and assay my battle prowess."
So he spoke, and goodly swift-footed Achilles
Smiled, rejoicing in Antilochus, much beloved
Of his heart; and responded he in wingèd words:
"Antilochus, should you bid me give Eumēlus 610
Whatever else as further prize from out my hut,
This even shall I do. His shall be the corselet
From Asteropaeus taken; of bronze it is,
And bright, with circleted patterns of outpoured tin.
And plainly precious shall he reckon it." He spoke, 615
And directed his companion Automēdon
To fetch it forward, which he did, conferring it
On Eumēlus who delighted receiving it.
Then in turn uprose Menelaus among them,
Sorely vexed at heart, enraged at Antilochus; 620
And a herald conveyed the sceptre to his hand,
A token of reverence amid the Danaans,
Whereupon the godlike warrior addressed them thus:
"Antilochus, wise erstwhile, account for yourself!
Staining my esteem have you sabotaged my steeds, 625
Frenziedly driving your own, inferior far.

Come now, you Achaean captains and commanders,
Impartially adjudge this matter, lest someday
One of the bronze-panoplied Danaans declare:
'Antilochus by deceit o'er Menelaus   630
Prevailed, acquiring the mare as prize, his horses
Worse, yet worthier he in virtue and degree.'
But aright shall I adjudge it myself, biding
No disapproval whate'er from the Danaans,
Sound my judgment deemed.
                          Zeus-nurtured Antilochus,   635
Approach as befits and stand you a'fore your steeds
And car, and grasp the slender lash which aforetime
You smartly applied; and thus reposing your hand
On your horses, swear by earth shaker Poseidon
That you stymied me without subterfuge or scheme."   640
Then in return answered prudent Antilochus:
"Patience now, for younger am I than you, O King,
And you elder and better born. You know youth's flaws,
Their nature and source, for thoughtless are youthful ways,
And faulty young minds withal. Thus govern patience   645
Your heart. I consign you the mare I have taken.
And should you require whatever worthier else
Of my possessions, for the asking be it yours,
Lord Menelaus, Lest enduringly I stand
The outcast of your heart and knave before the gods."   650
So great-hearted Nestor's son declared, entrusting
The mare to Menelaus' command. And gladdened
His spirit, even as stalks in a quavering
Cornfield, its kernels moisture-kissed to ripeness grown;
Thus did your heart, Menelaus, rejoice within.   655

Then to Antilochus addressed he wingèd words:
"Antilochus, my indignation now subsides
Since ne'er earlier wast reckless or unruly
Though youth in this instance over reason prevailed.
Think not again a superior to outwit.   660

In truth, by another were I not persuaded,
But for my sake have you endured and labored much,
You, your father, and your family. So, rightly
Accept I your apology, surrendered now
The mare, though mine from the outset, that these regard   665
Me dutiful at heart and never overproud."
He spoke, giving the mare to Noēmōn, comrade
Of Antilochus, to lead off, and Nestor's son
Thereafter claimed the bright cauldron, third prize, as his.
And received Mēriones two talents of gold   670
For his finish as fourth, but the fifth place remained
Unclaimed, even the two-handled urn. On Nestor
Achilles conferred it, through the Achaean throng
Conveying it; and, arrived at his side, enjoined:
"Take this now, dear elder, and reckon it treasure,   675
A remembrance of buried Patroclus, for ne'er
Again shall we greet him among the Achaeans.
This tribute I give for the giving, for nowise
In boxing will you contend; neither in wrestling,
Nor enter the ranks of the javelin hurlers,   680
Nor run the race; for grievous old age besets you."
So saying he presented the urn, and Nestor
Received it gladly, responding with wingèd words:
"My son, all have you verily spoken aright,
For my limbs, each and in the aggregate, dear friend,   685
No longer as aforetime thrive; nor do my arms
Dart lightly from my shoulders. Would I were youthful
And firm my strength, as when the Epeians buried
Lord Amaryncēs at Buprasium, and his sons
Appointed prizes honoring the king. Then proved   690
Nobody my peer, not one of the Epeians,
Nor of the Pylians, nor of the proud Aetolians.
In boxing I beat Clytomēdēs, Ēnops' son,
And in wrestling Ancaeus of Pleurōn, risen
Against me; Iphiclus in racing I outran,   695
Able though he was; and outthrew Polydorus

BOOK XXIII

And Phyleus in casting of lances. In chariot
Alone the two sons of Actōr exceeded me,
Crowding me out with their horses—outsizedly
Keen for success, the best prizes lying at hand. 700
Twin brothers were they: the one drove working the reins,
The other applying the goad. Thus earlier.
But now let younger men the like tasks undertake,
Assured my resignation to relentless years
Though once 'mid warriors I prospered preeminent. 705
But come, for your companions recommence these trials,
Whilst I happily take this urn, rejoiced my heart
That you remember me, nor am I forgotten,
Either as Danaan or friend for the honor
Befitting me. And may the gods reciprocate 710
With soul-sustaining courtesy." So he professed,
And traversed Achilles the vast Achaean throng,
Close harkening unto Nestor's commendation.

And next placed he prizes for batter of boxing.
A drudging mule he brought and tethered to its place 715
Amid the gathering, six years old, unbroken,
And most burdensome to break; and for the worsted
A twin-handled goblet appointed. Then among
The Danaans he stood and said: "Son of Atreus
And you other Argives well-greaved, for these prizes 720
Bid we two warriors, the best among us, upraise
Their hands and have at it. To whom lord Apollo
Grants persistence amid the assembled Argives,
With burly burro head he to his hut; but he
Who is bettered the two-handled beaker shall bear." 725
So he spoke, and instantly stood a dauntless man,
Self-confident in boxing, even Epeius,
Panopeus' son; and slapped he the muscular mule
And speaking, said: "Let him approach who will homeward
Bear the two-handled cup as prize. With the mule, will 730
No other Danaan, I determine, depart,

Flattening me with fists, for best I boast to be.
Admittedly is battle not my bent; one proves,
As it appears, not peerless in every pursuit.
For thus I aver, and eventuate it thus,   735
His flesh will I flatten, breaking him bone from bone;
So tarry here his relatives, hightailing him
Away, when hammered by my hands." He spoke, and hushed
They remained, quite speechless. Euryalus alone,
A godlike man, uprose opposing him, offspring   740
Of Mecisteus, offspring of Talaüs who once
Journeyed to Thebes for Oedipus' funeral rites—
After Oedipus' demise—and there had bested
Cadmus' every son. And spear-famed Diomedes
Readied undaunted Euryalus, heart'ning him   745
With words and wishing him the winner absolute.
About him he girded a waistband, thereafter
Attaching thongs, leather-wrought, of a rustic ox.
Thus readied both, they entered upon the contest,
And raising rugged hands against the other each,   750
Headlong hurtled, exchanging blows, their hands a blur.
Grim their grinding jaws and slid the sweat profusely
From their limbs. But seeking an opening, goodly
Epeius pounced, pummeling his foe on the cheek;
Nor upright managed he longer, for even there   755
His glorious limbs toppled groundward. Even as when
A northerly wind extracts a fish from shallows
Onto weed-entangled sand, and dusky the wave
O'er blanketing it; so floundered Euryalus
When battered. But great-souled Epeius uplifted   760
Him, setting him aright, and surrounding him his
Comrades thronged, escorting him through the assembly
As he trailed his feet, spat clotted blood, and sideward
Drooped his head; and they straightened him lamebrained and dazed,
And themselves went procuring the two-handled cup.   765

Then for the Achaeans Achilles selected

BOOK XXIII

Additional prizes, a third competition
For wrestling's travail: for the winner a tripod
Firepit-worthy, by the Danaans determined
A dozen oxen's worth. And a woman, mistress   770
Of manifold handiworks, the value assessed
Of heifers three, he allotted to the loser.
And he uprose, to the Danaans announcing:
"Advance, whoever you be, this undertaking
To accomplish." Thus he asserted, and arose   775
Great Ajax, Telamon's son, and many-minded
Odysseus adept in advantage. Then the twain,
Having girt them, entered upon the assembly,
Closely grappling one with the other and mighty
The clamp of their muscular hands, their feet planted   780
Firmly apart like to rafters forward slanting
Atop a tow'ring roof by some famed craftsman fit
To afford him a refuge from furious winds.
And creaked their backbones neath the strenuous tugging
Of meaty hands, and sweated they in rivulets;   785
And many the welt raised crimson on their shoulders
And ribs emergent, as ever toward victory
They struggled amain for the tripod's possession.
Succeeded not Odysseus to trip and topple
Ajax; nor Ajax him, for the firm Odysseus   790
Held fast. But when at length they had likely fatigued
The well-armored Danaans, then to Odysseus
Spoke towering Ajax, Telamon's son, saying:
"Zeus-born son of Laërtes, devious Odysseus,
Lift you me, or I you; the matter rests with Zeus."   795
He spoke and lifted him, but Odysseus forgot
Not his craft and squarely crimped the back of Ajax'
Knee, unsteadying him, that he was backward thrown;
And toppled Odysseus on his chest; and fully
Flabbergasted stood the folk. And next Odysseus   800
Much-enduring hefted Ajax up, moving him
Slightly from the ground, but managed not to lift him;

However, within Ajax's knee crooked his own,
And tumbled they groundward, one aside the other,
The twain in dust befouled. And now again wrestled   805
They incessantly had not Achilles himself
Arrested them, commanding: "Compete you no more
Nor suffer this travail; the victory is shared.
Step with equal prizes each aside, allowing
Other Argives to compete." So he protested,   810
And they attended and complied and, toweling
Off the dust and grime, were fitted to their tunics.

Achilles next promptly provided the prizes
For fleetness of foot: a silver-fashioned mixing
Bowl, six measures its fill, and far fairest of all   815
Was its finish, since Sidonian men well skilled
In striking handiwork had cannily conceived it,
And Phoenicians o'er the clouded deep had borne it
And, to harbor come, had gifted it to Thoas;
And as ransom for Lycaōn, Priam's offspring,   820
Jason's son Eunēus gifted it Patroclus.
And presently set Peleus' son the bowl as prize,
Honoring his dear companion, for whoever
Fleetest proved in speed of foot. And for second place
He proffered a splendid fatted ox and, for last,   825
A half-talent of gold. And, speaking, uprose he
Amid the Argives: "Up now, you that would venture
Your skills contending thus." So he spoke, and uprose
Swift Ajax, Oïleus' son, immediately,
And many-minded Odysseus, and thereafter   830
Antilochus, Nestor's son, surpassingly swift
Among youths when they raced.
                            Assumed they their stances,
And Achilles signaled the goal and marked the course
From the turning post. Then quickly Oïleus' son
Surged forward, and hastened close after him goodly   835
Odysseus, near as the weaving rod to the breast

Of a fair-girdled woman handily drawing
It in her palms, the spool positioned past the warp,
The rod proximate her breast; even so near ran
Odysseus behind, and his feet trod Ajax' tracks 840
Ere the tracks collected dust. And lit his breathing
On Ajax' ample shoulders the while Odysseus
Ran swiftly behind him. And the Argives shouted,
Cheering wily Odysseus to the limit strained.
But now, come to the competition's final stretch, 845
Odysseus straightway to Athena offered prayer:
"Hear me, goddess, as teammate to my feet attend!"
So he prayed, and listened the goddess Athena
And lightened his limbs throughout, hands and feet alike.
But as finish line and prize approached, then stumbled 850
Ajax—for Pallas Athena impeded him—
Where fallen lay the dung of the bellowing bulls
That Achilles swift-footed had slain for his friend,
And with bulls' ordure were his nose and mouth befouled.
Thus ever-enduring Odysseus claimed the bowl, 855
Being first to finish; and famed Ajax, the ox.
By the horn he stood, holding the hard-working ox
And, spewing excrement, addressed the Argives thus:
"For goodness' sake, the goddess has hampered my run,
She that succors and ever mothers Odysseus." 860
So he declared to their merry amusement all.

Antilochus then laid claim to the final prize,
Smiling the while, thus speaking among the Argives:
"This to you I affirm, my friends, who already
Comprehend it, that the gods to this present day 865
Most deference afford to elders. For Ajax
But slightly my elder is, whereas Odysseus
From an earlier time and generation hails,
An active senior, as they say; yet difficult
For another Argive in racing to engage 870
With exception of resolute Achilles here."

So he declared, paying homage to swift-footed
Peleus' son. And Achilles responded, speaking
To him thus: "Antilochus, not vainly conferred
This compliment of yours, addition deserving 875
Of half a golden talent's worth unto your purse."
This said, Antilochus gladly accepted it,
Placed within his palm.
                      And Achilles thereafter
Conveyed and set before them a far-shadowing
Spear, together with helmet and shield, the weapons 880
Of Sarpēdōn, Zeus' son, purloined by Patroclus.
And arising he spoke to the Argives, saying:
"To collect these prizes combatants twain we call,
Exceptional, to array themselves in armor,
Taking body-rending bronze to hand, making trial 885
Each of the other before the assembled host.
And whoever first reaches the other's fair flesh,
Once incising his armor and drawing blood, him
Will I cede this silver-studded sword—a solid
Thracian sword I procured from Asteropaeus; 890
And retain the twain in partnership the weapons,
And fully feast their heart's content within our huts."
So he spoke, and great Telamonian Ajax
Uprose the first, and opposing uprose stalwart
Diomedes, Tydeus' son. And having armed them 895
At th' assembly's either side, resolutely strode
Centerward for confrontation, glowering grim;
And amazement enthralled the Danaans. And drawn
In their advance toward the other each, thrice engaged
They at close quarters, and thrice together clashed. Then 900
Upon the shield well balanced about thrust Ajax,
Attaining not the flesh for saved him the corselet
Behind his shield. But o'er the shield strained Tydeus' son,
Ever seeking to light upon Ajax's neck
With taper of luminous spear. Then verily, 905
Apprehensive for Ajax, the Argives bade them

BOOK XXIII

Stop, equal prizes taking. And to Tydeus' son,
Achilles, the long sword allotted, conferring
It with scabbard and decorate belt.
       Then offered
Achilles a quantum of iron crudely cast   910
Which the fearsome Ëëtiōn was aforetime wont
To hurl; but him had swift-footed Achilles slain,
Loading the iron upon his ships with other
Possessions. Then stood he, announcing to the men:
"Up now, you entrants to this contest. The taker   915
Of this shall five years full sufficient iron have.
Remote though his farmstead, his shepherd need nowise
Procure iron from town. His needs will this suffice."
So he apprised, and staunch Polypoetēs arose,
And godlike and stalwart Leonteus, and Ajax,   920
Son of Telamon, and persistent Epeius.
Took they their stand in order arrayed, whereupon
Epeius grasped the mass and whirling flung it forth,
And chortled the Argives seeing it. Then in turn
Did Leonteus, scion of Ares, cast. And third   925
Hurled Ajax, son of Telamon, from meaty hand,
Surpassing the others' casting points. But when next
Polypoetēs battle-staunch took hold the iron,
Then, as herdsman flings his staff afar, and flies it
O'er trundling folds of kine; just so far released he   930
The iron beyond the assembled, and clamored
The folk aloud. And Polypoetēs' companions
Arising, to their hollow ships carted the prize.

For archery, Achilles next reckoned prizes,
Iron-dark axes, ten twin-headed, ten single,   935
And taking the mast of a dark-prowed ship, drove it
Into the sand, and binding twine about its foot,
Attached a trembling dove, bidding the Danaans
Aim and shoot: "Whoever shall strike the fearful dove,
Collect he the double axes, taking them home;   940

And who sunders the thread while avoiding the bird,
Less accomplished his shot, worth single axe alone."
So he spoke, and king Teucer uprose enormous,
And uprose Mēriones valiant attendant
Of Idomeneus. And next from a brazen helm   945
Withdrew they lots, Teucer shooting first, and awesome
The release. However, having failed to commit
To Phoebus Apollo his share of firstling lambs,
Begrudged him lord Apollo and missed he the bird
Although splitting the twine beside its foot wherewith   950
The bird was bound, and the bitter dart utterly
Loosened the line. And upward flew the dove, the line
Languishing below, and loud shouted the Argives.
Mēriones, at the ready, speedily snatched
The bow from Teucer's hand—having held an arrow   955
As Teucer took aim—and vowed timely sacrifice
Unto Apollo far-shooting: a glorious
Hecatomb of firstling lambs.
                              High beneath a cloud
He eyed the timorous dove, there circling about,
And to the center despatched her beneath the wing;   960
And piercingly traversed the shaft, and when fallen,
It fastened, grounded, afore Mēriones' feet.
But lighted the dove atop the towering mast,
Where dangled her head and drooped her layered plumage,
And abruptly departed the life from her limbs   965
As she plunged to the ground, at which the Argives gaped.
And Mēriones commandeered the twin axes,
And the singles bore Teucer, returned to his ships.

Then amid the gathered Peleus' son presented
A far-shadowing spear and a cauldron unfired,   970
Flower-embossed, an ox's worth, and javelin
Hurlers arose. Uprose the scion of Atreus,
Wide-ruling Agamemnon, and Mēriones
Idomeneus' valiant squire. And among them spoke

Goodly swift-footed Achilles: "Son of Atreus, 975
The measure of your manliness we know, and how
Superior in javelin and hardihood you are;
So accept you this cauldron and with it be pleased.
But give we the spear to warrior Mērionēs,
If so you quiesce. So at least would I have it." 980

So he spoke, and Agamemnon Atreïdēs
Failed nowise to hearken, and to Mērionēs
Accorded the weapon, but on Talthybius,
Atreïdēs' squire, Achilles conferred the cauldron.

~ Book XXIV ~

The Ransoming of Hector's Body, the Immolation of Hector

THE GODS DELIBERATE the return to Priam of Hector's body. Zeus sends Thetis to Achilles to persuade his doing so, and Iris to Priam to encourage his entreating Achilles face to face. The old king, despite his queen's objections, prepares to go, encouraged by an omen from Zeus. He first enters his treasure room, selecting finely woven garments and other prized possessions, and departs at night by wagon bearing the ransom—himself like one already dead. The Trojan herald Idaeus drives; and Hermes, herald of the gods, descends in a young man's guise to lead the way. Hermes, as herald, traverses inaccessible spaces and realms, here the deadly no-man's-land of the battle plain of Troy. Putting Priam at ease, Hermes speaks solicitously, expressing concern for Priam's advanced age and the danger in which he places himself.

Catching Achilles and his attendants unawares in Achilles' tent, Priam throws himself at Achilles' knees, clasping them, and begging for his son's return. All are stupefied at Priam's sudden appearance. Submissively kissing Achilles' hands, he seeks pity—doing, he says, what no man has ever done: kiss the hands of the man who has slain his sons (Hector and others). Alternatively (as some interpret the line), Priam extends his hands, in supplication, toward the mouth or chin of the man who has slain his sons. Either way, the scene is wrenching, overwhelming.

Priam looks upon Achilles and marvels at his mass and stature. Achilles regards and marvels at Priam, recollecting his own aged father, who will never see him returned from Troy. The two break into tears—Priam recollecting Hector; Achilles, Peleus and Patroclus. Moved to compassion, Achilles agrees to the ransom, his handmaidens cleansing Hector's corpse outside of

Priam's view. Achilles bids Priam sup, since one must eat (the mythical paradigm of Niobe follows) and would have Priam spend the night, but Hermes hastens Priam's departure.

As they enter the city, the Trojans run forth to meet the wagon. The lamentations of Andromache, Hecuba, and Helen follow. A truce (arranged during the visit) is held for the gathering of wood and burning of Hector's body, his ashes collected and interred. "Done so the rites for Hector, tamer of horses." So ends the book and poem.

❦

Then were the games concluded, and scattered the men
To their separate ships. The others of supper
Took thought and of balmy slumbers, their enjoyments.
But Achilles wept, his dear friend remembering,
Nor the least to o'erpowering sleep surrendered,   5
But persistently turned to either side, longing
For Patroclus' manliness and valorous might,
Recalling their experiences together,
All the tribulations in warfare encountered
And upon the embattled brine. Thus brooding, shed   10
He abundant tears, now lying upon his side,
Now prone, and now upon his back; and then again
Would he rise and wander o'erwhelmed along the shore.
Nor did Dawn, peering o'er sea and shore, escape him,
But neath his chariot yoked he horses twain, binding   15
Hector thereto, to be dragged along. And, having
Haled him thrice about the tomb of dead Patroclus,
Reposed he again within his hut, to the dust
Abandoning Hector outstretched upon his face.
But Apollo disallowed decomposition,   20
Pitying the man though dead, and with the golden
Aegis protecting him about, lest Achilles
Rend him asunder, dragging him time and again.
Thus provoked, Achilles beleaguered brave Hector.

BOOK XXIV

But the blessed gods, beholding him, took pity, 25
Rousing Hermes, keen-sighted Argeïphontēs,
To steal the corpse away. And the plan contented
The others, excepting Hera, lord Poseidon
And flashing-eyed Athena; for they persisted,
Even as when Ilium first aroused their ire, 30
And Priam and his folk, for Alexander's fault,
That he demeaned those goddesses first approaching
His dwelling, adulating her that engendered
His fateful lustfulness. But when the twelfth dawning
Thereafter appeared, among the immortals scoffed 35
Phoebus Apollo: "E'er heartless you immortals
And workers of woe. Has Hector never offered
You the fatted thighs of bulls and unblemished goats?
You now disdain to save him—though reposing dead—
For his wife, his mother, and child to look upon, 40
For Priam, his father, and all the Trojan folk
Who yearn to enkindle his pyre and obsequies
Confer. No, sooner, you remorseless gods, would you
Succor the vile Achilles, his mind unsteadied
And resistant, nor pliant the plan he presents; 45
But lion-like his heart is set on cruelty,
A beast whose lordly strength and forceful gait impels
Him forth against the keeper's flocks for feeding's gain;
Even so has pity eluded Achilles,
And lodges no shame in his heart, a condition 50
That greatly injures men, while aiding them withal.
And although a person forfeit one dearer far
Than comrade—a brother, of the selfsame mother
Born, or an offspring's love; yet having lamented
And bewailed him, he tethers his torment, endowed 55
By the blessèd gods with sturdy disposition.
But this man, having looted goodly Hector's life,
To his chariot attaches him, running circles
'Round the risen mound of his beloved companion,
From which arises nor honor nor advantage, 60

But our rebuke alone, no matter be he good,
For foul disdain to senseless clay his savagery."

Then to ire aroused responded white-armed Hera:
"Be this all as you profess, O silver-quivered
Lord, if indeed you gods the like in honor grant 65
Both Hector and Achilles: Hector but mortal
And nurtured at a woman's breast; but Achilles,
Offspring of a goddess whom I fostered and reared
Myself, giving her as wife to warrior Peleus,
Belovèd of the gods. And all you immortals 70
Attended the festivities, and amid them
Yourself, lyre-practiced Apollo, colleague to louts
And traitorous to boot."
                    Then cloud-gathering Zeus
Responded and spoke: "Hera, with the gods be you
Not over angered; the like honor shall these twain 75
Be lacking. And yet Hector was surely dearest
To the gods of all mortal men in Ilium,
And no less to me, for constant were his bounteous
Gifts, and my altar never lacked for feasting's fair
Proportion—for bounty of drink or for savored 80
Offerings burnt, the very worship we require.
"However, of bold Hector's corpse condone we no
Retaking, for constant is Thetis' wakefulness.
But I would some god despatch, summoning Thetis
To acknowledge my omniscient command, whereby 85
Pēleïdēs, accepting ransom from Priam,
Return him his son." So he spoke, and the tidings
Took storm-footed Iris, leaping and entering
The water between Samos and Imbros midway,
The billows about her resounding aloud. Sped 90
She the briny like plummet of lead, the which, strung
High from horn of pasturing ox, descends, bearing
Death to ravenous fish. And there she encountered
Thetis, ensconced within her cave, and 'round about

BOOK XXIV

Reposed the other sea goddesses assembled. 95
And she amid them wailed for her peerless offspring,
To her sorrow decreed to die in deep-soiled Troy,
Far from his native land. And swift-footed Iris
Approached and announced: "Up now, Thetis, father Zeus
Whose counsels are unwavering commands you come." 100
Then answered Thetis, the silver-footed goddess:
"Why summons me that godhead immortal? Chagrined
Am I among the gathering gods to mingle,
Now that sorrow unceasing unsettles my heart.
But I come, for his word once spoken is fulfilled." 105
So saying, the goddess seized a dark-colored veil,
Darker than which no raiment were wrought, and set forth.
And afore her wind-footed Iris led the way.
And sundered the sea surging sideward about them;
And setting briefly on land, sped they heavenward, 110
Lighting on father Zeus, far-resounding his voice,
And 'round him gathered together sat the other
Gods all, their beings immortal.
                              Then aside Zeus
Assumed Thetis her place, Athena ceding hers,
And Hera set a fair golden cup in her hand, 115
Speaking words of cheer, and Thetis drank returning
The cup. And among them the sire of men and gods
Commenced speaking: "To Olympus you come, goddess
Thetis, for all that you sorrow anguished at heart,
Uncomforted; this I well discern. Nonetheless, 120
I now reveal the reason for my summons here.
For nine days full has strife suffused the immortals
O'er Hector's corpse and Achilles, the city's scourge.
They urge Hermes, keen-sighted Argeïphontes,
To steal the corpse away. Yet, here to Achilles 125
I yield, valued hereafter your love and regard.
Get you quickly to the host, conveying my word
To your offspring, that the immortals are enraged
With him, myself especially, since, angered thus,

He sequesters Hector aside the ships, freeing 130
Him not for concern or any reproach of mine.
But to great-hearted Priam I will Iris send,
Bidding him approach the Achaeans to ransom
His son, gifting Achilles to gladden his heart."

He spoke, and the goddess silver-footed Thetis 135
Failed not to attend, but darted the pinnacle
Down of Olympus, and came to Achilles' hut.
There she found him groaning endlessly, and 'round him
Busily hastened his companions, preparing
Breakfast, and in the hut a great and shaggy ram 140
Lay slaughtered before them. Then his queenly mother
Seating herself aside him, stroked him with her hand
And spoke, addressing him by name: "Dear child of mine,
How long sorrowing and tearful will you weary
Your heart, unmindful alike of dalliance or food. 145
Good for you were woman's embrace, for I tell you
Not long among the living is your lot, and death
And mighty fate even now approach. But hearken
Directly, for I am messenger come from Zeus.
He asserts that the gods immortal are angered, 150
And surpassing all is he overcome with rage,
That you sequester Hector in hatred of heart
At the hollow ships and return him not. But come,
Releasing him take ransom for the dead." To her
Swift-footed Pēleidēs responded: "So be it. 155
Whoso ransom brings, let him bear the dead away,
If father Cronidēs, thus determined, commands."

Thus aside the gathered ships did son and mother
Many wingèd words exchange, one to the other,
But Cronidēs despatched Iris to sacred Troy: 160
"Up, go, swift Iris; leave your Olympian abode,
To Troy bearing word unto great-hearted Priam
To near the Argive ships, there ransoming his son,

BOOK XXIV

Bearing gifts to Achilles to gladden his heart.
Alone let him go, fully unaccompanied;   165
But a guide may attend him, an elder person
Escorting the donkeys and light-running wagon,
And return to the city transporting the dead,
Even him by Achilles slain. Nor unsettle
Him danger or alarm whatever; such a guide   170
Will we furnish him, even Argeïphontes,
Who shall lead him 'til to Achilles led. And come
To the hut, Achilles shall nowise misuse him
Nor suffer another's misuse; for not lacking
In wisdom is he, nor purposeless, nor hardened   175
Withal. With kindness shall he spare the suppliant."
So he spoke, and storm-footed Iris sped bearing
His message. Arriving at Priam's house, she found
Clamor and yowling throughout, his sons in the court
'Round their father collected, damp'ning their garments   180
With tears. And among them the elder, his mantle
About him, his head and neck with refuse suffused
Which he had gathered up a'grovel on the ground.
And lamented his daughters and daughters-in-law
Throughout the residence, mindful of the warriors,   185
Many and valiant, by Greek hands slain and despatched.
And encountering Priam, Zeus' messenger spoke.
Mildly she spoke, yet foreboding o'erwhelmed his limbs:
"Stand courageous, O Priam, Dardanus' offspring,
And nowise be affrighted. Not as misfortune's   190
Harbinger arrive I here, but with good intent.
A herald from Zeus I come who, though distant far,
Exceedingly regards and pities and you. Commands
He you ransom Hector anon, your goodly son,
Bearing gifts to Achilles to gladden his heart;   195
Sole your journey, entirely unaccompanied.
But a guide may attend you, an elder person
Escorting the donkeys and light-running wagon,
And return to the city transporting the dead,

601

Even him by Achilles slain. Nor unsettle 200
You danger or alarm whatever; such a guide
Shall we furnish you, even Argeïphontes,
Who shall lead you 'til to Achilles led. And come
To the hut, Achilles shall nowise misuse you
Nor suffer another's misuse; for not lacking 205
In wisdom is he, nor purposeless, nor hardened
Withal. With kindness shall he spare the suppliant."
Thus speaking, the swift-footed Iris departed.
But Priam bid his sons make the wagon ready,
Affixing thereon a coffer of wicker-work, 210
And himself descended to the vaulted treasure
Room—redolent with cedar, loftily o'er-roofed,
Harboring hoarded riches, and called Hecuba,
His wife, and spoke: "Lady, an Olympian herald
Arrives from Zeus, bidding that I ransom Hector, 215
Bearing gifts to Achilles to gladden his heart.
But come, afford me this: how appears it to you?
For as concerns myself, my inclination bids
Me entirely comply, 'mid the vessels and camp
Of the Argives."
           Thus he, but uttered his wife 220
A coagulate cry, and spoke responding thus:
"Ah, woe unto me, where now the circumspection
By which among strangers aforetime you excelled,
And among them held command, that you now propose
To approach the Achaean ships, meeting the eyes 225
Of the man who has butchered your offspring, many
And valiant? The heart within you is iron wrought.
For should he behold you and pounce, so murderous
Stands the man, and unsparing, that neither will he
Pity you nor elsewise regard your plight. Rather, 230
From afar observe we our mourning and complaint,
Here within our porticoes. Thus did mighty Fate
Spin thread upon his birth when I delivered him,
That he glut swift-footed dogs, from his kin afar,

O'erseen by a savage on whose inmost liver   235
I were fain to feed, my teeth deeply fastening,
Thus doing in fit retribution for my son
Who nowise shrank being slain by him, but stalwart
Stood, defending the men and deep-bosomed women
Of Troy, without thought of escaping whatever."   240

Then spoke the elder, godlike Priam, responding:
"Attempt not to dissuade me from my intention,
Nor, ill-omened bird, flit you here in my abode.
For had another of earthbound men commanded
Thus, whether a sacrifice-discerning prophet   245
Or priest, a falsehood might we fathom it, and turn
The more therefrom; but now—myself distinguishing
The goddess' disclosure and demeanor—I leave,
Nor vainly spoken shall she be. And if my fate
Decrees harsh death aside the bronze-mailed Argive ships,   250
So be it, and Achilles quickly slay me then,
Once I have clasped my son and wailing's want fulfilled."
He spoke, laying open the goodly coffer lid,
Upgathering twelve beauteous robes and twelve single-
Folded cloaks, and no fewer the coverlets all,   255
And as many white mantles and tunics alike.
And sequestered he gold, ten talents counting out,
Two gleaming tripods, four cauldrons, and a chalice
Exceedingly fair—gifted him by men of Thrace
Upon occasion of his embassy. Treasured   260
The cup, nor this did the elder withhold, wanting
Ever to ransom his son. Then the gathered crowd
Dispersed he from the portico, rebuking them,
Calumnious his words: "Vile miscreants, away!
Degenerates! Endure you no household laments   265
Of your own that you gather here to annoy me?
Or find you it insufficient that Cronidēs
Thus crushes me with sorrow, that I should forfeit
My unsurpassèd son? But you shall know it too,

For readier rank you as Argive prey for want 270
Of my valiant son. But for me, shielded my eyes
From Troy's desecration, the sooner take me Hell."

He spoke and threatened among them, cudgel in hand,
And hastening they sidestepped the elder's approach.
Then loud summoned he his sons, chiding Helenus, 275
And Paris, and goodly Agathōn, and Pammōn,
Politēs, good at warcry, and Antiphonus,
Deïphobus, Hippothous and lordly Dius.
To these nine calling aloud, the elder enjoined:
"Haste you, base offspring of my begetting, better 280
Had you perished all aside the Danaan ships,
To the man, instead of Hector. Woe unto me
Who am hapless most, having true sons begotten
Throughout expansive Troy, of whom, I vow, remains
Not one alive—not godlike Mēstōr, nor Troilus 285
Chariot-champion; nor Hector, a very god
Among men, appearing of no man begotten
But of immortals, offspring by Ares despatched.
But you delinquent scrounge about—fraudulent tongues,
Twinkling twirlers pirouetting the dancing floor, 290
Brigands of cattle among your own folk. Ready
Me a wagon, straightway— will you not?—thereupon
Resting this ransom, and embark we on our way."

So he spoke, and they, affrighted by their father's
Upbraiding, conveyed the mule-drawn lightly trundling 295
Car, newly constructed, binding the wicker box
Thereon, and from its peg unfastened the mule-yoke,
Of boxwood the yoke with a knob affixed thereon,
Well fitted with guiding-rings, and nine full cubits
The yoke-banding overall, and finally the yoke. 300
Positioned they the yoke upon the polished pole,
At the furthest point thereof, and upon the pin
They cast the ring, attaching it fast to the knob,

Thrice turning it leftward and right and, next, secured
It to the post and guided the hook thereunder.   305
Then brought they from the treasure-room a boundless store,
Upon the polished wagon placing it, ransom
For Hector's head, and to the harness strong-hoofed mules
Attached, which the Mysians had once given Priam,
A wondrous gift. And they guided Priam's horses   310
Beneath the yoke, horses the elder kept and reared
In his lustrous stalls. Thus the twain their wagon yoked
Beneath the tow'ring portico, even Priam
And his aide, prudent their planning withal—when nigh
Approached Hecuba, stricken in spirit, bearing   315
A golden cup of honey-hearted wine, to pour
Libation ere they left, and before the horses
Standing, spoke: "Pour you libation to father Zeus,
And entreat a safe return from amid the foe,
Seeing your spirit compels you toward the vessels,   320
My protests notwithstanding. Thereafter offer
Prayer to Zeus Cronidēs, lord of concealing cloud,
The god of Ida, surveying Ilium entire,
And a bird of omen request from him, even
That swiftest messenger, dearest of birds to him,   325
And mightiest in strength; let it rightward appear,
Visual assessment of guidance providing,
And shipward proceed to the horse-swift Danaans.
But if far-seeing Zeus his messenger withhold,
Then I, for one, would disavow your shipbound course,   330
Impatient though your objective."
                                    Then spoke Priam,
Answering her: "Wife, this bidding of yours I'll not
Discard; for helpful our supplications to Zeus,
If thus he take pity." So pronounced the elder
And bade the attendant pour water, undefiled,   335
On his hands; and the maid approached bearing pitcher
And basin together. Then, cleansing himself, took
Priam the cup from his consort, offering prayer,

And, positioned in the courtyard, outpoured the wine,
Gazing heavenward as he spoke aloud: "Father   340
Zeus, regent of Ida, greatest, most glorious,
Grant my coming to Achilles' hut be welcome,
And pitied I, and send a bird of omen, e'en
That swiftest messenger, dearest of birds to you,
And mightiest in strength; let it rightward appear,   345
That sighting the portent, assurance manifest,
I shipbound proceed to the horse-swift Achaeans."
So he spoke praying, and hearkened counselor Zeus.
Forthwith despatched he an eagle, surest wingèd
Omen, the dusky hunter, sable its plumage;   350
Wide as the well-bolted door of a high-vaulted
Treasure room; even so expansive its plumage
Leftward and to right; and rightward it presented,
Tearing through the town. And gladdened they glimpsing it,
And exulted their spirits within. Then hastened   355
The elder—to his wagon stepping, exiting
The gateway and echoing portico, the mules
Dragging the four-axled wagon by Idaeus
Driven, wise-hearted; and behind hoofed the horses
That the elder, applying the lash, urged onward   360
Through the town; and his kinsfolk followed lamenting,
As for one faring forward to death.
                            But when gone
From the city downward to the plain, returned his
Sons and sons-in-law to Troy. But Zeus Cronidēs,
Whose voice is borne afar, discerned them descending 365
The plain, and observing the elder took pity,
And straightway called Hermes, his cherished son: "Hermes,
Because dearest you deem the conveyance of men,
And safeguard whomever you desire, hasten you
And guide Priam to the hollow vessels, that none   370
Amid the Danaans detect or regard him
'Til making his way to the tent of Pēleidēs."

BOOK XXIV

So he spoke, and the herald Argeïphontēs
Failed not to obey and straightway fastened sandals
To his feet, dazzling footwear of gold, immortal, 375
That over seas and limitless land transport him
With the instancy of wind. And he took the wand
Wherewith enthralleth he the eyes of whom he will,
While others again he awakens though sleeping.
This clasping, soared the mighty Argeïphontēs, 380
Quickly arriving to Troy and the Hellespont.
Thence he proceeded, likened to a princely youth,
The down first nascent on his lip, by which youthful
Charm Is signaled most. Now when the others had passed
Beyond the great barrow of Ilus, King Priam's 385
Grandsire, they stood the mules and horses riverside
To drink; for nighttime had darkened the earth. Then glanced
The herald, recognizing Hermes, and addressed
Priam, saying: "Take you counsel, Dardanus' son.
Something's afoot. Let prudence guide your reaction. 390
I see a man, and fear our fortune determined.
Come, haste we fleeing in our car, or at least clasp
His knees, as supplicants, if thus he show mercy."
Thus he spoke, and quaked the elder, his mind confused,
And on his pliant limbs uprose the hair aright, 395
And he stood dismayed. But the Helper, swift Hermes,
Approaching took the elder's hand and inquired:
"Whither drive you, dear father, your horses and mules
Throughout the ambrosial night whilst others sleep?
Stand you unfazed before the fury-breathing foe, 400
Implacable men encompassing you about?
Should one behold you hauling such load of treasure
Through the darkful night, what, pray, is your strategy?
No young man yourself, old your attendant nearby,
Deficient protection against brash importuning. 405
But no trouble from myself will you encounter;
No, help against another would I grant—so much
Like my father's your aspect revealed before me."

Then the elder, godlike Priam, offered response:
"As you reck them, dear son, so prevail these matters.　　　　410
However, a god yet extends his hand o'er me
Who has sent me a wayfaring helper like you,
Propitious and beauteous in form and comportment,
Most heartful, and of blessèd parents begotten."
Then answered the messenger Argeïphontēs:　　　　415
"Truly, dear elder, you relate this correctly.
But come, tell me and truly declare it, whether
To foreigners you transport this plenteous treasure
For safe storage's need, or whether fearfully
You forsake the sacred town—so deft a fighter　　　　420
Now absent, unfailingly fine, your very son,
Attentively ever combatting the Argives."
And the elder, godlike Priam, responded thus:
"Who are you, dear lad, and of what stock begotten
Who thus tellingly speaks of my ill-fated son?"　　　　425
Then answered the messenger Argeïphontēs:
"Trial wouldst make of me, sire, inquiring of Hector?
Oft have I observed him in fame-conferring fight,
When, having repelled the Achaeans to their ships,
He decimated them decisively with bronze.　　　　430
And we, confounded, watched, for Achilles, wrathful
With Atreidēs, suffered us nowise to engage.
I am his squire, and the same well-crafted vessel
Brought us here. From among the Myrmidons my stock.
My father, Polyctōr, in opulence abounds,　　　　435
And even as you is he agèd. And boasts he
Six sons, the seventh myself, and chosen was I
By casting of lots to accompany him here.
And now from the vessels come, I traverse the plain,
For come daybreak, the quick-eyed Achaeans commence　　　　440
Their attack against Troy. For it distresses them
To be sitting idly by, and little avail
The Argive kings to stay their impatience for war."
And the elder, godlike Priam, responded thus:

"If you be helper to Achilles, Peleus' son, 445
Then truly tell me everything, whether my son
By the ships yet abides or whether Achilles
Has already made of him limb-meal for mongrels."
Then responded the herald Argeïphontes:
"Old sire, vultures and curs have yet not consumed him, 450
But aside Pēleïdēs' ships he reposes,
Amid the huts, the like as when there first conveyed,
And there now recumbent lies upon this twelfth day
And molders not away, nor do worms consume him,
Such as fester on the flesh of battle's fallen. 455
Yes, Achilles drags him remorselessly about,
Circling the barrow of his beloved Patroclus
As oft as sacred Dawn appears, but disfigures
Him not. Yourself would you marvel, coming to see
How dew-like-to-fresh he appears, being clean cleansed 460
Of blood and lacking defilement; and closed the wounds
Wherewith he was afflicted, for many there were
That embedded their bronze in his flesh. Even thus
The Olympian gods have attended to your son,
Though a corpse; thus highly respected in their hearts." 465

So he spoke, and the elder, heartened, responded:
"Truly befits it, my child, to tender the gods
Their due, for ne'er my son—as sure as e'er he was—
Within our halls forgot the Olympian gods;
Thus have they remembered him, reciprocally, 470
Though at rest reposed. But accept you this fair cup
And guard me close, with godspeed guiding me aright,
'Til reaching the hut of Peleus' son Achilles."
And again spoke the herald Argeïphontes:
"Trial wouldst make of me, old sire, exploiting my youth 475
To little avail, seeking acceptance of gift
Of which Achilles gathers not. Heartfelt wonder
And fear have I of him, lest he be embezzled,
And befall me misfortune thereafter. Your guide,

However, would I be, even unto glorious   480
Argos, with kindly care attending you by ship
Or by stride, disallowing provocation all."

So spoke the Helper, and leaping upon the car
Seized lash and reins, with constancy enspiriting
Horses and mules. But when come to the walls and trench   485
That protected the ships, even as the watchers
Bustled about their supper, Hermes the Helper
Suffused them with slumber, and straightaway opened
The gates, dislodging the restraints, and brought Priam
Within, his wondrous gifts on the wain. But when come   490
To the hut of Achilles—the high-vaulted hut
That the Myrmidons labored making for their king,
Cleaving lintels of fir therefor, o'er-roofing it
With downy meadow-gathered thatch, 'round it rearing
For him, their king, a spacious court with stakes thick-set,   495
Fastening its entrance with single latch of fir
That three Achaeans were wont to insert, and three
Others at least from its fastening to extract,
The expanse of which Achilles alone controlled—
Then for the elder Helper Hermes oped the door,   500
The glorious gifts delivering for swift-footed
Achilles, and from the chariot stepped he groundward
And spoke: "Old sire, a deathless god come I to you,
Even Hermes, whom father Zeus retains to guide
Your way. But now I return, not encountering   505
Achilles. Grounds for his displeasure would it be
That god immortal by mortal thus be hosted.
But enter you clasping the knees of Achilles,
Entreating him by his father, fair-haired mother,
And offspring, bestirring his soul to compassion."   510

So spoke Hermes, departing to high Olympus.
And Priam descended his chariot, there leaving
Idaeus, who stood holding the horses and mules.

BOOK XXIV

But proceeded the elder straightway to the hut
Where Achilles, beloved of Zeus, was wont to sit.   515
There he found Pēleïdēs, sitting apart his
Comrades, two only, the warrior Automedōn,
And Alcimus, of Ares' root, who busily
Attended him. And now had he finished eating,
Even of viands and drink, and stood the table   520
Nearby. And by these unnoted entered Priam,
Approaching Achilles and encircling his knees,
And kissed the hands, the hideous man-slaying hands
That had slaughtered his many sons. And as when sheer
Madness of spirit o'ertakes a man who at home   525
Another slays—escapes he to a distant land,
To a wealthy person's dwelling place, and wonder
O'erwhelms those witnessing it; so seized with wonder
Was Achilles, espying the godlike Priam,
And astonished alike were the others, glancing   530
In each direction. But Priam entreated him,
Addressing Achilles thus: "Remember your sire,
O godlike Achilles, whose years, as mine, progress
In senescence and grievous dissolution, whom
Dwellers 'round about with jeers abjure, nor finds he   535
Refuge from ruin and debasement; yet, learning
You thrive, his heart uplifts, and therewithal he hopes
To see his belovèd son from Troyland returned.
But accursed of men am I, having the bravest
Begotten of sons throughout Troy, of whom, I vow,   540
Not one survives. Fifty I had when the Argive
Host arrived, nineteen from the selfsame belly born;
And others did women about the palace bear.
These, then, in all their numbers furious Ares slew,
And he that alone persisted, who by himself   545
Defended town and folk, him you despatched, fighting
For his country, even Hector. For his sake come
I now to these Achaean ships, bearing ransom's
Bounty to reclaim him. But respect you the gods,

611

O Achilles, and pity me, recollecting 550
Your own father—the more piteous I than he,
Enduring what no other man alive endures:
My hands to the very lips of the man outstretched
Who has slaughtered my sons."
                So he spoke, instilling
Want in Achilles for lamenting his father; 555
And taking Priam by the hand, Achilles urged
Him gently back. So recollected they and wept,
The one for man-slaying Hector, close cowering
At Achilles' feet; the other, for his father
And next for Patroclus, the pangs of their anguish 560
Suffused throughout the dwelling. But when Pēleidēs
Had sated his despondency, and the longing
Had at length from his body and heart abated,
Forthwith he leapt from his seat, raising the elder
By his hand, pitying his agèd head and beard, 565
And spoke, addressing him wingèd words: "Unhappy
One, relentless trauma have you at heart endured.
Where, tell me, found you fortitude alone to near
The Danaan ships, confronting the countenance
Of him who has slaughtered your sons in abundance? 570
Iron-resolved is your heart.
                But here be seated,
And within your spirit lie wretchedness reposed,
Despite woe; for none the profit in chill lament.
For thus have the gods immortal unwound the thread
For piteous man: that he abide disheartened; 575
But divinity, wanting of care. For double
The urns of offerings upon Zeus' doorstep set:
The one of blessings bestowed, the other of bane.
On whom thunderbolted-hurling Zeus a tandem
Lot bestows, encounters he now blessing, now bane; 580
But whom with unrelenting ill he overwhelms,
Reviled that man becomes, and dreadful the madness
That driveth him o'er sacred earth, and ranges he

BOOK XXIV

Regarded nor of gods nor mortal man. Just so,
Peerless the gifts god-granted to Peleus from birth,   585
He in kindness surpassing mankind and in wealth:
Over Myrmidons they enthroned him, with goddess
Spouse provided, being himself but corporal.
The Olympians, howe'er, meted mishap as well:
The lack of princely offspring to manhood nurtured   590
In his halls; but bore he a solitary son,
One only, foretold his demise. Nor might I tend
To his worsening condition, since I abide
Far distant from my native domain, here in Troy,
Irritant to your race. And of you, agèd sire,   595
We hear you resided aforetime blessed; how once
O'er all that Lesbos, Macar's seat, contains within,
O'er Phrygia northward and the boundless Hellespont,
How o'er this all, old sire, you were once reported
To rule, in offspring and fortune felicitous.   600
But, from the time the immortal gods rained sorrow
On your being, unending war and butchery
Afflict the town. But abide, nor unabated
Be the heartbreak for your son; nor will you restore
Him, enduring some other misfortune ere then."   605
And thus responded the elder, godlike Priam:
"Bid me not be seated, Zeus-fostered Achilles,
So long as Hector lies discarded by the huts.
No, sooner return him, by mine own eyes beheld,
And accept you a copious ransom conferred,   610
Possessing its advantages once delivered
To your native land, recompense for sparing me."

Then with angered glance from neath his brows, addressed him
Swift-footed Achilles: "Provoke me no longer,
Old man; even now am I inclined to return   615
Brave Hector to your keeping; for from Zeus arrived
A messenger, even the mother that bore me,
Daughter of Nereus, elder of the sea. Some god,

Moreover, as I surmise, has guided you here
Amid the Achaean ships. For no mortal man, 620
However valiant and vigorous, would dare thus
Venture among the host, nor seek to circumvent
The watch, nor handily uplift the entrance latch.
Wherefore, renounce this incitement unto sorrow,
Old man, lest even here within the hut I spare 625
Thee not, though being my suppliant, and transgress
Cronidēs' command." So he spoke, and the elder
Swooned with misgiving and hearkened to the command.
But like to a lion leapt Pēleidēs forth,
Leaving the hut—not alone, for with him henchmen 630
Twain, even brave Automedōn and Alcimus,
Acclaimed by Achilles past all his companions,
With exception of Menoetius' son. From beneath
Their yokes they unleashed the horses and mules, leading
The herald within, the old king's crier, and sat 635
Him on a chair; and from the pine-polished wain
Took plenteous bounty for Hector's head. But left
They a tunic and two deftly embroidered robes,
That Achilles might cloak the corpse therein and thus
Homeward consign it to be borne. Then Achilles 640
Summoned the handmaidens forth and directed them
Cleanse and anoint the corpse, bearing it distantly
Apart, lest Priam perceive his offspring, and grief
Of heart curtail forbearance at the sight of him,
And Achilles' own heart to wrath be excited, 645
And he slay him, thuswise defying Zeus' edict.
So once the handmaids had cleansed the corpse, with unguents
Anointed, in tunic and comely robes enwrapped,
Achilles, himself uplifting it, reposed it
Upon a bier and, thus positioned, his helpers 650
To the lustrous wain entrusted it. Then uttered
He a groan, his companion invoking by name:
"Be not angry, Patroclus, should you ascertain,
Though hallowed in Hades' halls, that I have released

BOOK XXIV

The valiant Hector unto his sire. Befitting 655
The ransom he has specified, and unto you,
In turn, shall I apportion allocation's right."

So spoke dread Achilles, returning to his hut,
And from the wondrous chair where earlier he reposed,
By the hut's remotest wall ensconced, addressed he 660
Lord Priam thus: "Your offspring, old sire, is ransomed,
Even as you requested, rested on a bier.
And at daybreak shall you view him, bearing him hence.
But think we presently of supper. For even
The fair-haired Niobē remembered sustenance 665
Though twelve the sprightly offspring slaughtered in her halls,
Daughters six and six luxuriant sons: the sons
Apollo of the silver bow despatched, angered
At Niobē; and the archeress Artemis,
The daughters, since Niobē had compared herself 670
To fair-faced Leto, claiming the goddess had borne
But children twain, while she herself had many borne.
Wherefore they, though being but two alone, destroyed
The lot of them. Bloodied they lay for fully nine
Days' time, nor hastened to inter them anyone, 675
For Cronidēs had to granite transformed the folk.
But the heavenly gods interred them on the tenth,
And Niobē bethought herself of sustenance,
Exhausted by tears outflown. And now, somewhere 'mid
The rocks, on the desolate slopes of Sipylus, 680
Where, men relate, those goddesses relish repose—
The nymphs around Achelōus' stream quick circling
In dance—there, though to stone transformed her progeny,
She bears the gods' allotted pain. But come, do we
The twain alike, old noble sire, take sustenance; 685
And your son will you lament thereafter, Troyward
Taking him, and greatly mourned his arrival there."
Therewith upsprung rapid Pēleïdēs, slaying
A white-fleeced sheep, and his comrades flayed it about,

Fittingly preparing it; then deftly sliced it, 690
Spitted the pieces, and set them a'roast with care.
The meat from prongs extracted, Automedōn placed
Plenteous baskets of bread, apportioned it
About the board, whilst Achilles allotted meat.
And they extended their hands to the victuals there 695
Readied before them.
                 But next having satisfied
Their need of food and drink, then was Dardanian
Priam dumbfounded at Pēleidēs, his goodly
Appearance and demeanor, for godlike imbued
Was he to contemplate. And warrior Pēleidēs 700
Stood stunned at Dardanian Priam, beholding
His kindly mien and sympathetic to his words.
But the pleasures of contemplation satisfied,
Each on the other intent, the elder, godlike
Priam, next addressed Achilles: "Quickly show me 705
My sleeping place, O nurtured of Zeus, that restful
Slumber provide me composure and readiness,
Since nowise neath my withered eyes has slumber long
Resided, the while wasted my offspring, forfeit
To your hands, but ever lament I and ponder 710
My pain, groveling in the filth of my courtyards.
But now, ingesting sustenance and flaming wine,
Relinquish I constraint, naught consuming earlier."

He spoke, and Achilles bade his comrades and maids
Set bedsteads neath the portico, purple blankets 715
And opulent coverlets arraying thereon,
And fleecy cloaks for coverings withal. So labored
The handmaids, their torches aflame, throughout the hall,
And straightway two bedsteads most agilely prepared.
Then mockingly remarked swift-footed Achilles: 720
"Here, outdoors, repose you, old sire, lest Achaean
Counselors approach my tent, that ever upon me
Seeking advice descend, as befits. If any

Of these through the swiftly shadowed night espy you,
Soon might he tell Atreidēs, shepherd of the host, 725
And thus delay betide deliv'ry of the corpse.
But come, relate me this, and truthfully recount:
The amount of time for Hector's funeral planned,
That I myself forbear and keep the host away."
And the elder, godlike Priam, responded thus: 730
"If you envisage good Hector's rites accomplished,
Attend you, Achilles, that which my heart requires.
Fully discern you our constraint within the town,
And from mountain altitudes firewood here descends,
And great is Trojan dread. For nine days full within 735
The halls be our lament, and upon the tenth his
Funeral, and feast the folk, and on th' eleventh
High build we a mound upon him, and on the twelfth
Do battle, if we must." Then goodly swift-footed
Achilles responded: "So be it, then, old sire, 740
Even as you request; and let hostilities
Relinquished be throughout th' entreated duration."
Thus speaking, clasped he by the wrist the elder's hand,
Quieting the fear within him. So they slumbered
In the dwelling's courtyard, the herald and Priam, 745
Harboring wisdom in their hearts; but Achilles
Slept in the innermost part of the well-built hut,
And full length aside him the fair-faced Brisēis.

Now all the other gods and chariot-lording men
Reposed throughout the night, settled in gentle sleep; 750
But Helper Hermes remained withdrawn from slumber,
As he pondered Priam's departure from the ships,
Unperceived by the gate's stalwart keepers. Taking
Position above his head, he thus addressed him:
"Old sire, fear you no evil, thus soundly asleep 755
Midst the foe, that Achilles has spared you? Ransomed
Is Hector. But thrice the sum will surviving sons
Of yours for your life provide, should Atreïdēs

Agamemnon or the Argives discover you."
So he spoke, and the elder fearfully wakened 760
The herald. And Hermes yoked the horses and mules,
Circumspectly conducting the twain through the camp,
Nor did anyone detect them. But once arrived
At the stream and ford of fair flowing Scamander,
The stream of Zeus begotten, then returned Hermes 765
To tow'ring Olympus, as saffron-robèd Dawn
About the face of earth entire beflamed herself.

So wailing and bemoaning they approached the town,
And the mules transported the corpse. Nor were others
Ware of them, nor warrior nor fair-girdled woman; 770
Yet Cassandra, peer to golden Aphrodite,
Ascending Troy's citadel, marked her dear father
And marked the herald, crier of Troy; and remarked
She that other, transported on the carriage bier,
Whereat she shrieked, throughout the city bellowing: 775
"Come, you men and women of Troy, behold Hector,
In whose steadfast presence aforetime you rejoiced
When he returned from battle, since great the comfort
He afforded to Troy and its inhabitants."
So she proclaimed, nor within Troy itself remained 780
A solitary person, for upon them all
Had grief unbearable come, but they assembled
At the gate as Priam brought Hector's body home.

First darted Hector's mother and adorèd spouse
Toward the wheel-fitted wain and, fully overwrought, 785
Embraced his head and uprooted their hair; and the folk
In tears encircled them. And now throughout the day
'Til lowering of sun had lasted their lament
Aside the gates, had not old Priam from the wain
Addressed them thus: "Allow me passage for the mules; 790
Thereafter, once reposed within the house he be,
Your fill of wailing take." So he spoke, and parted

BOOK XXIV

They, permitting the wagon's passage. But th' others,
Having borne him to the glorious house, reposed him
On a bedstead strung tight with cord, and aside him   795
Were singers set, leaders of the dirge, commencing
The lament, the women of Troy participant.

And foremost wailed white-armed Andromachē, cradling
The man-slaying Hector's head: "Perished, dear husband,
Are you from among the living, though youthful yet,   800
Myself widowed at home, orphaned your infant son,
To our haplessness born. Nor count I his coming
To manhood, for sooner be wasted the city,
Since you of its dutiful wives were protector
And guardian of its young before meeting your fate.   805
With these shall I shortly ascend the hollow ships.
And you, my child, with me shall destination reach
Where, dwelling in dreadful servitude, you labor
Afore the face of unforgiving overlords,
Or else will some Danaan, dragging you away,   810
Hurl you pitifully forward from the parapet,
Enraged, perhaps, that Hector had slain his sibling,
Son, or sire, seeing that Hector slew numerous
Argives gorging on gravelly earth, for ruthless
Your father in heart-rending war; so sorrows Troy.   815
And accursèd misfortune your parents endure,
Dear Hector, and me past others all abhorrent
Woe bestrides. For in dying reached you not abed
For me nor soft uttered some endearment, whereby
The better to attend this lasting tearfulness."   820

So wailing she spoke, waking the women's lament.
And among them Hecuba led the dismal dirge.
"Hector, to my heart far dearest of all my sons,
Of the immortals beloved whilst living, wherefore
Have they loved you even upon your departure.   825
For, the other sons of mine whom he captive took

Would Achilles barter o'er the bountiful sea
On Samos, Imbros, or smoke-blanketed Lemnos;
But purloining your life with razored pointy bronze,
He repeatedly dragged you about the barrow   830
Of his dear companion Patroclus, whom you slew;
Though availed he not to upraise him even so.
Now dewy fresh within my halls, resembling one
New slain you lie, like one whom Apollo silver-
Bowed with gentle shaft assails and slays." So speaking,   835
Engendered she lament and sorrow uncontrolled.

And third did Argive Helen raise the threnody:
"Hector, dearest to me of all my husband's kin!
Truly is godlike Alexander my husband,
Who Troyward bore me—O, would I had perished first!   840
For now have twenty years transpired since I disowned
My native land, though never once met with evil
Or hurtful word from you, when others reproved me
In the halls, be it brother of yours, or sister,
Or fair-robèd sister-in-law, or your mother—   845
But e'er gentle was your father, as though my own—
But restrained you and deterred them with reprimand,
With gentleness of spirit and genial address.
Wherefore, alike for you and my destitute self
I lament, craving someone in Troy your equal   850
In kindheartedness; but all recoil before me."

Thus she intoned, and moaned the thronging multitude.
Thereafter the agèd Priam addressed the folk:
"Men of Troy, gather you wood into Ilium,
Nor bethink you of dire Danaan ambuscade,   855
For Achilles verily committed—sending
Me back from the hollow ships—to constraint, doing
No ill 'til the twelfth dawn be revealed." So he spoke,
And they yoked mules and oxen to carriages, fast
Gathering afore the town. For nine days entire   860

BOOK XXIV

They collected wood in countless store, but when Dawn
On the tenth arose lending light to mortalkind,
Conveyed they dauntless Hector, shedding tears the while,
And to the topmost pyre upheaved the corpse aflame.
But when rosy-fingered Dawn appeared, early-born,   865
Then gathered they 'round glorious Hector's pyre,
And once assembled and concertedly come, quenched
The pyre with sparkling wine throughout, wherever flame
Had blazed upon it; and thereafter his brethren
And comrades, tearfully bent, upgathered the bones.   870
They placed the bones in a golden urn, o'ercov'ring
It with silken purple robes, reposing the urn
In a hollow grave, o'ercovering it with great
Stones closely set. Then quickly heaped they up a mound,
And 'round about were watchmen placed to every side,   875
Lest the well-greaved Achaeans too early approach.
And piling the barrow they returned, gathering
In Priam's abode to partake of lavish feast.
Done so the rites for Hector tamer of horses.

—fin—

Map of Ancient Greek world highlighting sites significant to Homer, Sappho, and other Greek lyric poets, and places of general interest.